Macs

ALL-IN-ONE

FOR

DUMMIES®

3RD EDITION

by Joe Hutsko and Barbara Boyd

WILEY

John Wiley & Sons, Inc.

Macs® All-in-One For Dummies®, 3rd Edition

Published by
John Wiley & Sons, Inc.
111 River Street
Hoboken, NJ 07030-5774
www.wiley.com

Copyright © 2012 by John Wiley & Sons, Inc., Hoboken, New Jersey

Published by John Wiley & Sons, Inc., Hoboken, New Jersey

Published simultaneously in Canada

For general information on our other products and services, please contact our Customer Care Department within the U.S. at 877-762-2974, outside the U.S. at 317-572-3993, or fax 317-572-4002.

For technical support, please visit www.wiley.com/techsupport.

Wiley publishes in a variety of print and electronic formats and by print-on-demand. Some material included with standard print versions of this book may not be included in e-books or in print-on-demand. If this book refers to media such as a CD or DVD that is not included in the version you purchased, you may download this material at http://booksupport.wiley.com. For more information about Wiley products, visit www.wiley.com.

Library of Congress Control Number: 2012931839

ISBN 978-1-118-12961-6 (pbk); ISBN 978-1-118-22565-3 (ebk); ISBN 978-1-118-23843-1 (ebk); ISBN 978-1-118-26305-1 (ebk)

Manufactured in the United States of America

10 9 8 7 6 5 4 3 2 1

WILEY

About the Authors

Joe Hutsko is the author of *Green Gadgets For Dummies, Flip Video For Dummies* (with Drew Davidson), and *iPhone All-in-One For Dummies* (with Barbara Boyd). For more than two decades, he has written about computers, gadgets, video games, trends, and high-tech movers and shakers for numerous publications and websites, including the *New York Times, Macworld, PC World, Fortune, Newsweek, Popular Science, TV Guide,* the *Washington Post, Wired,* Gamespot, MSNBC, Engadget, TechCrunch, and Salon. You can find links to Joe's stories on his blog, JOEyGADGET.com.

As a kid, Joe built a shortwave radio, played with electronic project kits, and learned the basics of the BASIC programming language on his first computer, the Commodore Vic 20. In his teens, he picked strawberries to buy his first Apple II computer. Four years after that purchase (in 1984), he wound up working for Apple, where he became the personal technology guru for the company's chairman and CEO. Joe left Apple in 1988 to become a writer and worked on and off for other high-tech companies, including Steve Jobs' one-time NeXT. He authored a number of video game strategy guides, including the bestsellers *Donkey Kong Country Game Secrets: The Unauthorized Edition,* and *Rebel Assault: The Official Insiders Guide.*

Joe's first novel, *The Deal,* was published in 1999, and he recently rereleased a trade paperback edition of it with a new foreword by the author (tinyurl.com/hutskodeal).

Barbara Boyd writes about food, gardens, travel, and technology. She's written for *Chile Pepper Magazine, Islands,* and *BeeCulture.* With Joe, she just finished *iPhone All-in-One For Dummies.*

Barbara worked at Apple from 1985 to 1990, beginning as Joe's assistant and the first network administrator for the executive staff. She then took a position as an administrator in the Technical Product Support group. Barbara recalls working with people who went on to become top names in technology — it was an exciting time to be in Silicon Valley and at Apple in particular. That experience instilled a lifelong fascination with technology and Apple products. Her interest and experience led to subsequent jobs in marketing and publishing at IDG (International Data Group) and later for a small San Francisco design firm. In 1998, she left the corporate world to study Italian, write, and teach.

Presently, Barbara stays busy writing, keeping up with technology, growing olives, and beekeeping. (She's a certified honey taster.) Her next writing project — barring any unforeseen *For Dummies* books — will be a memoir of building a farm and house in Italy. Barbara divides her time between city life in Rome and country life on an olive farm in Calabria, which she blogs about at http://honeybeesandolivetrees.blogspot.com.

Dedication

Joe dedicates this book to: My fabulously thoughtful, kind, caring, smart, creative, beautiful, and amazing co-author — and lifelong friend (and karmic life preserver) — Barbara Boyd.

Barbara dedicates this book to: My sweet, patient husband, Ugo de Paula, who appreciates my inner geek and keeps me on my toes by asking complicated and challenging technical questions. And to my talented, inspiring, since-childhood friend Joe Hutsko, without whom I wouldn't be doing any of this techie stuff.

Authors' Acknowledgments

You see the author's names on the cover, but these books (like any book) are really a collaboration, an effort of a many-membered team. Thanks go to Bob Woerner at Wiley for trusting Joe's judgment and taking a chance on an unknown author. We couldn't have completed this book without our terrific project editor, Jean Nelson, who kept track of everything and kept everything on track. We truly appreciated our sharp-eyed, guitar-playing copy editor, Barry Childs-Helton, for polishing our book with his precise edits. A big hats off to Dennis R. Cohen for his insightful and accurate technical editing and witty comments that often made us laugh out loud during author review. Thanks, too, to the anonymous people at Wiley who contributed to this book — not just editorial, but tech support, legal, accounting, even the person who delivers the mail. We don't know you, but we appreciate the job you do; it takes a lot of worker bees to keep the hive healthy, and each task is important to the whole.

We want to thank our literary agent, Carole Jelen, for her astute representation and moral support. Carole plays a key role in our success, promoting us and keeping an eye out for new opportunities.

Thanks to the folks at Apple who developed such cool products, and specifically to Keri Walker for her ongoing editorial product support. Also, a special thanks to the app developers who shared their products and their time — their names are too many to list here, but please take our word for it when we say this book wouldn't have been complete without your support.

Joe adds: Major thanks to my dear, long-time friend Barbara Boyd, who stepped up to the plate as co-author on both this book and *iPhone All-in-One For Dummies* when my life and work focuses shifted to other time-sensitive projects and matters; writing and making deadlines on both books would have been impossible without Barbara's contribution. I mean it quite literally when I say both books are more Barbara's than mine, from perspectives of total word count, attention to detail, and commitment. Lastly, I am pleased to see Barbara managed to slip in a reference to her beloved bees in our Acknowledgments.

Barbara adds: Not a day goes by that I'm not grateful to my dear, long-time friend, and co-author, Joe. I love my job and working with him is a joy, but the real reason is that by asking me to write this book, I've gotten back in the habit of writing every day and there aren't enough thanks for that. Through the years, I've gotten several jobs by following in Joe's footsteps, but this one is by far the best. And a heartfelt "thank you" to my sister, Bonnie, whose enthusiasm was perhaps more than my own about writing this book. She's my biggest fan and personal cheerleader.

Publisher's Acknowledgments

We're proud of this book; please send us your comments at http://dummies.custhelp.com. For other comments, please contact our Customer Care Department within the U.S. at 877-762-2974, outside the U.S. at 317-572-3993, or fax 317-572-4002.

Some of the people who helped bring this book to market include the following:

Acquisitions, Editorial

Project Editor: Jean Nelson

Executive Editor: Bob Woerner

Senior Copy Editor: Barry Childs-Helton

Technical Editor: Dennis R. Cohen

Editorial Manager: Jodi Jensen

Editorial Assistant: Amanda Graham

Sr. Editorial Assistant: Cherie Case

Cover Photo: © iStockphoto.com / StockLib

Cartoons: Rich Tennant (www.the5thwave.com)

Composition Services

Project Coordinator: Nikki Gee

Layout and Graphics: Carl Byers, Amy Hassos, Joyce Haughey, Laura Westhuis

Proofreaders: Melissa Cossell, Bonnie Mikkelson

Indexer: BIM Indexing & Proofreading Services

Publishing and Editorial for Technology Dummies

    Richard Swadley, Vice President and Executive Group Publisher

    Andy Cummings, Vice President and Publisher

    Mary Bednarek, Executive Acquisitions Director

    Mary C. Corder, Editorial Director

Publishing for Consumer Dummies

    Kathleen Nebenhaus, Vice President and Executive Publisher

Composition Services

    Debbie Stailey, Director of Composition Services

Contents at a Glance

Table of Contents

Introduction

Whether you're a beginner, an intermediate user, or a seasoned computer expert, you can find something in *Macs All-in-One For Dummies,* 3rd Edition, for you. This book is divided into six minibooks so you can focus on the topics that interest you and skip over the ones that don't. We explored every menu and button of the Mac, its operating system, and Apple's iLife and iWork applications and wrote about most of them, focusing on the functions and features we think you'll use frequently or that will help you get the most out of your Mac and the applications. However, if you find that you want more detailed explanations on specific topics than this book provides, you should look into a more specialized book, such as *iWork '09 For Dummies* by Jesse Feiler or *iLife '11 For Dummies* by Tony Bove (both published by John Wiley & Sons, Inc.).

About This Book

This book focuses on the basics for all the aspects of using a Mac, from turning it on and using the mouse and trackpad to connecting your Mac to the Internet and e-mail to organizing your digital pictures and videos to creating photo albums and home movies with fancy captivating special effects to . . . you get the idea.

This book also shows you how to use and take advantage of Apple's iWork suite, which provides word processing, desktop publishing, a presentation program, and a spreadsheet program for calculating formulas and displaying your data as 3D charts. Whether you use a Mac for work, school, or just for fun, you'll find that with the right software applications, your Mac can meet all your computing needs.

If you're migrating to a Mac from a Windows desktop or notebook PC, this book can show you how to install Windows on your Mac so you can run your favorite Windows programs. By running Windows on a Mac, you can turn your Mac into two computers for the price of one.

If you're new to the Mac, you'll find that this book introduces you to all the main features of your Mac. If you're already a Mac user, you'll find information on topics you might not know much about. After reading this book, you'll have the foundation and confidence to move on to more advanced books, or delve deeper into your Mac's bundled applications and others you can buy for experimenting on your own.

Foolish Assumptions

In writing this book, we made a few assumptions about you, dear reader. To make sure that we're on the same page, we assume that

✦ You know something, but not necessarily a whole lot, about computers and you want to find out the basics of using a Mac or doing more with your Mac than you are already.

✦ You have at least a general concept of this wild and crazy thing called the Internet — or more precisely, the phenomenon known as the Web (or, more formally, the World Wide Web).

✦ You'll turn to the introductory chapters if you find yourself scratching your head at such terms as *double-click, drag and drop, scroll,* and *Control-click* — or any other terms that sound like things we think you should know but you don't.

✦ You appreciate the speed at which technology-based products like the Mac (and the programs you can run on it) can change in as little as a few months, with newer, sleeker, faster models and application versions replacing previous versions.

✦ You acknowledge that it's up to you to go on the Web to find updated information about the products described throughout this book.

✦ You know that keeping up with the topic of all things high-tech and Mac (even as a full-time job, as it is for us) still can't make a guy or gal the be-all and end-all Mac Genius of the World. You will, therefore, alert us to cool stuff you discover in your Mac odyssey so that we can consider including it in the next edition of this book.

✦ You're here to have fun, or at least try to have fun, as you dive into The Wonderful World of Mac.

Conventions Used in This Book

To help you navigate this book efficiently, we use a few style conventions:

✦ Terms or words that we *truly* want to emphasize are *italicized* (and defined).

✦ Website addresses, or URLs, are shown in a special monofont typeface, `like this`. If you're reading this book as an e-book, URLs will be active hyperlinks like this: `www.dummies.com`.

✦ Numbered steps that you need to follow and characters you need to type are set in **bold**.

✦ *Control-click* means to hold the Control key and click the mouse. If you're using a mouse that has a left and right button, you can right-click rather than Control-click. If you have one of Apple's trackpads, tap with two fingers.

What You Don't Have to Read

You don't have to read anything that doesn't pertain to what you're interested in. In fact, you can even skip one or more chapters entirely. We hope you don't skip too many, though, because we bet some of the chapters you think you might not be interested in might surprise you and be interesting after all.

That said, if you're absolutely, totally, 100 percent new to computers, we suggest that you read (or at least scan) Book I, and then move on to the minibooks you're interested in reading in any order you want.

As for the occasional sidebar you encounter in this book, feel free to ignore them because they contain, for the most part, tangential thoughts, miniature essays, or otherwise forgettable blathering that you're just as likely to forget anyway after you read them. Ditto for any of the text you see alongside the Technical Stuff icon.

How This Book Is Organized

Don't be afraid of this book because of its hefty bulk. You won't necessarily need (or want) to read this whole thing from cover to cover, and that's fine. Think of this book more as a reference along the lines of an encyclopedia or a dictionary than as step-by-step operating instructions that require you to read every page in sequence.

To help you find just the information you need, this book is divided into six minibooks, where each minibook tackles a specific topic independent of the other minibooks. Any time you have questions, just flip to the minibook that covers that particular topic.

Each minibook introduces a specific topic and then explains the details and procedures for doing the focus of that particular minibook. Here's a brief description of what you can find in each minibook.

Book 1: Mac Basics

This minibook explains everything you need to know just to use your Mac, such as how to turn it on and off, how to use the mouse, trackpad, keyboard, and multi-touch gestures to interact with the Mac user interface. Even if you're familiar with using a Mac, you might want to skim through this mini-book to pick up tidbits of information you might not know.

Book 11: Online Communications

This minibook shows you how to connect your Mac to the Internet and what you can do after you're connected. This minibook gives you the basics of using the Safari web browser, using e-mail with the Mail program, using iChat and FaceTime to conduct video conferences and phone calls, and taking steps to protect your Mac from online security threats, such as junk e-mail and malicious software known as malware and viruses.

Book III: Beyond the Basics

This minibook is the one to read if you want to go beyond the basics and do more with your Mac. This minibook contains explanations for backing up your Mac with Time Machine so your important information and programs are always safe and sound, and using iCloud to sync your Mac with other devices such as your mobile phone or iPad. Look here for troubleshooting advice and how to run Windows on your Mac. Windows programs? Yes, you read right — your Mac is an Equal Opportunity Computer, and running Windows on your Mac is easy thanks to the Boot Camp application that turns your Mac into two computers in one.

Book IV: Your Mac As a Multimedia Entertainment Center

This minibook takes entertainment to a new level. Here, entertaining topics are explained, such as organizing digital photographs, listening to audio files of your favorite songs, reading books, listening to podcasts, and watching movies, videos, and even university lectures. In this minibook, you also discover how to make movies and music and save it all on CDs or DVDs.

Book V: Taking Care of Business

This minibook is about the business applications that came with your Mac. This minibook shows you how to store names and addresses with Address Book, track appointments with iCal, even build a website with iWeb. If you want to write reports, create presentations, or crunch numbers, this minibook has your name written all over it. From using Keynote to turn out crowd-pleasing presentations loaded with charts and videos to using Numbers to crunch numbers every which way to your heart's delight (and your accountant's) to writing the next Great American Dummies Book by using Pages, this minibook is all about getting down to business — and having a little fun along the way.

Book VI: Mac Networking

This minibook explains what you need to know to set up a network of Mac computers so you can share hard drives, folders, and printers with other Mac computers. In this minibook, you also discover how to use your Mac's built-in Wi-Fi and Bluetooth features to connect to wireless keyboards and mice, and even your smartphone and other Mac and Windows computers so you can send information over the air between your Mac and other devices and computers. Look, Ma, no wires!

Icons Used in This Book

To help emphasize certain information, this book displays different icons in the page margins.

The Tip icon points out useful nuggets of information that can help you get things done more efficiently or direct you to something helpful that you might not know.

Watch out! This icon highlights something that can go terribly wrong if you're not careful, such as wiping out your important files or messing up your Mac. Make sure that you read any Warning information before following any instructions.

This icon points out some useful information that isn't quite as important as a Tip but not as threatening as a Warning. If you ignore this information, you can't hurt your files or your Mac, but you might miss something useful.

This icon highlights interesting information that isn't necessary to know but can help explain why certain things work the way they do on a Mac. Feel free to skip this information if you're in a hurry, but browse through this information when you have time. You might find out something interesting that can help you use your Mac.

Where to Go from Here

If you already know what type of help you need, jump right to that particular minibook and start reading. If you just want to know more about your Mac, feel free to skip around and browse through any minibook that catches your eye.

For starters, you might want to begin with Book I and find out about the basics of using your Mac. This first minibook will likely show you new or different ways to do something and help you fully take control of your Mac.

No matter what your experience is with the Mac, don't be afraid to explore and keep making new discoveries. While you expand your growing knowledge, you'll find that the capabilities of your Mac expand right along with you. If you know what you want to do, your Mac can probably help you, and this book can show you how.

Book I

Mac Basics

The 5th Wave   By Rich Tennant

"I'm ordering our new MacBook. Do you want it left-brain or right-brain oriented?"

Contents at a Glance

Chapter 1: Starting to Use Your Mac

Before you can use your Mac, you have to start it up — which makes perfect sense. Now, get ready for the counterintuitive part. After you have your Mac up and running, you can just leave it on.

In this chapter, we show you how to start and restart your Mac, and how to put it to sleep and shut it down completely. Sprinkled throughout this chapter is technical information about the various Mac models and what goes on inside that makes your Mac tick — we tried to make our explanations as clear and simple as possible. At the end of the chapter, we show you how to find out precisely which features your Mac has.

Starting Your Mac

Here's the simple way to start your Mac — the way you'll probably use 99 percent of the time: Press the Power button.

Depending on the type of Mac you have, the power button might be in back (Mac mini and some iMacs), front (Mac Pro and some iMacs), or above the keyboard (on notebook models, MacBook Air and MacBook Pro).

A few seconds after you press the power button, your Mac chimes to let you know that it's starting. (Techie types say *booting up*, a term derived from the phrase "to lift yourself up by the bootstraps.")

The moment electricity courses through, your Mac's electronic brain immediately looks for instructions embedded inside a special Read-Only Memory (or ROM) chip. While your computer is reading these instructions (also known as *firmware*), it displays the Apple logo on the screen to let you know that the computer is working and hasn't forgotten about you.

The firmware instructions tell the computer to make sure that all of its components are working. If some part of your computer (say a memory chip) is defective, your computer will stop. Unless you know something about repairing the physical parts of a Macintosh, this is the time to haul your Mac to the nearest Apple Store or authorized repair shop, or to call Apple Support to arrange shipping your bummed-out Mac directly to Apple for repair (800-275-2273 in the United States).

Sometimes a Mac might refuse to start correctly because of software problems. To fix software problems, check out Book III, Chapter 3, which explains how to perform basic troubleshooting on a Mac.

After your computer determines that all components are working, the last set of instructions on the chip tells the computer, "Now that you know all your parts are working, load an operating system."

When you unpack your Mac and turn it on for the very first time, it asks you to type your name and make up a password to create an account for using your Mac. To guide you through the process of setting up a Mac for the first time, a special application called the Setup Assistant runs, which asks for your time zone, the date, and whether you want to transfer files and applications from another Mac to your newer one. Normally, you need to run through this initial procedure only once, but you also have to perform this procedure if you reinstall your operating system, which we refer to as OS throughout this book. We explain reinstalling the OS in Book III, Chapter 3, too. The most important part of this initial procedure is remembering the password you choose because you'll need it to log in to your account, change some of the settings in System Preferences, or install new software.

An operating system is the program that controls your computer and is almost always stored on your computer's built-in hard drive (rather than on an external drive). On the Mac, the operating system is named Mac OS X (for Macintosh Operating System number ten) and is followed by a version number, such as 10.7.

Apple code-names each version of OS X. The current version is OS X 10.7 Lion, which succeeds OS X 10.6 Snow Leopard, which succeeded 10.5 Leopard, which in turn succeeded 10.4 Tiger, which was preceded by 10.3 Panther, and so on.

After the operating system loads and you log in, you can start using your computer to run other applications so you can write a letter or send an e-mail, browse the web, calculate your taxes, or play a game. (You know, all the things you bought your Mac for in the first place.)

Putting a Mac in Sleep Mode

After you finish using your Mac, you don't have to turn it off and then turn it on when you want to use it again. To save time (and do the "green" thing by conserving energy!), put your Mac into Sleep mode instead. When you put your Mac to sleep, it shuts down almost every power-draining component of your Mac, and draws only a teensy trickle of power so you can instantly wake it up with a touch of the keyboard or click of the mouse. Presto change-o: Your Mac immediately returns to the same state you left it in, without making you wait the minute or more it takes to power on when it's completely shut down.

To put your Mac to sleep, you have a choice of doing it manually or automatically. When you need to be away from your Mac for a short period (such as pouring a second cup of joe), you might want to put your Mac to sleep manually. If you suddenly bolt to the kitchen to tend to a smoking stovetop emergency without putting your Mac to sleep, your Mac can thoughtfully put itself to sleep for you, automatically.

To put your Mac to sleep manually, choose one of the following three actions:

✦ **Choose ⌥Sleep.**

✦ **Press the power button or Control+Eject** and, when a dialog appears, shown in Figure 1-1, click the Sleep button (or press the S key on your Mac's keyboard).

Figure 1-1:
Put your
computer in
Sleep mode.

✦ **Press ⌘+Option+Eject.** (If you have a MacBook Air, your Mac doesn't have an eject key because it doesn't have a disk drive.)

✦ **If you have a MacBook, just close its lid.** When a MacBook is sleeping, you can safely move it without worrying about jarring the built-in hard drive that spins most of the time your MacBook is "awake" and in use.

The Apple menu is located in the upper-left corner of the screen.

To put your Mac to sleep automatically, you set the amount of time your Mac sits idle before it goes to sleep. Follow these steps:

1. **Click the Apple (🍎) menu, choose System Preferences, and then click the Energy Saver icon in the Hardware section or right-click (control-click on a trackpad) the System Preferences icon on the Dock and choose Energy Saver from the menu that appears.**

   The Energy Saver window appears, as shown in Figure 1-2.

2. **On the timescale next to Computer Sleep, click and drag the slider to the amount of time you want your Mac to sit idle before it goes to sleep. The exact time is shown on the right, above the timescale, as you move the slider.**

   This setting puts the hard drive to sleep. You may want to set a longer time interval for Computer Sleep than for Display Sleep because it will take your Mac slightly longer to wake from its Computer Sleep than its Display Sleep.

3. **On the timescale next to Display Sleep, click and drag the slider to the amount of time you want your Mac to sit idle before the screen saver plays on the display.**

   This setting puts the display to sleep. A screen saver is an image that appears when your Mac is inactive after the time interval you set here. It hides whatever you were working on from peering eyes when you're away from your Mac. You can find out how to choose a special image for your screen saver and set a password for it in Book I, Chapter 5.

   If your computer is doing a task, such as downloading a sizeable file, set Computer Sleep to Never and set only Display Sleep with a time interval. This way your Mac continues to do the task at hand even though the display is sleeping.

4. **(Optional) Select the check boxes next to the other options to choose other circumstances when your Mac goes to sleep or wakes.**

5. **(Optional) Click the Schedule button.**

   A pane opens that lets you schedule the days and times you want your Mac to start or wake up and go to sleep. This is convenient if you don't want to accidently leave your Mac on when you leave your home or office or want to find it awake and waiting for you when you arrive.

6. **Click the Lock icon at the bottom of the pane if you want your changes to be password protected.**

7. **Choose Systems Preferences⇨Quit System Preferences or click the red button in the upper-left corner, which closes the window.**

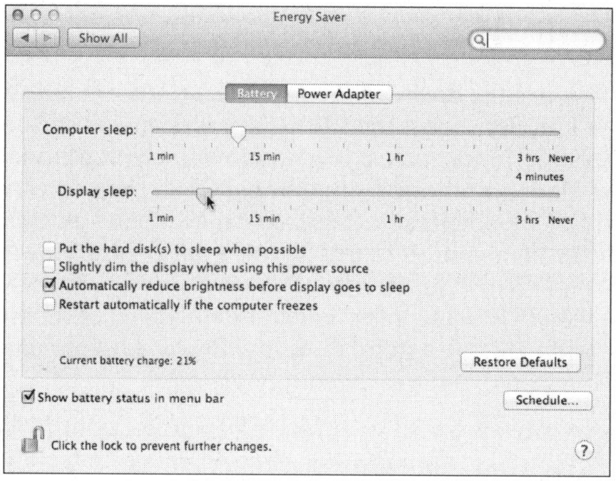

Figure 1-2:
Use the
Energy
Saver
System
Preferences
to put your
Mac on
a sleep
schedule.

If you have a MacBook Air or MacBook Pro, click the Battery and Power Adapter tabs at the top of the pane to choose different settings for when your Mac is running on battery power and when it's connected to a power adapter (refer to Figure 1-2). When powered by the battery, you may want your Mac to go to sleep after 5 minutes to make the battery charge last longer. When your Mac is connected to a power source, you could set it to go to sleep after 15 minutes. You can also select the Show Battery Status In Menu Bar check box to see an icon, at the top of your Mac's screen, that indicates how much charge is left on your battery.

To wake a sleeping Mac, click the mouse button or tap any key. To keep from accidentally typing any characters into a currently running application, press a noncharacter key, such as Shift or an arrow key. Open the lid on your sleeping MacBook to wake it up.

Depending on which Mac model you own, you may notice a built-in combination power/sleep indicator light that softly pulses like a firefly when your Mac is in Sleep mode. On the MacBook Pro, the power/sleep indicator light is on the front edge below the right wrist rest. On the Mac mini, the indicator light is in the lower-right corner. No such light is anywhere on the iMac or the latest MacBook Air, which appear to be totally in the dark when they're asleep.

Shutting Down Your Mac

When you shut your Mac down, all open applications are automatically closed, Internet and network connections are disconnected, and all logged-in users are logged out. It may take a few minutes for your Mac to shut down. You know your Mac is shut down completely when the screen is black, the hard drive and fan are silent, and there are no blinking lights anywhere. There are a few circumstances in which you want to shut down your Mac:

✦ When you won't be using it for an extended length of time. Turning your Mac completely off can extend its useful life, waste less energy, and save you a few bucks on your yearly energy expense.

✦ When you're traveling with your Mac and putting your MacBook Air, MacBook Pro, or Mac Mini in your wheeled carry-on trolley. (Sleep mode is fine if you're carrying your Mac in a laptop bag or backpack.)

Make sure that your MacBook Air or MacBook Pro is completely shut down before closing the cover or it may not shut down properly.

✦ If you want to open your Mac to install a new battery, additional memory, or a video graphics card.

✦ To resolve weird situations, such as unresponsive or slow-running applications, because your Mac runs a number of behind-the-scenes file system housekeeping chores every time you start it.

You have three ways to shut down your Mac:

✦ **Choose **✦⟳**Shut Down,** as shown in Figure 1-3. A dialog appears, asking if you're sure that you want to shut down. (Refer to Figure 1-1.) Click Cancel or Shut Down. (If you don't click either option, your Mac will shut down automatically after one minute.)

Figure 1-3:
Use this menu to turn off your computer.

Holding the Option key and then choosing Shut Down bypasses the prompt asking if you're sure that you want to shut down. (Yes, Mr. Mac, I'm *sure* I'm sure, but thank you for your concern.)

✦ **Press Control+Eject or press the power button** and when a dialog appears, click the Shut Down button, or press the Return key.

Select the Reopen Windows When Logging Back In check box if you want everything you're working on to be open when you turn your Mac on the next time.

✦ **Press and hold the power button** to force your Mac to shut down after a few seconds' wait (or press and hold ⌘+Control and then press the power button to force your Mac to shut down immediately).

The last option, a *force shutdown,* forces all running applications to shut down right away. A force shutdown is your last resort if your Mac appears to have frozen and is unresponsive. If only a single application is freezing or acting flaky, it's better to force quit that single application instead of shutting down your entire computer. (See Book III, Chapter 3 for information about how to force quit a single application.) Performing a force shutdown can cause you to lose any changes you've made to a letter or other file you're working on since the last time you saved it before the lockup. That's why you should use force shutdown only as a last resort.

Restarting a Mac

Sometimes the Mac can start acting sluggish, or applications might fail to run. When that happens, you can choose Shut Down or Restart to properly shut down or restart your Mac and then start it again, which essentially clears your computer's memory and starts it fresh.

To restart your computer, you have three choices:

✦ **Press the power button or Control+Eject** and, when a dialog appears, click the Restart button (refer to Figure 1-1) or press the R key.

✦ **Choose Restart**.

✦ **Press Control+⌘+Eject.**

When you restart your computer, your Mac closes all running applications; you will have the chance to save any files you're working on. After you choose to save any files, those applications are closed and then your Mac will shut down and boot up again.

Different Macintosh Models

Apple's Macintosh computer — Mac for short — enjoys the reputation of being the easiest computer to use in the world. Additionally, Macs are dependable, durable, and so beautifully designed, they incite techno-lust in gadget geeks like us, and ordinary Joes alike. For those doubly good reasons, you probably won't buy a new Mac to replace your old one because you *have* to, but because you *want* to.

The Macintosh has been around since 1984, and since that time, Apple has produced a wide variety of Mac models. Although you can still find and use older Macs (although many are not compatible with the latest and greatest OS or applications), chances are good that if you buy a newer Mac, it will fall into one of three categories:

✦ **Desktop:** Mac mini or Mac Pro, which require a separate display.

✦ **All-in-one desktop:** iMac, which houses the display and computer in one unit.

✦ **Notebook:** MacBook Air or MacBook Pro, which have built-in keyboards, trackpads that work like a mouse at the touch of your fingertip, and bright displays; a clamshell design lets you close and tote them in your backpack, messenger bag, or briefcase.

Like today's iMac, the original Mac came with a built-in display, a keyboard, and a mouse. The Mac Pro also comes with a keyboard and mouse, but no display, whereas the Mac Mini has neither keyboard, mouse, nor display sold with it. When you buy a Mac desktop, you can connect a display you already own, or you can buy a new one, such as Apple's LED Cinema Display. This LED display consumes 30 percent less power than conventional LCD displays, and it lights to full brightness when powered on (without needing time to warm up). What's more, the same LED-type display is standard equipment on every MacBook model.

By understanding the particular type of Mac that you have and its capabilities, you'll have a better idea of what your Mac can do. No matter what the capabilities of your Mac are, chances are good that it will work reliably for as long as you own it.

The Mac Mini and Mac Pro

The biggest advantage of both the Mac Mini and the Mac Pro are that you can choose the type of display to use and place it anywhere you want on your desk as long as you have a cable that can reach. The Mac Mini, however, is small enough to hide under your desk, or situate in a corner of your desktop.

The Mac Mini is a lower-priced, consumer version designed for people who want an inexpensive Mac for ordinary uses, such as word processing and writing, sending e-mail, browsing the web, and playing video games. Alternatively, it can function as a terrific, cost-effective server for home or small business networks.

The Mac Pro is a higher-priced, professional version with multiple drive bays and lots of expandability, as well as greater graphics and processing capabilities because of its advanced graphics processor and use of multiple processors.

The iMac

The all-in-one design of the iMac is an evolutionary extension of the original — 1984-era — Mac design. The iMac combines the computer with a built-in display and speakers. On iMac models, it's possible to connect external speakers and a second external display if you want.

The advantage of the all-in-one design of the iMac is that you have everything you need in a single unit. The disadvantage is that if one part of your iMac fails (such as the display, or the internal DVD drive), you can't easily replace the failed part.

Mac Mini, Mac Pro, and iMac models use an external wireless or wired (usually USB) keyboard and a mouse or trackpad (sold separately from the Mini). Apple's Magic Trackpad lets you use all the new multi-touch gestures such as swipe, pinch, and flick to control the cursor and windows on whichever Mac desktop model you choose. If you use a trackpad, you don't need a mouse but you can use both if you prefer.

The MacBook Air and MacBook Pro

MacBook Air and MacBook Pro are the notebook members of the Mac family. The MacBook Air comes with an 11-inch or 13-inch screen, and the MacBook Pro models come in three screen sizes: 13-inch, 15-inch, and 17-inch. All the MacBook models run on rechargeable battery packs or external power.

To make the MacBook Air as thin as a magazine, Apple did not include a built-in DVD drive. An optional external DVD drive, or connecting to another computer on a network to use its DVD drive, are how the MacBook Air can access CDs, DVDs, and software applications on discs. MacBook Pro models come with built-in DVD drives. If you need to take your Mac everywhere you go, you can choose from the ultralight MacBook Air or one of the MacBook Pro models.

With a fast Internet connection, many data transfer functions such as downloading applications or sharing photos and documents can take place online, making the DVD drive even more optional than before. Apple's latest OS, Mac OS X 10.7 Lion was initially delivered via the Internet rather than on an installation disc, although you can also purchase it on a USB memory stick.

The main differences in the MacBook Air and MacBook Pro are weight and storage. The MacBook Air may not weigh much but it's no lightweight when it comes to features. The latest models are fast and even the 11-inch model offers a display so crisp and brilliant you hardly notice the size. The downside is that the maximum storage is 256 gigabytes on the high-end 13-inch model. MacBook Air uses SSD (solid state drive) storage, which is fast and stable. The MacBook Pro models use HDD (hard disk drive) storage, which holds between 320 and 750 gigabytes. Pro models also have built-in double-layer CD/DVD drives, and Ethernet, Firewire, and audio line in ports (in addition to the USB, Thunderbolt, and audio line out ports and SDXC card slot that all MacBook models have). The downside of the MacBook Pro is that extra stuff adds weight. We didn't realize quite how much weight until we switched from a Pro to an Air. Although both MacBook Air and MacBook Pro models have full-size keyboards, neither includes the extra numeric keypad found on most external keyboards or on larger Windows notebooks. Instead of the mouse that comes in the box with every desktop Mac (or Windows computer, for that matter), the MacBooks use a built-in trackpad, which responds to all the multi-touch gestures you can use to control the cursor and windows on your Mac.

If you find the keyboard or trackpad of your notebook Mac too clumsy to use, you can always plug an external keyboard and mouse into your notebook.

The Thunderbolt port is standard on all newer Macs. Thunderbolt is a data-transfer protocol used to connect peripheral devices such as displays or hard drives. Thunderbolt transfers data faster than either USB or FireWire protocols.

Understanding Mac Processors

The *processor* acts as the brain of your Mac. A computer is only as powerful as the processor inside. Generally, the newer your computer, the newer its processor and the faster it will run.

In Spring 2006, Macs started shipping with Intel processors, which are the same type of processors used in many Windows PCs. Intel processors are less expensive than earlier Macs' PowerPC processors and more powerful. Intel processors also give the Mac the capability to run the Microsoft Windows operating system (although dyed-in-the-wool Mac loyalists would wryly consider that a drawback — if not outright blasphemy!).

The type of processor in your Mac can determine the applications (also known as *software*) your Mac can run. Before you buy any software, make sure that it can run on your computer.

To identify the type of processor used in your Mac, click the Apple menu in the upper-left corner of the screen and choose About This Mac. An About This Mac window appears, listing your processor as Intel Core 2 Duo, Core i3, Core i5, Core i7, or Xeon. If your Mac doesn't have one of these processors, you won't be able to run Mac OS X 10.7 Lion. This means Core Solo and Core Duo models can't run Lion. To use Lion, you also need at least 2GB RAM (Random Access Memory).

The Intel family of processors includes the Core Solo, Core Duo, Core 2 Duo, dual-core i3, dual-core i5, quad-core i7, and Xeon, where the Core Solo is the slowest and the Xeon is the fastest. Every processor runs at a specific speed, so a 2.0-gigahertz (GHz) Core 2 Duo processor will be slower than a 2.4 GHz Core 2 Duo processor. However, the type of storage your Mac has can skew this theory. The newest MacBook Air has a 1.7- or 1.8 GHz processor, but uses FlashMemory (the same kind of memory in your USB flash drive), so in benchmarking tests, the MacBook Air at 1.7 GHz is about as fast as the MacBook Pro at 2.2 GHz. If understanding processor types and gigahertz confuses you, just remember that the most expensive computer is usually the fastest.

Move the cursor over the More Info button and click to see an expanded window of information about your Mac, as shown in Figure 1-4. Click each of the buttons at the top of the window to open panes that show more information about your Mac: Displays, Storage (shown in Figure 1-5), and Memory. Click the Support button at top right for links to the Help Center and user manuals. Click the Service button to access links to information about your Mac's warranty and AppleCare Protection.

Figure 1-4:
The About
This Mac
window
identifies
the
processor
used in your
Mac.

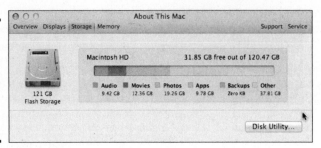

Figure 1-5:
About This
Mac panes
tell you how
your Mac's
storage is
used.

Identifying the Parts of Your Mac

By looking at your Mac, you can tell whether it's an all-in-one design (iMac), a notebook (MacBook Air or MacBook Pro), or a desktop unit that lacks a built-in screen (Mac mini or Mac Pro). However, looking at the outside of your Mac can't tell you the parts used on the inside. To identify the parts and capabilities of your Mac, follow these steps:

1. **Click the Apple menu in the upper-left corner of the screen and choose About This Mac.**

   An About This Mac window appears (refer to Figure 1-4).

2. **Click More Info, and then click System Report.**

   A System Report window appears.

3. **Click the Hardware option in the category pane on the left to view a list of hardware items.**

   If the list of hardware items (such as Bluetooth, Memory, and USB) already appears under the Hardware category, skip this step.

4. **Click a hardware item, such as Memory or Disc Burning.**

   The right pane of the System Profiler window displays the capabilities of your chosen hardware, as shown in Figure 1-6.

5. **You can also click the disclosure triangle next to Network or Software in the category pane on the left to see information about networks you are connected to or software installed on your Mac.**

Don't worry if the information displayed in the System Information window doesn't make much sense to you right now. The main idea here is to figure out a quick way to find out about the capabilities of your Mac, which can be especially helpful if you have a problem in the future and a technician asks for information about your Mac.

If you really want to know, pick through the technical details to find the parts that you understand — and search the Internet to look up the details that you don't understand.

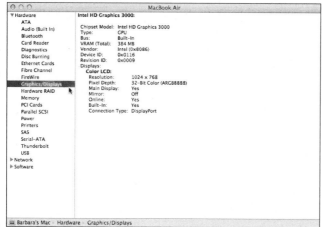

Figure 1-6:
The System
Report
identifies
the type and
capabilities
of the
hardware in
your Mac.

6. **When you finish scouting the contents of the System Report window, click the red circle in the upper-left corner to close the System Report window and return to the About This Mac window, or choose System Information⇨Quit System Information from the menu bar to close both the System Report and About This Mac.**

If you're going to look at anything in the System Report window, check out Disc Burning and Graphics/Displays under the Hardware option:

✦ **Disc Burning** tells you all about your DVD/CD–burning hardware, including general info about all the different types of CDs and DVDs your Mac can read and write to, so you'll know exactly which type to buy. (If you have a MacBook Air, you won't see this item unless you connect an external drive.)

✦ **Graphics/Displays** tells you whether your Mac has a separate graphics card. If you see *shared* in the VRAM category (Video RAM), your Mac doesn't have a separate graphics card and shares the main memory, which means its graphics capabilities will (usually) be slower than a Mac that has a separate graphics card. If you do not see *shared,* the VRAM category simply lists the amount of memory used by the separate graphics card. The more memory, the better your graphics capabilities.

If you have a Mac Pro, you have the option of replacing your graphics card with a better one. If you have any other type of Mac (iMac, MacBook Air, MacBook Pro, or Mac mini), your Mac's built-in graphics capabilities can't be upgraded with a more powerful graphics card.

Chapter 2: Getting Acquainted with the Mac User Interface

In This Chapter

✔ Using the mouse, trackpad, and keyboard

✔ Perusing menus and windows

✔ Getting familiar with the parts of the Desktop

✔ Working with Dashboard Widgets

✔ Getting help from your Mac

*T*heoretically, using a computer is simple. In practice, using a computer can cause people to suffer a wide range of emotions from elation to sheer frustration and despair.

The problem with using a computer stems mostly from two causes:

✦ Not knowing what the computer can do

✦ Not knowing how to tell the computer what you want it to do

In the early days of personal computers, this communication gap between users and computers arose mostly from ordinary people trying to use machines designed by engineers for other engineers. If you didn't understand how a computer engineer thinks (or doesn't think), computers seemed nearly impossible to understand.

Fortunately, Apple has solved this problem with the Mac. Instead of designing a computer for other computer engineers, Apple designed a computer for ordinary people. And what do ordinary people want? Here's the short (but definitely important) list:

✦ Reliability

✦ Ease of use

From a technical point of view, what makes the Mac reliable is its operating system, Mac OS X. An operating system is nothing more than an application that makes your computer actually work.

An operating system works in the background. When you use a computer, you don't really notice the operating system, but you do see its *user interface* — which functions like a clerk at the front desk of a hotel: Instead of talking directly to the housekeeper or the plumber (the operating system), you always talk to the front desk clerk, and the clerk talks to the housekeeper or plumber.

Apple designed a user interface that everyone can understand. With Mac OS X 10.7 Lion, Apple added multi-touch interface, which makes the user interface even more intuitive and hands-on, literally.

Mastering the Mouse, Trackpad, and Keyboard

To control your Mac, you use the mouse or trackpad and the keyboard. Using both the mouse or trackpad and the keyboard, you can choose commands, manipulate items on the screen, or create such data as text or pictures.

Using the mouse

A typical mouse looks like a bar of soap. The main purpose of the mouse is to move a pointer on the screen, which tells the computer, "See what I'm pointing at right now? That's what I want to select." To select an item on the screen, you move the mouse (which in turn makes the onscreen pointer move), put the pointer on that item, and then press and release (click) the mouse button, or press down the top, left side of the mouse if you have a mouse, such as Apple's Mighty Mouse or Magic Mouse, that doesn't have buttons.

The whole surface of the Apple Magic Mouse uses touch-sensitive technology that detects your fingertip gestures just like the MacBook trackpads. These are the basic mouse gestures:

✦ **Clicking (also called single-clicking)** is the most common activity with a mouse. With the Magic Mouse, move the mouse and tap anywhere on the surface. If you have an older mouse with buttons or an Apple Mighty Mouse, pressing the left mouse button, or the left side of the mouse, is clicking.

✦ **Double-clicking:** If you point at something and tap twice in rapid succession on the surface (that is, you *double-click* it), you can often select an item and open it at the same time. (Click the left mouse button or the mouse's single button twice in rapid succession on an older mouse.)

✦ **Dragging:** Another common activity with the mouse is *dragging* — pointing at an item on the screen, holding down the left mouse button or the mouse's single button, moving the mouse, and then releasing the button. Dragging is often the way to move items around onscreen.

✦ **Control-clicking/right-clicking:** Holding down the Control key while you click, or clicking the right button on the mouse, commonly displays a menu of commands (called a contextual or shortcut menu) at the point you clicked to do something with the item that the mouse is currently pointing at. For example, if you point at a misspelled word, right-clicking that misspelled word can display a list of properly spelled words to choose from, as shown in Figure 2-1.

On the MagicMouse, hold down the Control key and tap to click. To simulate a right-click with a single-button mouse, hold down the Control key and click the mouse button. On a two-button mouse, hold the right button and click the left (press and hold the right side of a MightyMouse surface and press the left side).

You can set up the Magic Mouse to function like an old-style two-button mouse by clicking on the Apple menu and selecting System Preferences. Click Mouse in the Hardware section, and then select the Secondary Click check box. You can even choose left or right side, making it more natural if you're left-handed.

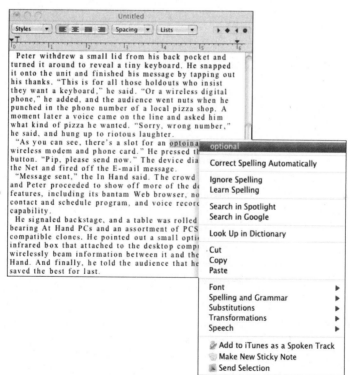

Figure 2-1:
Right-
clicking
typically
displays
a list of
commands
that you can
choose to
manipulate
an item.

✦ **Scrolling:** The surface of the MagicMouse has the sensitivity of a track-pad so you can move a finger up or down to scroll up and down the onscreen image (say, a word-processing document or a web page). Hold down the Control key while you scroll with one finger to zoom in on items on the screen.

✦ **Swipe:** Swipe two fingers left and right on the MagicMouse surface to move back and forth through web pages or to browse photos in iPhoto.

If you don't like the mouse that came with your Mac, you can always buy a replacement mouse or trackball. Some mice are molded to be a better fit for the shape of your hand, so find a mouse that you like and plug it into the USB port of your Mac, or get a wireless mouse that connects to your Mac using your Mac's Bluetooth wireless connection feature.

The trackpad

All of Apple's current MacBook models sport trackpads that can do more than most advanced multi-button mice. If you have a desktop model or find the trackpad on a MacBook model inconvenient, you can opt for the Magic Trackpad, which will give you all the multi-touch gestures.

Thanks to the trackpad's smart sensing abilities, *point-and-click* has a whole new meaning because you're often using your index (or pointer) finger to move the pointer and then tapping once on the trackpad to "click." A double-tap is the same as a double-click. Other gestures you can use with the trackpad are

✦ **Scroll:** Move what you see on the screen up and down or left to right is as easy as sliding or swiping two fingers up and down or across the trackpad. The items in the window follow the movement of your fingers, the window contents move up when you move your fingers up.

✦ **Rotate:** Move the window contents 360 degrees by placing two fingers on the trackpad and making a circular motion.

✦ **Swipe:** Swipe the tips of three or four fingers across the trackpad to perform various tasks:

  • Swipe up with three or four fingers to open Mission Control (see Book I, Chapter 3).

  • Swipe down with three or four fingers to open Mission Control (see Book I, Chapter 3).

  • Swipe left and right with three or four fingers to switch between full-screen applications or Spaces (see Book I, Chapter 3).

✦ **Pinch:** Place three fingers and your thumb slightly open on the track-pad, and then bring them together as if picking up a small item; doing so opens the Launchpad (see Book I, Chapter 3).

✦ **Unpinch:** Place three fingers and your thumb together on the trackpad and open them to move everything off the Desktop.

✦ **Control-click:** Hold the Control key and tap the trackpad.

✦ **Two-finger tap:** Tap the trackpad once with two fingers to Control-click/ right-click.

✦ **Two-finger double-tap:** Tap the trackpad twice with two fingers to zoom in on a web page.

✦ **Three-finger double-tap:** Tap the trackpad twice with three fingers to look up a word in the dictionary.

✦ **Three-finger drag:** Move the pointer to the title bar of a window and move it around on the desktop with three fingers.

Click System Preferences and choose Mouse or Trackpad in the Hardware section to specify how you want to use the mouse or trackpad and to see examples of how the multi-touch gestures work, as shown in Figure 2-2.

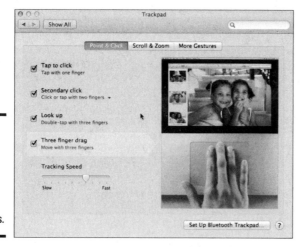

Figure 2-2:
See multi-touch gestures in action in System Preferences.

The parts of the keyboard

The primary use of the keyboard is to type information. However, the keyboard can also select items and menu commands — sometimes more quickly than using the mouse. Figure 2-3 shows that the keyboard groups related keys together. The next few sections cover each group of keys in detail.

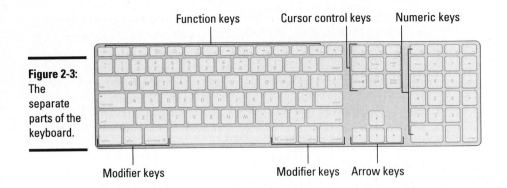

Figure 2-3:
The
separate
parts of the
keyboard.

Function keys   Cursor control keys   Numeric keys

Modifier keys   Modifier keys   Arrow keys

Special feature and function keys

Depending on your particular keyboard, you might see 12 to 20 function keys running along the top of the keyboard. These function keys are labeled F1 through F12/F19, along with an Escape key — brilliantly abbreviated "Esc" — and an Eject key that looks like a triangle on top of a horizontal line.

By default, every new and recent Mac's function key labels are tiny and shared by larger icons that represent special feature keys that you press to do things like turn down the screen brightness (F1), play or pause music you're listening to in iTunes (F8), or open your Mac's Dashboard Widgets application to check the weather forecast (F4). Although the icons on each of these special feature keys are self-evident, check out Table 2-1 to find out what all your Mac's special features keys do when you press them.

Table 2-1	Mac Assigned Commands
Function Key	*What It Does*
F1	Decreases display brightness
F2	Increases display brightness
F3	Displays Mission Control (displays Dashboard on older Macs)
F4	Displays Launchpad
F5	Decreases keyboard backlight brightness
F6	Increases keyboard backlight brightness
F7	Video and audio rewind
F8	Video and audio play/pause
F9	Video and audio fast-forward
F10	Mutes sound
F11	Decreases sound volume
F12	Increases sound volume

You actually select the Mac's application-specific function keys by pressing and holding the Fn key and *then* pressing one of the function keys on the upper row of the keyboard. In Microsoft Word, for instance, pressing Fn+F7 tells Word to run the spell checker; pressing Fn+F5 opens the Find and Replace dialog.

In other words, holding down the Fn key tells your Mac, "Ignore the special feature controls assigned to that function key listed in Table 3-1 and just behave like an old-fashioned function key."

To reverse the way the Mac's function keys work when you press them, choose ⌘⇨System Preferences and click the Keyboard icon. Click the Keyboard tab at the top of the window, and then select the check box next to Use All F1, F2, Etc. Keys as Standard Function Keys. When you activate this option, you *must* hold down the Fn key to perform the commands shown in Table 3-1, but you don't have to hold down the Fn key to use application-specific function keys as just described.

Pressing Fn+F10 shows you all windows that belong to the active application (this feature is called Exposé). You can identify the active application by looking for its name on the left side of the menu bar. Pressing Fn+F11 or ⌘+F3 shoves all windows out of the way so you can see the Desktop.

Pressing Fn+F12 (F3 on older Macs) displays the Dashboard application and its widgets, which are simple mini-applications, such as a calculator, calendar, or a display of your local weather forecast. You find out more about Dashboard in the later section, "The Dashboard."

As for the other keys — F1 through F7 and (possibly) F13 through F19 — holding the Fn key and pressing these fellows can carry out shortcut commands on a by-application basis. For instance, pressing Fn+F7 in Microsoft Word for the Macintosh opens the application's spelling and grammar checker.

Originally, function keys existed because some applications assigned commands to different function keys. Unfortunately, every application assigned different commands to identical function keys, which sometimes made function keys more confusing than helpful. You can assign your own commands to different function keys, but just remember that not every Mac will have the same commands assigned to the same function keys. (Not everyone thinks exactly like you, as amazing as that might seem.) To customize which function keys perform which commands, choose ⌘⇨System Preferences⇨Keyboard, and then click the Keyboard Shortcuts tab at the top of the window and adjust your Mac's keyboard shortcuts to your heart's content.

Turning to the two other keys grouped with the function keys, here's what you need to know. The Esc key often works as a "You may be excused" command. For example, if a pull-down menu appears on the screen and you want it to go away, press the Esc key. The Eject key ejects a CD or DVD from your Mac. (If you have a MacBook Air, there's no Eject key because there's no disk drive.)

Typewriter keys

You use the typewriter (also known as the *alphanumeric*) keys to create *data* — the typing-a-letter-in-a-word-processor stuff or the entering-of-names-and-addresses-into-the-Address-Book-application stuff. When you press a typewriter key, you're telling the Mac what character to type at the cursor position, which often appears as a blinking vertical line on the screen.

You can move the cursor by pointing to and clicking a new location with the mouse or by pressing the arrow keys as explained in the upcoming "Arrow keys" section.

One typewriter key that doesn't type anything is the big Delete key that appears to the right of the +/= key. The Delete key deletes any characters that appear to the left of the cursor. If you hold down the Delete key, your Mac deletes any characters to the left of the cursor until you lift your finger.

Two other typewriter keys that don't type anything are the Tab key and the Return key, which is sometimes labeled Enter on third-party external keyboards you can buy to use with your Mac. The Tab key indents text in a word processor, but it can also highlight different text boxes, such as ones in which you type your shipping address on the web page form of an online bookstore or another merchant.

The Return key moves the cursor to the next line in a word processor, but can also choose a default button (which appears in blue) on the screen. The default button in the Print dialog is labeled Print, and the default button in the Save dialog is labeled Save.

Holding Shift, Option, and Shift+Option while pressing another key on the keyboard results in different symbols or letters, such as uppercase letters or the symbol for trademark or square root. To see all the key combinations, choose ⌘➪System Preferences, and click Language & Text. Click Input Sources, and select the Keyboard & Character Viewer check box. Close System Preferences. An icon for the Keyboard and Character Viewer appears in the status bar at the top of your screen. Click the Keyboard & Character Viewer icon➪Show Keyboard Viewer. A graphic representation of the keyboard appears on your screen. Hold down the Shift, Option, or Shift+Option keys. The keyboard changes to show the letter or symbol that will be typed when you hold down Shift, Option, or Shift-Option and type a letter or number. Refer to the Cheat Sheet at `www.dummies.com/cheatsheet/macsaio` for more information about typing special characters.

Numeric keys

The numeric keys appear on the right side of the keyboard (if yours has them!) and arrange the numbers 0 through 9 in rows and columns like a typical calculator keypad. The main use for the numeric keys is to make typing numbers faster and easier than using the numeric keys on the top row of the typewriter keys.

On earlier MacBook keyboards, the numeric keys were assigned to a section of keys on the normal typewriter keys. To switch the numeric keys on, you had to press the Num Lock key (or press the Fn key with the desired numeric key). To switch the numeric keys off, you had to press the Num Lock key again. Recent and new MacBooks no longer sport these numeric keys.

Arrow keys

The cursor often appears as a vertical blinking line and acts like a place-holder. Wherever the cursor appears, that's where your next character will appear if you press a typewriter key. You can move the cursor with the mouse or trackpad, or you can move it with the arrow keys.

The up arrow moves the cursor up, the down arrow moves the cursor down, the right arrow moves the cursor right, and the left arrow moves the cursor left. (Could it be any more logical?) Depending on the application you're using, pressing an arrow key might move the cursor in different ways. For example, pressing the right arrow key in a word processor moves the cursor right one character, but pressing that same right arrow key in a spreadsheet might move the cursor to the adjacent cell on the right.

On some Mac keyboards, you might see four additional cursor-control keys labeled Home, End, Page Up, and Page Down. Typically, the Page Up key scrolls up one screen, and the Page Down key scrolls down one screen. Many applications ignore the Home and End keys, but some applications let you move the cursor with them. For example, Microsoft Word uses the Home key to move the cursor to the beginning of a line or row and the End key to move the cursor to the end of a line or row, and ⌘+Home/End moves the cursor to the beginning, or end, of a document.

Just because you might not see the Home, End, Page Up, and Page Down keys on your Mac or MacBook keyboard doesn't mean those command keys aren't there. On the MacBook that I'm using to write this, holding down the Fn key and then pressing the left arrow key acts as the Home key, which moves the cursor to the start of the line I'm on. Pressing Fn+→ jumps the cursor to the end of the current line, Fn+↑ scrolls the chapter up one page, and Fn+↓ scrolls the text down one page. Because seeing is believing, try it on your own Mac keyboard so you can see what I mean — even if you don't see keys bearing those actual labels, and ⌘+Fn+←/→ moves the cursor to the beginning or end of the document.

To the left of the End key, you might find a smaller Delete key. Like the bigger Delete key, this smaller Delete key also deletes characters one at a time.

The big Delete key erases characters to the *left* of the cursor. The small Delete key erases characters to the *right* of the cursor.

Modifier keys

Modifier keys are almost never used individually. Instead, modifier keys are usually held down while tapping another key. The five modifier keys are the Function (Fn) keys mentioned in a few of the previous sections: Shift, Control (Ctrl), Option, and ⌘ (Command).

If you press the S key in a word-processing document, your Mac types the letter "s" on the screen, but if you hold down a modifier key, such as the Command key (⌘), and then press the S key, the S key is modified to behave differently. In this case, holding down the ⌘ key followed by the S key (⌘+S) tells your word processing application to issue the Save command and save whatever you typed or changed since the last time you saved the document.

Most modifier keystrokes involve pressing two keys, such as ⌘+Q (the Quit command), but some modifier keystrokes can involve pressing three or four keys, such as Shift+⌘+3, which saves a snapshot of what you see on your screen as an image file, which is commonly referred to as a *screenshot*.

The main use for modifier keys is to help you choose commands quickly without fumbling with the mouse. Every application includes dozens of such keystroke shortcuts, but Table 2-2 lists the common keystroke shortcuts that work the same in most applications.

Table 2-2	Common Keystroke Shortcuts
Command	*Keystroke Shortcut*
Copy	⌘+C
Cut	⌘+X
Paste	⌘+V
Open	⌘+O
New	⌘+N
Print	⌘+P
Quit	⌘+Q
Save	⌘+S
Select All	⌘+A
Undo	⌘+Z

Most Mac applications display their keystroke shortcuts for commands directly on their pull-down menus, as shown in Figure 2-4.

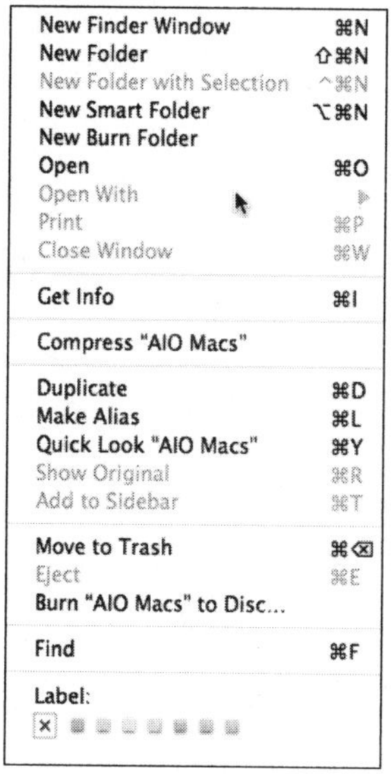

New Finder Window	⌘N
New Folder	⇧⌘N
New Folder with Selection	^⌘N
New Smart Folder	⌥⌘N
New Burn Folder	
Open	⌘O
Open With	▶
Print	⌘P
Close Window	⌘W
Get Info	⌘I
Compress "AIO Macs"	
Duplicate	⌘D
Make Alias	⌘L
Quick Look "AIO Macs"	⌘Y
Show Original	⌘R
Add to Sidebar	⌘T
Move to Trash	⌘⌫
Eject	⌘E
Burn "AIO Macs" to Disc...	
Find	⌘F
Label:	

Figure 2-4:
Most
pull-down
menus list
shortcut
keystrokes
for
commonly
used
commands.

Instead of describing the modifier keys to press by name (such as Shift), most keystroke shortcuts displayed on menus use cryptic graphics. Figure 2-5 displays the different symbols that represent shortcut commands.

Figure 2-5:
A guide to
symbols for
keystroke
commands.

⌘	Command
⌫	Delete
⌥	Option
⎋	Esc
⇧	Shift
^	Ctrl

Looking At Menus and Windows

The Mac user interface acts like a communication pathway between you and the operating system and serves three purposes:

✦ To display all the options you can choose

✦ To display information

✦ To accept commands

One of the most crucial parts of the Mac user interface is an application called the Finder, which displays files stored on your Mac. You find out more about the Finder later in this chapter.

The menu bar

The menu bar provides a single location where you can find nearly every possible command you might need. Think of the menu bar as a restaurant menu. Any time you want to order another dish, you can look at the menu to see what's available. Likewise, when using a Mac, you always know the menu bar will appear at the top of the screen. The menu bar consists of three parts, as shown in Figure 2-6:

Figure 2-6:
The three parts of the menu bar.

Apple menu   Menulets

Application menu

- ✦ **The Apple menu:** This menu always appears on the menu bar and gives you one-click access to commands for controlling or modifying your Mac.

- ✦ **The Application menu:** Here's where you find the name of the active application along with several menus that contain commands for controlling that particular application and its data. (If you don't run any additional applications, your Mac always runs the Finder, which you find out more about in this chapter.)

- ✦ **Menulets (Icons):** *Menulets* act like miniature menus that perform one or more functions for specific applications or system features, such as providing fast access to a troubleshooting utility, adjusting the volume, or displaying the current time. Clicking a menulet displays a small pull-down menu or control, as shown in Figure 2-7.

Figure 2-7:
Menulets let you control application functions.

If you don't want a menulet cluttering up the menu bar, you can typically remove it by holding down the ⌘ key, moving the pointer over the menulet you want to remove, dragging (moving) the mouse pointer off the menu bar, and then releasing the mouse button.

Understanding menu commands

Each menu on the menu bar contains a group of related commands. The File menu contains commands for opening, saving, and printing files, and the Edit menu contains commands for copying or deleting selected items. The number and names of different menus depend on the application.

To give a command to your Mac, click a menu title on the menu bar (such as File or Edit) to call up a pull-down menu listing all the commands you can choose. Then click the command you want the computer to follow (File⇨Save, for example).

Working with dialogs

When your Mac needs information from you or wants to present a choice you can make, it typically displays a *dialog* — essentially a box that offers a variety of choices. Some common dialogs appear when you choose the Print, Save, and Open commands.

Dialogs often appear in a condensed version, but you can blow them up into an expanded version, as shown in Figure 2-8. To switch between the expanded and the condensed version of the Save dialog, click the disclosure button, which looks like triangle to the right of the Save As field.

Whether expanded or condensed, every dialog displays buttons that either let you cancel the command or complete it. To cancel a command, you have three choices:

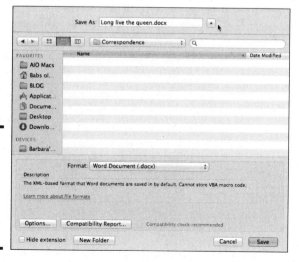

Figure 2-8:
When expanded, the Save dialog offers more options.

✦ Click the Cancel button.

✦ Press Esc.

✦ Press ⌘+. (period).

To complete a command, you also have two choices:

✦ Click the button that represents the command that you want to complete, such as Save or Print.

✦ Press Return or Enter to choose the default button, which appears in blue.

Viewing data in a window

Every application needs to accept, manipulate, and/or display data, also referred to as information. A word processor lets you type and edit text, a spreadsheet application lets you type and calculate numbers, and a presentation application lets you display text and pictures. To help you work with different types of information (such as text, pictures, audio, and video files), every application displays information inside a rectangular area called a *window,* as shown in Figure 2-9.

Figure 2-9: Multiple applications are displayed in windows onscreen at the same time.

Dividing a screen into multiple windows offers several advantages:

✦ Two or more applications can display information on the screen simultaneously.

✦ A single application can open and display information stored in two or more files or display two or more views of the same file.

✦ You can copy (or move) data from one window to another. If each window belongs to a different application, this action transfers data from one application to another.

Of course, windows aren't perfect. When a window appears on the screen, it might be too big or too small, hard to find because it's hidden behind another window, or display the beginning of a file when you want to see the middle or the end. To control the appearance of a window, most windows provide the built-in controls shown in Figure 2-10. The following sections show you what you can do with these controls.

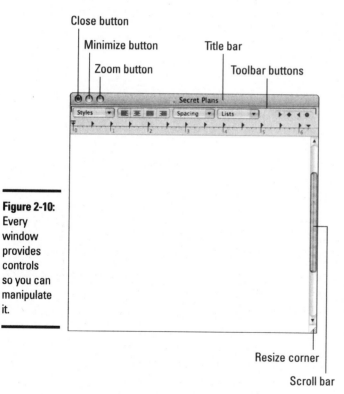

Close button

Minimize button

Zoom button

Title bar

Toolbar buttons

Figure 2-10:
Every
window
provides
controls
so you can
manipulate
it.

Resize corner

Scroll bar

Moving a window with the title bar

The title bar of every window serves two purposes:

✦ Identifies the filename that contains the information displayed in the window.

✦ Provides a place to grab when you want to drag (move) the window to a new location on the screen.

If you want to move a window on the screen, you can typically do so by dragging its title bar. Here's how:

1. **Move the pointer over the title bar of the window you want to move.**

2. **Hold down the mouse button and drag the mouse.**

If you have a two-button mouse, hold down the left mouse button.

The window becomes the active window and moves wherever you drag the mouse. If you want to move the window without moving it to the forefront, hold down the ⌘ key while clicking and dragging the title bar.

3. **Release the mouse button when you're happy with the new location of the window.**

With a trackpad, move the pointer over the title bar, and then drag the window with two fingers to its new location.

Resizing a window

Sometimes a window might be in the perfect location, but it's too small or too large for what you want to do at that moment. To change the size of a window, follow these steps:

1. **Move the pointer over any corner or edge of the window to reveal a resizing widget. It looks like a dash with arrows on both ends if you can make the window larger or smaller; it has just one arrow if the window has reached its size limits and can only be made smaller (or larger).**

2. **Hold down the mouse or trackpad button and drag the mouse or your finger to move the resizing widget.**

• If you have a two-button mouse, hold down the left mouse button.

• If you have a trackpad, tap when the pointer becomes a resizing widget, and then with three fingers swipe in the direction you want the window to grow or shrink or click and hold the bottom part of the trackpad with your thumb and drag your finger across the upper part of the trackpad to resize the window.

The window grows or shrinks while you drag or swipe.

3. **Release the mouse or trackpad button (or tap in the window if you're swiping) when you're happy with the new size of the window.**

Closing a window

When you finish viewing or editing any information displayed in a window, you can close the window to keep it from cluttering the screen. To close a window, follow these steps:

1. **Click the Close button (the little red button) of the window you want to close.**

If you haven't saved the information inside the window, such as a letter you're writing with a word processing application, the application displays a dialog that asks whether you want to save it.

2. **In the dialog that appears, click one of the following choices:**

- *Don't Save:* Closes the window and discards any changes you made to the information inside the window.

- *Cancel:* Keeps the window open.

- *Save:* Closes the window but saves the information in a file. If this is the first time you've saved this information, another dialog appears, giving you a chance to name the file and to store the saved information in a specific location on your hard drive.

Computers typically offer two or more ways to accomplish the same task, so you can choose the way you like best. As an alternative to clicking the Close button, you can also click inside the window you want to close and then choose File⇨Close or press ⌘+W.

Minimizing a window

Sometimes you might not want to close a window, but you still want to get it out of the way so it doesn't clutter your screen. In that case, you can *minimize* a window, which tucks the window (displayed as a tiny icon) into the right side of the Dock, shown in Figure 2-11, or into the icon of the application on the dock (depending on what you choose in ⬢⇨ Dock⇨Dock Preferences).

Figure 2-11:
Minimized window icons on the Dock.

A minimized window icon on the Dock actually displays the contents of that window, and sometimes continues playing the content. If you squint hard enough (or have a large enough screen), you can see what each minimized window contains.

To minimize a window, choose one of the following:

✦ Click the Minimize button of the window you want to tuck out of the way.

✦ Click the window you want to minimize and choose Window⭢Minimize (or press ⌘+M).

✦ Double-click the window's title bar.

To open a minimized window, follow these steps:

1. Move the mouse over the minimized window on the Dock.

2. Click the mouse button.

Your minimized window pops back onto the screen.

Zooming a window

If a window is too small to display information, you can instantly make it bigger by using the Zoom button — the green button in the upper-left corner of most windows. (When you move the mouse over the Zoom button, a plus sign appears inside.)

Zooming a window makes it grow larger. Clicking the zoom button a second time makes the window shrink back to its prior size.

Full-screen view

Most Apple applications and some third-party applications offer full-screen view. On Apple applications like Safari, Mail, FaceTime, and the iWork suite of applications, a zoom/unzoom widget (a line with an arrow on each end) appears when you hover the pointer over the upper-right corner of the title bar of the application window, and in a few like iPhoto and Pages, it is always present in the upper-right corner. Click the zoom widget and the application fills the screen and the menu bar is hidden from view. Hover the pointer at the very top of the screen to reveal the menu bar so you can point and click to use the menus. Move the pointer back to the window and the menu bar disappears again. Press the Esc key to return to normal view or hover the pointer over the upper-right corner again to see the unzoom widget. If you use several applications in full-screen view, you can swipe left or right with four fingers across the trackpad to move from one application to another.

Scrolling through a window

No matter how large you make a window, it may still be too small to display the entire contents of the information contained inside. Think of a window as a porthole that lets you peek at part, but not all, of a file's contents. If a window isn't large enough to display all the information inside it, the window lets you know by displaying vertical or horizontal scroll bars. If you set the General Preferences to show scroll bars when scrolling, you see the scroll bars only when you move the cursor over the section you want to scroll and begin scrolling.

You can scroll what's displayed in a window two ways:

✦ **Mouse or trackpad scrolling:** Move one finger (MagicMouse) or two fingers (trackpad) up and down and left and right to move the contents of the window up and down, left and right.

✦ **Scroll bars:** You can adjust the scroll bars' appearance — or eliminate them altogether — which we explain in Book I, Chapter 4. If you use scroll bars you can move the contents by

- *Dragging the scroll box:* Scrolls through a window faster
- *Clicking in the scroll bar:* Scrolls up/down or right/left in large increments or directly to the spot where you click

Depending on your Mac model, your Mac's keyboard may have dedicated Page Up and Page Down keys, which you can press to scroll what's displayed up and down. Not seeing Page Up and Page Down keys on your Mac or MacBook keyboard doesn't mean they aren't there. To use your Mac's invisible Page Up and Page Down keys, refer to the earlier section, "Arrow keys."

Getting to Know the Parts of the Desktop

The Desktop is always onscreen, although open windows cover up part or all of it. In the old days, placing application and file icons on the Desktop for quick access was common, much like placing an important book or day planner in one corner of your desk so you can grab it easily.

Unfortunately, the more icons you store on the Desktop, the more cluttered it appears, making it harder to find anything. Although you can still store application and file icons on the Desktop, storing application and folder icons in the Dock and in folders in the Finder is more common.

The Desktop generally shows an icon that represents your hard drive. If you have any additional storage devices attached to your Mac (such as an external hard drive, a CD or DVD, or a USB flash drive), you typically see icons for those storage devices on your Desktop, too.

You can change what your Mac displays on the Desktop. To do so, click the Finder icon in the Dock, click the Finder menu, and then choose Preferences. In the Finder Preferences window, shown in Figure 2-12, check, uncheck, or change the different options to suit your style.

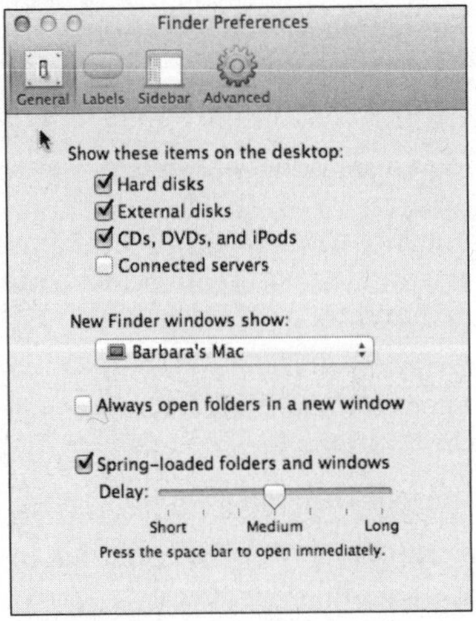

Figure 2-12:
Select what you want to see on the Desktop with Finder Preferences.

The Dock

The Dock is a rectangular strip that contains both application icons and file and folder icons. To help keep your icons organized, the Dock places application icons on the left side of a divider and file icons on the right side (refer to Figure 2-11). If you move the Dock to the side of the screen, the application icons are above the divider and the file icons are below.

Moving the Dock

The Dock appears initially at the bottom of the screen, but you can move it to the left or right of the screen.

To move the Dock to a new location, follow these steps:

1. Choose ⌘⇨Dock.

A submenu appears, as shown in Figure 2-13.

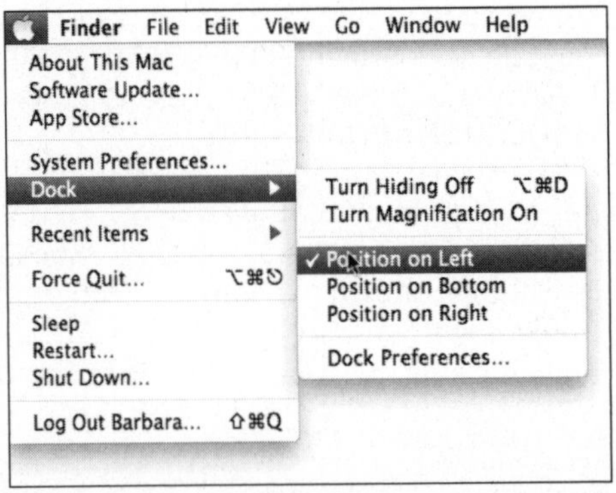

Figure 2-13:
The Dock submenu lets you change the position of the Dock on the screen.

2. **Click a new position — Position on Left, Position on Bottom, or Position on Right.**

A check mark appears next to your selection, and the Dock makes its move.

Changing the Dock's appearance

The Dock grows each time you add more applications and file icons to it. However, you may want to modify the size of the icons on the Dock so that the Dock as a whole doesn't appear too small or too large.

When you shrink the size of the Dock to hold more icons, the icons can appear too small, and it can be hard to see which icon the mouse is pointing at. Fortunately, the name of the application beneath the pointer appears to tell you what application it is. To make Dock icons zoom in size when you move the pointer over them, you can turn on magnification.

To resize the Dock and turn magnification on, follow these steps:

1. **Choose ⬆︎⇨Dock⇨Dock Preferences.**

The Dock preferences pane appears, as shown in Figure 2-14.

2. **Drag the Size slider to adjust the size of all the icons on the Dock.**

3. **Select (or clear) the Magnification check box.**

4. **Drag the Magnification slider to adjust the magnification of the Dock.**

5. **Click the Close button of the Dock preferences window.**

For a fast way to turn Magnification on or off, choose ⬆︎⇨Dock⇨Turn Magnification On (Off).

Hiding the Dock

The Dock might be convenient, but it can take up precious screen real estate when you view web pages or work with lengthy word processing documents. To get all the advantages of the Dock without the disadvantage of using extra screen space to display the Dock all the time, you can hide the Dock.

Figure 2-14:
The Dock preferences pane lets you control the appearance and position of the Dock.

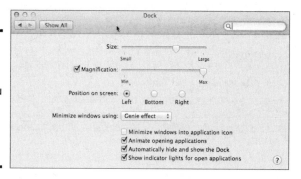

Hiding the Dock means that the Dock tucks itself out of sight, but as soon as you move the mouse near the edge of the screen where the Dock is located (bottom, left, or right), the Dock pops into view.

To hide (or show) the Dock, click the Apple menu and choose Dock⇨Turn Hiding On (Off).

You find out how to customize the icons on the Dock in Book I, Chapter 3.

The Finder

The Finder is an application that lets you find, copy, move, rename, delete, and open files and folders on your Mac. You can run applications directly from the Finder, but the Dock makes finding and running applications much more convenient.

The Finder runs all the time. To switch to the Finder, click the Finder icon in the Dock (the Picasso-like faces icon on the far left of the Dock).

Sometimes when you switch to the Finder, you may not see a Finder window. Clicking the Finder icon a second time in the Dock opens a new Finder window. You can also open a new Finder window by choosing File⇨ New Finder Window or choosing New Finder Window from the Finder's Dock menu. You can open as many Finder windows as you want, although it's common just to have one or a few Finder windows open at a time.

Because the Finder helps you manage the files stored on your hard drive, a Finder window consists of two panes, as shown in Figure 2-15.

Figure 2-15: The Finder displays two panes to help you navigate to different parts of your hard drive.

The left pane, called the Sidebar, displays three different categories:

+ **Favorites:** Lists the Desktop, Home, Applications, and Documents folders, which are the default folders for storing files, as well as any others you drag to Places so you can access them more quickly

+ **Devices:** Lists all the storage devices connected to your Mac, such as hard drives, flash drives, and CD/DVD drives

+ **Shared:** Lists all shared storage devices connected on a local area network

The right pane displays the contents of an item selected in the left pane. If you click the hard drive icon in the left pane, the right pane displays the contents of that hard drive. All applications and files displayed in a Finder window appear as icons with text labels, regardless of which type of view you chose to view the Finder window.

You find out how to use the Finder in more detail in Book I, Chapter 4.

The Dashboard

Many applications have so many features crammed into them that succeeding versions get more bloated and harder to use. If you only want to perform a simple task, such as adding a few numbers together or printing an envelope, you probably don't need to load a full-blown spreadsheet or word-processing application. Instead, you're better off using a much simpler application specifically designed to solve a single task.

That's the idea behind Dashboard. Dashboard provides you with quick access to a collection of small, simple-task applications called *widgets*. Some typical widgets display a calendar, weather forecasts for your city, a calculator, stock market quotes, and movie times for your neighborhood movie theaters.

Widgets are designed to simplify your life, and Dashboard is the feature that helps you display, manage, and hide widgets. By using Dashboard, you can be more productive without having to master an entirely new application to do so.

Viewing Dashboard widgets

The Dashboard can be a Desktop unto itself or you can view widgets on top of whatever windows are open on your Desktop. As a Desktop space, it resides to the left of the first Desktop (discover how to add more Desktop spaces in Book I, Chapter 3). To choose where you want to view your widgets, choose ⌘⇨System Preferences, and then click Mission Control in the Personal section or right-click (two-finger tap on the trackpad) the Dashboard icon on the Dock. Click the box next to Show Dashboard as a Space to give Dashboard its very own Desktop space. Deselect the box to make widgets appear on top of the open windows on your Desktop.

To view your widgets, open Dashboard in one of the following ways:

+ **Press the Dashboard key**: Depending on the keyboard you use, Dashboard may have its very own key — it has a little clock on it and shares space with one of the function keys.

+ **Press Fn+F12**: Do this if your keyboard doesn't (or does) have a dedicated Dashboard key.

+ **Click the Dashboard icon on the Dock.**

+ **Open the Launchpad and click the Dashboard icon.**

+ **If your Dashboard has its own space (as it does by default), you can do any of the above or swipe from left to right with four fingers on the trackpad or hold the Control key and press the left arrow.**

When you finish using a widget, you close it (and the Dashboard) the same way: by pressing the Dashboard key or Fn+F12, or press Esc. If your widgets are on top of your windows, click anywhere on the Desktop. If you gave Dashboard its own space, you can use the keys or click the arrow in the lower-right corner, swipe from right to left with four fingers on the trackpad, or press Control+→.

While most MacBook keyboards have a Function (Fn) key, other Mac keyboards don't always have the Fn key. If your Mac's keyboard doesn't have an Fn key, you can just press whatever function key we tell you to press and ignore our mention of Fn key whenever you encounter it.

As soon as you open Dashboard, several widgets pop into view, as shown in Figure 2-16. The default widgets that appear are the calendar, clock, calculator, and weather widgets.

The calendar widget lets you view dates for different months and years. The clock widget displays the time in a big clock, which can be easier to read than the tiny time display in the right end of the menu bar. The calculator widget acts like a typical four-function calculator, and the weather widget offers forecasts for a city of your choosing.

If you don't like the position of your widgets on the screen, you can always move them to a new location. To move a widget, click it and drag it to its new position. After you use a widget, you can hide Dashboard and all its widgets are out of sight once more.

Many widgets, including the weather widget, rely on an Internet connection. If you aren't connected to the Internet when you display such a widget, the widget can't display the latest information.

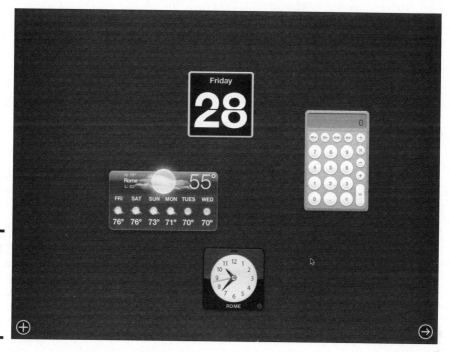

Figure 2-16:
Dashboard
displays
widgets on
their own
desktop.

Customizing a widget

Some widgets always appear the same way, such as the calculator widget.
Other widgets let you customize them to change their appearance or the
type of data they display. To customize a widget, follow these steps:

1. **Press the Dashboard key to open Dashboard and display all your
widgets (or press Fn+F12).**

2. **Hover the mouse on the widget you want to customize and then click
the Information button, as shown in Figure 2-17.**

The *i* button (the Information button) appears only for widgets you can
customize, such as the weather widget.

Figure 2-17:
Customize a
widget.

Information button

3. **Click any check boxes the widget may provide to display additional information, type the new information you want the widget to display, and then click Done.**

In this case, type the city and state or zip code of a city whose weather forecast you want to keep track of, shown in Figure 2-18, and check the Include Lows in 6-Day Forecast if you want to see that information as well.

Figure 2-18: Widget options you can modify.

Displaying and then clicking a widget changes or expands the information that appears. For instance, clicking the weather widget shows or hides the six-day forecast, and clicking the day/date display of the calendar widget toggles the month-at-a-glance and upcoming appointments displays. Click other widgets to discover whether they offer other additional displays.

Adding and removing widgets

When you open Dashboard, you see several widgets, even if you actually want to use just one widget. In case you don't want to see a particular widget, you can remove it from Dashboard. (Don't worry; you can always put it back on Dashboard again.) Conversely, you can also add more widgets to your Dashboard.

Removing a widget from Dashboard

When you remove a widget from Dashboard, you don't physically delete the widget. Instead, you just tuck the widget into storage where you can retrieve it later. To remove a widget from Dashboard, follow these steps:

1. **Press the Dashboard key or Fn+F12 to open Dashboard and display all your widgets.**

2. **Click the plus sign button that appears inside a circle in the bottom-left corner of the screen to display Close buttons in the upper-left corner of every widget, as shown in Figure 2-19.**

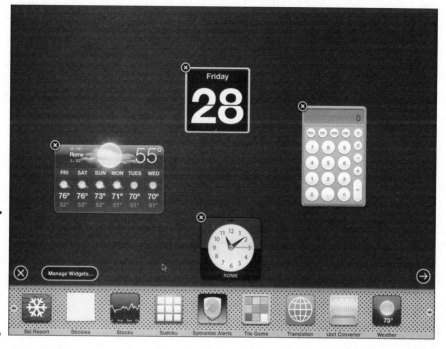

Figure 2-19:
Click the
Close button
to remove a
widget you
no longer
want to see.

If you hover the pointer on the widget you want to remove and hold down the Option key, a Close button appears in the upper-right corner of just that one widget (and you don't have to click the circled plus sign icon).

3. **Click the Close button of the widget you want to remove to make it disappear from the screen.**

4. **Press the Dashboard key or Fn+F12 to close Dashboard.**

Clicking anywhere on the screen except on another widget is another way to close Dashboard.

Displaying more widgets in Dashboard

When you open Dashboard, you see only a handful of all the widgets in the Dashboard's library of widgets that come with every Mac. Table 2-3 lists all of Dashboard's available widgets that you can choose to display every time you open Dashboard, some of which are shown in Figure 2-19. (*Note:* Apple may have changed the lineup since we wrote this, so keep in mind that your collection may vary.)

Table 2-3	Dashboard's Library of Widgets
Widget	*What It Does*
Address Book	Lets you search for names stored in your Address Book
Business	Displays a Yellow Pages directory for looking up business names and phone numbers
Calculator	Displays a four-function calculator
Dictionary	Displays a dictionary and thesaurus for looking up words
ESPN	Displays sports news and scores
Flight Tracker	Tracks airline flights
Google	Displays a text box to send a query to Google and display the results in Safari (or your preferred web browser)
iCal	Displays a calendar and any appointments stored within iCal
iTunes	Lets you Pause, Play, Rewind, or Fast Forward a song currently playing in iTunes
Movies	Displays which movies are playing at which times at a certain zip code
People	Displays a White Pages directory that lets you search for a person's name and address to find his or her telephone number
Ski Report	Displays the temperature and snow depth at your favorite ski resort
Stickies	Displays color-coded windows for jotting down notes
Stocks	Displays stock quotes
Tile Game	Displays a picture tile game in which you slide tiles to re-create a picture
Translation	Translates words from one language to another, such as from Japanese to French
Unit Converter	Converts measurement units, such as inches to centimeters
Weather	Displays a weather forecast for your area
Web Clip	Displays parts of a web page that you've clipped from Safari (see Book II, Chapter 1 for more information about creating Web Clips)
World Clock	Displays the current time

To display a hidden Dashboard widget, follow these steps:

1. **Press the Dashboard key or Fn+F12 to open Dashboard, and then click the plus sign that appears inside a circle in the bottom-left corner of the screen to display a list of widgets.**

2. **Click a widget that you want to display in Dashboard, such as ESPN or Stocks, to make it appear onscreen.**

    Click the left or right arrows on either side of the widget list to scroll through all the widgets your Mac has to offer.

3. **Move the cursor to the widget, click and drag the widget to wherever you want it to appear on your screen, and release the mouse button.**

4. **Press the Dashboard key or Fn+F12 to close Dashboard.**

    All your widgets disappear. The next time you open Dashboard, your newly added widgets appear onscreen.

You can have multiple instances of the same widget opened at the same time. For instance, to track the weather in two or more cities, you can just repeat Step 2 in the preceding steps for each additional instance of the Weather you want to display.

To create your own widgets from a section of a web page you're viewing with Safari, choose File➪Open in Dashboard and then drag the selection box to the section you want to turn into a Dashboard widget, as we explain in more detail in Book II, Chapter 1.

Finding new widgets

Dashboard comes with a library of widgets, but people are always creating more, which you can browse and download by visiting Apple's website. To find the latest widgets, follow these steps:

1. **Visit Apple's website (**`www.apple.com/downloads/dashboard`**), using your favorite browser (such as Safari) to access the widget download page, as shown in Figure 2-20.**

2. **Scroll down to see the Widget Browser or click the Categories, Just Added, or Top 50 tab to display a list of the widgets.**

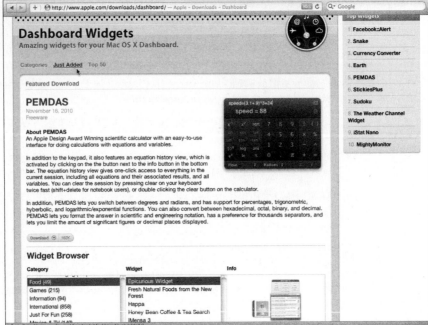

Figure 2-20: Download more widgets from Apple's Dashboard website.

3. **Click a widget in the Widget Browser or one of the lists to display details about the widget and then click the Download button if you decide to add the widget to your Mac's library of Dashboard widgets.**

   Your Mac downloads the chosen widget to the Downloads folder and displays a dialog asking whether you want to install your newly downloaded widget in Dashboard (as shown in Figure 2-21).

4. **Click the Install button to give your Mac permission to open Dashboard and install the new widget; click the widget and drag it to where you want it to appear on your screen.**

Figure 2-21: You can install your new widget right away.

Disabling and deleting widgets from Dashboard

If you keep installing new widgets, eventually your list of available widgets can get crowded and overwhelming. To reduce the number of available widgets, you can disable or delete them.

Disabling a widget hides it from view but keeps it stored on your hard drive in case you change your mind and decide to display it after all. *Deleting* a widget physically removes it from your hard drive.

Disabling a widget

To disable a widget and temporarily remove it from view, follow these steps:

1. **Press the Dashboard key (or Fn+F12) to open Dashboard and then click the plus sign that appears in a circle in the bottom-left corner of the screen to display a list of installed widgets.**

2. **Click the Manage Widgets button in the lower-left corner to open a list of installed widgets, as shown in Figure 2-22.**

3. **Deselect the check box in front of any widgets you want to disable.**

   If its check box is deselected, the widget is disabled and isn't available for display through Dashboard.

4. **Click the Close button of the Manage Widgets window and then press the Dashboard button (or Fn+F12).**

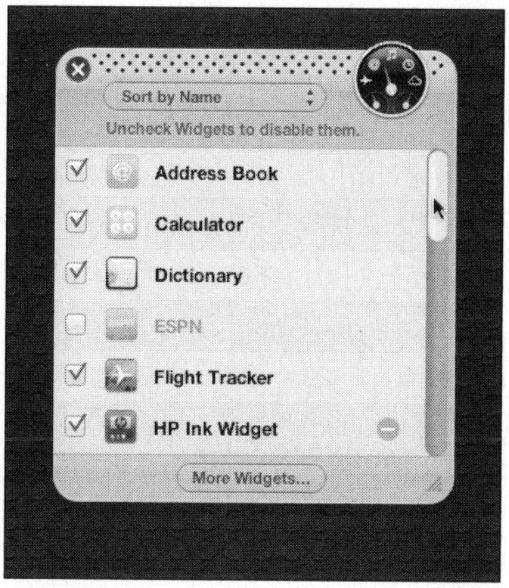

Figure 2-22:
A window
lists all
installed
widgets
with a
check box
next to each
one.

To reenable a widget you disabled, repeat these same steps *except* click any unchecked widgets to enable them again so they reappear in the row of available widgets you can display when you activate Dashboard.

Deleting a widget

You can delete any widgets that you install (see the "Finding new widgets" section, earlier in this chapter, for more about downloading additional widgets), although you can't delete the widgets that came with your Mac. To delete a widget, follow these steps:

1. **Press the Dashboard key or Fn+F12 to open Dashboard and then click the plus sign that appears in a circle in the bottom-left corner of the screen to display a list of installed widgets.**

2. **Click the Manage Widgets button in the lower-left corner to open a list of installed widgets (refer to Figure 2-22) and then click the minus sign that appears to the right of the widget you want to delete.**

   A dialog appears, asking whether you really want to move the widget to the Trash.

3. **Click OK to delete the widget and then click the Close button of the Manage Widgets window.**

4. **Press the Dashboard key (or Fn+F12).**

Getting Help

Theoretically, the Mac should be so easy and intuitive that you can teach yourself how to use your computer just by looking at the screen. Realistically, the Mac can still be confusing and complicated — there'd be no need for this book otherwise. Any time you're confused when using your Mac, try looking for answers in the Help Center — you just might find the answer you're looking for!

Your Mac offers two types of help. First, it can point out specific menu commands to choose for accomplishing a specific task. For example, if you want to know how to save or print a file, Mac Help will point out the Save or Print command so you know which command to choose.

Second, the Help Center can provide brief explanations for how to accomplish a specific task. By skimming through the brief explanations, you can (hopefully) figure out how to do something useful.

Pointing out commands to use

To use the Help Center to point out commands you can use with the Finder or an application you're running, follow these steps:

1. **Click the Help menu at the right end of the menu bar for any application you're running (or click the Finder icon to switch to the Finder and then click Help).**

A Search text box appears.

2. **Begin typing a word or phrase.**

If you want help on working with using printing, type **print**. While you type, a list of possible topics appears, as shown in Figure 2-23.

Help topics for the application you're running appear first under the Menu Items category, followed by the Help Topics category, which lists topics for the Finder and any other applications stored on your Mac.

3. **Move your pointer over a Menu Items topic.**

A floating arrow points to the command on a menu to show you how to access your chosen topic for the application you are running, as shown in Figure 2-24.

Figure 2-23:
While
you type,
Help lists
possible
topics.

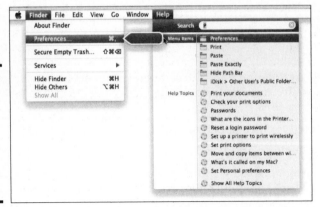

Reading Help topics

To read brief explanations of different topics, follow these steps:

1. **Click the Finder icon in the Dock.**

2. **Click the Help menu and then choose Help Center.**

   The Help Center window appears, as shown in Figure 2-25.

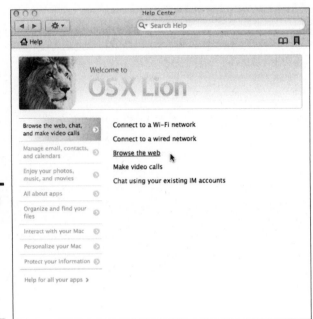

3. **Click a subject in the left column, and then click a topic in the right column.**

   Alternatively, click the option Help for All Your Apps at the bottom of the left column to reveal the window shown in Figure 2-26.

   Click the icon for the application you need help with to open a list of help topics for that application.

4. **Mac Help displays additional information about your chosen topic.**

   Click the Bookmark icon at the upper-right of the help window to book-mark that particular help explanation. Click the Book icon to the right of the bookmark icon to see explanations you bookmarked.

5. **Click the Back (or Forward) button to jump to a previously viewed topic or click the Home button to return to the original Mac Help window.**

6. **Click the Close button to close the Mac Help window.**

Figure 2-26:
Access help for all your applications from the Help Center.

Chapter 3: Managing Applications on the Dock, Launchpad, and Desktop

In This Chapter

✔ **Running applications from the Dock**

✔ **Running applications on the Launchpad**

✔ **Switching between applications**

✔ **Shutting down applications**

✔ **Organizing multiple desktops with Mission Control**

✔ **Shopping at the App Store**

✔ **Installing, updating, and uninstalling applications**

*A*fter you power on your Mac and have the OS X operating system up and running, you have to use applications (sometimes called *software* or *programs* or *apps*) to actually do anything with your Mac, such as write a letter with a word processor, play a video game, browse the web, or read and write e-mail. The number of applications you can load and run simultaneously is limited only by the amount of hard-drive space and memory installed inside your Mac.

This chapter explains how to run, install, and uninstall applications for your Mac. Most of the time, you start or launch an application from the Dock or Launchpad, so we explain how to use and manage those functions in this chapter too. We also give you pointers for finding new applications and take you window-shopping in the App Store (purchasing is optional).

Because you have a physical limit on the amount of software and data you can install on your Mac, you have two choices:

✦ You can get another hard drive (an external drive or a larger internal drive) to store big byte-consuming files, such as videos or graphic-heavy documents, so you can keep installing more applications.

✦ You can delete some applications or files that you don't want or need, which makes room for more applications that you do want and need.

Launching an Application

Running an application is also referred to as launching an application or starting up an application. Very hip Mac users shorten the term by saying they run this app or that app.

To start an application, you can choose any of the five most common methods:

+ Click an application or document icon in the Dock.

+ Click Launchpad in the Dock and click the application.

+ Double-click an application or document icon in the Finder.

+ Choose an application name from the Apple menu's Recent Items.

+ Find the application with the Spotlight search feature and then select it to run.

The Dock is the strip of animated icons that appears when you hover the pointer over the bottom of your Mac's screen (on the left or right side if you changed the Dock's position by choosing ⌘➪Dock➪Position).

The next few sections take a closer look at each one of these methods.

Two other not-so-obvious but nifty ways to launch applications include attaching a device (such as a digital camera or mobile phone with a camera to automatically launch iPhoto) or inserting a disc (such as a DVD or CD to automatically launch iTunes), and then Control-clicking (or right-clicking, if your mouse has a right button, or tapping with two fingers on a trackpad, Magic Trackpad or Magic Mouse) on a document and choosing Open or Open With from the shortcut menu.

From the Dock

To run an application from the Dock, just click the application icon that you want to run. (What? Were you expecting something difficult?) The Dock contains icons that represent some (but not all) of the applications installed on your Mac. When you turn on your Mac for the first time, you see that the Dock already includes a variety of applications that Apple thinks you might want to use right away. However, you can always add or remove application icons from the Dock (that's next in this section).

When using applications, you can use the Dock in several ways:

+ To gain one-click access to your favorite applications.

+ To see which applications are running. You see a small white dot next to the application icon (see Figure 3-1) if you turn on the Dock indicator lights. Go to ⌘➪System Preferences, click the Dock icon, and then select Show Indicator Lights for Open Applications.

**Book I
Chapter 3**

**Managing
Applications on the
Dock, Launchpad,
and Desktop**

✦ To switch between different applications quickly.

✦ To see which windows you have minimized. (Minimized windows are tucked out of sight on the Dock but still open.)

✦ To view a specific application window.

✦ To go to a specific window of a running application.

✦ To perform specific tasks of an application.

✦ To hide all windows that belong to a specific application.

Figure 3-1:
The Dock
identifies
running
applications
with a
glowing dot.

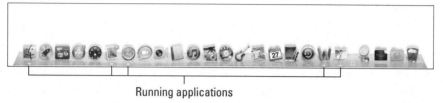

Running applications

Clicking a running application's Dock icon makes it easy to switch among all the applications you're running at the same time. So, if you want to switch to the iTunes application from the GarageBand application, you just click the iTunes application icon. Doing so immediately displays the iTunes window(s) and displays the iTunes application name in the Application menu on the menu bar at the top of the screen. (Clicking the iTunes application icon brings iTunes to the forefront, but the GarageBand application doesn't close or quit on you; it just moseys to the background, waiting for its turn to step into the limelight again.)

Optionally, the Dock identifies running applications by displaying a glowing dot underneath (next to, if you position the Dock on the side of the screen) the icon of each running application. The Application menu on the menu bar identifies the active application. You can have multiple applications running and windows open showing active files created with those applications, but you can have only one active window, and therefore one active application. The *active application* is the one that is front and center on your screen, ready to accept any data or commands you give. The window of the active application is on top of any other application windows that are open.

You can add or remove application icons from the Dock so it contains only the applications you use most often, and you can arrange the icons in the Dock to suit yourself and make starting applications even easier. The following sections give you all you need to know about the relationship between the Dock and its icons.

Adding application icons to the Dock

The Dock includes several applications already installed on your Mac, but if you install more applications, you might want to add those application icons to the Dock as well. One way to add an application icon to the Dock is to click and drag the icon onto the Dock. Here's how that's usually done:

1. **Click the Finder icon in the Dock and then click the Applications folder in the Finder window's sidebar.**

   The Finder displays the contents of the Applications folder.

2. **Click the application icon and hold down the mouse or trackpad button, drag the pointer where you want to place the icon in the Dock, and then release the mouse button.**

   Your chosen application icon now has its own place in the Dock.

Make sure that you drag application icons in the Dock to the left of the divider (or above it if you have the Dock on the left or right side of the screen), which appears as a gap near the Trash icon. To the left of (or above) the divider, you see application icons. To the right of (or below) the divider, you can store file or folder icons.

Be careful not to drag the application icon to the Trash bin unless you really want to delete it from your hard drive.

When you drag an application icon to the Dock, you aren't physically moving the application from the Applications folder onto the Dock; you're just creating a link, or *alias,* from the Dock to the actual application (which is still safely stashed in its folder).

You can also add an application icon to the Dock right after you load an application. Remember that the Dock displays the icons of all running applications at all times, but when you exit an application, that application's icon — if it's not a Dock resident — will disappear from the Dock. To keep an icon of a running application in the Dock so it stays there when you quit the application, Control-click the running application's icon in the Dock — or click and hold down on the application icon — and choose Options⇨Keep in Dock from the shortcut menu, as shown in Figure 3-2. Now when you exit from this application, the application icon remains visible in the Dock.

Rearranging application icons in the Dock

After you place application icons in the Dock, you may want to rearrange their order. How you rearrange your Dock is up to you! To rearrange application icons in the Dock, click the application icon that you want to move and drag the mouse or trackpad sideways (or up and down) to where you want to move it, and then release the mouse or trackpad button.

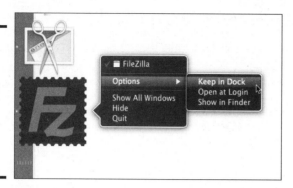

Book I
Chapter 3

Managing
Applications on the
Dock, Launchpad,
and Desktop

Figure 3-2:
Control-
click an
application
icon in the
Dock to
display a
shortcut
menu.

You notice that while you move an application icon, the existing icons move to the side to show you where the icon will appear when you let go of the mouse button. Neat effect, right?

You can rearrange application icons on the Dock how you want, but one icon you can't move or remove is the Finder icon, which won't budge no matter how hard you try to drag it from its Number One position on the Dock.

Removing application icons from the Dock

If you keep adding application icons to the Dock, eventually, you find that you rarely use some of these applications. Rather than let them clutter your Dock, it's better to get rid of them. You have two ways of removing an application icon from the Dock:

✦ Click the application icon that you want to remove from the Dock and drag it up and away from the Dock, and then release the mouse button. Your unwanted application icon disappears in an animated puff of smoke.

✦ Control-click the application icon and choose Options⇨Remove from Dock from the shortcut menu.

Note: Removing an application icon from the Dock doesn't remove or delete the actual application. To do that, see the "Uninstalling Applications" section, later in this chapter.

If you like having an application icon in the Dock but want to make room for other applications, you can store application icons in a folder and then store that folder on the right of the divider in the Dock, thanks to a feature called Stacks. Now to load that application, you can click its folder icon in the Dock and then click the application icon. To find out more about using Stacks to add, remove, and work with folders on the Dock, check out Book I, Chapter 4.

A couple of things you can't do with icons on the Dock:

✦ You can never remove the Finder and Trash icons from the Dock.

✦ You can't remove an application icon from the Dock if the application is still running.

From the Launchpad

If the application you want to open isn't stored on the Dock, you can go to the Launchpad. Click the Launchpad icon on the Dock, or press the F4 key, to open the Launchpad, as shown in Figure 3-3. (On older Macs, F4 may not open Launchpad.) If you use a trackpad, with three fingers and your thumb slightly open, place your fingers and thumb on the trackpad and bring them together as if you were to pick up a small object. Voila! Launchpad launches. (Sorry — there's no default mouse equivalent, although if you have a multibutton mouse, you can assign that function to one of the buttons.) Launchpad shows all the applications that are in the applications folder. That means all the applications that came with your Mac and all applications you install have an icon on the Launchpad.

Figure 3-3: Applications stored in the Applications folder on your Mac appear on the Launchpad.

Book I
Chapter 3

Managing
Applications on the
Dock, Launchpad,
and Desktop

Each Launchpad screen can hold up to 40 applications or folders. Each folder can hold up to 32 apps. You can have multiple Launchpad screens. To move from one Launchpad screen to another, hold the mouse button and move the mouse left or right, swipe left and right with two fingers on the trackpad, or use the left and right arrows on the keyboard.

To open an application, just click on the application icon in Launchpad and the application opens.

To leave the Launchpad without opening an application, simply click anywhere on the background or press Esc.

You can do the following to manage the appearance of the Launchpad:

✦ Click and drag an icon to move it on the Launchpad; drag it to the very right or left edge to move the icon to another screen. You can only move one icon at a time.

✦ Click and drag one icon over another to create a folder that holds both icons, and then drag other icons into the folder. Click on the folder once to open it, and then double-click the name to highlight the name and type in a new name. To remove an icon from a folder, just drag it out onto the Launchpad.

You can drag an icon from the Launchpad to the Dock to add the icon to the Dock.

By double-clicking icons

The Mac represents a file as a graphically descriptive icon with a name. Icons can represent two types of files: applications and documents.

Application files represent applications that actually do something, such as play a game of chess or send, receive, and organize your e-mail. *Document files* represent data created by applications, such as a letter created by a word processor, a business report created by a presentation application, or a movie created by a video-editing application.

Application icons are often distinct enough to help you identify the type of application they represent. For example, the iTunes application icon appears as a musical note over a CD, the iPhoto icon appears as a camera over a photograph, and the Mail application icon (for sending and receiving e-mail) appears as a postage stamp.

Document icons often appear with the icon of the application that created them or as thumbnail images of their content, as shown in Figure 3-4. So, if you save a web page in Safari, your file appears as a page with the Safari icon over it.

Figure 3-4:
Document
icons
display
thumbnails
of their
content
or the
application
icon.

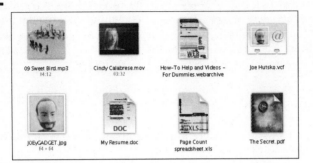

09 Sweet Bird.mp3
04:12

Cindy Calabrese.mov
03:32

How-To Help and Videos –
For Dummies.webarchive

Joe Hutsko.vcf

JOEyGADGET.jpg
64 × 64

My Resume.doc

Page Count
spreadsheet.xls

The Secret.pdf

A third type of icon you might see is an *alias* icon, which represents a link to an application icon or a document icon. You find out more about alias icons in the "Working with Alias Icons" section, later in this chapter.

Double-clicking an application icon

Because an application's icon might not appear in the Dock, you have to be able to access icons another way. You can find applications stored in the Applications folder on the Launchpad, but the Finder can help you find any applications that are stored in another folder.

It's actually possible to store an application icon in any folder on your hard drive, but you should store applications in the Applications folder. That way, if you need to find that application again, you just have to look on the Launchpad or in the Applications folder instead of trying to remember where else you stored it.

To run an application by double-clicking its icon, follow these steps:

1. **Click the Finder icon in the Dock, and then click the Applications folder in the Finder window's sidebar to display the applications installed on your Mac.**

2. **Scroll through the Applications folder window until you see the application icon you want and double-click the icon to run the application.**

   (You might have to double-click a folder that contains an application icon and then double-click the application icon.) Alternatively, you can choose File➪Open or press a keyboard shortcut such as ⌘+O or ⌘+↓.

   Your chosen application appears, typically with a blank window, ready for you to do something application-y, such as typing text.

Typing the first letter of an application file or document you are looking for in any Finder window will instantly jump to and select the first icon that matches the letter you type. For instance, to locate Safari in the Applications folder quickly, press S to jump to and select Safari (or another application icon whose name starts with S that might come before Safari, if one is present).

Book I
Chapter 3

Managing
Applications on the
Dock, Launchpad,
and Desktop

Double-clicking a document icon

When you double-click an application icon, you start (that is, *run* or *launch*) that particular application. If you want to use your newly opened application to work on an existing file, you then have to search for and open that file by using the application's File➪Open command.

As an alternative to running an application and then having to find and open the file you want to work with, the Mac gives you the option of double-clicking the document icon you want to open. This opens the application with your chosen document ready for action. Here's how to do it:

1. **You have four ways to find a document icon to double-click:**

   • Control-click the Documents icon in the Dock and choose Open Documents (or click and hold on the Documents icon to see the folders and documents inside it, move the pointer to the one you want to open, and then let go of the mouse button).

   • Click the Finder icon in the Dock, and then click the Documents folder in the sidebar to open the Documents window.

   • Click the Desktop and press ⌘+Shift+D to open the Desktop window and click the Documents folder in the sidebar.

   • Click the Finder icon in the Dock, and then click All My Files from the sidebar. You see all the documents on your Mac displayed. You can choose how to sort them — by Name, Kind, Date Last Opened, and so on, as shown in Figure 3-5.

2. **Scroll through the Documents window until you see the document icon you want and double-click it.**

   (You might need to double-click one or more folders until you find the document you want.)

   Your Mac loads the application that created the document (if it's not already running) and displays your chosen document in a window. If your Mac can't find the application that created the document, it might load another application, or it might ask you to choose an existing application on your Mac that can open the document.

   Sometimes if you double-click a document icon, an entirely different application loads and displays your file. This can occur if you save your file in a different file format. For example, if you save an iMovie project as a QuickTime file, double-clicking the QuickTime file opens the QuickTime Player rather than iMovie.

Figure 3-5:
See all the
files on your
Mac with
the Finder's
All My Files
feature.

From the Apple menu's Recent Items

This one's a no-brainer: Choose ♠⇨Recent Items, and then choose the application you want to run from the list of recently run applications. You can also choose a recently created or viewed document or other file to automatically launch the associated application and load the document or file.

With Spotlight

As an alternative to clicking an application's Dock or Launchpad icon, or locating an application or document by clicking through folders, you can use your Mac's handy Spotlight feature to quickly open applications or documents for you. We explain Spotlight in detail in Book I, Chapter 4. You can use Spotlight to run applications and open documents in two ways:

✦ Click the Finder icon in the Dock, click in the Search text box and type all or part of a document name (or the contents of a document you want to open), and then press Return. Double-click the document you want to open from the list of results.

✦ Click the Spotlight icon in the far-right corner of your Mac's menu bar (or press ⌘+spacebar) and begin typing the first few letters of the application name or file (or contents of a file) you're looking for. Move the pointer to the application or document you want to open and click the mouse.

Working with Alias Icons

Book I
Chapter 3

Managing
Applications on the
Dock, Launchpad,
and Desktop

An *alias icon* acts like a link to another icon. Double-clicking an alias icon works identically to double-clicking the actual application or document icon. The biggest advantage of alias icons is that you can move and place alias icons anywhere you want without physically moving (and perhaps losing) an application or document icon.

One way to use alias icons is to create alias icons to your application icons, store those alias icons in a folder, and store that folder to the right of the divider in the Dock. This gives you easy access to lots of application icons without cluttering the Dock.

You can do the following things with alias icons:

✦ **Create an alias icon.** Click the Finder icon in the Dock, click the icon you want to select, and then choose File➪Make Alias. (You can also Control-click it and choose Make Alias, or press ⌘+L.) A copy of your chosen icon appears in the window with an arrow and *alias* added to its name, as shown in Figure 3-6.

✦ **Move an alias icon.** Because it's pointless to store the original icon and the alias icon in the same location, you should store the alias icon in a new location. To move an alias icon, click it to select it and drag it to the Desktop or folder you want to move it to.

✦ **Create and move an alias icon in one step.** Hold ⌘+Option when you click on the icon you want to create an alias of and then drag it to the new position. The alias is created and positioned in the new location.

✦ **Delete an alias icon.** Simply Control-click it and choose Move to Trash, or press ⌘+Delete. Note that deleting an alias icon never deletes the original icon — meaning that if you delete an alias icon that represents an application, you never delete the actual application. The only way to delete an application or document is to delete the original application or document icon.

You can store alias icons on the Desktop for fast access or in specific folders to organize applications and documents without moving them to a new location. (Essentially, the Dock replaces the need to place alias icons on the Desktop, and Smart Folders duplicate the process of creating and storing alias icons in a folder. You can delve into Smart Folders in Book I, Chapter 4.)

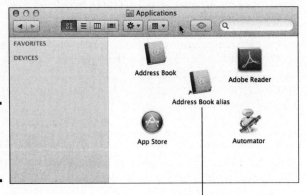

Figure 3-6:
A tiny arrow
identifies an
alias icon.

Address Book alias

Switching among Applications

When you run multiple applications, you have multiple windows from different applications cluttering your screen, much like covering a clean tabletop with piles of different papers. To help keep your screen organized, you can switch between different applications (say a word processor and a web browser) as well as switch to different windows displayed by the same application (such as a word processor displaying a window containing a letter of resignation and a second window containing a résumé).

Your Mac offers quite a few different ways to switch among different applications, including using the Dock, using the Application Switcher, clicking a window of a different application, using Mission Control, or by hiding applications or entire Desktops, which we explain in the section "Organizing Multiple Desktops with Spaces," later in this chapter.

We discuss the first three ways of switching between running applications in the following list:

✦ **Using the Dock:** Click an application icon in the Dock that has a dot underneath it (as long as you have indicator lights on in Settings➪Dock). That's all there is to it! If you want to switch to a specific document window opened by a certain application, you can switch to that application and that document window at once. Control-click the icon of the application you want to switch to and then click the name of the document you want to open.

✦ **Using the Application Switcher:** Press ⌘+Tab to open the Application Switcher, which displays icons of all non-hidden active applications. After you open the Application Switcher, choose the icon of the application you want to use by holding down the ⌘ key and pressing the Tab key repeatedly to move left to right from one running application to the next, as shown in Figure 3-7. When you release the ⌘ key, the chosen application moves to the front of your screen.

Book I
Chapter 3

Managing
Applications on the
Dock, Launchpad,
and Desktop

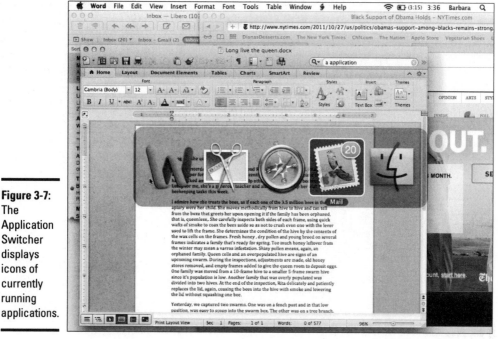

Figure 3-7:
The
Application
Switcher
displays
icons of
currently
running
applications.

Pressing the Shift key while holding down ⌘ and pressing Tab will move the selection from right to left. You can also press ⌘+Tab and then let go of the Tab key and use the arrow keys to navigate left and right.

If an application has several files open in different windows, the Application Switcher just switches you to that application, but you still have to find the specific window to view.

✦ **Clicking different windows:** A fast, but somewhat clumsier way to switch between applications is to rearrange your windows so you can see two or more windows at one time. To switch to another window, click anywhere inside that window.

✦ **Going to Mission Control:** To see all the open windows on your Desktop, as well as other Desktops Spaces and the Dashboard, press F3, flick up on the trackpad with three fingers, or press Ctrl+Shift+↑ to open Mission Control, as shown in Figure 3-8. Then click on the window you want to work in.

TIP

If you want to switch between two or more open windows from the same application, press ⌘+`. If you want to see all the windows from the same application, press fn+F10 or Control+Shift+↓ to open Exposé, as shown in Figure 3-9. Exposé shows you thumbnail versions of all the open windows from one running application. Then all you have to do is click the exact window you want to use.

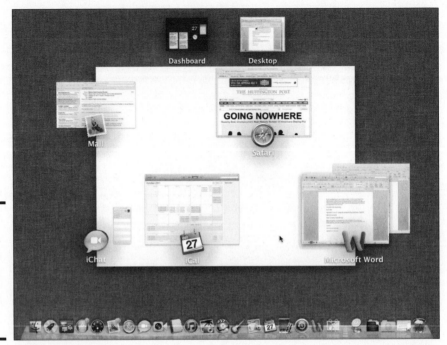

Figure 3-8:
Mission
Control
shows
everything
that's open
on your
desktop.

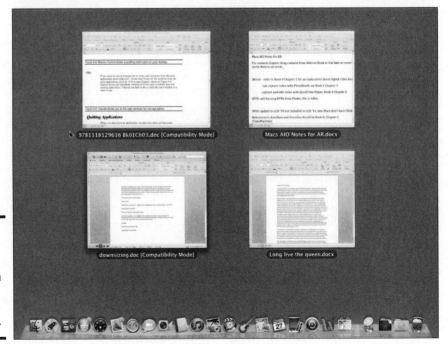

Figure 3-9:
Exposé
shows you
all the open
windows
for one
application.

Book I
Chapter 3

Managing
Applications on the
Dock, Launchpad,
and Desktop

Quitting Applications

When you shut down an application, you also shut down all document windows that application may have open. However, if you only shut down a document in an open application, the application keeps running.

If you leave applications running when you shut down your Mac or log out of your account, when you start your Mac the next time, the running applications will open automatically, letting you pick up where you left off.

Closing a document

If you want to stop working with or viewing a specific document but want to keep the application running, you can close just that particular document. You have three different ways to close a document window:

+ Choose File⇨Close.

+ Press ⌘+W.

+ Click the red Close button of the document window.

If you click the yellow button, the window is hidden on the Dock but isn't closed. Click the document icon on the Dock to quickly reopen it.

If you try to close a window before saving the file, a dialog appears, asking whether you want to save your file.

Shutting down an application

When you finish using an application, it's a good idea to shut it down to free up your Mac's memory to run other applications. The more applications you have running at the same time on your Mac, the slower your Mac can become, so always shut down applications if you don't need them anymore.

To shut down an application, you have three choices:

+ Choose the menu associated with the application and choose Quit (such as iPhoto⇨Quit iPhoto to shut down the iPhoto application).

+ Press ⌘+Q.

+ Control-click the application icon in the Dock and choose Quit from the contextual menu that appears.

If you try to shut down an application that displays a window containing a document that you haven't saved yet, a dialog appears, asking whether you want to save your file.

Force-quitting an application

Despite the Mac's reputation for reliability, there's always a chance that an application will crash, freeze, or hang, which are less-than-technical-terms for an application screwing up and not reacting when you click the mouse or press a key. When an application no longer responds to any attempts to work or shut down, you might have to resort to a last-resort procedure known as a *force quit.*

As the name implies, force-quitting makes an application shut down whether it wants to or not. Here are the two easiest ways to force quit an application:

✦ **Choose ⇨Force Quit (or press ⌘+Option+Esc).** The Force Quit dialog appears, as shown in Figure 3-10. Frozen or crashed applications might appear in the Force Quit dialog with the phrase Not Responding next to its name. Just click the application you want to force-quit and click the Force Quit button.

✦ **Control-click an application icon in the Dock and choose Force Quit from the shortcut menu that appears.** If the application hasn't really crashed or if your Mac thinks the application hasn't crashed, you won't see a Force Quit option in this pop-up menu. In that case, you may want to wait a minute or so to give your Mac time to correct the seemingly hung-up application. If, after you've waited awhile, the application still appears stuck but you don't see the Force Quit option, hold down the Option key, Control-click an application icon in the Dock, and then choose Force Quit.

If you force-quit an application, you will lose any data you changed right before the application suddenly froze or crashed. For instance, if we just performed ⌘+S to save this chapter before writing this sentence, and then performed a force-quit, this sentence would be missing the next time we reopened this chapter.

Figure 3-10: The Force Quit dialog shows you all currently running applications.

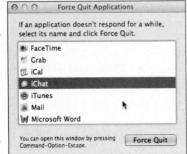

Organizing Multiple Desktops with Spaces

Book I
Chapter 3

Managing
Applications on the
Dock, Launchpad,
and Desktop

Spaces multiplies your Mac's single display into up to 16 separate virtual screens, or Desktops. The main purpose of Spaces is to help organize multiple applications running at the same time. Rather than cram multiple application windows on a single screen (Desktop), Spaces lets you store multiple applications in separate Desktops. One Desktop might contain only Internet applications, such as Safari and Mail, whereas a second Desktop might contain only Microsoft Word and the Mac's built-in Dictionary application. Each Desktop can have its own desktop picture and a customized Dock.

If one application has multiple windows open, you can store each application window on a separate Desktop. For example, if you have a word processor and open a personal letter and a business letter, you could store the personal letter's window on one Desktop and the business letter's window on a second Desktop.

You manage each Space individually, but you can see all of them and move windows from one Space to another in Mission Control.

Creating Desktops

Your Mac comes with one Desktop, also called a Desktop Space or Space, plus the Dashboard (see Book I, Chapter 2). You can see both by opening Mission Control, which is where you create additional Desktops. To create a Desktop, follow these steps:

1. **Open Mission Control by using one of these methods:**

- Press F3.

- Click the Mission Control icon in the Dock.

- Press Ctrl+Shift+↑.

- Swipe up on the trackpad with three or four fingers.

2. **Move the pointer to the upper-right corner until you see a plus sign. (If you have the Dock on the right, the plus sign will be in the upper-left corner.)**

3. **Click or tap the plus sign.**

A new Desktop Space appears with the name Desktop 2. Subsequent desktops will be named Desktop 3, Desktop 4, and so on up to Desktop 16, as shown in Figure 3-11.

Figure 3-11:
Create
additional
desktops
from
Mission
Control.

You can give each Desktop Space a personal desktop image and Dock. Open Mission Control and click the desktop you want to work in. Then do the following:

✦ **Set the desktop picture for that desktop.** Go to ⇨System Preferences⇨ Desktop and Screensaver, as explained in Book I, Chapter 5.

✦ **Choose which icons you want in the Dock for that Desktop.** Click and hold an icon in the Dock and choose Options⇨This Desktop (to use the icon only on this Desktop), All Desktops (to use the icon on every Desktop), or None (to not use this icon on the Dock in any Space).

Switching Desktops

Applications used in full-screen mode are treated as Desktop Spaces. When you create multiple desktops and/or use applications in full-screen mode, you want to be able to move from one Space to another. To move from one Desktop Space to another, you can do the following:

✦ **Use the trackpad.** Swipe left or right with three or four fingers to move from one Desktop to another.

✦ **Use Mission Control.** Enter Mission Control and click the Desktop you want.

Book I
Chapter 3

Managing
Applications on the
Dock, Launchpad,
and Desktop

✦ **Switch between Desktops.** Hold the Control key and press the left or right arrow keys.

✦ **Switch to the first Desktop.** Press Control+1.

Moving application windows to different Desktops

When you run an application, it appears in the Desktop you're working in. So, if you're in Desktop 1 and you run the Safari web browser, Safari appears on Desktop 1. You can switch to another Desktop to launch another application that appears on that Desktop. Or you can move an application's window from one Desktop to another, so the window appears where you want, by doing one of the following:

✦ Go to Mission Control and drag the window from the active Desktop (the one you were most recently on) to the thumbnail of the Desktop where you want to move the window to.

✦ From the Desktop, click the title bar of the window you want to move and drag to the far left or right edge of the screen until it shifts to the neighboring Desktop. Release the mouse or trackpad button or keep going until you reach the Desktop you want to move the window to.

Setting Mission Control preferences

Mission Control lets you choose some of the ways you view and interact with it. Select ⌘➪System Preferences and click the Mission Control icon in the Personal section (see Figure 3-12).

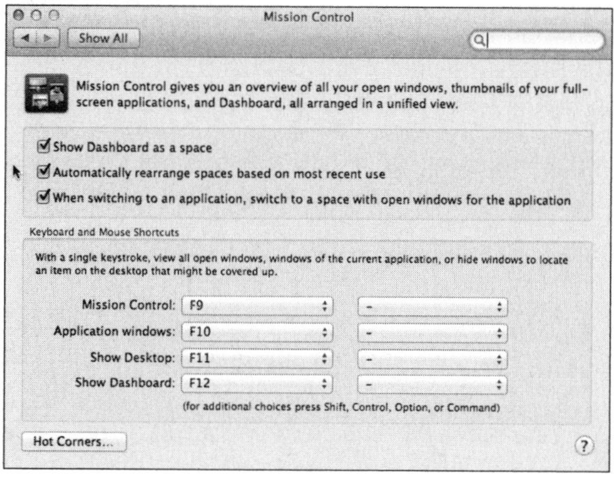

Figure 3-12:
Mission
Control
preferences.

Select the check boxes next to the features you want to activate:

✦ **Show Dashboard as a Space:** Shows Dashboard in Mission Control.

✦ **Automatically Rearrange Spaces Based on Most Recent Used:** Moves your Desktop Spaces around so the most frequently used are first. If you're a creature of habit and like to find things where you put them, leave this check box deselected.

✦ **When Switching to an Application, Switch to a Space with Open Windows for That Application:** When you open an application, your Desktop scrolls automatically to the Desktop that has a window open and uses that application.

In the Keyboard and Mouse Shortcuts section of the Mission Control dialog, you can use the pop-up menus to set keyboard (left column) or mouse command (right column) shortcuts to access Mission Control, to see Application Windows, to Show Desktop, and to Show Dashboard.

Acquiring New Applications

You can find the more popular Mac applications packaged in pretty boxes that typically contain a single CD/DVD, a thin manual (if any), and a lot of air. Big companies, such as Microsoft, Omni Group, Symantec, and Adobe write and sell most of these commercial applications.

No matter how big your local computer store is, it can offer only a fraction of all available Macintosh applications. For a much greater selection of software, you have to browse for Mac applications in the App Store (see the next section, "Shopping in the App Store") or on the web where you can find three types of software: commercial, shareware, and freeware/open source. The following list spells out how they differ:

✦ **Commercial:** Most companies that sell software through stores also sell the same commercial applications on the web. Sometimes you can even get a discount if you buy the application directly from the publisher and download it via the Internet.

As a further enticement, many commercial applications on the w often offer a trial version that you can download and use for a limited time, such as 30 days. After your trial period is over, the application will either stop working or run with many features turned off. If you pay for the software, the publisher will send you a registration key that converts the trial application into a fully functional version. To find trial versions of applications, just visit the websites of different software publishers.

✦ **Shareware:** Usually, shareware applications are limited functionality, time-limited trial versions, or fully functional applications written by individuals or small companies. The idea is for you to try out the application, and if you like it, you're then supposed to pay for it.

✦ **Freeware:** Freeware applications are typically simple utilities or games, although some commercial companies distribute freeware applications to promote their other products. Sometimes companies offer a freeware version of an application and then sell a more advanced version of that same application. As the name implies, freeware applications are available for you to copy and use at no cost. *Donationware* is a term for a freeware application whose creator welcomes donations to help the developer cover the cost of maintaining and developing new versions of the application.

A variation of freeware applications is *open source*. Like freeware applications, open source applications can be copied and used without paying for them. The main difference is that open source applications let you modify the application yourself if you know the specific application programming language that the application is written in.

Table 3-1 lists some popular open source applications and their commercial equivalents.

Book I
Chapter 3

Managing
Applications on the
Dock, Launchpad,
and Desktop

Table 3-1	Popular Open Source Applications and the Commercial Applications They Can Replace	
Open Source Application	*Purpose*	*Commercial Equivalent*
NeoOffice (www. neooffice.org)	Office suite containing word processing, spreadsheet, presentation, drawing, and database applications	Microsoft Office
OpenOffice.org (www. openoffice.org)	Office suite containing word processing, spreadsheet, presentation, drawing, and database applications	Microsoft Office
AbiWord (www. abisource.com)	Word processor	Microsoft Word
Firefox (www. mozilla.com)	Web browser	Safari
Camino (www.camino browser.org)	Web browser	Safari
Thunderbird (www. mozilla.com)	E-mail application	Mail
Tux Paint (www. tuxpaint.org)	Children's painting application	Broderbund Kid Pix
Paintbrush (http:// paintbrush. sourceforge.net)	Basic image editing	Adobe Photoshop Elements

(continued)

Table 3-1 *(continued)*

Open Source Application	Purpose	Commercial Equivalent
Nvu (www.nvu.com)	Web page designing	Adobe Dreamweaver
Audacity (http://audacity.sourceforge.net)	Audio editing	Adobe SoundBooth
ClamXav (www.clamxav.com)	Antivirus scanner	Norton AntiVirus
Celtx (www.celtx.com)	Screenplay word processor	Final Draft

Besides being free, many open source applications offer additional features that their commercial rivals lack.

For example, the Safari web browser comes free with every Mac, but many websites are designed to work only when viewed through Internet Explorer or Firefox. If you use Safari, it's possible that you won't be able to view some websites correctly, so you might want to switch to Firefox (or at least keep Firefox on your hard drive) and if you run across a website that Safari can't open, you can view that website in Firefox.

To find more shareware, freeware, and open source applications for your Mac, visit the following sites:

+ Open Source Mac (www.opensourcemac.org)
+ CNET Download (http://download.cnet.com/mac/)
+ MacShare.com (www.macshare.com)
+ Pure-Mac (www.pure-mac.com)
+ MacForge (www.macforge.net)
+ Tucows (www.tucows.com)
+ MacUpdate (www.macupdate.com)

Shopping in the App Store

Encouraged perhaps by the success of the iPhone/iPad App Store on iTunes, Apple opened the App Store for Mac in January 2011. The App Store application arrives as a free software update with Mac OS X 10.6.6 or later, so if you have an older Mac but have run Software Update (details are in this section) regularly, you have the App Store on the Dock. If you bought a Mac after January 2011, the App Store application came with your Mac.

Book I
Chapter 3

Managing
Applications on the
Dock, Launchpad,
and Desktop

The App Store is a great place to begin looking for new applications to add to your Mac. In this section and the next section, we give you a quick run-down of how the store is organized and how to purchase and download applications from the App Store.

Like the iTunes Store, the App Store is an online service, so you need to have an active Internet connection to browse, purchase, and/or download applications.

Although you can browse the App Store as much as you want, to download even free apps, you need an Apple ID. You can use your iTunes Apple ID, an iCloud Apple ID, or set up a new Apple ID by choosing Store⇨Create Account and following the onscreen instructions, which basically ask for an e-mail address and a password.

When you first click the App Store from the Dock or Launchpad, a window opens similar to the one shown in Figure 3-13.

The opening window of the App Store is updated weekly. Across the top, you see rotating banner ads. Below the banner ads, the left three-quarters of the window is occupied by more app ads, divided in three sections (you have to scroll down the window to see the sections you don't see in Figure 3-13):

Figure 3-13:
The App
Store
window.

✦ **New & Noteworthy:** These are a mix of the latest arrivals to the App Store and those that have generated user and shopper interest.

✦ **What's Hot:** These apps are being downloaded like hotcakes, well, they're being downloaded a lot.

✦ **Staff Favorites:** These apps are the ones that Apple staff like the most this week.

The column running down the right side of the window is divided into sections too:

✦ **Quick Links:** Tap any of these items to Sign In, go to your Account, Redeem iTunes or Apple gift cards, and go to the Support page.

✦ **Categories:** Next down the list is a pop-up menu that lets you choose the category of apps you want to view. This helps narrow your choices when you're looking for a specific type of app. Choose from categories such as Business, Games, Medical, Lifestyle, and Utilities. The Categories pop-up menu is followed by apps or groups of apps that Apple thinks will be useful to get you started, such as OS X Lion, iLife, and iWork.

✦ **Top Paid/Top Free:** These two lists show the top ten most downloaded apps divided by paid apps and free apps. Click See All to view an expanded list of the top paid and free apps for the week.

✦ **Top Grossing:** These apps are the apps that made the most money so you usually find higher-priced apps in this category, unless there's a low-priced app that's sold thousands of copies. Again, click See All to view an expanded list.

You can change the view of the opening window by clicking the tabs across the top. Featured is the opening that we described at the beginning. The others are

✦ **Top Charts:** Shows an expanded view of Top Paid, Top Free, and Top Grossing.

✦ **Categories:** Displays a grid with an icon for each category and the names of three apps in that category. This can help you choose which category best suits your shopping needs.

✦ **Purchased:** When you sign in to your account, you can see all the apps you purchased in your App Store history.

You can consult your past purchases by clicking the Purchased tab at the top of the window or by choosing Store➪Purchased. You can also download purchases again to another Mac or if you accidentally delete it — when you buy something in the App Store, it's yours forever.

✦ **Updates:** Lets you know if any apps you purchased in the App Store have updates available. If you do have updates, you need only click the Download Updates button, and the updates are downloaded immediately and applied to the apps in Launchpad.

Book I
Chapter 3

Managing
Applications on the
Dock, Launchpad,
and Desktop

As you browse through top ten lists and ads, when you find an app that interests you, click on the app name or icon to open the app information screen.

These are the parts of an information screen:

✦ **Name and description for the current version of this app.**

✦ **Buy/Free button**: Click to download the application.

✦ **Pop-up menu:** Click the triangle next to the price/free button for a pop-up menu that has options to tell a friend about it or copy the link, which you can then paste somewhere else, such as an e-mail or a status update on a social network.

✦ **Links to developers website and app-specific support website:** Click either to go to those websites.

✦ **Information box:** Check here for the category, release date and version number, the language used, a rating, and system requirements.

✦ **More By:** Lists other apps by the same developer.

✦ **Sample images:** In the center of the window, you see several sample images that you can click through to see what the app looks like and get an idea of how it works.

✦ **Reviews:** (Not shown in the figure.) Users can give a simple star rating, from zero to five, or write a review. Reviews help you decide if the item is worth downloading or purchasing.

At the bottom, lists show items by the same software developers and other items purchased by people who bought that particular item.

Downloading apps

When you find something you like, click the price or the Free button, and it's downloaded to the Launchpad on your Mac. Some apps have "in-app purchases," which you buy while using the app. Examples of in-app purchases are additional functions or features, chips for online poker games, or music for instrument apps.

You can switch over to Launchpad to see the app downloading or updating and pause or resume the download if you want. Most app downloads and updates are so quick, you won't have any reason to pause and resume. If, however, the power goes out or your Wi-Fi router dies in the middle of the download, when you're back up and running, clicking the app in Launchpad will resume the download at the point it was interrupted. Choose Store➪Check for Unfinished Downloads.

Of course, when you buy, you have to pay from your Apple ID account. This happens two ways:

✦ **Credit Card:** Enter your credit card information into your Apple ID account. If you didn't enter credit card information when you created an Apple ID, you can do so by choosing Store⇨View My Account and clicking Edit to the right of Payment Information. A window opens where you can choose your preferred payment method, such as credit card or Paypal, and type in the necessary information: account number, expiration date, billing address, and so on.

✦ **Redeem:** You can redeem Apple or iTunes gift cards, gift certificates, or allowances. Choose your Apple ID⇨Redeem. Type in the code from the card or certificate. The amount of the card or certificate is added to your account and appears to the left of the Apple ID account tab.

If you ever have a problem with a purchase, choose Store⇨View My Account. Click Purchase History, and then click the Report a Problem button next to the item that isn't working.

If you want to limit the types of downloads that others who use your Mac can make, you can set up separate user accounts and apply Parental Controls. If you apply Parental Controls to your account, those controls apply to you as well. See Book II, Chapter 4.

Installing Applications

Although purchasing, downloading, and installing applications from the App Store is one-stop shopping, if you purchase a packaged application from a store or download an application from a website, you have to install it yourself.

The most common place to install software is inside the Applications folder, so you should specify that folder when installing software. Some applications store their application icon inside the Applications folder plain as day, but others hide their application icons within another folder.

An application icon actually represents a folder containing multiple files. Hiding these details from you and letting you treat a folder of files as a single application icon ensures that you can't accidentally delete or move a single crucial file that the entire application needs to work. For the technically curious, you can see the hidden files tucked inside an application by Control-clicking the application icon and choosing Show Package Contents from the shortcut menu. You're free to look around, but we strongly advise that you don't delete, move, modify, or rename any of the files you see, because doing so might render the application inoperable.

Installing an application from a CD/DVD

Software bought from a store will probably come on a CD/DVD. When you insert the CD/DVD into your Mac, you might see nothing but a single application icon, along with several other files labeled Read Me or Documentation.

Book I
Chapter 3

Managing
Applications on the
Dock, Launchpad,
and Desktop

Other times, you might insert a CD/DVD and see an icon labeled Install. When you see an Install icon, you need to run this installation application to install the application on your hard drive.

When installing software, your Mac might ask for your password — the one you set up when you created your user account. (For more on user accounts, see Book I, Chapter 5.)

Requiring your password to install an application keeps unauthorized people (such as your kids) from installing applications that you might not want on your Mac, or applications you want to approve of before allowing another user to install on your Mac. (We write about parental controls and password protection in Book II, Chapter 4.)

Dragging an application icon off the CD/DVD

If you insert an application's CD/DVD into your computer and just see an application icon, you install the application by dragging the application icon into your Applications folder. To do this, follow these steps:

1. **Insert the software CD/DVD into your Mac or an external drive if you have a MacBook Air.**

   A window appears, showing the contents of the CD/DVD, as shown in Figure 3-14.

2. **Click the Finder icon in the Dock and then choose File⇨New Finder Window (or press ⌘+N).**

   A second Finder window appears, and is ready to do your bidding.

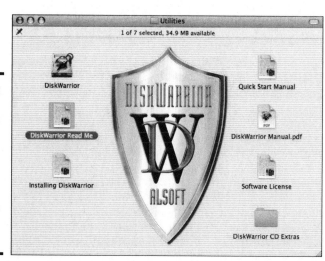

Figure 3-14: A CD/DVD contains an application icon along with other document icons that contain info about the application.

3. **Move the CD/DVD window and the Finder so they appear side by side.**

4. **Click and drag the application icon displayed in the CD/DVD window to the Applications folder in the Finder Sidebar.**

   Doing so copies the application icon from the CD/DVD to the Applications folder.

Running an installer application

Instead of displaying an application icon, a CD/DVD might display an Install icon. The installer is simply a special application designed to copy an application from the CD/DVD and place it in your Applications folder, as well as other files to other folders on your Mac.

To install software by using an installer application on a CD/DVD, follow these steps:

1. **Insert the software CD/DVD into your Mac and look for an icon labeled Install in the window that appears showing the contents of the CD/DVD.**

   The Install icon typically looks like a cardboard box with its top opened up.

2. **Double-click this Install icon and click Continue on the dialog that appears asking whether you really want to continue installing.**

3. **Follow the onscreen instructions.**

   If you have multiple hard drives, the installation application might ask where to install the application. (Generally, you should choose your Mac's built-in hard drive unless you have a reason to store the application elsewhere.) Right before the application installs, you're asked for your password.

Installing an application from the web

Although you can buy software in a box from your local computer store, it's becoming far more common to buy software directly from the web. Not only does this save the publisher the time and expense of packaging an application in a fancy box and shipping it to a store, but it also gives you the software to use right away.

When you download an application off the Internet, the application usually arrives as a DMG (disc image) file. Safari, Mac OS X's default web browser, stores all downloaded files in a special Downloads folder in your Home folder (unless you direct it to your Mac's Desktop or another folder of your choosing). The Downloads folder also appears right next to the Trash icon in the Dock. (If you're using a different browser, such as Firefox, you might need to define where it stores downloaded files.)

Book I
Chapter 3

Managing
Applications on the
Dock, Launchpad,
and Desktop

Distributing software as a DMG file is the most common way to compress files for sending via the Internet. A DMG file essentially copies the contents of an entire folder and smashes it into a single file. You can always identify a DMG file because its icon appears with a hard drive icon, and the name includes the three-letter .dmg extension.

After you have a DMG file on your Mac, you're set to install the software inside it. Just follow these steps:

1. Double-click the DMG file that contains the application you want to install on your Mac. (If a License Agreement window appears, click the Agree button.)

The DMG file displays a device icon on the Desktop and displays a Finder window that contains either the application icon or installer stored inside the DMG file, as shown in Figure 3-15.

2. Click the Finder icon in the Dock, choose File➪New Finder Window, and then click and drag the application icon in the DMG Finder window to the Applications folder in the second Finder window or simply double-click the installer and let it do its thing.

Doing so installs the application in your Applications folder.

3. Control-click the DMG device icon on the Desktop, and when a shortcut menu appears, choose Eject.

When you open a DMG file, it creates a *device icon*, a space that acts like a separate storage device — specifically, a temporary disk from which you can copy files. After you install an application from the DMG file, you might want to eject the DMG device icon just to clear it out of the way. (Leaving it on your Desktop won't hurt anything.)

Figure 3-15:
Expanding a DMG file displays an application icon or installer.

After you install an application on your Mac, you can always find it again by looking in the folder where you stored it, which is usually the Applications folder. At this point, you might want to add the application icon to the Dock or place an alias icon on the Desktop (see the earlier section, "Working with Alias Icons"). As long as it's in the Applications folder, you find in on the Launchpad too.

The first time you run a newly installed application, one of the following dialogs might pop up (see Figure 3-16), reminding you to be sure the application came from a secure source, informing you that the application was downloaded from the Internet, and/or you are running the application for the first time. To run the application, click Open. These dialogs pop up as a way of trying to protect you from malicious applications that might try to install and run themselves automatically. If you didn't try to run an application and see this dialog pop up, click Cancel.

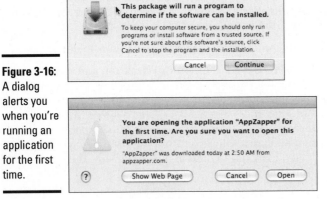

Figure 3-16: A dialog alerts you when you're running an application for the first time.

Updating Applications and System Software

Developers are constantly working to improve and enhance their applications or fix bugs that have been pointed out by disgruntled customers. You want to keep your applications up to date to take advantage of these improvements.

You see a badge on the App Store icon in the Dock to let you know when any applications you downloaded from the App Store have been updated. Simply click the Update button on the App Store and the updates will be downloaded.

You can set up your Mac to automatically check for updates to the Mac OS by choosing ❖⇨System Preferences, and then choose Software Update in the System section. As shown in Figure 3-17, select the Check for Updates check box, and then choose the frequency you want to check from the pop-up menu: Daily, Weekly, or Monthly. You can also leave the box unchecked and check manually by choosing ❖⇨Software Update, but we suggest that you let your Mac worry about checking for updates for you. Click the Installed Software tab to see a list of all the system software and version numbers installed on your Mac.

When new software is available, a message arrives, as shown in Figure 3-18.

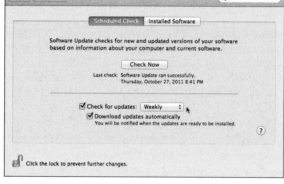

Figure 3-17: Let Software Update check automatically for system software updates.

Figure 3-18: Your Mac lets you know when updates are available.

Other applications also have automatic software updates available. You usually find them either under the Help menu or in the Application menu. If you're having problems with a particular application, go to the developer's website to see if there is an update. If you're having a problem, others probably are too, and an update can often be the remedy.

Uninstalling Applications

If you no longer use or need an application, you can always remove it from your hard drive. By uninstalling an application, you can free up space on your hard drive.

Don't uninstall an application that you might need after all because if you don't have the original installation disc, you may have to purchase the application again.

Uninstalling an application can involve three parts:

✦ **Uninstalling the application:** Uninstalling an application, either by dragging it to the Trash or running an accompanying uninstaller application, physically removes the application from your hard drive.

✦ **Deleting application icons/alias icons:** When you delete an application, you don't necessarily delete that application's icon from the Dock or any alias icons that you created from that application icon. To delete an application's alias icon from the Dock, click and drag the alias icon up and away from the Dock; then let go to make the alias icon disappear in a puff of smoke. To delete an application's alias icon from the Desktop or inside a folder, click and drag the alias icon to the Trash; choose Finder⇨Empty Trash to delete the alias icon (and any other items you may have dragged into the Trash bin).

Deleting the alias is *not* the same as deleting the application because the alias is only a pointer to the application, not the application itself. Removing the alias is useful to eliminate clutter but won't eliminate the application.

✦ **Deleting application settings:** Most applications store user settings in the Library folder, which is located inside your Home folder. The Library folder is invisible, but if you want to see it, hold down the Option key while clicking the Go menu, and choose Library. When you uninstall an application by dragging it to the Trash, its user settings files — also referred to as *application preferences* — remain on your hard drive. Uninstalling an application by using an accompanying uninstaller application sometimes deletes your user settings files automatically, or offers you the option to do so if you want. Although not necessarily harmful, you might want to delete an application's user settings files off your hard drive to free up space for more applications or documents, and to protect potentially personal information from prying eyes if you are giving away or selling the computer to another person. To delete an application's user settings files from your Mac's hard drive, check out the upcoming "Removing user setting files" section.

VMB Uninstaller

If an application you want to uninstall comes with an uninstaller application, such as this one that comes with Vodafone Mobile Broadband (shown in the margin), double-click it to uninstall your application instead of dragging it to the Trash. However, the next few sections give you a more detailed look at what's involved when you uninstall an application by dragging it to the Trash.

Book I
Chapter 3

Managing
Applications on the
Dock, Launchpad,
and Desktop

Uninstalling an application

Uninstalling a Mac application is typically as simple as dragging and dropping its application icon into the Trash. Applications that are pre-installed on your Mac are extremely difficult to remove; we suggest that you don't try to remove them.

To uninstall an application, follow these steps:

1. **Make sure that the application you want to uninstall isn't running. If it is running, shut it down by choosing the Quit command (⌘+Q).**

2. **Click the Finder icon in the Dock.**

   The Finder appears.

3. **Click the Applications folder in the Finder Sidebar to display the applications installed on your Mac, and then click the application icon or folder that you want to uninstall.**

4. **Choose File⇨Move to Trash.**

   Alternatively, you can also drag the application icon or folder to the Trash icon in the Dock, or press ⌘+Delete to move the application icon or folder to the Trash.

   In some cases, you might be prompted for your password when you move an application file to the Trash. If so, type in your password and then click OK or press Return.

   The Trash icon displays an image showing the Trash filled with crumpled papers.

   Before emptying the Trash, make sure that you want to permanently delete any other applications or documents you might have dragged into the Trash. After you empty the Trash, any files contained therein are deleted from your hard drive forever.

5. **Choose Finder⇨Empty Trash.**

   Alternatively, you can Control-click the Trash icon and choose Empty Trash, or press ⌘+Shift+Delete to empty the Trash.

   Adios, application!

From the Launchpad, you can delete applications purchased in the App Store. Press the Option key and all the icons begin to wiggle and jiggle. Those you can delete from the Launchpad have an "x" on the upper left of the icon. Click the "x." A message asks if you really want to delete the application. Click Delete if you do; click Cancel if you don't.

Removing application alias icons from the Dock and Desktop

After you uninstall an application, it's also wise to remove all Dock or alias icons because those icons will no longer work. To remove an application icon from the Dock, click the application icon that you want to remove, drag the icon up and away from the Dock, and then release the mouse button. Your chosen application disappears in a puff of animated smoke.

If you created multiple alias icons of an application, click the Finder icon to open a new Finder window, click in the Spotlight text box, and then type the name of the application you uninstalled followed by the word *alias,* such as **PowerPoint alias** or **Stickies alias**. The Finder will display the location of the specified alias icons, as shown in Figure 3-19. Hold down the ⌘ key, click each alias icon you want to delete, and then press ⌘+Delete to move them to the Trash. *Au revoir!*

Spotlight text box

Figure 3-19: Spotlight can help you find all alias icons.

Removing user setting files

Almost every application creates special user setting files that contain custom settings and preferences for the application, such as the default font used to type text when you use the application or your choice of toolbar icons displayed by the application. When you uninstall an application by dragging it to the Trash, the application's user setting files remain on your computer.

Book I
Chapter 3

Managing
Applications on the
Dock, Launchpad,
and Desktop

The more unnecessary files you have cluttering your hard drive, the slower your Mac might perform because it needs to keep track of these unused files even though it isn't using them anymore. To keep your Mac in optimum condition, you should delete the user setting files of applications you uninstall from your computer. You can do that manually or you can buy an application to do it for you automatically. We explain both ways.

Manually removing user setting files

Manually removing user setting files requires deleting individual files or entire folders from your Mac's hard drive. This process isn't difficult, though it can be tedious.

If you feel squeamish about deleting files that you don't understand, don't delete them without an expert's help. If you delete the wrong files, you could mess up the way your Mac works.

Many applications store their user setting files in one or both of two folders: the Application Support folder and the Preferences folder. To find these two folders, click anywhere on the Desktop, and then hold down the Option key and choose Go⇨Library. Look inside the Application Support and Preferences folders and click any icons or folders bearing the name of the application you uninstalled; drag them to the Trash and choose File⇨Empty Trash (or press ⌘+Shift+Delete).

Automatically removing user setting files

Because manually deleting user setting and preference files might seem scary and intimidating, you may prefer to remove these files automatically. To do so, you have to buy and install a special uninstaller application. When you run an uninstaller application, you tell it which application you want to uninstall and the uninstaller application identifies all the files used by that application, as shown in Figure 3-20.

Figure 3-20:
An uninstaller application finds and deletes all application files.

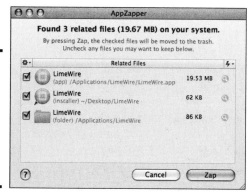

Some popular uninstaller applications include

✦ AppZapper (`www.appzapper.com`)

✦ Spring Cleaning (`http://my.smithmicro.com/mac/springcleaning`)

✦ Uninstaller (`http://macmagna.free.fr`)

Chapter 4: Working with Files and Folders

In This Chapter

✔ Using the Finder

✔ Organizing and viewing folders

✔ Creating folders

✔ Manipulating files and folders

✔ Searching with Spotlight

✔ Setting up Smart Folders

✔ Putting folder and file icons on the Dock

✔ Deleting files and folders

*W*hen you need to organize stuff scattered around the house, one strategy would be to toss everything in the middle of the floor. However, it's probably easier to take a more organized approach by storing off-season clothes in one box, retired gadgets in another box (to be taken to the local recycling center), bills in one file folder, and new books you want to read — or your e-book reader — on your nightstand.

Computers work in a similar way. Although you *could* dump everything on the top level of your hard drive, it's more helpful to divide your hard drive in a way that can help you sort and arrange your stuff in an orderly, easy-to-get-to fashion. Instead of boxes or shelves, the Mac uses *folders* (which tech-types like Joe also refer to as *directories*). In a nutshell, a folder lets you store and organize related files.

This chapter is dense with information, but familiarizing yourself with the way your Mac organizes documents, applications, and files will make everything you do on your Mac a lot easier. We tell you several ways to do the same thing so you can choose the way that's easiest for you to do and remember. We begin by explaining the Finder, the tool you use to organize your files and folders. Next, we show you how to create and manage folders. We then shine a light on your Mac's search tool, Spotlight Search. At the end of the chapter, we spell out the procedure for deleting files and folders.

Using the Finder

The Finder manages drives, files, and folders on your Mac. To access the Finder, click the Finder icon (the smiley face icon on the far left) in the Dock. The Finder is divided into two parts, as shown in Figure 4-1:

✦ A left pane showing the *Sidebar,* which is where you find a list of connected storage devices as well as commonly used folders.

✦ A right pane showing the contents of the selected drive or folder (or search results if one was performed). If you switch to List, Column, or Cover Flow view, which we explain in the section "Organizing and Viewing a Folder," the right pane also shows a hierarchy of files stored inside folders.

Understanding devices

The Devices category of the Sidebar lists all removable or nonremovable storage devices you can use for storing and saving files. *Nonremovable devices* are always connected to your Mac. Every Mac has one nonremovable device, which is the drive that your Mac boots from; typically, it's an internal hard disk drive (HDD) or solid state drive (SSD), which is named Macintosh HD.

A *removable drive* is any additional drive that you plug into your Mac, such as an external hard drive. If your desktop Mac has a second hard drive installed, it also appears in the list of devices. You can eject a removable drive when you no longer need to access it or want to take it with you. Ejecting a removable hard drive or USB flash drive removes its icon from the Finder. However, you can't eject a nonremovable drive (makes sense, right?). After you eject a removable external hard drive or USB flash drive, you can physically disconnect it from your Mac.

If you physically try to disconnect a removable drive before you eject it, your Mac might mess up the data on that drive. Always eject removable drives before physically disconnecting them.

Removable devices can be attached and disconnected at any time. Common types of removable devices are external hard drives, USB flash drives, and digital cameras.

To connect a removable device to your Mac, just plug it in with the appropriate FireWire, Thunderbolt, or USB cable.

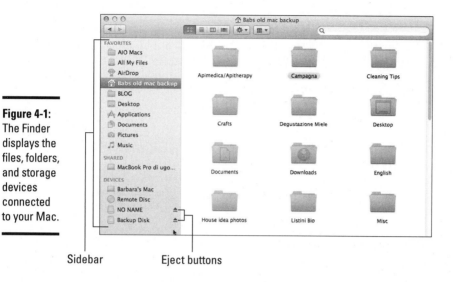

Figure 4-1:
The Finder
displays the
files, folders,
and storage
devices
connected
to your Mac.

Sidebar   Eject buttons

To remove a removable device from a Mac, follow these steps:

1. **Click the Finder icon in the Dock to open the Finder window, and
    then click the Eject button next to the connected drive you want to
    remove in the Finder window sidebar.**

    If the removable device is a CD/DVD, your Mac ejects it. If the removable
    device is plugged into a USB (Universal Serial Bus) port or a FireWire
    port on your Mac, you have to physically disconnect the device.

2. **Wait until the device's icon disappears from the Finder.**

3. **Physically disconnect the device from your Mac.**

Some other ways to choose the Eject command are

✦ Click the device icon on the Desktop and choose File⇒Eject.

✦ Click the device icon and press ⌘+E.

✦ Control-click the device icon and choose Eject from the shortcut menu
   that appears.

✦ Drag the device icon to Trash on the Dock (it turns into an Eject button);
   then let go of the mouse.

Understanding folders

All the data you create and save by using an application (such as a word-processing document or a photograph you copy from your digital camera to your Mac's hard drive) is stored as a file. Although you can store files on any storage device, the more files you store on a single device, the harder it is to find the one file you want at any given time.

Folders help you organize and manage files on a storage device in a logical way. You can even store folders inside other folders. Initially, every Mac hard drive contains the following folders:

✦ **Applications:** Contains all the software applications installed on your Mac. When you open the Launchpad, you also see all the applications that are stored in the Applications folder.

✦ **Library:** Contains data and settings files used by applications installed on your Mac, fonts, and plug-ins used by the Internet.

✦ **System:** Contains files used by the Mac OS X operating system. You can't change this folder.

Never delete, rename, or move any files or folders stored in the Library or System folders, or else you might cause your Mac (or at least some applications on your Mac) to stop working. Files in the Library and System folders are used by your Mac to make your computer work. If you delete or rename files in either folder, your Mac might not operate the way it's supposed to, or (worse) grind to a halt.

✦ **Users:** Contains any files you create and save, including documents, pictures, music, and movies.

✦ **Home:** Kept in the Users folder, each account on your Mac is assigned a Home folder when the account is set up. (See Book I, Chapter 5 for more information about creating accounts.) The Home folder has the same name as the account and can't be renamed. The Home folder of the user who is logged in looks like a little house (refer to Figure 4-1).

Each Home folder automatically contains the following folders when an account is set up. Notice that these folders have icons on them.

• *Desktop:* Contains any application and document icons that appear on your Mac's Desktop.

• *Documents:* Contains any files you create and save by using different applications. (You'll probably want to organize this folder by creating multiple folders inside it to keep all your files organized in a logical, easy-to-manage way.)

• *Downloads:* Contains any files you download from the Internet.

✦ **Library:** Contains folders and files used by any applications installed on your Mac. (***Note:*** There are three Library folders, one stored on the top level of your hard drive, another inside that Library folder, and one hidden inside your Home folder, which you can see by holding the Option key and choosing Go➪Library.)

✦ **Movies:** Contains video files created by iMovie and certain other applications for playing or editing video, such as Final Cut Pro X or QuickTime Player.

✦ **Music:** Contains audio files, such as music tracks stored in iTunes, or created by GarageBand or another audio application such as Audacity.

✦ **Pictures:** Contains digital photographs, such as those you import into iPhoto.

✦ **Public:** Provides a folder that you can use to share files with other user accounts on the same Mac, or with other users on a local area network.

✦ **Sites:** Provides a folder for storing any web pages, such as those created with iWeb.

Every drive (such as your hard drive) can contain multiple folders, and each folder can contain multiple folders. A collection of folders stored inside folders stored inside other folders is a *hierarchy*. It's important to know how to view and navigate through a folder hierarchy to find specific files.

Setting Finder preferences

You can choose the items you see in the Finder Sidebar and also how the Finder behaves in certain situations by setting the Finder preferences to your liking. Follow these steps, and remember you can always go back and change them later if you think of a better setup:

1. **Click the Finder icon in the Dock.**

A Finder window opens.

2. **Choose Finder➪Preferences.**

The Finder Preferences window opens.

3. **Click the General button at the top, if it isn't selected.**

4. **Select the check boxes next to the items you want to see on your Desktop.**

You can select any or all of the following: Hard Disks, External Disks, CDs, DVDs, and iPods, and/or Connected Servers.

5. **From the New Finder Windows Show pop-up menu, choose which window you want to open when you open the finder.**

6. **(Optional) Select the Always Open Folders in a New Window check box if you want to see a new window each time you click a folder.**

   This means that your Desktop gets cluttered with open windows pretty quickly if you have a deep hierarchical system; we suggest leaving this option deselected.

7. **Click the Sidebar button.**

   The Sidebar preferences pane opens, as shown in Figure 4-2.

8. **Select the check boxes next to the items you want to see in the Finder Sidebar.**

   When the Finder is open, you can show and hide the items in each category by clicking the Show/Hide button that appears when you hover to the right of the category title in the Sidebar.

9. **Click the Labels button to assign names to each color label, such as Urgent to Red or Energy Saving Tips for Green.**

10. **Click the Advanced button to activate the following options:**

    - *Show All Filename Extensions* displays the file extension on every file-name on your Mac. File extensions are the two or three letters after a file name, such as `.doc` or `.xls`.

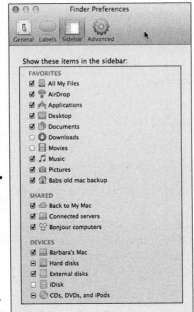

Figure 4-2: Choose the items you see listed in the Finder Sidebar in Finder Preferences.

- *Show Warning before Changing an Extension* opens a dialog if you save a file as a different type, such as saving a .doc file as .txt.

- *Show Warning before Emptying the Trash* gives you time for second thoughts before you throw a document away.

- *Empty Trash Securely* overwrites files when you empty the trash so a savvy hacker can't rebuild your documents. This is sort of like shredding your credit card bills before recycling the paper they're printed on.

You can also set the search level for Spotlight search, which we discuss in the "Spotlight Preferences" section, later in this chapter.

11. **Click the red button in the upper-left corner to close the window.**

Navigating through the Finder

To access files you've stored on your Mac, you navigate through the different folders and devices by using the Finder. To navigate, you must first choose a connected drive or device, and then you can open and exit folders or jump between specific folders. We explain each of these methods throughout these sections.

To open the Finder, click the Finder icon on the Dock or click the background of your Desktop and choose File⇨New Finder Window. The Finder opens when you double-click a folder too, but it opens at the level of that specific folder, not at the highest point of the folder (or directory) hierarchy.

Opening a folder

After you choose a device, the Finder displays all the files and folders stored on that device. To open a folder (and move down the folder hierarchy), you have five choices:

✦ Double-click the folder.

✦ Click the folder and choose File⇨Open.

✦ Click the folder and press ⌘+O.

✦ Click the folder and press ⌘+↓.

✦ Control-click the folder and choose Open from the shortcut menu that appears.

Each time you open a folder within a folder, you're essentially moving down the hierarchy of folders stored on that device.

Exiting a folder

After you open a folder, you might want to go back and view the contents of the folder that encloses the current folder. To view the enclosing folder (and move up the folder hierarchy), choose one of the following:

✦ Choose Go⇨Enclosing Folder.

✦ Press ⌘+↑.

✦ Hold down the ⌘ key, click the Finder title bar to display a list of enclosing folders, and then click an enclosing folder.

Click the Finder icon in the Dock, and then choose View⇨Show Path Bar to display the series of folders that lead to a folder you're currently viewing. Double-click any of the folders in the series to switch to that folder's view.

Jumping to a specific folder

By moving up and down the folder hierarchy on a device, you can view the contents of every file stored on a device. However, you can also jump to a specific folder right away by choosing one of these options:

✦ Choose a folder from the Go menu, such as your Mac's Utilities folder, for example, by choosing Go⇨Utilities, or press ⌘+Shift+U. Other folders listed in the Go menu can also be accessed by pressing the appropriate shortcut keys, which appear next to the folder name on the menu.

✦ By clicking a folder displayed in the Sidebar.

✦ Using the Go⇨Recent Folders command to jump to a recently opened folder. (Using this command sequence displays a submenu of the last ten folders you visited.)

If you display the contents of a folder in List, Column, or Cover Flow views, you can view folder hierarchies directly in the Finder. (You find out more about using the List, Column, and Cover Flow views later in the "Organizing and Viewing a Folder" section.)

Jumping back and forth

While you navigate from one folder to the next, you might suddenly want to return to a folder for a second look. To view a previously viewed folder, you can choose the Back command in one of three ways:

✦ Click the Back arrow.

✦ Choose Go⇨Back.

✦ Press ⌘+[.

A command that lets you jump back to a previously opened folder is not the same thing as the Go➪Enclosing Folder command. If you opened an external drive and then switched to the Utilities folder on your hard drive, the Back command would return the Finder to the external drive, but the Go➪Enclosing Folder command would open the Applications folder.

After you use the Back command at least once, you can choose the Forward command. The Forward command reverses each Back command you choose. To choose the Forward command, pick one of the following ways:

✦ Click the Forward arrow.

✦ Choose Go➪Forward.

✦ Press ⌘+].

Organizing and Viewing a Folder

The Finder shows the contents stored on a device, such as a hard drive, which acts like a giant folder. If your Mac's hard drive contains a large number of files and folders, trying to find a particular file or folder can be frustrating. To organize a folder's contents, the Finder can display the contents of a folder in five views (shown in Figure 4-3), which we discuss throughout this section.

To switch to a different view in the Finder, choose View and then choose As Icons, As Lists, As Columns, or As Cover Flow — or just click one of the view icons shown in Figure 4-3.

Selecting items in the Finder

No matter how you view the contents of a folder, selecting items remains the same. You always have to select an item before you can do anything with it, such as copy or delete it. You can select items three ways:

✦ Select a single item (file or folder) by clicking it.

✦ Select multiple items by holding down the ⌘ key and clicking each item.

✦ Selecting a range of items by clicking and dragging the mouse or by using the Shift key.

The Shift key trick works only in List, Column, or Cover Flow view. Just click the first item you want to select in your particular view, hold down the Shift key, and then click the last item in the range that you want to choose. Your desired range is selected, just like that.

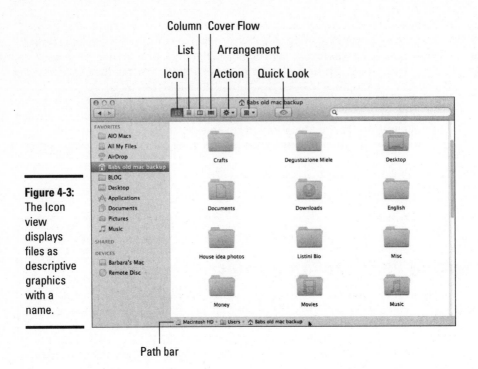

Figure 4-3:
The Icon
view
displays
files as
descriptive
graphics
with a
name.

Path bar

Using Icon view

Icon view displays all files and folders as icons. To organize files in Icon view, you can manually drag icons around, or you can have your Mac automatically arrange icons based on certain criteria, such as name or date modified.

To arrange icons within Icon view manually, follow these steps:

1. **Move the pointer over an icon you want to move.**

   You can select two or more icons by holding down the ⌘ key and clicking multiple icons.

2. **Click and drag the mouse.**

   Your selected icon(s) moves when you move the mouse.

3. **Release the mouse button when you're happy with the new location of your icon(s).**

When you arrange icons manually, they might not align with one another. To fix this problem, make sure that no items are selected and then choose View➪Clean Up Selection to straighten them up.

Manually arranging icons can be cumbersome if you have dozens of icons you want to arrange. As a faster alternative, you can arrange icons automatically in Icon view by following these steps:

1. **Click the Arrangement button in the toolbar of the Finder window to open the pop-up menu shown in Figure 4-4. (Or choose View⇨Arrange By).**

2. **Choose one of the following options:**

   • *Name:* Arranges icons alphabetically.

   • *Kind:* Arranges items alphabetically by file extension, clustering together Microsoft Word files, JPG picture files, and music tracks, for instance.

   • *Application:* Arranges items by application type.

   • *Date Last Opened:* Puts files and folders you opened today in the Today section, those you opened yesterday in the Yesterday section, and so on for the Previous 7 Days, Previous 30 Days, and Earlier.

   • *Date Added:* Same type of sorting as Date Last Opened but by when you added the file or folder. Added files may be ones that were copied or downloaded from another source as well as files or folders you created.

   • *Date Modified:* Arranges the most recently modified items at the top of the window and divides the others in the time intervals as Date Last Opened.

   • *Date Created:* Arranges the most recently created items at the top of the window and divides the others in the time intervals as with Date Last Opened.

   • *Size:* Arranges the largest sized files and folders at the top of the window. Files are grouped by size divisions such as 100MB to 10GB, 1MB to 100MB, and 10KB to 1MB.

   • *Label:* Arranges icons alphabetically by color. Icons with no color appear near the top of the window followed by icons colored blue, gray, green, orange, purple, red, and yellow.

Figure 4-4:
The
Arrangement
button
opens a
menu that
lists ways
to organize
your icons.

TIP

If you don't see the buttons we describe in the toolbar, choose View⇨ Customize Toolbar. Click and drag the buttons you want to see from the bottom pane to the Finder toolbar. To delete those you don't want to see, simply click and drag them down to the bottom pane and they disappear in a puff of smoke.

Using List view

By default, List view displays each item by name, size, date it was last modified, and the kind of item it is, such as a folder or a PDF (Portable Document Format) file. The biggest advantages of List view are that it always displays more items in the same amount of space than the Icon view, it displays hierarchies of folders as indented items (shown in Figure 4-5), and you can select items from multiple folders at the same time.

You can change the width of the columns by hovering the cursor over the line between to headers until it becomes a vertical line crossed by a double-ended arrow. Click and drag left or right to make the columns wider or narrower. Rearrange the order of the columns by clicking and dragging the header title. Only the Name column must remain as the first column.

The List view makes it easy to select multiple folders at one time by holding down the ⌘ key and clicking each folder you want to select. When you're done selecting folders, you can then click and hold on one of the folders and drag them to wherever you want to move them.

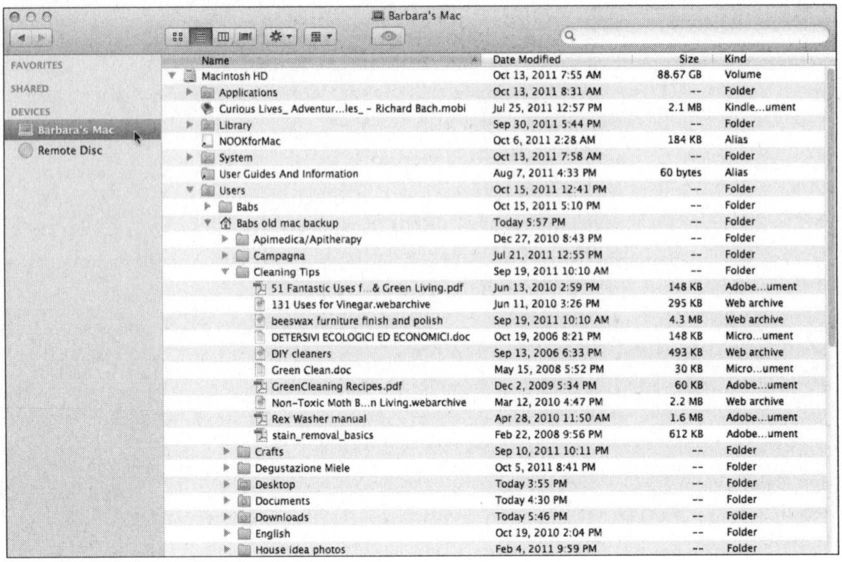

Figure 4-5:
List view displays items in rows and folders as hierarchies.

Name	Date Modified	Size	Kind
▼ 🖥 Macintosh HD	Oct 13, 2011 7:55 AM	88.67 GB	Volume
▶ 📁 Applications	Oct 13, 2011 8:31 AM	--	Folder
📄 Curious Lives_ Adventur...les_ – Richard Bach.mobi	Jul 25, 2011 12:57 PM	2.1 MB	Kindle...ument
▶ 📁 Library	Sep 30, 2011 5:44 PM	--	Folder
📄 NOOKforMac	Oct 6, 2011 2:28 AM	184 KB	Alias
▶ 📁 System	Oct 13, 2011 7:58 AM	--	Folder
📄 User Guides And Information	Aug 7, 2011 4:33 PM	60 bytes	Alias
▼ 📁 Users	Oct 15, 2011 12:41 PM	--	Folder
▶ 📁 Babs	Oct 15, 2011 5:10 PM	--	Folder
▼ 🏠 Babs old mac backup	Today 5:57 PM	--	Folder
▶ 📁 Apimedica/Apitherapy	Dec 27, 2010 8:43 PM	--	Folder
▶ 📁 Campagna	Jul 21, 2011 12:55 PM	--	Folder
▼ 📁 Cleaning Tips	Sep 19, 2011 10:10 AM	--	Folder
📄 51 Fantastic Uses f...& Green Living.pdf	Jun 13, 2010 2:59 PM	148 KB	Adobe...ument
📄 131 Uses for Vinegar.webarchive	Jun 11, 2010 3:26 PM	295 KB	Web archive
📄 beeswax furniture finish and polish	Sep 19, 2011 10:10 AM	4.3 MB	Web archive
📄 DETERSIVI ECOLOGICI ED ECONOMICI.doc	Oct 19, 2006 8:21 PM	148 KB	Micro...ument
📄 DIY cleaners	Sep 13, 2006 6:33 PM	493 KB	Web archive
📄 Green Clean.doc	May 15, 2008 5:52 PM	30 KB	Micro...ument
📄 GreenCleaning Recipes.pdf	Dec 2, 2009 5:34 PM	60 KB	Adobe...ument
📄 Non-Toxic Moth B...n Living.webarchive	Mar 12, 2010 4:47 PM	2.2 MB	Web archive
📄 Rex Washer manual	Apr 28, 2010 11:50 AM	1.6 MB	Adobe...ument
📄 stain_removal_basics	Feb 22, 2008 9:56 PM	612 KB	Adobe...ument
▶ 📁 Crafts	Sep 10, 2011 10:11 PM	--	Folder
▶ 📁 Degustazione Miele	Oct 5, 2011 8:41 PM	--	Folder
▶ 📁 Desktop	Today 3:55 PM	--	Folder
▶ 📁 Documents	Today 4:30 PM	--	Folder
▶ 📁 Downloads	Today 5:46 PM	--	Folder
▶ 📁 English	Oct 19, 2010 2:04 PM	--	Folder
▶ 📁 House idea photos	Feb 4, 2011 9:59 PM	--	Folder

Because List view can display the contents of two or more folders at one time, you can select files from multiple folders. Additionally, if you click a column heading in List view (such as Name or Date Modified), the Finder sorts your items in ascending or descending order.

List view identifies folders by a folder icon and a triangle symbol (which Apple officially refers to as a *disclosure triangle*) pointing to it. Clicking that triangle symbol expands that folder to display its contents — files, more folders, whatever. Clicking the triangle again collapses that folder to hide its contents.

Using Column view

Column view initially displays files and folders in a single column. As with List view, all folders display a triangle next to the folder name. (Okay, okay, in List view, the triangle is just to the left of the folder name, and Column view has the triangle at the far right, but you get the idea.) Clicking a folder displays the contents of that folder in the column to the right, as shown in Figure 4-6.

When you reach an application or document file, the rightmost column shows a preview of the application or document.

You can adjust the width of the columns by clicking and dragging the short, vertical lines at the bottom of the column divider. You can rearrange the order of the columns by dragging the headers, as in List view.

Figure 4-6: Column view displays the folder contents in adjacent columns.

In any view, click the Arrangement button to change the sorting criteria.

Using Cover Flow view

Cover Flow view combines List view with the graphic elements of Icon view, as shown in Figure 4-7. Cover Flow originated from jukeboxes that let you pick songs by viewing and flipping through album covers. In the Finder, Cover Flow lets you choose files or folders by flipping through enlarged icons of those files or folders, which can make finding a particular file or folder easier.

To scroll through items in the Cover Flow view, you have a number of choices:

✦ Click the left and right scroll arrows on the Cover Flow scroll bar (which appears below the enlarged icon preview images).

✦ Drag the scroll box in the Cover Flow scroll bar.

✦ Click in the scroll area to the left or right of the scroll box on the Cover Flow scroll bar.

✦ Click an icon on either side of the icon preview image that appears in the middle of the Cover Flow view.

✦ Press the up- and down-arrow keys to select a different file or folder in the list portion of the Cover Flow view. Each time you select a different file or folder, the Cover Flow icon for that file or folder appears.

If you don't have many files or folders (or you just like everything sort of thrown together), the Finder has an All My Files option, which displays documents from your user account on your Mac, in the view you choose, sorted by the criteria selected from the Arrangement pop-up menu.

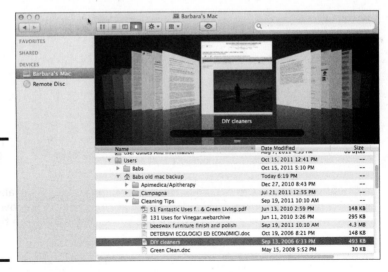

Figure 4-7: The Cover Flow view displays both icons and item names.

Changing your view options

In any view of the Finder or any folder — Icon, List, Column, or Cover Flow — you can change the view options. You can also choose to make one style view the default for every folder you open in a finder or you can set different views for different folders. Follow these steps:

1. **From any of the four views, choose View⇨Show View Options.**

   The View Options window opens, shown in Figure 4-8, displaying these choices from left to right:

   - *Icon View* lets you scale the size of the icons and the grid spacing, adjust the text size and position, and add color to the background.
   - *List/Cover Flow View* have the same options. Choose small or large icons, the text size, and the columns you want to see displayed.
   - *Column View* lets you choose the text size and whether you want to see icons and the preview column.

   In any of the View Options windows, you can choose how to Arrange or Sort the folders and files.

2. **Select Always Open in Icon/List/Column/Cover Flow View if you want to see the selected folder in that view.**

3. **Select Browse in Icon/List/Column/Cover Flow View if you want sub-folders of this folder to open in the same view.**

4. **Click Use as Defaults if you want the Finder and any folders to always open with this view.**

Using Quick Look to view file contents

Quick Look is a nifty feature that enables you to see the contents of a file for many file types without having to run the application you would normally use to create, view, and save it. Just select a file icon and then click the Quick Look view button (or press the spacebar) to display an enlarged preview icon of the selected file, as shown in Figure 4-9. You have three options to close the Quick Look display:

✦ Click the Close button in the upper-left corner.

✦ Press the spacebar.

✦ Press the Escape key.

You can resize the Quick Look display by clicking and dragging any edge or corner of the Quick Look display or by clicking the Zoom arrows icon (bottom center of the display), which fills the entire screen with the Quick Look display.

Figure 4-8:
Use View
Options to
customize
how you
view the
Finder and
folders.

Figure 4-9:
Click a file
icon and
press the
spacebar
to preview
the file's
contents
with Quick
Look.

The Quick Look view behaves differently, depending on the type of file you're peeking into:

✦ An audio file plays in its entirety so you can hear its contents.

✦ A full-size picture file appears in a window so you can see what the picture looks like.

✦ A movie file plays in its entirety so you can see and hear its contents.

✦ PDF (Portable Document Format) files and HTML files (web pages) appear in a scrollable window that lets you read their contents.

✦ A document file (created by other applications such as spreadsheets and word processors) is scrollable if it is a format that QuickLook recognizes or displays the first screen of its contents along with a listing of its name, size, and date of last modification.

✦ A folder appears as an icon listing its name, size, and last modified date.

✦ An application icon is displayed along with a name, size, and last modified date.

If you don't have the application that a file was created in, chances are that you can view it as an image by using the Preview application. From Preview, you can search, copy, and print — but not edit — image and PDF documents. Click the Preview icon on the Launchpad. Choose File➪Open, and then click the file you want to view in the chooser.

You can also sign PDF documents, which we explain in the section about sending a file or photo attachment in Book II, Chapter 2.

Creating Folders

In addition to letting you navigate your way through different folders, the Finder also lets you create folders. The main purpose for creating a folder is to organize related files and folders together. You create a folder in the Finder or the Save As dialog. The next sections walk you through each method.

Creating a folder by using the Finder menu

You can create a folder anywhere, although the first place you're likely to create a folder is inside the Documents folder to organize your files. You might create multiple folders named Word Processor Files, Spreadsheets, and Databases. Or, you might create multiple folders based on topics, such as 2012 Tax Info, which might contain a mix of word processor, spreadsheet, and database files. You decide how to organize your folders.

To create a folder by using the Finder menu, follow these steps:

1. **Click the Finder icon in the Dock.**

   The Finder appears.

2. **In the Sidebar of the Finder, click the location (for example, Desktop or Macintosh HD) or device (such as an external USB flash drive) where you want to create a folder.**

3. **Navigate to and open the folder where you want to store your new folder, such as inside the Documents folder.**

4. **Choose File⇨New Folder (or press ⌘+N).**

   An untitled folder icon appears with its name selected.

5. **Type a descriptive name for your folder and then press Return.**

   Your new folder is christened and ready for use.

Creating a folder through the Save As dialog

The Finder isn't the only way to create a new folder. When you save a file for the first time or save an existing file under a new name (using the Save As command, which is the Duplicate command in apps that support Versions such as Pages or Numbers), you can also create a new folder to store your file at the same time. To create a folder within the Save or Save As dialog, follow these steps:

1. **Create a new document in any application, such as MS-Word or Pages.**

2. **Choose File⇨Save if this is the first time you are saving the document (choose Save As or Duplicate if you already saved the document because Save will only save changes to the current document without opening a dialog).**

   A Save As dialog appears, as shown in Figure 4-10.

3. **Click the Arrow button to the right of the Save As text box.**

   The Save As dialog expands to display your Mac's storage devices and common folders in a Finder-like presentation.

4. **In the Sidebar of the dialog, click the device where you want to create a folder and open the folder where you want to create a new folder.**

5. **Click the New Folder button.**

   A New Folder dialog appears, as shown in Figure 4-11.

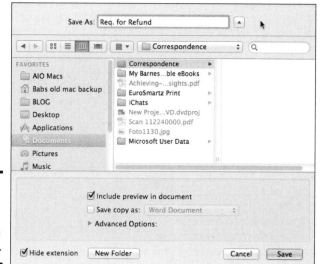

Figure 4-10:
Create a
new folder
while you're
saving a file.

Figure 4-11:
The New
Folder
dialog lets
you name
your folder.

6. **Type a name for your folder in the dialog's text box and then click Create.**

A new folder is created in the location you specified.

This name can't be identical to the name of any existing folder in that location.

7. **In the main window of the Save As dialog, type a name for your document in the Save As text box and click Save.**

Your new document is stored in your new folder.

Using Versions

If you're using an application that supports Versions in Mac OS X 10.7 Lion, the first time you save the document, you see Save in the File menu. After you save the document for the first time, you see Save a Version in the File menu. Versions automatically saves a copy of the file you're working on once an hour while you're working on it. If you want to save a version in the interim, choose File⇨Save a Version. Versions keeps your current document, creates a snapshot of the changed document, and saves a version of the changed document. The new version doesn't have a different name. You access the different versions from within the document and restore an older version if you don't like the changes you made to a more recent version. To see the previous versions of a document, choose File⇨Revert Document. Scroll through the stack of versions that appears and click Restore when you find the version you want to use.

If you want to save a copy of the document and create a new folder in which to place it, choose File⇨Duplicate, and then choose File⇨Save. Create a folder as explained previously and save the duplicated document in the newly created folder.

Manipulating Files and Folders

After you create a file (by using an application such as a word processor) or a folder (by using the Finder or a Save As dialog from an application), you might need to change or edit the name of that file or folder to correct a misspelling or to change the name altogether. Additionally, you might need to move or copy that file or folder to a new location or delete it altogether.

To make sure that you're copying, moving, or changing the correct file, you may want to open it first. However, this can take time, and a faster way to view the contents of a file is to click that file in the Finder window and then click the Quick Look icon (or press the spacebar) to take a peek into the file's contents (refer to Figure 4-9).

Renaming a folder

The only limitation on naming a file or folder is that a name can't be longer than 255 characters. One folder can't have the same name as another folder in that same location. For example, you can't have two folders named Tax Info stored in one folder (such as the Documents folder). You can have two folders with the same name in two different locations, and if you try to move one of them to the same place as the other, your Mac asks whether you want to merge or replace the two folders into one folder with the same name.

You can have two identically named files stored in different folders, and if you try to move a file into a folder that already contains a file with the same name, a dialog will ask whether you want to replace the older file with the new one or keep the new one with the word copy appended to the name.

You can't use certain characters when naming files or folders, such as the colon (:). Additionally, some applications might not let you use the period (.) or slash (/) characters in a filename.

You *can* also store identically named files in the same location if a different application created each file. That means you can have a word processor document named My Resume and a spreadsheet file also named My Resume stored in the same folder.

The reason for this is that a file's complete name consists of two parts: a name and a file extension. The name is any arbitrary descriptive name you choose, but the file extension identifies the type of file. An application file actually consists of the .app file extension, a Microsoft Word file consists of the .doc or .docx file extension, a Pages file consists of the .pages file extension, and a Keynote file consists of the .key file extension.

Therefore, a My Resume file created by Microsoft Word is actually named My Resume.doc, and the identically named file created by Pages is actually named My Resume.pages.

Not all files may have file extensions. It's possible to save a file without a file extension, although this can make it difficult to determine what type of file it is.

To view a file's extension, click that file and choose File⇨Get Info (or press ⌘+I). An Info window appears and displays the file extension in the Name & Extension text box, as shown in Figure 4-12. To view the file extensions for this file, deselect the Hide Extension check box. To view extensions for all files in the Finder, follow the instructions as explained in the earlier section, "Setting Finder preferences."

Folders don't need file extensions, because file extensions identify the contents of a file, and folders can hold a variety of different types of files.

For a fast way to rename a file or folder, follow these steps:

1. **Click a file or folder that you want to rename and then press Return.**

   The file or folder's name appears highlighted.

2. **Type a new name (or use the left- and right-arrow keys and the Delete key to edit the existing name) and then press Return.**

   Your selected file or folder appears with its new name.

When editing or typing a new name for a file, changing the file extension can confuse your Mac and prevent it from properly opening the file because it can no longer identify which application can open the file.

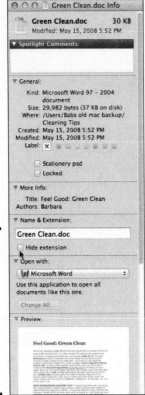

Figure 4-12:
You can
choose to
display file
extensions
of individual
files by
using
the Info
window.

Copying a file or folder

At any time, you can copy a file or folder and place that duplicate copy in
another location. When you copy a folder, you also copy any files and folders
stored inside. To copy a file or folder, you can use either menus or the mouse.

Using menus to copy a file or folder

To copy a file or folder by using menus, follow these steps:

1. **Click the Finder icon in the Dock.**

   The Finder appears.

2. **Navigate to (and open) the folder that contains the files or folders you
   want to copy.**

   Use the Sidebar and the various other navigation techniques outlined
   earlier in this chapter to find what you want.

3. **Select one or more files or folders you want to copy and then choose
   Edit⇒Copy (or press ⌘+C).**

4. **Navigate to (and open) the folder where you want to store a copy of the file or folder.**

5. **Choose Edit⇨Paste (or press ⌘+V).**

   You have your own cloned file or folder right where you want it.

Using the mouse to copy a file or folder

Using the menus to copy a file or folder is simple, but some people find clicking and dragging items with the mouse to be more intuitive. How clicking and dragging works depends on whether you're dragging between two separate devices (such as from a flash drive to a hard drive) or between different folders on the same device.

If you want to use the click-and-drag method to copy a file or folder *from one device to a second device,* follow these steps:

1. **Click the Finder icon in the Dock.**

   The Finder shows its face.

2. **Navigate to (and open) the folder where you want to store your copied files or folders.**

3. **Choose File⇨New Finder Window.**

   A second Finder window appears.

4. **In the Sidebar of the new Finder window, click a device.**

   This device must be different from the device you choose in Step 2.

5. **In this second Finder window, navigate to (and open) the folder containing the file or folder you want to copy.**

6. **Using your mouse, click or drag to select one or more files or folders.**

   If you want to drag a file or folder to a new location on the same device, hold down the Option key while dragging the mouse.

7. **Move the pointer over one of your selected items and then click and drag the selected items into the first Finder window and onto the folder that you opened in Step 2.**

   Notice that a green plus sign appears near the pointer while you drag the mouse.

8. **Release the mouse button.**

   Your selected files and folders appear as copies in the folder you selected.

Copying (or moving) a file or folder from one device (or folder) to another without having to open two windows, described in the steps below, is easy to accomplish thanks to your Mac's *spring-loaded folders* feature. Drag and hold the file or folder you want to copy (or move) over the icon of the device or folder you want to copy to and wait a moment or two until the folder will spring open. (You can keep springing folders open this way until you reach the one you want.) Let go of the mouse button to copy (or move) the file or folder. To adjust how long it takes for folders to spring open, click the Finder, choose Finder⇨Preferences and click the General tab, and then drag the slider at the bottom of the window to adjust how quickly (or slowly) folders spring open when you hover over them with a selected file or folder.

If you want to use the click-and-drag method to copy a file or folder from one folder to another folder *on the same device,* you need to use the Option key. If you don't hold down the Option key in Step 4, you move your selected items rather than copy them.

Moving a file or folder

Dragging a file or folder to a new location on the same device (such as from one folder to another on the same hard drive) always moves that file or folder (unless you hold down the Option key, which ensures that the original stays where it is and a copy is created in the new location). On the other hand, dragging a file or folder from one device to another (such as from a USB flash drive to a hard drive) always copies a file or folder — unless you use the ⌘ key, which puts a halt to the cloning business and moves the file or folder to a new location.

Grouping files

You can select several files from different locations and move them into a folder by holding the ⌘ key and clicking each file, or by holding the Shift key while clicking the first and last file in a list to select all the files between the first and last file selected. Click and hold one of the selected files and begin to drag them toward the folder where you want to place them. They will be grouped together and the number of files appears in a red circle on top of the group. Drag the group over the folder where you want to place them until the folder is highlighted, and then release the mouse or track pad.

If you want to create a new folder for a group of files, select the files as described in the previous paragraph, and then from the Desktop choose File⇨New Folder with Selection. A new folder is created called New Folder with Items, which you can rename as explained previously in the "Renaming a folder" section.

Archiving Files and Folders

Files and folders take up space. If you have a bunch of files or folders that you don't use, yet want or need to save (such as old tax information), you can archive those files. *Archiving* grabs a file or folder (or a bunch of files or folders) and compresses them into a single file that takes up less space on your hard drive than the original file(s).

After you archive a group of files, you can delete the original files. If necessary, you can later *unarchive* the archive file to retrieve all the files you packed into it.

You have two common ways to archive files and folders:

✦ **Creating ZIP files:** ZIP files represent the standard archiving file format used on Windows computers. (By the way, ZIP isn't an acronym. It just sounds speedy.)

✦ **Creating DMG files:** DMG files (DMG is an abbreviation of *disc image*) are meant for archiving files to be shared only with other Mac users. Generally, if you want to archive files that Windows and Mac users can use, store them in the ZIP file format. If you want to archive files just for other Mac users, you can use the ZIP or DMG file format.

The ZIP file format is faster and creates smaller archives than the DMG file format. However, the DMG file format offers more flexibility by allowing you to access individual files in the archive without having to unzip everything the way you must with a ZIP file. Most people use ZIP archives to store data. The most popular way to use DMG files is for storing and distributing software.

Creating a ZIP file

A ZIP file can contain just a single file or folder, or dozens of separate files or folders. To create a ZIP file, follow these steps:

1. **Click the Finder icon in the Dock.**

The Finder comes to the fore.

2. **Navigate to (and open) the folder that contains the file or folder you want to archive.**

3. **Select one or more items you want to archive.**

4. **Choose File⇨Compress.**

If you select three items in Step 3, the Compress command displays `Compress 3 items`.

An archive file named `Archive.zip` appears in the folder that contains the items you selected to compress, as shown in Figure 4-13. (You can rename this file to give it a more descriptive name.)

To open a ZIP file, just double-click it. Doing so creates a folder inside the same folder where the ZIP file is stored. Now you can double-click this newly created folder to view the contents that were stored in the ZIP file.

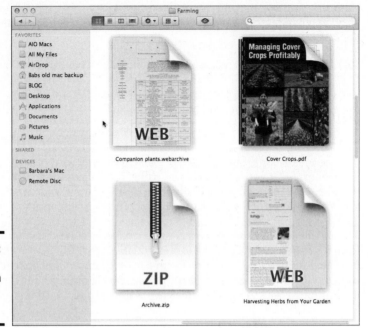

Figure 4-13:
ZIP files
appear with
a zipper
icon.

Creating a DMG file

Although ZIP files are handy for storing files, DMG files more often are used to compress and store large items, such as the contents of an entire folder, CD, or hard drive. To create a DMG file, follow these steps:

1. **Click the Finder icon in the Dock.**

The Finder appears.

2. **Move or copy the files you want to store in the DMG file into a single folder.**

3. **Choose Go⇨Utilities and double-click the Disk Utility application icon.**

The Disk Utility application loads and displays its window.

4. **Choose File⇨New⇨Disc Image from Folder.**

The Select Folder to Image dialog appears.

5. **Using the Select Folder to Image dialog, navigate to and then select the folder containing the files you chose in Step 2.**

6. **Click Image.**

A New Image from Folder dialog appears, as shown in Figure 4-14.

Figure 4-14:
Name and
define the
location of
your disk
image file.

7. **Click in the Save As text box and type a name for your disk image file.**

8. **(Optional) Click the Where pop-up menu and choose a folder or device to store your disk image.**

9. **Click the Image Format pop-up menu and choose one of the following:**

   • *Read-Only:* Saves files in the DMG file, but you can never add more files to this DMG file later.

   • *Compressed:* Same as the Read-Only option, except squeezes the size of your DMG file to make it as small as possible.

   • *Read-Write:* Saves files in a DMG file with the option of adding more files to this DMG file later.

   • *DVD/CD Master:* Saves files for burning to an audio CD or a video DVD.

   • *Hybrid Image (HFS + ISO/UDF):* Saves files in a DMG file designed to be burned to a CD/DVD for use in computers that can recognize Hierarchical File Structure (HFS), ISO 9660 (International Organization for Standardization), or Universal Disk Format (UDF) for storing data on optical media. (Most modern computers can recognize HFS and UDF discs, but older computers might not.) Also saves files in a DMG file designed for transfer over the Internet.

10. **(Optional) Click the Encryption pop-up menu and choose None, 128-bit AES, or 256-bit AES encryption.**

    If you choose encryption, you have to define a password that can open the DMG file.

    AES stands for Advanced Encryption Standard, the American government's latest standard for algorithms that scramble data ✓oose one of these options if you want to prevent prying eyes from viewing your disk image file's contents (unless you share the password with those you trust).

11. **Click Save.**

    Disk Utility displays a progress message while it compresses and stores the files in your chosen folder as a DMG file.

12. **When the disk imaging is complete, choose Disk Utility⇨Quit Disk Utility to exit the application.**

Double-clicking a DMG file displays the contents of that DMG file in the Finder.

Searching Files

No matter how organized you try to be, there's a good chance you might forget where you stored a file. To find your wayward files quickly, you can use the Spotlight feature.

Spotlight lets you type a word or phrase to identify the name of the file you want or a word or phrase stored inside that file. Then Spotlight displays a list of files that matches what you typed. Therefore, if you want to find all the files related to your baseball collection, you could type **baseball** and Spotlight would find all files that contain *baseball* in the filename — or in the file itself, if it's one your Mac can peer into (such as a Word document or an Excel spreadsheet).

Using Spotlight

Spotlight searches for text that matches all or part of a filename and data stored inside of a file. When using Spotlight, search for distinct words. For example, searching for *A* will be relatively useless because so many files use *A* as part of the filename and in the content. However, searching for *ebola* will narrow your search to the files you most likely want.

To use Spotlight, follow these steps:

1. **Click in the Spotlight icon, which looks like a magnifying glass in the upper-right corner of the status bar. Alternatively, press ⌘+spacebar.**

   If you are using an application in full-screen mode, move the pointer up to the upper-right corner of your screen and the status bar appears so you can click the Spotlight icon.

2. **Type a word or phrase.**

   While you type, Spotlight displays the files that match your text, dividing by file type. If you click one of the matching files, a quick view window opens, as shown in Figure 4-15.

3. **Click a file to open it or click Show All In Finder at the top of the list to see the entire list of matches in a Finder window.**

   Narrow your search by setting more limited criteria in the Show All in Finder window.

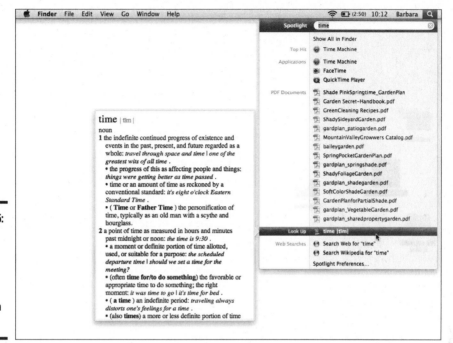

Figure 4-15:
Click one
of the
matching
files in the
Spotlight
list to see a
preview.

4. **Click the plus button next to Save on the right side to open two criteria fields, as shown in Figure 4-16.**

5. **In the first field, choose from Kind, Name, Contents, Visibility, and Creation and Modification Dates. Click Other to open a window that lets you choose more specific attributes to search by.**

6. **Enter information in the successive field (or fields) or pop-up menus to complete the search criteria, and then type the word or words in the file(s) you're seeking.**

   For example, if you choose Name in the first field, the second field enables you to select Matches, Contains, Begins With, and so on.

7. **Repeat Steps 4 through 6 to add another rule for the search criteria.**

8. **When you find the file you're looking for, click the item to open it or drag and drop it to a new location.**

   You can even drop the files in an AirDrop box on a different Mac — read about AirDrop in Book VI, Chapter 2.

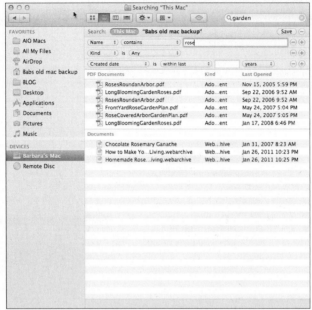

Figure 4-16:
Use specific
criteria to
narrow your
search.

Spotlight Preferences

In Finder⇨Preferences⇨Advanced, you can specify whether you want Spotlight
to perform searches by looking through your entire Mac or only in the active
folder. You can also set preferences for the types of results Spotlight gives you.
Choose ⌘⇨System Preferences and click Spotlight in the Personal section.
Select the check boxes next to the types of files you want Spotlight to include
when searching, as shown in Figure 4-17. Deselect check boxes next to types of
files you want Spotlight to ignore. Then click and drag the names to put them in
order of priority. For example, you may want documents listed before folders,
and you may not want applications to be included in your search results.

Using Smart Folders

Spotlight can make finding files and folders fast and easy. However, if you
find yourself searching for the same types of files repeatedly, you can create
a Smart Folder.

A Smart Folder essentially works behind the scenes with Spotlight to keep
track of a bunch of files that share one or more common characteristics. For
example, you can tell a Smart Folder to store info about only those files that
contain *rose* in the filename or the file; and from now on, you can look in that
Smart Folder to access all files and folders that match *rose* without having to
type the words in the Spotlight text box.

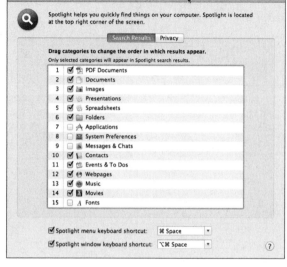

Figure 4-17:
Set
Spotlight
Preferences
to obtain
better
search
results.

Think of Smart Folders as a way to organize your files automatically. Rather than take the time to physically move and organize the files, you can have Smart Folders do the work for you.

A Smart Folder doesn't physically contain any files or folders. Instead, it contains only links to files or folders. This saves space by not duplicating files.

Creating a Smart Folder with Spotlight

To create a Smart Folder, follow these steps:

1. **Click the Finder icon in the Dock.**

The Finder appears.

2. **Choose File⇨New Smart Folder.**

3. **Click in the Spotlight text box and type a word or phrase.**

4. **Click the plus button next to Save on the right side to open two criteria fields. (Refer to Figure 4-16.)**

5. **In the first field, choose from Kind, Name, Contents, Visibility, and Creation and Modification Dates.**

Click Other to open a window that lets you choose more specific attributes to search by.

6. **Enter information in the successive field (or fields) or pop-up menus to complete the search criteria, and then type the word or words in the file(s) you're seeking.**

7. **Click the Save button that appears underneath the Spotlight text box.**

A Save As dialog appears, as shown in Figure 4-18.

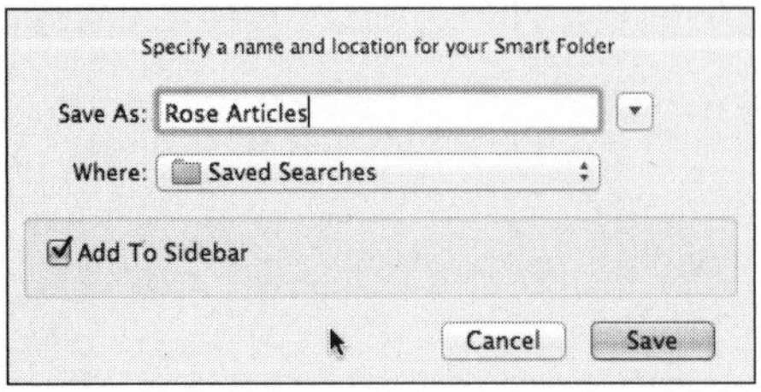

Figure 4-18: Name your Smart Folder and define where to store it.

Specify a name and location for your Smart Folder

Save As: Rose Articles

Where: 📁 Saved Searches

☑ Add To Sidebar

Cancel   Save

8. **Click in the Save As text box and type a descriptive name for your Smart Folder.**

9. **Choose a location to store your Smart Folder from the Where pop-up menu (or click the down arrow and navigate to the location where you want to save your Smart Folder).**

10. **(Optional) Select or deselect the Add to Sidebar check box.**

Select the check box if you want the Smart Folder to appear in the Sidebar in the Searches section near the bottom. Deselect the check box if you don't want to see your Smart Folder in the Sidebar.

11. **Click Save.**

Your Smart Folder appears in your chosen location. Instead of displaying an ordinary folder icon, Smart Folder icons always show a gear inside a folder.

After you create a Smart Folder, it automatically keeps your list of files and folders up to date at all times. If you create new files or folders that match the criteria used to define a Smart Folder, that new file or folder name will appear in the Smart Folder automatically. Delete a file, and the Smart Folder deletes its link to that file as well.

Storing Files and Folders in the Dock

You can always find the files and folders you want by using the Finder. However, you might find that switching to the Finder constantly just to access the contents of a particular folder can be tedious. As a faster alternative, you can store pointers to files and folders directly in the Dock.

Storing files in the Dock

If you have a file that you access regularly, consider placing an icon for that file directly in the Dock. That way, the file icon remains visible at all times (as long as the Dock is visible), and gives you one-click access to your frequently used files.

To place a file icon in the Dock, follow these steps:

1. **Click the Finder icon in the Dock and navigate to the folder containing the file you use frequently.**

2. **Click and drag the file to the Dock into any space to the left of the Trash icon and release the mouse button.**

The icons in the Dock slide apart to make room for the icon. To open this file, just click its file icon.

A file icon in the Dock is just a link to your actual file. If you drag the file icon off the Dock, your physical file remains untouched.

Creating Stacks in the Dock

Rather than clutter the Dock with multiple file icons, consider storing a folder in the Dock. A folder icon, when stored in the Dock, is called a *Stack*. After you create a Stack in the Dock, you can view its contents by clicking the Stack.

To store a Stack in the Dock, follow these steps:

1. **Click the Finder icon in the Dock to open a new Finder window, and then navigate to a folder you use frequently.**

2. **Click and drag the folder to the Dock into any space to the right of the divider and release the mouse button.**

The Dock icons slide apart to make room for your Stack to give your folder a place all its own.

A Stack in the Dock is just a link to your actual folder and files. If you drag the Stack off the Dock, your folder and its file contents remain untouched.

Opening files stored in a Stack

After you place a Stack on the Dock, you can view its contents — and open a file in that Stack — by following these steps:

1. **Click a Stack folder on the Dock.**

The documents in the stack appear.

Control-click (two-finger tap on a trackpad) a Stack icon to display a shortcut menu of options you can choose to customize the way a Stack folder appears in the Dock (as a Stack or Folder) and how its contents are displayed when you click it, as shown in Figure 4-19.

2. **Click the file you want to open in the fan, grid, or list.**

   Your chosen file opens.

Figure 4-19:
Control-click a Stack to display a shortcut menu.

Deleting a File or Folder

To delete a file or folder, you first have to place that item in the Trash. But putting an item in the Trash doesn't immediately delete it. In fact, you can retrieve any number of files or folders you've "thrown away." Nothing is really gone — that is, permanently deleted — until you empty the Trash.

Deleting a folder deletes any files or folders stored inside. Therefore, if you delete a single folder, you might really be deleting 200 other folders containing files you might not have meant to get rid of, so always check the contents of a folder before you delete it, just to make sure it doesn't contain anything important.

To delete a file or folder, follow these steps:

1. **Click the Finder icon in the Dock to open a new Finder window, and then navigate to (and open) the folder that contains the file or folder you want to delete.**

2. **Select the file or folder (or files and folders) that you want to delete.**

3. **Choose one of the following:**

- Choose File⇨Move to Trash.

- Drag the selected items onto the Trash icon in the Dock.

- Press ⌘+Delete.

- Control-click a selected item and choose Move to Trash from the shortcut menu that appears.

Retrieving a file or folder from the Trash

When you move items to the Trash, you can retrieve them again as long as you haven't emptied the Trash since you threw them out. If the Trash icon in the Dock appears filled with a pile of crumbled up paper, you can still retrieve files or folders from the Trash. If the Trash icon appears empty, there are no files or folders there that you can retrieve.

To retrieve a file or folder from the Trash, follow these steps:

1. **Click the Trash icon in the Dock.**

A Finder window appears, showing all the files and folders you deleted since the last time you emptied the Trash.

2. **Select the item (or items) you want to retrieve, drag them onto a device or folder in which you want to store your retrieved items, and then release the mouse button.**

Emptying the Trash

Every deleted file or folder gets stored in the Trash, where it eats up space on your hard drive until you empty the Trash. When you're sure that you won't need items you trashed any more, you can empty the Trash to permanently delete the files and free up additional space on your hard drive.

To empty the Trash, follow these steps:

1. **Click the Finder icon in the Dock (or click the Desktop) and choose File⇨Empty Trash.**

A dialog appears, asking whether you're sure that you want to remove the items in the Trash permanently.

2. **Click OK (or Cancel).**

If you open the Finder and choose Finder⇨Secure Empty Trash, your Mac will write over the deleted files with random data to foil any attempt to recover deleted files later with a special file recovery application. If you want to delete something sensitive that you don't want to risk falling into the wrong hands, choose Finder⇨Secure Empty Trash.

For a faster way of emptying the Trash, Control-click the Trash icon in the Dock and choose Empty Trash from the shortcut menu that appears, or click the Finder icon (or the Desktop) and press ⌘+Shift+Delete.

Chapter 5: Customizing Your Mac and Adjusting Settings

In This Chapter

✔ Changing the Desktop and display

✔ Customizing the screen saver

✔ Setting the date and time

✔ Adjusting sounds

✔ Making Mac more accessible for people with special needs

✔ Talking to your Mac

The Mac user interface functions the same way regardless of the model you have, but that doesn't mean they all have to look and feel the same. To personalize your Mac, you can change the way it looks and even how it behaves.

By customizing your Mac — and adjusting to how it works to make things easier on your eyes, ears, or hands — you can stamp it with your personality and truly turn your Mac into a personal computer that feels like it's working with you and for you, rather than against you.

When you have a choice about how an application or function looks or responds, Preferences are where you go to specify your choices. There are two places to find preferences on your Mac:

✦ **⬤⇨System Preferences** gathers all the preferences settings for your Mac operating system in one place. This is where you set up your Mac's appearance, choose the type of sound your Mac plays when an e-mail message arrives, or connect to a network or printer.

✦ *Application menu*⇨**Preferences** lets you set application-specific preferences.

In this chapter, we discuss the System Preferences. We show you how to customize your Desktop image, set up screen savers, and adjust the screen resolution. We explain how to select different sounds your Mac uses to alert you to new information and how to set the date and time. At the end of the chapter, we introduce you to the Universal Access functions, the preferences you can choose to make working with your Mac easier if you have trouble with your vision, hearing, or movement.

Changing the Desktop

The Desktop fills the screen in the absence of any application windows. Generally, the Desktop displays a decorative background image, but you can display any image, such as a picture captured with a digital camera or a favorite picture you downloaded from the Internet.

Choosing a bundled Desktop image

Your Mac comes with a variety of images stored and organized into different categories. To choose one of these images as your Desktop image, follow these steps:

1. **Control-click anywhere on the Desktop and choose Change Desktop Background from the shortcut menu that appears.**

   The Desktop preferences pane appears, as shown in Figure 5-1.

2. **Click Desktop Pictures to browse images, or click Solid Colors to pick a solid background color.**

3. **Click the image (or color) that you want to adorn your Desktop, and then click the Close button to close the preferences pane.**

   If you want to set your favorite color, say poppy red, as your desktop, click Solid Colors, and then click the Custom Color button under the color chips. The color picker opens; click to choose your preferred shade and click the Close button.

4. **Click the red Close button to close the System Preferences window.**

Figure 5-1: Desktop preferences let you choose a different background image.

The Desktop preferences pane offers other options, which you can see near the bottom of Figure 5-1:

✦ **Change Picture:** Click the pop-up menu to tell your Mac to change the Desktop background picture to another one in the selected category based on a time interval, when you log in to your Mac, or when you wake it from Sleep mode.

✦ **Random:** Randomly changes the Desktop background image.

✦ **Translucent Menu Bar:** Gives your Mac's menu bar a translucent "see through" effect.

Choosing an iPhoto image for the Desktop

If you capture images with a digital camera and store those images in iPhoto, you can choose one of your iPhoto images to appear on your Desktop by following these steps:

1. **Control-click anywhere on the Desktop and choose Change Desktop Background from the shortcut menu.**

   The Desktop preferences pane appears (refer to Figure 5-1).

2. **Click the disclosure triangle that appears to the left of iPhoto in the left column, click an iPhoto category, such as Photos, and then click the image you want to display as your new Desktop background.**

   Your chosen iPhoto image appears on the Desktop as the background image, and a new pop-up menu appears above your iPhoto images.

3. **Click the pop-up menu above your iPhoto images and choose from the following options:**

   • *Fill Screen:* Expands or contracts the image to fill the screen but might cut off edges, depending on the aspect ratio of the original image.

   • *Fit to Screen:* Expands the image to fill most of the screen, but might leave edges uncovered, depending on the aspect ratio of the original image; click the menu to the right of this option to choose the color of the border that may surround the image.

   • *Stretch to Fill Screen:* Stretches a picture to fill the entire screen, which might distort the image similar to the way a carnival mirror can.

   • *Center:* Places the image in the middle of the screen at its original size, and might leave edges uncovered, depending on the image's dimensions; click the menu to the right of this option to choose the color of the border that may surround the image.

   • *Tile:* Duplicates the image in rows and columns to fill the screen.

4. **Click the Close button of the System Preferences window.**

Choosing your own image for the Desktop

You might have images stored on your hard drive that you have not imported into iPhoto. To display non-iPhoto images on the Desktop background, follow these steps:

1. **Control-click (two-finger tap on a trackpad) anywhere on the Desktop and choose Change Desktop Background from the shortcut menu to open the Desktop preferences pane (refer to Figure 5-1).**

2. **Click the triangle symbol that appears to the left of Folders in the left column.**

   You have two options:

   • Click the Pictures folder to display any pictures you've stored in your Pictures folder. Any images stored in separate folders inside the Pictures folder will not initially be visible.

   • Click the Add (+) button in the lower-left corner and use the dialog that appears to navigate to the folder that contains the image you want to use.

3. **Click the image that you want to use for the Desktop background and then click the Close button to close the preferences pane.**

Customizing the Screen Saver

A *screen saver* is an animated image that appears on the screen after a fixed period when your Mac doesn't detect any keyboard, trackpad, or mouse activity. When selecting a screen saver, you can choose an image to display and the amount of time to wait before the screen saver starts.

For an eco-friendlier alternative to using the screen saver, check out the Energy Saver setting described in the section about putting your Mac in sleep mode in Book I, Chapter 1.

To choose a screen saver, follow these steps:

1. **Choose ⚫⇨System Preferences from the Finder menu and click the Desktop & Screen Saver icon in the Personal section or Control-click the System Preferences icon in the Dock and choose Desktop & Screen Saver from the menu that opens.**

   The Desktop & Screen Saver preferences pane appears.

2. **Click the Screen Saver tab to display the Screen Saver preferences pane, shown in Figure 5-2, and then click one of the screen savers listed in the Apple or Pictures category in the left column.**

Figure 5-2:
Screen
Saver
preferences
let you
define an
image and
an inactivity
time.

The preview pane shows you what your screen saver will look like. (If you select the Use Random Screen Saver check box, your Mac will pick a different screen saver image every time the screen saver starts. After your randomly chosen screen saver starts, that same animated image appears until you press a key to turn off the screen saver.)

Under the Pictures category, you can choose the Pictures folder, an iPhoto album, or click the Add (+) button in the lower-left corner and use the dialog that appears to navigate to the folder that contains the image you want to use.

Choose Shuffle under the Pictures category and a window opens that lets you choose which images you want played randomly and gives you options for how the images are displayed. (As opposed to Use Random Screen Saver, where your Mac chooses from all the images.)

3. **Drag the Start Screen Saver slider to specify an amount of time to wait before your screen saver starts.**

    A short amount of time can mean the screen saver starts while you're reading a web page or document, so you might have to experiment a bit to find the best time for you.

4. **(Optional) Select the Show with Clock check box to display the time with your screen saver.**

5. **Click one of the buttons under Display Style to choose how you want the screen saver to appear onscreen.**

6. **(Optional) Click Options.**

    A dialog appears that gives you additional choices for modifying the way your screen saver appears, such as changing the speed that the screen saver image moves.

7. **(Optional) Click Test to preview the way your Screen Saver will look when it turns itself on.**

   Moving the mouse or tapping a key gets you out of test mode.

8. **(Optional) Enable Hot Corners.**

   a. *Click the Hot Corners button (refer to Figure 5-2).*

   b. *Click one (or each) of the four pop-up menus and choose a command that your Mac will carry out when you move your pointer to the specified corner, as shown in Figure 5-3.*

      Two common uses for a hot corner are to turn on the screen saver, or to put your Mac's display to sleep to save energy.

      You can define multiple hot corners to do the same task, such as defining the two top corners to start the screen saver and the two bottom corners to put the display to sleep.

   c. *Click the OK button to close the Hot Corner dialog.*

9. **Click the Close button in the Desktop & Screen Saver preferences pane.**

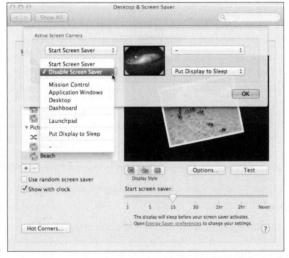

Figure 5-3: Each pop-up menu defines a function for a hot corner.

Changing the Display and Appearance

Because you'll be staring at your Mac's screen every time you use it, you might want to modify the way the screen displays information. Some changes you can make include changing the Desktop size (resolution), or selecting another color scheme of your various menus, windows, and dialogs. The next sections show you how.

Changing the screen resolution

The display defines the screen resolution, measured in *pixels* — the dots that make up an image. The higher the display resolution, the more pixels you have and the sharper the image — but everything on your screen might appear smaller.

Selecting your Mac display's highest resolution generally puts your Mac's best face forward, so to speak, when it comes to making everything look sharp and correct on your screen.

To change the screen resolution, follow these steps:

1. **Choose ⌐System Preferences and click the Displays icon in the Hardware section, or Control-click the System Preferences icon in the Dock and choose Displays from the menu that opens.**

The Display preferences pane opens, as shown in Figure 5-4.

2. **Click the Display tab (if it isn't already selected), and then choose a screen resolution from the Resolutions list.**

Your Mac immediately changes the resolution so you can see how it looks. If you don't like the resolution, try again until you find one that's easy on your eyes.

3. **Slide the brightness tab to adjust the luminosity of your screen or select the Automatically Adjust Brightness check box to have your Mac adjust the screen brightness based on the ambient light.**

4. **(Optional) Click the Color tab, click the Calibrate button, and then follow the steps that appear to tweak the way your Mac displays colors; click the Done button when you reach the final step to return to the Display preferences pane.**

5. **Click the Close button in the System Preferences window when you're happy with the screen resolution.**

**Book I
Chapter 5**

Customizing
Your Mac and
Adjusting Settings

Figure 5-4:
Display
preferences
let you
choose a
different
screen
resolution.

Changing the color of the user interface

Another way to change the appearance of the screen is to modify the colors used in windows, menus, and dialogs. To change the color of these user interface items, follow these steps:

1. **Choose ⌘⇨System Preferences and click the General icon in the Personal section or Control-click the System Preferences icon in the Dock and choose General from the menu that opens.**

   The General preferences pane appears, as shown in Figure 5-5.

2. **Use the Appearance and Highlight Color pop-up menus to choose your color variations.**

   The Appearance pop-up menu defines the colors that normally show up on windows, buttons, and so on, whereas the Highlight Color pop-up menu defines the color of items that you select.

3. **Select the radio buttons and check boxes to adjust how the scroll bars work.**

   These changes will be seen only in applications that support these features. Here are your choices:

   - *Automatically Based on Input Device* reveals scroll bars only when the window is smaller than its contents. This gives you a visual clue that there's more than meets the eye.

   - *When Scrolling* uses a shadowy black oblong that appears only when you are hovering over the right edge of the window if you're scrolling up and down, or on the bottom of the window if you're scrolling left to right. The advantage is that scroll bars don't take up precious window real estate.

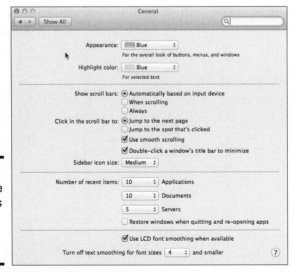

Figure 5-5:
Appearance preferences let you modify colors.

- *Always* puts right side and bottom scroll bars on your windows whether you need them or not.

- *Jump to the Next Page* moves your document up or down one page when you click above or below the scroller in the scroll bar.

- *Jump to the Spot That's Clicked* takes you to the position in your document more or less in relation to where you clicked the scroll bar. If you click near the bottom of the scroll bar, the window jumps toward the end of the document.

- *Use Smooth Scrolling* scrolls through the document or window without jumping.

- *Double-Click a Window's Title Bar to Minimize* works like the yellow button at the top of the window; the window is minimized and an icon appears on the right end of the Dock (or on the lower end if you use the Dock in vertical position).

4. **Use the pop-up menu next to Sidebar Icon Size to choose the size of icons in the sidebar of the Finder window.**

5. **Use the pop-up menus to choose how many items you want to appear in the Recent Items list under the menu.**

6. **Select the Restore Windows When Quitting and Re-opening Apps check box so that when you open an application after quitting, the document you were working on when you quit the application opens automatically.**

7. **Choose Font Smoothing to make fonts appear smoother.**

   Font smoothing can make small fonts hard to read, so if you use a lot of small fonts, choose the size limit for font smoothing from the pop-up menu. Font smoothing will be applied only to font sizes larger than the number you choose.

8. **Click the Close button to close the General preferences pane.**

To move quickly between one System Preferences pane and another, click and hold the Show All button to reveal a pop-up menu that lists all the preferences items in alphabetical order.

Changing the Date and Time

Keeping track of time might seem trivial, but knowing the right time is important so your Mac can determine when you created or modified a particular file and keep track of appointments you've made through applications, such as iCal.

Of course, keeping track of time is useless if you don't set the right time to begin with. To set the proper date and time, follow these steps:

1. **Choose ¢⇨System Preferences and click the Date & Time icon in the Systems section or Control-click the System Preferences icon in the Dock and choose Date & Time from the menu that opens.**

   The Date & Time preferences pane appears, as shown in Figure 5-6.

2. **Select (or deselect) the Set Date & Time Automatically check box. If you select this check box, click the drop-down list to choose a location.**

   This feature works only if you're connected to the Internet. If you aren't connected to the Internet, click the calendar to pick a date and click the clock to pick a time.

3. **(Optional) If you didn't select the Set Date & Time Automatically check box in Step 2, click the Time Zone tab at the top of the window, and click near your home city on the map.**

   You can also click in the Closest City field and begin typing the name of the city nearest you, or click the drop-down list and select the city nearest you, as shown in Figure 5-7.

   Click the Set Time Zone Automatically Using Current Location if you want the clock to change automatically when you travel to a different time zone. This feature works when you have an Internet connection.

4. **Click the Clock tab and select (or deselect) the Show Date and Time in Menu Bar check box, as shown in Figure 5-8.**

   If selected, this displays the time in the right side of the menu bar. After you make your selection, you can select the other options to change the appearance of the clock, such as choosing between a digital or analog clock, and choosing whether to show the day of the week.

Figure 5-6:
Date & Time
preferences
let you set
the clock in
your Mac.

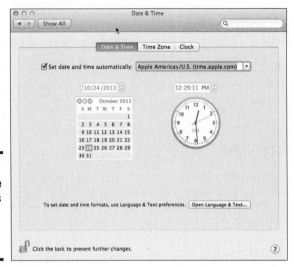

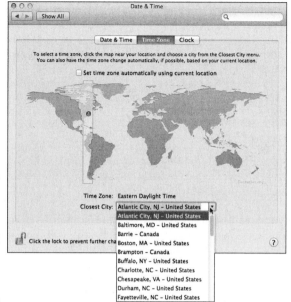

Figure 5-7:
The Time
Zone pane
lets you pick
the closest
city in your
time zone.

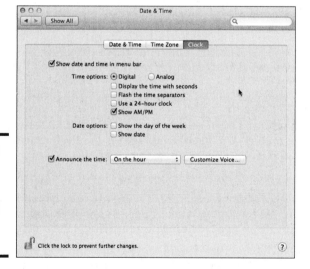

Figure 5-8:
The Clock
pane lets
you pick
the type of
clock you
want.

5. **Select (or deselect) the Announce the Time check box if you want
your Mac to recite the time by using a synthesized voice every hour,
half-hour, or quarter hour.**

   The associated pop-up menu lets you specify when announcements are
   made; the Customize Voice button is what you click to choose what kind
   of voice is used and how quickly and loudly it utters the time.

6. **Click the Close button to close the Date & Time preferences pane.**

You can customize the layout of the System Preferences window by choosing View➪Customize. Deselect the check box next to the items you don't want to see.

Adjusting Sounds

Every Mac can play sound through speakers (built-in or external) or headphones, from making the simplest beeping noise to playing audio CDs like a stereo. Three primary ways to modify the sound on your Mac involve volume, balance, and input/output devices.

Volume simply means how loud your Mac plays sound by default. Many applications, such as iTunes, also let you adjust the volume, so you can set the default system volume and then adjust the volume within each application, relative to the system volume, as well.

Balance defines how sound plays through the right and left stereo speakers. By adjusting the balance, you can make sound louder coming from one speaker and weaker coming from the other.

Depending on your equipment, it's possible to have multiple input and output devices — speakers and headphones as two distinct output devices, for example. By defining which input and output device to use, you can define which one to use by default.

To modify the way your Mac accepts and plays sound, follow these steps:

1. **Choose ➪System Preferences and click the Sound icon in the Hardware section or Control-click the System Preferences icon in the Dock and choose Sound from the menu that opens.**

   The Sound preferences pane appears, as shown in Figure 5-9.

2. **Click the Sound Effects tab if it isn't already selected and choose the sound your Mac will play when it needs your attention, such as when you're quitting an application without saving a document.**

3. **(Optional) Click the Play Sound Effects Through pop-up menu to choose whether your Mac plays sounds through its built-in Internal Speakers or through another set of speakers you might have connected to your Mac.**

4. **(Optional) Drag the Alert Volume slider to the desired location to set how loudly (or softly) your Mac will play the alert when it needs to get your attention.**

Figure 5-9:
Sound
Effects
preferences
let you
define
which
sound to
use as an
alert.

5. **(Optional) Select (or deselect) either of the following check boxes:**

   - *Play User Interface Sound Effects:* Lets you hear such sounds as the crinkling of paper when you empty the Trash or a whooshing sound if you remove an icon from the Dock.

   - *Play Feedback When Volume Is Changed:* Beeps to match the sound level while you increase or decrease the volume.

6. **(Optional) Drag the Output Volume slider.**

   Output volume defines the maximum volume that sound-playing applications can emit, so if you set Output volume at 75 percent and then play a song in iTunes with the iTunes volume at 50 percent, the song pays at 37.5 percent of the Mac's maximum output capacity.

7. **Click the Output tab to display the Output preferences pane, as shown in Figure 5-10.**

8. **Click the output device you want to use if you have another output option connected to your Mac, such as headphones or external speakers.**

9. **(Optional) Drag the Balance slider to adjust the balance.**

10. **(Optional) Select (or deselect) the Show Volume in Menu Bar check box, which, when selected, lets you see and adjust your Mac's volume with the menulet in the menu bar.**

11. **Click the Input tab to open the Input preferences pane, shown in Figure 5-11, and then click the input device you want your Mac to use to receive sound, such as the built-in microphone, or the Line In port.**

    Your Mac may not have a Line In port — the MacBook Air does not. You can use the Line In port to plug a TV or stereo into to record sound.

12. **(Optional) Drag the Input Volume slider to adjust the default input volume.**

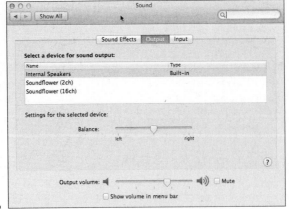

Figure 5-10:
Output
preferences
let you
define how
to play
sound.

13. **(Optional) Select (or deselect) the Use Ambient Noise Reduction check box to eliminate background noise.**

    Select this option if someone you're having a voice or video chat with iChat complains that they can't hear you clearly.

14. **Click the Close button to close the Sound preferences pane when you finish making adjustments.**

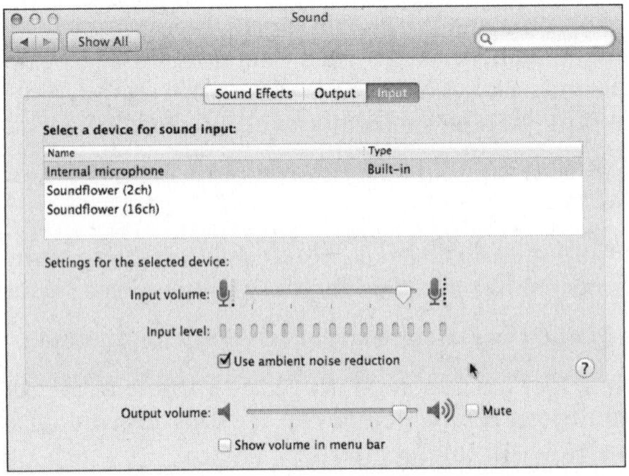

Figure 5-11:
Input
preferences
let you
define how
to record
sound.

Using Your Mac's Accessibility Features

Unfortunately, not everyone has perfect eyesight, hearing, or eye-hand coordination. If you have trouble with your vision, hearing, or ability to use the keyboard, trackpad, or mouse (or all three), using a computer can be difficult. That's why every Mac comes with special universal access features that you can turn on and modify. These universal access features fall under four categories — seeing, hearing, keyboard, and mouse and trackpad — all of which we introduce you to on the following pages. If you are interested in getting the most out of the Universal Access features, especially VoiceOver, we recommend that you read Apple's extensive, if not exhaustive, instructions for all the Universal Access features on both the Help menu and online at (www.apple.com/support/).

Mitigating vision limitations

To help the visually impaired, every Mac includes a VoiceOver feature, which lets your Mac read text, e-mail, and even descriptions of the screen in a computer-generated voice. VoiceOver can speak 22 languages and analyzes text paragraph by paragraph, so the reading is more natural and, well, humanlike. You can set up preferences for specific activities; for example, reading headlines at a quicker speaking rate than the article itself. And there are special commands to make browsing web pages easier. For partially sighted users, the Mac can magnify images on the screen or change the contrast of the screen to make it easier to read. To modify the vision assistance features of your Mac, follow these steps:

1. **Choose ➪System Preferences and click the Universal Access icon in the Personal section to open the Universal Access preferences pane, as shown in Figure 5-12.**

2. **Click the Seeing tab and select the options you want to activate, which include:**

   - *VoiceOver:* Allows your Mac to describe what's on the screen and assist you in using the Macintosh menus. Click the Open VoiceOver Utility button to customize such options as how fast your Mac speaks and whether it speaks with a male or female synthesized voice. (See Figure 5-13.)

   - *Zoom:* Allows you to magnify the screen around the cursor by pressing Option+⌘+= (equal sign) or return to normal by pressing Option+⌘+− (minus sign).

   - *Display:* Select either the Black on White (the default option) or White on Black (which gives a photographic negative effect) radio button.

     Select the Use Grayscale option if you want to make your Mac's screen have the look and feel of a black-and-white photograph. Drag the Enhance Contrast slider to increase/decrease the screen contrast.

   - *Enable Access for Assistive Devices:* Check this option to allow external devices (such as unique keyboards or mice) to use AppleScript to control the Mac user interface.

   - *Show Universal Access Status in the Menu Bar:* If selected, this option displays a Universal Access menulet on the menu bar, allowing you to turn Universal Access features on or off.

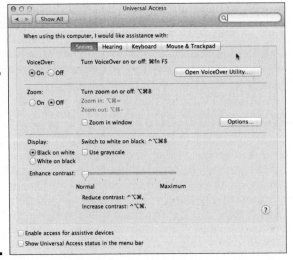

Figure 5-12:
The Seeing preferences pane displays options for making the Mac easier to use for the visually impaired.

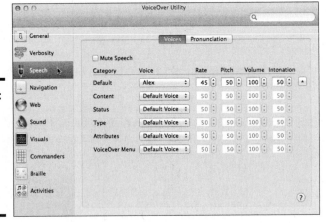

Figure 5-13:
Use the VoiceOver Utility to customize the VoiceOver settings.

3. **Click the Close button to close the Universal Access Preferences pane or press ⌘+Q to quit System Preferences.**

Mac OS X 10.7 Lion provides built-in support for many Braille tablets and offers Brailled verbosity settings, which allow you to specify how much information you want to receive about what's on the screen.

Compensating for hearing limitations

To adjust for hearing impairments, you can increase the volume for your various system alerts or you can have your Mac flash the screen to catch your attention. To have the Mac flash the screen rather than make a beeping noise, follow these steps:

1. Choose ⌘⇨System Preferences and click the Universal Access icon in the Personal section to open the Universal Access preferences pane (refer to Figure 5-12).

2. Click the Hearing tab to display the Hearing preferences pane, as shown in Figure 5-14.

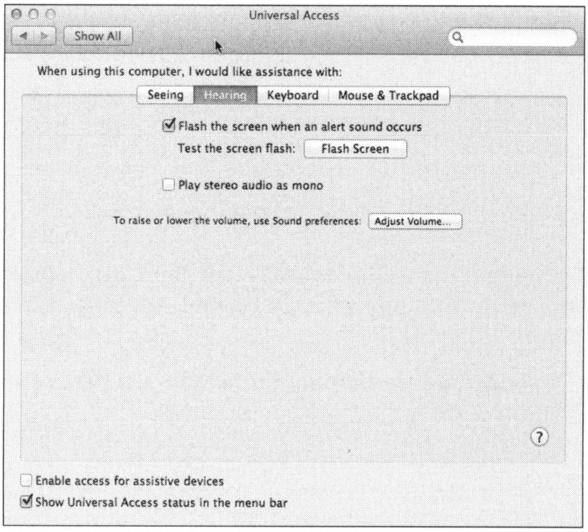

Figure 5-14:
The Hearing preferences pane gives you the option to set a flashing screen to alert you.

3. Select the Flash the Screen When an Alert Sound Occurs check box.

4. Select the Play Stereo Audio as Mono check box to remove the stereo effect from music or other stereo-enabled sounds your Mac plays.

5. (Optional) Click the Adjust Volume button to open the Sound Preferences dialog, where you can adjust the system volume to suit your hearing needs.

Refer to the earlier section, "Adjusting Sounds."

6. Click the Close button or press ⌘+Q to close the Universal Access Preferences pane.

Your Mac can work with www.purple.us so you can better see onscreen hand motions when having iChat conversations.

If you're watching movies, TV shows, or other video in one of your Mac's media player applications such as iTunes, QuickTime, or DVD Player, you may have closed caption options available, depending on the source of the video.

Easing keyboard limitations

If you have physical limitations using the keyboard, the Mac offers two solutions: the Sticky Keys feature and the Slow Keys feature. Sticky Keys can help you use keystroke shortcuts, such as ⌘+P (Print), which usually require pressing two or more keys at the same time. By turning on Sticky Keys, you can use keystroke shortcuts by pressing one key at a time in sequence. Press the modifier key first, such as the ⌘ key, and it "sticks" in place and waits until you press a second key to complete the keystroke shortcut.

The Slow Keys feature slows the reaction time of the Mac every time you press a key. Normally when you press a key, the Mac accepts it right away, but Slow Keys can force a Mac to wait a long time before accepting the typed key. That way, your Mac will ignore any accidental taps on the keyboard and patiently wait until you hold down a key for a designated period before it accepts it as valid.

To turn on Sticky Keys or Slow Keys, follow these steps:

1. **Choose ⌂⇨System Preferences and click the Universal Access icon in the Personal section to open the Universal Access preferences pane (refer to Figure 5-12).**

2. **Click the Keyboard tab to display the Keyboard preferences pane, as shown in Figure 5-15.**

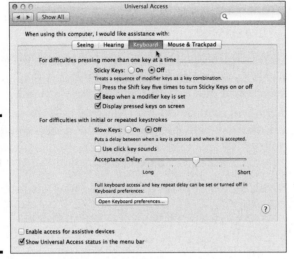

Figure 5-15: Keyboard preferences let you adjust the behavior of the keyboard.

3. **Select the On radio button to turn on Sticky Keys, which lets you press key combinations in a sequence instead of trying to hold down two or three keys at the same time, and then select any additional options you want to activate, including**

   • *Press the Shift key Five Times to Turn Sticky Keys On or Off:* Lets you turn the Sticky Keys feature on or off with the keyboard.

- *Beep When a Modifier Key Is Set:* Alerts you when you've pressed a so-called "modifier" key — a key such as Option or ⌘ — which is used in combination with another key to modify how that key works.

- *Display Pressed Keys On Screen:* When activated, any modifier keys you press (such as the ⌘ or Option key) display onscreen in the upper-right corner of the screen, so you can verify that you've pressed the right key.

4. **Select the On radio button to turn on Slow Keys (which adjusts the amount of time that passes from when you touch a key and when it's activated), and then choose or adjust additional options you want to activate, including these:**

- *Use Click Key Sounds:* This option causes your Mac to make a clicking sound every time you press a key to give you audible feedback.

- *Acceptance Delay:* Dragging this slider to the left lengthens the time it takes your Mac to recognize when you press and hold down a key; dragging the slider to the right shortens the time your Mac waits to recognize when you press and hold down a key.

- *Set Key Repeat:* Click this button to turn on, turn off, and adjust how slowly (or quickly) your Mac repeats a key when you hold it down.

5. **Click the Close button or press ⌘+Q to close the Universal Access preferences pane.**

Safari offers Universal Access functions to make web browsing more accessible. Choose Safari➪Preferences, and then click the Advanced icon. You can define a minimum font size up to 24 points and choose to press the Tab key to highlight items on a web page.

Dealing with mouse limitations

If you have physical limitations using the mouse, you can turn on the Mouse Keys feature, which lets you control the mouse through the numeric keys, as shown in Table 5-1.

Table 5-1	Mouse Key Commands
Numeric Key	*What It Does*
9	Moves the pointer diagonally up to the right
8	Moves the pointer straight up
7	Moves the pointer diagonally up to the left
6 or o	Moves the pointer to the right
5 or I or m then .	"Clicks" the mouse button
4 or u	Moves the pointer to the left

(continued)

Table 5-1 *(continued)*

Numeric Key	What It Does
3 or l	Moves the pointer diagonally down to the right
2 or k	Moves the pointer down
1 or j	Moves the pointer diagonally down to the left
0	"Right-clicks" the right mouse button

The Mouse Keys feature is really designed for keyboards that have a separate numeric keypad. If you're using a laptop or other keyboard that doesn't have a separate numeric keypad, the numeric keys might be embedded in the regular typewriter keys. To control the mouse pointer, you have to turn on the Num Lock key to use the numeric keys to move the mouse pointer. Then you have to press the Num Lock key again to use the keys for typing ordinary letters.

New MacBook and desktop Mac compact keyboards (without dedicated numeric keypads) do not have Num Lock keys and corresponding numeric key overlays on their keyboards. When Mouse Keys is turned on, you can use the letters as shown in Table 5-1 or you might want to consider buying an optional external numeric keypad, such as the one sold by Logitech (www.logitech.com) shown in Figure 5-16.

No matter how you plan to move the mouse, you might still have trouble finding the pointer on the screen. Fortunately, you can enlarge the size of the pointer to make it easy to spot and use.

To turn on the Mouse Keys feature or change the size of the pointer, follow these steps:

1. **Choose ⌘⇨System Preferences and click the Universal Access icon in the Personal section to open the Universal Access preferences pane.**

2. **Click the Mouse (or Mouse & Trackpad) tab and select the On radio button to turn on the Mouse Keys feature, as shown in Figure 5-17.**

3. **Choose or adjust any other Mouse Keys options you want to activate, including:**

   • *Press the Option Key Five Times to Turn Mouse Keys On or Off:* Lets you turn the Mouse Keys feature on or off from the keyboard.

   • *Initial Delay:* Drag the slider to define how long the Mac waits before moving the pointer with the numeric key. A short value means that the Mac might immediately move the pointer as soon as you press a number key. A long value means that you must hold down a numeric key for a longer period before it starts moving the pointer.

   • *Maximum Speed:* Drag the slider to adjust how fast the Mouse Keys feature moves the pointer with the keyboard.

Figure 5-16:
An external
numeric
keypad lets
a MacBook
play the
numbers.

Figure 5-17:
The Mouse
& Trackpad
pane lets
you adjust
the size
of the
pointer and
determine
whether
to control
the mouse
pointer
with the
keyboard.

- *Cursor Size:* Drag the slider to adjust the size of the pointer on the screen. Enlarging the size of the pointer can make it easier to spot and use.

4. **Click Trackpad Options to set trackpad speed and coordinate trackpad and mouse use.**

   The Trackpad options pane opens, as shown in Figure 5-18.

   - *Double-Click Speed* and *Scrolling Speed:* Drag the slider to adjust the double-click and scrolling speeds.

- *Scrolling:* Use the pop-up menu to choose scrolling with inertia (scrolling continues after you lift your finger) or without inertia (scrolling stops when you lift your finger).

- *Dragging:* Use the pop-up menu to choose Without Drag Lock, in which you place the pointer on the item, tap the trackpad twice, and then drag the item without removing your finger from the trackpad, or With Drag Lock, in which you click and drag an item and even if you lift your finger from the trackpad, the item remains locked to the dragging maneuver until you tap the trackpad once.

- *Ignore Built-In Trackpad When Mouse Keys Is On* or *Ignore Built-In Trackpad When Mouse or Wireless Trackpad Is Present:* Selecting either of these options prevents your MacBook trackpad from detecting your fingertips and misinterpreting those touchy moments as mouse commands. Click the Done button to close the Trackpad Options pane.

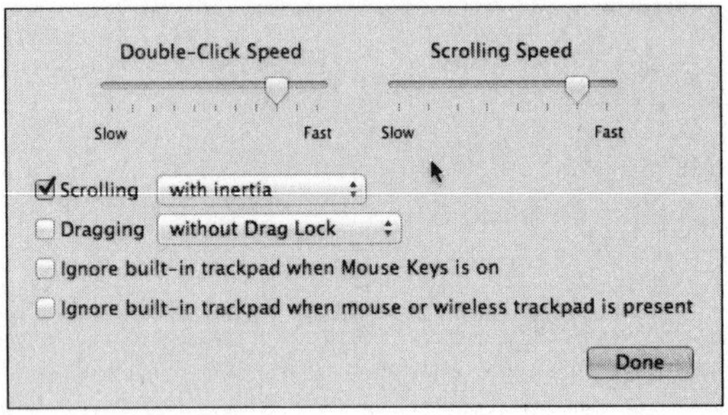

Figure 5-18:
Trackpad
Options
let you
customize
trackpad
behavior.

5. **Click Mouse Options to set the Double-Click and Scrolling Speed by dragging the respective sliders, as shown in Figure 5-19.**

   Click the Done button to close the Mouse Options pane.

6. **Click the Close button or press ⌘+Q to close the Universal Access preferences pane.**

Figure 5-19:
Set your
mouse's
double-
clicking and
scrolling
speeds.

Using Voice Recognition and Speech

Your Mac offers both voice recognition and speech capabilities. The voice-recognition feature lets you control your Mac by using spoken commands, and the speech capability lets your Mac read text or beep to alert you when something happens (for example, when a dialog pops up onscreen).

Even if you don't have an impairment, your Mac's voice recognition and speech capabilities can be useful for controlling your Mac, or listening to text you've written to catch typos or other errors you might miss by only reading what you've written rather than hearing it aloud.

Setting up Speech Recognition

To use the Mac's built-in voice recognition software, you have to define its settings and then assign specific types of commands to your voice. You define the Speech Recognition settings to choose how to turn on voice recognition and how your Mac will acknowledge that it received your voice commands correctly. For example, your Mac may wait until you press the Esc key or speak a certain word before it starts listening to voice commands. When it understands your command, it can beep.

To define the Speech Recognition settings, follow these steps:

1. **Choose &⇨System Preferences and click the Speech icon in the System section to open the Speech preferences pane.**

2. **Click the Speech Recognition tab, shown in Figure 5-20, and select the On radio button to turn on the Speakable Items feature.**

3. **Choose an appropriate device for accepting your spoken commands from the Microphone pop-up menu.**

   Internal Microphone would be an obvious choice here unless you happen to have an external microphone connected to your Mac.

4. **Click Calibrate to open the Microphone Calibration dialog, as shown in Figure 5-21.**

5. **Recite the phrases displayed in the Microphone Calibration dialog and if necessary, adjust the slider until your Mac recognizes your spoken commands.**

   Each command phrase in the listing blinks when your Mac successfully recognizes your phrasing of the command.

6. **When all phrases are recognized by your Mac, click Done to return to the Speech Recognition preferences pane.**

7. **(Optional) Click the Change Key button if you want to choose a key other than Esc (shown in Figure 5-22), which, when you press it, tells your Mac to begin listening for your spoken commands.**

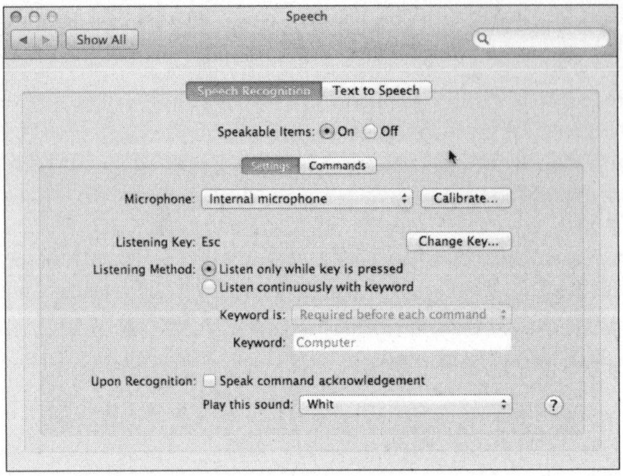

Figure 5-20:
Speech
Recognition
preferences
let you
define how
your Mac
recognizes
spoken
commands.

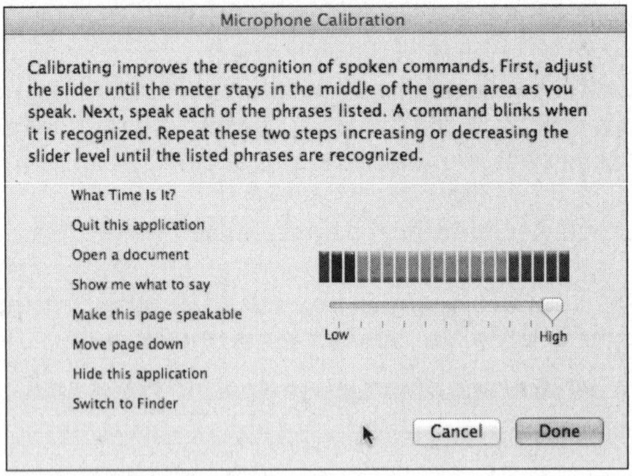

Figure 5-21:
The
Microphone
Calibration
dialog lets
you train
your Mac to
recognize
your voice.

8. **Press a key (such as ` or one of your Mac keyboard function keys) and click OK to return to the Speech Recognition dialog.**

9. **Select one of the following radio buttons in the Listening Method category:**

   - *Listen Only while Key Is Pressed:* Your Mac accepts only spoken commands as long as you hold down the Escape key, or a different listening key you defined in Step 8. If you choose this radio button, go to Step 12.

   - *Listen Continuously with Keyword:* Your Mac waits to hear a spoken keyword (such as "Computer" or "Yoohoo!") before accepting additional spoken commands. If you choose this radio button, go to Step 10.

10. **Click the Keyword Is pop-up menu and choose one of the following:**

- *Optional before Commands:* Your Mac listens for spoken commands all the time. This can make it easier to give spoken commands, but it also means that your Mac might misinterpret the radio or background conversations as commands.

- *Required before Each Command:* You must speak the keyword before your Mac will accept spoken commands.

- *Required 15 Seconds after Last Command:* You must repeat the keyword within 15 seconds after each command.

- *Required 30 Seconds after Last Command:* Same as the preceding option except the Mac waits up to 30 seconds for the next spoken commands.

Figure 5-22:
Define a
listening
key to start
giving
spoken
commands.

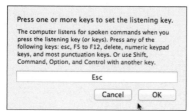

Press one or more keys to set the listening key.

The computer listens for spoken commands when you press the listening key (or keys). Press any of the following keys: esc, F5 to F12, delete, numeric keypad keys, and most punctuation keys. Or use Shift, Command, Option, and Control with another key.

Esc

Cancel   OK

11. **Click the Keyword text box and type your keyword if you don't want to use the default keyword (Computer) to speak to your Mac.**

12. **(Optional) Make choices in the Upon Recognition area.**

If you want your Mac to use the voice Whit to confirm commands it successfully recognizes, select the Speak Command Acknowledgement check box. If you prefer to hear an alert sound rather than Whit's voice, click the Play This Sound pop-up menu and choose the alert sound you want.

13. **Click the Commands tab to open the Commands preferences pane, as shown in Figure 5-23.**

14. **Select the check boxes for one or more of the following command sets:**

- *Address Book:* Listens for names stored in your Address Book. Select Address Book and click the Configure button to specify which names in your Address Book you want recognized.

- *Global Speakable Items:* Listens for common commands applicable to any situation, such as asking your Mac, "What time is it?" or "Tell me a joke" — and that's no joke! Select Global Speakable Items and click the Configure button to turn off the Speak Command Names Exactly As Written. When this command is turned off, you can ask the same question in more than one way, such as asking "What is the time?" rather than "What time is it?"

Click the Open Speakable Items Folder to open a Finder window containing file icons of all the commands you can say to your Mac, as shown in Figure 5-24.

- *Application Specific Items:* Listens for commands specific to each application. A word processor might have a Format menu, but an audio-editing application might not.

- *Application Switching:* Listens for commands to switch between, start, or quit applications.

- *Front Window:* Listens for the commands to control specific items in the displayed window, such as telling your Mac to click a button or check box.

- *Menu Bar:* Listens for commands to display pull-down menus and choose a command.

Figure 5-23: Speech Recognition feature's Commands options let you assign different actions to voice commands.

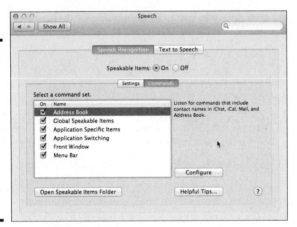

Figure 5-24: The Speakable Items Folder contains file icons of commands your Mac can recognize.

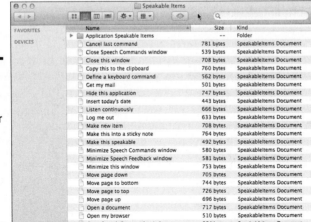

15. **Click the Close button or press ⌘+Q to close the Speech preferences pane.**

If you find the Mac's built-in voice recognition features inadequate for your special needs, consider buying a different application that lets you control your Mac with your voice. Nuance Communications, Inc., (www.nuance. com) offers voice-recognition applications for the Mac.

Setting up speech capabilities

Your Mac has a collection of different computer-synthesized voices that can read text to you or alert you when something occurs, such as when you try to quit an application without saving a document. To define the speech capabilities of your Mac, follow these steps:

1. **Choose ➪System Preferences and click the Speech icon to open the Speech preferences pane.**

2. **Click the Text to Speech tab to open the Text to Speech preferences pane, as shown in Figure 5-25.**

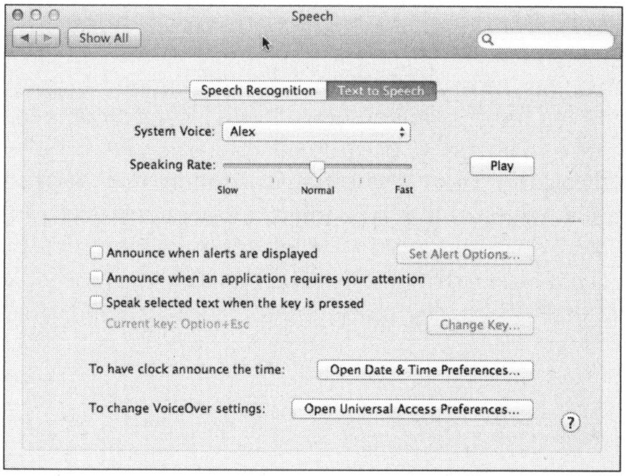

Figure 5-25: Text to Speech preferences let you define the synthesized voice characteristics of your Mac.

3. **Click the System Voice pop-up menu and choose the voice you want to hear when your Mac speaks to you.**

Choose Customize to see a larger selection of voices, including some that you can download (Samantha, Jill, and Tom), which have a more natural way of speaking. (Our personal favorite is Samantha.)

4. **Drag the Speaking Rate slider to a desired speed and click Play to hear your chosen synthesized voice at the specified speaking rate.**

Drag the Speaking Rate slider to the left to slow how quickly your Mac speaks; drag the Speaking Rate slider to the right to make your Mac speak more quickly.

5. **Select the check boxes for any of the following additional Text to Speech options you want to enable:**

- *Announce When Alerts Are Displayed:* Makes your Mac speak when it needs your attention. It might utter a message saying that you don't have enough room on your hard drive to save a file, for instance.

- *Set Alert Options*: When you select Announce When Alerts Are Displayed, click this button to open a dialog and define how your Mac should speak an alert, as shown in Figure 5-26. Make any changes you want in the Set Alert Options dialog and then click OK to return to the Text to Speech preferences pane.

- *Announce When an Application Requires Your Attention*: Makes your Mac speak when a specific application needs additional information from you, such as when you try to close a file without saving it first.

- *Speak Selected Text When the Key Is Pressed:* Allows you to press a key combination (Option+Esc is the default) to tell your Mac when to start reading any text you select. Click Change Key to open a dialog that lets you change the key combination to one that's easier for you.

6. **Click the Close button or press ⌘+Q to close the Speech preferences pane.**

To find different types of keyboards and mice designed to make controlling your computer even more comfortable, search for *ergonomic input devices* by using your favorite search engine, such as www.google.com, www.yahoo.com, or www.bing.com. Search results will contain a list of product reviews and websites selling everything from left-handed keyboards and mice to foot pedals and keyboards designed to type letters by pressing multiple keys like piano chords. For a little extra money, you can buy the perfect keyboard and mouse that can make your Mac more comfortable for you to use.

Figure 5-26:
You can customize which voice and phrase to speak, along with a delay time.

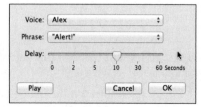

Book II

Online Communications

The 5th Wave   By Rich Tennant

"Wow, I didn't know OS X could redirect an e-mail message like that."

Contents at a Glance

Chapter 1: Connecting to the Internet and Browsing the Web

In This Chapter

✔ **Setting up an Internet connection**

✔ **Browsing websites**

✔ **Creating a reading list**

✔ **Keeping up with RSS feeds**

✔ **Searching a web page**

✔ **Saving web pages**

✔ **Viewing and playing multimedia files**

✔ **Downloading files**

For most people, an Internet connection is no longer an option but a necessity. You can use a computer all by itself, but to get the most out of your Mac, you need an Internet connection. The Internet can open a whole new world for you by letting you research fun facts, virtually visit museums around the world, read news from mainstream and obscure outlets, watch movies, listen to radio stations, find and download new applications, update versions of your existing applications, shop online, and make reservations for everything from local restaurants to far-flung ferries.

In this chapter, we explain how to connect your Mac to the Internet. Then we go through Safari, showing you Safari's many features for browsing, searching, and reading on the Internet. We give you a few tips and tricks to make your surfing experience more fun and productive.

Setting Up an Internet Connection

From a technical point of view, to connect to the Internet, your Mac must connect to another computer, run by a company called an Internet Service Provider (ISP); it's through the ISP that your Mac actually connects to the Internet.

To connect your Mac to an ISP, you have two options:

✦ Ethernet (also called *high-speed broadband*)

✦ Wireless (also called *Wi-Fi high-speed broadband*)

Ethernet connection

A broadband Ethernet connection is the fastest way to connect to the Internet. The two most common broadband connections are through cable modems or DSL (Digital Subscriber Line) modems.

Your Mac can connect to a cable modem or DSL modem with an Ethernet cable, which plugs into the Ethernet port with a plug that looks like a wider version of a telephone plug. (If you have a MacBook Air, you need the USB-to-Ethernet adapter.) After you connect your Mac to a cable or DSL modem, you can usually start using the Internet right away.

Your Mac can also connect to your broadband modem wirelessly if the modem you buy (or rent from your cable or phone provider) has a built-in Wi-Fi router, which your Mac's built-in AirPort Wi-Fi feature can access.

When you connect your Mac to a broadband modem by using your Mac's Ethernet port, your Mac can recognize the Internet connection right away through the Dynamic Host Configuration Protocol (DHCP): Your Mac automatically figures out the proper settings to connect to the Internet without making you type a bunch of cryptic numbers and fiddle with confusing technical standards.

For more information about setting up a network and sharing a single Internet connection with multiple computers, see Book VI, Chapter 1.

Wireless (Wi-Fi) access

Wireless broadband access is popular because it allows you to connect to the Internet without stringing cables across the room to trip over. Every new and recent Mac comes with a built-in wireless capability called AirPort Wi-Fi.

You need to connect to a wireless network in your home, or out of the house at another location if you're using a MacBook that you can take wherever you go. Public libraries and many coffee houses offer free wireless Internet access, as do many hotels and motels, which is handy when you're travelling. You can set up your own wireless network at home or work by using a wireless router that lets several computers and other Wi-Fi-able gadgets (such as video game consoles, iPhones, and some printers) share a single Internet connection.

Choosing a wireless router

A *wireless router* connects to your cable or DSL modem and broadcasts radio signals to connect your Mac wirelessly to the Internet. Most cable and DSL modems come with built-in Wi-Fi transmitters, which means that one device does the job of two Wi-Fi devices.

If you choose to use a separate Wi-Fi router to connect to your cable or DSL modem, Apple sells three wireless router models:

✦ **AirPort Express:** Small and ideal for small homes, apartments, and dorm rooms.

✦ **AirPort Extreme:** Ideal for homes; four Ethernet ports to connect to Macs in the same room with an Ethernet cable; a built-in USB port lets you connect a printer or hard drive to share wirelessly with other people in your house or workplace.

✦ **Time Capsule:** Same features as AirPort Extreme but also includes a built-in hard drive for wirelessly backing up one or more Macs that connect to it.

Apple's Wi-Fi routers are nice, and the admin tools of Apple's AirPort make management and setup easy. You can buy any brand of wireless router to connect to your DSL or cable modem and create a home Wi-Fi network. The brand name of your wireless router is less important than the speed offered by the router, which is determined by the wireless standard the router uses. A *wireless standard* simply defines the wireless signal used to connect to the Internet. Table 1-1 lists the different wireless standards.

Table 1-1   Wireless Standards and Speeds of Different Routers

Wireless Standard	Speed	Indoor Range
802.11a	Up to 54 Mbps	30 meters (98 feet)
802.11b	Up to 11 Mbps	35 meters (114 feet)
802.11g	Up to 54 Mbps	35 meters (114 feet)
802.11n	Up to 248 Mbps	70 meters (229 feet)

The upload/download speed of wireless standards is measured in megabits per second (Mbps), although this maximum speed is rarely achieved in normal use. The speed and range of a wireless Internet connection also degrade with distance or if obstacles, such as walls or heavy furniture, stand between the Wi-Fi router and your Mac.

To connect to a wireless network, you need to make sure that your router and your Mac's built-in wireless use the same wireless standard. All new and recent Macs connect to Wi-Fi routers that use one or up to all four types of the wireless network standards.

The 802.11g wireless standard is the most popular wireless standard, but the newer 802.11n standard is becoming more popular because it offers greater range and higher speeds. Most routers are compatible with multiple standards,

such as 802.11a, 802.11b, and 802.11g. The newer routers also include compatibility with the 802.11n standard.

Connecting to a Wi-Fi network

You can connect your Mac to a wireless network (say, at a café or a Wi-Fi network in your home) by following these steps:

1. **Click the Wi-Fi icon in the right corner of the menu bar to open a pull-down menu displaying a list of any Wi-Fi networks within range of your Mac, and then select the network name you want to connect to, as shown in Figure 1-1.**

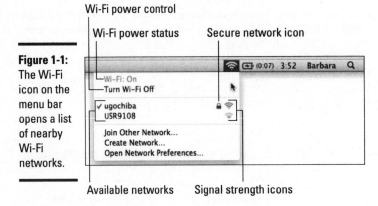

Wi-Fi power control
Wi-Fi power status   Secure network icon

Figure 1-1:
The Wi-Fi icon on the menu bar opens a list of nearby Wi-Fi networks.

Available networks   Signal strength icons

Note: If you see WiFi: Off when you click the Wi-Fi icon on the menu bar, choose Turn WiFi On and then click the Wi-Fi menu icon again to display a list of any nearby wireless networks (refer to Figure 1-1).

If you don't see the Wi-Fi icon on the menu bar, choose ⌘⇨System Preferences, click the Network icon in the Internet & Wireless section, and then select the Show Wi-Fi Status in Menu Bar check box.

The signal strength icon next to a Wi-Fi network name shows how strongly you're receiving that network router's wireless signal (stronger signal strength means faster, more reliable connections).

A lock icon to the left of the network's signal strength indicates a *secured* (also known as *encrypted*) wireless network that is protected by a password. You must know what password to enter when prompted if you try to connect to a secured network.

2. **If a dialog appears indicating that the network you selected requires a password to connect to it (shown in Figure 1-2), type the password and click OK.**

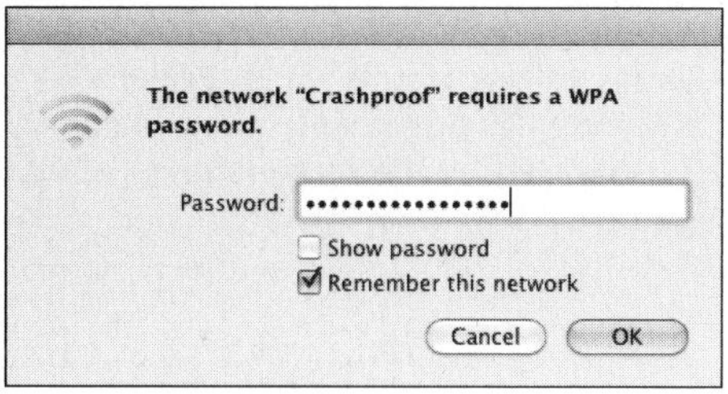

Figure 1-2:
A secure
Wi-Fi
network
requires a
password
to connect
to it.

> The network "Crashproof" requires a WPA
> password.
>
> Password: ••••••••••••••••
>
> ☐ Show password
> ☑ Remember this network
>
> (Cancel) (OK)

3. **(Optional) Select the following options on the password dialog
prompt:**

- *Show Password*: Displays actual characters you type instead of dots
  that hide your password in case anyone is looking over your shoulder.

- *Remember This Network:* Remembers you connected to the selected
  network and connects to it automatically whenever you're within
  range of its signal. (If you chose to remember more than one wireless
  network, your Mac always connects to the one with the strongest
  signal first.)

The Wi-Fi icon on the menu bar shows black bars to indicate the strength of
the Wi-Fi network signal your Mac is connected to — as with mobile phone
reception, and gold, more bars are better.

You're now free to choose any activity that requires an Internet connection,
such as running Safari to browse the news on The New York Times website
(www.nytimes.com), or launching iChat to partake in a video chat with a
friend who's also connected to the Internet and signed in to iChat.

When you connect to a wireless network that doesn't require you to enter a
password, your Mac essentially broadcasts any information you type (such as
credit card numbers or passwords) through the airwaves. Although the likelihood of anyone actually monitoring what you're typing is small, tech-savvy
engineers or hackers can "sniff" wireless signals to monitor or collect information flowing through the airwaves. When you connect to a public Wi-Fi network, assume that a stranger is peeking at your data. Then only type data that
you're comfortable giving away to others. Connecting to a secured network
that requires you to type a password to connect to it can lessen the likelihood
that anyone is monitoring or collecting what you're typing.

Broadband wireless modem

If you're on the move a lot and go to places that don't have Wi-Fi service and
you take your MacBook with you, a broadband wireless modem may be a
good solution. These devices, which look like thumb or flash drives, hold a

SIM card just like the one in your cellphone — and use your selected cellular carrier to connect to the cellular broadband network. Keep in mind that they are significantly slower than cable or DSL Wi-Fi and relatively expensive. Most are *plug-and-play:* You plug the device into your Mac's USB port, enter the associated password (provided by the modem and cellular service provider), and voilá! You're online.

Browsing Websites

After you connect to the Internet with one of the methods explained previously, you can run a web browser application to browse websites that interest you. The most popular browser for the Mac is the one that comes with it: Safari. Besides Safari, you can download and run another web browser, such as Firefox (`www.mozilla.org/en-US/firefox/new`), Google Chrome (`www.google.com/chrome`), Camino (`http://caminobrowser.org`), OmniWeb (`www.omnigroup.com/products/omniweb`), or Opera (`www.opera.com`).

Setting Safari's home page

The first time you open Safari, the Apple website appears because it is set as the default Home page. Subsequent times you open Safari, the website you were browsing when you last closed or quit Safari (or shutdown and restarted your Mac) reopens. You can change Safari's Home page to whatever you want — even a blank page, if that's what you prefer.

Throughout this chapter, all step-by-step instructions are given for Safari. Just keep in mind that other browsers (Firefox, Chrome, Camino, and so on) work in relatively similar ways.

To define a home page in Safari, follow these steps:

1. **Click the Safari icon in the Dock or Launchpad to run Safari and display the home page window.**

2. **Choose Safari⇨Preferences to open the General preferences pane, and then type a website address (such as** `www.nytimes.com`**), shown in Figure 1-3, in the Home Page field.**

    If you click the Set to Current Page button, you can make the currently displayed web page your new home page without having to type the web page's address. To use this feature, visit your favorite website immediately after Step 1. Then when you click the Set to Current Page button, the current website address instantly fills in the Home Page field as if you typed it yourself.

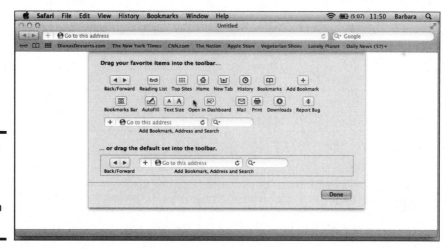

Figure 1-3:
Safari's
General
preferences
let you
change your
home page.

If you want Safari to open to your Home page or a blank page when you restart or reopen Safari (instead of opening the most recent web page you visited), choose Homepage or Empty Page from the pop-up menu next to New Window Open With.

3. **Click the Close button to close the Safari preferences pane.**

You can go to the Home page by choosing History⇨Home. If you want a Home button, or other navigation buttons, on the Safari Toolbar, choose View⇨Customize Toolbar, and then drag the Home icon to the Toolbar. A pane opens, as shown in Figure 1-4. Click and drag the icons to and from the toolbar and the pane to create a toolbar that meets your browsing needs.

Figure 1-4:
Customize
the toolbar
for easier
browsing in
Safari.

Visiting a website

To visit a website, you use the website's *address* (also known as a *URL*, which stands for Uniform Resource Locator).

Most website addresses, such as `http://www.dummies.com`, consist of several parts:

✦ **`http://www:`** Identifies the address as part of the World Wide Web that uses the HyperText Transfer Protocol (http). Some websites omit the www portion of the name. Other websites use something else like `mobile`. Just keep in mind that www is common, but not always necessary for many website addresses.

✦ **The domain name of the website (`dummies`):** Most website names are abbreviations or smashed-together names of the website, such as white-house for the White House's website.

✦ **A three-letter identifying extension, such as `.com`:** The extension identifies the type of website, as shown in Table 1-2. Many websites in other countries end with a two-letter country address, such as `.uk` for the United Kingdom, `.ca` for Canada, `.fr` for France, and `.eu` for Europe.

Table 1-2	Common Extensions Used in Website Addresses	
Three-Letter Extension	Type of Website	Examples
`.com`	Often a commercial website, but can be another type of website	`www.apple.com`
`.gov`	Government website	`www.nasa.gov`
`.edu`	School website	`www.mit.edu`
`.net`	Network, sometimes used as an alternative to the `.com` extension	`www.earthlink.net`
`.org`	A nonprofit organization website	`www.redcross.org`
`.mil`	Military website	`www.army.mil`

When visiting different web pages on a site, you might see additional text that identifies a specific web page, such as `www.dummies.com/how-to/computers-software.html` or `www.apple.com/iphone`.

To visit a website by typing its website address, follow these steps:

1. **Click the Safari icon in the Dock or Launchpad to run Safari.**

2. **Click the Smart Address Field and type an address (such as www. joeygadget.com), shown in Figure 1-5, and then press Return.**

   As you begin to type an address, Safari completes it automatically with a likely match, usually based on your viewing history, and highlights the part it added. Press the Return key if the highlighted address is the one you want. Otherwise, continue typing or choose from the pop-up list that appears, if the website you want is listed there.

   Safari displays the website corresponding to the address you typed, as shown in Figure 1-6.

   In Mac OS X 10.7 Lion, Safari supports full-screen view. Click the Full Screen View toggle switch in the upper-right corner to take advantage of your entire screen. To return to partial-screen view, press the Esc button or hover the pointer in the upper-right corner until you see the Full Screen View toggle switch and click it once.

   If you don't see all the things mentioned in Figure 1-5, choose Safari⇨ Preferences and click the Bookmarks tab. Select the Include Reading List and the Include Top Sites check boxes.

Figure 1-5: Begin typing an address and Safari suggests potential matches.

Bookmarks bar

Forward

Reader view

Reload/Stop

Top Sites view

Private Browsing

Full Screen view

Back

Smart Address field

Reader

Search

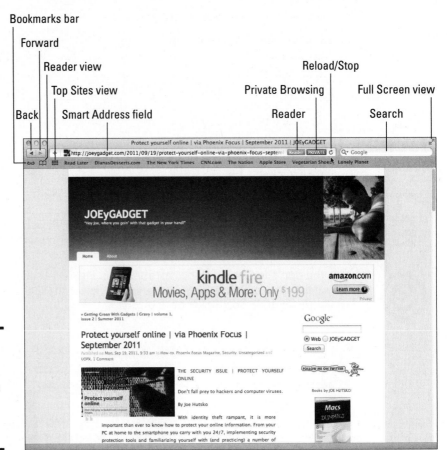

Figure 1-6:
Type an address in the address bar to go to another website.

3. **Move about the web page by using the mouse, trackpad, or arrow keys to scroll up and down. Move the pointer over images, buttons, and bold text to click links that open other web pages of the same website or open other websites.**

   Double-tap with two fingers on the trackpad or Magic Mouse to zoom in or out of the web page.

4. **(Optional) Click the Navigation buttons if you want to:**

   • *Go Back:* Takes you to the previous web page; click again to go back another page, and so on, until you wind up on the first page you viewed when you launched Safari.

   • *Go Forward:* Moves you forward to a page you backed away from; click again to advance to the next page you backed away from, and so on, until you wind up on the last page you visited before you clicked the Back button.

- *Reload/Stop:* Clicking the little arrowed-circle icon on the right side of the address bar reloads the current web page and displays any new information that changed since you arrived on the web page (such as breaking news on The New York Times home page). When Safari is loading or reloading a web page, the arrowed-circle turns into an X icon. Clicking the X icon stops Safari from loading or reloading the web page.

If you use a MacBook or a Magic Mouse or Trackpad with desktop Mac model, you can use the three-finger swipe gesture to move back and forward between web pages that you visited.

5. **(Optional) Click the Reader/RSS button.**

    If either the Reader or RSS options are available (we explain both in the sections "Reading in Reader" and "Tracking breaking news with RSS feeds," respectively), clicking the button will activate the option that's available.

6. **(Optional) Choose Safari⇨Block Pop-Up Windows.**

    Some windows "pop up," or appear, on top of the open Safari window. Pop-up windows are often advertisements. This option will block pop-up windows.

You may encounter a web page that has fields where you type limited information, such as your name, address, and billing information to make an online purchase. Other fields are meant for typing in longer passages, such as comments about a blog post. Resize the second type of field by clicking and dragging the bottom-right corner, allowing you to see more of what you type.

7. **When you finish, click the Close button (the red circle in the upper-left corner) to simply close the Safari window or choose Safari⇨Quit Safari to completely exit the application.**

If you type a website address and see an error message, it might mean one of a few things: You typed the website address wrong, your Internet connection isn't working, or the website is temporarily (or permanently) unavailable.

Reading in Reader

If Safari perceives a readable article on the page you are viewing, the Reader button is active in the Smart Address Field and you have the option to open the article in Reader. Safari aims to be elegant and clutter free, so Reader removes all the ads, buttons, bells, and whistles from the web page and shows you only the article as one continuous page. Even the scroll bar appears only when you hover the mouse pointer near the edge of the Reader "page," as shown in Figure 1-7. To display an article in Reader, do the following:

1. **Click the Safari icon in the Dock or Launchpad to run Safari.**

2. **Type in the URL for the website you want to visit; for example, The New York Times (**`www.nytimes.com`**).**

3. **Click the article you want to read.**

   You see the article with various advertisements, banners, photos, links, and so on.

4. **Click the Reader button in the Smart Address Field or press ⌘+Shift+R (it must be a capital *R*).**

   If the article runs over several pages, Reader displays it as one continuous page so you need only scroll down, not click from one page to the next.

5. **Hover over the bottom-center part of the window to open a heads-up display.**

   The buttons here let you zoom in or out on the text, print, or e-mail the article.

6. **Click the X in the heads-up display or press the Esc key to exit Reader and return to the normal Safari view of the article.**

   Click the Back button to return to the original site, in our example, The New York Times front page.

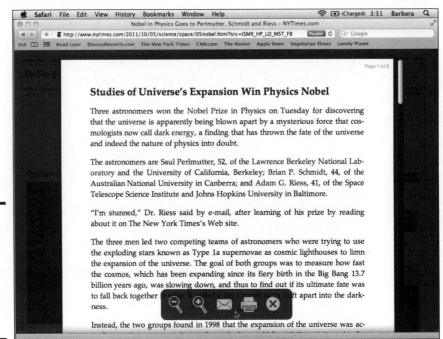

Figure 1-7: Reader dispays multipage articles as one continuous page.

In both Reader and normal Safari view, press ⌘++ (plus-sign key without Shift) or ⌘+- (minus-sign key) to zoom in or out on the text. If you have a Magic Mouse or Trackpad or a MacBook that recognizes multi-touch gestures, you can also pinch in or out to zoom.

Creating a Reading List

Sometimes you find a great article that you really, really want to read but you just don't have time. Instead of bookmarking the page (we tell you all about bookmarks later on in this chapter; bear with us), you can save the article to a reading list. Here's how to save and manage articles in the Reading List:

1. **In Safari, with the article or web page you want to read later open, choose Bookmarks⇨Add to Reading List.**

   The article is added to your reading list.

2. **When you're ready to read one or more of your saved articles, click the Reading List icon in the toolbar (it looks like a pair of eyeglasses).**

   The Reading List, down the left side of the Safari window, shown in Figure 1-8, shows the title of the article, the website it's from, and a two-line preview.

   To make the Reading List pane wider or narrower, move the pointer to the right edge of the Reading List until it becomes a vertical line with an arrow on one or both sides, and then click and drag. Use the scroll bar or multi-touch scrolling gestures on the trackpad to see articles farther down on your list.

3. **Click the article you want to read (which could be a web page with more than one article, such as the cover page of a newspaper).**

   The web page opens in the main part of the Safari window to the right of the Reading List.

   Reading List is basically a list of links to websites, so you have to have an Internet connection to see the articles on your Reading List.

4. **Click the All or Unread buttons to change which articles you see in the Reading List.**

5. **To delete an article from the list, click the article and then click the X in the upper-right corner near the name of the selected article.**

6. **To delete the whole list, click the Clear All button.**

7. **Click the Reading List button again to close the Reading List.**

You can read articles from your reading list in Reader view. If you're reading in Reader view and go to a different article, that one opens in Reader view too.

Book II Chapter 1

Connecting to the Internet and Browsing the Web

Figure 1-8: The Reading List stores articles you want to read at a later date.

Tracking breaking news with RSS feeds

Safari comes with a built-in RSS (Really Simple Syndication) reader. Whether you're a news junkie and don't want to miss anything — or you want an overview of worldwide happenings so you can follow dinner-party conversations — RSS feeds meet your needs. Essentially, an *RSS feed* is a continually updated list of headlines followed by a brief description of the article and a link to access the entire article. Most daily news outlets have RSS feeds, as do many blogs; you know when you see the RSS button in the Smart Address Field. Click this button to view the RSS feed for that site, as shown in Figure 1-9.

Setting RSS preferences

Safari's built-in RSS helps you sift through the myriad articles that appear on an hourly — if not minute-by-minute — basis. By setting RSS preferences, you can expand or limit how much information you receive. Do the following:

1. **Choose Safari⇨Preferences and click the RSS tab.**

The RSS preferences pane appears, as shown in Figure 1-10.

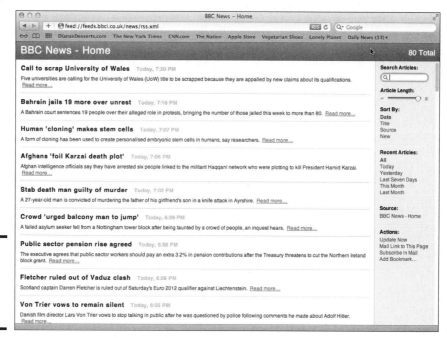

Figure 1-9:
The
newsfeed
for one
website.

Figure 1-10:
Use RSS
preferences
to choose
where
and when
you see
RSS feed
updates.

2. **Choose from the following settings so you see the RSS feeds when and where you want.**

   • *Default RSS Reader:* Choose Safari or Mail as the application where you see RSS feeds. If you choose Mail, you should set RSS preferences from the Mail preferences.

- *Automatically Update Articles In:* If you bookmark RSS feeds (which we explain in the "Using bookmarks to create an aggregated RSS feed" section of this chapter), you can choose to update the feeds automatically, depending on where you keep them. Perhaps the RSS feeds you check most often you put in the Bookmarks bar and you want to update automatically, whereas those in the Bookmarks menu you check less frequently and will update manually.

- *Check for Updates:* Select the interval at which you want Safari to check for updates from the pull-down menu.

- *Mark Articles as Read:* Safari indicates how many new articles have appeared since you last opened the RSS reader by putting a number next to the bookmarked source either in the Bookmarks Bar or Bookmarks Menu, as shown in Figure 1-11. Choose After Viewing the RSS Page from the pop-up menu if you want the number to zero out after you open the RSS reader, or choose After Clicking Them if you want them to be deleted from the new articles count only after you have actually opened the article.

- *Highlight Unread Articles:* Select this check box if you want to easily see which articles are new in the RSS reader. This is helpful if you view your articles by source because you'll see which sources have updated feeds.

- *Remove Articles:* Establish the interval when you want articles removed from the RSS feeds.

3. **Click the close button to close the RSS preferences pane.**

Figure 1-11:
Safari
notifies you
when new
RSS articles
are posted
by websites
you've
bookmarked.

Sorting and searching RSS feeds

Whether you open an RSS feed for one website or for a folder of bookmarked websites, Safari offers many options for sorting and searching the RSS feeds so you can see the information that's most important to you first. These are your RSS options (refer to Figure 1-9):

✦ **Search Articles:** Type a keyword or phrase to search all the current articles. The results show articles that contain that word or phrase.

✦ **Article Length:** Drag the slider to the left to see more feeds in one screen's space but less information about each one. Drag to the right to see more information but fewer feeds on the screen; use the scroll bar to see subsequent feeds.

✦ **Sort By:** Click Date, Title, Source, or New to sort by that category. Titles and Sources are sorted alphabetically.

✦ **Recent Articles:** Choose how much history you want to see. For example, if you check in with the newsfeed on a weekly basis and want to see a week's worth of articles, choose Last Seven Days. If you check on a daily basis, Today or Yesterday probably gives you enough information.

✦ **Source:** Shows the name of the website or websites from which the newsfeed appears. If you create an aggregated RSS feed, you see more than one source and can choose whether to see all newsfeeds or limit the newsfeed to one website by clicking its name in the list.

✦ **Actions:** Click Update Now to refresh the RSS feed. Click Mail Link to This Page to send an e-mail with a link to this collection of RSS feeds. Click Subscribe in Mail (which only appears if you are looking at the RSS feed for one website) to see the RSS feeds in Mail. (See Book II, Chapter 2 to find more about Mail and this particular feature.)

Book II
Chapter 1

Connecting to the Internet and Browsing the Web

Searching for websites

Typing a long website address can get tedious, and sometimes you don't even know what website you want. That is, you know what kind of information you want, just not where to find it.

One way to find a website that can contain information of interest to you is to use a *search engine,* which is a behind-the-scenes technology used by special websites that can look for other websites and the information they contain based on a word or phrase you enter.

Because search engines are so convenient, Safari (and most other browsers) offers a built-in search engine text box in its upper-right corner. By typing a word or phrase that describes the kind of website or information you want, the search engine can find a list of related web search results (referred to as *hits* or *links*) that you can click to go to a web page containing more information about what you're trying to find.

You can choose Google (which is the default search engine), Yahoo!, or Bing as your search engine. Click the triangle next to the magnifying glass in the Search field to select the search engine you want, as shown in Figure 1-12.

Figure 1-12:
Choose
Google,
Yahoo!, or
Bing.

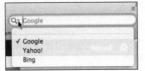

To search for a website that might contain information that you're looking for, follow these steps:

1. **Click the Safari icon in the Dock or Launchpad to run Safari.**

2. **Click the Search text box (refer to Figure 1-6), enter a word or phrase, and press Return.**

   The Safari window displays a web page of links your chosen search engine found based on contents that match or relate to the word or phrase you typed, as shown in Figure 1-13.

3. **Click the website you want to visit.**

Figure 1-13:
Words or
phrases you
search for
appear as
web links in
a new web
page.

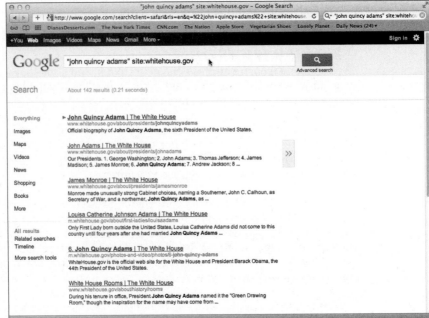

Searching tips

Given the billions of websites on the World Wide Web, your search can turn up more exact results if you better define your search terms. Here are a few ways you can specify your search terms:

✔ Use quotation marks around a phrase to find the words exactly as you typed them. For example, if you want type **John Quincy Adams** in the search field, your result contains references for **John** Smith and Jane **Adams** in **Quincy**, Massachusetts, as well as references to the former president, whereas if you type **"John Quincy Adams"**, your search results contain only websites that contain the name as you typed it.

✔ Confine your search to a specific website by adding *site:domain.* For example, if you want references to John Quincy Adams from the White House website, type **"John Quincy Adams" site:whitehouse.gov.**

✔ Exclude certain common usages by placing a hyphen before the word you want to exclude.

✔ Don't worry about small articles and prepositions like *a, the, of, about,* or using capital letters.

✔ Check your spelling. If you mistype a word or phrase, the search engine might offer suggestions for the correct spelling and look for websites that contain that misspelled word or phrase, which probably won't be the website you really want to see.

Every time you type a word or phrase in the Search text box, Safari (and most other browsers) saves the last ten words or phrases you searched. If you want to search for that same word or phrase later, just click the downward-pointing arrow that appears in the left side of the Search text box to display a pull-down menu. Then click the word or phrase you want to search for again.

Returning to website search results with SnapBack

If you search for websites and find yourself wandering down a number of blind alleys because the web pages you navigate to aren't what you're looking for, the SnapBack feature can catapult you to where you began before losing your web-footed way.

To try out the SnapBack feature, follow these steps:

1. **Click the Search field, type a word or phrase that describes a website you want to find, and then press Return.**

The Safari window displays a web page of web links the search engine found, all based on contents that match or relate to the word or phrase you typed (refer to Figure 1-13).

2. **Click the website you want to visit to display its web page in the Safari window.**

3. **Click any link on the web page to navigate to another web page.**

The new web page opens in the Safari window and an orange left-pointing SnapBack icon appears in the far right of the Search text box, as shown in Figure 1-14.

Figure 1-14:
Return to
your search
results.

4. **Click the SnapBack button to return to the web page displaying your initial search results.**

   The SnapBack icon disappears from the Search field. Welcome back!

Searching previously viewed websites

If you visit a website and find it interesting, you might want to visit it again later. Fortunately, Safari stores a list of your previously visited websites in its History menu for up to one year.

To view a list of the websites you visited, follow these steps:

1. **In Safari, click History on the menu bar.**

   A pull-down menu appears, displaying the most recent websites you visited. Additionally, the History menu lists the past week's dates so you can view websites that you visited several days ago, as shown in Figure 1-15.

2. **Choose a website to have Safari display your selected site.**

Although the History menu only displays the past seven days, you can choose History⇨Show All History to view a list of all the websites you visited in the period specified by the Remove History Items pop-up menu in the General preferences pane.

You can define how long Safari stores your previously visited websites by following these steps:

1. **Choose Safari⇨Preferences to open the preferences window, and then click the General tab to open the General preferences pane.**

2. **Click the Remove History Items pop-up menu and choose an option, such as After One Month or After One Day, as shown in Figure 1-16.**

   You can also erase your web-browsing history at any time by choosing History⇨Clear History.

Figure 1-15:
The History menu lets you revisit previously viewed websites.

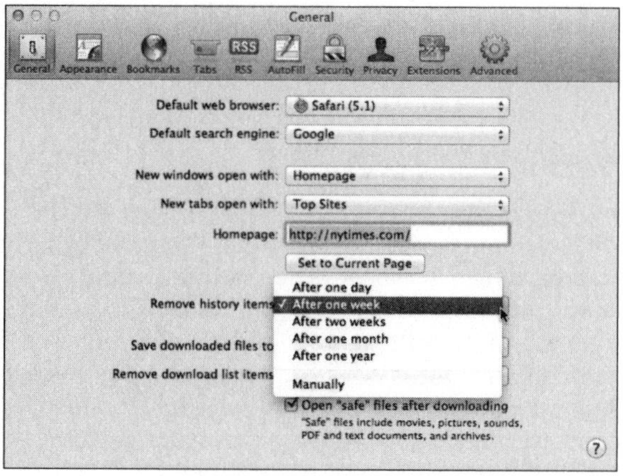

Book II
Chapter 1

Connecting to
the Internet and
Browsing the Web

Figure 1-16:
Define how long Safari keeps track of websites you visit.

3. **Click the Close button to close the Safari preferences pane.**

Protecting your web-browsing privacy

Safari has many built-in security and privacy features. When you open a website that Safari finds suspicious, you receive a warning before Safari will open the page. Safari encrypts your web browsing to help avoid Internet eavesdropping and potential digital theft. And, instead of letting websites access your information automatically when you fill out forms, Safari detects forms and presents your information in drop-down fields so you can choose which information to insert.

As a rule, Safari keeps track of your browsing history, but if you use Safari on a shared Mac, either at home or in a public setting such as a library, you may not want to leave a trace of where you've been. Choose Safari⇨Private Browsing and Safari keeps your browsing secrets safe. In a nutshell, turning on the Private Browsing keeps your web-browsing history usage private by

✦ Not tracking which websites you visit

✦ Removing any files that you downloaded from the Downloads window (Window⇨Downloads)

✦ Not saving names or passwords that you enter on websites

✦ Not saving search words or terms that you enter in the Google search box

In other words, the Private Browsing feature gives Safari a case of amnesia when you turn it on, making Safari mind its own business until you turn off Private Browsing. You know Private Browsing is active because you see the word Private in the address field. You can use the navigation buttons during the session but when you close Safari, your viewing history is erased.

When Private Browsing is turned off, Safari goes back to thoughtfully keeping track of the websites you visit and the terms you type into the search box so you can easily return to those sites or searches later.

 If you don't share your Mac and you visit a lot of websites that require usernames and passwords, Safari can remember and automatically fill in the username and password for you when you open those websites. Safari encrypts this information, so even though it's remembered, it's safe. Choose Safari⇨Preferences and click the AutoFill tab. Select the User Names and Passwords check box. The first time you visit a website that requires a username and password, Safari asks whether you want it remembered. If you choose Yes, your username and password are filled in automatically the next time you visit the website. You can see the list of websites any time by clicking the Edit button next to User Names and Passwords in the AutoFill preferences pane. You can also choose to AutoFill information about you on website forms such as your address and telephone number, which will be taken from Address Book, and AutoFill other forms, which will remember what you enter the first time you fill in a form and use it if the same website asks for the same information again. Click the Edit button next to any of the options to see, and remove, websites for which AutoFill has been enabled.

We talk about securing the files on your Mac in Book II, Chapter 4, but there are also privacy and security options in Safari's preferences. Do the following to set these up:

1. **Choose Safari⇨Preferences and click the Privacy tab.**

The Privacy preferences pane opens, as shown in Figure 1-17.

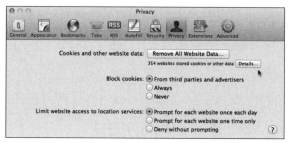

Figure 1-17:
Specify
your privacy
settings
in Safari
preferences.

2. **Tighten your web-browsing security by clicking the Remove All Website Data button to remove cookies.**

Safari keeps a list of websites that keep track of information about you. This data is stored on your Mac in different places and used in different ways. You can click the Remove All Website Data button, but that may lead to problems with loading your favorite web pages until Safari builds up the information again. You can click the Details button and see who's tracking what (shown in Figure 1-18), and then select which you would like to remove. The three basic types of information are

- *Cache* is information your Mac stores and remembers about your Safari usage so Safari runs faster; things like web page address. You can empty the cache by choosing Safari⇨Empty Cache. A dialog will ask if you really want to do this because it can slow down your browsing.

- *Cookies* are pieces of information about you that websites you visit use to track your browser usage. Cookies may also be used for user authentication or specific information. When you sign up with a website, that site gives you a cookie so that the next time you go to that website, it recognizes you because it sees you have one of its cookies.

- *Local storage* is information about you that's used by the websites you visit.

3. **Select an option to block cookies: Always, Never, or From Third Parties and Advertisers.**

If you selectively block cookies by selecting the From Third Parties and Advertisers option, you are less likely to have trouble with online stores that use cookies to keep your shopping cart information.

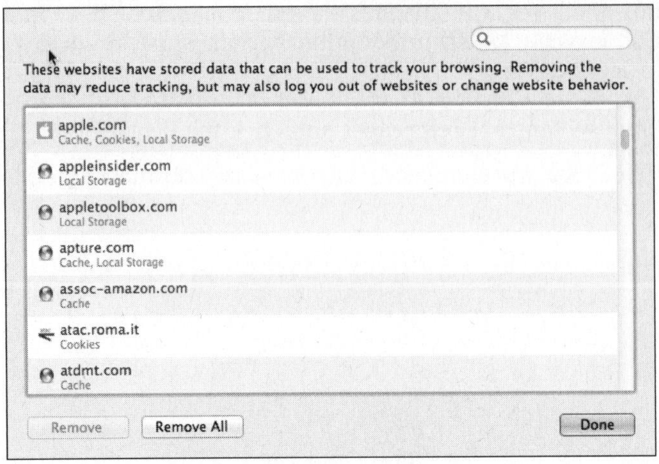

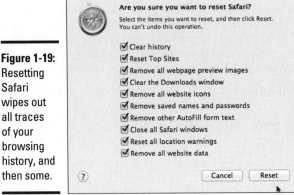

Figure 1-18:
Safari
tracks
which
websites
have
stored data
about your
computer.

4. **Select an option to limit location services.**

   Some websites ask to identify your physical location, which they can access based on your Internet connection. You can select when you want to be asked by selecting the Prompt for Each Website Once a Day or the Prompt for Each Website Once Only options; if you want to tacitly deny access to everyone, select the Deny without Prompting option.

5. **Click the close button when you have selected the Privacy preferences you want.**

If you have reason to believe that your Mac or your Internet browsing have been tampered with, you can reset Safari. To do this, choose Safari➪Reset Safari. A dialog opens with a series of check boxes, as shown in Figure 1-19. You can't undo this procedure; so *carefully* choose the items you want to reset.

Figure 1-19:
Resetting
Safari
wipes out
all traces
of your
browsing
history, and
then some.

Searching within a web page

You can search for a word or phrase within the text on a web page. Safari will find and highlight each occurrence of the word or phrase. Here's how:

1. **From the web page you want to search, choose Edit⇨Find⇨Find.**

Under the toolbar, a banner appears that has a search field and navigation buttons.

2. **Type in the word or phrase you want to find.**

3. **Click the small triangle next to the magnifying glass to choose whether you want to find text that starts with the word you entered or contains the word you entered, as shown in Figure 1-20.**

The results are immediately highlighted in the text and the number of hits is shown to the left of the search field.

4. **Use the navigation arrows to go to the next or previous occurrence of the search term.**

5. **Click Done to close the Find banner.**

Figure 1-20:
Search for words within a web page with the Find command.

Using the Top Sites view to display favorite sites

While you browse the web and go from one site to another to another, Safari pays attention behind the scenes to which websites you visit most. By tracking the websites you visit most frequently, Safari can display a selection of Top Sites that you can browse through to return to what Safari deems to be your favorite websites, as shown in Figure 1-21.

To display the Top Sites view of websites you visited, that Safari believes are your favorite websites, follow these steps:

1. **In the Safari window, click the Top Sites icon in the Bookmarks bar to open the Top Sites display window.**

   You see thumbnail views of the sites you visit most frequently. A star appears in the upper-right corner of the thumbnail of sites that have been updated since you last visited.

2. **Click a Top Sites thumbnail image of a website you want to visit.**

   Safari goes to that web page.

3. **(Optional) Click the Edit button in the lower-left corner to turn on the Top Site display's view options, as shown in Figure 1-22:**

Figure 1-21: The Top Sites view displays thumbnail images of your favorite websites.

Figure 1-22:
The Top
Sites editing
options let
you add
or remove
Top Sites
choices.

- *Thumbnail size:* Click the Small, Medium, or Large buttons in the lower-right corner to change the size of the Top Sites thumbnail images to display 24, 12, or 6 thumbnail images, respectively.

- *Exclude website:* To exclude a Top Sites selection that Safari deemed a favorite, click the X in the upper-left corner of that Top Sites thumbnail image.

- *Permanent website:* To mark a Top Sites selection as a permanent top site, click the black pushpin icon next to the X in the upper-left corner of the Top Sites thumbnail image. The pushpin icon turns blue to indicate that the website is a permanent top site. Click a blue pushpin icon to reverse the action: The page is no longer a permanent fixture in the Top Sites display and is replaced by a website you visit more frequently.

- *New website:* To add a new website to the Top Sites display window, type a website address in the address bar, click the tiny icon to the left of the address, and then drag and drop it into the Top Sites display window where you want it to appear. ***Note:*** You can drag a link from another source directly into the Top Sites display window, such as a website link in an e-mail message, or from another open Safari web page window. When you aren't in Top Sites view, you can also drag the address or link to the Top Sites icon in the toolbar.

- *Rearrange thumbnails:* To rearrange the order in which your Top Sites thumbnail images appear, click a top site and drag and drop it to the location where you want it to appear.

- *Done:* Click the Done button in the lower-left corner to close the Top Sites display view options and return to the main Top Sites display window.

4. **(Optional) Click the History button at the top of the Top Sites display or the Search History field in the lower-right corner of the Top Sites display window to switch to the History view, and then choose from these options:**

- *Search box:* Begin typing a word or phrase in the Search box to search for frequently viewed websites that match your search criteria.

- *Scroll bar:* Drag the Scroll button beneath the search view left or right to flip through your Top Sites favorite websites, as shown in Figure 1-23.

- *Clear History:* Click Clear History in the lower-left corner to clear your Safari viewing history; a dialog appears asking whether you're sure that you want to clear Safari's history of previously visited websites. Before clicking the Clear button, you can select the Also Reset Top Sites check box if you want to erase Safari's memory of websites it deems favorites. Click the Clear button to clear the history of previously visited websites.

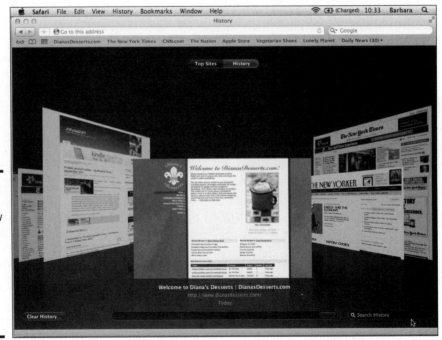

Figure 1-23: Use the History view in Top Sites to browse through websites you previously visited.

5. **Click the Top Sites button at the top to return to the Top Sites view.**

6. **To exit the Top Sites display window, type a web address in the address bar and press Return to go to that website.**

   You can also click one of the thumbnails in the Top Sites to go to that website or click a bookmark button in the toolbar to close the Top Sites view and go to that bookmarked website, which we show you how to do in the next section.

Using bookmarks

Bookmarks let you store and organize your favorite websites into groups, such as news sites, book review sites, or gadgets sites. By organizing your favorite websites into groups, you can quickly find them again. You can save and view bookmarks in either the Bookmarks menu or the Bookmarks bar, as shown in Figure 1-24.

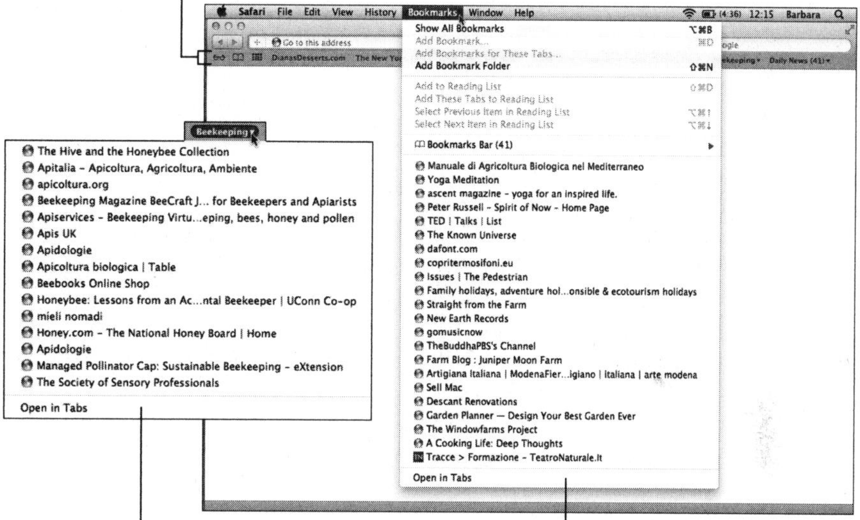

**Book II
Chapter 1**

**Connecting to
the Internet and
Browsing the Web**

Figure 1-24:
The Bookmarks menu is a pull-down menu. The Bookmarks bar displays bookmark quick-link buttons and folders.

Storing bookmarks on the Bookmarks menu tucks them out of sight. The drawback is that you must click the Bookmarks menu to find your bookmarks.

Storing bookmarks on the Bookmarks bar keeps bookmarks buttons for websites you visit often visible and within easy access at all times. The drawback is that the Bookmarks bar can display only a limited number of bookmark buttons that link to your favorite websites.

Generally, use the Bookmarks bar for one-click access to your favorite web-sites and use the Bookmarks menu to store websites that you don't access as often.

One way to cram more bookmarks onto the Bookmarks bar is to create a folder based on a particular category on the Bookmarks bar, which you can fill with more bookmarks related to that particular category (refer to Figure 1-24). Clicking a Bookmarks bar folder opens a menu of all the bookmarks saved in that bookmark folder. For instance, you can create a Lunch Joints folder on the Bookmarks bar and then bookmark the websites of nearby res-taurants you frequent for lunch inside the folder. Today's lunch specials are now only two clicks away.

Bookmarks behave the same whether they appear on the Bookmarks menu or on the Bookmarks bar.

By default, Safari comes with several bookmarks already placed on the Bookmarks bar. If you saved bookmarks on both the Bookmarks menu and Bookmarks bar (see the next section, "Adding bookmarks"), you can choose bookmarks from either location (refer to Figure 1-24).

To choose a bookmark on the Bookmarks bar, do either of the following:

✦ Click a bookmark on the Bookmarks bar to view your chosen web page.

✦ Click a bookmark folder on the Bookmarks bar to view a pull-down menu of additional bookmarks or folders. Then click the bookmark you want to view.

To choose a bookmark on the Bookmarks menu, click the Bookmarks menu and do either of the following:

✦ Click a bookmark on the Bookmarks menu to view your chosen web page.

✦ Click a bookmark folder on the Bookmarks menu to view a submenu of additional bookmarks or folders. Then click the bookmark you want to view.

Adding bookmarks

To bookmark a website address in either the menu or the bar, follow these steps:

1. **In Safari, visit a website that you want to store as a bookmark.**

2. **Choose Bookmark⇨Add Bookmark (or click the plus-sign button that appears to the left of the address bar) to open the dialog shown in Figure 1-25.**

Figure 1-25:
Safari
names
a new
bookmark
based on
the website,
or you can
give it a new
name.

By default, the Name text box displays the current web page's title —
which is typically the main website's name.

3. **(Optional) Type a new name for the bookmark if you don't want to keep the default name.**

4. **Click the Location pop-up menu and choose a location for storing your bookmark.**

   You can choose the Bookmarks bar, Bookmarks menu, or a specific folder stored on the Bookmarks bar or Bookmarks menu. (You discover how to create a bookmark folder in the "Storing bookmarks in folders" section, later in this chapter.) Notice that you can also add this website to your Reading List or Top Sites.

5. **Click the Add button.**

You can also add a website to the Bookmarks bar by simply clicking and dragging the icon to the left of the URL up to the Bookmarks bar.

Deleting bookmarks

After you start saving bookmarks of your favorite websites, you may find that you have too many bookmarks that you don't use anymore. To delete a bookmark, follow these steps:

1. **In Safari, choose Bookmarks⇨Show All Bookmarks or click the Bookmark button in the toolbar (it looks like a little open book).**

Safari displays a window divided into three panes, as shown in Figure 1-26. The left pane displays a list of bookmark collections followed by Bookmark folders. Collections include the Bookmarks bar, the Bookmarks menu, your History, and All RSS feeds).

The right panes display the contents of the currently selected bookmark folder or individual bookmark, displaying a Cover Flow thumbnail view in the upper-right pane, and a list of bookmark folders and individual bookmarks in the lower-right pane.

If you don't see the Cover Flow thumbnails, move the pointer over the black strip at the top of the right pane until it becomes a hand. Then click and drag down to pull open the Cover Flow view. Likewise, if you want to hide the Cover Flow view, click and drag the hand up from the bottom of the Cover Flow area.

2. **Click the folder in the left pane that contains the bookmark you want to delete.**

The right panes display the contents of your chosen bookmark folder, which might include bookmarks and additional folders that contain other bookmarks (refer to Figure 1-26).

Figure 1-26:
The Show All Bookmarks window displays your bookmarks and bookmark folders.

3. **(Optional) Click the triangle that appears to the left of any folder displayed in the lower-right pane to display the bookmarks and any other folders in that particular folder.**

   You may need to repeat this step several times to find the bookmark you want.

4. **Click the bookmark name that you want to delete and press the Delete key.**

   You can also Right-click a bookmark and, when a pop-up menu appears, choose Delete, or choose Edit⇨Delete.

   Your chosen bookmark disappears.

   To restore a bookmark you mistakenly deleted, press ⌘+Z or choose Edit⇨Undo Remove Bookmark.

5. **Choose Bookmarks⇨Hide All Bookmarks or click the Bookmarks button in the toolbar.**

Book II Chapter 1

Connecting to the Internet and Browsing the Web

Moving bookmarks and bookmark folders

Your browser saves your bookmarks and bookmark folders in the order you create them. However, chances are you want to rearrange your bookmarks or bookmark folders and put them in a more logical order. You can move a bookmark and bookmark folder by following these steps:

1. **Choose Bookmarks⇨Show All Bookmarks to display your saved bookmarks (refer to Figure 1-26).**

2. **Click the folder in the left pane that contains the bookmark or bookmark folder you want to move.**

   The right panes display the contents of your chosen bookmark folder.

3. **(Optional) Click the triangle that appears to the left of any folder that appears in the lower-right pane to display the contents of the folder.**

   You may need to repeat this step several times to find the bookmark you want.

4. **Drag and drop the bookmark or bookmark folder you want to move onto a folder in the left or right pane.**

   Safari moves your chosen bookmark to its new location.

5. **Click and drag bookmarks up and down within the collection or folder to change the order in which they are displayed.**

6. **Choose Bookmarks⇨Hide All Bookmarks (or press Option+⌘+B).**

Storing bookmarks in folders

After you save many bookmarks, you might find that they start to clutter the Bookmarks menu or Bookmarks bar. To organize your bookmarks, you can store related bookmarks in folders. To create a bookmark folder, follow these steps:

1. **In Safari, choose Bookmarks⇨Show All Bookmarks to display your saved bookmarks.**

2. **Click Bookmarks Bar or Bookmarks Menu in the left pane to choose a location to store your folder.**

3. **(Optional) Click the triangle that appears to the left of a folder that appears in the lower-right pane to display the contents of the folder.**

4. **Click any bookmark or a specific bookmark folder in the right pane.**

   When you create a bookmark folder, it appears inside the same folder that holds the bookmark or folder you click in this step.

5. **Choose Bookmarks⇨Add Bookmark Folder, or click the plus sign button in the bottom corner of the left or right pane, depending on where you'll store your new folder.**

   An untitled bookmark folder appears.

6. **Type a descriptive name for your bookmark folder in the text field and press Return.**

7. **Choose Bookmarks⇨Hide All Bookmarks or click the Bookmarks button in the toolbar.**

After you create a bookmark folder, you can copy or move existing bookmarks into that folder, or move the folder into another folder.

Using bookmarks to create an aggregated RSS feed

We explain how to view the RSS feed for a news outlet earlier in this chapter in the "Tracking breaking news with RSS feeds" section. The timesaver is when you bookmark RSS feeds from several sources and search those aggregated sources for the topics that interest you. Here's how to make Safari your personal clipping service:

1. **Click the Safari icon in the Dock or Launchpad to run Safari.**

2. **Choose Bookmarks⇨Add Bookmark Folder.**

   The Bookmark browser opens with an Untitled Folder at the bottom of the Bookmarks section.

3. **Type a name for the folder, for example** Daily News.

4. **In the Collections list, click Bookmarks Bar or Bookmarks Menu, whichever one you want the folder to appear in.**

   Bookmarks in the Bookmarks Bar run across the toolbar at the top of the Safari window and those in the Bookmarks Menu appear when you pull down the Bookmarks menu.

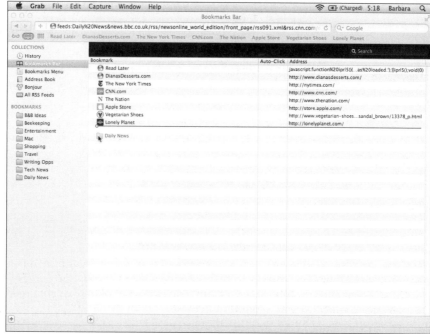

Figure 1-27:
Create
a folder
for your
bookmarked
RSS feeds.

5. Click and drag the new folder to the right where either Bookmarks Bar or Bookmarks Menu is opened, as shown in Figure 1-27.

6. Click the Back button to return to your home page.

7. Type in the URL for the website that has an RSS feed you want to bookmark, for example the MacWorld page, www.macworld.com.

8. Click the RSS button.

   The RSS newsfeed opens.

9. Choose Bookmarks⊅Add Bookmark.

   A dialog appears, asking where you want to store the bookmark.

10. Choose the new folder you just created (refer to Figure 1-25).

11. Click Add.

   Safari creates a bookmark for the RSS feed and places it in the folder you chose.

12. Repeat Steps 7 through 11 for each of the RSS feeds you want placed together.

13. To see a cumulative RSS newsfeed of the bookmarks you placed in the folder, choose Bookmarks⊅*Your Folder*⊅View All RSS Articles, or choose Bookmarks⊅Bookmarks Bar⊅View All RSS Articles.

Alternatively, click the triangle next to the folder's tab in the Bookmarks Bar and choose View All RSS Articles, as shown in Figure 1-28.

Figure 1-28:
Choose
View All
RSS Articles
to see
all your
bookmarked
RSS feeds
together.

Importing and exporting bookmarks

After you collect and organize bookmarks, you might become dependent on your bookmarks to help you navigate the web. Fortunately, if you ever want to switch browsers, you can export bookmarks from one browser and import them into another browser.

To export bookmarks from Safari, follow these steps:

1. **In Safari, choose File⇨Export Bookmarks to open the Export Bookmarks dialog.**

2. **(Optional) Type a descriptive name for your bookmarks if you don't want to keep the default, Safari Bookmarks.**

3. **Click the Where pop-up menu to choose where you want to store your exported bookmarks file.**

    If you click the arrow button that appears to the right of the Save As text box, a window appears displaying all the drives and folders that you can choose in which to store your bookmarks.

4. **Click Save.**

After you export bookmarks from one browser, it's usually a snap to import them into a second browser. To import bookmarks into Safari, follow these steps:

1. **In Safari, choose File⇨Import Bookmarks to open the Import Bookmarks dialog and navigate to the folder where the exported bookmarks file is stored.**

2. **Click the bookmark file you want to use and click the Import button.**

Your imported bookmarks appear in an Imported folder that includes the date you imported the folder. At this point, you can move this folder or its contents to the Bookmarks bar or Bookmarks menu to organize them (see the earlier section, "Moving bookmarks and bookmark folders).

Using tabbed browsing

One problem with browsing websites is that you might want to keep track of more than one website while browsing a second, third, or fourth site. Although you could open two (or three or four) separate browser windows, Safari and most other browsers offer a handy *tabbed browsing* feature. Essentially, tabbed browsing lets you easily jump around among multiple web pages in a single window — all you have to do is click the tab associated with the web page. (See Figure 1-29.)

**Book II
Chapter 1**

**Connecting to
the Internet and
Browsing the Web**

Figure 1-29:
Tabbed browsing lets you juggle multiple web pages inside a single window.

Creating new tabs

When you load Safari, you see a single web page displayed. To create a tab, follow these steps:

1. **Choose File⇨New Tab (or press ⌘+T) to open a new tabbed window.**

2. **Click a bookmark (or type a website address into the address bar and press Return) to display your chosen web page in your new tab.**

Managing tabs

When you open 3, 4, or 15 tabbed windows, you can do things such as rearrange the way they are ordered, close tabs, and save a group of tabs as a bookmark that you can reopen all at once with a single click of your mouse, or add them to your Reading List.

Some cool things you can try doing with tabbed windows include

+ Add a new tab by pressing ⌘+T, or if two tabs are already open, clicking the plus sign at the far right of the Tab bar.

+ Switch from tab to tab by pressing ⌘+Shift+→ or ⌘+Shift+←.

+ Close a tab by moving your mouse over the tab and clicking the Close icon that appears (or press ⌘+W). You can also right-click a tab and choose Close Tab or Close Other Tabs.

+ Rearrange the order of your tabs by dragging and dropping a tab to the left or right of another tab.

+ Move a tab to a new window by dragging it below the Tab bar and then letting go of your mouse button, or by right-clicking a tab and choosing Move Tab to New Window.

+ Save your collection of every currently loaded tabbed window as a bookmark by right-clicking any tab and choosing Add Bookmark for These Tabs.

+ Save the articles of every currently loaded tabbed window in the Reading List by right-clicking any tab and choosing Add These Tabs to Reading List.

+ Merge a bunch of open web page windows into a single web page with tabs for each of the windows by choosing Windows⇨Merge All Windows.

+ View tabs that get shoved off the row of visible tabs when you've opened too many tabs to display them all by clicking the double right-pointing arrows on the rightmost tab.

Capturing Web Clips

Rather than view an entire web page, you might really care about only a certain part of a web page that's frequently updated, such as status updates on such social networking sites as Twitter or Facebook, traffic reports on local highways, or breaking news. Fortunately, Safari lets you copy part of a web page and store it as a Dashboard widget called a *Web Clip*.

Dashboard widgets are applications that perform a single task and pop up whenever you choose the Dashboard from the Dock or press Fn+F12. You find out more about Dashboard widgets in Book I, Chapter 3.

To create a Web Clip, follow these steps:

1. **In Safari, go to the web page you're interested in and choose File⇨ Open in Dashboard.**

The web page darkens and highlights a portion of the currently displayed web page.

2. **Move your pointer over the part of the web page that you want to view as a Dashboard widget, and then click the mouse to create a selection box, as shown in Figure 1-30.**

3. **(Optional) Click one of the selection box handles surrounding the selection box and drag your mouse to make the box bigger or smaller around the section of information you want to capture.**

4. **Click the Add button in the upper-right corner to save your Web Clip as a Dashboard widget.**

Dashboard automatically opens and displays your newly created Web Clip widget.

**Book II
Chapter 1**

**Connecting to
the Internet and
Browsing the Web**

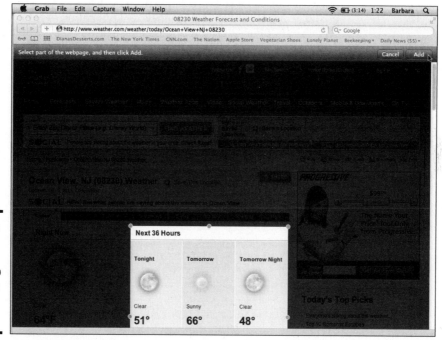

Figure 1-30:
Click a
section of a
web page to
turn it into a
Dashboard
Web Clip.

To delete a Web Clip, click the Dashboard icon in the Dock (or press Fn+F12 to display your Dashboard widgets), hold down the Option key, move your pointer over the widget you want to delete, and then click the Close button that appears in the upper-left corner. Adios, Web Clip.

Saving and Sharing Web Pages

When you come upon a web page containing a story or a recipe that you want to share with friends, you can save, print, or e-mail the web page to your friends so they can have a look at what you find so interesting.

Saving a web page as a file

When you save a web page as a file, you store the complete text and graphics of that web page as a file on your Mac's hard drive. Safari gives you two ways to save a web page:

✦ **As a Web Archive:** A *web archive* is meant for viewing a web page only in the Safari browser.

✦ **As an HTML Source File (called Page Source):** If you view a web page saved as Page Source, you won't see any of the graphics, but you will see text references to the graphics and each one's associated URL address. Saving a web page as an HTML source file lets you view and edit that file in any browser or web page authoring application — which is helpful if you want to figure out how someone designed that particular web page.

HTML stands for *HyperText Markup Language,* which is a special language used to specify the layout and behavior of web pages.

To save a web page as a file, follow these steps:

1. **In Safari, find the web page that you want to save and choose File⇨Save As.**

The Save As dialog opens, as shown in Figure 1-31.

Figure 1-31:
The Save As dialog lets you choose where to save a file.

2. **(Optional) Type a new descriptive name in the Export As field if you don't want to keep the one Safari automatically fills in for you.**

3. **Click the Where pop-up menu and choose where you want to store your file on your Mac's hard drive.**

   If you click the Expand (downward-pointing arrow) button to the right of the Export As field, the Save As dialog expands to let you choose more folders to store your file.

4. **Click the Format pop-up menu, choose Web Archive or Page Source, and then click Save.**

After you save a file as a Web Archive or a Page Source, you can view it by double-clicking the file icon in the folder where you saved the Web Archive or Page Source file.

Only Safari can view a Web Archive file, but any browser can view a Page Source file.

Saving a photo from the web

Websites are full of graphics and photos. There are times that you want to save an image and Safari makes it easy to do — just make sure that you keep the image to yourself if you don't have the rights to it. To save an image to iPhoto, do the following:

1. **In Safari, find the image on a web page that you want to save.**

2. **Right-click the image and choose Add Image to iPhoto Library, shown in Figure 1-32, or choose one of the other saving options from the menu.**

   Some websites "protect" against copying the images by using a transparent overlay that prevents your click from being on, and selecting, the image you want to copy.

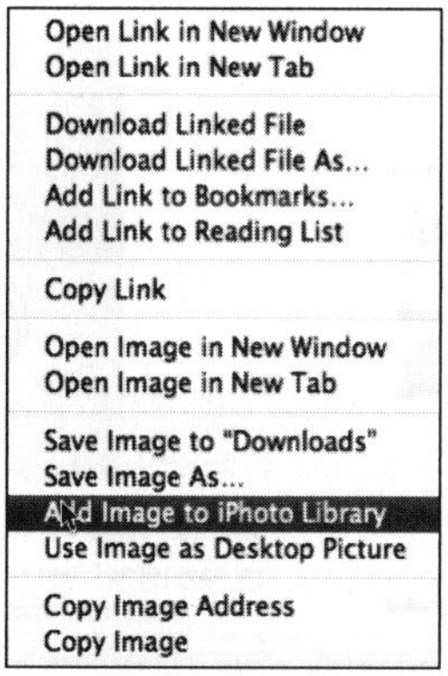

Figure 1-32:
Right-click
to save an
image from
a web page.

```
Open Link in New Window
Open Link in New Tab

Download Linked File
Download Linked File As...
Add Link to Bookmarks...
Add Link to Reading List

Copy Link

Open Image in New Window
Open Image in New Tab

Save Image to "Downloads"
Save Image As...
Add Image to iPhoto Library
Use Image as Desktop Picture

Copy Image Address
Copy Image
```

3. **iPhoto opens automatically and the image is imported.**

   You can adjust, share, or print the image. (See Book IV, Chapter 3 for details on using iPhoto.)

Printing a web page

Rather than save a web page as a file, you might just want to print it instead. To print a web page, follow these steps:

1. **In Safari, find the web page you want to print and choose File⇨Print to open the Print dialog.**

2. **Click the Printer pop-up menu and select the printer to use.**

   If you click the PDF button, you can save your web page as a PDF file. If you click the Expand button (downward-pointing arrow) to the right of the Printer pop-up menu, the Print dialog expands to let you select which pages to print and other print-related options.

3. **Click Print.**

Sending a web page by e-mail

After saving a web page as a separate file, you can then attach that file to an e-mail message to send it to a friend. An easier way to send a web page to one or more people is to send the web page in an e-mail message. (You can also just send a link to the web page rather than the entire web page itself, which is quicker because you don't have to send the space-consuming megabytes of data.)

To send a web page (or just a link to a web page) in an e-mail message, follow these steps:

1. **In Safari, click the File menu and choose one of these options:**

   - *Mail Contents of This Page:* Sends the entire web page in an e-mail message.

   - *Mail Link to This Page:* Sends a link to the web page that the recipient can click to open the web page with his or her web browser.

   The Mail application loads and opens a new e-mail message containing your web page or your web page link, depending on which command you select.

2. **In the To: field that's automatically selected, type the e-mail address (or addresses) of the person or people that you want to send the web page to.**

3. **Type your message (if desired), and click the Send button.**

   The Mail application sends your e-mail message.

If you send a link to a web page and that web page or website is changed or is no longer available, anyone who clicks the link will see an error message instead of the web page you wanted him or her to see. And if you send the page contents, the recipient may not be able to view the page if the e-mail application used doesn't display web pages.

Viewing and Playing Multimedia Files

The most basic web pages consist of mainly text and sometimes graphics. However, most websites offer robust content beyond simple words and pictures, including content stored as video, audio, and other types of common files, such as PDF (Portable Document Format) files. Although your Mac includes many applications for viewing and listening to video, audio, and PDF files, you might still need additional software to view some websites.

Watching video

Many news sites offer videos that require Adobe Flash, Windows Media Player, or RealPlayer.

To download the necessary application so you can play Windows Media video content, go to `www.microsoft.com/mac/products/flip4mac.mspx`. Microsoft actually gives you two choices. First, you can download the Windows Media Player for the Mac. However, Microsoft has stopped developing this application, so as a second choice, Microsoft offers a free application called Flip4Mac.

Some websites won't work unless you're using Microsoft Windows. In this case, you might need to run Windows on your Mac with one of the applications described in Book III, Chapter 4.

The Flip4Mac application allows the QuickTime Player that comes with your Mac to play most video files designed to run with the Windows Media Player.

Besides downloading and installing the Flip4Mac application, you should also download and install the RealPlayer application (`www.real.com`) and Adobe Flash (`www.adobe.com`). After you have Flip4Mac, Flash, and RealPlayer installed, you should be able to watch videos on most every website you visit.

Listening to streaming audio

Many websites offer audio that you can listen to, such as live interviews or radio shows. Such audio is often stored as *streaming audio,* which means that your computer downloads a temporary audio file and begins playing it almost instantly but doesn't actually save the radio application as a file on your hard drive.

Sometimes you can listen to streaming audio through the iTunes application, sometimes you need a copy of Windows Media Player (or Flip4Mac), and sometimes you need a copy of RealPlayer.

Viewing PDF files

Some websites offer downloadable documents, booklets, brochures, eBook editions of *The New York Times* best-selling nonfiction and fiction titles, and user guides as a PDF (Portable Document Format) file, which is a special file format for storing the layout of text and graphics so they appear exactly the same on different computers. If a website offers a PDF file as a link you can click to open, you can view and scroll through it directly within Safari.

You can save a PDF document you're viewing to look at later by clicking the document displayed in the Safari web browser window and choosing File⇨Save As. If you double-click a PDF file icon, you can view the contents of that PDF file by using the Preview application included with every Mac.

You can also view PDF files by using the Adobe Reader application — a free download from Adobe (www.adobe.com) — which offers the basic features of the Preview application plus extra features for opening and viewing PDF documents. If you have problems printing certain PDF files with the Preview application, try printing them with the Adobe Reader application instead.

Downloading Files

Part of the web's appeal is that you can find interesting content — music tracks, or free demos of applications you can try before you buy, for example — that you can download and install on your own computer. (When you copy a file from the web and store it on your computer, that's *downloading*. When you copy a file from your computer to a website — such as your electronic tax forms that you file electronically on the IRS's website — that's *uploading*.)

Only download a file if you trust the source. If you visit an unknown website, that unknown website might be trying to trick you into downloading a file that could do harmful things to your Mac, such as delete files, spy on your activities, or even bombard you with unwanted ads, so be careful. Safari has built-in protections that scan websites and downloads to warn you of potential dangers. To discover ways you can protect your Mac (and yourself) from potentially dangerous Internet threats, take a look at Book II, Chapter 4.

To download a file, click a link or button on a website that offers downloadable content, such as MacUpdate (www.macupdate.com), or Apple's Downloads web page (www.apple.com/downloads). When you find a file you want to download, follow these steps:

1. **Click the Download link or button to begin downloading the file you want to save on your Mac's hard drive.**

An arrow button appears next to the search field with a small blue progress bar. Clicking the progress bar opens a list of past and current downloads and their status, as shown in Figure 1-33. You can also view downloads from the Downloads stack in the Dock and from there, open them in the Finder.

2. **When the file has completely downloaded, double-click the file icon in the Downloads progress list to open the file.**

Alternatively, you can go to the Downloads stack in the Dock and open the file from there, as shown in Figure 1-34.

If you downloaded an application, that application might start running or installing itself on your Mac, so follow the onscreen instructions.

If you click the magnifying glass icon to the right of a file displayed in the Downloads progress window, Safari opens a Finder window and displays the contents of the Downloads stack.

3. **(Optional) Choose Safari⇨Preferences and click the General tab to select where files are saved when they are downloaded and when to remove downloaded files from Safari.**

Figure 1-33:
The
Downloads
progress
bar shows
you how
much longer
you'll need
to wait
to finish
downloading
a file.

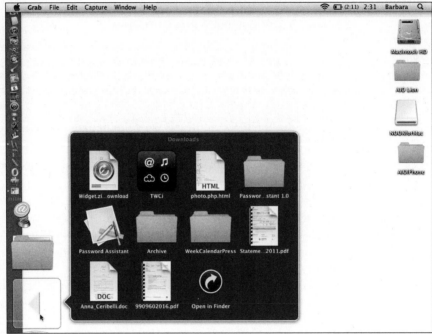

Figure 1-34:
The
Downloads
stack in the
Dock shows
the files
you have
downloaded.

4. **(Optional) Choose to open "safe" files, such as PDFs, photo, and movies, as soon as the download is finished by selecting the check box next to Open "Safe" Files After Downloading.**

5. **Click the Close button to close the Safari preferences pane.**

Using Extensions

You can enhance your Safari Internet navigation experience by adding extensions, which are add-ons applets designed by developers and approved by Apple. To find and install extensions, follow these steps:

1. **Click the Safari icon on the Dock or Launchpad.**

2. **Choose Safari⇨Safari Extensions.**

   The Safari Extensions Gallery on the Apple website opens, as shown in Figure 1-35.

Figure 1-35:
Safari
Extensions
automate
and add
features to
your web
browsing
activities.

3. **Search for extensions by scrolling through the extensions on the opening page or clicking a category and scrolling through the results.**

4. **When you find a useful or entertaining extension, click the Install Now button.**

   The extension is installed in the Library to be accessed by Safari. Depending on the type of task the extension performs, it may appear as a banner under the toolbar, as a button on the toolbar, or it might show up on-call, for example as password manager.

5. **To manage your extensions after you install them, choose Safari⇨Preferences and click the Extensions tab.**

   The Extensions pane opens, as shown in Figure 1-36.

6. **Click the extension you want to manage and choose settings from the menus offered. Click Uninstall if you want to remove the extension.**

7. **Click a bookmark or enter a new URL in the Smart Address Field when you're finished visiting the Extensions Gallery.**

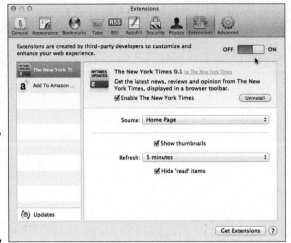

Figure 1-36:
Manage
Safari
Extensions
from
Preferences.

Chapter 2: Corresponding with Mail

In This Chapter

✔ Configuring an e-mail account

✔ Writing e-mail

✔ Receiving and reading e-mail

✔ Organizing e-mail

✔ Cleaning up junk e-mail

✔ Using RSS and Notes

Some futurists say e-mail, like its paper-based predecessor, is being replaced — in this case, by social networks and by text messages exchanged via mobile phone. No doubt there are examples of a start-up receiving funding after a Facebook exchange; however — for now anyway — e-mail remains the professional, not to mention private, secure, and trackable, method of electronic communication. E-mail is fast (almost always) free, and accessible to anyone with a computer, smartphone, tablet, or e-reader and an Internet connection.

When you have an e-mail account, you have two choices for reading and writing messages:

◆ Through a web browser, such as Safari or Firefox

◆ Through an e-mail application, such as the Mac's free Mail application

Accessing an e-mail account through a web browser is simple because you don't need to know how to use another application, and you don't have to worry about knowing the technical details of your e-mail account. You do need Internet access every time you want to read or respond to messages.

Accessing an e-mail account through an e-mail application lets you download messages so you can read or respond to them even if you aren't connected to the Internet. (Of course, you won't be able to send or receive any messages until you connect to the Internet again.)

If you plan to access your e-mail account only through a browser, such as Safari, you can skip this entire chapter because this chapter explains how to use Mail. If you want to use Mail, read on. In this chapter, we explain how to send and receive e-mail. First, though, we show you how to set up an e-mail account. Then we take you through Mail, the e-mail application that came with your Mac. Mail not only sends and receives messages but is also a veritable filing cabinet for your documents; you can use it to organize and store your correspondence to make later searches easier when you need to find an old "letter" or contract.

Setting Up an E-Mail Account

The three types of e-mail accounts you can set up are POP (Post Office Protocol), IMAP (Internet Message Access Protocol), and Exchange. A POP e-mail account usually transfers (moves) e-mail from the POP server computer to your computer. An IMAP or Exchange e-mail account stores e-mail on its server, which allows access to e-mail from multiple devices. Most individuals have POP accounts, whereas many corporations have IMAP or Exchange accounts.

You can use dozens of e-mail applications, but the most popular one is the free Mail application that comes with your Mac. If you don't like Mail, you can download and install a free e-mail application, such as Thunderbird (www.mozilla.org/en-US/thunderbird or Mailsmith.

You can access your e-mail from Mail (or a different e-mail application) on your Mac, from a web browser on your Mac or on another computer, such as at your friend's house, or in an Internet café. When you use a web browser, you go to the e-mail provider's website.

Gathering your e-mail account information

To make an e-mail application work with your e-mail account, you need to gather the following information:

✦ **Your username (also called an account name):** Typically a descriptive name (such as nickyhutsko) or a collection of numbers and symbols (such as nickyhutsko09). Your username plus the name of your e-mail or Internet Service Provider (ISP) defines your complete e-mail address, such as nickyhutsko@gmail.com or lilypond@comcast.net.

✦ **Your password:** Any phrase that you choose to access your account. If someone sets up an e-mail account for you, he or she might have already assigned a password that you can always change later.

✦ **Your e-mail account's incoming server name:** The mail server name of the computer that contains your e-mail message is usually a combination of POP or IMAP and your e-mail account company, such as `pop.comcast.net` or `imap.gmail.com`.

✦ **Your e-mail account's outgoing server name:** The name of the outgoing mail server that sends your messages to other people. The outgoing server name is usually a combination of SMTP (Simple Mail Transfer Protocol) and the name of the company that provides your e-mail account, such as `smtp.gmail.com` or `smtp.comcast.net`.

If you don't know your account name, password, incoming server name, or outgoing server name, ask the company that runs your e-mail account or search on the provider's website. If for some reason you're unable to find the information, chances are you might still be able to set up your e-mail account on your Mac, thanks to the Mail application's ability to detect the most popular e-mail account settings, such as those for Gmail or Yahoo!.

Apple has created a nice PDF form that, when filled out, will have all the information you need to set up your e-mail account manually: `http://support.apple.com/library/APPLE/APPLECARE_ALLGEOS/HT1277/What-to-ask.pdf`.

If you use Apple's iCloud service and typed your me.com (or mac.com) account name and password when you completed the Welcome setup process, Mail is already configured to access your me.com e-mail account.

Configuring your e-mail account

You can set up your Mail account when you first set up your Mac or by using one of the following two procedures. The first procedure sets up your e-mail account from within the Mail application, and the second way to set up your e-mail account is to use System Preferences.

Using Mail

After you collect the technical information needed to access your e-mail account, you need to configure Mail to work with your e-mail account by following these steps:

1. **Click the Mail icon in the Dock to open the Welcome to Mail dialog.**

The Welcome to Mail dialog prompts you to enter your name, e-mail address, and password, as shown in Figure 2-1.

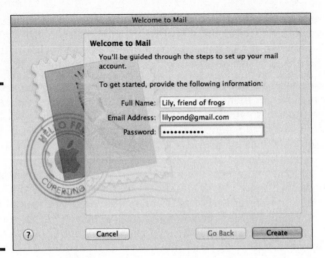

Figure 2-1:
The New
Account
dialog
asks for
your name,
e-mail
address,
and
password.

2. **Enter your full name, e-mail address, and password in the text boxes and click Create.**

   Your full name is any name you want to associate with your messages. If you type `Lily, friend of frogs` in the Full Name text box, all your messages will include `From: Lily, friend of frogs`. Your e-mail address includes your username plus ISP name, such as `lilypond@ gmail.com`. Your password might be case-sensitive (most are), so type it exactly.

   Mail connects to your email account and attempts to fill in your e-mail account settings automatically.

   • If Mail succeeds in detecting your e-mail account's settings, Mail displays an account summary window with two check boxes that you can choose to set up Calendars or Chat information, as shown in Figure 2-2. Select these check boxes if you want Mail to set up Calendar and Chat information associated with this account. Click Create and the Mail window opens.

     (Read the rest of these steps if you want to find out about additional settings that you can adjust to gain greater control over how Mail handles your e-mail.)

   • If Mail doesn't automatically detect your e-mail account settings, continue following these steps to configure Mail to work with your e-mail account.

3. **Click Continue.**

   An Incoming Mail Server dialog appears, as shown in Figure 2-3.

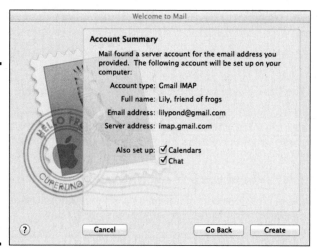

Figure 2-2:
Choose
to have
Mail set up
Calendar
and Chat
information
associated
with your
e-mail
account.

Figure 2-3:
The
Incoming
Mail Server
dialog lets
you specify
where to
retrieve
your e-mail.

4. **Choose your incoming mail server type from the Account Type pop-up menu.**

   Your choices here include POP, IMAP, Exchange 2007, Exchange IMAP, and (if you typed in an @me.com e-mail address) iCloud.

5. **(Optional) Click the Description text box and type a description of your account.**

   This description is for your benefit only, so feel free to type anything you want. Because you can configure Mail to access two or more e-mail accounts, you may want to identify an account as a Work account or a Gmail account.

6. **Click the Incoming Mail Server text box and type the name of your server.**

   If you don't know this name, you'll have to ask your ISP or e-mail account provider.

7. **Click the User Name text box and type your username.**

   Depending on your e-mail account provider, your username may be a standalone word or combination of letters and numbers, such as lilypond, or it may also include the e-mail account provider's Internet domain, such as lilypond@gmail.com or lilypond@earthlink.net.

8. **Click the Password text box and type your password.**

   Your password appears onscreen as a series of dots to keep anyone peeking over your shoulder from seeing your password.

9. **Click Continue to display the Outgoing Mail Server dialog, as shown in Figure 2-4.**

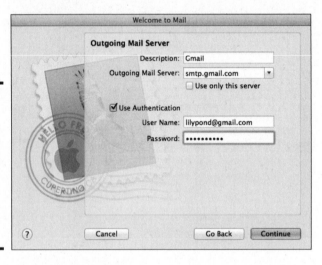

Figure 2-4:
The Outgoing Mail Server asks for the name of the server to send your e-mail through.

10. **(Optional) Click the Description text box and type a description of your account.**

    This description is for your benefit only, so feel free to type anything you want. If you type in the technical support number of your ISP as the outgoing mail server, you'll know whom to call if you're having trouble.

11. **Click the Outgoing Mail Server text box and type the name of your outgoing mail server.**

    If you don't know this name, you'll have to contact your ISP or e-mail account provider.

12. **Click the User Name text box and type your username.**

13. **Click the Password text box and type your password.**

14. **Click Continue.**

The Account Summary dialog appears, as shown in Figure 2-5.

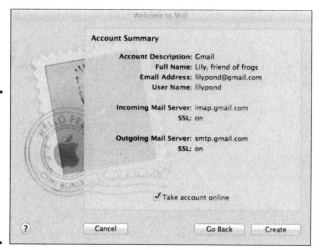

Figure 2-5:
The
Account
Summary
dialog
shows
your e-mail
account
settings.

15. **Click Create.**

The Mail window appears.

You can configure Mail to retrieve e-mail from multiple e-mail accounts. To add more e-mail accounts, choose File⇨Add Account and repeat the preceding steps to add one or more additional e-mail accounts.

Using System Preferences

With the technical information needed to access your e-mail account, you can configure Mail to work with your e-mail account by following these steps:

1. **Right-click (two-finger tap the trackpad) the System Preferences icon on the Dock and choose Mail, Contacts & Calendars from the pop-up menu, or choose ⬛⇨System Preferences and click the Mail, Contacts & Calendars icon in the Internet and Wireless section.**

The Mail, Contacts & Calendars pane opens as shown in Figure 2-6.

2. **Click Add Account in the list on the left side.**

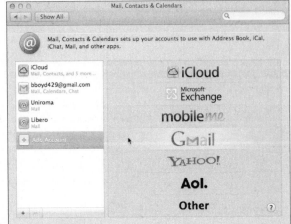

Figure 2-6:
Set up
your Mail
account
in System
Preferences.

3. **Click the type of e-mail account you have, such as Gmail or Yahoo! in the list on the right side.**

   Click Other if the e-mail service you use isn't in the list. Then click the button next to Add a Mail Account and click Create.

   An initial setup dialog appears.

4. **Type in your name, e-mail address, and password, and then click Setup or Continue (depending on which type of account you chose).**

   Mail goes online and tries to discover the settings for the server.

   If the settings can't be found, you are re-directed to Mail. Follow from Step 3 onward in the previous section.

Looking at the Mail Window

In the next few sections, we refer to buttons and panes in the Mail window. There are five parts to the mail window, as shown in Figure 2-7:

✦ **Toolbar:** Runs across the top of the window and holds the buttons that you click to take an action, such as write a new message, send a message, or even throw a message away. You can customize the Toolbar with the buttons you use most by choosing View➪Customize Toolbar. Click and drag the buttons until the Toolbar has the tools you need. At the bottom, choose from the pop-up menu to show Text and Icon, Icon Only, or Text Only.

New Message

Forward   Get Messages

Favorites bar   Reply All   New Note

Toolbar   Trash Reply   Related Messages

Show/Hide Mailboxes Junk   Flags

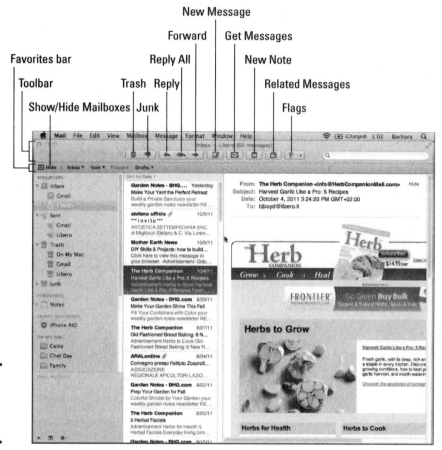

Figure 2-7:
The Mail
window has
five parts.

✦ **Favorites Bar:** Here you find buttons that quickly open your favorite mailboxes. To customize the Favorites Bar, drag the mailboxes from the Mailbox list to the Favorites Bar; to delete a button from the Favorites Bar, click and drag the undesired button out of the Favorites Bar, and it disappears in a puff of smoke.

✦ **Mailboxes:** The first column on the left shows a list of your mailboxes — if you don't see this column, click the Show button on the left of the Favorites Bar. If you have more than one account, each account will have an item in the Inbox, Sent, Trash, and Junk sections. If you click the topmost button of the section, say Inbox, you see all the messages in your Inbox listed in the center column. If you click Gmail in the Inbox section, you see only the messages on your Gmail e-mail account. If you have just one e-mail, you will see only the categories. Click the disclosure triangles to the left of the category names to show or hide the subcategories. (For example, Junk is hidden but there are junk bins for both Gmail and Libero in there.)

✦ **Message Preview List:** The second column (which is the first if the mail-boxes column is hidden) shows your messages. Click Sort By at the top of the column to choose how you want to sort your messages (shown in Figure 2-8), or choose View⇨Sort By. Choose View⇨Message Attributes and choose what information you want to see about each message in the preview.

Figure 2-8:
Sort messages in a way that makes sense to you.

Hover the pointer over the scroll bar on either column to show a vertical line with an arrow. Click and drag to make the columns wider or narrower.

✦ **Message:** The largest part of the Mail window shows your active message. This is the message that you click on in the Message List. Mail gives you the option of viewing your messages in a Conversation format. When you view a conversation, you see the thread of messages with the same subject, even if they were exchanged between more than one recipient. This way, you don't have to scroll through to find responses from different people on different days, but can follow the "conversation" exchanges as they occurred. To view your messages in conversation mode, choose View⇨Organize by Conversation. See Figure 2-8 for an example.

The number to the right of the preview in the Message Preview List shows how many exchanges make up the conversation. You can also see the "speakers" in the conversation by clicking the arrow next to the number; the active message in Figure 2-9 is expanded. To expand all the messages in Message Preview List, choose View⇨Expand All Conversations. Choose View⇨Collapse All Conversations to condense them again.

If you prefer the "classic" version of Mail, with your messages displayed in a single line across the top and the active message below, choose Mail⇨ Preferences, click the View tab, and choose Classic Layout.

Mail supports full-screen viewing. Just click the full-screen toggle switch in the upper-right corner and take advantage of your Mac's whole screen.

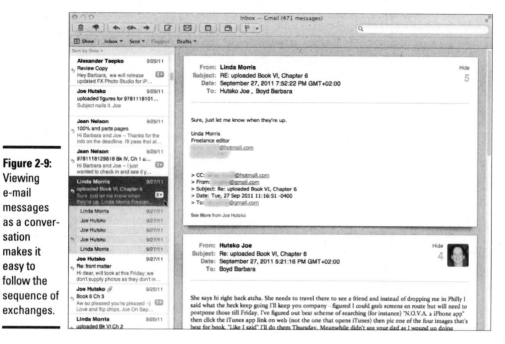

Figure 2-9:
Viewing
e-mail
messages
as a conver-
sation
makes it
easy to
follow the
sequence of
exchanges.

Writing E-Mails

After you configure Mail and are familiar with the buttons and panes, you
can start writing and sending e-mail to anyone with an e-mail address. In this
section, we describe the three ways to write and send an e-mail, how
to attach files and photos, and how to customize the appearance of your
messages.

Creating a new e-mail

When you write a message to someone for the first time, you have to create
a new message by following these steps:

1. **In Mail, choose File⇨New Message or click the New Message button.**

   The New Message button looks like a piece of paper with a pencil on it. A
   New Message window appears.

2. **Click the To text box and type an e-mail address, or just begin typing
   someone's name you have stored in Address Book and Mail will automatically fill in that person's e-mail address.**

   You can type multiple e-mail addresses in the To text box by separating
   them with a comma, such as steve@apple.com, bill@microsoft.com.

3. **Click the Subject text box and type a brief description of your message for your recipient.**

4. **Click the Message text box and type your message.**

If you want to add a signature to your e-mail that shows up at the bottom of your message, choose Mail➪Preferences and click the Signatures tab. If you have multiple e-mail accounts, you can assign a different signature to each account. Click the account name in the first column, click the + (plus sign) at the bottom of the second column. Mail makes a signature suggestion such as your first name or your first and last name with your e-mail address. If you want to sign with something different, click the text to select it and retype what you want to appear as your signature.

5. **Click the Send button, which looks like a paper airplane, in the upper-left corner.**

Replying to a message

You'll often find yourself responding to messages others send to you. When you reply to a message, your reply can contain the text that you originally received so the recipient can better understand the context of your reply.

To reply to a message, you need to receive a message first. To receive messages, just click the Get Mail button, which looks like an envelope. You find out more about receiving messages later in this chapter.

To reply to a message, follow these steps:

1. **In Mail, click the Inbox button in the Favorites bar.**

The left column lists all the messages stored in your Inbox folder.

2. **Select a message in the Inbox that you want to reply to.**

3. **Reply to the message in the following ways:**

- *If you want the original message to appear in your reply, choose Message➪Reply or click the Reply button in the toolbar.*

  The Reply button contains a left-pointing arrow. Hover over the center of the line between the address information and message to reveal the heads-up display that contains the Trash, Reply, Reply All, and Forward buttons.

- *If you want to include only a portion of the original message, highlight the portion of the message you want to appear in your reply, and then click the Reply button.*

  Only the highlighted text appears in your message.

- *If you don't want any of the original message in your new message, choose Mail⇨Preferences and then click the Composing tab. Click the check box next to Quote The Text Of The Original Message to deselect it, or click the Reply button and press ⌘+A followed by the Delete key to select all the quoted text and then delete it.*

- *If you're replying to a message that was sent to you and several other people, you can reply to everyone who received the same message by choosing Message⇨Reply All or by clicking the Reply All button, which is the double left-pointing arrow.*

Whichever way you chose to reply, a new Message window appears with the e-mail address of your recipient(s), the subject already entered, and the text of the message so that the other person can understand the context of your reply, as shown in Figure 2-10.

4. **Click the Message text box and type a message.**

5. **Click the Send button.**

Book II
Chapter 2

Corresponding
with Mail

Figure 2-10:
When you
reply to
an e-mail,
all, part,
or none of
the original
message
can appear
in your
reply.

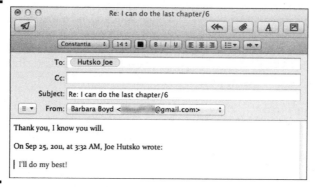

Forwarding a message

Sometimes you might receive a message and want to send that message to someone else. When you *forward* (send a copy of) a message, that message appears directly in the Message text box.

To forward a message, follow these steps:

1. **In Mail, click the Inbox button in the Favorites bar.**

   The left column lists all the messages stored in your Inbox folder.

2. **Select a message in the Inbox that you want to send to someone else.**

3. **Click the Forward button in the Toolbar or hover over the center of the line between the address and the message to bring up the heads-up display that contains the Trash, Reply, Reply All, and Forward buttons.**

4. **Click the To text box and type an e-mail address.**

5. **Click above the content of the forwarded message to type a message to accompany the forwarded message.**

6. **Click the Send button.**

Sending a file or photo attachment

When you send an e-mail, you're sending text. However, sometimes you might want to send pictures, word-processing documents, or videos and links to websites you think others may want to visit. Anyone receiving your message and file attachment can then save the file attachment and open it later. Because so many people need to share Microsoft Word files or digital photographs, file attachments are a popular way to share files with others.

Your e-mail account may have a maximum file size limit you can send, such as 10MB. If you have a file larger than 60 to 70 percent of the maximum limit, you might have to send your files through a free, separate file-delivery service, such as YouSendIt (`www.yousendit.com`), SendThisFile (`www.send thisfile.com`), or BigUpload (`www.bigupload.com`).

To attach a file to a message, follow these steps:

1. **In Mail, open a new Message window as described in one of the preceding sections.**

   You can open a new Message window to create a new message, reply to an existing message, or forward an existing message.

2. **Choose File⇨Attach Files or click the Attach button, which looks like a paper clip.**

   A dialog appears.

3. **Navigate through the folders to get to the file you want to send and click it.**

   To select multiple files, hold down the ⌘ key and click each file you want to send. To select a range of files, hold down the Shift key and click the first and last files you want to send.

4. **Click Choose File.**

   If you have just one file, it is pasted into your message. If you paste multiple files, or the file is particularly large, you see an icon for the attached file in the message window.

5. **Choose Edit⇨Attachments and select one or more of the following to set rules for attachments:**

   - *Include Original Attachments In Reply:* Attaches the original attachment to your reply to the message it came with. This is usually best left unchecked because it only creates bigger messages that take longer to send and the person who sent you the attachment should have it anyway.

   - *Always Send Windows-Friendly Attachments:* Makes sure that Windows users can read your attachment. This option is best selected because you can never be 100 percent sure which operating system your recipient will use to read your attachment.

   - *Always Insert Attachment at End of Message:* Inserts the attachment at the bottom, so the recipient may have to scroll down to get to the attachment. Whether you select this option is really a personal preference. If you want the attachment in the middle of the message, a photo for example, don't select this check box.

6. **Click the Message text box and type your message.**

7. **Click the Send button.**

You could use the preceding steps to attach a photo to your message, or you can go directly to the Photo Browser, which shows photo previews instead of a list of names like DSC174 that don't mean anything to you until you open them. To use the Photo Inspector, do the following:

1. **In Mail, open a new Message window as described in one of the preceding sections.**

   You can open a new Message window to create a new message, reply to an existing message, or forward an existing message.

2. **Click the Photo Browser button, which has an image of a mountain with a tiny moon over it.**

   The Photo Browser opens, as shown in Figure 2-11. Click and drag the bottom-right corner to enlarge the browser.

3. **Scroll through thumbnails from your iPhoto photos, events, and albums until you find the photo you want.**

4. **Double-click an event or album to see the photos in the event or album; double-click a photo to see an enlarged preview in the bottom half of the browser window.**

5. **To select multiple photos, hold down the ⌘ key and click each photo you want to send. To select a range of photos, hold down the Shift key and click the first and last photos you want to send.**

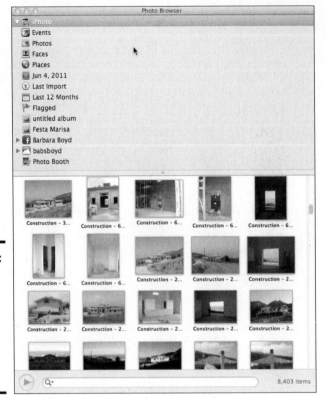

Figure 2-11:
Choose
photos
to attach
to your
messages
from the
Photo
Browser.

6. **Drag the selected photo or photos into your message.**

   The photos are pasted into your message.

7. **Adjust the image size by selecting Small, Medium, Large, or Actual Size from the pop-up menu on the bottom right of the new message window, as shown in Figure 2-12.**

   The larger the photo, the larger the message file will be, making it potentially slower to send and receive, although the better resolution is useful if the photo is destined to be printed or used as wallpaper.

8. **Click in the Message text box to type in a message.**

9. **Click the Send button.**

Figure 2-12:
Adjust the size of the photo you want to send.

Sending a message to multiple recipients

If you want to send the same message to several people, you can type multiple e-mail addresses, separated by a comma, in one or more of the following fields:

✦ **To:** The To field is where you type e-mail addresses of people who you want to read — and possibly reply to — your message.

✦ **Carbon copy (Cc):** The Cc field is where you type e-mail addresses of people who you want to keep informed, but who don't necessarily need to write a reply.

✦ **Blind carbon copy (Bcc):** The Bcc field sends a copy of your message to e-mail addresses that you type here, but those e-mail addresses will not be visible in the message to the recipients you enter in the To: and Cc: fields.

When sending out a particularly important message, many people type the recipient's e-mail address in the To field and their own e-mail address in the Cc: or Bcc: fields. This way, they can verify that their message was sent correctly.

When someone receives an e-mail message, he or she can read all the e-mail addresses stored in the To and Cc fields. If you don't want anyone else to know who received your message, use Bcc. (It's possible to use both Cc and Bcc in the same message.)

Whenever you write a message, the To field is always visible because you need to send your message to at least one e-mail address. However, Mail can hide and display both the Cc and Bcc fields because you don't always want or need them in every message you write.

To send multiple copies of the same message as Cc or Bcc, follow these steps:

1. **In Mail, open a new Message window as described in one of the preceding sections.**

   You can open a new Message window to create a new message, reply to an existing message, or forward an existing message.

2. **Click the Cc and/or Bcc text box and type an e-mail address.**

3. **Click in the Message text box to type in a message and add any attachments or photos you want.**

4. **Click Send.**

If you rarely use Cc or Bcc, you can customize the header layout to keep your outgoing message workspace free of clutter. Do the following:

1. **Click the New Message button to open a new message.**

2. **Click the Header Fields button to the left of the From field.**

3. **Choose Customize.**

   The header appears, as shown in Figure 2-13.

4. **Select the check boxes next to the fields you want to appear on your messages.**

   The To and Subject fields are mandatory.

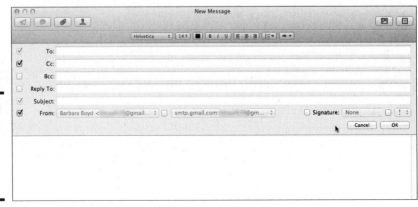

Figure 2-13: Customize the header fields you see on new messages.

If you only want to show or hide the Cc, Bcc, or Reply To field, you can also choose View⇨Cc Address Field/Bcc Address Field/Reply To Address Field. Those with a check mark appear in your new messages.

5. **Click OK.**

   You will see only the fields you selected in this and future new messages, replies, or forwarded messages that you create.

Using fonts, colors, and stationery

Even if you set your favorite font (choose Mail⇨Preferences⇨Fonts and Colors) as the standard for your outgoing messages, sometimes you may want to spruce up a message to have a greater impact on the recipient (provided the recipient uses an e-mail application that can read HTML messages). You can customize the appearance of your message by using different fonts, colors, and even stationery templates.

Book II
Chapter 2

Corresponding
with Mail

To simply change the fonts and colors and insert a few emoticons — those little smiley faces and hearts — do the following:

1. **In Mail, choose File⇨New Message or click the New Message button to open a New Message window.**

2. **Type in the recipient's address, any Ccs or Bccs you want to include, and a subject.**

3. **Click in the message text box to type your message and use the menus and buttons at the top of the message (see Figure 2-14) to create a personalized look:**

Figure 2-14:
Customize
the typeface
and layout.

- Use Font, Size, and Color menus at the top of the message to personalize your message. You might want to choose Chalkboard to make your message look handwritten.

- Click the Style and Alignment buttons to choose Bold, Italic, or Underline and Left, Center, or Right alignment.

- Create a bulleted or numbered list.

- Indent or outdent your paragraphs.

- Choose Edit⇨Special Characters to insert symbols, as shown in Figure 2-15. Scroll through the categories and double-click the one you want to use; it will be inserted in your message. (As previously noted, the recipient must use an e-mail app that can read the characters you use.)

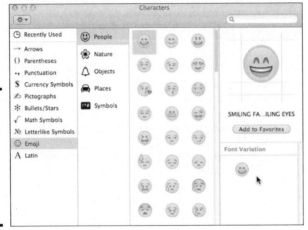

Figure 2-15: Symbols and special characters add a nice touch to your message.

4. **Click Send when you're satisfied with your message's appearance.**

Picking a stationery design

E-mail stationery consists of graphic designs and formatted text that you can edit. By using stationery, you can create e-mail messages that look more interesting than plain text. Keep in mind, however, that all those pretty accents increase the size of any e-mail messages you create with stationery and may not be legible if the recipient uses an e-mail application that doesn't support HTML. To use the Mail application's Stationery feature to create a new message, follow these steps:

1. **In Mail, choose File⇨New Message or click the New Message button to open a New Message window.**

2. **Click the Show Stationery button in the upper-right corner of the new message window.**

    A list of stationery categories (Birthday, Photos, and so on) appears in the upper-left pane and a list of stationery designs appears in the upper middle of the New Message window.

3. **Click a Stationery category, such as Sentiments or Birthday.**

    Each time you click a different category, the Mail window displays a list of stationery designs in that category.

4. **Click the stationery design that you want to use.**

   Your chosen stationery appears in the main section of the New Message window.

5. **Click any placeholder text and edit or type new text.**

Modifying photographs in a stationery design

After you choose a stationery design, you can edit the text and replace it with your own message. If the stationery displays a photograph, you can replace the photograph with another picture stored in iPhoto or somewhere else on your hard drive.

To add your own pictures to a stationery design, follow these steps:

1. **Make sure that Mail displays a stationery design that includes one or more pictures.**

2. **Click the Photo Browser button.**

   The Photo Browser window appears, containing all the photographs you've stored in iPhoto.

3. **Scroll to the folder that contains a photograph that you want to use in your stationery.**

4. **Click and drag your chosen photograph onto the picture in your stationery design.**

5. **Release the mouse button.**

   Your chosen picture now appears in your stationery, as shown in the lower part of Figure 2-16.

6. **Click the Close button of the Finder or Photo Browser window.**

Spelling and grammar checking

Although e-mail is considered less formal than many other forms of communication, such as letters or a last will and testament, you probably don't want your e-mail message riddled with spelling errors and typos that can make you look like, well, a dummy. That's why Mail provides a spelling and grammar checker.

To use the built-in spelling and grammar checker, you need to configure it to define whether you want it to check while you type or wait until you finish typing.

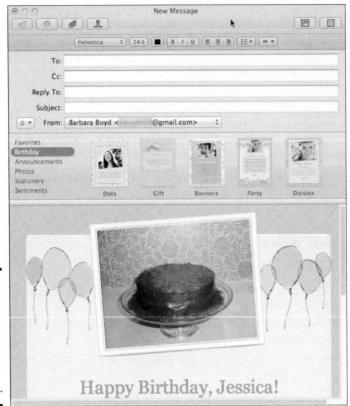

Figure 2-16:
Click and drag to replace stationery pictures with your own images.

Configuring the spelling and grammar checker

By default, Mail has its spell checker turned on to check misspellings while you type. When Mail finds a misspelled word, it underlines the word in red so you can right-click on the underlined word and then choose another word from the shortcut menu of best guesses. Or you can choose Learn Spelling from the shortcut menu to add the word to your Mac's list of correctly spelled words if your Mac doesn't already have it in its own list of spell checker words. If you find the red underline feature annoying or want to turn on the grammar checker, too, you need to configure the spelling and grammar checker. If you're happy with the way the spell checker works, you don't have to configure the spelling and grammar checker at all.

To configure the spelling and grammar checker, follow these steps:

1. **Open a new Message window as described earlier in this chapter, click in the Message text box, and enter some text or an actual e-mail message you want to send.**

You can open a new Message window to create a new message, reply to an existing message, or forward an existing message.

2. **Choose Edit⇨Spelling and Grammar⇨Check Spelling and choose one of the following from the submenu, as shown in Figure 2-17:**

   - *While Typing:* Underlines possible misspellings and grammar problems while you write.

   - *Before Sending:* Spelling and grammar checks your message before it's sent.

   - *Never:* Doesn't perform spelling and grammar checking.

Figure 2-17:
The Check
Spelling
menu
provides
spelling and
grammar
checking
options.

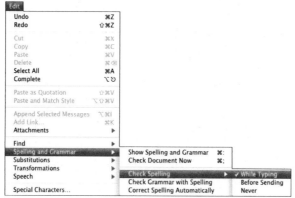

3. **(Optional) Choose Edit⇨Spelling and Grammar⇨Check Grammar with Spelling if you want to have Mail flag potential grammatical errors.**

4. **(Optional) Choose Edit⇨Spelling and Grammar⇨Correct Spelling Automatically if you want Mail to automatically correct words it deems incorrect.**

Checking spelling and grammar

If you have spell checking turned on while you type, the spell checker will underline suspected misspelled words in red to help you find potential problems easily. If you want to spell-check and grammar-check your entire message, follow these steps:

1. **Open a new Message window as described earlier in this chapter.**

   You can open a new Message window to create a new message, reply to an existing message, or forward an existing message.

2. **Type your message.**

3. **Choose Edit⇨Spelling and Grammar⇨Show Spelling and Grammar.**

The spelling and grammar checker does it thing, with a Spelling and Grammar dialog appearing each time Mail finds a potentially misspelled word.

4. **Click one of the following buttons:**

   - *Change:* Changes the misspelled word with the spelling that you choose from the list box on the left.

   - *Find Next:* Finds the next occurrence of the same misspelled word.

   - *Ignore:* Tells Mail that the word is correct.

   - *Learn:* Adds the word to the dictionary.

   - *Define:* Launches Mac's Dictionary application and looks up and displays the word's definition in the Dictionary's main window.

   - *Guess:* Offers best-guess word choices.

5. **Click Send.**

The spelling and grammar checker can't catch all possible errors (words like *to* and *two*, or *fiend* and *friend* can slip past because the words are spelled correctly), so make sure that you proofread your message after you finish spell-checking and grammar-checking your message.

Receiving and Reading E-Mail

To receive e-mail, your e-mail application must contact your incoming mail server and download the messages to your Mac. Then you can either check for new mail manually or have Mail check for new mail automatically.

Retrieving e-mail

To check and retrieve e-mail manually in Mail, choose Mailbox⇨Get New Mail or click the Get Mail icon. The number of new messages appears next to the Inbox icon, and in a red circle on the Mail icon in the Dock.

Checking for new e-mail manually can get tedious, so you can configure Mail to check for new mail automatically at fixed intervals of time, such as every 5 or 15 minutes. To configure Mail to check for new messages automatically, follow these steps:

1. **In Mail, choose Mail⇨Preferences to open the Mail preferences window.**

2. **Click the General icon to display the General pane, as shown in Figure 2-18.**

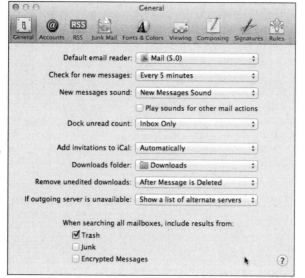

Figure 2-18:
The General pane lets you define how often to check for new e-mail.

3. **From the Check for New Messages pop-up menu, choose an option to determine how often to check for new messages.**

You can check Every Minute, Every 5 Minutes, Every 15 Minutes, Every 30 Minutes, or Every Hour.

4. **(Optional) Choose a sound to play when you receive new messages from the New Messages Sound pop-up menu.**

You can also choose None in case any sound bothers you.

5. **Click the Close button of the Mail preferences window.**

Mail can check for new messages only if you leave Mail running. If you quit Mail, it can't check for new messages periodically.

Reading e-mail

After you start receiving e-mail, you can start reading your messages. When you receive a new message, Mail flags it with a dot in the Message Preview column, as shown in Figure 2-19. If you have the Mailboxes column showing, the number next to each mailbox indicates the number of unread messages.

To read a message, follow these steps:

1. **In Mail, click the Inbox icon in the Favorites bar.**

A list of messages stored in the Inbox appears in the Message Preview column.

2. **Click a message to read the message in the message pane, or double-click a message to display and read a message in a separate window.**

Figure 2-19:
Mail shows
you which
messages
you haven't
read yet.

The advantage of the message pane is that you can scan your messages quickly by clicking each one without having to open a separate window. The advantage of reading a message in a separate window is that you can resize that window and see more of the message without having to scroll as often as you would if you were reading that same message in the message pane.

Viewing and saving file attachments

When you receive a message that has a file attachment, you see a paper clip next to the sender's name in the Message Preview column, and on the actual message, Mail identifies how many attachments there are and displays a Save button and a Quick Look button, as shown in Figure 2-20.

To save a file attachment, follow these steps:

1. **In Mail, click the Inbox icon in the Favorites bar.**

   A list of messages stored in the Inbox appears.

Book II
Chapter 2

Corresponding
with Mail

Figure 2-20:
Save and
Quick Look
buttons
appear
whenever
a message
includes
a file
attachment.

2. **Click a message in the Message Preview column.**

   If the message has a file attachment, the number of attachments, the amount of space they take up, the Save button, and the Quick Look button all appear in the message previews that list who sent the message, the date sent, the message subject, and the first two lines of the message.

   If the attachment is a picture or video clip, the image or clip will appear in the body of the e-mail message (refer to Figure 2-19).

3. **(Optional) Click the Quick Look button (refer to Figure 2-20).**

   A window appears, displaying the contents of your file attachment (or playing the file if it's a music or video file). If there are multiple images, click the arrows to move from one image to the next or click the thumbnail view button to see all the images at once. Click the Close box of the Quick Look window when you finish looking at its contents.

4. **Click the Save button, or click and hold down the Save button to display a list of attachments, and then choose either Save All to save all attachments or Add to iPhoto if the attachments are images.**

   If the e-mail message contains more than one attachment, choose an individual attachment to save it but not the others.

You can also just click and drag attachments from the message body to the Desktop or a Finder window. To do so, hold down the ⌘ key to select more than one attachment; then click and drag any one of the selected attachments to the Desktop or a Finder window.

Mail saves your attachments into the Downloads stack in the Dock.

Storing e-mail addresses

Typing an e-mail address every time you want to send a message can get tedious — if you can even remember the address. Fortunately, Mail lets you store names and e-mail addresses in the Address Book on your Mac so your addresses are all in one place. Then you can just click that person's name to send a message without typing that person's entire e-mail address.

Adding an e-mail address to the Address Book

When you receive an e-mail from someone you like, you can store that person's e-mail address in the Address Book by following these steps:

1. **In Mail, click the Inbox icon in the Favorites bar.**

2. **In the Message Preview column, select a message sent by someone whose e-mail address you want to save.**

3. **Choose Message⇨Add Sender to Address Book.**

Although nothing appears to happen, your chosen e-mail address is now stored in the Address Book.

To view your list of stored names and e-mail addresses, you can retrieve information from Address Book by choosing Window⇨Address Panel.

Retrieving an e-mail address from the Address Book

When you create a new message, you can retrieve an e-mail address from your Address Book. To retrieve an e-mail address, follow these steps:

1. **In Mail, choose File⇨New Message or click the New Message button.**

A New Message window appears.

2. **Click the Address button, which looks like the silhouette of a person, or choose Window⇨Address Panel.**

The Addresses panel appears, as shown in Figure 2-21.

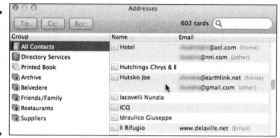

Figure 2-21:
The Addresses window lets you pick an e-mail address.

3. **Select the name of the person you want to send a message to.**

   To select multiple addresses, hold down the ⌘ key and click each address you want to send the message to. To select a range of addresses, hold down the Shift key and click the first and last address you want to send to. If you have groups in your Address Book, you can also select the group and the e-mail will be sent to everyone in that group, provided each card has an e-mail address. (See Book V, Chapter 1 to find more about working with Address Book.)

4. **Click the To button.**

   Your chosen e-mail address appears in the To text box. (If you click the Cc or Bcc buttons, you can add an e-mail address to the Cc or Bcc text boxes, respectively.)

5. **Click the Close button of the Addresses window.**

A shortcut to sending an e-mail from your Address Book is to choose Window⇨ Address Panel and double-click the name of the person you want to send a message to. A new message opens addressed to the person you double-clicked. If you have Address Book open, you can double-click or right-click the e-mail address to which you want to send an e-mail.

Deleting messages

After you read a message, you can either leave it in your Inbox or delete it. Generally, it's a good idea to delete messages you won't need again, such as an invitation to somebody's birthday party back in the summer of 2008. By deleting unnecessary messages, you can keep your Inbox organized and uncluttered — and if you're using an IMAP or Exchange account, free up space on the mail server where your e-mail messages are stored.

To delete a message, follow these steps:

1. **In Mail, click the Inbox icon in the Favorites bar.**

   A list of messages stored in the Inbox appears.

2. **Click the message you want to delete.**

To select multiple messages, hold down the ⌘ key and click additional messages. To select a range of messages, hold down the Shift key, click the first message to delete, click the last message to delete, and then release the Shift key.

3. **Choose Edit⇨Delete (or click the Delete button).**

Deleting a message doesn't immediately erase it, but stores it in the Trash folder. If you don't "empty the trash," you still have the chance to retrieve deleted messages, as outlined in the next section.

Retrieving messages from the Trash folder

Each time you delete a message, Mail stores the deleted messages in the Trash folder. If you think you deleted a message by mistake, you can retrieve it by following these steps:

1. **In Mail, click the Trash folder.**

   A list of deleted messages appears.

2. **Click the message you want to retrieve.**

3. **Choose Message⇨Move To⇨Inbox.**

You can set up Mail to automatically move deleted messages to the trash and permanently erase those trashed messages after a month, a week, a day, or upon quitting Mail. To configure this option, choose Mail⇨Preferences, click the Accounts tab, click a mail account in the Accounts column, and then click Mailbox Behaviors and adjust the settings for Trash to suit your e-mail housekeeping style.

Emptying the Trash folder

Messages stored in the Trash folder continue to take up space, so you should periodically empty the Trash folder by following these steps:

1. **In Mail, choose Mailbox⇨Erase Deleted Messages.**

   A submenu appears, listing all the e-mail accounts in Mail.

2. **Choose either In All Accounts (to erase all deleted messages) or the name of a specific e-mail account (to erase messages only from that particular account).**

Archiving messages

If you want to reduce the number of messages you see in your mailboxes but not delete the messages, say at the end of the year or when a project is complete, you can create an archive of those messages. Archived messages are kept in a folder in Mail but removed from active mailboxes. To archive messages, do the following:

1. **Click the mailbox that contains messages you want to archive.**

2. **Right-click the messages you want to archive or choose Edit⇨Select All if you want to archive all messages in the mailbox.**

3. **Choose Message⇨Archive.**

   The selected messages are moved to the Archive file in Mail.

Organizing E-Mail

To help you manage and organize your e-mail messages, Mail lets you search and sort your messages. Searching lets you find specific text stored in a particular message. When you find the messages you want, you may want to group them together in a folder. You can also establish smart mailboxes so Mail automatically puts related messages in the same folder or establish rules for what mail goes to which mailbox.

Searching through e-mail

To manage your e-mail effectively, you need to be able to search for one message (or more) you want to find and view. To search through your e-mail for the names of senders, subjects, or text in a message, follow these steps:

1. **In Mail, click the Spotlight text box in the upper-right corner.**

2. **Type a word, phrase, or partial phrase that you want to find.**

   When you type, Mail displays a list of messages that match the text you're typing in the Message Preview column and indicates where the text was found (for example People, Subject, Mailboxes, or Attachments), and the word Search appears next to the buttons in the Favorites bar, as shown in Figure 2-22.

3. **Click one of the buttons in the Favorites bar or the mailboxes in the Mailbox column (click Show to see it) to narrow your search.**

   Your options are to search through All Mailboxes, the Inbox, or one of the account-specific inboxes or in Sent or one of the account-specific outboxes.

   To include the Trash, Junk, or Encrypted Messages in your search, choose Mail⇨Preferences⇨General and select the Trash, Junk, and/or Encrypted Messages check boxes.

4. **(Optional) Click the Save button in the upper-right corner to open a Smart Mailbox window, type in a name for your new Smart Mailbox search, choose any options you want to customize your search, and then click OK to save your Smart Mailbox search.**

   We explain smart mailboxes in depth in the "Automatically organizing e-mail with smart mailboxes" section, later in this chapter.

5. **Click a message to read it.**

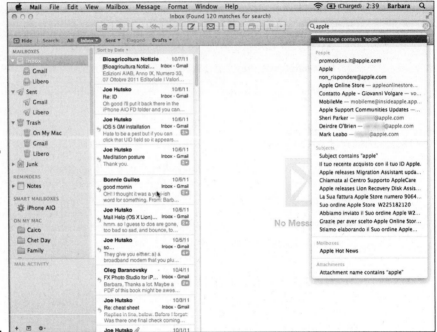

To change the appearance of how messages are viewed in Mail, choose Mail⇨ Preferences and click the Viewing tab. If you liked the pre-Lion layout of Mail, select the Use Classic Layout check box. Select the other check boxes to change the display of how message previews appear in the message list and how conversations are managed.

Organizing e-mail with mailbox folders

When you receive e-mail, all your messages are dumped in the Inbox. If you have multiple accounts, the Inbox shows messages from all accounts, while clicking a specific account in the Favorites bar or Mailbox Column shows only the messages in that account. Organizing your messages by conversation (choose View⇨Organize By Conversation) helps, but after a while, you might have so many messages stored there that trying to find related messages can be nearly impossible.

To fix this problem, you can create separate folders for organizing your different e-mails. After you create a folder, choosing to organize by conversation keeps related messages together so you can quickly find them later.

One common type of e-mail to organize is junk e-mail, which you can route automatically to the Trash folder, as we write about in the upcoming "Dealing with Junk E-Mail" section.

Creating a mailbox folder

To create a mailbox folder, follow these steps:

1. In Mail, choose Mailbox⇨New Mailbox.

A New Mailbox dialog appears, as shown in Figure 2-23.

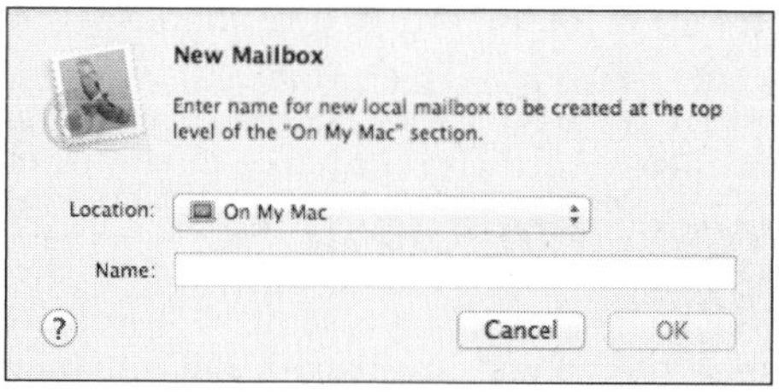

Book II
Chapter 2

**Corresponding
with Mail**

Figure 2-23:
The New
Mailbox
dialog lets
you choose
a name
for your
mailbox
folder.

> **New Mailbox**
>
> Enter name for new local mailbox to be created at the top
> level of the "On My Mac" section.
>
> Location: ▢ On My Mac ⬍
>
> Name:
>
> ?   Cancel   OK

2. In the Name text box, type a descriptive name for your mailbox folder and click OK.

Your mailbox folder appears in the Mailbox column of the Mail window.

3. (Optional) Drag the folder into the Favorites bar if you want.

Storing messages in a mailbox folder

When you create a mailbox folder, it's completely empty. To store messages in a mailbox folder, you must drag those messages manually to the mailbox folder. Dragging moves your message from the Inbox folder to your designated mailbox folder.

To move a message to a mailbox folder, follow these steps:

1. In Mail, click the Inbox icon in the Mailboxes column or Favorites bar to view your e-mail messages.

2. Click a message and drag it to the mailbox folder you want to move it to, and release the mouse.

Your selected message now appears in the mailbox folder.

If you hold down the ⌘ key while clicking a message, you can select multiple messages. If you hold down the Shift key, you can click one message and then click another message to select those two messages and every message in between.

Deleting a mailbox folder

You can delete a mailbox folder by following these steps:

1. **In Mail, click the mailbox folder you want to delete.**

2. **Choose Mailbox⇨Delete.**

A dialog box appears, asking whether you're sure that you want to delete your folder.

When you delete a mailbox folder, you delete all messages stored inside.

3. **Click Delete.**

Automatically organizing e-mail with smart mailboxes

Mailbox folders can help organize your messages, but you must manually drag messages into those folders or set up rules to automate the process. As an alternative, to make this process automatic, you can use *smart mailboxes*.

A smart mailbox differs from an ordinary mailbox in two ways:

✦ A smart mailbox lets you define the type of messages you want to store automatically; that way, Mail sorts your messages without any additional work from you.

✦ A smart mailbox doesn't actually contain a message but only a link to the actual message, which is still stored in the Inbox folder (or any folder that you move it to). Because smart mailboxes don't actually move messages, it's possible for a single message to have links stored in multiple smart mailboxes.

Creating a smart mailbox

To create a smart mailbox, you need to define a name for your smart mailbox along with the criteria for the types of messages to store in your smart mailbox. To create a smart mailbox, follow these steps:

1. **In Mail, choose Mailbox⇨New Smart Mailbox.**

A Smart Mailbox dialog appears, as shown in Figure 2-24.

2. **Click the Smart Mailbox Name text box and type a descriptive name for your smart mailbox.**

3. **Click the Match pop-up menu and choose All (of the Following Conditions) or Any (of the Following Conditions).**

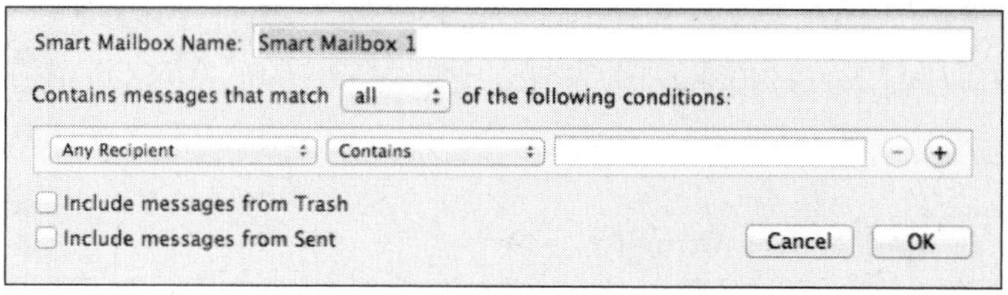

Figure 2-24:
Define the
types of
messages to
automatically
store.

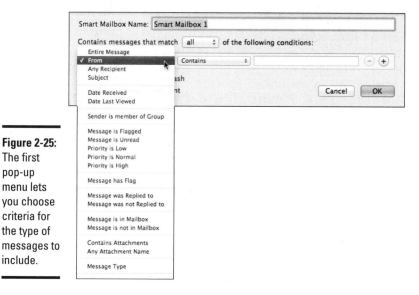

4. **Click the first criterion pop-up menu and choose an option, such as From or Date Received, as shown in Figure 2-25.**

Figure 2-25:
The first
pop-up
menu lets
you choose
criteria for
the type of
messages to
include.

5. **Click the second criterion pop-up menu and choose how to apply your first criterion (for example, Contains or Ends with).**

6. **Click the Criteria text box and type a word or phrase that you want to use for your criterion.**

7. **(Optional) Click the Add Rule icon (the plus-sign button) and repeat Steps 3 through 6.**

8. **Click OK.**

Your smart mailbox appears in the Mailboxes column of the Mail window. If any messages match your defined criteria, you can click your smart mailbox's icon to see a list of messages.

The messages stored in a smart mailbox are just links to the actual messages stored in your Inbox folder. If you delete a message from a smart mailbox, the message remains in the Inbox; if you delete a message from the Inbox, it is also deleted from the smart mailbox.

Deleting a smart mailbox

Deleting a smart mailbox doesn't physically delete any messages because a smart mailbox only contains links to existing messages. To delete a smart mailbox, follow these steps:

1. **In Mail, click the smart mailbox folder you want to delete.**

2. **Choose Mailbox⇨Delete.**

   A dialog appears, asking whether you're sure that you want to delete your smart mailbox.

3. **Click Delete (or Cancel).**

Automatically organizing e-mail with rules

Smart mailboxes provide links to e-mail messages that actually remain in your Inbox folder. However, you may want to actually move a message from the Inbox folder to another folder automatically, which you can do by defining rules.

The basic idea behind rules is to pick criteria for selecting messages, such as all messages from specific e-mail addresses or subject lines that contain certain phrases, and route them automatically into a folder.

To create a rule, follow these steps:

1. **Choose Mail⇨Preferences to open the Mail preferences window.**

2. **Click the Rules icon.**

   The Rules window appears.

   If you click an existing rule and click Edit, you can modify an existing rule.

3. **Click Add Rule.**

   The Rules window displays pop-up menus for defining a rule, as shown in Figure 2-26.

4. **Click the Description text box and type a description of what your rule does.**

5. **Click one or more pop-up menus to define how your rule works, such as what to look for or which folder to move the message to, as shown in Figure 2-27.**

Description: Rule 2
If any of the following conditions are met:
Any Recipient
Contains
@gmail.cor
Perform the following actions:
Move Message
to mailbox:
Joe
Cancel
OK

Figure 2-26: Clicking different pop-up menus lets you define a rule for routing your messages.

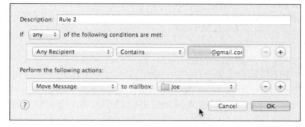

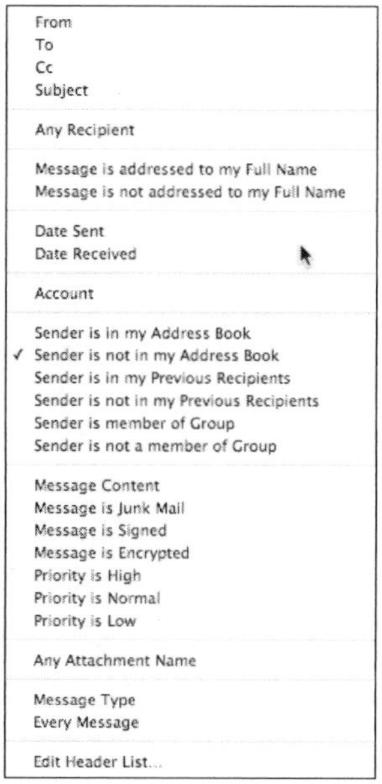
From
To
Cc
Subject
Any Recipient
Message is addressed to my Full Name
Message is not addressed to my Full Name
Date Sent
Date Received
Account
Sender is in my Address Book
✓ Sender is not in my Address Book
Sender is in my Previous Recipients
Sender is not in my Previous Recipients
Sender is member of Group
Sender is not a member of Group
Message Content
Message is Junk Mail
Message is Signed
Message is Encrypted
Priority is High
Priority is Normal
Priority is Low
Any Attachment Name
Message Type
Every Message
Edit Header List...

Figure 2-27: Pop-up menus provide different options for selecting messages to sort by your rule.

6. **(Optional) Click the Plus Sign button to define another sorting criterion for your rule and repeat Steps 5 and 6 as often as necessary.**

7. **Click OK when you finish defining your rule.**

   A dialog appears, asking whether you want to apply your new rule to your messages.

8. **Click Apply.**

9. **Click the Close button of the Rules window.**

   Mail now displays your messages sorted into folders according to your defined rules.

Flagging your messages

Sometimes you receive a message that contains a task you must attend to later. You could print the message and hang it on a bulletin board in your office or on your refrigerator so you don't forget, or you can flag it in Mail. You can choose from seven colors so you can use different colors for different types of e-mails, say all e-mails related to one project, or to give the task a priority. Here's how to work with flags:

1. **Click Inbox in the Favorites bar or Mailboxes column.**

2. **Select the message you want to flag.**

3. **Click the Flag pop-up menu in the toolbar, or choose Message➪Flag, and select the color flag you want to assign to that message.**

   A little colored flag appears next to the message in the Message Preview column and next to the From field in the message itself.

4. **To see your flagged messages all together, do one of the following:**

   • Click Flagged under Reminders in the Mailboxes column (click Show to the left of the Favorites bar to see the Mailboxes column). These Reminders can be synced via iCloud to iOS devices, such as an iPhone or iPad, which use the Reminders app and Notification Center.

   • Click the Flagged button in the Favorites bar (if you don't see the button, drag it from the Mailboxes column).

   • Choose Flags in the Sort By menu at the top of the Message Preview column to see the flagged messages all together in the mailbox that you are viewing.

5. **To remove the flag, select the message and select Clear Flag from the flag pop-up menu.**

Flags are named by their color, but you can rename them; for example, name the red flag "Urgent" rather than "red." Click the disclosure triangle next to Flagged in the Reminders section of the Mailboxes column. Double-click the flag color to select the word, and then type the name you want, as shown in Figure 2-28.

You can set up rules (choose Mail➪Preferences➪Rules) to automatically flag messages that meet certain criteria.

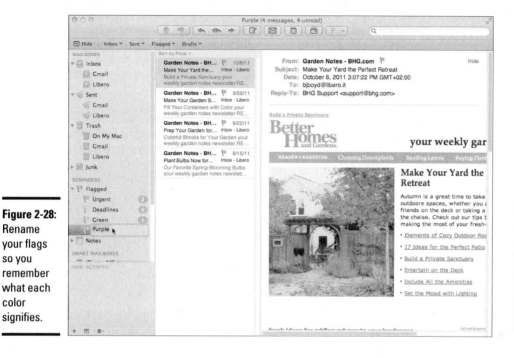

**Book II
Chapter 2**

Corresponding
with Mail

Figure 2-28:
Rename
your flags
so you
remember
what each
color
signifies.

Dealing with Junk E-Mail

Just like you receive junk mail in your paper mailbox, soon after you get
an e-mail address, you're going to start receiving junk e-mail (or *spam*).
While you can't entirely stop it, Mail has filters that help limit the inevitable
flow of junk e-mail so you can keep your e-mail account from getting over-
whelmed, and — perhaps more important — limit the dispersion of your
e-mail address and the personal information on your computer that can be
accessed through your e-mail.

Most junk e-mail messages are advertisements trying to sell you various
products, but some junk e-mail messages are actually scams to trick you into
visiting bogus websites that ask for your credit card number or (worse) try
to trick you into giving your bank-account info. This form of spam is called
phishing. Other times, junk e-mail might contain an attachment masquerading as a free application that secretly contains a computer virus. Or, a junk
e-mail might try to trick you into clicking a web link that downloads and
installs a computer virus on your Mac. By filtering out such malicious junk
e-mail, you can minimize potential threats that can jeopardize your Mac's
integrity or your personal information.

Filtering junk e-mail

Filtering means that Mail examines the content of messages and tries to determine whether the message is junk. To improve accuracy, Mail allows you to train it by manually identifying junk e-mail that its existing rules didn't catch.

After a few weeks of watching you identify junk e-mail, the Mail application's filters eventually recognize common junk e-mail and route it automatically to a special junk folder, keeping your Inbox free from most junk e-mail so you can focus on reading the messages that matter to you.

To train Mail to recognize junk e-mail, follow these steps:

1. **In Mail, click the Inbox button in the Favorites bar or click Show to reveal the Mailboxes column, and then click the Inbox icon.**

   A list of messages appears in the Message Preview column.

2. **Click a message that you consider junk.**

3. **Choose Message⇨Mark⇨As Junk Mail.**

   This tells the Mail application's filters what you consider junk e-mail. The message is moved to the Junk mailbox.

4. **Click the Junk mailbox.**

   Mail displays the messages in the Message Preview column and the message information is written in brown.

5. **Click the message you marked as Junk.**

   A banner runs across the top of the message, as shown in the top of Figure 2-28. If you accidentally marked the message as Junk, click Not Junk and drag the message back to the inbox it came from.

6. **Click the Delete icon.**

   This deletes your chosen message and "trains" Mail to recognize similar messages as junk.

   Sometimes legitimate e-mail messages can wind up in Junk in Mail or in the Spam folders of web-based e-mail providers, such as Gmail, Yahoo! Mail, and Microsoft Live Hotmail. If there are messages in your Junk or Spam mailboxes that shouldn't be there, click the message. A banner runs across the top of the message, as shown in the bottom of Figure 2-29. Click Not Junk and drag the message to your inbox. This way, Mail learns that messages from this sender are not junk mail.

Figure 2-29:
Click Not
Junk for
legitimate
messages.

You marked this message as Junk Mail.   ?   Load Images   Not Junk

Mail thinks this message is Junk Mail.   ?   Load Images   Not Junk

Using advanced filter rules

If you find that you're still getting a lot of junk mail or that it arrives from a specific source, you can set the Junk mail preferences to better manage junk mail by following these steps:

**Book II
Chapter 2**

**Corresponding
with Mail**

1. **Choose Mail⇨Preferences and click the Junk button.**

The window shown in Figure 2-30 opens.

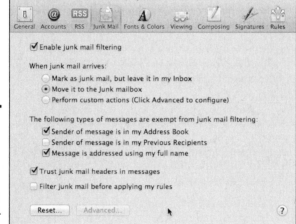

Figure 2-30:
Help Mail
learn which
messages
are Junk by
setting Junk
preferences.

2. **Make sure that the Enable Junk Mail Filtering check box is selected.**

3. **Select one of the following choices to indicate where you want Junk mail to go when it arrives: Mark as Junk Mail, But Leave It in My Inbox, or Move It to the Junk Mailbox.**

Selecting Mark as Junk Mail, But Leave It in My Inbox puts junk mail in with all your good mail. Selecting Move It to the Junk Mailbox nicely separates junk mail for you and puts it in its own mailbox.

4. (Optional) Select Perform Custom Actions to activate the Advanced button. Click Advanced.

A pane opens, as shown in Figure 2-31.

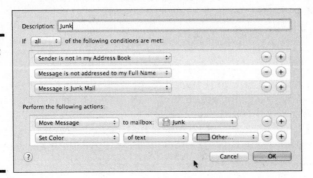

Figure 2-31:
Advanced
Junk
settings
can better
eliminate
unwanted
e-mail.

a. Use the pop-up menus to set up rules for filtering incoming mail. Use the plus and minus buttons to the right of each rule to add or delete a rule. (Refer to Figure 2-26 to see the choices you have.)

b. Use the pop-up menus under the Perform the Following Actions section to indicate what you want Mail to do when a message arrives that meets the established rules.

c. Click OK.

d. Click the close button of the Preferences window.

5. Select one or more of the following choices for the types of messages to exempt from the junk mail filter, which helps keep legitimate messages out of your Junk mailbox:

- *Sender of Message Is in My Address Book*

- *Sender of Message Is in My Previous Recipients* even if the sender isn't in your Address Book, if you received a message from the sender in the past, it won't be considered junk

- *Message Is Addressed Using My Full Name*

6. Select Trust Junk Mail Headers in Messages to have Mail trust the mail that your e-mail provider identifies as junk.

Many web-based e-mail providers have special applications running on their e-mail servers that try to sniff out junk e-mail before it lands in your Inbox.

7. Select Filter Junk Mail before Applying My Rules to give precedence to Mail's filter before applying your custom filter rules.

Although Mail's built-in junk e-mail filters can strip away most junk e-mail, consider getting a special junk e-mail filter as well. These e-mail filters strip out most junk e-mail better than Mail can do, but the Mail application's filters might later catch any junk e-mail that slips past these separate filters, which essentially doubles your defenses against junk e-mail. Some popular e-mail filters are SpamSieve (`http://c-command.com`) and Purify (`www.hendricom.com`). Spam filters cost money and take time to configure, but if your e-mail account is overrun by junk e-mail, a separate junk e-mail filter might be your only solution short of getting a new e-mail account.

Other Mail Features

Mail has a lot of features and functions — enough for a book of its own really — two, however, are worth mentioning: RSS feeds and Notes.

RSS Feeds

We explain RSS feeds in depth in Book II, Chapter 1. RSS feeds, which stands for Real Simple Syndication, are communications that are released by websites that are frequently updated, such as newspapers or blogs. If you subscribe to an RSS feed, that is you want to be notified when something new is published, you can receive the feed on Safari and/or Mail. If you spend more time in Mail than Safari, you may want to see RSS feeds in Mail. To do that, follow these steps:

1. **Choose Mail⇨Preferences and click the RSS button.**

2. **Choose Mail from the pop-up menu next to Default RSS Reader.**

3. **Choose the intervals you want from the pop-up menus for Check for Updates and Remove Articles.**

4. **Choose File⇨Add RSS Feeds and do one or both of the following:**

- *Browse feeds in Safari bookmarks:* If you have already set up RSS feeds in Safari, you can choose the ones you want to see in Mail by selecting the check box next to the feed name, as shown in Figure 2-32.

- *Specify the URL for a Feed:* Type in the URL for the RSS feed you want. You can also open Safari, go to the RSS source, and copy and paste the URL.

5. **Click Add.**

6. **The RSS feeds you chose appear under the RSS section of the Mailboxes column.**

If you don't show the Mailboxes column, you may want to drag the RSS icon to the Favorites bar so you can quickly see how many RSS updates have arrived and click the button to see them.

Notes

You can use notes in Mail to organize your thoughts, keep lists, or even as a fun format for sending messages. Notes are stored under the Reminders section of the Mailboxes column, although you can create a button in the Favorites bar so you have quick access to all of them. To use notes, do this:

1. **In Mail, choose File⇨New Note or click the New Note button in the toolbar, which looks like a lined notepad.**

   A new lined, yellow page opens.

2. **Type whatever you want and do one or more of the following:**
   - *Click the "A" to change the font style.*
   - *Click the paper clip to attach a file or photo to your note.*
   - *Click the Send button to send your note to someone's e-mail address.*

3. **Click the close button on the note, and it's stored in the Notes section.**

4. **Click Notes in the Mailbox column to see your saved notes displayed as a list in the Message Preview column.**

5. **Click the note you want to read or edit, and it opens in the message pane.**

6. **To delete a note, select it in the list and press the Delete key.**

Chapter 3: Instant Messaging and Video Chatting with iChat

In This Chapter

✔ Setting up an account

✔ Finding people to chat with

✔ Chatting via text, audio, and video

✔ Saving and recording chats

✔ Sharing pictures, files, and screens with iChat Theater

✔ Calling other Apple devices with FaceTime

✔ Chatting about other chat applications

The idea behind instant messaging is that you can communicate with someone over the Internet by using text, audio, or even video — and it's all free. (Well, it's sort of free, when you ignore the fact that you're probably paying your broadband Internet provider a pretty penny every month so you can access the Internet.)

Now you can swap messages with your friends, chat in real time across the planet, and even see each other through live video windows while you speak. Instant messaging offers another way for you to communicate with anyone in the world, using an Internet connection and your Mac.

By using your Mac's iChat application, you can conduct basic text chat messages with others instantly. And iChat also makes integrating live video, audio, and sharing files with others you connect to practically as easy as chatting over the telephone. If you have friends or family with a Mac or iPhone 4 or 4S, iPad 2, or iPod touch (fourth generation or newer), you can use FaceTime to conduct a video chat from your Mac to your friend's Apple device.

In this chapter, we show you how to set up an iChat account and use iChat to have instant message, audio, and video chats. We also explain how to share files, images, and even your Mac's screen with iChat. We give you all the tips and tricks to set up and use FaceTime too. If that's not enough, we also list some other chatting options so you're never out of touch with your friends, family, and colleagues.

Setting Up an iChat Account

If you have an existing instant-messaging chat account with one of the following services, you're ready to set up iChat and start chatting in a matter of minutes. If you don't have a chat account, you need to set up an account with at least one of the following services:

+ **iCloud:** When you sign up for an Apple ID, which you use for your interactions on iTunes, the App Store, and to register your Mac, you can set up an iCloud account, which gives you an e-mail such as babsboyd@ me.com. See Book III, Chapter 2 for details about iCloud. If you already have a me.com or mac.com account name, you can use that. You use this account name when you sign in to iCloud and you can also use it for iChat.

   We explain how to do this in Step 3 of the step-by-step directions following these bullets.

+ **AOL Instant Messenger (AIM):** Available free at www.aim.com, existing AIM account users and new users are warmly welcome to use their account name with iChat.

+ **Google Talk:** Got a Google Gmail account? If so, you have a Google Talk account, which lets you send and receive text messages or conduct video conferences with other Gmail account holders from your Gmail web page (http://gmail.google.com). Having a Google Gmail account also means that you can use it to set up iChat to send and receive text messages and connect with other Gmail account buddies with iChat's audio and video chat, and screen-sharing feature. Google Talk usernames end with @gmail.com.

+ **Jabber:** The original IM service, based on XMPP, the open standard for instant messaging, you can create a Jabber account by visiting http:// register.jabber.org or one of the other public XMPP services, and then use your Jabber account, which ends with @jabber.org, to log in and start chatting.

+ **Yahoo! Messenger:** If you use have a Yahoo! Messenger account, you can create a Yahoo! Messenger account directly in iChat as long as you have your Yahoo! Messenger ID and password. iChat will take care of the rest. Set up an account through iChat (as explained a little later in this chapter) or go directly to Yahoo!'s website (http://messenger. yahoo.com).

To understand which chat accounts can communicate with which other chat accounts, check out the nearby sidebar, "Can't we all just get along?"

Can't we all just get along?

You can only use some of iChat's livelier features, like video chatting and screen sharing, when you connect to friends using the same kind of account as you. That means iCloud and MobileMe account users can send text messages and video chat with one another and with AIM users, but they can't conduct video chats with Google Talk, Jabber or Yahoo! users.

On the other hand, Google Talk accounts act as Jabber accounts, and Jabber accounts act as Google Talk accounts. That is, Google Talk and Jabber account holders running iChat get along to take advantage of iChat's audio and video chat, and screen-sharing features, in addition to text chat.

To get the most from using iChat with friends, you want to sign in with an account that matches the ones your friends are using. If your friends use Google Talk to sign in to iChat and you use Yahoo! Messenger, you might want to create a Google Gmail account and add your Google Talk account to iChat so you can audio chat and video chat with your friends who sign in with a Google Talk account name.

To add additional account names to iChat, check out the nearby sidebar, "Managing multiple chat personalities and options."

After you create a chat account, you can set up an iChat account by following these steps:

1. Click the iChat icon in the Dock or Launchpad to launch iChat.

An iChat welcome window appears.

2. Click Continue.

The Account Setup window appears, ready to receive your account type, name, and password information, as shown in Figure 3-1.

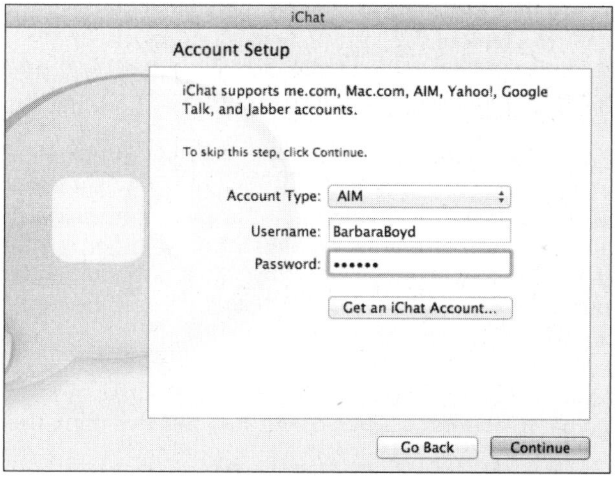

Figure 3-1:
The iChat window prompts you for your account information.

3. **Click the Account Type pop-up menu and choose your account type.**

   Your choices here include iCloud, AIM, Jabber, Yahoo! Messenger, and Google Talk accounts.

   If you don't have one of these accounts, in the Account Type pop-up menu, choose AIM to set up an AOL ID or iCloud to set up an Apple ID, and then click the Get an iChat Account button to launch Safari, which takes you to the service's website and new account sign-up form that you can fill out to create your own chat account name.

4. **Type your account username in the first text box.**

   The name to the left of the text box changes, depending on which account type you select in Step 3. In Figure 3-1, the name reads Username, but it may say Account Name if you choose another service.

5. **Type your password in the Password text box.**

6. **Click Continue to take you to a third iChat pane informing you that you've successfully set up your iChat account, and then click Done to close the iChat window.**

7. **The iChat Buddy List window appears and iChat automatically logs in to your account.**

   If you sign in by using an existing instant-messaging account, the iChat Buddy List window displays a list of any buddies who are online when you are.

If you sign in to iChat by using an existing chat account, you can go about your merry way and communicate with the friends, family, and co-workers you previously added whenever they're online and you want to get in touch with them (or vice versa).

If you're brand new to instant messaging, setting up a chat account is only half the process to using iChat. Your next step is to contact your friends and other contacts you want to chat with, to exchange instant-messaging account names. Think of account names as telephone numbers; you can't call a friend without first knowing her phone number, and similarly, you can't chat with someone if you don't know her account name.

If you're not brand new to instant messaging, but the instant-messaging account you use isn't one that works with iChat, you can install and run other chat applications to send and receive instant messages and conduct voice and video chats with your buddies who use other chat accounts and chat applications. To find more about the most popular chat accounts and applications, check out the "Taking a Look at Other Chat Applications" section at the end of this chapter.

If, like us, you have more than one chat account, you can add your additional chat accounts to iChat, and iChat displays them together in one unified Buddy List so you see and manage your accounts in one window. If you want to see a separate window for each account, choose iChat⇨Preferences⇨General and deselect Show All My Accounts in One List. To add or delete more than one iChat chat account, check out the nearby sidebar, "Managing multiple chat personalities and options."

Storing names in a buddy list

A *buddy list* lets you store the account names of your friends. Stored names automatically appear in your iChat buddy lists whenever your friends log in to their particular chat application (which can be an application other than iChat, such as AOL Instant Messenger for Mac or Windows, or even a mobile chat application running on a smartphone).

To add a name to your buddy list, follow these steps:

1. **Click the iChat icon in the Dock or Launchpad to launch iChat.**

The iChat Buddies window opens automatically (and if you've already used iChat, your status is as it was when you last closed iChat).

If you don't see a Buddy List window, choose Window⇨iChat Buddies.

2. **Choose Buddies⇨Add Buddy, or click the Add (+) button in the lower-left corner of the iChat Buddy List window and select Add Buddy from the pop-up menu.**

A dialog appears, as shown in Figure 3-2.

Figure 3-2:
Add a buddy by chat account name or e-mail address.

3. **If you have multiple iChat accounts, choose the iChat account — AIM, GoogleTalk, and so on — to which you want to add the buddy from the Add To pop-up menu.**

Make sure that your account type and your buddy's account type are compatible.

4. **Fill in your buddy's chat account name and real name.**

You have two ways to do so:

- *Type your buddy's account name and real name in the three text boxes shown in Figure 3-2.* Depending on the chat account your buddy has, the account name might be a single word or an e-mail address.

  Filling in your buddy's first and last name is for your convenience only. If you don't know someone's first or last name, or if you prefer to see his chat account name rather than his real name in your buddy list, just leave the name fields blank.

- *Add contacts from your Address Book.* Click the down-arrow button next to the Last Name field (refer to Figure 3-2) to expand the Add Buddy dialog and show your Mac's Address Book contacts. Use the search field or click the scroll arrows — both are visible in Figure 3-3 — to locate your buddy's contact card and then click your buddy's name to select him or her.

  Your buddy's account name, first name, and last name automatically fill in the related fields of the Add Buddy dialog.

  If your Address Book holds many records, it might be easier to search for a name rather than scroll through. In the search field, type in the first few letters of the name of the person you want to add as a buddy. Potential matches appear in the names list. The more letters you type, the narrower the results.

Figure 3-3:
Clicking a buddy's contact card automatically fills in the blanks.

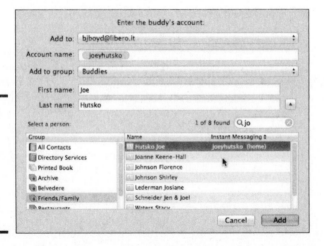

5. (Optional) Click the column heading to the right of the Name column (named Instant Messaging in Figure 3-3) to open a pop-up menu that lets you choose among displaying, phone numbers, e-mail addresses, or instant messaging.

6. (Optional) Click the Add to Group pop-up menu (which only appears if more than one group is available), and then choose the group

category where you want to store your friend's name, such as Buddies, Family, or Co-Workers.

You can change which group your buddy appears in at any time.

7. **Click the Add button.**

Your new buddy appears in your buddy list.

8. **Repeat Steps 2 through 7 to add other people to your buddy lists.**

If a buddy has more than one account type, add a new buddy for each account. Each account will appear in the group where you store it.

If you don't see your newly added buddy (or buddies you previously added) in your buddy list, chances are that you might have inadvertently chosen an iChat option to hide offline buddies from your buddy list. To show offline buddies in your buddy list, choose View⇨Show Offline Buddies. Conversely, if you only want your buddies to appear in the iChat Buddy List window when they're online, choose View⇨Show Offline Buddies to deselect it. A check mark appears next to the item in the menu when that feature is active.

The names of buddies who are online when you're online appear as normal text with an accompanying generic chat icon or a custom icon of your buddy's choosing (if he uses a custom icon with his chat application). The names of buddies who are offline when you're online appear dimmed on your iChat buddy list.

Organizing a buddy list

When you add a name to your buddy list, you have to store it within an existing group, such as Buddies, Family, or Co-Workers. If you want, you can always move or copy a buddy's chat account name to a different group or even create completely new groups, such as a group of people involved in a specific project. For instance, a community recycling team that you organize in a group named WeCyclers, or new acquaintances you met at that Jack Russell Terriers for National Office conference you recently attended, all of whom you can organize in a buddy list group called JRT4NO.

Moving a name to another group

The first time you add a chat name to your buddy list, you might have unintentionally put the name in your Family group when you really want the name in the Co-Workers group. To move a name to another group, follow these steps:

1. **Click the iChat icon in the Dock or Launchpad to launch iChat.**

The iChat Buddies window opens automatically (and if you've already used iChat, your status is as it was when you last closed iChat).

If you don't see a buddy list window, choose Window⇨iChat Buddies.

2. **Click the triangle to the left of a group name in the Buddy List window to reveal all the names stored within that group.**

3. **Click and drag a name to a new group name and let go of the mouse button to make the name appear in the new group.**

   If you hold down the Option key when you drag a name to another group, you create a duplicate copy of the name instead of moving it from one group to the other.

Creating a new group

iChat includes Buddies, Co-Workers, and Family groups, but you might want to create new groups of your own. To create a group, follow these steps:

1. **Click the Add (+) button in the bottom-left corner of the Buddy List window to open a pop-up menu and then select Add Group.**

   A dialog appears, asking for a group name.

2. **Type a descriptive name for your group in the Enter Group Name text box and click the Add button.**

   Your new group appears in the buddy list, ready for you to copy or move names into your newly created group.

You can rename a group by right-clicking the group name and choosing Rename Group from the shortcut menu that appears.

Sorting names in a buddy list

To customize the appearance of your buddy lists, you can sort the names by first or last name alphabetically, by availability, or manually.

To sort names in your buddy list, follow these steps:

1. **Choose View⇨Sort Buddies to open a submenu, as shown in Figure 3-4.**

2. **Choose one of the following:**

   - *By Availability:* Groups all buddies who are online and available for chatting when you are.

   - *By Name:* Sorts buddies by name; use the lower part of the menu to choose *First Name, Last Name* (to sort buddies alphabetically by first name) or *Last Name, First Name* (to sort buddies alphabetically by last name).

   - *Manually:* Lets you drag names to sort them any which way you want.

Book II
Chapter 3

Instant Messaging
and Video Chatting
with iChat

Figure 3-4:
The Sort
Buddies
submenu
lets you
rearrange
your buddy
list.

Shortening names in a buddy list

iChat can display names as full names (Joe Hutsko), as shortened names
(Joe), or by nicknames (GadgetJoey). For friends, it might be fun to display
names based on nicknames, but for business use, you may prefer to stick
with full or shortened names.

To define how names should appear in your buddy list, follow these steps:

1. **Choose View⇨Buddy Names to open a submenu.**

2. **Choose one of the following:**

- Show Full Names

- Show Short Names

- Show Handles (*handle* is chat-speak for nickname)

Deleting names and groups in a buddy list

Eventually, you might want to prune names from your buddy lists to make it
easier to keep track of people you actually chat with on a regular basis.

To delete a name from your buddy list, follow these steps:

1. **In the iChat Buddy List window, click the disclosure triangle next to a
group to display the names in that group.**

2. **Click the name you want to delete.**

3. **Choose Buddies⇨Remove Buddy (or press the Delete key).**

A dialog appears, asking whether you really want to delete the name.

4. **Click the Remove button (or Cancel if you suddenly change your mind before giving your buddy the axe).**

Rather than delete names one by one, you can also delete a group and all names stored in that group. To delete a group from your buddy list, follow these steps:

1. **In the iChat Buddy List window, right-click a group that you want to delete to open a shortcut menu.**

2. **Choose Delete Group from the shortcut menu.**

   A dialog opens, asking whether you really want to delete this group and all names in the group.

3. **Click Delete (or Cancel).**

iChat requires at least one buddy list group to exist in order to operate. If you delete all but one buddy list group, you can't delete the remaining group. If you don't like the name of the necessary group you're stuck with, Right-click the group name, choose Rename Group, and then type a name that you can live with for your one and only group.

Chatting with Others

After you store your friends in your buddy lists and give your account name to others to store in their buddy lists, you're ready to start chatting. Of course, before you can chat, you have to find someone who wants to chat.

You can chat with someone in five ways:

✦ **Text:** You type messages back and forth to each other.

✦ **Audio:** You can talk to and hear the other person, much like a telephone.

✦ **Video:** You can talk to, hear, and see the other person in a live video window.

✦ **Screen Sharing:** You can talk to and hear the other person while you take over her screen, mouse, and keyboard to fill your screen as though you're sitting in front of her computer. Likewise, your chat partner can take over your screen and control your keyboard or mouse as if she were sitting in front of your computer.

Screen sharing can be especially handy for helping family members or friends solve a problem with their Mac. If you can't easily travel to the person in need, use screen sharing. We show you how in the "Using iChat Theater to shareg files, photos, and screens" section, later in this chapter.

✦ **iChat Theater:** You can talk and hear each other while you share a file (or files), such as a document, a Keynote presentation, or photos in your iPhoto library. The files you want to share appear on your chatting partner's screen. Likewise, if your chatting partner is sharing photos (or other files) with you, you see them on your screen.

Anyone on your buddy list can use text chatting because it requires only an Internet connection and a keyboard.

To participate in audio chatting, each person (there can be up to ten chat participants) needs a microphone and speakers or headphones. Most Macs come with a built-in microphone, but you might want an external microphone, such as one built into a headset, to capture your voice (and hear the other person's side of the conversation) more clearly.

**Book II
Chapter 3**

**Instant Messaging
and Video Chatting
with iChat**

Participating in a video chat with a buddy (or up to three buddies in a multi-person video chat) requires a video camera, such as the iSight video camera built in to all new and recent iMacs and MacBooks. If your Mac is a model without a video camera (or if you want to connect a different kind of video camera to your Mac that has a built-in iSight video camera), you can buy and connect an external video camera that is USB Video Class (UVC), such as one of the models offered by Microsoft (`www.microsoft.com/hardware`), Creative Labs (`www.creative.com`), or Logitech (`www.logitech.com`).

If your Internet connection is too slow, iChat might refuse to let you start an audio or video chat.

Initiating a text chat

To begin a text chat (or any kind of chat) with someone, you must first make sure that the person is online and available when you are online. The easiest way to find someone to chat with is to look at your buddy list. If you use the Offline group (choose View⇨Use Offline Group), all names displayed in the Offline group are people unavailable and all names displayed in other groups, such as Family or Co-Workers, are connected to the Internet and might be available for chatting. Otherwise, if Use Offline Group isn't selected, the names of available people in each group are bold; unavailable people's names are grayed.

Someone being connected to the Internet doesn't necessarily mean that he's in front of his computer and/or wants to chat. So if you find your instant messages are falling on deaf ears (or fingertips) and the person is not bothering to reply to your messages or chat requests, chances are that the buddy you're trying to chat with has gone fishing or is otherwise away from his computer.

Starting a text chat

To initiate a chat with someone listed in your buddy list, follow these steps:

1. **In the Buddy List window, double-click the name of a buddy who is online (or click the Text Chat button — it looks like the letter A — at the bottom of the Buddy List window) to open a new chat window.**

2. **Type a message in the text box at the bottom of the chat window and press Return to send your message, as shown in Figure 3-5.**

Figure 3-5:
The chat window lets you type a message in the bottom text box.

The recipient of your message will see your message, as shown in Figure 3-6. The recipient can choose to Block, Decline, or Accept your invitation. (We talk more about blocking and accepting invitations in the section "Making Yourself Available (Or Not) for Chatting," later in this chapter.) If the recipient accepts your invitation to chat, you can start typing messages back and forth to one another. You type in the lower text box, and your dialogue with the other person appears in the main text box.

Figure 3-6:
An invitation to chat.

If you want to insert emoticons — those little smiley faces — in your text message, choose Edit⇨Insert Smiley or click the triangle at the right end of the text-entry box where you also see the key sequences that create that emoticon (refer to Figure 3-5). Choose iChat⇨Preferences⇨Messages to change the colors and fonts used for your text chats. Choose View⇨ Messages to choose how you see balloons, boxes, names, and pictures in text chats.

Starting a group text chat

Instead of chatting with a single person, you may want to chat with multiple people at the same time. To create a group text chat, follow these steps:

1. **Hold down the ⌘ key, click each online buddy's name in the Buddy List window who you want to invite to your group chat, and press Return (or click the Text Chat button at the bottom of the Buddy List window).**

   A chat window appears (refer to Figure 3-5).

2. **Type a message that you want everyone in the group to see and press Return.**

3. **To see who is participating in the chat, choose View⇨Show Chat Participants.**

Initiating an audio chat

To initiate an audio chat, everyone needs a microphone and speakers, which are standard equipment on iMacs and Macbooks (add-ons for Mac Minis or MacPros) and on most Windows PCs (if that's what the person or people you want to chat with are using). You can initiate an audio chat by following these steps:

1. **Click the name of your online buddy in the Buddy List window and click the Audio Chat button (it looks like a telephone receiver) at the bottom of the Buddy List window (or choose Buddies⇨Invite to Audio Chat).**

   A message appears, informing you that your audio chat invitation is sent and that iChat is waiting for a reply, as shown in Figure 3-7.

   If this feature is dimmed, you don't have a microphone on your Mac or you don't have a fast enough Internet connection to support audio chatting.

2. **When a buddy you invited to an audio chat clicks the Accept button, your audio chat begins and you can both start talking as though you were speaking over a telephone.**

Figure 3-7:
A message
informs you
when you're
sending an
audio chat
invitation.

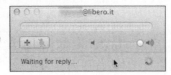

You might need to drag the volume slider to adjust the sound level. If you click the plus-sign button, you can invite another person into your chat. If you click the mute button, you can mute your microphone during the audio chat in case you need to shout at your dog to stop barking at the cat, or whatever else you want to say but don't want your audio chat partner to hear.

Initiating a video chat

To initiate a video chat, everyone's computer needs a microphone and a video camera. Macs with a built-in iSight video camera can use that, but for Macs without a built-in iSight camera, you have three options:

✦ Plug a digital video camcorder into your Mac's FireWire port (if your Mac model has a FireWire port; some don't).

✦ Buy a USB Video Class (UVC) video camera from Logitech (www.logitech.com), Creative Labs (www.creative.com), or Microsoft (www.microsoft.com/hardware) and plug it into your Mac.

✦ Conduct a one-way video chat in which you see the other person but the other person only hears your voice. If the person you're chatting with doesn't have a video camera but you do, the opposite occurs in which she sees you but you only hear her.

After everyone (up to three people) has a video camera connected to their Macs along with a fast Internet connection (a minimum of 100 Kbps), you can participate in a video chat.

Possibly, your Mac has a camera and a fast Internet connection, but someone you want to connect with in a video chat does not. In that case, you might be limited to using an audio or text chat instead.

You can initiate a video chat by following these steps:

1. **Click your online buddy's name in the Buddy List window and click the Video Chat icon to the right of your buddy's name to send a video chat invitation (or click the Video Chat icon at the bottom of the Buddy List window, or choose Buddies➪Invite to Video Chat).**

Your invitation is sent, and a video-chat window appears, showing how you will look to the other person you want to video chat with, as shown in Figure 3-8.

If you don't see a Video Chat icon next to your buddy's name in the Buddy List window, your buddy does not have a video camera built-in or connected to his computer. If you see a Video Chat icon next to your buddy's name but it is dimmed, your buddy is currently in a video chat with another buddy or group of buddies.

Figure 3-8:
A preview window appears so you can see how you will look to others.

2. **When your buddy accepts your invitation, your buddy's live video fills the video-chat window and a small window showing your live video appears in a corner of the window, as shown in Figure 3-9.**

Figure 3-9:
A video chat lets you see and speak to another person.

You can click and hold on your live video-chat window and drag it to any corner in your buddy's live video window.

3. **(Optional) Click the Effects button in the bottom-left corner of the video chat window.**

   Doing so opens a window showing several different visual effects you can choose to change the way your live video appears on your buddy's screen, as shown in Figure 3-10.

Figure 3-10: You can pick a unique visual effect to spice up your appearance.

4. **(Optional) Click a visual effect to select it and then click the Close button to close the visual effects window.**

5. **(Optional) Use the three buttons centered beneath the main video chat window:**

   • *Add*: Click the plus-sign button to invite one or more additional buddies to join the video chat, or start and stop iChat Theater (see the "Using iChat Theater to share files, photos, and screens" section).

   • *Mute:* Click the Mute button to stop your microphone from sending sound to your buddy on the other end of the video chat.

   • *Zoom:* Click the Zoom button (double arrows) to make the video chat window fill your Mac's entire screen. Press the Escape key to close the full-screen view and return to the window view.

Using iChat Theater to share files, photos, and screens

Some fun things you can try with a selected online buddy (or buddies) include sharing a file (such as a document or picture), sharing a web page, sharing an album or your entire iPhoto images collection, and sharing your screen. If you choose to share your screen, you let your buddy control it as though it were her screen (or vice versa, if a buddy shares her screen with you).

To share files, photos, and screens with iChat, click an online buddy in your buddy list and then choose

✦ **File⇨Share a File with iChat Theater:** Locate and select a file you want to share in the file window that opens, click the Share button, follow the iChat Theater prompts, and then click the Video Chat icon next to your buddy's name in the Buddy List window to initiate the iChat Theater connection.

✦ **File⇨Share a Webpage with iChat Theater:** Type in or copy and paste the web page you want to share in the dialog that opens, and then click the Share button. Follow the iChat Theater prompts, and then click the Video Chat icon next to your buddy's name in the Buddy List window.

✦ **File⇨Share iPhoto with iChat Theater:** Select an album name (or the Photos icon to share your entire iPhoto library) in the iPhoto window that opens, and then click the Share button. Click the Video Chat icon next to your buddy's name in the Buddy List window to show off your selected photos. Click the control buttons in the iPhoto control window that appears to move forward and backward through your photos, shown in Figure 3-11, or to pause or quit sharing your photos with your buddy.

**Book II
Chapter 3**

Instant Messaging and Video Chatting with iChat

Figure 3-11: Show off your iPhoto collection with the iChat Theater feature.

✦ **Buddies⇨Share My Screen or Buddies⇨Ask to Share Screen:** Choosing Share My Screen fills your buddy's screen with your screen, as though he's seated in front of your Mac, which he can now control with his mouse and keyboard. Choosing Ask to Share Screen fills your screen with your friend's screen as though you're seated in front of his Mac and controlling it with your keyboard and mouse (assuming your buddy has granted you permission to do so).

To end any of the sharing sessions listed here, press Right+Escape.

To take a snapshot during a video chat, ⌘-click in the center of the video and drag the image out of the window. The file will be on the Desktop or in whichever folder you dragged it to and named Image.tiff.

Saving or recording your chats

If you have romantic chats with your sweetheart, you might want to save them much as you would a bundle of letters tied together with a lavender ribbon. Likewise, if you use audio or video chat for business meetings, you can record the chat so you have a record of what occurred and who agreed to do what at the "meeting." Do the following to save or record your text chats:

1. **Click the iChat icon on the Dock or Launchpad to open iChat.**

2. **Choose File⇨New Chat and choose Text, and then type in the name of the person you want to chat with or double-click a buddy's name in the Buddies List to initiate a new chat.**

3. **When the chat is finished, before closing the chat window or exiting iChat, choose File⇨Save a Copy As and give your chat a name and choose a folder where you want to store it.**

4. **To save all chats, choose iChat⇨Preferences⇨General.**

5. **Select the Save Chat Transcripts To check box, and leave the folder as the iChats folder (which is in the Documents folder) or use the pop-up menu to choose another folder.**

6. **Select the In New Chat Windows, Show check box and choose The Last Chat or a set number of messages from the pop-up menu.**

A transcript of all your chats will be kept in the designated folder. You can open and read them from iChat at a later date by choosing File⇨ Open and selecting the chat you want to read from the Finder that opens.

To record audio or video chats, do the following:

1. **Click the iChat icon on the Dock or Launchpad to open iChat.**

2. **Choose File⇨New Chat and choose Audio or Video chat, and then type in the name of the person you want to chat with or double-click a buddy's name in the Buddies List to initiate a new chat.**

3. **When your buddy has accepted your invitation, choose Video⇨ Record Chat.**

   A request to record the chat appears on your buddy's screen.

4. **If the buddy clicks Allow, recording begins.**

5. **Click the red Stop button or close the chat window to stop recording.**

6. **The recorded audio or video chat is kept in the iChats folder in the Documents folder, as well as in the Chats playlist in iTunes.**

Interpreting status indicators

When you look at your buddies list, you see different icons next to the names of your buddies. The colored bullets let you know your buddy's status; a phone or video icon tells you the type of chat her computer supports.

✦ **Red bullet:** Your buddy has an Away status and is unavailable to receive messages.

✦ **Yellow bullet:** Your buddy is available but hasn't used his computer for 15 minutes or more.

✦ **Green bullet:** Your buddy is available.

✦ **Gray bullet:** Your buddy's status can't be determined.

✦ **Telephone:** Your buddy's computer has a microphone and she can have audio chats. If the telephone icon has depth, her computer supports multi-person audio chats.

✦ **Video camera:** Your buddy's computer has a video camera and he can have video chats. If the video icon has depth, his computer supports multiperson video chats.

✦ **Wi-Fi:** If you see the Wi-Fi symbol, your buddy receives notifications of chat requests on her mobile phone.

Making Yourself Available (Or Not) for Chatting

As soon as you connect to the Internet, your Mac broadcasts your availability to all the friends in your buddy lists. The moment someone wants to chat with you, you'll see a window and maybe hear an audible alert. Choose iChat⇨Preferences⇨Alerts to choose the sounds you hear when different events happen, such as a buddy coming online or an incoming invitation to a chat. Choose the event from the Event pop-up menu, and choose the action you want to occur from the choices below, as shown in Figure 3-12.

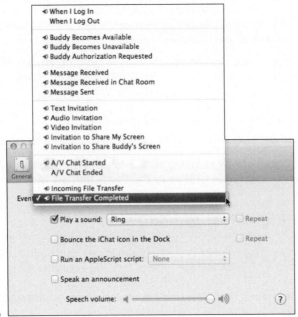

Figure 3-12:
Choose
how iChat
alerts you
to events in
Preferences.

Chat invitations can be fun to receive, but sometimes they can be distracting if you're trying to get work done and don't want to stop what you're doing to chat with someone. One thing you can do is change the status description others see next to your name in their own buddy lists.

Changing your status description to Away or something that indicates you're not in a chatting mode can discourage others from sending you chat invitations until they see that you've set your status to Available again.

Changing your status

To let others know that you're busy, you can change your status message to indicate that you're out to lunch, on the phone, or revising a big book and not really in the mood to chat with others unless it's about something *really* important. (Otherwise, you might as well just exit iChat altogether.)

Although you change your status to indicate you are away or unavailable to chat, you can still receive chat messages and invitations your buddies send if they choose to disregard your status message. Therefore, you still need to click Accept or Decline for each invitation you receive.

Alternatively, you can change your status to make yourself *invisible,* which means that you don't appear in your friends' Buddy List windows. However, you still see your friends in your Buddy List window (unless they choose to make themselves invisible, in which case neither of you can see the other).

To change the status friends see about you in their buddy list, click the arrow button beneath your name in the Buddy List window to open the My Status menu. (Alternatively, you can choose iChat⇨My Status to open the My Status menu.) Choose a status line, shown in Figure 3-13, and your chosen status now appears in your friends' buddy lists.

If you have multiple accounts, you can choose a different status for each account; for example, on the account you use with colleagues and associates, you may want your status to say "Emergencies Only" or "On the Phone"; whereas for your friends, you may want to say something clever like "Should be working." You can also opt to use the same status for all accounts by choosing Use Same Status for All Accounts at the bottom of the My Status menu on the iChat Buddies window.

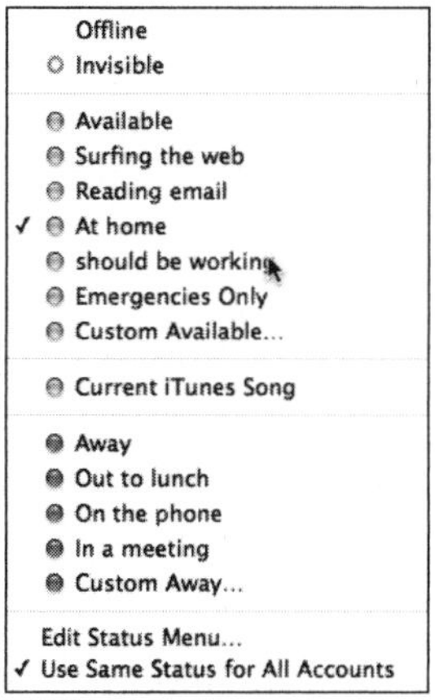

Book II
Chapter 3

Instant Messaging
and Video Chatting
with iChat

Figure 3-13:
The My
Status menu
provides a
variety of
statuses you
can display.

```
     Offline
  ○  Invisible

  ◒  Available
  ◒  Surfing the web
  ◒  Reading email
✓ ◒  At home
  ◒  should be working
  ◒  Emergencies Only
  ◒  Custom Available...

  ◒  Current iTunes Song

  ●  Away
  ●  Out to lunch
  ●  On the phone
  ●  In a meeting
  ●  Custom Away...

     Edit Status Menu...
✓  Use Same Status for All Accounts
```

You can also choose a status that lets your buddies know you are available and what you are doing, such as surfing the web or reading e-mail. If you choose Current iTunes Song, people can see the name of the song you're listening to. If you choose Custom Available, you can type your own message that others will see. Choosing Custom Away lets you type your own Away message.

Becoming invisible

The AIM and iCloud accounts give you the option of making yourself invisible to your buddies. Being invisible lets you see who on your buddy lists might be available to chat, but when other people see your name on their buddy lists, your name appears as though you are offline.

To make yourself invisible in iChat, click the arrow beneath your name in the Buddy List window to open the My Status menu and choose Invisible.

To make yourself visible again, open the My Status menu and choose a status that indicates you are online and available or away, such as Available or On the Phone.

For GoogleTalk, Jabber, and Yahoo! Messenger accounts, you must choose Offline to be invisible to your buddies with iChat or go to the Google, Jabber, or Yahoo! websites to set your status to invisible. If you choose one of the red statuses such as Away or In a Meeting, your buddies see you as unavailable but can still send you chat requests and you can see their statuses.

If you want to leave iChat running but sign out so that you are truly offline and unavailable, open the My Status menu beneath your name in the Buddy List window and choose Offline or iChat⇨Log Out.

As an alternative to taking time to click Decline on every chat invitation you receive, iChat offers several ways to decline invitations automatically.

Accepting (or blocking) chat invitations with privacy levels

Rather than block invitations from everyone, you may want to accept chat invitations from some people but block them from others. For example, an old flame might be harassing you so you want to block that person, but someone close to you, such as a family member or good friend, might need to reach you so you want that person to get through at any time.

To set your privacy level, follow these steps:

1. **Choose iChat⇨Preferences to open the iChat preferences window.**

2. **Click the Accounts icon to open the Accounts preferences pane.**

3. **If you added more than one chat account, click the account whose privacy level you want to change and click the Security tab.**

   Only AIM and iCloud accounts offer iChat Security preferences.

   You see the Security pane, shown in Figure 3-14, showing these options:

   • *Allow Anyone:* Allows anyone to send you a chat invitation, close friends or complete strangers alike.

   • *Allow People in My Buddy List:* Allows only people in your buddy lists to contact you.

   • *Allow Specific People:* Allows you to create a list of specific people who have permission to contact you. Click the Edit List button to open the Allow Specific People window, and then click the plus sign and type in the name of the person you want to allow to contact you.

- *Block Everyone:* Stops all chat invitations from friends, family, co-workers, and everyone else in the world.

- *Block Specific People:* Allows you to create a list of specific people you always want to keep from contacting you. Click the Edit List button to open the Block Specific People window, and then click the plus sign and type in the name of the person you want to block from contacting you.

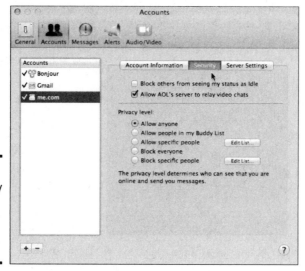

**Book II
Chapter 3**

**Instant Messaging
and Video Chatting
with iChat**

Figure 3-14:
The Security
pane lets
you choose
a privacy
level.

4. **In the Privacy Level section, select the radio button that corresponds to the privacy level you want to use.**

   For general privacy, you may want to choose the Allow People in My Buddy List option.

   Note: If you select the Allow Specific People or Block Specific People radio buttons, you need to click the Edit List button and type the exact account names of the people you want to allow or block.

5. **Click the Close button to close the iChat preferences window.**

If you want to control how others use chat on your Mac, read about Parental Controls in Book II, Chapter 4.

Using preferences to block requests

If you receive a lot of chat invitations, you may want iChat to reply automatically when you're really busy. You have a couple settings in preferences to help limit interruptions. Choose iChat➪Preferences, and try these settings:

✦ **General:** Select the Keep My Status As Away radio button under the option labeled When I Return to My Computer, If My Status Is Away.

✦ **Messages:** Select the Auto-Reply with My Away Message check box, and iChat will send an Away message to people who send you invitations.

Calling iPhones, iPods, iPads, and other Macs from Your Mac with FaceTime

Your Mac came with an application called FaceTime installed. If your Mac runs OS X 10.6.6 or later and has a built-in or external camera and microphone, FaceTime lets you place video calls with the following Apple devices:

✦ iPhone 4, 4S, and newer running iOS 4.1 or later

✦ iPod touch fourth generation and newer running iOS 4.1 or later

✦ iPad 2 and newer running iOS 4.1 or later

✦ Intel-based Mac running OS X 10.6.6 or later with camera and microphone

FaceTime uses your contacts in Address Book to call iPhone 4s and 4Ses with a phone number and iPod touches, iPad 2s, or other Macs with an e-mail address. Any edits you make to Address Book in FaceTime appear when you open Address Book on its own; addresses in FaceTime reflect the preferences you set up in Address Book (see Book V, Chapter 1 to get a closer look at Address Book). You also need an Internet connection and an Apple ID (your iTunes Store account or iCloud account work too). If you don't have an Apple ID, you can set one up in FaceTime.

Signing in to FaceTime

To use FaceTime to make or receive calls on your Mac, you have to turn FaceTime on and sign in to your account. To sign in to FaceTime, follow these instructions:

1. **Click the FaceTime icon in the Dock or Launchpad.**

The FaceTime window opens and you see yourself in the video pane.

2. **Click the FaceTime button On or choose FaceTime⇨Turn FaceTime On.**

3. **Enter your Apple ID in the User Name field and the associated password in the Password field.**

If you don't have an Apple ID, click Create New Account and fill in the form that appears to the right of the video window, and then click Next to finish setting up an Apple ID.

4. **Click Sign In.**

FaceTime signs you in and asks for an e-mail address that other people with FaceTime can use to call you on your Mac.

5. **Type in the e-mail address associated with your Apple ID account.**

6. **Click Next.**

   The calling pane opens.

7. **You can close the FaceTime window, but you remain signed in so you can receive calls.**

Making a call with FaceTime

After you turn FaceTime on and sign in to your account, you can make and receive calls. To make a call, follow these steps:

1. **Click the FaceTime icon in the Dock or Launchpad.**

   The FaceTime window opens and you see yourself in the video pane.

2. **Click the Contacts button at the bottom of the pane.**

   Your Address Book information appears in the calling pane. If you have groups, you see a list of your groups. If your contacts are in one All Contacts group, you see an alphabetical list of your contacts, as shown in Figure 3-15.

Book II
Chapter 3

Instant Messaging
and Video Chatting
with iChat

Figure 3-15: FaceTime uses your Address Book to make phone calls.

3. **Click the name of the person you want to call.**

   That person's Info appears.

4. **Click the e-mail address to call the person on an iPod touch, iPad, or Mac. Click the person's mobile phone number to call the mobile phone.**

   You hear the phone ringing on the other end.

   The person you're calling has to have FaceTime activated on her device (unless it's an iPhone) for the call to go through. If she doesn't have FaceTime turned on, you receive a message that she is unavailable.

   When the person accepts your phone call, you see her face in the main part of your screen and a small window appears where you see yourself, which is what the person you called sees, as shown in Figure 3-16.

Figure 3-16: You see the person you're talking to in the large window and yourself in the picture-in-picture window.

5. **You have a few options while you're talking:**

- Click the full-screen toggle to see the person you called fill the whole screen.

- Click and drag any edge of the window to resize it.

- Click the Landscape/Portrait toggle on your image to rotate the image that the person you called sees. Landscape can be a better view if the person is using an iPad, iPod touch, or iPhone. You can also drag your image around to place it where it doesn't block your view of the person you called.

- Pause a call by choosing FaceTime⇨Hide or Window⇨Minimize. Click the FaceTime icon in the Dock to return to the paused call.

- Click the Mute button if you don't want the person you're speaking with to hear you. Click the Mute button again to unmute.

6. **When you finish your call, click the End button or close the FaceTime window.**

Receiving a FaceTime call

You can receive calls when you turn FaceTime on and sign in, as described in the first part of this section. If someone calls you, FaceTime automatically opens and you see yourself in the video pane, the name or phone number of the person who is calling you, and two buttons, which give you the option to accept or decline the phone call, as shown in Figure 3-17. Click Accept to open the video call.

Figure 3-17: You can Accept or Decline incoming calls.

If you don't want to receive FaceTime video call invitations, choose either FaceTime⇨Turn Off FaceTime or FaceTime⇨Preferences and turn the switch off or sign out.

Managing your Apple ID settings

You can make changes to your Apple ID settings in FaceTime or change the country where you are located. To access your Apple ID settings, do the following:

1. **Click the FaceTime icon in the Dock or Launchpad.**

   The FaceTime window opens and you see yourself in the video pane.

2. **Choose FaceTime⟹Preferences.**

   Your FaceTime Preferences appear in the pane to the right of the video pane (replacing the Address Book list that usually appears there).

3. **Click your account name.**

   The Account pane appears, as shown in Figure 3-18.

4. **Click Change Location to change the country where you are using your Mac and FaceTime, and then click Save.**

5. **Click View Account to see your Apple ID account information and make changes, such as changing your password or your birthday, and then click Done.**

6. **Click the Preferences button to return to the main Preferences pane.**

7. **Click Done to close Preferences.**

   The Address Book list appears again.

Figure 3-18: FaceTime Preferences let you change the country you're in and Apple ID account information.

Adding contacts and favorites to FaceTime

FaceTime uses the contacts in Address Book to make calls. Any time you add, delete, or edit a contact in Address Book, the information appears in FaceTime, too. You can also add a contact to Address Book from FaceTime by following these steps:

1. **Click the FaceTime icon in the Dock or Launchpad.**

The FaceTime window opens and you see yourself in the video pane.

2. **Choose the group you want to add the new contact to or choose All Contacts if you don't have groups.**

3. **Click the plus sign in the upper-right corner.**

4. **Enter the person's first and last name, company name if you want, phone number, and e-mail (as shown in Figure 3-19).**

5. **Click Done.**

The new contact is added to your Address Book. If you want to add other pertinent information such as a street address or birthday, go to Address Book to edit this contact's information (as explained in Book V, Chapter 1).

Figure 3-19:
Add new
contacts to
Address-
Book from
FaceTime.

If you have people you call frequently, you may want to add them to your Favorites list so you don't have to scroll through your entire Address Book to find them each time you want to call. To select a contact as a favorite, do this:

1. **In All Contacts or a Group, find the person you want to add as a favorite.**

You can use the Search field to find a person quickly — scroll to the very top of the list of contacts to see it. Just type in the first letters of the first or last name. The more letters you type, the narrower the results in the list.

2. **Click the name of the person you want to make a favorite.**

3. **Click the Add to Favorites button.**

A list of the person's phone numbers and e-mail addresses appears.

4. **Click the phone number or e-mail address you use to call this person from FaceTime.**

A star appears next to the phone number or e-mail address you chose, as shown in Figure 3-20.

Figure 3-20:
Make the people you call the most your FaceTime Favorites.

5. **Click the Favorites button at the bottom of the pane.**

   The person is now in your Favorites list.

6. **To call someone from the Favorites list, click the Favorites button and click the name of the person you want to call.**

   To see more information about that person, click the arrow to the right of the name.

Book II
Chapter 3

Instant Messaging
and Video Chatting
with iChat

Chapter 4: Protecting Your Mac against Local and Remote Threats

In This Chapter

✔ Locking your Mac

✔ Adding passwords

✔ Encrypting your documents with FileVault

✔ Configuring Firewall and Privacy settings

✔ Adding other users to your Mac

✔ Switching between user accounts

✔ Using parental controls

One of the Mac's advantages is that it (seems to be) a minor target of viruses, but that certainly doesn't make it immune. With the world-wide connectivity of the Internet, everyone is vulnerable to everything, including malicious software (known as *malware*) and malicious people with above average computer skills (known as *hackers*). Worse are those hackers who like to use e-mail and websites to steal your personal identity information, such as credit card accounts or social security numbers (known as *phishing*) or those who send out software masquerading as one thing but, as soon as you open it, you discover it is harmful (*Trojan horses* disseminating malware). Although threats over the Internet attract the most attention, your Mac is also vulnerable from mundane threats, such as thieves who might want to steal your computer.

No matter how much you know about computers, you can always become a victim if you're not careful. Therefore, this chapter looks at the different ways to protect your Mac from threats — physical and cyber, local and remote. Of course, keeping a backup of your files is a good insurance policy; we talk about that in Book III, Chapter 1.

Locking Down Your Mac

Most people lock their cars and house doors when they're away, and your Mac should be no exception to this practice. To protect your Mac physically, you can get a security cable that wraps around an immovable object (like that heavy rolltop desk you have in the den) and then attaches to your Mac. You can attach it by threading it through a handle or hole in your Macintosh case, or if you have a MacBook Pro, by connecting it to your Mac's built-in security slot, which is a tiny slot that a security cable plugs into. If you have a MacBook Air, don't bother searching because there is no security slot, but Maclocks makes an unobtrusive "security skin."

Some companies that sell security cables are

+ **Kensington** (`www.kensington.com/kensington/us/us/home.aspx`)

+ **Targus** (`www.targus.com`)

+ **Maclocks** (`www.maclocks.com`)

+ **Tryten** (`www.tryten.com/categories/Mac-Computer-Locks`)

+ **Belkin** (`www.belkin.com`)

Of course, security cables can be cut. The main purpose of a security cable is to deter a thief who isn't carrying a pair of bolt cutters.

After protecting your Mac physically, you have other ways to lock down your Mac and keep other people out. Use a password to stop intruders from sneaking into your computer if you step away from your desk, encrypt the files, and use a software or hardware firewall, or both, to stop intruders from sneaking into your computer over the Internet.

Anyone with enough time, determination, and skill can defeat passwords and firewalls. Security can only discourage and delay an intruder, but nothing can ever guarantee to stop one.

Using Passwords

Before you can ever use your Mac, you must configure it by creating an account name and password. If you're the only person using your Mac, you'll probably have just one account (although we encourage you to have two: one for admin and one for everyday use). If you disable automatic login, your password can keep others from using your Mac without your knowledge.

As a rule, your password should be difficult for someone to guess but easy for you to remember. Unfortunately, in practice, people often use simple — as in, lousy — passwords. To make your password difficult to guess but easy to remember, you should create a password that combines upper- and lowercase letters with numbers and/or symbols, such as `OCHSa*co2010alum!` (which abbreviates a phrase, in this case "Ocean City High School all-star class of 2010 Alumnus!").

TIP

One way to create passwords is to combine the first letters of the words in a phrase that you'll never forget with the name of a dearly departed pet. By picking a memorable phrase or lyric, such as "I'm walkin' on sunshine" and turning it into a nonsensical combination of letters, paired with the name of your long-gone pet hermit crab, Louise (Iw0sLou!se), you'll easily remember your password, but others won't easily guess it. Presumably, someone would have to know you very well to guess which phrase you use with which pet. Pairing these two things that are unique to you makes for a password that's easy for you to remember but hard for someone to guess.

Changing your password

Many online banking and credit card services require you to change your password every so often, some as often as once a month, which certainly keeps password generating apps popular. They have reason to require you to change — it increases security. To increase your file security, you should change the password on your Mac periodically too. To change your password, follow these steps:

1. **Choose System Preferences.**

The System Preferences window appears.

2. **Click the Users & Groups icon in the System section to open the Users & Groups preferences pane, as shown in Figure 4-1.**

REMEMBER

If the lock icon in the lower-left corner of the preferences window is locked, you must unlock it to make changes to your Mac's user account details. Click the lock icon, type your password in the dialog that appears, and then press Return to unlock your Mac's user account details.

**Book II
Chapter 4**

Protecting Your Mac against Local and Remote Threats

Figure 4-1:
Users & Groups preferences let you change your user account details.

3. **Click your username under Current User in the left pane (or another account name under Other Users that you want to modify).**

   If you haven't created any additional users, you see only yourself listed.

4. **Click the Change Password button.**

   A dialog appears, displaying text boxes for typing your old password and typing a new password twice to verify that you typed your new password correctly.

5. **Enter your current password in the Old Password text box.**

6. **Enter your new password in the New Password text box.**

   If you want your Mac to evaluate your password or invent a password for you, click the key icon to the right of the New Password text box. The Password Assistant opens, as shown in Figure 4-2. Type in a password that you invent (Manual), and the Password Assistant rates the security level of your password. Or, you can choose from five types of passwords and choose one of the suggestions given. Click the Close box and the chosen suggestion is inserted as bullets in the New Password text box.

7. **Enter your new password in the Verify text box.**

8. **Enter a descriptive phrase into the Password Hint text box.**

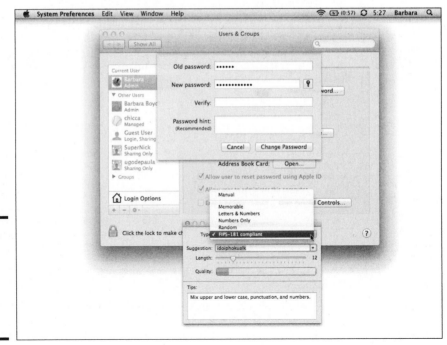

Figure 4-2:
The
Password
Assistant
helps you
choose a
password.

Adding a hint can help you remember your password, but it can also give an intruder a hint on what your password might be. Using our Iw0sLou!se example, you might use the phrase "favorite song crab." The intruder would have to know you pretty darn well to figure out that one!

9. **Click Change Password.**

   The password dialog disappears.

10. **Click the Close button to close the Users & Groups preferences window.**

Applying password protection

Normally, you need your password to log in to your account. As we mention earlier, we recommend creating an admin account that you use to make changes to your Mac, such as installing new software or changing certain settings, and a user account with a different username and password for your day-to-day Mac activities. The two account names and passwords should be different. Of course, after you log in to either account, anyone can use your Mac if you walk away and don't log out.

If you leave your Mac without logging out, your Mac will either go to sleep or display a screen saver. At this time, anyone could tap the keyboard and have full access to your Mac. To avoid this problem, you can password-protect your Mac when waking up from sleep or after displaying a screen saver.

For further protection, you can also password-protect your Mac from allowing an unauthorized person to make any changes to your Mac's various System Preferences. By applying password protection to different parts of your Mac, you can increase the chances that you'll be the only one to control your computer.

If you're the only person who has physical access to your Mac, you won't have to worry about password protection, but if your Mac is in an area where others can access it easily, password protection can be one extra step in keeping your Mac private.

To password-protect different parts of your Mac, follow these steps:

1. **Choose ⬛⇨System Preferences.**

   The System Preferences window appears.

2. **Click the Security & Privacy icon to open the Security & Privacy preferences pane.**

   If the lock icon in the lower-left corner of the preferences window is locked, you must unlock it to make changes to your Mac's user account details. Click the lock icon, type your password in the dialog that appears, and then press Return to unlock your Mac's user account details.

3. **Click the General tab.**

The General preferences pane appears, as shown in Figure 4-3.

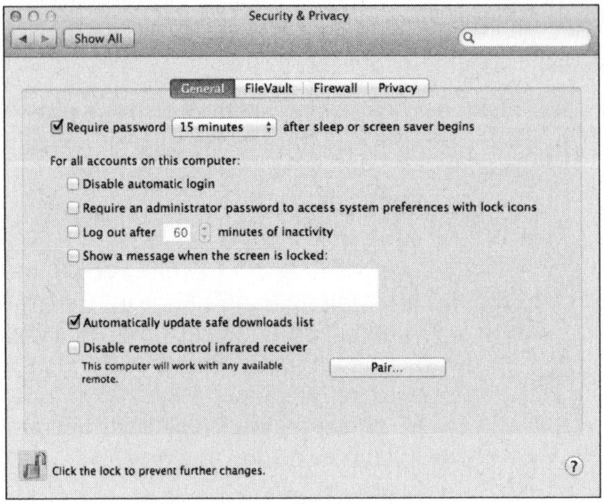

Figure 4-3: General Security & Privacy preferences let you choose different ways to password-protect your computer.

4. **(Optional) Select (or deselect) the Require Password *<immediately>* after Sleep or Screen Saver Begins check box.**

You can also choose to require the password at an interval between 5 seconds and 4 hours after your Mac goes to sleep.

5. **(Optional) Select (or deselect) the Disable Automatic Login check box.**

If this check mark is selected, your Mac asks for a password before logging in to your account. If it's deselected, you don't enter a password to log in.

6. **(Optional) Select (or deselect) the Require an Administrator Password to Access System Preferences with Lock Icons check box.**

If this check box is selected, nobody can modify a number of your Mac's System Preferences (such as the one you're adjusting right now!) without the proper password.

7. **(Optional) Select (or deselect) the Log Out after ___ Minutes of Inactivity check box.**

If selected, this option logs off your account after a fixed period so anyone trying to access your computer will need your password to log in to and access your account.

8. **(Optional) Select (or deselect) the Show a Message When the Screen Is Locked check box.**

Write a message in the text box that will be displayed when your Mac is locked. It could be something witty or appropriate for someone who attempts to log in to your Mac or contact information if the Mac is found.

9. **(Optional) Select (or deselect) the Automatically Update Safe Downloads List check box.**

10. **(Optional) Select or deselect the Disable Remote Control Infrared Receiver check box.**

Disabling this option simply keeps someone from controlling your Mac with an infrared remote control. (This option won't appear if your Mac doesn't have an infrared receiver.)

11. **Click the Close button of the Security preferences window.**

Encrypting Data with FileVault

Encryption physically scrambles your files so that even if people can access your files, they can't open or edit them unless they know the correct password. When you use FileVault, your Mac encrypts your entire drive, which means everything on your Mac is secure.

FileVault uses an encryption algorithm called Advanced Encryption Standard (AES), which is the latest American government standard for scrambling data that even national governments with supercomputers can't crack — at least not in a realistic time frame.

Setting up FileVault

FileVault scrambles your files so that only your password (or the system's Master Password) can unlock the files so you — or someone you trust and give the password to — can read them. When you type in a password, you can access your files and use them normally, but as soon as you close a file, FileVault scrambles it once more. FileVault works in the background; you never even see it working.

FileVault uses your *login* password to encrypt your data. For added safety, FileVault creates a recovery key that can decrypt any encrypted files for all user accounts and the files for each account that you have stored on your Mac. If you forget your login password and your recovery key, your data will be encrypted forever with little hope of unscrambling and retrieving it again. You can opt to store your recovery password with Apple. Should you lose it, you can retrieve it from Apple by giving the correct answers to three specific, pre-established questions.

To turn on FileVault, follow these steps:

1. **Choose System Preferences and click the Security icon to open the Security preferences pane.**

   The Security preferences pane appears.

2. **Click the FileVault tab to open the FileVault preferences pane, as shown in Figure 4-4.**

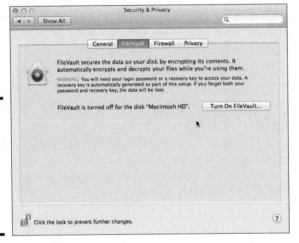

Figure 4-4: The FileVault pane lets you turn on FileVault and set a password.

   If the lock in the lower-left corner of the FileVault preferences pane is locked, click it, enter your password when prompted, and then click OK.

3. **Click the Turn On FileVault button, enter your login password when prompted, and then click OK.**

   The recovery key appears, as shown in Figure 4-5.

4. **Write down your recovery key, and then click Continue.**

   The recovery key changes if you turn FileVault off and then on again.

5. **If you want to store your recovery key with Apple, click Store the Recovery Key with Apple and options for three questions appear, as shown in Figure 4-6.**

   You must answer all three questions correctly for Apple to release your recovery key.

   If you don't want to store your recovery key with Apple, click Do Not Store the Recovery Key with Apple.

6. **Select a question from each of the three pop-up menus, and type the answers for the questions in the text boxes. Click Continue.**

   A dialog opens, instructing you to click the Restart button to begin the encryption process.

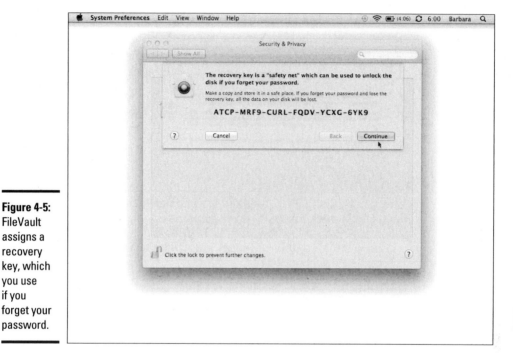

Figure 4-5:
FileVault assigns a recovery key, which you use if you forget your password.

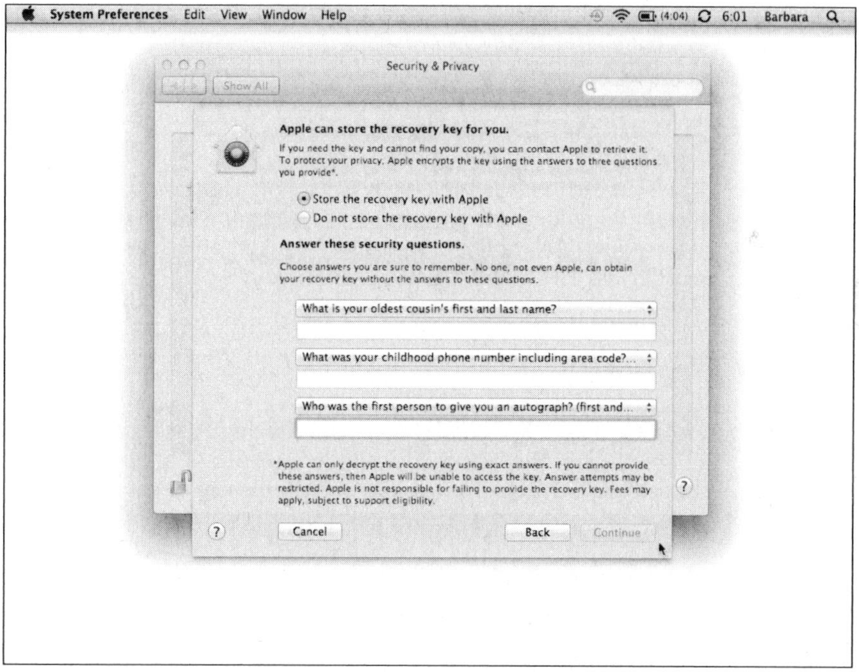

Figure 4-6:
Store your recovery key with Apple to protect against (your) memory loss.

7. **Click the Restart button to encrypt (or Cancel if you changed your mind).**

   Your Mac restarts and begins the encryption process. You can work while the encryption takes place. You can return to FileVault in System Preferences to check on the status.

FileVault also works with external USB, FireWire, and Thunderbolt drives (as well as SCSI and eSATA for MacPro users who have cards installed for those types of drives) so your data is safe wherever it's stored.

Turning off FileVault

In case you turned on FileVault and later change your mind, you can always turn off FileVault by following these steps:

1. **Choose ⬛⇨System Preferences and click the Security icon to open the Security preferences pane.**

   The Security preferences pane appears.

2. **Click the FileVault tab to open the FileVault preferences pane, (refer to Figure 4-4).**

   Note that when FileVault is turned on, the Turn Off FileVault button appears.

3. **Click the Turn Off File Vault button, enter your login password, and then click OK.**

   A dialog appears, informing you that you are about to turn off FileVault.

4. **Click the Turn Off FileVault button.**

If you decide to sell or give your Mac to someone, you can use FileVault's Instant Wipe function to completely *clean* your Mac's drive. Technically, Instant Wipe eliminates the FileVault 2 key, making the data inaccessible, and then overwrites the data with an illegible pattern.

Using Firewalls

Padlocks and FileVault protect your Mac against local threats, but when you connect your Mac to the Internet, you essentially open a door to remote threats. A highly technical person (such as a hacker) situated anywhere in the world could access your computer, copy or modify your files, or erase all your data. To keep out unwanted intruders, every computer needs a special program called a *firewall*.

A firewall simply blocks access to your computer, while still allowing you access to the Internet so you can browse websites or send and receive e-mail. Every Mac comes with a *software* firewall that can protect you whenever your Mac connects to the Internet.

Many people use a special device, called a *router,* to connect to the Internet. A router lets multiple computers use a single Internet connection, such as a high-speed broadband cable or DSL Internet connection. Routers include built-in *hardware* firewalls, and using one in combination with your Mac's *software* firewall can provide your Mac with twice the protection of using only one of these types of firewalls. For more about how to configure your router's firewall settings, refer to the router's user guide or look for more information in the support section of the router manufacturer's website.

Configuring a firewall

Although the default setting for your Mac's firewall should be adequate for most people, you might want to configure your firewall to block additional Internet features for added security. For example, most people will likely need to access e-mail and web pages, but if you never transfer files by using FTP (File Transfer Protocol), you can safely block this service.

Don't configure your firewall unless you're sure that you know what you're doing. Otherwise, you might weaken the firewall or lock programs from accessing the Internet and not know how to repair those problems.

To configure your Mac's firewall, follow these steps:

1. **Choose ⇨System Preferences to open the System Preferences pane.**

2. **Click the Security & Privacy icon to open the Security & Privacy preferences pane.**

If the lock icon in the lower-left corner of the preferences window is locked, you must unlock it to make changes to your Mac's user account details. Click the lock icon, type your password in the dialog that appears, and then press Return to unlock your Mac's user account details.

3. **Click the Firewall tab.**

The Firewall preferences pane appears.

4. **Click the Start button to turn on your Mac's firewall if it isn't already turned on.**

5. **Click the Advanced button to display the firewall's advanced preferences, as shown in Figure 4-7.**

The dialog that appears offers three check boxes.

In the center list box, you might see one or more sharing services you turned on by using the Sharing preferences pane (⇨System Preferences⇨Sharing). Find out how to share in Book VI, Chapter 2.

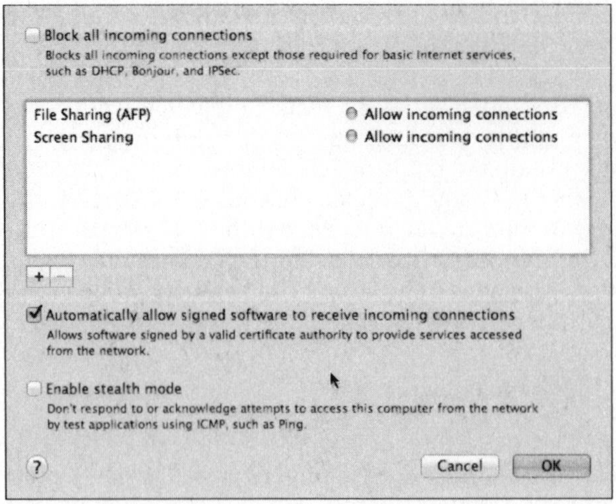

Figure 4-7:
The
Advanced
preferences
pane offers
additional
firewall
security
options.

6. **Select (or deselect) the following check boxes:**

    • *Block All Incoming Connections:* Allows only essential communica-
      tions for basic Internet and Web access, and blocks sharing services,
      such as iTunes music sharing or iChat screen sharing. When you
      select this option, any services or applications listed in the pane
      disappear, replaced with a static warning that indicates all sharing
      services are being blocked.

    • *Automatically Allow Signed Software to Receive Incoming Connections:*
      Allows typical commercial applications such as Microsoft Word to
      check for software updates, for Safari to access the Web, and for Mail
      to allow you to send and receive e-mail messages.

    • *Enable Stealth Mode:* Makes the firewall refuse to respond to any
      outside attempts to contact it and gather information based on its
      responses.

7. **Continue to Step 8 if you want to make additional adjustments to your
    Mac's firewall feature; otherwise skip to Step 13.**

8. **(Optional) Click the Add (+) button to add applications that you want
    to allow or block from communicating over the Internet.**

    A dialog appears, listing the contents of the Applications folder.

9. **Click a program that you want to allow to access the Internet.**

10. **Click Add.**

    Your chosen program appears under the Applications category.

11. **(Optional) Click the pop-up button to the right of an application in the applications list and choose Allow Incoming Communications or Block Incoming Communications.**

12. **(Optional) To remove a program from the applications list, click the program name to select it and click the Delete (–) button below the program list.**

13. **Click the Close button of the Security preferences window.**

Mac OS X 10.7 Lion enhanced your Mac's security with two features: ASLR (Advanced Space Layout Randomization), which makes your applications more resistant to malicious attacks, and *sandboxing,* which limits the types of operations an application can do, thereby making it difficult for a threat to take advantage of an application and, consequently, affect the whole operating system. Think of it as strengthening a potential weak link.

Dealing with nasty malware and RATs

There are two big threats that exploit personal computers that aren't protected by properly configured firewall preferences or properly configured router firewall settings. The first of these threats, *malware*, consists of programs that sneak on to your computer and then secretly connect to the Internet to do merely annoying (and offensive) things like retrieve pornographic ads that appear all over your screen, or do more serious things like infect your computer with a virus that can erase your personal data. Or, they can keep track of every keystroke you type on your computer, which in turn is transmitted to a snooping program on a malevolent person's computer so the hacker can find out things like your credit card numbers, usernames, and passwords.

A second type of program that requires an outgoing Internet connection is a *RAT* (Remote Access Trojan). Malicious hackers often trick people into downloading and installing a RAT on their computer. When installed, a RAT can connect to the Internet and allow the hacker to completely control the computer remotely over the Internet, including deleting or copying files, conducting attacks through this computer, or sending junk e-mail (spam) through this computer.

Although computer malware and RATs written and released by hackers typically target PCs running Windows, security experts agree that it's only a matter of time before the same digital nastiness begins infecting Macs. To guard against potential viruses, spyware, and RATs, your Mac displays a dialog that alerts you when you run a program for the first time. This feature can alert you if a virus, spyware, or a RAT tries to infect a Mac, but for further protection, consider purchasing a router with built-in firewall features, or installing an antivirus and antimalware program. (See the "Buying a firewall" section for recommendations.)

Buying a firewall

Although the built-in Mac firewall blocks incoming connections well, it allows all outgoing connections. Allowing all outgoing connections means that a malicious program you might inadvertently download could communicate via the Internet without your knowledge. To prevent this problem, you need a firewall that can block both incoming and outgoing connections.

You should use only one software firewall at a time, although it's possible to use one software firewall and a hardware firewall built into your router. If you use two or more software firewall programs, they may interfere with each other and cause your Mac to stop working correctly.

If you want a more robust firewall than the one that comes with the Mac (and the added security of antivirus and antimalware protection), consider one of the following:

✦ **ClamXav:** Available for free at `www.clamxav.com`

✦ **Intego VirusBarrier or Internet Security Barrier:** Costs between $50 and $100; available at `www.intego.com`

One problem with a firewall is that, in the normal scheme of things, you never really know how well it's working. To help you measure the effectiveness of your firewall, visit one of the following sites that will probe and test your computer, looking for the exact same vulnerabilities that hackers will look for:

✦ **Audit My PC:** `www.auditmypc.com`

✦ **HackerWatch:** `www.hackerwatch.org/probe`

✦ **Shields Up!:** `https://www.grc.com/x/ne.dll?bh0bkyd2`

✦ **Symantec Security Check:** `http://security.symantec.com/sscv6/WelcomePage.asp`

Because each firewall-testing website might test for different features, testing your Mac with two or more of these sites can help ensure that your Mac is as secure as possible. Figure 4-8 shows the results of a Symantec Security Check test of the Mac's built-in firewall feature.

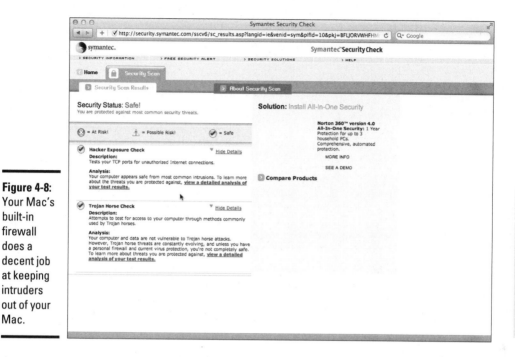

Figure 4-8:
Your Mac's built-in firewall does a decent job at keeping intruders out of your Mac.

Selecting Privacy Settings

If you belong to a social network such as Facebook or LinkedIn, you might know a little bit about privacy settings and how confusing they can be. Seems like everyone wants to know where you are and what you're doing. Maybe that's okay with you, maybe it's not. Either way, you can set privacy settings on your Mac, too. Follow these steps:

1. **Choose ⇨System Preferences to open the System Preferences pane.**

2. **Click the Security & Privacy icon to open the Security & Privacy preferences pane.**

    If the lock icon in the lower-left corner of the preferences window is locked, you must unlock it to make changes to your preferences. Click the lock icon, type your password in the dialog that appears, and then press Return to unlock your preferences.

3. **Click the Privacy tab.**

    The Privacy preferences pane appears, as shown in Figure 4-9.

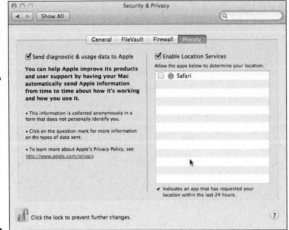

Figure 4-9:
The Privacy preferences let you choose who sees where you are and what you've been up to.

4. **You have two privacy options to configure:**

   • *Send Diagnostic & Usage Data to Apple:* Select this check box if you want to send a message to Apple when you have a problem, such as Safari crashing, or let your Mac send a message about how you're using it from time to time. The information is sent anonymously, so you don't have to worry about being spammed or anything.

   • *Enable Location Services:* Select this check box to allow applications that use your location to access it. You can selectively allow access only to certain applications or websites or deselect the check box and prohibit access altogether. The applications and websites use your location anonymously to gather consumer data.

5. **Click the Close button to close the Security & Privacy preferences window.**

Creating Multiple Accounts

Every Mac has at least one account that allows you to use your computer. However, if multiple people need to use your Mac, you probably don't want to share the same account, which can be like trying to share the same pair of pants.

One problem with sharing the same account is that one person might change the screen saver or delete a program that someone else might want. To avoid people interfering with each other, you can divide your Mac into multiple accounts.

Essentially, multiple accounts give your Mac a split personality. Each account lets each person customize the same Mac while shielding other users from these changes. Therefore, one account can display pink daffodils on the screen, and a second account can display pictures of Mt. Rushmore.

To access any account, you need to log in to that account. To exit an account, you need to log out.

Not only do separate accounts keep multiple users from accessing each other's files, but creating multiple accounts also gives you the ability to restrict what other accounts can do. That means you can block Internet access from an account, limit Internet access to specific times, or limit Internet access to specific websites. (It's great for parents, of course, which is why such limits are referred to as *parental controls.*)

Creating a new user account

To protect your files and settings, you should create a separate account for each person who uses your Mac. You can create four types of accounts:

✦ **Administrator:** Gives the user access to create, modify, and delete accounts. Typically, you have only one Administrator account; however, another user you trust implicitly, such as your partner or spouse, might also have an Administrator account.

✦ **Standard:** Gives the user access to the computer and allows them to install programs or change their account settings, but doesn't let the user create, modify, or delete accounts or change any locked System Preferences settings.

✦ **Managed with Parental Controls:** Gives the user restricted access to the computer based on the parental controls defined by an Administrator account.

✦ **Sharing Only:** Gives the user remote access to shared files but not the access to log in or change settings on your computer.

You can set up a Managed with Parental Controls account from the Users & Groups System Preferences or directly from the Parental Controls System preferences. To set up a new user account, follow these steps:

1. **Choose ⌘⇨System Preferences.**

The System Preferences window appears.

2. **Click the Users & Groups icon in the Systems section to open the Users & Groups preferences pane (refer to Figure 4-1).**

If the lock icon in the lower-left corner of the preferences window is locked, you must unlock it to make changes to your Mac's user account details. Click the lock icon, type your password in the dialog that appears, and then press Return to unlock your Mac's user account details.

Book II
Chapter 4

Protecting Your
Mac against Local
and Remote Threats

3. **Click the Add (+) button in the lower-left corner (above the lock icon).**

A New Account dialog appears, as shown in Figure 4-10.

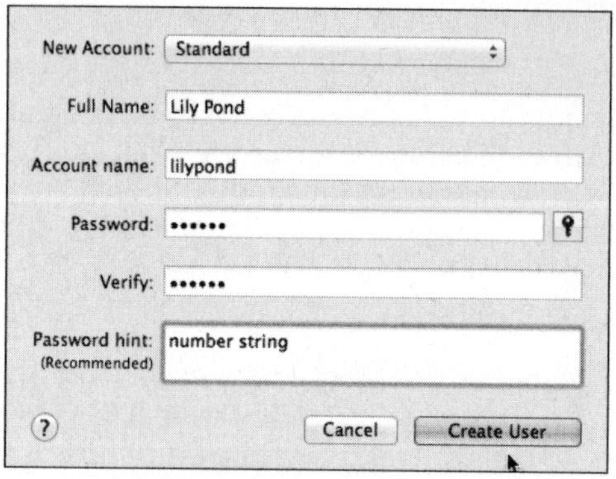

Figure 4-10:
The New
Account
dialog lets
you define
your new
account.

New Account:	Standard
Full Name:	Lily Pond
Account name:	lilypond
Password:	••••••
Verify:	••••••
Password hint: (Recommended)	number string

Cancel   Create User

4. **Choose the type of account you want to set up from the New Account pop-up menu.**

5. **Enter the name of the person who'll be using the account into the Full Name text box.**

6. **(Optional) Click the Account Name text box and edit the short name that your Mac automatically creates.**

7. **Enter a password for this account into the Password text box.**

If you click the key to the right of the password text box, your Mac will generate a random password that may be more difficult to guess than your doggie's name, but also harder to remember.

8. **Re-enter the password you chose in Step 7 into the Verify text box.**

9. **(Optional) In the Password Hint text box, enter a descriptive phrase to help remind you of your password.**

10. **Click the Create User button.**

The Users & Groups preferences pane displays the name of your new account.

11. **(Optional) To assign an image to a user, follow these steps:**

a. *Hover over the image above the name, and then click the disclosure triangle to reveal a selection of images you can assign to that user.*

b. *Click Edit Picture to assign a custom photo to the User.*

    c. Click the camera icon next to Take Photo Snapshot to take a photo with your Mac's iSight camera or another external camera connected to your Mac, or click Choose to open the Finder, and then scroll through the files and directories to select a photo stored on your Mac. Click Open to view the photo.

    d. When you have a photo you like, click the Set button to assign the photo to the user.

12. **Click the Close button of the Users & Groups preferences window.**

Setting up a master password

If you have many user accounts set up on your Mac and each has a password, you should have a plan if someone forgets his or her password. By setting up a master password, the administrator of the Mac (probably you), can override any encrypting that the user may have set up and reset the password. To create a master password, follow these steps:

1. **Choose ⇨System Preferences.**

The System Preferences window appears.

2. **Click the Users & Groups icon in the Systems section to open the Users & Groups preferences pane (refer to Figure 4-1).**

If the lock icon in the lower-left corner of the preferences window is locked, you must unlock it to make changes to your Mac's user account details. Click the lock icon, type your password in the dialog that appears, and then press Return to unlock your Mac's user account details.

3. **Click the Action button (it looks like a gear) at the bottom of the user list.**

4. **Choose Set Master Password.**

A dialog opens, as shown in Figure 4-11.

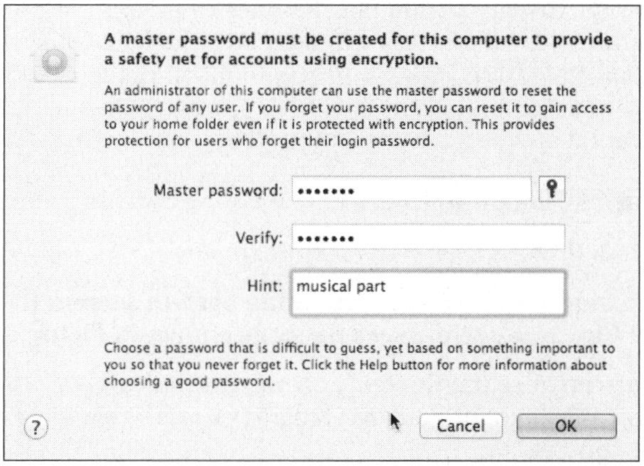

Figure 4-11:
Set a
Master
Password
so the
Admin-
istrator
can reset
other users'
passwords.

> A master password must be created for this computer to provide a safety net for accounts using encryption.
>
> An administrator of this computer can use the master password to reset the password of any user. If you forget your password, you can reset it to gain access to your home folder even if it is protected with encryption. This provides protection for users who forget their login password.
>
> Master password: ●●●●●●●
>
> Verify: ●●●●●●●
>
> Hint: musical part
>
> Choose a password that is difficult to guess, yet based on something important to you so that you never forget it. Click the Help button for more information about choosing a good password.
>
>   [Cancel] [OK]

5. **Type in a password in the Master Password text box.**

If you want help inventing a password, click the key to the right of the text field.

6. **Retype the password in the Verify text box.**

7. **Type a hint to help you remember the Master Password.**

8. **Click OK.**

9. **Click the Close button to close Users & Groups preferences.**

Defining parental controls

There are plenty of reasons you might want to use parental controls, not only to protect your children from seeing things they may not be mature enough to see, but also to restrict what guest users might do with your Mac. You apply limits or restrictions to a Managed with Parental Controls account, even if the person who accesses that account isn't your child. You can place several types of restrictions on an account. Following are the categories of limits you find in the Parental Controls preferences:

✦ **Apps:** Select Use Simple Finder to create a Finder that's easier for novice Mac users to work with. Choose Limit Applications to restrict which programs the account can run and restrict accessibility to apps in the App Store to a specific age group. Choose whether this use may modify the Dock or not.

✦ **Web:** Limits which websites the account can access.

✦ **People:** Limits the account to sending and receiving e-mail and instant messages from a fixed list of approved people. You can also receive an e-mail when the user tries to exchange e-mail with a non-approved contact.

✦ **Time Limits:** Prevents accessing the account at certain times or on certain days.

✦ **Other:** Select the associated check boxes to hide profanity, prevent modifications to the printers connected to the Macintosh, prevent saving data to a CD or DVD, or prevent changing the account password.

To apply parental controls to an account, follow these steps:

1. **Choose ⇨System Preferences.**

The System Preferences window appears.

2. **Click the Parental Controls icon in the System section to open the Parental Controls preferences pane, as shown in Figure 4-12.**

If there are no Parental Control accounts, a dialog gives you the option to convert the account you are using or create a new user account with parental controls.

Figure 4-12:
Parental
Controls
preferences
let you
define
restrictions
for an
account.

If the lock icon in the lower-left corner of the preferences window is locked, you must unlock it to make changes to your Mac's user account details. Click the lock icon, type your password in the dialog that appears, and then press Return to unlock your Mac's user account details.

3. **Click the account icon in the left list to which you want to apply parental controls.**

4. **Click the Apps tab (if it isn't already selected).**

   The Apps preferences pane appears, as shown in Figure 4-13.

5. **(Optional) Select the Use Simple Finder check box.**

   This creates a Finder that's easier for novice Mac users to work with.

6. **Select the Limit Applications check box.**

7. **Click the gray triangle to the left of each application category to display a list of programs for the selected category, and then select or deselect the programs you want to allow or disallow the user from accessing.**

   Selecting or deselecting the check box for an entire application category, such as iLife, Internet, or Utilities, gives you a single-click way to allow user access to all or none of the programs in that selected category.

8. **Click the Web tab to open the Web preferences pane, as shown in Figure 4-14.**

Figure 4-13:
Choose
which
applications
the user
can use in
the Apps
preferences.

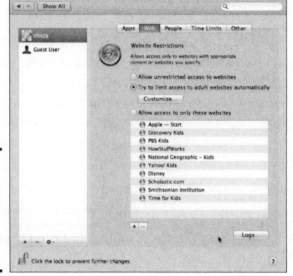

Figure 4-14:
Content
preferences
let you
restrict
what users
can see.

9. **Select one of the following radio buttons under the Website Restrictions section:**

   • *Allow Unrestricted Access to Websites:* Selecting this option allows users to access any website they want to visit.

- *Try to Limit Access to Adult Websites Automatically:* If you select this option, you can click the Customize button so that you can type the websites the account can always access and the websites that the account can never access.

  In both cases, you must type the address you chose to allow or block (such as www.nytimes.com or www.playboy.com). Although the Try to Limit Access to Adult Websites Automatically option can attempt to block most adult websites automatically, you need to enter additional addresses for particular websites that slip past the adult-website filter.

- *Allow Access to Only These Websites:* If you select this option, you can then specify which websites the user can access by clicking the "+" (plus-sign) button and adding websites you permit the user to visit. You can also remove websites you no longer want guest users to access by clicking on the website in the list of allowed websites, and then clicking the "–" (minus sign) to remove the website.

Click the Logs button if you want to see which websites this user accessed in the past.

10. **Click the People tab.**

The People preferences pane appears, as shown in Figure 4-15.

**Book II
Chapter 4**

Protecting Your
Mac against Local
and Remote Threats

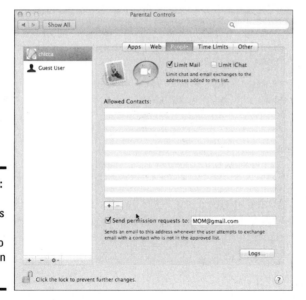

Figure 4-15: People preferences lets you restrict who the user can contact.

11. **Select the Limit Mail and/or Limit iChat check boxes.**

These features let you define which e-mail or iChat addresses the account can access; however, it doesn't limit the people they can converse with on FaceTime.

12. **Click the Add (+) button.**

    A dialog appears, as shown in Figure 4-16.

Figure 4-16: You can specify the name and e-mail or instant messaging addresses of approved people.

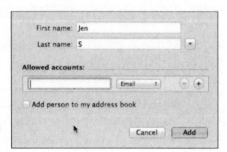

13. **Enter the first and last name of a person that you approve of into the First Name and Last Name text boxes.**

    Access your Address Book by clicking the triangle to the right of the last name field. Select multiple addresses by holding down the ⌘ key.

14. **Enter an e-mail or instant messaging address of the approved person into the Allowed Accounts text box.**

    The iChat program can connect with anyone who has an AIM (AOL Instant Messenger), iCloud, MobileMe, Mac.com, Google Gmail, or Jabber instant messaging chat account.

15. **Choose the account type (Email, AIM, or Jabber, for example) from the Allowed Accounts pop-up menu.**

    If you click the Add Person to My Address Book check box, the instant messaging address and name of the approved person will be added as a contact to your Address Book program.

16. **(Optional) Click the Add (+) button and repeat Steps 13 through 15 to specify another person and the associated e-mail or instant messaging chat account address.**

17. **Click Add.**

    If you want to remove someone from the Allowed Contacts list, click the name and press the Delete key or click the "–" button.

18. **Click the Time Limits tab to open the Time Limits preferences pane, as shown in Figure 4-17.**

19. (Optional) Select the Limit Computer Use To check box under the Weekday Time Limits category and drag the slider to specify how much time the account can use your Mac.

Figure 4-17: Time Limits preferences let you specify certain days or times the account can be used.

20. (Optional) Select the Limit Computer Use To check box under the Weekend Time Limits category and drag the slider to specify how much time the account can use your Mac.

21. (Optional) Select the School Nights and Weekend check boxes under the Bedtime category and select the start and end times of when you don't want the account to use your Mac, such as between 9:00 p.m. and 9:00 a.m.

The School Nights option defines Sunday–Thursday. The Weekend option defines Friday and Saturday; however, this option pays no mind to exceptions such as holidays, school vacations, snow days, and other potential nonschool-night calendar dates.

22. Click the Other tab to open the Other preferences pane, as shown in Figure 4-18.

Select the check boxes next to the limits you want to set:

• Hide Profanity in Dictionary

• Limit Printer Administration

• Limit CD and DVD Burning

• Disable Changing the Password

23. Click the Close button of the Parental Controls preferences window.

Figure 4-18:
The Others
pane
offers four
additional
parental
controls.

Monitoring a parental control managed account

After you create a Managed with Parental Controls account, you can view
what that user has been doing on your Mac by reviewing the log files. The
log files keep track of all the websites the user visited and tried to visit
(blocked by the Mac parental controls), the programs the user ran, and the
people the user contacted through iChat or e-mail. To view these log files,
follow these steps:

1. **Choose É➪System Preferences.**

The System Preferences window appears.

2. **Click the Parental Controls icon to open the Parental Controls preferences pane.**

If the lock icon in the lower-left corner of the preferences window is
locked, you must unlock it to make changes to your Mac's user account
details. Click the lock icon, type your password in the dialog that appears,
and then press Return to unlock your Mac's user account details.

3. **Click the account icon in the list on the left whose log files you want
to examine.**

4. **Click the Web tab to open the Web preferences pane, and click the
Logs button, as shown in Figure 4-19.**

5. **Choose a period from the Show Activity For pop-up menu, such as
viewing everything the user did in the past week or month.**

Figure 4-19:
Logs
preferences
let you
investigate
what the
user does
on your
Mac.

6. **Choose Website or Date from the Group By pop-up menu.**

7. **Click Websites Visited, Websites Blocked, Applications, or iChat in the Log Collections list box to review the selected log.**

Not all blocked websites are necessarily pornographic. Sometimes a blocked website could just be a blocked pop-up ad from an acceptable site, or an educational or reference site with keywords that trigger the block.

8. **Click the Close button of the Parental Controls preferences window.**

Creating a Sharing Only account

Your Mac comes with a pre-established Guest User account. This account lets friends or clients use your Mac temporarily but nothing they do is saved on your Mac, although it could be saved to a Shared file or to a DropBox or external drive.

You can create only one Guest account because multiple users will access the same Guest account. To create a Guest account, follow these steps:

1. **Choose ➪System Preferences.**

The System Preferences window appears.

2. **Click the Users & Groups icon in the System section to open the Accounts preferences pane (refer to Figure 4-1).**

If the lock icon in the lower-left corner of the preferences window is locked, you must unlock it to make changes to your Mac's user account details. Click the lock icon, type your password in the dialog that appears, and then press Return to unlock your Mac's user account details.

3. **Click the Guest User icon that appears in the list box on the left to open the Guest User dialog, as shown in Figure 4-20.**

Figure 4-20:
When you create a Guest account, you can define additional options for how the Guest account works.

4. **Select the Allow Guests to Log In to This Computer check box, which allows anyone to use your Mac's Guest account without a password.**

5. **(Optional) Click the Open Parental Controls button if you want to specify which programs guests can use (or not use) and whether they can access the Internet.**

   We wrote about adjusting these settings in the earlier section, "Defining parental controls."

6. **(Optional) Select or deselect the Allow Guests to Connect to Shared Folders check box.**

   If this option is selected, a Guest account can read files created by other accounts and stored in a special shared folder or the other users' Public folder.

7. **Click the Close button of the Accounts preferences window.**

Switching between accounts

The Mac offers several ways to switch between accounts. The most straightforward way is to log out of one account and then log in to a different account. A faster and more convenient way is to use Fast User Switching, which essentially lets you switch accounts without having to log out of one account first.

To log out of an account, simply choose ⇨Log Out (or press ⌘+Shift+Q). After you log out, the login window appears, listing the names and user icons of all accounts. At this time, you can click a different account name to log in to that account.

Before you can log out, you must close any files and shut down any running programs. If you use Fast User Switching, you won't have to bother with any of that, because Fast User Switching gives the illusion of putting the currently active account in "suspended animation" mode while your Mac opens another account.

Enabling Fast User Switching

Before you can use Fast User Switching, you have to turn on this feature. Log in as Administrator and then follow these steps:

1. **Right-click the System Preferences icon on the Dock and choose Users and Groups, or choose ⬤⬦System Preferences and click the Users and Groups icon in the Systems section.**

The Users and Groups pane opens.

2. **Click the Lock icon (if it is locked) in the lower-left corner of the Users & Groups window to allow you to edit your accounts, type your password into the dialog that appears, and then click OK.**

3. **Click the Login Options icon at the bottom of the list of users on the left side of the pane to display the Login Options pane, as shown in Figure 4-21.**

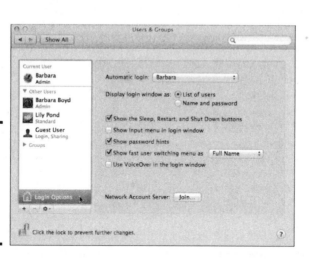

Figure 4-21: Login Options is where you can turn on Fast User Switching.

4. **Select the Show Fast User Switching Menu As check box, click the pop-up menu, and choose how you want to display the Fast User Switching Menu: Full Name, Short Name, or Icon.**

These options display what appears on the menulet. Full Name displays full account names, Short Name displays abbreviated account names, and Icon displays a generic icon that takes up the least amount of space in the menu bar.

5. **Click the Close button to close the Users & Groups preferences pane.**

Changing accounts with Fast User Switching

When you enable Fast User Switching, the Fast User Switching menulet appears in the right side of the menu bar, as shown in Figure 4-22. The menulet displays the names of accounts you can choose.

Figure 4-22:
The Fast
User
Switching
menulet.

To switch to a different account at any time, follow these steps:

1. **Click the Fast User Switching menulet on the right side of the menu bar and then click the account name you want to use.**

2. **Type the account password in the dialog that appears and press Return.**

   Your Mac switches you to your chosen account.

Deleting an account

After you create one or more accounts, you might want to delete an old or unused account. When you delete an account, your Mac gives you the option of retaining the account's Home folder, which might contain important files. To delete an account, follow these steps:

1. **Make sure that the account you want to delete is logged out and you are logged in to your Administrator account.**

2. **Right-click the System Preferences icon on the Dock and choose Users and Groups, or choose ⌥System Preferences and click the Users and Groups icon in the Systems section.**

3. **Click the Lock icon in the bottom-left corner of the Users & Groups preferences pane to allow you to edit your accounts, type your password into the dialog that appears, and click OK.**

4. **Select the account you want to delete in the accounts list and click the Delete Account (–) button in the lower-left corner of the Accounts preferences pane.**

A dialog appears, asking whether you really want to delete this account and presents options to save the Home folder of the account, as shown in Figure 4-23. Select one of the following radio buttons:

- *Save the Home Folder in a Disk Image:* Saves the home folder and its contents in a compressed disk image (DMG) file. This keeps the files compressed, so they take up less space on the hard drive than if you choose the next option (which does not compress the files contained in the Home folder). Choosing this option is like stuffing things in an attic to get them out of sight, but still keeping them around in case you need them later.

- *Don't Change the Home Folder:* Keeps the Home folder and its contents exactly as they are before you delete the account, so you can browse through the files contained within the folder at any time.

- *Delete the Home Folder:* Wipes out any files the user might have created in the account.

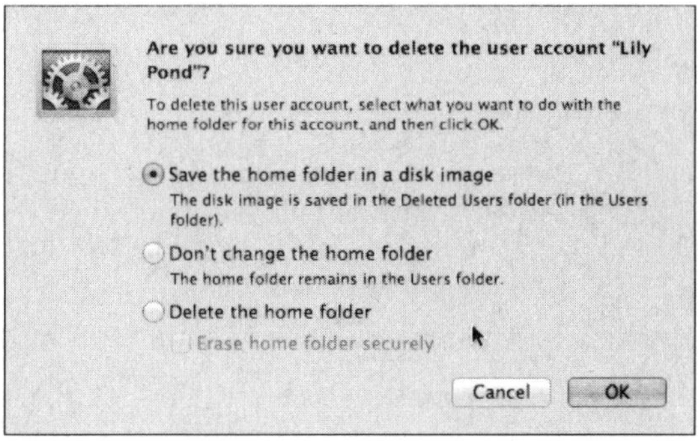

Figure 4-23:
Do you
really want
to delete?

Are you sure you want to delete the user account "Lily Pond"?

To delete this user account, select what you want to do with the home folder for this account, and then click OK.

◉ Save the home folder in a disk image
 The disk image is saved in the Deleted Users folder (in the Users folder).

○ Don't change the home folder
 The home folder remains in the Users folder.

○ Delete the home folder
 Erase home folder securely

[Cancel]   [OK]

5. **Click OK.**

Your Mac deletes the specified account.

A Few Final Security Tips

We want to give you a few extra security tips to keep your Mac and your documents safe:

✦ From the Desktop, choose Finder➪Secure Empty Trash when eliminating old files, especially if you have sensitive documents. This feature is more incinerator than simple trash can.

✦ Avoid suspicious websites. If you open a website and a gazillion other pages open, quit Safari and re-open. Mac OS X Lion screens downloads from Safari, Mail, and iChat and offers to move potential malicious files directly to the trash — usually a good idea.

✦ If an e-mail arrives that *seems* to be from your bank or credit card provider but the domain is @hotmail.com or @gmail.com, don't respond, mark it as Junk, and move on. Sorry to disappoint, but they really *didn't* find $14 million that belongs to you.

Banks don't send or ask for sensitive financial information via e-mail, maybe because they know that an ordinary e-mail message is about as secure as a postcard — as in, *not secure*.

✦ Although it's tempting, don't use the same password for everything. Use Password Assistant to generate passwords, and then track those passwords by using Keychain Access (choose Go⇨Utilities and click Keychain Access).

Book III

Beyond the Basics

The 5th Wave   By Rich Tennant

"Don't laugh. It's faster than our current system."

Contents at a Glance

Chapter 1: Backing Up and Restoring Your Data with Time Machine

In This Chapter

✔ **Understanding backup options**

✔ **Using Time Machine**

✔ **Transferring your data to a new Mac with Migration Assistant**

✔ **Working with data-recovery applications**

*B*acking up data is something that many people routinely ignore, like changing the oil in the car on a regular basis. The only time most people think about backing up their data is after they've already lost something important, such as a business presentation, or a folder full of close-to-the-heart family photos. Of course, by that time, it's already too late.

Backing up your data might not sound as exciting as playing video games or browsing the web, but it should be a part of your everyday routine. If you can't risk losing your data, you must take the time to back it up. The good news is that your Mac came with Time Machine, the application that makes backing up a routine that your Mac can do on its own.

In this chapter, first we explain some of the different backup options. Next, we show you how to set up Time Machine to perform regular, automatic backups. We also talk about recovering an individual file and restoring your Mac with the Time Machine backup in the unfortunate event that you lose all your files. We include a brief explanation Mac OS X 10.7 Lion's new AutoSave and Versions features.

Understanding Different Backup Options

Backing up is, essentially, duplicating your data — making a copy of every important file. You could duplicate each file as you create it and keep a copy on your hard drive, although this doesn't solve the problem if your hard drive crashes or your Mac is stolen. Ideally, you back up to one of the following external sources (we explain each of these in the following sections):

✦ External hard drive — personal or networked, such as Time Capsule

✦ Remote storage, such as iCloud

✦ Flash drive

✦ CD-R or DVD-R

You must make sure to back up periodically, such as at the end of every week or even every day if you update and create new files often. If you forget to back up your files, your backup copies could become woefully outdated, which can make them nearly useless.

Depending on the value of your files, you may want to consider using more than one backup method. For example, you may want to use Time Machine to completely back up your Mac, and iCloud to back up only critical documents. The idea here is that if catastrophe falls and you lose your Mac, you can replace the applications, but you can't retake family photos or rewrite your unfinished novel. The more backup copies you have of your critical files, the more likely it is that you'll never lose your data no matter what might happen to your Mac.

Backing up with external hard drives

To prevent the loss of all your data if your hard drive should suddenly bite the dust, you can connect an external hard drive to your Mac's USB, FireWire, or Thunderbolt port with a cable that's typically included with the hard drive.

USB (Universal Serial Bus), FireWire, and Thunderbolt ports connect peripherals to a computer. USB ports commonly connect a mouse, printer, or digital camera. FireWire ports often connect video camcorders or other computers. Thunderbolt connects displays and storage devices. The FireWire port transfers data at least twice as fast as the USB 2.0 port, whereas Thunderbolt is incredibly fast but because it's a new technology, there are fewer devices that support it. Earlier-model MacBooks and MacBook Airs lack a FireWire port. The newest Macs have both FireWire and Thunderbolt ports.

The main advantage of external hard drives is that copying large files is much faster and more convenient than copying the same files to CD/DVD discs, and they offer more capacity than USB drives. Additionally, external hard drives are easy to unplug from one Mac and plug into another Mac. Because of their low cost, fast copying speed, and ease of moving and plugging into any Mac, external hard drives are the most popular choice for backing up files.

You can also put an external hard drive on your network. For example, Apple's Time Capsule provides external storage and functions as a Wi-Fi hub so multiple computers can back up to the Time Capsule. (There are 1- and

2-terabyte versions, so you probably won't have to worry about storage space.) Any networked drive must use AFP (Apple File Protocol) file sharing.

Perhaps the biggest drawback of external hard drives is that they can't protect against a catastrophe near your computer, such as a fire burning down your house or a flood soaking your computer desk and office. If a disaster wipes out the entire area around your computer, your external hard drive might be wiped out in the catastrophe as well.

You can treat an external hard drive as just another place to copy your files, but for greater convenience, you should use a special backup application, such as Time Machine, which we get to in shortly in the section "Blasting into the Past with Time Machine." Backup applications can be set to run according to a schedule (for example, to back up your files every night at 6:00 p.m.)

If the files haven't changed since the last time you backed them up, the backup application saves time by skipping over those files rather than copying the same files to the external hard drive again.

To retrieve files, you could just copy the files from your external hard drive back to your original hard drive, but be careful! If you changed a file on your original hard drive, copying the backup copy can wipe out the most recent changes and restore an old file to your hard drive, which probably isn't what you want. To keep you from accidentally wiping out new files with older versions of that same file, backup applications always compare the time and date a file was last modified to make sure that you always have copies of the latest file.

Storing backups off-site

Backing up your Mac's important files to an off-site storage service virtually guarantees that you'll never lose your data.

Low-cost (and even free) off-site storage options are available for Mac users. Many companies sell off-site storage space for a monthly fee. However, to entice you to try their services, they often provide a limited amount of free space that you can use for an unlimited period at no cost whatsoever. To get your free off-site storage space, sign up with one or more of the following off-site data-backup sites, each of which offers a paid version with more storage space:

✦ **iCloud (**www.icloud.com**):** Free 5GB storage space plus up to 1,000 photos and any purchased media, apps, and books. Automatically synchronizes your Mac's Address Book contacts, iCal calendar events, Safari bookmarks, as well as backup files and folders between multiple Macs or between your Mac and your iPhone, iPad, iPod Touch, or Windows PC that you might also use. iCloud provides online backup storage space that you can access from the Finder just like a hard drive; however, copying files to and from iCloud may be slower than copying to a locally connected drive, depending on your Internet connection speed.

✦ **SugarSync** (`www.sugarsync.com`): Free 5GB storage space.

✦ **MediaMax** (`www.mediamax.com`): Free 5GB storage space.

✦ **Syncplicity** (`www.syncplicity.com`): Free 2GB storage space.

✦ **Mozy** (`http://mozy.ie`): Free 2GB storage space.

✦ **ElephantDrive** (`www.elephantdrive.com`): Free 2GB storage space.

Storing backups on USB flash drives

Low cost and high storage capacity make USB flash drives an attractive alternative to using CDs for backing up your most crucial files. USB flash drives offer ease of use because you can plug them into any open USB port in a Mac and move them to another Mac. Many USB flash drives have built-in keyrings. Carrying one in your pocket or purse is not only convenient, but also ensures that your data is always safe and on your person should something happen to your Mac's hard drive at home or in the office, where your backup drive's original files are stored.

The biggest drawback of USB flash drives is their somewhat limited storage capacities, which typically range from 1GB to 64GB or sometimes more. While USB flash drives in those capacity ranges can usually cost between $5 and $100, a whopping 256GB model sold by Amazon (`www.amazon.com`) costs around $300 as of this writing. Whatever the capacity, USB flash drives are especially convenient for carrying your most critical files but not necessarily for backing up all your important files. In contrast to the hassles of writing (or *burning*) data to a CD or DVD, saving files to a USB flash drive is speedier and as simple as saving a file to a backup folder on your hard drive.

Backing up to CDs/DVDs

Every Mac that has an optical disc drive can write to CDs, and most Macs can write to DVDs. (If you're the proud owner of a MacBook Air or Mac mini, you need an external optical disc drive.) As a result, storing backups on CDs or DVDs is a popular option because CDs and DVDs are easy to store and are durable. The biggest drawbacks of CDs and DVDs are their limited storage capacities. CDs can store up to 700MB of data, single-layer DVDs can store 4.7GB of data, and dual-layer DVDs store up to 8.5GB of data.

A *dual-layer* disc employs a second physical layer within the disc, which the drive accesses by shining its laser through the disc's first, semitransparent layer.

If you need to back up only word-processor or spreadsheet files, a single CD should be sufficient. However, music, video, and digital photographs take up more space, which means that you might need to use several CDs or DVDs to back up all your files of those types.

DVDs can store much more data than CDs, but even they can be limited when you're backing up hard drives that contain several gigabytes worth of files. The more discs you need to back up your files completely, the harder it is to keep track of all the discs — and the slower (and more tedious) your backups are to make. In view of all this hassle, you might not back up your data as often as you should; eventually your backup files fall too far out of date to be useful — which defeats the purpose of backing up your data. So if your data frequently exceeds the storage limits of a single CD or DVD, you should probably rely on a different backup method.

Blasting into the Past with Time Machine

One problem with traditional backup applications is that they store the latest, or the last two or three previous, versions of your files. Normally this is exactly what you want, but what if you want to see an earlier version of a short story you began working on two weeks ago? Trying to find files created on certain dates in the past is nearly impossible, unless you do one of the following:

+ Keep a copy of the backup you made previously.

+ Save different versions of the document.

+ Use Lion and your application supports Versions (we explain this in the "Understanding Versions" section, later in this chapter).

Fortunately, that type of problem is trivial for your Mac's backup application, Time Machine. Unlike traditional backup applications that copy and store the latest or last one or two versions of files, Time Machine takes snapshots of your Mac's hard drive so that you can view its exact condition from two hours ago, two weeks ago, two months ago, or even farther back.

The external hard drive you use to back up your Mac with Time Machine should have oodles of storage space, and ideally, you use that drive *only* for Time Machine backups. The bigger the hard drive, the farther back in time you can go to recover old files and information.

By viewing the exact condition of what your Mac hard drive looked like in the past, you can see exactly what your files looked like at that time. After you find a specific file version from the past, you can easily restore it to the present with a click of the mouse.

**Book III
Chapter 1**

**Backing Up and
Restoring Your Data
with Time Machine**

Setting up Time Machine

To use Time Machine, you need to connect an external hard drive to your Mac with a USB, FireWire, or Thunderbolt cable, or have an additional hard drive installed in one of the additional drive bays inside your Mac Pro desktop computer.

To set up Time Machine to back up the data on your Mac's primary hard drive to an external hard drive, follow these steps:

1. **Connect the external hard drive to your Mac.**

When you plug in a new hard drive, the Time Machine backup feature typically starts automatically and asks whether you want to use the hard drive to back up your Mac, as shown in Figure 1-1.

Figure 1-1:
Time
Machine
offers to
back up
your Mac
when you
plug in an
external
hard drive.

If Time Machine automatically runs and prompts you as described, skip to Step 4. If Time Machine does not prompt you, continue to the next step.

2. **Choose ⌘⇨System Preferences and then click the Time Machine icon to open the Time Machine preferences pane, as shown in Figure 1-2.**

Figure 1-2:
To set
up Time
Machine,
turn it on
and choose
an external
drive to use.

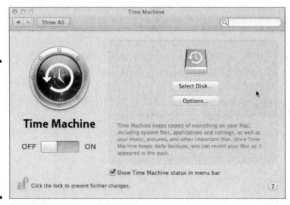

If the lock icon in the lower-left corner of the Time Machine preferences pane is bolted, click it, enter your password when prompted, and then click OK.

3. **Click the On button.**

   A dialog appears, listing all available external hard drives you can use, as shown in Figure 1-3.

Figure 1-3: You must choose an external hard drive to use with Time Machine.

4. **Select an external hard drive and check the Encrypt Backup Disk box if you want to encrypt your backup drive. (See Book II, Chapter 4 to discover more about encryption.)**

5. **Click the Use Backup Disk button.**

   The Time Machine pane appears again, listing your chosen external hard drive, shown in Figure 1-4, and after a short amount of time, the Time Machine application begins backing up your Mac's data to the external hard drive you selected.

Figure 1-4: The Time Machine pane can show how much free space remains on your external hard drive.

To find how frequently Time Machine backs up and manages your Mac's data, see the nearby sidebar, "How Time Machine does its backup thing."

6. **(Optional) Select the Show Time Machine Status on the Menu Bar check box if it isn't already checked.**

With this option checked, the Time Machine icon on the menu bar animates with a twirling arrow whenever Time Machine is backing up your Mac's data. Clicking the Time Machine icon at any time (see Figure 1-5) is how you can keep tabs on the status of an active backup, start or stop a backup, and choose the Enter Time Machine command to run the Time Machine recovery application, as described in the upcoming section, "Retrieving files and folders."

Figure 1-5:
Access your Mac's backup options from the menu bar.

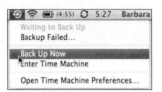

7. **Click the Close button to close the Time Machine preferences pane.**

How Time Machine does its backup thing

The first time you turn on and begin using Time Machine, it backs up your Mac's entire hard drive — which can take a long time if your Mac's hard drive contains lots of applications and data. One thing you can do is start the Time Machine backup before going to bed so when you wake the next morning, your Mac will be completely (or almost completely) backed up.

After its initial backup of your Mac's hard drive, Time Machine automatically performs an incremental backup of any data changed on your Mac's hard drive (providing the backup drive is attached) every hour. Time Machine saves hourly backups for the past 24 hours,

daily backups for the past month, and weekly backups for everything older than a month. Time Machine skips backing up files you create and then delete before the next hourly backup.

When your external backup hard drive starts running out of free space for more backups, Time Machine deletes the oldest files it finds in order to make room for the newer ones.

If you use a portable Mac, when the external drive isn't connected, Time Machine saves a snapshot on your Mac's internal drive; the next time you connect the external drive, the backup resumes.

Don't interrupt Time Machine during the first backup. You can continue working while Time Machine runs in the background.

Understanding Versions

Mac OS X 10.7 Lion added AutoSave and Versions to Time Machine, which automatically saves your files while you work. That is, when you're working in applications that support these features (as of the time of writing, only iWork, Preview, and TextEdit do, although other developers say they will be supported in future software updates), AutoSave saves your document every five minutes or when you pause. If you make a series of changes that you don't want to lose, you can choose File⇨Lock to lock the document at that point. You have to unlock it to make future changes or use it as a template for a new document. In the Time Machine preferences, you can also choose to Lock documents after two weeks (see Figure 1-6).

Versions takes a snapshot of your document when it's new, each time you open it, and once an hour while you're working on it. Versions keeps those hourly snapshots for a day, saves the day's last version for a month, and then saves weekly versions for previous months. If at some point you want to go back to an earlier version, choose File⇨Browse All Versions, and a list of snapshots of that document appear. You can make side-by-side comparisons and cut and paste between them.

Skipping files you don't want to back up

Unless you specify otherwise, Time Machine backs up everything on your Mac except temporary files like your web browser's cache. To save space, you can identify certain files and folders you're not concerned about losing that you want Time Machine to ignore. For example, you might not want to back up your Applications folder if you already have all your applications stored on separate installation discs or you purchased them through the App Store, which lets you download them again if necessary. Or you might choose to skip backing up media and apps you purchased and downloaded from iTunes because if you lose them you can download them again, so there's no need to waste that precious space on your Mac's backup drive.

To tell Time Machine which files or folders to skip, follow these steps:

1. **Choose ⌘⇨System Preferences and then click the Time Machine icon to open the Time Machine preferences pane (refer to Figure 1-4).**

2. **Click Options to open the Exclude These Items from Backups dialog, as shown in Figure 1-6.**

Click the plus sign (+) to open a dialog for choosing files you don't want to back up. Note the check box for locking documents that use AutoSave.

Figure 1-6:
Click the plus sign (+) to choose files you don't want to back up.

3. **Click the plus sign (+) and then navigate to the file or folder you want Time Machine to ignore, as shown in Figure 1-7.**

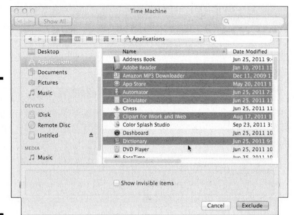

Figure 1-7:
Select the hard drive, folder, or files you want Time Machine to ignore.

You can select multiple drives, files, and folders by holding down the ⌘ key and then clicking what you want Time Machine to ignore.

4. **Click the Exclude button.**

   The Exclude These Items from Backups dialog appears again (refer to Figure 1-6).

5. **Select or deselect these additional optional Time Machine features if you want:**

   • *Backup While on Battery Power:* Allows Time Machine to back up your MacBook when it's running on battery power. Turning this option on will drain your MacBook's battery faster than if you turn this option off.

- *Notify After Old Backups Are Deleted:* Time Machine displays a dialog requesting your approval before it deletes any old backup files.

6. **Click the Done button and then click the Close button to close the Time Machine preferences pane.**

Retrieving files and folders

After you configure Time Machine to back up your Mac, you can use the Time Machine recovery application to retrieve old files or information you deleted or changed after Time Machine backed them up. The two ways to use the Time Machine recovery application to recover files, folders, or other pieces of information, such as address cards, e-mail messages, or iCal calendar items, are as follows:

✦ By running an application and then clicking the Time Machine icon in the Dock or Launchpad, or choosing the Enter Time Machine command from the Time Machine icon on the menu bar.

✦ By opening a new Finder window and then clicking the Time Machine icon in the Dock or on the Launchpad, or choosing the Enter Time Machine command from the Time Machine icon on the menu bar.

Time Machine consists of two components:

✦ The Time Machine preferences pane (described earlier in this section) that you use to turn the Time Machine backup feature on or off, or to adjust its settings.

✦ The Time Machine restore application is what you use to recover files you deleted or changed from earlier backups. You run the restore application by clicking the Time Machine icon in the Dock or on the Launchpad, or by choosing the Enter Time Machine command from the Time Machine icon on the menu bar.

Recovering data from within an application

To use Time Machine to retrieve a specific piece of information from within an application (such as an address card from your Mac's Address Book, which we use in this example), follow these steps:

1. **Click the Address Book icon in the Dock or on the Launchpad to launch Address Book.**

   The Address Book application opens and displays the Address Book window, which lists all your contacts.

2. **Click the Time Machine icon in the Dock or Launchpad (or click the Time Machine icon on the menu bar and choose Enter Time Machine) to run the Time Machine restore application.**

Your Mac's screen will appear to literally space out while it launches the Time Machine restore application — into another dimension known as The Time Machine Zone, as shown in Figure 1-8.

3. **Choose one of the following ways to select a contact card (or cards) that you want to restore from a past backup:**

   • *Click the Backward and Forward arrow buttons near the bottom-right corner of the screen.* Click the Backward button to move the Address Book window backward in time to earlier Time Machine backups. Click the Forward button to move forward to more recent Time Machine backups.

   • *Click an Address Book window in the stack of windows behind the frontmost Address Book window.* You can click the Address Book window directly behind the front Address Book window, or one behind it stretching farther back in time. Each time you click an Address Book window in the stack, Time Machine moves it to the front of the screen.

   • *Move the pointer to the Time Machine timeline along the right edge of the screen.* The timeline bars expand to display a specific date. To choose a specific date, click it.

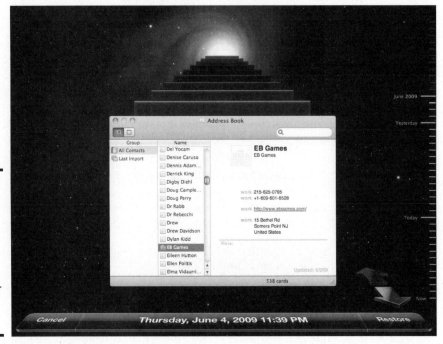

Figure 1-8: The Time Machine restore application displays a far-out view of your Address Book.

4. **When you locate the contact card you want to retrieve, click it, click the Restore button in the lower-right corner, and then proceed to Step 6.**

To select more than one contact card, hold down the ⌘ key and click each additional contact you want to recover.

5. **If the contact you want to restore is nowhere to be found in the Address Book windows — or if you change your mind and don't want to recover a backed up contact — click the Cancel button in the lower-left corner (or press the Escape key).**

Time Machine closes and returns you to the present.

6. **The Time Machine Address Book window zooms forward and then closes, returning you to the Address Book application window, which now includes the recovered contact card (or cards).**

That's it — you've been saved!

You can search within Time Machine to locate the file you want to retrieve from a previous backup by typing in a search term in the search field in the upper-right corner. You can also use Spotlight Search from the Finder, and then click the Time Machine icon in the Dock or Launchpad. When you find the file you want, select it and click the Restore button. The item is placed in its original location.

Retrieving files and/or folders by using the Finder

To use the Finder window to retrieve files, folders, or a combination of both with the Time Machine restore application, follow these steps:

1. **Click the Time Machine icon in the Dock or on the Launchpad (or click the Time Machine icon on the menu bar and choose Enter Time Machine) to run the Time Machine restore application, as shown in Figure 1-9.**

2. **Choose one of the following ways to locate the file or folder from the past that you want to recover by using the Finder window:**

- *Click the Backward and Forward arrow buttons near the bottom-right corner of the screen.* Click the Backward button to move the Finder window backward in time to previous Time Machine backups. Click the Forward button to work your way forward to more recent Time Machine backups.

- *Click a Finder window behind the frontmost Finder window.* Each time you click a Finder window, Time Machine moves it forward to the front of the screen.

- *Move the pointer to the Time Machine timeline along the right edge of the screen.* The timeline bars expand to display a specific date. To choose a specific date, click it.

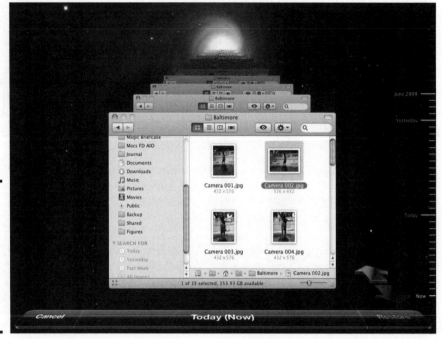

Figure 1-9:
Use Time
Machine's
Finder
window to
choose files
or folders
you want to
recover.

To take a peek at the contents of a particular document, picture, audio
track, or other file, click it and then press the Spacebar to open the
Quick Look view (see Figure 1-10), which gives you a speedy way to
view the contents of your selected file to make sure that it's the one
you really want to recover. The filetype needs to be one that QuickLook
understands. QuickLook can't read some database applications, such as
FileMaker and Bento, nor most CAD documents.

3. **When you locate the data you want to recover, select the file or folders, click the Restore button in the bottom-right corner of the screen,
   and then proceed to Step 5.**

   To select more than one file or folder, hold down the ⌘ key and click
   each additional item you want to recover.

4. **If the data you want to recover is nowhere to be found in the Finder
   windows — or if you change your mind and don't want to recover
   backup data — click the Cancel button in the bottom-left corner (or
   press the Escape key).**

   The Time Machine recovery application closes and you return to the
   present.

**Book III
Chapter 1**

Figure 1-10:
Select a
file icon
and then
press the
Spacebar
to preview
the file's
contents
with the
Quick Look
view.

5. **The Time Machine Finder window zooms forward and then closes, safely returning you to a Finder window that now includes your recovered file or folder.**

   Consider yourself saved!

Restoring your entire backup

If your system or start-up disk is damaged, you may have to restore your entire backup to your Mac. If you use Time Machine, you're worry free. Here's how to restore your Mac with Time Machine:

1. **Connect the backup drive to your computer.**

   If you use a networked drive, make sure that your computer and the drive are on the same network.

2. **Select menu⇨Restart and hold down ⌘+R while your Mac restarts.**

   If you can't access the menu, that is your Mac is off and won't boot, hold down ⌘-R and press the On button. See Book III, Chapter 3 for more information about troubleshooting.

Backing Up and
Restoring Your Data
with Time Machine

3. **Choose the language you use when the language chooser appears, and then click the arrow button (continue).**

4. **Select Restore from a Time Machine Backup, and click Continue.**

5. **Choose the drive where your backup is stored:**

   • Select the external drive and click Continue.

   • Select Time Capsule or the networked drive and click Connect to Remote Disk.

6. **Enter the username and password if requested.**

7. **Select the date and time of the backup you want to use.**

   Time Machine begins copying your backup from the drive to your Mac.

8. **Breathe a sigh of relief that you backup regularly!**

Moving Your Backup from an Old Mac to a New Mac

Sooner or later, your Mac will be outdated and you'll want to move your files to a new Mac. Apple has a handy application called Migration Assistant to perform this task. You can transfer your files directly by connecting one Mac to the other with a FireWire cable or over a network. If the old Mac is kaput, however, you can use your Time Machine to back up. Follow these steps:

1. **On the new Mac, click the Launchpad icon in the Dock, and then click the Utilities folder and click Migration Assistant.**

   The Migration Assistant Introduction dialog opens, as shown in Figure 1-11.

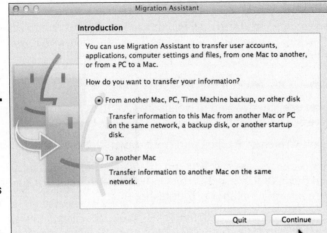

Figure 1-11: Migration Assistant transfers your existing files to your new Mac.

2. **Select the From Another Mac, PC, Time Machine Backup, or Other Disk option button and then click Continue.**

   Enter the password for your computer, if asked. The Select a Migration Method dialog opens.

3. **Choose the From a Time Machine Backup or Other Disk option button and click Continue.**

   Migration Assistant searches for external drives.

4. **Select the drive from which you want to transfer your backup.**

5. **Select the information you want to transfer, as shown in Figure 1-12.**

   - *Users* include all the user's media, documents, messages, contacts, and calendars.

   - *Applications* transfers applications that are compatible with the new Mac.

   - *Settings* transfers personal settings. Check Computer to transfer your desktop image and other personal settings, check Network (not shown in the figure) to transfer your network settings.

6. **Click Continue.**

   Migration Assistant begins transferring the selected files.

Book III
Chapter 1

Backing Up and Restoring Your Data with Time Machine

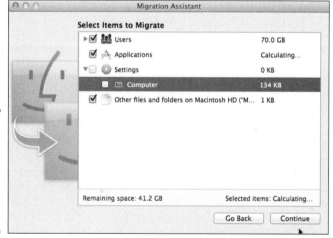

Figure 1-12: Choose the files, applications, and settings you want to transfer.

If your new Mac has a newer operating system than your old Mac, applications that aren't compatible with the new operating system may not work or even be transferred. Choose ⇨Software Update to find and install any application updates that are compatible with the operating system of your new Mac.

Working with Data-Recovery Programs

Data-recovery applications work by taking advantage of the way computers store and organize files by physically placing them in certain areas, known as *sectors,* on your Mac's internal hard drive (or removable storage device). To find out more about the nitty-gritty of how hard drives manage files, check out the nearby sidebar, "Hard drive: A tale of control, corruption, and redemption."

Suppose you're a well-protected Mac user who backs up your data regularly. You're completely safe, right, and you never have to worry about losing files you can't retrieve? Not exactly. Here are three situations where backup applications can't help you, and you might need to rely on special data-recovery applications instead:

+ **Accidentally deleted from the hard drive:** The most common way to lose a file is by accidentally deleting it. If you try to recover your lost file through a backup application, such as Time Machine, you might be shocked to find that your backup application can recover only a version of your file from the previous hour or older, but not from the span of time between Time Machine backups. So if you spent the last 45 minutes changing a file and accidentally deleted it before Time Machine could run its next automatic backup, you're out of luck if you want to recover the changes you made in the last 45 minutes.

+ **Hardware failure:** Another way to lose a file is through a hardware failure, such as your hard drive mangling portions of its disk surface. If a power outage knocked out your Mac without properly shutting it down first, any open files that you were working on or that were stored may be corrupted. Such a failure can go unnoticed because the hard drive still works. As a result, your backup application copies and saves these mangled versions of your file. The moment you discover your file is corrupted, you also find that your backup application has been diligently copying and saving the same corrupted version of your file.

+ **Deleted from removable media:** You might lose data by deleting it from removable media, such as a USB flash drive or digital camera flash memory card (such as a Compact Flash or Secure Digital card). Most likely, your backup applications protect only your hard drive files, not any removable storage devices, which means that you could take 20 priceless pictures of your dog doing midair back-flip Frisbee catches, only to delete all those pictures by mistake (and tanking your dog's chances at YouTube stardom). Because your backup application might never have saved those files, you can't recover what was never saved.

Even if you format and erase your entire hard drive, your files may still physically remain on the hard drive, making it possible to recover those files.

Hard drive: A tale of control, corruption, and redemption

To keep track of where each file is stored, your Mac maintains a directory that tells the computer the names of every file and the exact physical location where each file begins. Files are divided into blocks and (typically) the end of each block contains a pointer to the next block of that file. This division is transparent to you, the user, and when you open a file, you see all the blocks together. When different applications, such as word processors or spreadsheets, need to find and open a file, these applications depend on the Mac operating system to keep track of this directory so they know where to find a file.

When you delete a file, the computer simply removes that file's name from the directory. The blocks that make up your file still physically exist on the disk surface, but the computer can't find and assemble them again. Therefore data-recovery applications ignore the disk's directory listing and search for a file by examining every part of the entire storage device to find your missing files, locating the beginning of the first block and then following the pointers at the end of each block that indicate the beginning of the next one, creating a chain of blocks that make up the whole file.

If you didn't add any files since you last deleted the file you want to retrieve, a data-recovery application will likely retrieve your entire file again. If you saved and modified files since you last deleted a particular file, there's a good chance any new or modified files might have written over the area that contains your deleted file. In this case, your chances of recovering the entire file intact drops rapidly over time.

If a hardware failure corrupts a file, all or part of your file might be wiped out for good. However, in many cases, a hardware failure won't physically destroy all or part of a file. Instead, a hardware failure might physically scramble a file, much like throwing a pile of clothes all over the room. In this case, the file still physically exists, but the directory of the disk won't know where all the parts of the file have been scattered. So, to the computer, your files have effectively disappeared.

A data-recovery application can piece together scattered files by examining the physical surface of a disk, gathering up file fragments, and putting them back together again like Humpty Dumpty. Depending on how badly corrupted a file might be, collecting file fragments and putting them back together can recover an entire file or just part of a file, but sometimes recovering part of a file can be better than losing the whole file.

Some popular data-recovery applications include:

✦ **Disk Warrior 4 (**www.alsoft.com/DiskWarrior**; $100):** Builds a new replacement directory, using data recovered from the original directory, thereby recovering files, folders, and documents that you thought were gone forever.

✦ **FileSalvage (**www.subrosasoft.com**; $80):** FileSalvage retrieves deleted and corrupted files from your Mac's hard drive.

- ✦ **Stellar Phoenix Macintosh Recovery** (www.stellarinfo.com; **$99):** Stellar Phoenix Macintosh retrieves deleted and corrupted files.

- ✦ **Klix** (www.joesoft.com; **$20):** Specialized application for recovering lost digital images stored on flash memory cards, such as Secure Digital or Compact Flash cards.

- ✦ **Data Rescue III** (www.prosofteng.com; **$99):** This application recovers and retrieves data from a hard drive your Mac can no longer access because of a hard disk failure.

- ✦ **Mac Data Recovery** (www.macdiskrecovery.net; **$69):** This application specializes in recovering files from corrupted or reformatted hard drives.

The art of computer forensics

Most anything you store on your Mac can be recovered, given enough time and money. When most people lose data, they're thankful when a data-recovery application can retrieve their files. However, in the criminal world, people may want to delete files so that nobody can ever find them again, to hide evidence. To retrieve such deleted files, law enforcement agencies rely on something called computer forensics.

The basic idea behind computer forensics is to make an exact copy of a hard drive and then try to piece together the deleted files on that copy of the original hard drive. Some criminals have lit hard drives on fire, poured acid on them, and sliced them apart with a buzz saw — and law enforcement agencies still managed to read and recover portions of the files from the slivers of hard-drive fragments that contained magnetic traces of the original files.

The good news is that if you can't recover a file yourself by using a data-recovery application, you can often hire a professional service that can recover your data for you — but that data better be really important to you, because data-recovery services are very expensive.

Chapter 2: Syncing All Your Devices with iCloud

In This Chapter

↙ **Setting up an iCloud account**

↙ **Using iCloud to manage your data**

↙ **Considering other online storage solutions**

The days of writing birthdays into a new calendar and rewriting your address book over the course of several long winter evenings are gone. You may have replaced the paper-based agenda with a calendar and address book on your mobile phone or perhaps you use iCal and Address Book on your Mac. Maybe you use both but the information is a mixed bag of personal appointments on your Mac and business appointments on your mobile phone and current names and addresses scattered among your Mac, phone, and some scraps of paper stuck on the refrigerator with a smiley-face magnet.

If you use both a Mac and iPhone, you probably avoid this problem by connecting your iPhone to your Mac with the USB connector cable or via a Wi-Fi connection and syncing with iTunes. Now, Apple has made syncing automatic with iCloud. iCloud is a remote storage service for your Mac and other Apple devices, such as iPhones, iPads, and iPods, and PCs too. iCloud stores your iTunes collection of music and television shows, contacts, calendars, e-mail, notes, apps, and books. A free iCloud account gives you 5 gigabyes of storage — but your iTunes collection and photos don't count toward that amount. (You can purchase additional storage for a yearly fee if necessary.) In PhotoStream, iCloud stores up to 1,000 photos from the last 30 days. You can access all this data from your Mac, Windows computer, and other iOS 5 devices.

In this chapter, we show you how to set up and use iCloud. At the end of the chapter, we also give you some suggestions for other online storage options, in case iCloud doesn't quite meet your needs.

Keeping Your Data in the iCloud

If you were a MobileMe user, you already know a bit about iCloud because Apple made it possible to switch MobileMe accounts to iCloud accounts as of October 12, 2011. If you didn't have a MobileMe account, you may want to set up an iCloud account. Here are some situations where an iCloud can make your life easier:

✦ You want to keep a backup of your iTunes music and television show collections.

✦ You use both a Mac and an iOS 5 device such as an iPhone, iPad, or iPod.

✦ You want to access your Address Book, Calendar, and Mail from more than one computer — Mac or Windows — say one for work and one at home.

✦ You keep a calendar that other people need to see and maybe even edit.

Setting up an iCloud account

Before you can upload your songs, calendar, and contacts to iCloud, you have to set up an account. You can use your AppleID or iTunes Account as long as it uses an e-mail address format, such as *janedoe@me.com*. If not, you must set up an iCloud account. Follow these steps:

1. Choose ⌘⇨System Preferences and then click the iCloud button under the Internet & Wireless section.

The window shown in Figure 2-1 appears.

Figure 2-1:
Set up
an iCloud
account to
use iCloud.

2. Enter your Apple ID and password if you have one or click Create Apple ID.

If you create an Apple ID, the first window asks for your location and birthday. Use the pop-up menus to provide this information.

The second window asks if you want to use an existing e-mail address or create a free @me.com e-mail address. Enter an existing e-mail address or type in the e-mail address you'd like to have with @me.com, and then type in your first and last name, a password, and a secret question. If your name isn't available, Apple will give you a list of available e-mail addresses that are similar to your request.

3. **Click Next.**

   iCloud asks which services you want to use, as shown in Figure 2-2.

Figure 2-2: Choose which services you want to use with iCloud.

Book III Chapter 2

Syncing All Your Devices with iCloud

4. **Select the first check box to upload your contacts, calendars, and bookmarks to iCloud; select the second check box if you want iCloud to use your location to find your Mac, in the event you lose it.**

5. **Click Next.**

6. **The iCloud preferences window opens, as shown in Figure 2-3.**

7. **Place a check mark next to each type of data you want stored on iCloud for you.**

   The data is pushed to the iCloud storage on line.

8. **(Optional) Click Manage if you want purchase additional storage, see how much storage each section of iCloud occupies, or view your Apple ID account information.**

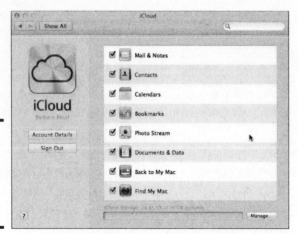

Figure 2-3:
Choose the
type of data
you want
to store on
iCloud.

Using iCloud

The initial setup on your Mac both activated your iCloud account and placed
a copy of the data you selected in iCloud preferences from your Mac to
the cloud. Here, we show you how to sign in to and use the iCloud website.
First, consider how the different types of data are treated in slightly
different ways:

✦ **Mail and Notes:** You can sign in to the iCloud website and do all your
  e-mail correspondence there. However, if you have multiple e-mail
  addresses, you may prefer to manage them all within Mail on your Mac.
  E-mail that you send and receive in the iCloud e-mail account will appear
  in Mail — not only on your Mac, but also on iCloud and your other iOS 5
  devices. In this case, you want to add the e-mail address you use for
  your iCloud account to Mail. Read about how to add accounts to Mail
  in Book II, Chapter 2. (If your iCloud e-mail account is already in Mail,
  you're set to go.)

  Mail on iCloud has a more simplistic user interface, as shown in Figure 2-4.
  Click the icons above the right pane to create new messages, reply, forward, and delete. Messages are managed in folders in the first column
  on the left. Clicking and dragging moves messages around. Any changes
  made on Mail in iCloud, on your Mac, or on another iOS device will
  appear in the other places simultaneously (as long as the other devices
  are connected to the Internet).

✦ **Contacts:** From this point forward, make any changes to Contacts
  (Address Book on your Mac) on the iCloud website. Contacts on iCloud
  looks and works just like Address Book on your Mac. Go to Book V,
  Chapter 1 to read about using Address Book.

Figure 2-4:
Mail on iCloud is a slimmed-down version of Mail on your Mac.

✦ **Calendars:** From this point forward, make any changes to iCal on the iCloud website. iCal on iCloud looks and works just like iCal on your Mac. Go to Book V, Chapter 2 to read about using iCal. You can set up public and private sharing privileges for your iCal calendars:

- *Public:* Your calendar may be viewed by anyone to whom you give the URL address for the public calendar.

- *Private*: Only other iCloud account holders can open your calendar. You can set View Only or View and Edit privileges for the calendar.

✦ **Bookmarks:** iCloud syncs bookmarks from Safari on your Mac with Safari on your iOS devices.

✦ **PhotoStream:** PhotoStream is activated in iPhoto. (See Book IV, Chapter 3 to find out about using PhotoStream in iCloud.)

✦ **Documents and Data:** iCloud stores any documents that are created in iOS 5-compatible apps, such as Pages, Keynote, and Numbers. Click and drag your documents from your Mac to the Documents section of iCloud. You can place MS-Office documents on iCloud, but they can then only be opened in the corresponding iWorks application.

After you place a document in iCloud, if you delete it from iCloud, it is also deleted from your Mac.

✦ **Back to my Mac:** This feature lets you see your Mac from another Mac. Click ⌘⇨System Preferences and choose Sharing under the Internet and

Wireless section. Choose the things you want to share, such as Screen Sharing and File Sharing. From the other Mac, choose Finder from the Dock (select File⇨New Finder Window if one doesn't appear). Click the disclosure button next to Shared in the sidebar, and then click your Mac. See Book VI, Chapter 2 for more information about sharing.

✦ **Find My Mac:** In the tragic event that your Mac is stolen or just lost beneath a pile of unfolded laundry on the bed, you can access your iCloud account from another computer or iOS 5 device and choose to make the Mac sound an alarm (to scare the thief or your laundry) or make a message appear across your Mac's screen that perhaps says "This Mac is lost, please call 555-1212 to return it to its rightful owner." Your Mac must be awake and connected to Wi-Fi for Find My Mac to work.

If you use a Windows PC in addition to your Mac, you can download the iCloud Control Panel for Windows (Vista SP2 or later or Windows 7) at `http://support.apple.com/kb/DL1455`, which enables iCloud storage and syncing in Windows. To manage your data on iCloud, you have to go to the iCloud website. Follow these steps:

1. **Click the Safari icon in the Dock or on the Launchpad. (Refer to Book II, Chapter 1 to read about getting on the Internet and using Safari.)**

2. **Type** `www.icloud.com` **in the URL field in Safari.**

The iCloud website opens with the sign in fields, as shown in Figure 2-5.

Figure 2-5:
Sign in to your iCloud account at www.icloud.com.

3. **Type in your Apple ID or the e-mail you used when you set up your iCloud account, and then type your password.**

4. **(Optional) Select the Keep Me Signed In check box if you want to stay connected to iCloud even when you go to other websites or quit Safari.**

5. **Press the Enter key or click on the arrow button.**

   Your name appears in the upper-right corner and icons that take you to your activated services appear in the window, as shown in Figure 2-6.

6. **Click any of the icons to go to the data you want. For example, click Mail.**

   The Mail window opens (refer to Figure 2-4).

7. **Click the cloud button in the upper-left corner to return to the opening iCloud web page.**

Figure 2-6: Click the icons to go the data you want.

Book III Chapter 2

Syncing All Your Devices with iCloud

What about iTunes?

You might have noticed that iTunes isn't mentioned in the iCloud preferences under System Preferences nor is there an iTunes icon on the iCloud website. Nonetheless, all your iTunes purchases are automatically stored in iCloud and you can set up iTunes to automatically download your purchases to all your devices, regardless of which device you use to make your purchase. Songs you didn't purchase through iTunes are not stored in iCloud. If you have a lot of songs that weren't purchased through iTunes, you may want to consider purchasing iTunes Match for $25 per year. iTunes Match downloads all songs you own that you didn't purchase from iTunes (but that exist in the iTunes Store) to your iTunes purchase history. You get the advantage of having iTunes quality songs included in the iCloud storage. See Book IV, Chapter 1 for more information about using iTunes.

Other Online Storage and Syncing Services

iCloud is fairly Apple specific when it comes to online storage. We think it's great for syncing your Mac with other Apple devices and data you have in iTunes, contacts, and calendars. However, there are other online storage and syncing services that might offer a better solution for your document storage and sharing, especially if you don't use iOS 5–compatible applications and if you want to remove documents from the online storage but keep them on your Mac. Most of the following websites have a free option that offers 5 gigabytes of storage and then paid options for more storage:

✦ **SugarSync:** www.sugarsync.com

✦ **Evernote:** www.evernote.com

✦ **Elephant Drive:** www.elephantdrive.com

✦ **Box.net:** www.box.net

If you don't use an iPhone but would still like to sync your mobile phone and your Mac, try these products:

✦ **The Missing Sync:** www.markspace.com

✦ **PocketMac:** www.pocketmac.com

Chapter 3: Maintenance and Troubleshooting

In This Chapter

✔ Taking care of application freezes and hang-ups

✔ Fixing startup troubles

✔ Troubleshooting disk problems and repairs

✔ Unjamming jammed CDs/DVDs

✔ Making your Mac perform routine maintenance

*N*o matter how well designed and well built a Mac is, it's still a machine, and all machines are liable to break down through no fault of yours. Many times, you can fix minor problems with a little bit of knowledge and willingness to poke and prod around your Mac. If your Mac isn't working correctly, you can check obvious things first, like making sure it's plugged in and that any connecting cables to your Mac are plugged in and secure. However, sometimes your Mac might be in more serious trouble than you can fix, so don't be afraid to take your Mac into your friendly neighborhood computer-repair store (one that specializes in repairing Macs, of course).

Luckily, Apple and third-party developers have created applications that analyze, diagnose, and repair problems on your Mac. In this chapter, we begin by addressing one of the most common problems — applications freezing. We then get down to more serious problems related to your Mac not starting up properly or your hard drive acting strangely. We explain how to use the Recovery and Disk Utility applications that came with your Mac and give you suggestions for third-party applications to consider. We close the chapter by showing you how to remove a jammed CD or DVD from the disc drive, and then give you suggestions for preventive maintenance.

 Only open your Mac if you know what you're doing. If you open the case and start fiddling around with its electronic insides, you might damage your Mac — and invalidate your Mac's warranty.

Shutting Down Frozen or Hung-Up Programs

Programs that always run perfectly might suddenly stop working for no apparent reason, and no matter which keys you press, where you click the mouse, or where you tap the trackpad, nothing happens. Sometimes you might see a spinning cursor (affectionately referred to as the "spinning beach ball of death"), which stays onscreen and refuses to go away until you take steps to unlock the frozen application.

Sometimes being patient and waiting a few minutes results in the hung-up application resolving whatever was ailing it as though nothing was wrong in the first place. More often, however, the spinning cursor keeps spinning in an oh-so-annoying fashion. To end the torment, you need to *force-quit* the frozen or hung-up application — basically, you shut the application down so that the rest of your Mac can get back to work. To force-quit an application, use one of the following methods:

✦ Right-click the application's icon on the Dock and choose Force Quit from the menu that appears. If you use a trackpad, hold down the Option key and perform a two-finger tap on the application icon in the Dock and choose Force Quit from the menu.

✦ Choose ⌘⊏➪Force Quit to display the Force Quit Applications dialog, as shown in Figure 3-1. Then select the name of the hung-up application and click the Force Quit button.

✦ Press ⌘+Option+Esc to display the Force Quit Applications dialog (see Figure 3-1). Then select the name of the hung-up application and click the Force Quit button.

✦ Load the Activity Monitor application (located inside the Utilities folder in the Launchpad), select the process name, and then choose View➪Quit Process. A Quit Process dialog appears. Click Force Quit.

One of the best ways to avoid problems with applications and the Mac operating system is to keep them updated. Set Software Update to check automatically for updates on a daily, weekly, or monthly basis. Choose ⌘⊏➪Software Update, and then choose Software Update➪Preferences to open the Software Update dialog, as shown in Figure 3-2. Choose the interval at which you want your Mac to check for updates. Some applications, such as MS-Office and HP Print Utility, have automatic-update options in their preferences, too. You can also check for updates in the App Store for any apps you downloaded from there. (See Book I, Chapter 3 for information about the App Store.)

Figure 3-1: Choose an application to force-quit.

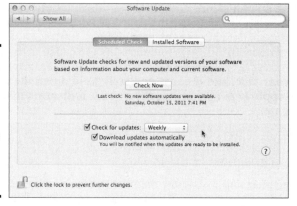

Figure 3-2:
Keeping your operating system and applications updated helps avoid problems.

Handling Startup Troubles

Sometimes you might press the power button to turn on your Mac and nothing seems to happen. Other times, you might press the power button and see the usual Apple logo on the screen, and *then* nothing happens from that point on.

Before you rush your Mac to the emergency room of Mac repairs, do some simple troubleshooting yourself. At the very least, be sure to back up your important files — before you have any troubles — so you won't lose them if you wind up sending your Mac to the repair shop. (Read about backing up in Book III, Chapter 1.)

Booting up in Safe Mode

If you turn on your Mac and you can't see the familiar Desktop, menu bar, and Dock, don't panic. The first thing to do is try to boot up your Mac in what's called *Safe Mode,* a boot sequence that loads the bare minimum of the Mac OS X operating system, just enough to get your computer running.

Many startup problems occur when nonessential applications, such as appointment reminders, automatically load at login time and wind up interfering with other startup applications, preventing your Mac from booting up correctly. Other startup applications load before you see the login screen or the Desktop (if you've set your Mac to bypass the login window automatically and go directly to the Desktop when it starts up). Booting up in Safe Mode cuts all the nonessential pre- and post-login applications out of the loop; only your core applications load. A successful boot in Safe Mode at least tells you that your Mac's core system hasn't been compromised.

By booting up your Mac in Safe Mode, you can remove any applications you recently installed, turn off any startup options you may have activated, and then restart to see whether that fixes the boot-up problems. If you remove recently installed applications and deactivate startup options and problems persist, copy any important files from your hard drive to a backup drive to protect your crucial data in case the hard drive is starting to fail (see Book III, Chapter 1). Follow these steps to determine the cause of the problem:

1. **Turn on your Mac, and then immediately hold down the Shift key until the Apple logo appears on the screen, indicating that your Mac is booting up.**

   If your Mac is on but not responding, hold down the power button until your Mac restarts, and then immediately hold down the Shift key until the Apple logo appears on the screen.

   If your Mac starts up, you know the problem isn't with the Mac OS itself but with something else on your Mac. Move on to Step 2 to repair it.

2. **To turn off startup options, go to ⌘⇨System Preferences and click Users & Groups in the System section.**

   The Users & Groups window, shown in Figure 3-3, opens.

3. **Click your username in the column on the left.**

4. **Click the Login Items tab at the top of the right side of the window.**

   A list of the items that open automatically when you log in appears (refer to Figure 3-3).

5. **Deselect one.**

6. **Click the Close button.**

7. **Choose ⌘⇨Restart.**

   If your Mac restarts without a problem, you know that the startup item you deselected was the problem.

   If your Mac doesn't restart, repeat Steps 1 through 5, each time deselecting the next login item on the list until your Mac restarts without a problem.

Figure 3-3: Deselect login items to determine which one might be causing problems.

Uninstalling applications

If the problem isn't resolved by removing startup items, the next thing to try is to uninstall any applications you recently installed. Sometimes uninstalling is as simple as dragging the application icon from the Applications folder to the Trash (we talk about that in Book I, Chapter 3) — sometimes that's not the case. Just as there are *installers* that install applications on your Mac, there are also *uninstallers*.

When you install an application, you see the application icon in the Applications folder (and on the Launchpad), but there are also files associated with the application that the installer places in other folders on your Mac, such as the System and Library folders. To make sure that you throw away all the associated files, you need to run the uninstaller. To find the uninstaller associated with the application you suspect is causing your problems, click the Spotlight Search button in the upper-right corner and type in Uninstall. A list appears similar to that in Figure 3-4. Double-click the uninstaller you want to run. A window may open, asking for your login password or telling you that your Mac has to reboot. Either way, follow the onscreen instructions. If your Mac reboots successfully afterward, you know that the removed application was causing the problems. At that point, before reinstalling, visit the website of the problematic application to determine whether there's an update or information about incompatibility with your Mac model or operating system version. Try reinstalling from the disc if that's what you have; otherwise try downloading the application anew and installing a new copy.

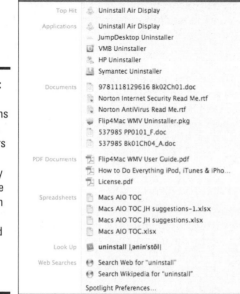

Figure 3-4: Some applications come with uninstallers that completely remove the application and associated files from your hard drive.

Repairing and Maintaining Hard Drives

If the problem isn't because of other applications trying to load when you turn on your Mac, you might have a more serious problem with your hard drive. Hard drives can fail for a number of reasons. A minor problem might involve scrambled data on your hard drive that confuses your Mac and makes it impossible to read data from it. If data is scrambled, you can often reorganize your data with a special utility diagnostic and repair application, such as Disk Utility on your Mac or DiskWarrior (www.alsoft.com/DiskWarrior) to get your hard drive back in working condition.

A more serious problem could be physical damage to your hard drive. If a disk utility application fails to repair any problems on your hard drive, this might be a sign that your hard drive's surface is physically damaged. When this occurs, your only option is to copy critical files from the damaged hard drive (if possible), replace it with a new one, and then restore your most recent Time Machine backup (you *are* backing up, aren't you?) to the new hard drive so you're back in business again as though nothing (or almost nothing) went kaput in the first place.

To find out how to use Time Machine to back up your Mac's hard drive, check out Book III, Chapter 1. As further loss prevention insurance, you can create a clone of your Mac's hard drive by using an application such as SuperDuper! (www.shirt-pocket.com/SuperDuper/SuperDuperDescription.html).

The Disk Utility application that comes free with every Mac — tucked away in the Utilities folder inside the Applications folder or on the Launchpad — can examine your hard drive. However, to fix any problems it might find, you have to boot your Mac from a different hard drive or bootable USB flash drive, from the Recovery drive, or from the Mac OS X Install DVD that came with your Mac.

Empty the Trash every now and then to eliminate files that you throw away from the Trash's temporary storage. Control-click or right-click (two-finger tap on the trackpad) the Trash icon on the dock and choose Empty Trash or choose Finder⇨Secure Empty Trash. You can't retrieve items thrown away with Secure Empty Trash unless they were backed up with an application like Time Machine.

Verifying a disk

If you suspect that your hard drive might be scrambled or physically damaged, you can run the Disk Utility application to verify your suspicions. When using Disk Utility, select a device and choose one of the following:

+ **Verify Disk:** Checks to make sure that all the files on that device are neatly organized.

+ **Verify Disk Permissions:** Checks to make sure that relevant files, installed with the operating system and with each application installed or updated by using Apple's Installer, maintain the permissions originally assigned. (Permissions apply only to your startup disc.)

The Disk Utility application can verify and repair all types of storage devices (except optical discs such as CDs and DVDs), including hard drives, flash drives, and other types of removable storage media, such as compact flash cards.

To verify a disk, follow these steps:

1. **Load the Disk Utility application stored inside the Utilities folder on the Launchpad or choose Go⇨Utilities from the Desktop.**

    The Disk Utility window appears.

2. **Click the device (hard drive, flash drive, and so on) that you want to verify in the left pane of the Disk Utility window, as shown in Figure 3-5.**

3. **Make sure that the First Aid pane is visible. (If not, click the First Aid tab to call it up.)**

4. **Click the Verify Disk button.**

    The Disk Utility application examines your chosen device. If Disk Utility can't verify that a device is working, you see a message informing you that First Aid feature of Disk Utility has failed, as shown in Figure 3-6.

5. **Click OK and then click the Repair Disk button.**

    You can do this step only with a non-startup disk — to repair your Mac's startup disk, skip ahead to the next set of steps.

    Disk Utility tries to fix your device. If it succeeds, you see a message informing you that the device is repaired.

You can verify your hard drive to identify any problems, but you cannot repair your startup hard drive by using the copy of Disk Utility stored on your startup hard drive. To repair your startup hard drive, you need to perform a Recovery Boot or reinstall the operating system, as described in the following sections.

Figure 3-5:
The Disk
Utility
window lets
you pick
a drive to
examine.

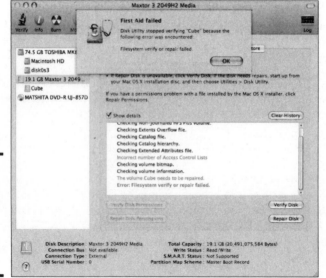

Figure 3-6:
Disk Utility
informs you
whether
a device
might need
repairing.

Performing a Recovery Boot

If you can't boot up from your hard drive, even in Safe Mode, or you can
boot in Safe Mode but can't boot in normal mode and any utility application
you run can't fix the problem, you might have to boot from the Recovery
drive. Mac OS X 10.7 Lion creates two partitions on your Mac's hard drive:

✦ One is what you see as your Mac hard drive, where everything you do with your Mac is stored.

✦ The other is the (unseen) Recovery drive, which contains a copy of the operating system and the Disk Utility application.

When you have problems, you can boot your Mac from the Recovery drive, which can then run the Disk Utility's Repair Disk feature on your Mac's primary hard drive, restore your hard drive from a Time Machine backup, or reinstall the operating system and return your Mac to its original out-of-the-box condition. (If you're using a Mac with an OS prior to OS X 10.7 Lion, see the sidebar "Booting from a DVD.")

To be on the safe side, you might want to download the Lion Recovery Disk Assistant (http://support.apple.com/kb/dl1433), which lets you create a Recovery Hard Drive on an external USB drive with least 1GB of storage. We advise you to have a dedicated USB thumb drive to store the Recovery Drive. In the event that your Mac won't boot at all, not even in Recovery mode, you can try booting from the Recovery Disk on the external drive. You can also purchase Lion on a USB thumb drive from Apple for $69.

Here's how to boot from the Recovery drive:

1. **Press the power key to turn on your Mac (or choose ⌘⇨Restart) and hold down ⌘+R until you see the Apple logo.**

The Mac OS X Utilities window opens, as shown in Figure 3-7.

2. **Select Disk Utility and then click Continue.**

3. **Select the Macintosh HD startup drive (or whatever your Mac's primary hard drive is named if you renamed it) in the left pane of the Disk Utility window.**

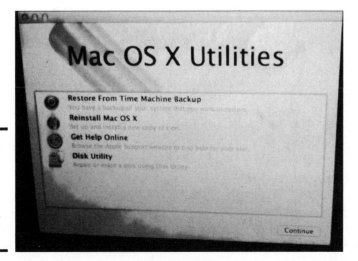

Figure 3-7: The Recovery drive may be able to repair your Mac.

The Mac OS X Base System is the Recovery Drive and you see that Repair Disk is gray because you can't repair the active system disk.

4. **Make sure that the First Aid pane is visible. (If not, click the First Aid tab to call it up.)**

5. **Click the Repair Disk button.**

   The Repair feature of Disk Utility does what it can to fix any problems on your hard drive and informs you of its success — or failure.

6. **Choose Disk Utility⇨Quit Disk Utility.**

   You see the Mac OS X Utilities window again.

7. **If the Disk Utility was able to repair your hard drive, choose ⌥⇨Restart.**

   Your Mac restarts and you continue doing what you were doing before the problems began.

If Recovery Boot doesn't solve your problem, you can boot from a troubleshooting disc that runs an application such as DriveGenius (www.prosofteng.com), TechTool Pro (www.micromat.com), or DiskWarrior (www.alsoft.com). By running any of these applications directly from the DVD or bootable USB flash drive, you can attempt to repair or resurrect any hard drive that fails to boot up on its own. Sometimes these troubleshooting DVDs can repair a hard drive, and sometimes they can't. If you have important files trapped on your hard drive, this option may be your only hope of retrieving your files to back them up before sending or taking your Mac to a repair service to repair or replace your Mac's hard drive.

You can use Safari to access the Internet from the Recovery disk. Before you go so far as reinstalling the operating system or erasing your Mac's hard drive, it's a good idea to consult the Apple Support website (www.apple.com/support) and discussion boards (http://discussions.apple.com/index.jspa) to see whether someone else has had the same problem you're having — and maybe solved it.

Reinstalling the operating system

If neither Disk Utility nor a troubleshooting application solves your problem, the next thing to try is reinstalling the operating system from the Recovery drive. To reinstall the operating system, follow these steps:

1. **Press the power key to turn on your Mac (or choose ⌥⇨Restart) and hold down ⌘+R until you see the Apple logo.**

   The Mac OS X Utilities window opens.

2. **Select Reinstall Mac OS X and click Continue.**

   You must be connected to the Internet to reinstall Mac OS X 10.7 Lion. Click the Wi-Fi icon in the status bar at the top of the screen to connect to your Wi-Fi network or connect via an Ethernet cable (see Book II, Chapter 1 to find out how to connect to the Internet).

3. **The installer verifies that you are a registered OS X Lion user.**

4. **Click Agree when the user agreement window appears.**

5. **Choose the hard drive where you want to reinstall and click Install.**

6. **Follow the onscreen instructions and type in any requested information such as username, e-mail, passwords, and so on.**

7. **When the installation is complete, your Mac restarts.**

Wipe out!

No one likes to reach this point, but if none of the procedures described in the earlier sections have solved your problem, you have to take drastic measures and completely erase (called *reformatting*) your hard drive, reinstall the operating system and applications, and restore your files from a backup. If you'd rather not take this step on your own, take your Mac to a trusted technician.

If you're ready to attempt to repair your Mac on your own by reformatting and starting over, here's how:

1. **Press the power key to turn on your Mac (or choose ⌘⇨Restart) and hold down ⌘+R until you see the Apple logo.**

   The Mac OS X Utilities window opens.

2. **Select Disk Utility, and then click Continue.**

3. **Select the Macintosh HD startup drive (or whatever your Mac's primary hard drive is named if you renamed it) in the left pane of the Disk Utility window.**

4. **Click the Erase tab at the top of the pane on the right.**

5. **Choose Mac OS Extended (Journaled) from the Format pop-up menu.**

6. **Click the Erase button.**

7. **When Disk Utility finishes erasing, choose Disk Utility⇨Quit Disk Utility.**

   The Mac OS X Utilities window appears.

8. **Click Reinstall Mac OS X, and then click Continue.**

   Follow Steps 3 through 7 in the preceding section, "Reinstalling the operating system."

   When your Mac restarts, it's as new as when you took it out of the box, a tabula rasa.

Booting from a DVD

If you're running Mac OS X 10.6.x or earlier, you might have to boot from a DVD. Use either the original Mac OS X Install disc that came with your Mac or the disc containing a newer version of Mac OS X that you used to upgrade your Mac's operating system.

Older Macs came with a DVD that contains the entire Mac OS X operating system. The purpose of this DVD is to let you run the Disk Utility application's Repair Disk feature on your Mac's primary hard drive, or to reinstall the operating system.

To boot your Mac from a DVD instead of letting your Mac attempt to boot from its own hard drive, follow these steps:

1. **Turn on your Mac.**

2. **Insert a DVD into your Mac, and wait for your Mac to boot up to the Desktop if it can.**

   If your Mac gets stuck and can't boot up to the Desktop, insert the DVD while your Mac is still on, hold down the Power button for five seconds until your Mac turns off, and then turn it on again and skip to Step 4.

3. **Choose ⇨ Restart.**

4. **After your Mac has shut down the Desktop and the screen goes blank, hold down the C key while your Mac restarts until you see the Apple logo, at which point you can release the C key.**

   This command tells your Mac to boot from the DVD instead of the hard drive.

5. **If you booted from a troubleshooting disc you purchased, follow the instructions on the screen.**

6. **If you booted from your Mac's original OS X Install disc (or a newer OS X Install disc**

you purchased to upgrade your Mac), continue here.

7. **Select the language you want to use and click the arrow button in the bottom-right corner of the window.**

   An OS X Installer Welcome window appears.

8. **Click the Utilities menu and choose Disk Utility.**

   The Disk Utility window appears.

9. **Select the Macintosh HD startup drive (or whatever your Mac's primary hard drive is named if you renamed it) in the left pane of the Disk Utility window.**

10. **Make sure that the First Aid pane is visible. (If not, click the First Aid tab to call it up.)**

11. **Click the Repair Disk button.**

    The Repair feature of Disk Utility does what it can to fix any problems on your hard drive and informs you of its success — or failure.

12. **Choose Disk Utility ⇨ Quit Disk Utility.**

    The Mac OS X Installer Welcome window appears again.

13. **Click the Mac OS X Installer menu, choose Quit Mac OS X Installer, and then click the Restart button to restart your Mac.**

14. **Hold down the Eject button while your Mac restarts to eject the Mac OS X Install disc.**

    If your Mac starts up normally and presents you with the Desktop, then Disk Utility managed to repair your Mac's hard drive successfully. Phew, crisis averted!

9. **Connect the external drive where your Time Machine backup is stored.**

10. **Restore your Time Machine backup to your Mac (as explained in Book III, Chapter 1).**

    Your Mac should be back to where it was before your problems began.

Erasing your hard drive and reinstalling the operating system from scratch will *also* wipe out any important files stored on your hard drive — *all* your files, in fact — so make sure that you're willing to accept this before erasing your hard drive. Ideally, you have a clone of your hard drive, or at least you should have all your important files backed up on a separate external drive, such as an external hard drive or a DVD, before wiping out your hard drive completely.

Another occasion when you may want to erase your hard drive and reinstall the operating system is if you plan on selling your Mac or giving it away. For security reasons, you want to wipe out your data with one of the secure-erase options in Disk Utility and return the Mac to its original condition so someone else can personalize the Mac.

Booting from another Mac through a FireWire cable

As an alternative to booting up from a DVD, you can also boot up from another Mac connected to your computer through a FireWire cable. A FireWire cable simply plugs into the FireWire ports of each Mac, connecting the two Macs together (provided, of course, that your Mac has a FireWire port; some models don't).

After connecting two Macs through a FireWire cable, you boot up the working Mac normally and boot up the other Mac in FireWire Target Mode. This makes the second Mac's hard drive appear as an external hard drive when viewed through the working Mac's Finder.

Using this approach, you can run a Disk Utility on the Target Mode Mac's hard drive (as described in the earlier section, "Verifying a disk") or you can run another hard-drive utility application (such as Tech Tools Pro, DriveGenius, or DiskWarrior) on the working Mac to rescue the hard drive of the defective Mac. This is much like jump-starting a car's dead battery by using a second car with a good battery.

To boot up from a second Mac connected by a FireWire cable, follow these steps:

1. **Connect the second Mac to your Mac with a FireWire cable.**

2. **Turn on the working Mac.**

3. **Turn on the Mac that's having startup troubles and hold down the T key.**

When the defective Mac's hard drive appears as an external drive on the working Mac, you can copy your important files from the hard drive or run a utility application to fix the hard drive on the defective Mac. After copying files or repairing the hard drive, you need to disconnect the FireWire cable and restart both Macs.

Verifying disk permissions

Disk permissions apply to your startup disk and define what each application's files are allowed to access and which users have access to which files. If permissions aren't correct, your files can become scrambled, which can cause your Mac to act erratically or prevent an application from launching.

Unlike repairing a hard drive, verifying and fixing disk permissions won't require you to boot up from a separate hard drive or DVD.

To verify disk permissions, follow these steps:

1. **Load the Disk Utility application (stored inside the Utilities folder in the Applications folder).**

The Disk Utility window appears.

2. **Select your Macintosh HD (or whatever you renamed your Mac's hard drive if you changed the name) in the left pane of the Disk Utility window.**

3. **Make sure that the window is on the First Aid pane. (If not, click the First Aid tab to call it up.)**

4. **Click Verify Disk Permissions.**

If Disk Utility finds any problems, it displays a message to let you know. Otherwise, it displays a message to let you know all permissions are okay, as shown in Figure 3-8.

5. **Click Repair Disk Permissions.**

Disk Utility displays any messages concerning permission problems it found and repaired.

6. **Choose Disk Utility➪Quit Disk Utility.**

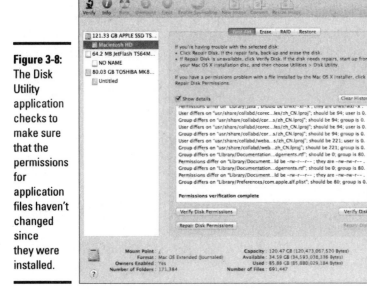

Figure 3-8:
The Disk
Utility
application
checks to
make sure
that the
permissions
for
application
files haven't
changed
since
they were
installed.

Removing Jammed CDs/DVDs

If a CD/DVD gets jammed in your Mac's CD/DVD drive, you can try one (or more) of the following methods to eject the stuck disc:

✦ Press the Eject key on your keyboard (if it has one, the MacBook Air, for example, does not because it doesn't have a disc drive).

✦ Drag the CD/DVD icon on the Desktop to the Trash icon in the Dock. (The Trash icon turns into an Eject icon to let you know that your Mac wants to eject the disc but does not intend to delete the information on the disc.)

✦ Choose ⚫➪Restart, and hold down the mouse or trackpad button while your Mac boots up.

✦ Click the Eject button next to the CD/DVD icon in the Sidebar of a Finder window (click the Mac-faced Finder icon in the Dock to open a new Finder window).

✦ Click the Eject button next to the CD/DVD icon in iTunes.

✦ Choose Controls➪Eject DVD from inside the DVD Player application.

✦ Load the Disk Utility application (located in the Utilities folder inside the Applications folder), click the CD/DVD icon, and click the Eject icon.

✦ Select the CD/DVD icon on the Desktop and choose File⬭Eject from the main menu.

✦ Select the CD/DVD icon on the Desktop and press ⌘+E.

✦ Control-click the CD/DVD icon on the Desktop and choose Eject from the menu that appears.

Although it might be tempting, don't jam tweezers, a flathead screwdriver, or any other object inside your CD/DVD drive to pry out a jammed disc. Not only can this scratch the disc surface, but also it can physically damage the CD/DVD drive.

Prevention is the best medicine, so here a few pointers on how to avoid getting discs jammed in the drive in the first place:

✦ Do not use mini or business card CDs/DVDs or any other non-119mm optical discs in slot-loading drives.

✦ Be careful of using hand-applied labels on discs you put in the drive. These can easily jam or make the disc too thick to eject properly.

✦ If your Mac's disc drive is repeatedly acting strange or not working properly when you try to play a music CD or watch a DVD, it's possible that your disc drive is on its last legs and might have to be repaired or replaced. Stop using the drive and take (or send) your Mac to Apple or an authorized service provider for a checkup.

✦ If you use a lot of optical media (those are your CDs and DVDs), you may want to purchase an external tray-loading drive, which is not only faster and robust, but also easier to repair if something goes wrong.

Automating Preventive Maintenance

Your Mac has daily, weekly, and monthly maintenance tasks that it runs periodically early in the morning if you leave your Mac on at night. However, if your Mac is asleep during this time, it won't run these maintenance tasks. You can get out of bed before dawn every day and wake your Mac so it can run its maintenance tasks, or you can set up your Mac to run its daily, weekly, and monthly maintenance tasks automatically.

To automate running your Mac's preventive maintenance applications, consider getting an application called MainMenu (`http://mainmenuapp. com/pro.php`).

To force your Mac to run its maintenance tasks automatically, follow these steps:

1. **Load the Terminal application (located in the Utilities folder inside the Applications folder or on the Launchpad).**

The Terminal window appears, as shown in Figure 3-9.

2. **Type** sudo periodic daily **and then press Return.**

The Terminal window asks for your password.

To make your Mac run weekly or monthly maintenance tasks, type **sudo periodic weekly** or **sudo periodic monthly**, respectively. Weekly and monthly tasks can take a long time to run. You'll know when a maintenance task is done when you see the cryptic-looking prompt (such as *mycomputer$*) reappear.

3. **Type your password and then press Return.**

Wait until you see the Terminal prompt (such as *mycomputer$*) reappear.

4. **Choose Terminal⇨Quit Terminal.**

Figure 3-9:
Use
Terminal
to run
maintenance
tasks.

Chapter 4: Running Windows on a Mac

In This Chapter

✔ **Understanding why you might need Windows**

✔ **Giving your Mac a split personality with Boot Camp**

✔ **Running virtual machines**

✔ **Using CrossOver Mac**

*A*s much as you might enjoy using your Mac, sometimes you might need to run Windows because you need to use an application that runs only on Windows. Many applications are Windows-only, such as a retail store point-of-sale (POS) system or stock-picking application, as are many custom applications developed by a company for in-house use. When faced with this dilemma, you have a choice:

✦ You can buy a Windows PC and use that computer just to run the Windows application you need.

✦ You can run Windows on your Mac. Ever since Apple started using Intel processors, you've been able to turn your Mac into a Windows PC.

Don't worry — you don't have to wipe out your hard drive and eliminate the Mac OS to run Windows. You have ways to run Windows on your Mac that still let you use all the features that made you want to use a Mac in the first place.

If you need Windows to access Microsoft Exchange services such as address lists, calendar events, and e-mail, Mac OS X 10.7 Lion gives you access to this information through Mail, iCal, and Address Book. Therefore you might not need to install Windows after all.

Giving Your Mac a Split Personality with Boot Camp

To install Windows on a Mac, you can split your hard drive in two parts (called *partitions*), using one partition to install and run Windows and a second to keep using Mac OS X the way you've been using it. By storing two different operating systems on your hard drive, you can choose which operating system to use every time you turn on your Mac. To divide your hard drive into partitions and install Windows, Apple provides an application called Boot Camp.

If your Mac has a Boot Camp partition with Windows XP or Windows Vista that you created by using a prior version of OX, such as Snow Leopard 10.6 that you upgraded to Lion OS X 10.7, you can continue to use your Boot Camp partition, but you can't upgrade to Boot Camp 4.0. Boot Camp 4.0 works with Windows 7 only.

If the Lion upgrade installation process discovers a Boot Camp partition with Windows XP or Windows Vista, Lion leaves the prior version of Boot Camp 3.0 on your Mac so you can continue using either of those Windows operating systems.

To use Boot Camp with Windows 7, you need the following:

✦ An Intel-based Mac

✦ 2GB (gigabytes) of RAM

✦ Internet access

✦ Mac OS X 10.6 Snow Leopard, or OS X Lion

✦ A USB keyboard and mouse or trackpad

✦ An authentic, single, full-installation, 32-bit or 64-bit Microsoft Windows 7 Home Premium, Professional, or Ultimate disc

✦ A built-in optical disc drive or a compatible external optical drive

✦ 16GB of available hard-drive space for 32-bit or 20GB of available hard-drive space for 64-bit

✦ Administrator account in Mac OS X to configure Boot Camp Assistant, located in `/Applications/Utilities`

✦ A blank CD or DVD, USB storage device, or external drive formatted as MS-DOS (FAT) to install the downloaded drivers

To format an external drive as MS-DOS (FAT), use Disk Utility in the Utilities folder.

Follow these basic steps to use Boot Camp:

1. **Make sure that your Mac can run Boot Camp.**

2. **Download and save the supplementary Windows drivers to a blank CD or DVD, USB storage device, or external drive formatted as MS-DOS (FAT).**

3. **Create a partition on your hard drive and install Windows.**

The following sections give the details you need to complete these steps.

Making sure that you can run Boot Camp

If you have a new Mac, chances are very good that you can run Boot Camp. However, the older your Mac is, the lower your chances of using this application.

Identifying the hardware capabilities of your Mac

To identify the processor, firmware version, and version number of the Mac OS X operating system running on your computer, follow these steps:

1. **Click the Apple menu and choose About This Mac.**

   An About This Mac window, shown in Figure 4-1, appears.

2. **Make sure that the processor type contains the word *Intel*, such as Intel Core 2 Duo.**

   If the processor type contains the term *PowerPC,* you can't use Boot Camp.

3. **Make sure that the version number for Mac OS X is 10.6 or higher to use BootCamp 4 (BootCamp 3 is compatible with Mac OS 10.5 or higher).**

   If the version number is lower, such as 10.4, you can't use Boot Camp until you acquire and install a newer version of Mac OS X.

4. **Click the Close button of the About This Mac window.**

**Book III
Chapter 4**

Running Windows on a Mac

Figure 4-1:
The About This Mac window identifies the processor type and version of Mac OS X.

Identifying the amount of free space on your hard drive

You need at least 16GB to 20GB of free space on your hard drive to install both Boot Camp and Windows. To find out how much free space you have on your hard drive, click the Finder icon in the Dock and, in the Finder window that opens, click the Macintosh HD icon in the sidebar. If you look at the status bar at the bottom of the Finder window, you can see how much space is available on your hard drive.

Installing Windows

When you confirm that your Mac can run Boot Camp, you need to go
through two more steps before you can install Windows. First, you need
to partition your hard drive. This reserves a chunk of your hard drive for
Windows. Some good news here: Creating a partition and installing Windows
on your computer are tasks you have to do only once (unless your hard
drive crashes and you have to reinstall everything).

Second, you need to install Windows on your newly created hard-drive partition. Installing Windows can be time consuming, but isn't necessarily difficult.
The two most technical parts of installing Windows on a Mac involve partitioning your hard drive and choosing the partition on which to install Windows.

Partitioning divides your hard drive in two parts: one part for Mac OS X and
the second part for Windows. Boot Camp uses *nondestructive partitioning*,
which means that you resize your hard drive's partitions without losing data.
After you partition your hard drive, you must tell Windows which partition to
install itself on — *and* you must specify the partition designated for Windows.

If you install Windows on the wrong partition, you'll wipe out everything on
your Mac. If you don't feel comfortable partitioning a hard drive and choosing the right partition on which to install Windows, get a more knowledge-
able friend to help you.

To install Windows, follow these steps:

1. **Open the Finder window by clicking the Finder icon on the Dock.**

2. **Choose Go⇨Utilities.**

   The contents of the Utilities folder appear in the right pane.

3. **Double-click the Boot Camp Assistant icon.**

   A Boot Camp Assistant Introduction window appears, informing you of
   the process of using Boot Camp, as shown in Figure 4-2.

4. **(Optional) If you want a printed copy of the Boot Camp installation
   process, perform the following steps (otherwise skip to Step 5 if you
   don't want to print the instructions):**

   a. *Click the Print Installation & Setup Guide button.*

      A Print dialog appears.

   b. *Change the default settings, such as changing the paper size, and
      click OK.*

      A second Print dialog appears, letting you choose a specific printer
      and number of copies to print.

   c. *Choose a printer and click the Print button.*

      The Installation & Setup Guide prints and then the Boot Camp
      Assistant window appears again (refer to Figure 4-2).

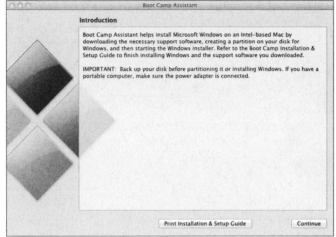

Figure 4-2:
The
introductory
Boot Camp
Assistant
window tells
you what
you need
to run Boot
Camp.

Reading the Installation & Setup Guide before you continue may provide you any newly updated instructions for installing Boot Camp that may have changed after we wrote this section.

5. **Click Continue.**

   The Download Windows Support Software window appears, with the Download Windows Support Software for this Mac option selected, as shown in Figure 4-3.

6. **Click Continue.**

   The Downloading Windows Software Support progress window appears as the download progresses, followed by the Save Windows Support Software window, which appears after the download completes. See Figure 4-4.

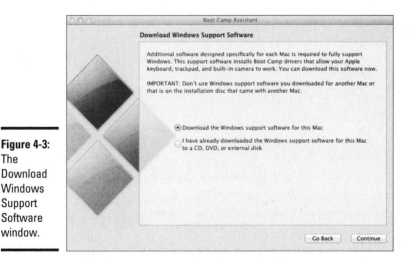

Figure 4-3:
The
Download
Windows
Support
Software
window.

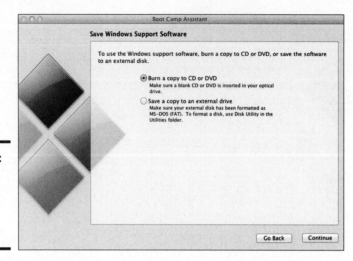

Figure 4-4:
The Save
Windows
Support
Software
window.

7. **Choose Burn a Copy to CD or DVD, or Save a Copy to an External Drive, depending on which you prefer, and then click Continue.**

   The Save Windows Support Software Status window appears as the support files are saved, followed by the Create a Partition for Windows window, as shown in Figure 4-5.

8. **Click and drag the divider between the Macintosh partition and the Windows partition left or right to choose a partition size.**

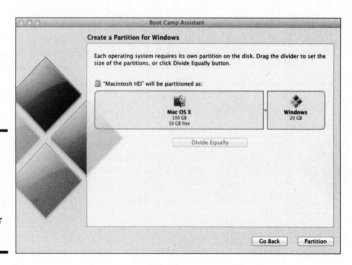

Figure 4-5:
Define
how much
hard-drive
space to
allocate for
Windows.

9. **Click the Partition button.**

Boot Camp partitions your hard drive. (This process might take a little while.) When partitioning is complete, the Start Windows Installation window appears, prompting you to insert your valid Windows installation disc in your Mac, as shown in Figure 4-6.

10. **Insert your Windows installation disc in your Macintosh and then click the Start Installation button.**

When the Windows installation application asks you which partition to install on, look for the partition size you specified in Step 8 that displays BOOT CAMP. If you choose the wrong partition, Windows might install on your Mac's partition — which could wreck your files and bring your entire Mac crashing to its knees. Refer to your printed Installation & Setup Guide for specific Windows 7 help.

11. **Follow the Windows installation instructions on the screen, and when the installation is finished, eject the disc.**

Be patient. Installing Windows can take time and Windows will reboot several times during installation, so don't panic if the screen suddenly goes blank.

12. **When prompted, insert the Windows Support Software disc or drive you saved in Step 7.**

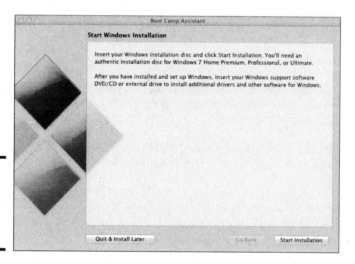

Figure 4-6:
Insert your
Windows
installation
disc.

13. **Follow the onscreen instructions to install the Windows Support Software files.**

   The Windows Support Software files allow certain Mac components to work in the Windows environment, such as AirPort, the built-in FaceTime camera, the trackpad on MacBooks or the Magic Trackpad accessory, and the function keys on your Mac's keyboard. A Windows control panel is also installed during the Windows Support Software installation process.

   Click Continue Anyway if you see a message that tells you the software you are installing has not passed Windows Logo testing. Do not click Cancel in any of the installer dialogs. Follow the instructions for any wizards that appear.

Choosing an operating system with Boot Camp

After you complete the Boot Camp installation process to install Windows on your Mac, you can choose which operating system you want to use when you start your Mac by following these steps:

1. **Restart your computer and hold down the Option key until two disk icons appear.**

   One disk icon is labeled Windows and the other is labeled Macintosh HD. (If you changed the name of your Mac's hard disk, you'll see this name displayed instead.)

2. **Click the Windows or Macintosh Startup Disk icon.**

   Your chosen operating system starts.

Holding down the X key after you power on your Mac tells your Mac that you want to load Mac OS X. You can let go of the X key as soon as you see the Mac OS X start-up screen.

To switch to a different operating system, you have to shut down the current operating system and repeat the preceding steps to choose the other operating system.

If you start your Mac without holding down the Option key, your Mac starts the default operating system. You can define the default operating system in Mac OS X by following these steps:

1. **Within Mac OS X, choose ⌘⇨System Preferences to open the System Preferences window.**

2. **Click the Startup Disk icon under the System category.**

   The Startup Disk window opens.

3. **Click the Mac OS X or Windows icon and click the Restart button.**

Sharing Mac and Windows files

With Mac OS X version 10.6 and later, whether you're running the Mac or Windows operating system, you can open and view files from the other operating system's hard-drive partition. To modify files, copy the file from the partition where the file is stored to the operating system partition you're using. For example, if you're in Windows and want to modify a file saved on your Mac partition, copy the file from the Mac partition to the Windows partition, and then make the changes.

Removing Windows from your Mac

If you want to wipe out the partition on your hard drive that contains Windows, you can do so by following these steps:

1. **Double-click the Boot Camp Assistant icon in the Utilities folder.**

   The Boot Camp Introduction window appears.

2. **Click the Continue button.**

   The Download Windows Support Software window appears.

3. **Choose the option I Have Already Downloaded the Windows Support Software for this Mac to a CD, DVD or External disk, and then click Continue.**

   The Select Task window appears.

4. **Choose the Create or Remove a Windows Partition option, and then click the Continue button.**

   The Restore Disk to a Single Volume window appears.

   Wiping out your Windows partition deletes all data stored on that partition that you created by using Windows.

5. **Click the Restore button.**

 Book III
Chapter 4

Running Windows on a Mac

Using Virtual Machines

Although you can share files between the Mac and Windows partitions as described previously in this chapter, you may still want to purchase a virtualization application, such as Parallels Desktop (`www.parallels.com`) or VMWare Fusion (`www.vmware.com`), to run Windows and Mac OS X at the same time and switch between the two.

 Another virtualization application that you can download and use free is VirtualBox (`www.virtualbox.org`).

Virtualization is a technology that lets you run multiple operating systems at the same time, where each operating system time-shares the computer's hardware. Because the active operating system isn't really controlling the computer's hardware completely, it is called a *virtual machine* (a part of your computer that works like some other real machine, such as a Windows PC).

Parallels Desktop, VMWare Fusion, and VirtualBox work in similar ways by creating a single file on your Mac hard drive that represents a virtual PC hard drive — which contains the Windows operating system plus any additional Windows applications you might install, such as Microsoft Office.

When you run Parallels, Fusion, or VirtualBox, the application boots up from this virtual hard drive while your original Mac OS X operating system continues to run. This lets you run another operating system, such as Windows, inside a separate Mac OS X window, as shown in Figure 4-7.

Rather than require you to load Windows and then load a specific application within Windows, virtualization applications let you store a Windows application icon directly on the Desktop or in the Dock so that it behaves like a Mac application icon.

Clicking a Windows application icon loads Windows and the Windows application at the same time without showing the Windows desktop or the Windows Start menu.

Figure 4-7:
Parallels
Desktop
application
lets you run
Windows
inside a
separate
Mac
window.

Because the operating system stored on the virtual hard drive has to share the computer's processor and memory with Mac OS X, operating systems running on virtual machines tend to run slower than when you run Windows and Windows programs within Boot Camp. In Boot Camp, the application has total access to your computer's hardware, meaning that the application runs as fast as it would on a stand-alone Windows PC.

To ease the migration from Windows to the Mac, virtualization programs can clone your existing Windows PC and duplicate it, with all your data and programs, on to the Mac. You can essentially use your old Windows PC as a virtual computer on your Mac.

Using CrossOver Mac

With Boot Camp, VirtualBox, Parallels, and Fusion, you need to buy a separate copy of Windows. CrossOver Mac lets you run Windows programs without a copy of Windows. The application works by fooling Windows programs into thinking that they're really running on a Windows PC.

CrossOver Mac lets you pop a Windows CD into your Mac and install the Windows application on a simulated PC that CrossOver Mac creates automatically on your Mac. After you install a Windows program, CrossOver Mac displays the normal Windows icons inside a Finder window. Double-clicking the Windows application icon runs that Windows application on your Mac, as shown in Figure 4-8.

Like Parallels, Fusion, and VirtualBox, CrossOver Mac runs only on Intel Macintosh computers. A more crucial limitation is that CrossOver Mac works with only a handful of Windows programs, so you can't run just any Windows application on a Mac with CrossOver Mac and expect it to run flawlessly.

To help you determine whether your favorite Windows application, such as Quicken or DirectX 8; or game, such as Wizard 101, World of Warcraft, or Alien Swarm, will work with CrossOver Mac, the product's website (www. codeweavers.com/compatibility/browse/name) lists all known programs that have been tested and verified to work correctly. If you need to run the latest Windows programs, a little-known Windows program, or a custom Windows program, CrossOver Mac probably won't let you run it. However, if you need to run only a handful of older or popular programs, CrossOver Mac might be the ideal solution.

Figure 4-8:
CrossOver
Mac lets
you run a
handful of
Windows
programs
without
running
Windows.

Book IV

Your Mac as a Multimedia Entertainment Center

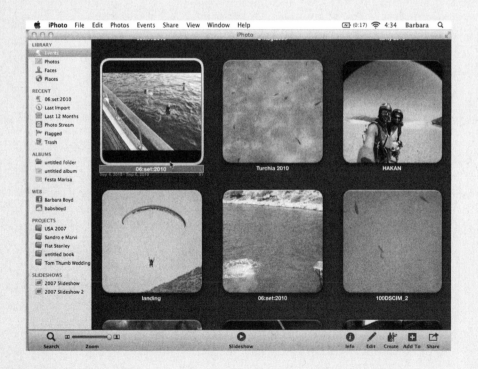

Contents at a Glance

Chapter 1: Listening, Watching, Reading, and Learning with iTunes

In This Chapter

✔ **Understanding audio file formats**

✔ **Moving media you already own to iTunes**

✔ **Managing your iTunes Library**

✔ **Creating playlists**

✔ **Playing audio and video**

✔ **Browsing and buying from the iTunes Store**

✔ **Sharing media**

✔ **Burning audio files to disc**

When iTunes first came on the scene in 2001, followed by the iTunes Store in 2003, it was all about music. Today, the iTunes Store is a one-stop media megastore — or mega media store. You can still buy music, choosing from over 18 million songs, but you also find music videos, movies, television shows, audio and video podcasts, audio books, electronic books, iOS apps, and lectures from some of the best universities in the world. All the more reason to have a sizeable hard drive!

The iTunes application that came with your Mac is a combination audio and video organizer, player, audio file converter, and disc-burning application. You can even listen to the radio with iTunes as long as you're connected to the Internet.

Digital files have all but replaced CDs, DVDs, and flash drives. Ubiquitous Wi-Fi, broadband cellular networks, and Apple's new iCloud service make accessing and sharing remote files between your Mac and other iOS devices, like an iPod touch or iPhone, quick and easy. If you find that you still want your music on a CD, you can use the iTunes disc-burning feature to copy your favorite audio files to a CD that you can play whenever you don't have the option of listening to music with iTunes on your Mac.

We begin this chapter with an explanation of different file formats and copying media you already own into iTunes on your Mac. We also explain how to convert files in iTunes. We go through how iTunes is set up and how to listen to music or watch a movie on iTunes. We show you how to set up playlists on your own or let iTunes do it for you with Genius. At the end of the chapter, we then take a tour of the iTunes Store so you can find out how to add other media to your Mac.

Understanding Audio File Compression Formats

Audio files offer tremendous advantages in storage and audio quality compared to previous forms of audio storage. However, dozens of different audio file compression types — the underlying conversion technology used to save audio as digital files — are out there. Therefore, to hear different audio files, you might need to use different applications. This would be like having to buy two separate radios where one radio receives only AM stations and the second radio receives only FM stations.

Different types of audio file compression formats exist because each file format offers certain advantages. The standard approaches to audio file compression are three schemes used for saving audio as digital files: lossless (no compression), lossless compression, and lossy compression.

Your Mac can play almost any audio file format as long as you install the right software.

Lossless audio files

The highest-quality audio files are called *lossless* because they never lose any audio data. As a result, lossless audio files offer the highest-quality sound, but they also create the largest file sizes.

The two most popular lossless audio file formats are WAV (Waveform audio format) and AIFF (Audio Interchange File Format). WAV files typically end with the .wav file extension and AIFF files typically end with the .aiff or .aif file extension.

Compressed lossless audio files

Lossless audio files take up large amounts of space, so compressed lossless audio files are designed to squeeze audio data into a smaller file size. Three popular compressed lossless audio file formats are FLAC (Free Lossless Audio Codec), Shorten, and Apple Lossless. FLAC files typically end with the .flac file extension, Shorten files typically end with the .shn file extension, and Apple Lossless files typically end with the .m4a file extension.

You can play Apple Lossless files in iTunes, but not FLAC or Shorten audio files. To play FLAC files, grab a free copy of SongBird (http://getsongbird.com) or VLC Media Player (www.videolan.org/vlc). To play Shorten files, use Audion (www.panic.com/audion), which is still available although not actively updated.

Compressed lossy audio files

A *lossy* audio file compresses audio files by stripping certain audio data to shrink the file size; it's much like pulling unnecessary clothing from a suitcase to lighten the load. The greater the audio quality, the more audio data the file needs to retain and the bigger the file. The smaller the file, the less audio data the file can hold, and the lower the audio quality. As a result, most audio file formats strive for an optimal balance between audio quality and file size.

The amount of data an audio file format retains is measured in kilobits per second (Kbps). The higher the kilobits, the more data is stored and the higher the audio quality. Table 1-1 shows approximate kilobit values and the audio quality they produce.

Table 1-1	Audio Quality Comparisons
Bit Rate (Kilobits per Second)	*Audio Quality*
32 Kbps	AM radio quality
96 Kbps	FM radio quality
128–160 Kbps	Good quality, but differences from the original audio source can be noticeable
192 Kbps	Medium quality, slight differences from the original audio source can be heard
224–320 Kbps	High quality, little loss of audio quality from the original source

The most popular compressed lossy audio file formats are MP3 (MPEG-1 Audio Layer 3), AAC (Advanced Audio Coding), and WMA (Windows Media Audio). You can recognize MP3 audio files by their .mp3 file extension.

The iTunes alternative to MP3 files is the AAC audio file format. AAC audio files offer greater audio quality and smaller file compression than equivalent MP3 files. The AAC format offers a Digital Rights Management (DRM) feature that allows copy protection; however, music you download today from iTunes is DRM-free (up until a few years ago iTunes music was DRM protected). AAC files typically end with the .aac or .m4a file extension (if it does not have DRM) or the .m4p file extension (if it does have DRM).

Book IV
Chapter 1

Listening,
Watching, Reading,
and Learning with
iTunes

Streaming media

Except for sound effects or mobile phone ring-tones, most audio files are 2 to 4 megabytes in size. Before you can play such an audio file or a larger movie or TV show file, you must first copy the entire file to your Mac. Normally, this isn't a problem except if you want to listen to audio or watch the video right away, such as a live radio broadcast on a radio station's website or a *Webinar* (a seminar that is broadcast on the Internet, which you watch as if you were attending in person) on a news website. These kinds of audio files are called *streaming audio*.

Two features distinguish streaming files from ordinary files. First, a streaming file plays while it's being downloaded — or *streamed* — to your Mac. Second, streaming files are not typically saved to your hard drive.

iTunes can play streaming media. Some other popular (and free) applications for listening to streaming audio include Audion (`www.panic.com/audion`), RealPlayer (`www.real.com`), and AOL Radio (`http://music.aol.com/radioguide/bb`).

Getting to Know the iTunes Window

You can use iTunes to play music on your Mac, but iTunes shows its real strength when you use it to organize your media files. iTunes has a system to make the Library of Congress envious — okay, maybe that's an exaggeration. If you tend to have CDs stacked in the cupboard under your stereo and others sliding around under the passenger seat of your car and still more CDs in a desk drawer at work, moving all your music into iTunes helps you manage your music in one place. Before we get into listening, watching, and learning, we want to explain how iTunes manages your media.

The iTunes window has four main parts, as shown in Figure 1-1.

✦ **Top Toolbar:** Across the top, you find the playback and volume controls, the status bar, the view buttons, and the search field. In the upper-right corner, the two-way arrow is the toggle to switch to full-screen viewing.

✦ **Source List:** Down the left side, iTunes displays the categories and sub-categories of sources where you can find media. We explain the functions of each of these categories throughout this chapter.

   • *Library* shows the media categories Music (which includes music videos), Movies, TV Shows, Podcasts, iTunes U, Books, Apps, Radio, and Ringtones, if you add any to the library. If your Library isn't divided by category, choose Files⇨Library⇨Organize Library. iTunes automatically divides your media by type.

   • *Store* has links to the iTune Store, Ping (the iTunes social network), and your purchased items.

   • *Devices* lists external devices such as optical discs, iPhones, or MP3 players connected to your Mac and accessed through iTunes.

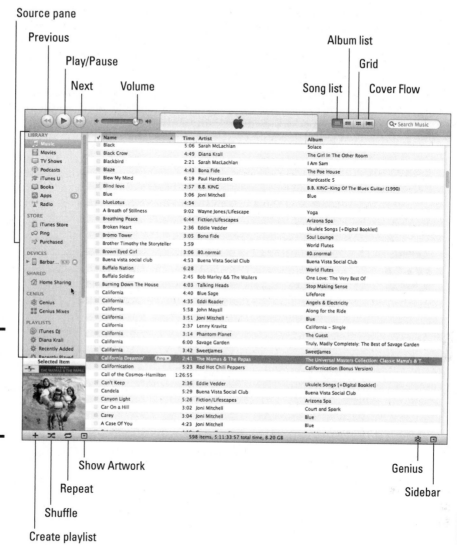

Figure 1-1:
Manage
your media
from the
iTunes
window.

Source pane

Previous

Play/Pause

Next   Volume

Album list

Grid

Song list   Cover Flow

Show Artwork

Repeat

Shuffle

Create playlist

Genius

Sidebar

Listening,
Watching, Reading,
and Learning with
iTunes

- *Shared* shows networks on which you share your iTunes libraries as well as the Home Sharing icon.

- *Genius* holds the Genius mixes and Genius playlists that iTunes creates for you.

- *Playlists* lists Smart Playlists and normal playlists you create, as well as folders of playlists.

✦ **Bottom Toolbar:** Running across the bottom of the window, you find the buttons Create a Playlist, Shuffle, Repeat, and Show Artwork on the left; the song number and playing time appear in the center; the Genius and Sidebar buttons are on the right side, where you also find an AirPlay menu if you use AirPlay.

✦ **Media Pane:** The media you select appear in the main center section of the window. If open, the Sidebar appears on the right. You can change the view by clicking the buttons in the top toolbar or choosing View⇨List/Album List/Grid/Cover Flow. View your media in four ways:

• *List* shows the content in a list without images. Click the heading of any part of the list and the list is sorted by that heading; for example, Name sorts alphabetically by artist name. Click the triangle to the right of the name to sort in the opposite direction, that is, from A to Z or Z to A.

To customize the way your List view displays your iTunes music collection, choose View⇨Column Browser and then select or deselect any columns you want to see in the List view. Choose On Top or On Left to choose how the columns you've selected appear — above the music tracks pane, or to the left of the Music Tracks pane, as shown in Figure 1-2.

Figure 1-2: The List view in iTunes with the Column Browser.

- *Album List* shows an album cover (when the list is sorted by album), book cover, movie, podcast, or TV show icon, along with a list of tracks on albums or episodes of TV shows. See Figure 1-3.

- *Grid* displays album covers, which can then be further sorted by album, artist, genre, or composer; or Grid view shows movie or TV show icons, which can be sorted by name, genre, and unwatched. If you don't see the sorting tabs at the top, choose View⇨Grid View⇨Show Header. See Figure 1-4. Move the slider in the upper-right corner to reduce or enlarge the size of the images.

- *Cover Flow* displays the album, book cover, or TV show icon in the top half of the screen and a list of the details in the bottom half (like the List view), as shown in Figure 1-5. Move from one item to another by clicking the item on the list or using scrolling gestures (if you have a trackpad, as explained in Book I, Chapter 2) or the scroll bar. Click the full-screen button to see the cover flow display on your entire screen. Double-click the album cover to begin playing that album.

Figure 1-3:
Album List
view.

**Book IV
Chapter 1**

**Listening,
Watching, Reading,
and Learning with
iTunes**

Figure 1-4:
The Grid view shows media artwork.

Figure 1-5:
Cover Flow view lets you flip through media to choose what you want.

You can choose different columns and views for each item in the Source List and iTunes remembers which view you like. You may want to view your Music as a List that shows the album, song title, and playing time, and TV Shows in a Grid. If you recognize your books by their covers, display them by using Cover Flow.

When you are browsing any item from the Source List, you can change the columns you see by opening the library you want and then choosing View➪View Options. The pane opens, as shown in Figure 1-6. Select the check box next to the columns you want to see and deselect those you want to hide, and then click OK.

Figure 1-6: Pick and choose the information you want to see for each category in the Library.

Adjusting iTunes General Preferences

Choosing how iTunes should respond when you insert a CD, what type of audio file format it uses to import your CD audio tracks, and which Library categories you want to display in the left-hand column of the iTunes application window are all options you can adjust by accessing the iTunes Preferences dialog. We go through the General preferences in this section, and throughout the chapter, we direct you to Preferences to adjust other aspects of iTunes. To open the iTunes's Preferences dialog and adjust the settings, follow these steps:

1. **Choose iTunes➪Preferences.**

The iTunes Preferences window appears.

2. **Click the General icon (if it isn't already selected) to display the General settings pane, as shown in Figure 1-7.**

**Book IV
Chapter 1**

**Listening,
Watching, Reading,
and Learning with
iTunes**

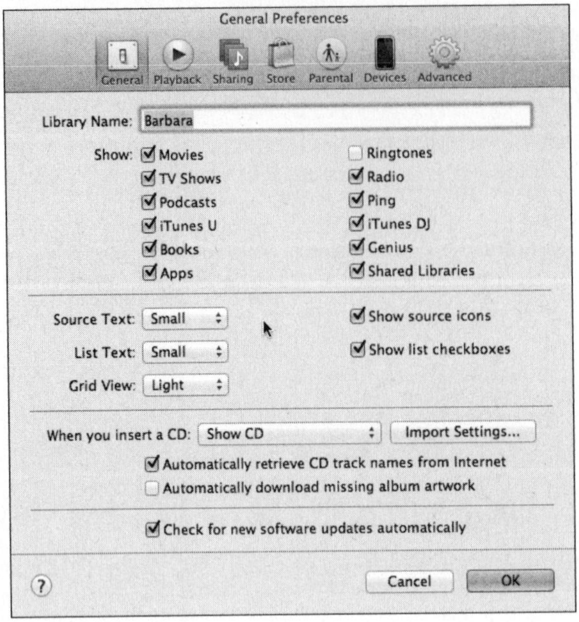

Figure 1-7:
The iTunes
Preferences
dialog lets
you tailor
iTunes to
your liking.

3. **(Optional) Select the Automatically Retrieve CD Track Names from Internet check box if you want iTunes to try to identify audio tracks by their song titles.**

   If this option isn't selected, each audio track will have a generic name such as Track 1.

4. **(Optional) To specify what you want to happen whenever you insert an audio CD into your Mac, click the When You Insert a CD pop-up menu and choose one of the following:**

   - *Show CD:* Displays a list of audio tracks.

   - *Begin Playing:* Displays a list of audio tracks and starts playing the first track.

   - *Ask to Import CD:* Displays a dialog, asking whether you want to import all audio tracks from the CD (this is the default setting).

   - *Import CD:* Automatically converts all audio tracks into digital files.

   - *Import CD and Eject:* Automatically converts all audio tracks into digital files and ejects the CD when it finishes without playing any tracks.

5. **(Optional) To specify the file format and audio quality of the audio files iTunes will create when importing CD audio tracks, click the Import Settings button.**

   The Import Settings preferences pane opens, as shown in Figure 1-8.

a. *Click the Import Using pop-up menu and choose one of the following:*

AAC Encoder: Stores audio tracks as AAC files.

AIFF Encoder: Stores audio tracks as AIFF files.

Apple Lossless Encoder: Stores audio tracks as a lossless compressed `.m4a` file.

MP3 Encoder: Stores audio tracks as MP3 files.

WAV Encoder: Stores audio tracks as WAV files.

b. *Click the Setting pop-up menu and choose the audio quality for your files.*

The higher the audio quality, the larger the file size.

c. *(Optional) Select the Use Error Correction When Reading Audio CDs check box to increase the chances that iTunes can retrieve and convert audio tracks from a damaged or scratched CD.*

d. *Click the OK button to close the Import Settings preferences pane and return to the General preferences pane.*

6. **(Optional) Click Check for New Software Updates Automatically to allow iTunes to check periodically for newer versions of the iTunes application.**

7. **(Optional) Click the other iTunes preferences icons in the iTunes Preferences dialog toolbar to explore any other options you might want to select, deselect, or adjust.**

8. **Click OK to close the iTunes Preferences dialog.**

You return to the main iTunes application window.

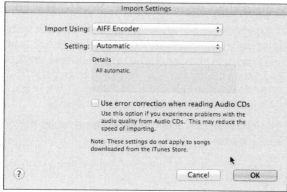

Figure 1-8:
In the Import Settings dialog, you choose the file format iTunes uses to convert audio tracks from your CD.

Book IV
Chapter 1

Listening,
Watching, Reading,
and Learning with
iTunes

Playing Audio with iTunes

Just as you need a turntable to play records or a cassette player to play cassettes, you need a specific application to play each type of audio file. Think of iTunes as one of those all-in-one stereo systems that have a turntable, cassette player, and radio all in one unit. iTunes plays the most common audio files (MP3, WAV, AAC, and AIFF) on your Mac.

You don't have to use iTunes to play audio CDs and digital audio files on your Mac. You can always use another audio player on your Mac (such as RealPlayer, which you can get free at www.real.com, VLC Media Player at www.videolan.org/vlc, or Audion at www.panic.com/audion). These other audio players can be especially useful if you want to play oddball audio formats like Ogg Vorbis or FLAC, but in most cases, you'll probably find that iTunes works just fine.

Listening to CDs

You probably have audio CDs of your favorite albums, but rather than play them in a CD player, you can play them in your Mac by using iTunes. Much like a CD player, iTunes can play audio tracks on a CD in order or randomly. Even better, iTunes lets you choose which audio tracks you want to hear. To play an audio CD in iTunes, follow these steps:

1. **Click the iTunes icon in the Dock or Launchpad to launch iTunes if it isn't already running.**

2. **Insert an audio CD into your Mac.**

   A dialog may appear (depending on the iTunes Preferences settings you choose), asking whether you want to import all audio tracks on the CD into iTunes. We discuss this process in the next section. For now, click No.

   If you're connected to the Internet, iTunes searches a website called GraceNote for information about the CD you inserted, based on multiple criteria, including the number, order, and length of tracks on the CD. If GraceNotes finds a match for your CD, iTunes displays that information, which can include the album name and artist, track titles, and, if available in the iTunes Store, the album's cover artwork.

3. **Click the Play button or press the spacebar to start playing your selected audio tracks.**

   The Play button turns into a Pause button (which you can click to pause the track you're listening to).

4. **When you finish listening to the CD, eject it by choosing Controls⇨ Eject Disc or by clicking the Eject Disc icon to the right of the CD icon.**

If you have a stereo, iTunes playback controls in the toolbar across the top of the window and below the Source List will look familiar. Refer to Figure 1-1. You have a few extra options, which you access from the iTunes menu and preferences:

✦ **Volume slider:** Drag the volume slider to adjust the sound.

✦ **Adjust play:** Click one of the following buttons:

- *Pause:* Temporarily stops playing audio. You can also press the spacebar to toggle the Play and Pause button.

- *Previous:* Starts playing the selected audio track from the beginning. Clicking the Previous button a second time starts playing the previous audio track from the beginning.

- *Next:* Skips the selected audio track and starts playing the next audio track.

✦ **Selective play:** Deselect the check boxes of any audio tracks you don't want to hear.

✦ **Random play:** Click the Shuffle button or choose Controls⇨Shuffle to play your audio tracks in random order. Choosing the Shuffle command again turns off random play. You can keep toggling this command off and on until you see a random order that you like.

✦ **Repeat-selection play:** Choose Controls⇨Repeat⇨All to play the selected audio tracks continuously on the CD or Repeat⇨One to repeat the same song. (Choose Controls⇨Repeat Off to turn off the Repeat Play feature.)

✦ **Equalizer:** Choose Window⇨Equalizer and select one of the 22 preset frequency options that's closest to the type of media you're listening too, such as R&B, Classical, Small Speakers, or Spoken Word. You can also adjust the equalizer settings manually (see Figure 1-9).

✦ **Preferences:** Choose iTunes⇨Preferences⇨Playback to adjust a few of your playback options.

- *Crossfade Songs*: Move the slider to set the length of silence between songs.

- *Sound Enhancer:* Move the slider from low to high to boost the sound quality.

- *Sound Check*: Sometimes songs play at different volumes. Select the Sound Check option so all songs are played at the same volume.

Control-click the iTunes icon on the Dock to bring up a playback controls menu.

**Book IV
Chapter 1**

**Listening,
Watching, Reading,
and Learning with
iTunes**

Figure 1-9:
Select
the type
of music
you're
listening
to with the
Equalizer.

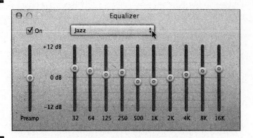

Importing Music into iTunes

Having to insert a CD into your Mac every time you want to hear a few songs can be cumbersome, which is why you might find it easier to store your favorite songs as digital audio files instead. You may also have music you purchased from other vendors, such as Amazon (www.amazon.com) or GoMusic (www.gomusic.com), that you'd like to store in iTunes so all your music is in one place. In the following sections, we explain the import options you have and give you the instructions for copying songs from CDs to iTunes on your Mac or moving digital files you already own into iTunes.

Importing a CD's audio tracks into iTunes

The process of converting audio tracks on a CD into digital audio files is known as *ripping*. After you adjust the iTunes import settings (see the earlier section, "Adjusting iTunes General Preferences"), you're ready to rip.

By default, iTunes saves songs imported from your CDs as high-quality iTunes Plus files in the 256 Kbps AAC format.

To convert an audio disc into digital files, follow these steps:

1. **Click the iTunes icon in the Dock or Launchpad to launch iTunes if it isn't already running.**

2. **Insert an audio CD into your Mac.**

   Depending on how you set the iTunes preferences, a dialog may appear, asking if you want to import all audio tracks on the CD into iTunes. Click Yes if you want to convert every audio track into a digital audio file and import it to iTunes. If you want to import only some of the songs, click No and continue with the following steps.

   If the tracks of the CD don't appear in the central pane of iTunes, click the name of the CD under Devices in the Source List, which runs down the left side of the iTunes window.

3. **If you want to choose which songs to import, deselect the check boxes of the tracks you don't want to import.**

   Check marks should appear in the check boxes of the audio tracks you want to import.

4. **Click the Import CD button in the lower-right corner of the iTunes window.**

   The iTunes application converts and copies all the CD's audio tracks into digital audio files and saves them to your Mac's hard drive in the Music folder.

   The status window indicates which track is being copied and how long it will take to copy. A white check mark in a green circle appears next to tracks that have been successfully imported.

5. **When iTunes finishes importing your CD's audio tracks, eject the CD by choosing Controls⇨Eject Disc or by clicking the Eject Disc icon to the right of the CD icon.**

6. **(Optional) To download album cover artwork for CDs that you import to your Mac, choose Advanced⇨Get Album Artwork.**

   You need an iTunes account or an Apple ID. If you have an iTunes account or Apple ID, choose Store⇨Sign In to sign in to your Apple or iTunes account. To create an Apple ID, choose Store⇨Create Account. Creating an account won't cost you anything, but you will need to enter a credit card number or iTunes Gift Card number in case you decide to buy anything from the iTunes online store.

   After you sign in, iTunes begins downloading album artwork. The status bar shows which album iTunes is working on and how much time remains.

Importing digital audio files

Besides ripping audio tracks from a CD and storing them on your Mac, you might also get digital audio files through the Internet or handed to you on a flash drive or external hard drive. Before you can play any digital audio files in iTunes, you must first import those files, which essentially copies them into the iTunes folder inside your Music folder.

You can simply drag files into your iTunes library, or you can follow these steps:

1. **Click the iTunes icon in the Dock or Launchpad to open iTunes if it isn't already running.**

2. **Choose File⇨Add to Library to open the Add to Library dialog.**

3. **Navigate to and select the folder, audio files, or files you want to import into iTunes, and then click the Choose button.**

   iTunes imports the folder, audio files, or files into your Music folder.

**Book IV
Chapter 1**

Listening, Watching, Reading, and Learning with iTunes

If you download music from an online source other than iTunes, select the Automatically Add to iTunes option when selecting the destination for saving a downloaded a file, and the file shows up in your iTunes library.

If you poke around in your Mac's folders and files and see two Library files in iTunes, don't delete one just because it *looks* like a duplicate. iTunes stores your media in two Library folders. One holds the actual media files, the other makes media available to other apps such as Keynote, iMovie, or iWeb.

Searching your iTunes library

After you copy music, and eventually other media, into iTunes, there may come a time when you can't find what you're looking for in your library. To find a song, podcast, TV show, or any other media you store on iTunes, you can search by typing some or all of a song, album, or show title, artist name, and so on. To search iTunes, follow these steps:

1. **Click the library you want to search in, for example Music or Podcasts.**

2. **Click the triangle next to the magnifying glass to choose which field you want to search or select All to search all fields associated with the library you chose in Step 1 (see Figure 1-10).**

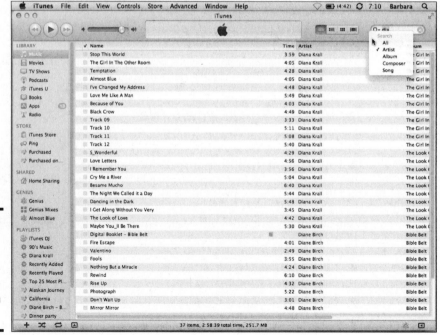

Figure 1-10: Choose to search all fields or specific fields within a library.

3. **Click the Search field in the upper-right corner of the iTunes window and type part of the title, album, television series, or other item that you want to find.**

   Each time you type a letter in the Search field, iTunes narrows the list of potential matches.

4. **Click the media you want to play.**

   Read the next section, "Playing digital audio files," to find out more about playback.

Playing digital audio files

After you import one or more audio files into iTunes, you can view your list of audio files within the iTunes media pane, as outlined in the beginning of this chapter in the "Getting to Know the iTunes Window" section. Refer to the earlier section, "Listening to CDs," for details on the playback controls. To play one or more audio files, follow these steps:

1. **Choose a view for displaying your audio file collection, such as List, Grid, or Cover Flow view.**

   Check marks appear in the check boxes of selected songs.

2. **Select the check boxes of the audio tracks you want to hear and deselect the check boxes of audio tracks you don't want to hear.**

   To deselect all audio tracks so you don't have to listen to them, hold down the ⌘ key and select a check box. To reselect all audio tracks, repeat the process.

3. **Click the Play button or press the spacebar to start playing your selected audio tracks.**

   The Play button turns into a Pause button.

If you have an Apple Remote, you can control iTunes playback with the remote control as long as you are in view of the infrared receptor on your Mac. If you don't have an Apple Remote or your Mac doesn't have an infrared receptor, but you do have an iPhone, iPad, or iPod touch and a Wi-Fi network, you can download the Remote app from the App Store and control iTunes with your device.

Choose View⇨Switch to Mini Player, or click the green zoom button at the top left of the window, to reduce the playback controls to a small window, shown in Figure 1-11, that you can leave on the Desktop so you can listen and control your music while you're using your Mac to do other things.

**Book IV
Chapter 1**

Listening, Watching, Reading, and Learning with iTunes

Figure 1-11:
The Mini
Player puts
controls
on your
Desktop.

Listening to the radio

Click Radio in the Library category of the Source List, and a list of streaming radio stations appears. Double-click the station that you want to listen to and the audio begins playing. You do have to be connected to the Internet.

If you have a favorite station that's not listed, locate the station on the Internet, and then choose Advanced➪Open Stream in iTunes and type or paste the URL for the station in the URL field. It's now added to the iTunes Radio.

Playing Around with Playlists

If you're a professional disc jockey or event planner, you know how the sequence and mix of songs can set the mood of a crowd. Some songs provide background music that unconsciously stimulates calm conversation, while other songs grab your attention or pull you to the dance floor. With iTunes, you create playlists from your music collection. Rather than go through the hassle of selecting the same group of songs over and over, you can select a group of songs once and store that list as a *playlist*. When you want to hear the group of songs, just select the playlist rather than each song. You might choose calming New Age instrumentals when you're studying, a classic rock jam to keep you moving while housecleaning, and a jazz or blues mix to play in the background at a dinner party.

iTunes offers five types of playlists. You create ordinary playlists or Smart Playlists; iTunes creates Genius mixes and playlists and a random, ever-changing playlist called iTunes DJ. An ordinary playlist is a list of favorite songs you select to include in that playlist. A Smart Playlist lets you define rules for which songs to include, such as only songs recorded by a specific artist. While your audio file collection grows, a Smart Playlist can automatically include any new songs by that specific artist or by whatever other criteria you define for the particular Smart Playlist. iTunes creates Genius playlists based on a song you choose.

When you create an ordinary playlist or a Smart Playlist, those playlists appear in the Playlist section of the Source list of the iTunes window. Genius playlists show up in the Genius section of the Source list. By default, iTunes already includes several Smart Playlists, including Recently Added, Recently Played, and Top 25 Most Played.

Creating an ordinary playlist

The simplest playlist to create is one that contains specific songs, such as a favorite album, a group of songs you want to listen to when you go for a run or workout, or perhaps every song by a particular artist. To create a playlist of particular songs you want to group, follow these steps:

1. **In iTunes, hold down the ⌘ key and click each song you want to store in your playlist.**

2. **Choose File⇨New Playlist from Selection.**

   An untitled playlist appears in the Source List under the Playlists category, and your chosen songs appear in the right pane.

3. **Type a name for your playlist and press Return.**

You can always edit a playlist name by double-clicking the name in the Source List.

Adding songs to a playlist

After you create a playlist, you can add to or remove songs from that playlist at any time. To add a song to a playlist, click a song you want to add and drag it to the playlist in the iTunes Source List. The song you added appears in the playlist.

Putting a song in a playlist doesn't physically move the song from the folder it's stored in on your Mac's hard drive.

Deleting songs from a playlist

To delete a song from a playlist, follow these steps:

1. **In iTunes, click the playlist that contains the songs you want to delete.**

   Your chosen playlist appears onscreen.

2. **Click a song to delete and then press the Delete key.**

   A dialog appears, asking whether you really want to remove the song from your playlist.

3. **Click Remove.**

Deleting a song from a playlist doesn't delete the song from your iTunes library.

To delete a song from your music collection, click Music under the Library category in the iTunes Source List, click a song you want to delete, and then press the Delete key. When a dialog appears, asking whether you want to delete the song from your Library, click Remove. When a second dialog appears, click Move to Trash if you want to delete the song track from your Mac's hard drive. Click Keep File if you want to keep the song track on your Mac's hard drive but no longer display it in your iTunes music library.

**Book IV
Chapter 1**

Listening,
Watching, Reading,
and Learning with
iTunes

Creating a Smart Playlist

Manually adding and removing songs from a playlist can get tedious, especially if you regularly add new songs to your iTunes audio collection. Instead of placing specific songs in a playlist, a Smart Playlist lets you define specific criteria for the types of songs to store in that playlist, such as songs recorded earlier than 1990 or songs under a particular genre, such as Blues, Country, Hard Rock, or Folk. To create and use a Smart Playlist, you tag songs, define rules to determine which songs to include, and finally, edit existing playlists.

Tagging songs

To sort your song collection accurately into Smart Playlists, you can tag individual songs with descriptive information. Most songs stored as digital audio files already have some information stored in specific tags, such as the artist or album name. However, you might still want to edit or add new tags to help Smart Playlists sort your song collection.

To edit or add tags to a song, follow these steps:

1. **In iTunes, click a song that you want to tag and choose File⇨Get Info (or press ⌘+I) to display the song track's information.**

2. **Click the Info tab to display text boxes where you can type in or change the song track's associated information, as shown in Figure 1-12.**

3. **Click a text field and edit or type new information.**

Figure 1-12: The Info pane lets you edit or type new labels to identify a song.

4. **In the same Info pane, click the Genre pop-up menu to add or change the song's genre.**

5. **Click the song track's other tabs, such as Sorting or Options, shown in Figure 1-13, to make additional adjustments to your selected audio file.**

6. **When you finish tagging the song track, click the OK button to close the dialog and return to the main iTunes window.**

Defining Smart Playlist rules

Smart Playlists use tags to sort and organize your song collection. You can use existing tags that are created for songs automatically (such as Artist and Album), as well as tags that you add to your songs to define the type of songs you want that Smart Playlist to store. A specific criterion for choosing a song is a *rule.*

To create a Smart Playlist, follow these steps:

1. **In iTunes, choose File⇨New Smart Playlist or Option-click the New Playlist button (+).**

    A Smart Playlist dialog appears, prompting you to define a rule for specifying which songs to store in the playlist.

2. **Click the first pop-up menu on the left and choose a category, such as Artist or Date Added, for deciding which songs the Smart Playlist will automatically choose.**

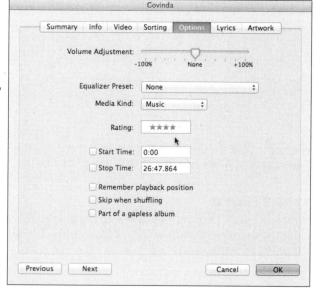

Figure 1-13: The Options pane lets you adjust volume, choose an equalizer setting, and rate audio files with one to five stars.

Book IV Chapter 1

Listening, Watching, Reading, and Learning with iTunes

3. **Click the second pop-up menu in the middle and choose how to use your chosen category.**

4. **Click the text box and type a criterion, such as a specific date or an artist name.**

5. **(Optional) Click the Plus sign to add another rule to the Playlist, as shown in Figure 1-14.**

6. **(Optional) Make other selections in the Smart Playlist dialog:**

   • *Limit To:* Select this option and enter a number to define the maximum number of (choose one) songs/file size/minutes/hours/items the Smart Playlist can hold; then choose an option that suits your desired Smart Playlist criteria in the Selected By pop-up menu.

   • *Match Only Checked Items:* If you want to store only songs that both match your criteria and are selected with check marks in the iTunes window, select this option.

   • *Live Updating:* Select this check box if you want the Smart Playlist to update its list of songs automatically each time you add or remove a song from your iTunes song collection library or change a tag (on a song) that's used in the rule.

7. **Click the OK button.**

   Your Smart Playlist appears in the list of playlists in the Source List of the iTunes window. Smart Playlists have a gear icon to the left of the name.

Figure 1-14:
Define a
rule for
automatically
choosing
certain
songs.

To rename any playlist, double-click the name in the Playlist list to highlight the name, and then type in a new name to replace the existing name.

Editing a Smart Playlist

After you create a Smart Playlist, you may want to modify the way it works, such as adding more rules or editing any existing rules. To edit a Smart Playlist, follow these steps:

1. **In iTunes, select the Smart Playlist that you want to edit in the iTunes Source List.**

2. **Choose File⇨Edit Smart Playlist.**

   The Smart Playlist dialog appears (refer to Figure 1-14).

3. **Make any changes to your Smart Playlist rule and click the OK button when you finish.**

If you have a lot of playlists, the Source pane can get pretty crowded. You can streamline your playlist list by filing similar playlists in folders. Choose File⇨New Playlist Folder. Double-click the folder to rename it with a meaningful name, and then click and drag the playlists you want to file to the folder.

Letting iTunes create a Genius playlist

If your guests are already ringing the doorbell and you don't have time to create the background music for your party, you can let iTunes create a Genius mix or a Genius playlist for you with songs iTunes thinks go well together. iTunes automatically creates Genius Mixes based on your existing collection, whereas a Genius playlist is created based on a song you choose. Genius also suggests new songs for you to purchase that it thinks you'll like based on your purchase history. Here's how to create Genius playlists:

1. **Choose Store⇨Turn On Genius.**

   iTunes accesses the iTunes Store so it can review your interests in music, movies, and TV shows and make informed suggestions about media you might like.

   A Genius Mixes item appears in the Genius section of the Source List. One or more Genius Mixes may be created, depending on how varied your music collection is.

2. **Click a song you like in your music collection and click the Genius button in the bottom-right corner.**

   A playlist is created from your music library with songs that iTunes thinks go well with the song you selected, as shown in Figure 1-15.

   Click the Sidebar button in the bottom-right corner to see a list of songs available in the iTunes Store that complements your Genius playlist. If the Sidebar doesn't display suggestions, the song you chose may not have tags that iTunes recognizes. Click another song in the playlist.

   If the artist of the song you chose is on Ping (iTunes social network, which we explain later in this chapter), the artist's Ping information is shown above the Genius recommendations list.

**Book IV
Chapter 1**

Listening,
Watching, Reading,
and Learning with
iTunes

Figure 1-15:
Genius creates a playlist based on a song selection; Ping information and Genius recommendations appear in the Sidebar.

3. **Click the pull-down menu next to Limit To to set how many songs you want in your Genius playlist: 25, 50, 75, or 100.**

4. **Click the Refresh button to update your Genius playlist after you add more music to your iTunes Music library.**

5. **Click Save Playlist to name and save the Genius playlist for future listening.**

Sometimes a message appears that there aren't enough related songs to create a playlist. Genius seems somewhat limited if you have non-English, classical, or pre-1960 music. Tagging your songs, as explained previously in the Smart Playlist section, can help Genius create playlists because tagging gives iTunes more information to work with.

iTunes DJ

iTunes DJ plays a random selection from the Music library or from a playlist that you select. The playlist is updated continuously, so while you might hear the same songs, you'll hear them in a different order. If you have the Remote app on your iPhone, iPad, or iPod touch, you or others with Remote can request songs and even vote on them. (Imagine how little work would get done in an office with iTunes DJ running!) Here's how to use iTunes DJ:

1. **Click iTunes DJ in the Playlists section of the Source pane.**

   If you don't see iTunes DJ, choose iTunes➪Preferences➪General and select the iTunes DJ check box.

   The first time you open iTunes DJ, click Continue when the dialog opens.

2. **Select the Source you want iTunes DJ to use to create the playlist from the pop-up menu at the bottom of the window.**

3. **Click the Settings button in the bottom-right corner.**

   The dialog appears, as shown in Figure 1-16. Use the pop-up menus to choose how many songs you want in the playlist and how you want guests to interact with iTunes DJ by using the Remote app on iPhone, iPad, or iPod touch.

4. **Click OK.**

5. **Click the Play button or spacebar to begin playing.**

6. **(Optional) To control iTunes DJ, make a request, or vote on a song from an iOS device, tap the Remote icon and choose iTunes DJ, which is under Playlists.**

Figure 1-16:
iTunes DJ plays a random, continuous playlist that you can control with Remote on an iOS device.

Book IV
Chapter 1

Listening,
Watching, Reading,
and Learning with
iTunes

Deleting a playlist

After you create a playlist or a Smart Playlist, you may want to delete that list later. To delete a playlist, follow these steps:

1. **In iTunes, click a playlist that you want to delete in the Source List of the iTunes window and press the Delete key.**

   A dialog appears, asking whether you really want to delete your playlist.

   Deleting a playlist doesn't physically delete the audio files from your iTunes library.

2. **Click the Delete button.**

If iTunes created a Genius Mix that you don't like, you can delete unwanted Genius Mixes by using the same procedure.

Publishing your playlist

If you create a really great playlist and want to publicize your secret inner DJ, you can share your playlist by publishing it on iTunes. iTunes can then provide a link to post your playlist on your website. Follow these steps:

1. **Click the playlist you want to share.**

   Only songs available in the iTunes Store can be shared.

2. **Choose Store⇨Share Playlist.**

   You have to be connected to the Internet to publish your playlist.

3. **Click Gift if you want to send the songs to someone.**

   iTunes opens and lists only the songs that are available in the iTunes Store. Fill out the onscreen form with the name and e-mail of the recipient (or recipients). You can also type in a personal message. Then click Continue to fill in the billing information — yes, you have to buy the songs you are gifting to someone.

4. **Click Publish to post your playlist to Ping profile.**

iTunes Store

If you have a thousand CDs, you're obviously enthusiastic about music and the iTunes Store can keep you informed of new releases or help you find rare recordings. If you have a small music collection, the iTunes Store can help you find music you like to expand your listening library. As we explain in the following sections, the iTunes Store isn't limited to music. You find movies, TV shows, audiobooks, electronic books, podcasts, and lectures from some of the top universities in the country. Have your Apple ID on hand when you want to shop the iTunes Store because that's what you use to sign in. To create an Apple ID, choose Store⇨Create Account.

For many purchases, you also have to authorize your computer. This helps with copyright issues. You can authorize up to five computers — you can also de-authorize computers, so don't worry about someone else using your iTunes account if you sell or give away your Mac. Other devices don't count as computers, so your iPad or iPhone aren't part of the five-computer limit. Choose Store⇨Authorize This Computer. That's it.

To open the iTunes Store, click the iTunes Store icon in the Source List in iTunes. With literally millions of digital media files to choose from, the initial impact can be overwhelming, but the iTunes Store organization helps you narrow your choices. When you first open the iTunes Store, the window you see is divided into sections that give you suggestions for music, movies, and television shows to download, rent, or purchase. See Figure 1-17.

At the top, you see rotating banner ads for songs, television shows, and movies. Scrolling down reveals other sections, such as Music, Genius Recommendations, Ping Artists and Music, Movies, TV Shows, Special Offers, and Free on iTunes. You also find one or two dividing strips, which advertise special iTunes offers. Clicking any of the ads or icons takes you to an information screen about that item.

In each section, you see two rows of icons. You can use the scroll bar underneath the selection to scroll horizontally, or click See All to see the entire selection from that section.

Figure 1-17: The iTunes Store lets you browse for music, movies, TV shows, and more.

Book IV Chapter 1

Listening, Watching, Reading, and Learning with iTunes

Across the top of the window are tabs for each type of media: Music, Movies, TV Shows, App Store (refer to Book I, Chapter 3), Books, Podcasts, and iTunes U. (There's also a tab for Ping, the iTunes social network, which we explain later in this chapter.) To the far right, you see your Apple ID, which is a tab, too. (The Apple ID in Figure 1-16 is `barbaradepaula`.) When clicked, each tab opens a pull-down menu, as shown in Figure 1-18. The choices on the menus take you to selections of new releases, special offers, or specific categories or genres available in that type of media. The pull-down menu from your Apple ID tab gives you options for managing your account.

Down the right side, you see two sections:

✦ **Quick Links:** This section is divided into two sections — the upper section lists options for searching, browsing, and buying; the lower section is related to your iTunes/Apple ID account so you can see a list of items you Purchased, your Wish List (a list you create of items you'd like to have), Recent Activity (which takes you to Ping), and Genius Recommendations, which are iTunes purchase recommendations based on items in your iTunes library.

✦ **Top Charts:** This section is divided into Singles, where you can view songs or music videos; and Albums, Movies, and TV Shows, which can be viewed by episode or season. Each has a See All option to view the top 200 in the category. Except for Songs, each See All selection can be sorted by Name, Bestseller, or Release Date.

Figure 1-18:
Click a media tab to open a pull-down menu with direct links to specific types of selections.

When you click a song or album icon or name from anywhere in the iTunes store, the album information window opens. Click a TV show and the season information screen opens. Click a movie and a movie information screen opens; Figure 1-19 shows an example. These are the parts of an information screen:

✦ **Name**

✦ **Genre**

✦ **Release date**

✦ **Buy button:** Click to download the media. Each option (for example, rent or buy, standard or high-definition) has its own button. Songs can be purchased singly or you can purchase the whole album; TV shows can be purchased singly or by season.

✦ **Pop-up menu:** Click the triangle next to the price for a pop-up menu that has options to gift the app to a friend, add it to your own wish list, tell a friend about it, copy the link, or share the app info via Facebook or Twitter.

✦ **Ratings:** For movies only. The ratings reflect the country the film is from.

✦ **Description:** The first few lines of the description are visible. If the description is longer, click More on the right side to expose the complete description.

✦ **Reviews:** (Not shown in Figure 1-19.) Users can give a simple star rating, from zero to five, or write a review. Reviews help you decide whether the item is worth downloading or purchasing.

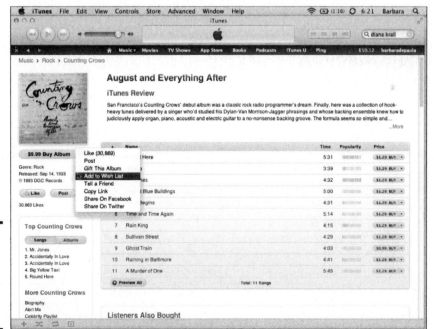

Figure 1-19: Information about the media item is displayed in iTunes.

Book IV Chapter 1

Listening, Watching, Reading, and Learning with iTunes

At the bottom, lists show items by the same performers and other items purchased by people who bought that particular item.

iTunes makes recommendations in the Sidebar while you browse your personal library. Click a song, movie, or show in your library and recommendations appear in the Sidebar. To open the Sidebar, click the Sidebar button or choose View⇨Show iTunes Sidebar.

When you know what you're looking for

You might know exactly what you're looking for. Maybe you heard an old favorite song on the radio or a new singer you want to hear more of. A quick search through iTunes offerings and you're one step closer to chilling with a great groove.

Type the name of the song or artist or a couple key words, say from an album title, in the Search field at the top right of the window. After you press Return, a list of matching results appears. The results are extracted from the entire iTunes Store but are divided by media category. If you click Music or Podcasts in the Filter by Media Type section, you'll only see that type of media.

Click See All next to the media title to see all the items found that meet your search criteria. If you want to narrow your search, click the Power Search button.

Power Search narrows your search by providing more detailed criteria, such as a singer's name or a genre. Adjust the criteria and click the Search button to come up with more precise search results.

To view a larger selection of just one type of media, click one of the media tabs at the top of the screen — Music, Movies, TV Shows. Click and hold the tab to open the pull-down menu, which displays genres or categories within a particular type of media.

Other media

There's so much more in iTunes than music and movies. iTunes is a warehouse of podcasts, books, and university courses. Here we run through what each category offers, but don't just take our word for it. Take a look for yourself at the vast assortment of media available.

iTunes U

Divided into 13 faculties, iTunes U features over 100,000 audio and video lectures from seminars and courses at universities around the world. This means that you can get an Ivy League education — but not the degree — without writing papers, taking exams, or paying tuition (the lectures are free)!

The opening screen is organized like the Music and Movies sections. Banner ads scroll across the top, Noteworthy and Categories sections follow, and Quick Links and Top Charts run down the right side. You can search by institution, by faculty, or, with the power search function, by description, institution, or title. In addition to lectures from universities and colleges, you find lectures from conferences and professional organizations in the Beyond Campus category and K-12 offers basic subjects such as math, science, and test preparation.

When you find a course you want to watch or listen to, subscribe to the entire course by clicking the Subscribe button or download one lecture from the course by clicking the name of the course, which opens the information screen and shows a list of lectures to choose from, as shown in Figure 1-20.

Books

The Books layout mimics the other media categories: banner ads, sections by category, and top charts down the right side. The iTunes top downloads are divided into paid and free; *New York Times* bestsellers are divided by fiction and nonfiction. The Books section of iTunes comprises electronic books, which — with the right app — you can download and read on your iPhone, iPad, or iPod touch, (Apple doesn't yet offer an app that can read e-books on your Mac) and audiobooks, which you listen to via iTunes on your computer or more likely, on your iPhone, iPod, or iPad. To switch between electronic books (iTunes refers to them just as "books") and audiobooks, click on one of the subheads in the Books or Audiobooks section to open that department of the iTunes Store.

Figure 1-20: iTunes U offers lessons and lectures from universities around the world.

Book IV Chapter 1

Listening, Watching, Reading, and Learning with iTunes

Podcasts

iTunes offers both audio and video podcasts in 16 categories (at the time of publication) and you can view the podcasts by audio or video only, by category, or by new releases. Apple's recommendations show up under the Staff Favorites link, and the Top Charts lists the most popular episodes. You can *stream* a podcast — that is, listen to it while it's downloading. If you want to download and listen later, click the Pause button; the podcast will download into the Podcast library and you can play it at a later time. Choose a single episode of a podcast or subscribe, in which case iTunes automatically downloads new episodes to your podcast library. And, as with iTunes U, podcasts are free.

Ping

The last tab you see on iTunes is Ping, iTunes' social network. The first time you click the Ping tab, you use your Apple ID and password to activate it, and then fill out the information requested: name, gender, hometown. The photo and personal description are optional. Choose three genres of music from the check boxes shown to give Ping an idea about what you like. Click Continue and select the privacy options you want from those offered, as shown in Figure 1-21.

Figure 1-21: Choose who sees what about you in the Ping privacy settings.

After you activate Ping, you can choose artists to follow, which means that when you open Ping, you'll see the latest activity about those artists, new releases, upcoming concert dates, and the like. You can also follow other people — friends, acquaintances, artists themselves — whose musical tastes interest you.

At any time, you can click on My Profile and make changes to your information or privacy settings. See Figure 1-22 for Ping on iTunes. To turn Ping off, choose Account from the pull-down menu that appears when you click your account name, which is on the tab on the far right of the window. Click Turn Off to turn Ping off. You can also reach your Ping profile by clicking Edit Profile.

In the iTunes Music library, click an item and a Ping button appears. Click this button to open a menu that gives you

✦ **Ping options:** Click Like to add a thumbs-up to the song, album, or artist, or Post to add a review or comment. People who follow you will see your likes and posts.

✦ **Show Artist Profile:** This takes you to the iTunes store and displays information about the artist.

✦ **iTunes:** Clicking this button gives you four other choices, each of which takes you to a destination in the iTunes store: The first takes you to the song itself; the second, to the artist; the third, to the album; and the fourth, to other albums in that genre.

Figure 1-22: The Ping screen on iTunes.

Downloading media from iTunes

When you find something you like, click the Buy button and it's downloaded to iTunes on your Mac. If you have other devices such as an iPad or iPhone, you can automatically download your purchases to the other devices at the same time. Choose iTunes⇨Preferences⇨Store and choose the media you want to download simultaneously, as shown in Figure 1-23.

Don't worry if you have to interrupt the download process or it's interrupted unexpectedly — iTunes remembers the point it reached; it will resume downloading when you open your iTunes account again and have an active Internet connection.

Of course, when you buy, you have to pay from your Apple ID account. This happens in either of two ways:

✦ **Credit Card:** Enter your credit card information into your Apple ID account. If you didn't enter credit card information when you created an Apple ID, you can do so by choosing Store⇨View My Account and clicking Edit to the right of Payment Information. A window opens where you can choose the type of credit card you want to use and type in the necessary information: account number, expiration date, billing address, and so on.

✦ **Redeem:** You can redeem Apple or iTunes gift cards, gift certificates, or allowances. Choose your Apple ID⇨Redeem. Type in the code from the card or certificate. The amount of the card or certificate is added to your account and appears to the left of the Apple ID account tab.

Yes, allowances. You can set up a monthly allowance for yourself or someone else. A set amount will be charged to your credit card and credited to the designated iTunes account.

Figure 1-23:
Automatic downloads puts your purchases on all your devices simultaneously.

All songs on iTunes are now in iTunes Plus format, which is 256 Kbps AAC without DRM (Digital Rights Management) limitations. Songs cost 69 cents, 99 cents, or $1.29, and most albums cost $9.99. If you buy a few songs from the same album and later decide you want the whole album, you can choose the Complete My Album option; iTunes deducts the cost of songs you already own from the album price. After you purchase and download music from iTunes, you can copy and play it on any of your devices — your Mac, iPod, iPad, smartphone, or MP3 player. (If you have pre-iTunes Plus audio files, you can upgrade them to iTunes Plus for 30 cents a song or 30 percent of the album price. Choose Upgrade Library from the account menu.)

Some albums on iTunes have an iTunes LP option. When you purchase an iTunes LP, you get liner notes, band photos, lyrics, and other bonus material along with the songs. You view everything in iTunes on your Mac.

If you want to build your video library, iTunes offers movies in both standard (SD) and high definitions (HD) formats. If you're a passionate movie buff, you may like iTunes Extra, which includes extra video such as director's comments or interviews with the actors along with the movie.

TV shows may be free — often to introduce a new series or season — or can be purchased singly or you can buy a season pass and download every episode. If not free, episodes start at $1.99 and you can choose standard or HD versions (HD begins at $2.99).

After you download the item, close the iTunes Store by clicking the X in the upper-left corner. You return to iTunes player, which is the non-store iTunes on your Mac. You can check in the Recently Added playlist to confirm that the items you rented or purchased were downloaded. Or, look in the section of the library related to the type of media you downloaded; for example, if you purchased and downloaded songs, click Music; if you downloaded podcasts, click Podcasts.

You can consult your past purchases on your iTunes account. Click Store⇨ View My Account. Sign in to iTunes with your Apple ID and choose Purchase History. You can also download purchases again — when you buy something in iTunes, it's yours forever.

If you ever have a problem with a purchase, choose Store⇨View My Account. Click Purchase History and click the Report a Problem button next to the item that isn't working.

Book IV
Chapter 1

Listening, Watching, Reading, and Learning with iTunes

Playing Digital Video Files

After you download movies, TV shows, lectures, or video podcasts, you want to watch them. To watch a video, follow these steps:

1. **Click the category of video you want to watch, for example TV Shows.**

   The list of videos you have in your library in that category appears in the media pane of the iTunes window. We like the Album List view for any of the video categories because you see artwork for the movie or series and the chapters or episodes listed to the right.

   Both Podcasts and iTunes U have Subscribe and Settings buttons at the bottom of the pane. Click Subscribe to receive other episodes of a podcast or lecture series automatically. Click Settings to establish how often you want iTunes to check for updates.

2. **Double-click the movie or episode you want to watch.**

   The video begins playing in the media pane.

3. **Move the pointer over the bottom of the video to see the playback controls.**

   You can also use the playback controls in the toolbar.

   If the item you are watching has chapters, a chapters menu appears next to the Windows menu.

To enhance your viewing experience, iTunes offers a few options under Preferences. Choose iTunes⇨Preferences⇨Playback. Choose the language you want to listen to and have subtitles in — these options work when other languages are available. You can also opt to watch HD video in standard and show closed captions when available.

It's Nice to Share

You put together a terrific music and movie library on iTunes and now you want your friends to know about the great new artist you heard or the quirky TV series you watch. You could just tell them or send them a link from the iTunes store; however, iTunes gives you a few options for directly sharing the media with your friends or family.

Sharing over a network

If your Mac is connected to a network, you can give access to your computer to other computers on the same network. Choose iTunes⇨Preferences⇨Sharing. You see the pane, as shown in Figure 1-24. Specify sharing your entire library or specific categories and playlists of your library. You can add a password too if you want to restrict who has access. Protected DRM content, such as movies and TV shows, can only be viewed on other "authorized" computers.

Figure 1-24:
Set up
Sharing
in iTunes
Preferences.

Home Sharing

If your household is like many today, you probably have more than one computer, not to mention other devices like smartphones, iPods, or iPads. HomeSharing lets you share the media you keep on iTunes — music, TV shows, apps, and so on — among up to five computers in your house. Click the Home Sharing icon in the Source pane and the dialog opens, as shown in Figure 1-25.

Use the same Apple ID on each computer, and anything you download from iTunes to one computer can then be shared with another computer, either over the network or set up iTunes to automatically download your purchases to all associated devices. Choose iTunes⇨Preferences⇨Store. Under Automatic Downloads, select the type of media you want downloaded on all devices that are signed in with the same Apple ID.

Sharing from the iTunes Store

When you click the Buy button on an item in the iTunes Store, a pop-up menu opens that gives you some sharing options in addition to buying the item. You can choose one or more of the following: Tell a Friend, Share on Facebook, Share on Twitter, or even Gift This to purchase the item for another person. Think how surprised and happy your friend, colleague, or relative will be when the gifted item shows up in the recipient's e-mail inbox.

**Book IV
Chapter 1**

Listening,
Watching, Reading,
and Learning with
iTunes

Figure 1-25:
Home
Sharing lets
you share
your media
with up to
five devices.

Burning an Audio CD

After you add your favorite songs to your iTunes music library, you can copy music tracks to a custom CD (often called a *mix CD* or just a *mix*) that you can play in your car or home stereo. To burn an audio CD, you first create a playlist, and then instruct iTunes to copy all the songs in the playlist to an audio CD.

CDs can hold approximately 70–80 minutes of audio. More stereos can recognize and play CD-Rs, although newer stereos can recognize and play CD-RWs as well. (CD-Rs let you write to them only once, whereas CD-RWs allow you to erase and reuse them.)

To burn a disc by using a playlist, follow these steps:

1. **Click the Playlist you want to burn to CD.**

2. **(Optional) Deselect the check boxes of any songs you don't want to burn to the CD.**

3. **(Optional) Arrange the songs in the order you want them to play on the CD.**

To arrange songs in a playlist, click in the first column (that displays the number of each song) and then drag a song up or down to a new position.

4. **Choose File⇨Burn Playlist to Disc.**

   A Burn Settings dialog appears, offering different radio buttons for choosing the type of CD you want to burn, such as Audio CD, MP3 CD, or Data CD or DVD, as shown in Figure 1-26. Audio CD is your best choice because only some players will recognize MP3 CDs and Data CD/DVDs won't be playable.

5. **Select a Disc Format radio button (Audio CD, MP3 CD, or Data CD or DVD).**

6. **(Optional) Click the Preferred Speed pop-up menu and choose a disc burning speed, such as Maximum Possible or 24x.**

   If the CDs you burn on your Mac don't play correctly on other CD players, choose a slower burning speed. Otherwise, use the Maximum Possible option.

   If you choose Audio CD, consider these additional options:

   - (Optional) Click the Gap between Songs pop-up menu and choose None or 1 to 5 Seconds to specify the amount of silence between song tracks.

   - (Optional) Select the Use Sound Check check box to instruct iTunes to ensure that all the song tracks play from the CD at the same volume level.

   - (Optional) Select the Include CD Text check box to display information about the CD on CD player models that offer a CD text information feature.

7. **Click the Burn button.**

8. **When prompted, insert a blank CD-R or CD-RW into your Mac.**

   The status bar of the iTunes window displays the progress of your disc burning. If you're burning more than one or two songs, you now have enough time to go get a cup of coffee, tea, or another beverage of your choosing.

**Book IV
Chapter 1**

Listening, Watching, Reading, and Learning with iTunes

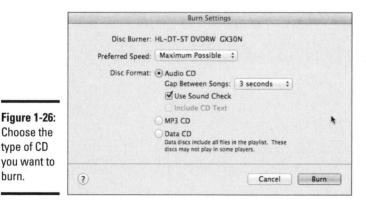

Figure 1-26: Choose the type of CD you want to burn.

Chapter 2: Watching Videos and Movies on Your Mac

In This Chapter

✔ Understanding movie formats

✔ Understanding digital movie formats

✔ Playing a digital video file

✔ Using QuickTime Player

✔ Playing a DVD with DVD Player

✔ Controlling your Mac with the Apple Remote

Looking to unwind after a busy day of work? Feel free to kick back, relax, and cozy up to a movie on your Mac. Want to watch your favorite scene again? Your Mac can bookmark and store your favorite scenes so you can easily watch your favorite parts of a movie. And, you can watch them in slow motion so you don't miss one second of the action.

Although many full-length movies appear on DVD, many shorter movies and videos — commercial or homemade — are stored entirely as digital video files either on your hard drive or the Internet. Whether a movie is stored on DVD or as a digital video file, your Mac can play it at your convenience.

In this chapter, we begin by explaining video disc formats and digital movie formats. We explain the options your Mac has for playing those formats — namely QuickTime and DVD Player. (A third option is iTunes, which Book IV, Chapter 1 is dedicated to.) At the end, we write about using the Apple Remote to control your movie viewing as well as some other functions and applications.

Understanding Video Disc Formats

The most common video disc format is DVD (Digital Video Disc). However, DVDs aren't the only video disc format. An earlier video disc format is VCD (Video Compact Disc), which essentially stores video files on ordinary CDs. VCDs typically offer lower video quality than DVDs (comparable to videotape) and offer much less storage capability than DVDs. Another popular format is DiVX, which many DVD players can play.

Although DVD is the common video disc standard, Blu-ray is the dominant high-definition digital disc format. The main advantage of Blu-ray discs is that they can store much more data than standard DVDs (25GB for a Blu-ray disc versus 4.7GB for a DVD or 8.55GB for a dual-layer — that is two layers recorded on the same side yet accessed separately — DVD). However, Blu-ray discs are also much more expensive to produce.

The Mac can play DVDs out of the box. If you want to watch Blu-ray discs, you need to buy a special Blu-ray disc drive and an application to use it or convert the file first by using an application like Pavtube to rip the Full Disc Copy and then Handbrake to convert the file.

Understanding Digital Video Formats

Video discs are popular for storing and distributing videos, but with high-speed Internet connections and lower hard drive storage costs, storing full-length movies as a single digital video file has become both popular and practical. The biggest problem with digital video is the wide variety of digital video formats available. To play a digital video file, you need a video-player application that accepts the type of video file you have. The following is a list of digital video file types and the applications you can use to play them:

✦ **QuickTime (.mov):** Playable by the QuickTime Player that comes with every Mac.

✦ **Audio/Video Interleaved (.avi):** An older video file format introduced by Microsoft in 1992, although still commonly used today.

✦ **Windows Media Video (.wmv):** Playable on a Mac if you first install the Flip4Mac application (www.flip4mac.com), which allows the QuickTime Player to open and play DRM-free Windows Media Video files.

✦ **DivX (.divx):** A high-quality video format known for storing DVD-quality video images in a digital video file format. DivX files can play on a Mac with the free DivX player (www.divx.com) or the free VLC media player (www.videolan.org).

Because DivX is a proprietary video file format, programmers have created a similar open source equivalent called Xvid (www.xvid.org).

✦ **Flash video (.flv):** A video file format commonly used on websites, such as news sites that offer video (CNN and Reuters) and YouTube, MySpace, and Yahoo! Video. You can play Flash videos by using the free Adobe Flash player (www.adobe.com).

✦ **RealVideo (.rm):** A video file format often used for streaming video. You can play RealVideo files by using the free Real Player application (www.real.com).

✦ **Moving Picture Expert Group (MPEG) (.mpg):** A video file format that consists of different versions, including

- *MPEG-1:* Used for storing video on VCDs

- *MPEG-2:* Broadcast-quality video used for storing video on SVCDs, DVDs, HD TV, HD DVDs, and Blu-ray discs

- *MPEG-3:* Originally designed for HD TV but now rarely used

- *MPEG-4:* For storing video on HD DVD and Blu-ray discs

You can view most MPEG-4 videos with the QuickTime Player; however, the free VLC media player (www.videolan.org) is a better solution because it reads all MPEG files as well as other video formats.

The QuickTime Player can't play MPEG videos if the audio is stored as AC3 (Dolby Digital) files.

Most video players are free because the companies developing and promoting a specific video file format want as many people as possible to use (and rely on) their particular video file format. Then these companies can make money by selling applications that create and store video in their specific file format.

You can download and install a free Mac video enabler (known as a *codec*) called Perian (www.perian.org) that can give QuickTime the capability to play lots of video file types it can't normally play without such an add-on.

Playing a Digital Video File

Playing a digital video file is as simple as double-clicking that file, which opens the appropriate video player on your Mac and displays your video file on the screen. If you find a video file on a website, you can usually click the video file directly on the web page to see it play within your browser.

Occasionally, you might find a video file format that you can't play on your Mac. In this case, you have two choices:

✦ Download and install a video player for that particular video file format.

✦ Convert the video file into a format that your Mac can play.

In our opinion, it's simpler just to download and install (yet another) free video player to watch video encoded in a different video file format. However, downloading and installing multiple video players can be annoying, so you may prefer to convert digital file formats instead. To convert digital video files, you need a special digital video file format conversion application.

To convert non-copy-protected (and most copy-protected) DVD videos to MPEG-4, you can use a free application called HandBrake (`http://hand brake.fr`). In case you need to convert one digital video file format into another one (such as converting a DivX file into a QuickTime file), grab a copy of the oddly named ffmpegX (`www.ffmpegx.com`) or MPEG Streamclip (`www.squared5.com`).

We won't go into how to use each application but the gist is that you go to one of the aforementioned websites, download and install the conversion application, open the application, and then open the file you want to convert and choose something like Convert To and choose a file type for which you have a player.

Converting digital video files lets you store all your videos in a single file format, such as QuickTime, and avoid having to download and install half a dozen video players. It's your call which tactic you prefer.

Using QuickTime Player

Your Mac came with QuickTime Player installed. If you're running Mac OS 10.7 Lion, you have a version of QuickTime Player that approaches QuickTime Pro. Not only can you play video, you can also record and edit movies with your Mac's built-in iSight camera — or with an external recording device, such as a camcorder or digital camera, that you connect to your Mac. We explain the movie-making capabilities of QuickTime Player in Book IV, Chapter 4.

In addition to QuickTime Movie (`.mov`), QuickTime Player supports MPEG-4 (`.mp4`, `.m4v`), MPEG-2, MPEG-1, 3GPP, 3GPP2, AVI, and DV files.

Follow these steps to use the playing part of QuickTime Player:

1. **Open QuickTime Player by doing one of the following:**

   - Drag the movie file over the QuickTime Player icon in the Dock.

   - Open QuickTime Player from the Dock or Launchpad and then choose File⇨Open File.

     Choose the file you want to view from the Open dialog. You may have to sift through directories or folders to find the file you're looking for.

   - Choose File⇨Open Location.

     An Open Location dialog appears, in which you can type the URL where the movie is located.

   - Choose File⇨Open Recent and select a file you recently viewed from the pop-up menu.

2. **Your selected movie opens.**

3. **Choose View and select one of the following viewing options:**

   - *Enter Full Screen:* Only your movie is seen, as large as possible, on the entire screen. No other windows or menus are visible.

   - *Float on Top:* Your movie plays on top of whatever else is on your desktop.

   - *Actual Size:* Displays movie at size it was recorded.

   - *Fit to Screen:* Your movie is adjusted to fit the screen while maintaining the height-to-width ratio. Other windows and the menu bar are visible.

   - *Fill Screen:* Your movie is adjusted to fill the entire screen, without borders. Some of the image may be lost or distorted because the height-width ratio is ignored to fill the screen (only in full-screen mode).

   - *Panoramic:* The movie is displayed with the outer horizontal edges compressed to avoid cropping (only in full-screen mode).

4. **(Optional) Choose other options from the View menu that may be available with your movie.**

   - *Show Closed Captioning* displays written dialogue.

   - *Subtitles* displays a written translation in a language other than the spoken dialogue.

   - *Languages* lets you choose a different language for the audio of your movie.

5. **(Optional) If your movie has chapters, you can choose View⇨ Show Chapters and select Next Chapter or Previous Chapter to go to a different part of your movie.**

6. **Click the Play/Pause button to view your movie.**

7. **Use the other playback controls, shown in Figure 2-1, to view your movie.**

   - Move the volume slider left or right to decrease or increase the audio.

   - Click the Rewind or Fast Forward buttons to go quickly back or ahead in your movie. Clicking a second or third time changes the speed from 2 to 4 to 8 times faster.

     Alternatively, drag the playhead slider left or right to go to another part of your movie. The time to the left of the playhead is how long your movie has played; the time to the right of the playhead indicates how much is left to play.

   - Click the Play/Pause button to stop your movie.

Figure 2-1:
QuickTime
Player lets
you view
movies from
many file
formats.

Playing a DVD

The most common video disc format is the DVD format. To play DVDs, just insert your DVD into your Mac. DVD Player loads and displays your DVD's main menu, as shown in Figure 2-2.

Click the menu options to select them (or use your Mac's arrow keys to move through the DVD's menu options and then press the Return key or spacebar to select them), such as Play Movie, or Special Features.

If you just want to watch a DVD from start to finish, you don't have to read the rest of this chapter. However, if you want to use some of the special features of DVD Player, keep reading.

Figure 2-2:
When DVD
Player
starts, it
displays the
inserted
DVD's main
menu.

Understanding full-screen mode and window mode

One of the simplest ways to enrich your viewing experience is to switch between full-screen mode and window mode. In full-screen mode, the video fills your entire computer screen. In window mode, the video fills only part of your computer screen while giving you access to the rest of your Mac Desktop, such as the Dock and other application windows, as shown in Figure 2-3.

Exiting and returning to full-screen mode

The first time you insert a DVD into your Mac, DVD Player displays your video in full-screen mode. To exit full-screen mode, choose one of the following:

+ Press Esc.

+ Press ⌘+F.

+ Click the Exit Full Screen button on the Controller, as shown in Figure 2-4.

In full-screen mode, you can view the DVD Player menu bar by moving the pointer to the top of the screen. You can also view the DVD Controller in full-screen mode by moving the pointer to the bottom of the screen.

To return to full-screen mode, choose one of the following:

+ Click the Full Screen button at the upper-right corner of the DVD Player window.

+ Press ⌘+F.

+ Choose View⇨Enter Full Screen.

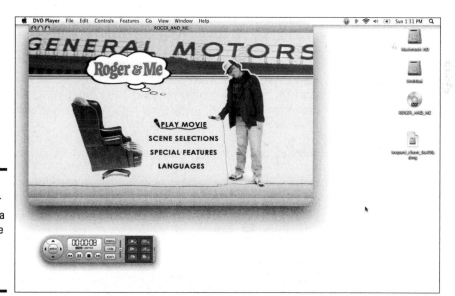

Figure 2-3: DVD Player can shrink a video inside a window on your Desktop.

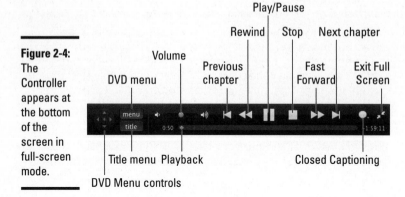

Figure 2-4: The Controller appears at the bottom of the screen in full-screen mode.

Viewing a video in a window

When you exit full-screen mode, your video appears in a window with the Controller displayed underneath the DVD window. (Refer to Figure 2-2.) By choosing the View menu, you can display a video in the following window sizes:

✦ Half Size

✦ Actual Size

✦ Double Size

✦ Fit to Screen

✦ Enter Full Screen

When viewing a video in a window, the Controller takes on a different *skin* (the display appearance), as shown in Figure 2-5. To open the drawer on the window-mode Controller, click and drag the handle down or toward the right (depending on how you choose to view the controller) or choose Controls⇨Open Control Drawer.

Although the Controller in both full-screen and window mode allows you to control a DVD, each Controller offers slightly different features. You can access some features in both full-screen and window mode, but many features are available only in one mode or the other.

In either viewing mode, click Option+cmd+C to show or hide the Controller.

To avoid letting any other window cover up part of your video window, choose View⇨Viewer Above Other Apps. To turn off this feature, choose the same command again.

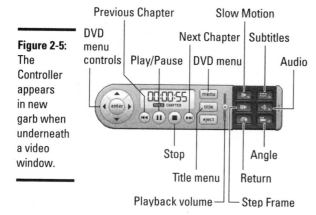

Figure 2-5:
The Controller appears in new garb when underneath a video window.

Previous Chapter

Slow Motion

DVD menu controls

Next Chapter | Subtitles

Play/Pause | DVD menu

Audio

Stop

Angle

Title menu | Return

Playback volume — └─ Step Frame

Viewing the DVD and Title menus

Most DVDs include an initial menu that lets you choose what to watch, such as the feature presentation or extra content such as interviews with the director and actors. Some DVDs also offer a Title menu that lets you pick different episodes, such as a DVD containing multiple episodes from a single season of a TV show. DVDs may offer both an initial menu and a Title menu. To jump to the initial DVD or Title menu (and note that not all DVDs have one), try clicking the Menu button (DVD menu) or the Title button on the Controller.

If at any time you want to start the DVD from the very beginning, choose Go⇨Beginning of Disc. (In full-screen mode, move the pointer to the top of the screen to display the DVD Player menu bar.) Alternatively, click the Stop button twice.

Skipping through a video

Sometimes you may want to skip over or replay part of a video. To skip backward or forward through a video, follow these steps:

1. **In full-screen mode, click one of the following buttons on the Controller:**

   - *Rewind:* Plays the video quickly in reverse
   - *Fast Forward:* Plays the video quickly going forward

   In DVD Player window mode, click and hold the Previous Chapter button to rewind, or the Next Chapter button to fast-forward.

2. **Click Play or press the spacebar when you want to resume viewing the video.**

Hold down the ⌘ key and press the left or right arrow keys to increase the rewind or fast forward speed incrementally by 2X, 4X, 8X, 16X, or 32X with each press of the arrow key. To stop rewinding or fast-forwarding and resume playing the video at normal speed, click the Play button or press the spacebar.

If you prefer menu commands, follow these steps:

1. **Choose Controls⇨Scan Forward (or Scan Backwards).**

   Your video continuously rewinds or fast-forwards.

2. **Change the scan rate by selecting Controls⇨Scan Rate⇨2/4/8/16/32x Speed.**

3. **Click the Play button or press the spacebar or choose Control⇨Play to resume playing the video at its normal speed.**

You can also drag the slider at the bottom of the Controller (in full-screen mode) to rewind or fast-forward a video.

Viewing frames in steps and slow motion

If you want to study a particular part of a video, the DVD Player lets you view individual frames one at a time or view your video in slow motion. To view individual frames, follow these steps:

1. **In window mode, click the Step Frame button on the Controller.**

   Each time you click the Step Frame button, the video advances one frame.

2. **Click the Play button on the Controller or press the spacebar to play the video at normal speed.**

Stepping through a video one frame at a time can be tedious, so an easier way to step through a video is in slow motion. To view your video in slow motion, follow these steps:

1. **Choose Controls⇨Slow Motion or click the Slow Motion button on the Controller in window mode.**

   The Slow Motion rate appears in the upper-left corner of the window. Select Controls⇨Slow Motion Rate⇨1/2, 1/4, 1/8 Speed to change how slow the video plays. In window mode, clicking the Slow Motion button again changes the rate of slow motion.

2. **Click the Play button on the Controller, or press the spacebar to play the video at normal speed.**

Skipping by chapters

Most DVD videos are divided into segments called *chapters*, which are usually listed somewhere on or inside the DVD case. If you want to view a favorite scene, just jump to the chapter that contains your favorite scene.

To move between chapters, choose one of the following:

✦ In full-screen mode, move your pointer to the top of the screen and then click the Chapters button (it looks like an open book) in the upper-left corner to open thumbnail images of the chapters. Click the chapter you want to skip to. Use the scroll bar to move forward and backward to other chapters.

✦ Click the Previous Chapter or Next Chapter button on the Controller.

✦ Press the left-arrow (previous) or right-arrow (next) key while the video is playing.

Placing bookmarks in a video

Sometimes your favorite parts of a movie don't correlate exactly to chapter sections on a DVD. In case you want to be able to jump to a specific part of a video, you can create a bookmark.

DVD Player saves your bookmarks on your Mac's hard drive, so if you pop the DVD out and back in again, your bookmarks are still preserved.

Creating a bookmark

To create a bookmark, follow these steps:

1. **Click the Pause button (or press the spacebar) to pause the video at the spot where you want to place a bookmark.**

2. **Choose Controls⇨New Bookmark or press ⌘+= to open the new bookmark dialog, as shown in Figure 2-6.**

3. **Enter a descriptive name for your bookmark in the text field and then click Add.**

If you select the Make Default Bookmark check box, you can jump to this bookmark in window mode by choosing Go⇨Default Bookmark.

Figure 2-6:
Enter a descriptive name for your bookmark.

Jumping to a bookmark

After you create at least one bookmark, you can jump to that bookmark by following these steps:

1. Choose Go➪Bookmarks.

A pop-up menu appears, listing all your saved bookmarks.

2. Click the bookmark name you want to jump to.

In full-screen mode, you can also click the Bookmarks button in the upper-left corner (under the Chapters button) and then click the bookmark you want to jump to.

Deleting a bookmark

After you create at least one bookmark, you can delete a bookmark by following these steps:

1. Choose Window➪Bookmarks.

A Bookmarks window appears, as shown in Figure 2-7.

2. Click to select the bookmark you want to delete and then click the Remove bookmark button (minus sign).

A dialog appears, asking whether you're sure that you want to delete your chosen bookmark.

3. Click OK (or Cancel) and then click the Close button to close the Bookmarks window.

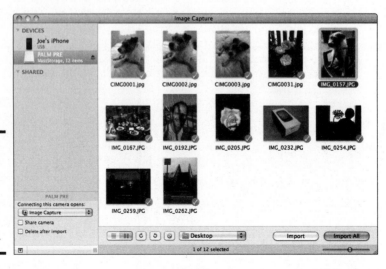

Figure 2-7:
The Bookmarks window shows you all your bookmarks.

You can Control-click in the viewing screen to open a shortcut menu, as shown in Figure 2-8.

Figure 2-8: Control-click to open a shortcut menu.

Viewing closed captioning

Many DVDs (but not all) include closed captioning and subtitles. Closed captioning displays written dialogue onscreen in the same language that's being spoken — English, for example — whereas subtitles give you a choice of reading dialogue onscreen in a language other than what's being spoken, such as French and Spanish.

To turn on closed captioning, choose one of the following:

✦ Choose Features⇨Closed Captioning⇨Turn On, and then choose Separate Window or Over Video to set where you want to see the captions.

✦ In full-screen mode, click the Closed Captioning button on the Controller and choose Turn On Closed Captioning. To view subtitles in different languages, choose one of the following:

• Choose Features⇨Subtitles and then choose a language, such as French or Spanish.

• In full-screen mode, click the Closed Captioning button on the Controller and choose a language under the Subtitles category.

Some DVDs have subtitle options in the DVD's interactive menu, which you access by clicking the Menu button on the controller.

Viewing different camera angles

Some DVDs, such as those containing video of concerts, offer a choice of multiple camera angles. This gives you a chance to view a DVD and, at a certain spot, switch from looking at the drummer to the lead guitarist.

To switch to a different camera angle, choose one of the following methods:

✦ Choose Features⇨Angle and then choose an angle.

✦ In window mode, click the Angle button on the Controller and then choose an angle. (If the DVD you're watching doesn't offer optional angles, the video will continue playing without changing the way it looks.)

✦ In full-screen mode, click the Streams/Closed Captioning button on the Controller and then choose an angle under the Angle category.

Choosing different audio tracks

Sometimes a DVD might offer multiple audio tracks, such as a default audio track and alternative audio tracks of foreign languages. To switch to different audio tracks, choose one of the following:

✦ Choose Features⇨Audio and then choose an audio track.

✦ In window mode, click the Audio button on the Controller and then choose an audio track. (If the DVD you're watching has only one audio track, the audio will continue playing without changing how you're hearing the audio.)

✦ In full-screen mode, click the Streams/Closed Captioning button on the Controller and then choose an audio track under the Audio Streams category.

To reveal DVD Player menus in full-screen mode, move the pointer to the top of the screen.

Enhancing your viewing experience

DVD Player has a few options to take full advantage of both your Mac's capabilities and the DVD that you're watching. You can adjust the video color quality, screen size, and audio to better suit your viewing needs. Follow these steps:

1. **Choose Window⇨Video Zoom.**

The Video Zoom inspector opens.

2. **Select the On check box.**

3. **Click the pop-up menu next to Manual, as shown in Figure 2-9.**

4. **Choose the preset zoom setting that you want.**

The width and height sliders move according to the type of display you choose.

Figure 2-9:
Video Zoom
lets you
change
the display
set up for
watching
your movie.

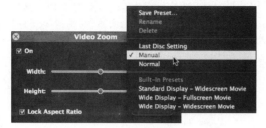

To adjust the color of your video, do this:

1. **Choose Window⇨Video Color.**

The Video Color inspector opens.

2. **Select the On check box.**

3. **Click the pop-up menu next to Manual, as shown in Figure 2-10.**

4. **Choose the preset setting that you want: Brighter, Deeper, or Richer.**

The brightness, contrast, color, and tint sliders move according to the type of color you choose.

You adjust the volume in DVD Player with the volume sliders on the controllers or by selecting Controls⇨Volume Up/Volume Down/Mute. You can control more than just the volume of the audio, however. For example, if you are watching a DVD on your Mac, you might want to set up the audio for small speakers. Follow these steps to adjust the audio:

1. **Choose Window⇨Audio Equalizer.**

The Audio Equalizer inspector opens.

2. **Select the On check box.**

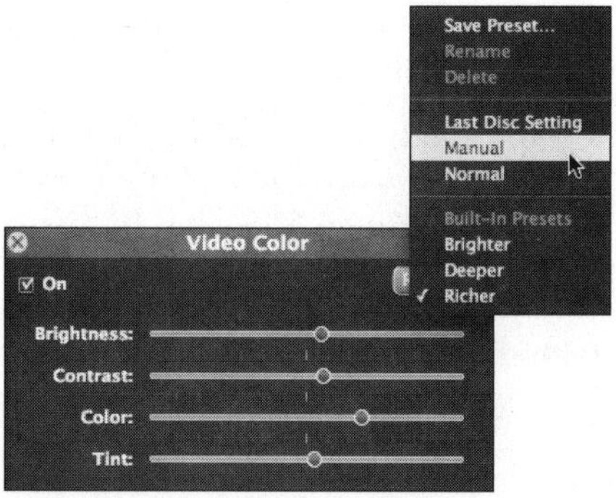

Figure 2-10:
Video Color
lets you
brighten or
enrich the
color of your
video.

3. **Click the pop-up menu next to Normal, as shown in Figure 2-11.**

4. **Choose the preset setting that you want: Bass and Vocal Boost, Bass Boost, Small Speakers, Vocal Boost.**

   The equalizing sliders move according to the type of audio you choose.

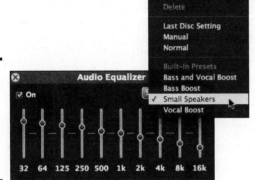

Figure 2-11:
The Audio Equalizer enhances the sound quality of your video.

Using DVD Player's Timer

If you're in the habit of falling asleep while watching a television show or film, you'll like DVD Player's Timer control. Like the sleep function on a clock radio, you set a time for how long you want your DVD to play and what action you want to take place when the time's up. Follow these steps:

1. **Choose Controls⇨Timer⇨Set Timer. Your DVD can be playing or stopped.**

   The Timer dialog opens, as shown in Figure 2-12.

2. **Type in the time limit you want to set (30 minutes is the default), or select the At End of Current Title option.**

   Use At End of Current Title if you want the action to take place when the DVD finishes playing (for example, so you don't have to get out of bed to turn your Mac off when the DVD finishes).

3. **Choose the action you want to happen when the time expires from the Action pop-up menu: Quit DVD Player, Sleep, Shut Down, Log Out.**

4. **Click OK.**

   The Timer appears briefly in the upper-left corner of the window. The other Timer options are activated in the Controls menu: Display Time, Resume, or Cancel Timer.

Figure 2-12:
Use the
Timer to
turn DVD
Player off
after a set
interval.

Ejecting the DVD

When you finish watching your DVD, you probably want to eject it from your Mac. Some Macs have an Eject key on the keyboard, which you can press to eject your disc. Otherwise, there are three ways to eject your DVD:

✦ From DVD Player, select Controls⟶Eject DVD.

✦ In window mode, click the Eject button on the controller.

✦ From the Finder, choose File⟶Eject *disc title*.

You can connect your Mac to a television, monitor, or projector and watch your DVD on a bigger screen. First, see what kind of port your television, monitor, or projector has, and then look through the Apple Online Store or visit your local Apple reseller to find the cable and adapter that matches your Mac. Attach the adapter to your Mac and then connect an HDMI or VGA cable from the adapter to your television, monitor, or projector. If your movie doesn't appear automatically on the external device, choose ⟶System Preferences⟶Displays and click Detect Displays to sync your Mac and the television, monitor, or projector.

Customizing DVD Player

Normally, you can pop a DVD into your Mac and watch it play right away. However, you might want to take some time to customize DVD Player to change how it plays.

Parental controls

If you don't want your children watching certain DVDs, you can turn on DVD Player's parental controls. These parental controls are designed either to block certain types of DVDs from playing or to prevent certain objectionable scenes from appearing, while allowing the rest of the movie to be seen.

Because of the extra expense involved in adding parental control features to a DVD, many DVDs don't support parental controls. If you turn on parental controls, it's entirely possible to watch an inappropriate DVD on your Mac if the DVD isn't programmed to implement the parental control features.

To turn on (or off) parental controls, follow these steps:

1. **Choose Features⇨Enable Parental Control.**

A dialog appears, asking for your password.

2. **Type your password and then click OK.**

3. **To see whether parental controls are enabled and set preferences, choose File⇨Get Disc Info⇨Parental Control.**

The Parental Control pane appears, as shown in Figure 2-13.

4. **If the DVD has parental controls enabled, the first time a DVD is inserted, you have to authorize it with the administrator password in order to play the DVD.**

In the dialog that appears, choose Play Once if you want to require the administrator name and password each time the DVD is inserted, or select Always Allow to play the DVD whenever it is inserted.

If you want to change the authorization, when the DVD is playing, choose File⇨Get Disc Info and click Parental Control. Select Always Ask for Authorization if you want to require the administrator name and password to play the DVD or Always Allow to be Played to let the DVD be played without being authorized again. You can also choose Features⇨Deauthorize Media. Enter the administrator name and password to immediately stop playback and eject the DVD.

Figure 2-13:
Parental
Control lets
you choose
which
DVDs your
children can
watch.

To disable parental controls, choose Features⇨Disable Parental Controls.

Defining DVD Player preferences

DVD Player offers six categories for modifying how to play DVDs:

✦ **Player:** Defines how DVD Player behaves when running, such as whether to start in full-screen mode. If you watch videos when your Mac isn't connected to a power source, select the Put the DVD Drive to Sleep check box next to When Playing Using Battery.

✦ **Disc Setup:** Allows you to change the language used to display audio, subtitles, and DVD menus. If you connect external speakers to your Mac, select the preferred Audio Output here.

✦ **Windows:** Defines how to display closed captioning in a window and whether or not to show the video status window.

✦ **Previously Viewed:** Defines how to handle a DVD that was ejected and inserted back into your Mac — for example, specifies whether to start playing the DVD at the beginning or at the last scene viewed before you ejected the DVD.

✦ **High Definition:** Defines how to play high-definition DVDs. You won't see this option if your Mac doesn't support HD.

If you aren't sure which DVD Player features your Mac supports, choose Help⇨Show Supported Features. A list appears on the screen; click the list to close it. To change DVD Player's preferences settings, follow these steps:

1. **Choose DVD Player — Preferences.**

A Preferences dialog appears, as shown in Figure 2-14.

2. **Click an icon at the top of the dialog, such as Player or Windows, and change any options.**

Some of these options let you mute sound in case you receive an iChat invitation or define colors for displaying closed captioning so it's easier to read on the screen. Feel free to experiment with different options to see which ones are most useful.

3. **Click OK (or Cancel) to close the DVD Player preferences dialog.**

Using Apple Remote

Although new Macs don't come with an Apple Remote control, some earlier model Macs do, and you can also buy one for your Mac (go to www.apple. com) if your Mac has an Infrared port. With the Apple Remote control, you can control many of your Mac's applications, including DVD Player, Keynote, iTunes, and iPhoto.

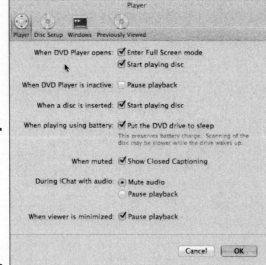

Figure 2-14:
Player
preferences
let you
customize
different
features of
DVD Player.

 If your Mac doesn't have a built-in Infrared port, you can buy an external
Infrared receiver called Mira (http://twistedmelon.com/mira) that
plugs into your Mac's USB port and gives it the same remote-control-friendly
capabilities as a Mac with a built-in Infrared port.

The Apple Remote works like the remote control that you use with your television or stereo, providing the following controls, as shown in Figure 2-15:

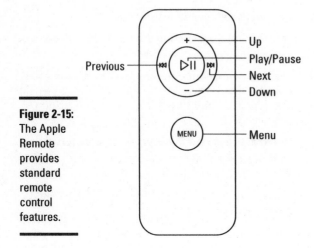

Figure 2-15:
The Apple
Remote
provides
standard
remote
control
features.

✦ **Up:** Moves the highlighting up one option.

✦ **Down:** Moves the highlighting down one option.

✦ **Next:** Fast-forwards a media file or selects the next item.

✦ **Previous:** Rewinds a media file or selects the previous item.

✦ **Play/Pause:** Toggles between playing and pausing a media file. Also used to select a highlighted option.

✦ **Menu:** Displays the main Front Row menu. Also used to go back to a previous menu.

For your Mac to pick up the Apple Remote's Infrared (IR) signal, your Mac must be in line-of-sight range when you point it at your Mac and press the remote control's buttons.

Pairing an Apple Remote with a Mac

If you have two or more Mac computers, an iPod, or an Apple TV unit in the same room, your Apple Remote can accidentally control multiple devices rather than only the one you want to control. To make sure that your Apple Remote works with only a particular Mac, you can pair the Apple Remote with that specific Mac.

To pair an Apple Remote to a specific Mac, follow these steps:

1. **Hold the Apple Remote 4 to 6 inches away from the Infrared (IR) port on the Mac you want to control and then press the Menu and Next buttons at the same time.**

2. **When a paired-remote icon appears a few seconds later, release the Menu and Next buttons.**

Your Apple Remote is now paired to work only with that specific Mac.

To unpair an Apple Remote from a specific Mac, follow these steps:

1. **Choose ⌘⇨System Preferences on the Mac that you want to unpair from an Apple Remote to open the System Preferences window.**

2. **Click the Security & Privacy icon to open your Mac's Security & Privacy preferences pane and then click the General tab (if it isn't already selected) to display the General options.**

3. **Deselect the Disable Remote Control Infrared Receiver check box to let your Mac work with any Apple Remote.**

**Book IV
Chapter 2**

Watching Videos
and Movies on
Your Mac

Controlling your Mac and applications

You can use Apple Remote to control applications and functions on your Mac. Remote control is handy when you're making a presentation and don't want to fumble with keyboard or menu commands, or any time your Mac is farther than arm's reach away.

Making a Mac go to sleep

To make your Mac go to sleep by using the Apple Remote, hold down the Play/Pause button until a sleeping Apple Remote icon appears on the screen and then release the Play/Pause button.

To wake up a sleeping Mac with the Apple Remote, just tap any button on the Apple Remote.

Booting up a Mac

If you've divided your hard drive into partitions and have installed two different operating systems (as when you use Boot Camp to run Windows), you can use the Apple Remote to help you choose which partition and operating system to use by following these steps:

1. **Hold down the Menu button on the Apple Remote and turn on (or restart) your Mac.**

   The hard-drive icons that appear list all the startup partitions you can choose.

2. **Press the Previous and Next buttons to select a hard drive and then press the Play/Pause button to start your Mac with the selected hard drive.**

Controlling applications

You can use the Apple Remote to control several popular applications, including Keynote, iTunes, iPhoto, and DVD Player.

The Apple Remote can control different applications, but it won't let you switch, open, or close applications. If you want to do this from a distance, use a wireless keyboard and mouse.

The Apple Remote is so simple to use, you can usually figure out how it works with a particular application by loading the application, pointing the Apple Remote at your Mac, and then pressing its couple of buttons to see what they do. Some applications you can control with the Apple Remote, and tips on how you can control these applications include

✦ **Keynote:** Press the Play/Pause button to begin viewing a presentation. To view the next (or previous) slide, press the Next (or Previous)
button. Press the Menu button to display thumbnails of your slides.
Holding down the Menu button exits your presentation and returns you
to the main Keynote screen.

✦ **iTunes:** Choose a playlist (or choose your entire music collection) and
then press the Play/Pause button to start listening to your selection.
Press the Previous button to restart the playing track from the beginning. Press the Previous button twice in rapid succession to start playing the previous audio track. Jump to the next song by pressing the Next
button. The Up and Down buttons control the volume level.

✦ **iPhoto:** Select an album that contains the pictures you want to see and
then press the Play/Pause button. To view the previous (or next) photograph, press the Previous (or Next) button. Exit from your slideshow by
holding down the Menu button.

✦ **DVD Player:** To start playing a DVD, press the Play/Pause button.
Choose an option from the DVD menus by pressing the Previous and
Next buttons and select an option by pressing the Play/Pause button.
Use the Up and Down buttons to adjust the volume.

If you don't have Apple Remote or an infrared port, but you do have an
iPhone, iPad, or iPod touch, iOSpirit (www.iospirit.com/products/
remotebuddyexpress) sells Remote Buddy Express in the App Store,
which turns your iPhone, iPad, or iPod touch into a remote control for
over 100 applications on your Mac.

Chapter 3: Importing, Viewing, Organizing, and Sharing Photos

In This Chapter

✔ Understanding digital photography

✔ Capturing images with Image Capture

✔ Snapping and sharing photos with Photo Booth

✔ Importing photos into iPhoto

✔ Organizing Events

✔ Organizing photos

✔ Organizing with Faces and Places

✔ Editing photos

✔ Sharing photos with others

*M*ore people are taking photos than ever before with digital cameras and mobile phones. Both gadgets let you capture a photo, see it right away, and then decide whether you want to save, eliminate, or share it. Even better, after you capture a photo, you can edit it to make it look better than the subject or scene did in real life. You can even alter a digital image with an image-editing application. You can use iPhoto, which is part of the iLife suite, not only for image editing but also for *managing* (an important part of digital photography because it's so easy to accumulate hundreds, if not thousands, of photos in a short time) and sharing your photos. We explain all these tasks in this chapter.

Understanding Digital Photography

Instead of using film, digital photography captures images on memory-storage devices. Not only does this make digital photographs easy to store on your Mac, but you can also make identical copies of your photos at any time without losing image quality.

When using a digital camera or mobile phone equipped with a camera, it's helpful to understand how digital cameras and mobile phones store images so you can transfer them to your Mac.

Megapixels

Digital photographs capture images as a collection of tiny dots called *pixels*. A single photo consists of hundreds, thousands, or (most commonly) millions of pixels. The greater the number of pixels used to create a photo, the sharper the overall image. To help you understand the capabilities of different digital cameras and mobile phones, manufacturers identify the gadgets by how many millions of pixels they can capture in each photo. This total number of pixels, called the *resolution,* ranges from as little as less than one megapixel (MP) to 16 megapixels or more. Figure 3-1 shows how pixels create an image.

Figure 3-1:
Every digital image consists of hundreds, thousands, or millions of pixels.

The more megapixels a digital camera has (and the better the lens), the sharper the image resolution. A photo captured with a 3-megapixel camera won't look as sharp as that same image captured with an 8-megapixel camera, especially if you enlarge it.

Flash memory cards

Every time you snap a digital photo, your camera or mobile phone needs to save that photo somewhere. Some digital cameras and mobile phones (such as the Apple iPhone) come with built-in memory, which can store any digital images that you capture. However, to store large numbers of photos, most digital cameras and some mobile phones can also store photos on removable storage devices called *flash memory cards.*

In no particular order, here are a few things to keep in mind about flash memory cards:

✦ **Reuse:** The biggest advantage of flash memory cards over film is that you can erase and reuse flash memory cards. You can take as many photos as the flash memory card can hold, copy your photos to your Mac's hard drive, and then erase the photos from the flash memory card so you can use it again.

✦ **Resolution versus storage:** The number of photos you can store on flash memory cards depends on the resolution of the photos you take. If you capture photos at a high resolution, you can store far fewer photos than if you capture those same photos at a lower resolution.

✦ **Storage and speed measurement:** Flash memory cards are often measured in terms of their storage size and speed. The amount of storage a flash memory card can hold is measured in megabytes (MB) and, most frequently today, gigabytes (GB), such as 512MB or 2GB. The greater the storage capability of a flash memory card, the higher the cost.

The speed of flash memory cards is often described as minimum read and write speeds, measured in megabytes per second (MB/sec) such as 10MB/sec. The higher the write speed of a flash memory card, the faster you can capture and store photos. Sometimes the speed of a flash memory card might also be described as a number — 60x, for example — which tells you the flash memory card is 60 times faster than the original flash memory cards.

✦ **Image recovery:** If you ever accidentally erase a photo from a flash memory card, don't panic (and don't store any more photos on that flash memory card). If you buy a special file-recovery application, such as MediaRECOVER (http://freshcrop.com) or Digital Photo Recovery (www.digitalphotorecovery.org), you can often retrieve deleted photos from any type of flash memory card. However, if you delete a photo and then store more photos on the flash memory card, the new photos will likely wipe out any traces of your deleted photos, making it impossible to retrieve the deleted photos ever again.

Many different types of flash memory cards exist because each design is meant to set the "standard" for flash memory cards. Unfortunately, every flash memory card has its limitations, so companies keep coming up with newer designs to overcome these limitations. Because so many "standards" exist, the result is that there is no standard. The following are the most popular flash memory cards:

✦ **Compact Flash Type I (CFI) and Compact Flash Type II (CFII):** Introduced in 1994, CompactFlash cards were one of the first flash memory cards available and one of the largest. There are two types of CompactFlash cards: Type I (3.3 mm thick), or CFI; and Type II (5.0 mm thick), or CFII.

Because of the thickness differences, make sure that you use the right CompactFlash cards for your digital camera and card reader. A digital camera and card reader that can use a CFII card can also use a CFI card, but the reverse isn't true.

✦ **Secure Digital (SD) and Plus Secure Digital (Plus SD):** SD cards are much smaller than CompactFlash cards and offer built-in encryption to prevent storing copyright-infringing materials, such as illegal songs, although this encryption feature is rarely used. Because of their small size, Secure Digital cards are slowly evolving into the standard for digital photography. Even smaller versions of Secure Digital cards include Mini and Micro SD cards, which are often the type of flash memory card used in mobile phones.

✦ **Memory Stick (MS), Memory Stick Pro (MS Pro), Memory Stick Duo (MS Duo), Memory Stick Pro Duo (MS Pro Duo), and Memory Stick Micro (MS Micro):** The Memory Stick format was developed by Sony, and, as of this writing, only Sony devices (digital cameras, video camcorders, and PlayStations) use Memory Sticks for storing digital images. The original Memory Stick stores up to 32GB of data, whereas the Memory Stick Pro purportedly can hold up to 2TB (that's *tetrabytes,* as in "thousand gigabytes") of data. The Memory Stick Duo and Memory Stick Pro Duo look like an original Memory Stick cut in half. Sony also makes the Memory Stick Micro, which holds up to 16GB.

Despite Sony's backing, the Memory Stick format has never gained popularity with other manufacturers. If you buy a Sony camera, you'll probably be stuck with using Memory Sticks, although some of the latest Sony cameras now use Secure Digital cards instead.

✦ **xD Photo Cards (xD):** Olympus and Fuji invented the xD Photo Cards to provide yet another standard. Fewer cameras use them — with the exception, of course, of Olympus cameras and some Fuji cameras. An xD Photo Card is often more expensive than other flash memory cards, making them less attractive.

Digital image file formats

When you take photos, your digital camera stores those photos in a specific graphics file format. The three most common file formats for storing digital photographs are

✦ **JPEG (Joint Photo Experts Group):** JPEG is the most common file format because it is recognized by most computers and offers the ability to compress images to shrink the overall file size. (*Compressing* a JPEG file means decreasing the number of colors used in an image, which shrinks the file size but lowers the visual quality.)

✦ **TIFF (Tagged Image File Format):** If photo quality is more important than file size, save your photos as TIFF files. You can still compress TIFF files slightly, but TIFF files always retain all colors. As a result, a compressed TIFF file is usually larger than an equivalent compressed JPEG file.

✦ **RAW (which doesn't stand for anything!):** RAW files offer greater visual quality but there is no single RAW file-format standard. As a result, every digital camera manufacturer offers its own RAW file format.

The biggest advantage is that RAW files allow for greater manipulation. As a result, professional photographers often use RAW files for greater control over manipulating their images. The biggest disadvantage is that RAW images take up a large amount of storage space and take longer for a consumer digital camera to store, which means that you can't capture images in rapid succession as you can with JPEG files. Some pricier dSLR (digital single lens reflex) cameras capture images in a "burst" mode, making them fast even in RAW format.

Ultimately, there is no single "best" file format. If a digital camera lets you save images in different file formats, experiment to see which one you like best. You might prefer one type of file format, such as JPEG, for ordinary use, but prefer RAW for capturing images in special situations that don't require capturing images quickly, such as taking photos of a landscape.

Transferring Digital Images to the Mac

To transfer photos from a digital camera to your Mac, you have two choices. First, you can connect your digital camera to your Mac by using a USB cable. Second, you can pop the flash memory card out of your digital camera and plug it into your Mac's built-in SDxD card reader (if your Mac has one) or a third-party card reader that connects to your Mac's USB port. No matter which method you use, your Mac then treats all the images stored on your digital camera's flash memory card as just another external drive that you can copy photos from to your Mac's hard drive (such as into the Photos folder).

When you connect a digital camera or a mobile phone to your Mac, it can automatically load an application to retrieve those images. Two applications included with your Mac that you can use to retrieve digital snapshots automatically are iPhoto and Image Capture.

If you organize photos in iPhoto, choose it as your default application to retrieve photos from a digital camera. (You can specify another application as the external editor.) If you use a different application to organize your photos, such as Adobe Photoshop, you can make that application your default application. If you use more than one application to organize your photos, you can make Image Capture your default application and then run the application you want to work with your imported photos, deciding what to use on an application-by-application basis.

Defining a default application for retrieving photos

If you need to transfer digital images from a camera to your Mac on a regular basis, you can define a default application to use for retrieving these images by following these steps:

1. **Double-click the Image Capture icon in the Applications folder or Launchpad.**

   The Image Capture window appears.

2. **Connect your camera or smartphone to your Mac's USB or FireWire port with the appropriate cable.**

   Your connected camera or smartphone will appear under the Devices group in the left pane, as shown in Figure 3-2.

   You can also define a default application by running iPhoto and choosing iPhoto⇨Preferences.

3. **Click the Connecting This [*your device name here*] Opens pop-up menu in the bottom-left corner and choose iPhoto or Image Capture (refer to Figure 3-2).**

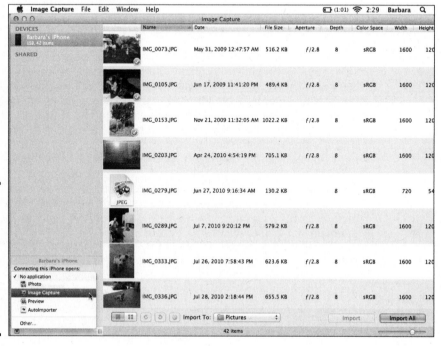

Figure 3-2:
Your camera or smartphone appears in the left pane under the Devices group.

You can choose another application listed on the pop-up menu, or click Other to choose an application in your Mac's Applications folder that isn't listed in the pop-up menu so it can run automatically when you connect your camera to your Mac.

4. **Choose the following options if you want to**

   - *Delete after Import:* Copies your photos from your connected device to your Mac's hard drive, and then deletes the photos from your camera or smartphone, freeing memory on the device so you can take more photos.

   - *Import To:* Click the pop-up menu to the right of Import To choose where you want Image Capture to save your imported photos.

5. **Choose File⇨Quit to exit the Image Capture application.**

Retrieving photos by using Image Capture

If you define Image Capture as the default application to run when you connect a digital camera to your Mac, follow these steps:

1. **Connect your digital camera or smartphone to your Mac with the appropriate cable.**

   The Image Capture window appears, displaying your camera or smartphone photos in the right pane (refer to Figure 3-2).

   You can also use the Image Capture application to capture and copy images from a scanner.

2. **(Optional) Before importing your photos, you can click the icons below the right pane of the Image Capture window, shown in Figure 3-3, to**

   - Switch between List view and Icon view.

   - Rotate a selected photo left.

   - Rotate a selected photo right.

   - Delete a selected photo.

   - Choose the location to which you want Image Capture to save your imported photos (click the pop-up menu).

Figure 3-3: Tweak a photo before importing.

Book IV
Chapter 3

Importing, Viewing, Organizing, and Sharing Photos

3. **(Optional) Click and drag the slider in the bottom-right corner of the Image Capture window left or right to increase or decrease the size of your photo icons.**

4. **Click a photo that you want to transfer and click Import, or click Import All to retrieve all photos stored on your camera or smartphone.**

   To select multiple images, hold down the ⌘ key and click each photo you want to import.

5. **Image Capture marks each photo with a check mark after it copies that photo to the location selected in the pop-up menu to the left of the Import button (refer to Figure 3-2).**

6. **Choose Image Capture➪Quit Image Capture.**

If you didn't select the Delete after Import check box, you have to erase the photos from your flash memory card after you import them to your Mac so the memory card has space to store more snapshots.

Retrieving photos by using iPhoto

If you want to use iPhoto as the default application to run when you connect a digital camera to your Mac, follow these steps:

1. **Connect your digital camera or smartphone to your Mac with the appropriate cable (or plug your memory card into your memory card reader).**

   iPhoto launches automatically if you chose it as your default (as explained in the section "Defining a default application for retrieving photos") and displays your camera or smartphone photos in the right pane, as shown in Figure 3-4.

   If you're running iPhoto for the first time and didn't choose a default application, two dialogs will appear, offering these options:

   • *Do you want to use iPhoto when you connect your digital camera?:* Click Yes if you want iPhoto to open automatically whenever you plug in your digital camera or camera-enabled smartphone. Click No if you don't want iPhoto to open automatically — or click Decide Later if you'd rather make this momentous decision another time.

   • *Look up Photo Locations:* Click Yes if you want iPhoto to automatically tag location information when it imports photos you snap with your GPS-capable camera or smartphone.

Figure 3-4:
iPhoto
displays
the photos
stored on
a camera,
smartphone,
or memory
card
plugged into
your Mac.

2. **(Optional) Before importing your photos, you can adjust or choose the following options in the upper area of the iPhoto window:**

   - *Event Name:* Click the text field and type a name for the batch of photos you're importing, such as **My Wedding Day** or **Summer Vacation**.

   - *Split Events:* Select this check box to make iPhoto automatically create separate event folders for photos you're importing based on the date you snapped the photos.

   - *Show All (number of) Photos:* Click the arrow to see all the photos that are still on your device but that you already imported to iPhoto.

3. **(Optional) Click and drag the slider in the bottom-left corner of the iPhoto window left or right to increase or decrease the size of your photo thumbnails.**

4. **Click a photo that you want to transfer and click Import Selected.**

   If you click Import All, iPhoto retrieves all photos stored on your camera or smartphone.

   To select multiple images, hold down the ⌘ key and click each photo you want to import.

Book IV
Chapter 3

Importing, Viewing,
Organizing, and
Sharing Photos

5. **When iPhoto finishes importing your photos, a dialog appears asking if you want to keep or delete the photos from your camera or smartphone.**

6. **If you want to delete the photos from your device to make room so you can take more photos, click the Delete Photos button. Otherwise, click the Keep Photos button to leave the photos on your camera or smartphone.**

7. **Choose iPhoto⇨Quit iPhoto to exit iPhoto.**

Moving photos from other folders into iPhoto

If you have photos or image files in other folders on your Mac or on an external hard drive or flash drive, follow these steps to bring the photos and images into iPhoto:

1. **Click the iPhoto icon in the Dock or Launchpad.**

2. **Choose File⇨Import to Library.**

   An Import Photos dialog appears, as shown in Figure 3-5.

Figure 3-5: The Import Photos dialog lets you choose the device and folder that contains photos.

3. **Click the drive or folder in the Source List that contains the photos you want to import.**

4. **Choose one of the following:**

   • *To import every photo file displayed on a drive or in a selected folder:* Proceed to Step 5.

- *To import individual files from a drive or folder:* Click the photo file(s) in the middle column that you want to import, or click a folder in the middle column that contains the photos you want to import and click the photo files that you want to import in the right column.

To select multiple photos, hold down the ⌘ key and click each photo you want to import. To select a range of photos, click the first photo you want to import, hold down the Shift key, and then click the last photo to include all the photos in between.

5. **Click Import.**

iPhoto imports your photos and organizes them into an Event, or several Events if the photo files you import are tagged with information about them, and/or if you import the contents of two or more separate folders.

A fast way to import photos into iPhoto is to drag and drop those photos to the iPhoto icon in the Dock, or to the Photos category under Library in the iPhoto Source List.

Retrieving photos by using the SDxD memory card reader

A second way to transfer digital images is to remove the memory card from your camera or smartphone and then plug it into the SDxD memory card reader port on your Mac, if your Mac has one. (You can also connect a card reader to the USB port and insert the card into the reader.) Your Mac displays the flash memory card icon on the Desktop and its contents in a Finder window the same way it displays an external hard drive.

Never yank a flash memory card out of the card reader port because doing so might cause your Mac to scramble the data on the memory card. Before physically removing a flash memory card from the port, choose one of the following ways to eject a flash memory card safely from your Mac:

- ✦ Drag the flash memory card icon to the Trash icon in the Dock to eject it.
- ✦ Click the flash memory icon and choose File⇨Eject.
- ✦ Click the flash memory icon and press ⌘+E.
- ✦ Control-click the flash memory icon and choose Eject from the shortcut menu that appears.
- ✦ Click the Eject button that appears to the right of the flash memory icon in the Source List of the Finder window.

Capturing Photos from Other Sources

If you don't have a separate digital camera, but you have a MacBook Air, MacBook Pro, or iMac, you have a built-in iSight digital camera in your Mac. You can also find a built-in iSight camera on Apple's LED Cinema Display external monitor that can connect to your Mac desktop computer, or act as a second display for your MacBook computer. To capture photos with this built-in camera, the simplest method is to use the Photo Booth application located in your Mac's Applications folder.

If you're the type who doesn't like taking photos, you may prefer to save photos you like from websites you visit or from friends' postings on social networks like Facebook and Flickr. By copying photos from websites, you can find images that you wouldn't normally capture yourself, such as images of fighting in the Middle East or photos of mountain climbers scaling Mount Everest, unless of course you're a courageous-and-adventurous type.

Photos stored on websites are usually copyrighted, so you can't legally copy those photos and reuse them for commercial purposes.

Capturing photos with Photo Booth

If your Mac has a built-in iSight camera, you can capture photos of yourself (or whoever or whatever is stationed in front of your Mac) by using the Photo Booth application. Photos you snap with Photo Booth save as JPEG files in a Photo Booth folder tucked inside your Photos folder.

You can plug in an optional external webcam, such as one of the models sold by Logitech (www.logitech.com) or Microsoft (www.microsoft.com/hardware), or plug in certain camcorders, to capture photos with Photo Booth. You can also use one of these optional external choices to conduct live, two-way video chats with friends and family, as we write about in Book II, Chapter 3.

To capture photos with Photo Booth, follow these steps:

1. **Click the Photo Booth icon on the Dock or Launchpad, or double-click the Photo Booth icon in the Applications folder.**

    The Photo Booth window appears, displaying the image seen through the iSight camera. Click the zoom widget in the upper-right corner to use Photo Booth in full-screen mode, as shown in Figure 3-6. That way you have those nice red theater curtains framing your image.

    If you click the Effects button, you can capture a photo by using visual effects (such as fish-eye) or in front of a background (such as the Eiffel Tower).

Figure 3-6:
Photo Booth
lets you
capture
photos with
your Mac's
built-in
iSight
camera.

Four-up   Video   Camera button
Photo

Single Photo

2. **Use the three buttons on the lower-left side to choose from three formats:**

   • *Four-up photo:* Click the left button to take four successive photos, just like an old-fashioned photo booth.

   • *Single photo:* Click the middle button to take a single photo.

   • *Video:* Click the right button to record video.

3. **Click the camera button in the middle of the iSight window (or press ⌘+T).**

   Photo Booth counts down from 3 (in seconds) before capturing your photo. If you choose four-up, Photo Booth snaps four successive shots. If you chose video, Photo Booth begins recording video. Click the camera button again to stop recording video.

   Each captured photo or video appears at the bottom of the Photo Booth window. Click a photo to see it in the Photo Booth viewing pane. Swipe

**Book IV
Chapter 3**

**Importing, Viewing,
Organizing, and
Sharing Photos**

left and right on the trackpad or with the Magic Mouse to move from one photo to the next.

If you hold down the Option key when you click the camera icon (or press ⌘+T), Photo Booth snaps your photo right away without going through the three-second countdown.

4. **You have five options for sharing your photos. If you are in normal view, click the icons underneath the viewing pane. If you are in full-screen view, click the Share button to reveal a pop-up menu that offers the same choices. Click a photo from the preview filmstrip and click one of the following buttons or choices from the Share pop-up menu:**

   - *E-mail* opens a new message in Mail with your selected photo pasted in the message.

   - *iPhoto* transfers the photo to your iPhoto library.

   - *User Photo* assigns the photo to your user account on your Mac. This is the photo that appears when you log in to your Mac.

   - *Buddy Icon* uses the photo as your buddy icon in iChat.

5. **Choose File⇨Export to export your photo to another folder.**

6. **Click the disclosure triangle next to the Save As field to see the Finder. Scroll through the directories and folders to choose the location to which you want to save the image.**

7. **To print your photo, click the photo you want to print in the preview filmstrip, and then choose File⇨Print.**

8. **Adjust any necessary settings in the print dialog, and then click the Print button.**

9. **When you finish snapping and sharing photos, choose Photo Booth⇨ Quit Photo Booth or press ⌘+Q to exit Photo Booth.**

   Photo Booth stores its photos in a Photo Booth Library inside the Photos folder.

You can delete photos you take with Photo Booth as follows:

✦ Open Photo Booth as described in the previous steps. In the preview filmstrip, click a photo that you want to delete, and then press the Delete key or click the "x" in the upper-left corner of the preview image.

✦ To delete all your Photo Booth photos at one time, choose Edit⇨Delete All Photos and click OK to confirm your choice.

When you choose the Delete All Photos command, you remove all photos stored in the Photo Booth folder inside the Photos folder.

Capturing photos from websites

By browsing through different websites, you can find a variety of images that you may want to use for personal use, such as adding them to an album in your iPhoto library of a movie star or public servant whose career you follow, or saving photos from the social network profiles of friends and relatives who live far away.

To save images from a web page, follow these steps:

1. **Load Safari by clicking the Safari icon in the Dock.**

You can use a different web browser for these steps if you prefer.

2. **Browse to a web page and Control-click a photo you want.**

Doing so opens a shortcut menu, as shown in Figure 3-7.

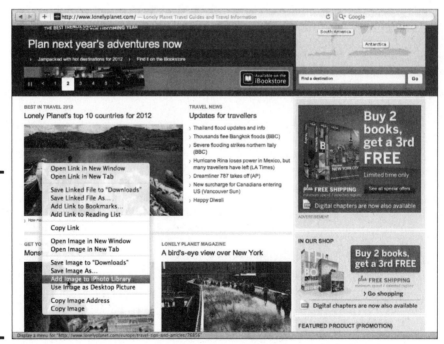

Figure 3-7:
Control-clicking a web page image gives you a variety of choices for saving the photo.

Generally, because of copyright rules, don't copy photos from websites for reuse on a commercial website.

3. **Choose one of the following commands from the shortcut menu:**

   • *Save Image to "Downloads":* Saves the photo in the Downloads folder, stored inside your Home folder.

   • *Save Image As:* Lets you choose a name for your photo and a folder where you want to save the photo.

   • *Add Image to iPhoto Library:* Saves the image in your iPhoto photo library.

   • *Copy Image:* Copies the image to the Mac's invisible clipboard so you can paste it into another document, such as an e-mail message or a letter to your mom.

The Save Image As option is the only one that lets you choose your own descriptive name for an image and specify the save location. All the other options save an image by using that image's original filename, which might be something cryptic like `wild_things_LJ-0187.jpg`, although you can always rename the file later if you want.

Clicking and dragging a web image to your Mac's Desktop (or to a Finder window) is one way to quickly capture photos from websites.

Organizing Photos with iPhoto

After you take photos with your digital camera, smartphone, or Photo Booth, download photos attached to e-mail messages, or copy photos from the web, you need to organize them in such a way that you can find the photos you want when you want to look at them again. This is where iPhoto comes in.

Think of iPhoto as a place where you can dump all your digital photographs so you can browse them again later. In iPhoto, all your photos are stored in a Library. The Library provides five ways to organize your photos:

✦ **Events** typically contain photos captured on the same day.

✦ **Albums** typically contain photos grouped by a common theme, such as photos of your commitment ceremony or vacation.

✦ **Faces** organizes your Library based on the faces of individuals you *tag* with a name; over time, iPhoto tries to identify faces in new photos you import and automatically tag them with the name of the person (or persons) in the photos.

✦ **Places** automatically tags and organizes your photos based on where you snapped them with your GPS-capable camera or mobile phone, like the Nikon Coolpix 6000 camera or the iPhone 4 smartphone, which both have built-in Global Positioning System (GPS) receivers. You can also tag photos with location information on an individual or group basis.

✦ **Folders** hold and organize multiple albums. You can create a folder called Animals, for instance, and then store albums, such as Goats, Monkeys, Terriers, and Hermit Crabs, inside your Animals folder.

If you work in normal view, the library categories run down the left side of the iPhoto window in what's called the Source List. However, iPhoto works in full-screen view (as long as you're using Mac OS X 10.7 Lion), in which case the library buttons along the bottom of the screen represent categories. Click the zoom widget in the upper-right corner to open iPhoto in full-screen view, which is great for working in iPhoto because it takes advantage of all the real estate of your Mac screen — no matter how big or small.

After importing your photos (following one or all of the procedures described in the first part of this chapter), iPhoto lets you edit your photos to modify colors, fix photos containing people afflicted by that vexing "red-eye" condition, or clip out unwanted portions. When your photos look perfect, you can print them on your printer or through a printing service (which can actually cost less than what you might spend on ink cartridges and glossy photo paper!). You can also share photos in your iPhoto Library with others via e-mail, or by posting them to websites, such as Facebook or Flickr, and you can back up your most recent 1,000 photos on iCloud by using Photo Stream. From start to finish, iPhoto can take care of organizing your photos so you can focus on taking even more photos.

Organizing Events in the Library

The iPhoto Library can store literally thousands of photos, which can soon become as disorganized as dumping a decade's worth of photographs in a box and then wondering why you can never find a specific photo easily.

Just as most people organize photos in albums, boxes, or bags, iPhoto can organize groups of photos in one place. In iPhoto, a group of related photos is an *Event*.

Two other ways you can organize and view photos is by using the Faces feature, which sorts photos by the faces of people in your photos, and the Places feature, which sorts photos based on the location where you capture them. Both of these other ways of organizing and viewing photos in your iPhoto Library are covered in later sections of this chapter.

The main purpose of Events is to group related photos together. One Event might contain photos you capture during your stay on a UFO, and a second Event might hold photos of your new puppy's first visit to the beach. After you group related photos in an Event, you quickly can find photos you want to look at again or share with others.

Creating an Event

When you import photos, iPhoto automatically organizes them as Events, based on the day the photo was captured. Organizing Events by day can automatically sort photos into one Event (the first day of your vacation when you visited London) and a second Event (the second day of your vacation when you visited Paris, and so on).

You can also create an Event manually by choosing Events⇨Create Events.

Browsing through an Event

An Event can represent a single photo you capture on a particular day, but more likely, an Event represents several photos. To view thumbnail previews of all the photos stored in an Event, hover the pointer over the Event icon and then slowly move the pointer left or right (or press the left and right arrow keys) to step through a thumbnail preview of each photo contained in the Event.

When you position the pointer over an Event, iPhoto displays the date of the event and the number of photos it contains, as shown in Figure 3-8.

Figure 3-8:
Hover on an Event to reveal its date and number of photos.

turchia2010
Sep 1, 2010 – Sep 3, 2010   57

If you'd rather see individual thumbnails of all the photos stored in a single Event, double-click the Event to display them, shown in Figure 3-9, which shows the full-screen view.

Figure 3-9:
Double-
clicking
an Event
expands all
the photos
in the iPhoto
window.

Click the All Events button to return to the iPhoto window.

Naming an Event

To make finding photos easier, you can give each Event a descriptive name so you have a rough idea what type of photos are stored in that Event without having to browse through them. To give your Event a descriptive name, follow these steps:

1. **Click the Events category under Library in the left pane (the Source List) of the iPhoto window or click the Events button at the bottom of the screen if you're working in full-screen view.**

iPhoto displays all your Events in the right pane. If you haven't named your Events, each Event may display the date when you captured those photos as its name.

2. **Click the Event name, which appears directly under the Event photo.**

A yellow box highlights the Event and a text box appears along with the number of photos stored in that Event, as shown in Figure 3-10.

Figure 3-10:
Clicking the
Event text
box lets
you type a
new name
or rename
an existing
Event.

3. **Type a new, descriptive name for your Event and press Return.**

Merging Events

You might have photos stored as separate Events, but you might later decide that the photos in both Events really should be grouped in a single Event. In this case, you can merge two Events into a single Event by following these steps:

1. **Click the Events category in the iPhoto Source List or the toolbar along the bottom of the full-screen iPhoto window.**

   iPhoto displays all your Events.

2. **Move the pointer over an Event you want to move or merge into another Event.**

3. **Click and drag the Event to the Event you want to merge it with.**

   The pointer turns into an arrow with a green plus sign.

4. **Release the mouse button when the pointer appears over an Event.**

   Your two Events now appear as a single Event.

Splitting an Event

Sometimes an Event might contain too many photos. In this case, you may want to store photos in separate Events. To split an Event, follow these steps:

1. **Click the Events category in the iPhoto Source List or the toolbar along the bottom of the full-screen iPhoto window.**

   iPhoto displays all your Events in the right pane.

2. **Double-click an Event you want to split.**

   The photos in your Event appear in the iPhoto window (refer to Figure 3-9).

3. **Hold down the ⌘ key and click each photo you want to add to your new separate Event.**

   A yellow border highlights each chosen photo.

4. **Choose Events⇨Split Event.**

   Your chosen photos now appear in a separate Event.

5. **Click the All Events button.**

   Your original and newly split Events appear highlighted with a yellow border.

Moving photos from one Event to another

If a photo appears in one Event but you think it should appear in a different Event, you can always move that photo. To move a photo from one Event to another, follow these steps:

1. **Click the Events category in the iPhoto Source List or the toolbar along the bottom of the full-screen iPhoto window.**

   iPhoto displays all your photos in the right pane.

2. **Choose View⇨Event List.**

3. **Click and drag the photo you want to move from one Event to the Event where you want it to be.**

   Click the disclosure triangle to the left of the Event name to see fewer open events.

   Hold down the Shift key to select a first and last photo and all the photos in between, or hold the ⌘ key and click the photos you want to move and then click and drag the group of photos.

4. **Release the mouse button.**

   Your chosen photo or group of photos now appears in the other Event.

5. **Click the All Events button to see all your Events again.**

Book IV
Chapter 3

Importing, Viewing, Organizing, and Sharing Photos

Sorting Events

The more Events you create to store your photos, the harder it is to find what you need. To help keep you organized, iPhoto gives you three options for sorting your Events:

✦ **Date:** Lets you sort Events by time.

✦ **Title:** Lets you sort Events by title.

✦ **Manually:** Lets you sort Events by clicking and dragging them.

You can also sort photos by rating and keywords, but you must first give a photo a rating or keyword, which you find out about later in this chapter.

Sorting by date or title

Sorting by date makes it easy to find photos based on the time you remember capturing those photos. Sorting by title is helpful after you give all Events a descriptive title and want to find a photo stored under a specific Event title.

To sort Events by date or title within the iPhoto window, follow these steps:

1. **Click the Events category in the iPhoto Source List or the toolbar along the bottom of the full-screen iPhoto window.**

iPhoto displays all your Events in the right pane.

2. **Choose View➪Sort Events.**

A submenu appears with a check mark next to the way you have your Events sorted, as shown in Figure 3-11.

Figure 3-11: The Sort Events submenu lists the different ways to sort Events.

3. **Choose By Date, By Title, Manually, and Ascending or Descending.**

Your Events sort by the criteria you choose.

If you choose Ascending or Descending, iPhoto sorts your Events based on the sorting method that appears with a check mark in the Sort Events submenu.

Sorting manually

Another way to sort Events is by clicking and dragging them within the iPhoto window. This gives you the freedom to arrange photos in Events based on your preferences, regardless of date or titles. For example, you might put all your family Events near the top of the iPhoto window, which makes it easy to find photos of different family members if you're putting together a newsletter for a family reunion.

To sort Events manually within the iPhoto window, follow these steps:

1. **Click the Events category in the iPhoto Source List or the toolbar along the bottom of the full-screen iPhoto window.**

iPhoto displays all your Events in the right pane.

2. **Click and drag an Event you want to move to its new location.**

When you move an Event between two other Events, the other Events slide out of the way to make room.

3. **Release the mouse button when you're happy with the new position of the Event.**

Organizing Photos

After you store photos in separate Events, you may want to view and organize individual photos stored in an Event.

Viewing photos stored in a single Event

If you want to view photos in only one Event, follow these steps:

1. **Click the Events category in the iPhoto Source List or the toolbar along the bottom of the full-screen iPhoto window.**

iPhoto displays all your Events in the right pane.

2. **Double-click an Event.**

All your photos in that Event appear in the iPhoto window. (Refer to Figure 3-9.)

3. **Click the All Events button in the upper-left corner of the iPhoto window to view all your Events again.**

Book IV
Chapter 3

Importing, Viewing,
Organizing, and
Sharing Photos

Viewing photos stored in all Events

Rather than view photos stored in a single Event, you may want to view all your photos in separate Events at the same time. To view photos in all Events, follow these steps:

1. **Click the Photos category in the iPhoto Source List. (There is no Photos choice in full-screen view.)**

   iPhoto displays all your photos. If you've hidden any photos from view (by choosing Photos⇨Hide Photos), you can view those hidden photos by choosing View⇨Hidden Photos and making sure that a check mark appears to the left of Hidden Photos.

2. **Choose View⇨Event Titles so a check mark appears to the left of Event Titles.**

   Note: If a check mark already appears to the left of Event Titles, skip this step.

   Displaying Event Titles lets you see how your photos are organized into different Events, as shown in Figure 3-12.

Figure 3-12: The Photos category lets you view all your photos.

3. **Click the triangle to the left of the Event title to display or hide photos in an Event.**

This step works only if a check mark appears to the left of Event Titles on the View menu.

Click the Slideshow icon beneath your photos or events to display the Slideshow options dialog, choose a slideshow theme shown in Figure 3-13, and then click Play to begin the (slide) show! Click the Music and Settings tabs at the top to add music and other controls to your slideshow.

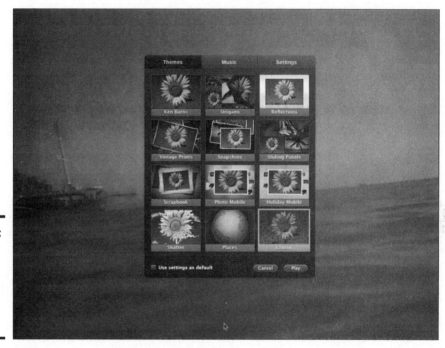

Figure 3-13:
Choose a theme and then click Play to enjoy a slideshow.

Naming photos

Every digital camera stores photos with generic filenames, such as DSC_846. Fortunately, you can replace these generic titles with more descriptive names.

In iPhoto, you can give descriptive names to your Events and descriptive names to individual photos as well. So an Event might be named "Spring Break," and photos stored in that Event might be named "Day 1: Arrival," "Day 2: Imbibing," and "Day 3: Recovering."

To name individual photos stored in an Event, follow these steps:

1. **Choose one of the methods mentioned earlier (in the section "Viewing photos in a single Event" or "Viewing photos stored in all Events") to view your photos.**

2. **Choose View⇨Titles.**

   Note: If a check mark already appears to the left of Titles, skip this step.

   Titles appear underneath every photo.

3. **Click the title that you want to change.**

   A text box appears, as shown in Figure 3-14.

4. **Type a new name for your photo or use the arrow and Delete keys to edit the existing name.**

5. **Press Return.**

After you name all photos in an Event, you can sort them by choosing View⇨ Sort Photos⇨By Title. Then you can choose View⇨Sort Photos⇨Ascending (or Descending) to sort by titles in ascending or descending order.

Figure 3-14: Descriptive titles can help you find photos easier.

Fresh From the Garden

Rating photos

Some photos are better than others, so another way to sort and organize photos is by rating them from zero to five stars. To rate photos, follow these steps:

1. **Choose one of the methods mentioned earlier (in the section "Viewing photos stored in a single Event" or "Viewing photos stored in all Events") to view your photos.**

2. **Choose View⇨Rating.**

   Note: If a check mark already appears to the left of Rating, skip this step.

   Ratings and titles appear underneath every photo if you select them in the View menu.

3. **Select the photo you want to rate.**

A row of five stars appears beneath your selected photo.

4. **Click the first, second, third, fourth, or fifth star to mark the photo with that number of stars, as shown in Figure 3-15.**

Figure 3-15:
You can rate each photo with zero to five stars.

You have other ways to rate photos:

✦ Choose Photos⇨My Rating and choose the number of stars you want to rate the photo with from the submenu.

✦ Control-click a photo and choose the My Rating submenu to pick a star rating.

✦ Click a photo and press ⌘+0 through ⌘+5 to rate a photo from zero to five stars.

After you rate some or all of your photos in an Event, you can sort them by choosing View⇨Sort Photos⇨By Rating. To change whether to sort by ascending or descending rating, choose View⇨Sort Photos⇨Ascending (or Descending).

Adding keywords to a photo

A *keyword* helps you organize photos based on categories, such as Cityscapes, Nature, or All in the Family. By placing keywords on photos, you can quickly find all your favorite outdoor photos or family photos.

To add a keyword to a photo, follow these steps:

1. **Choose one of the methods mentioned earlier (in the section "Viewing photos stored in a single Event" or "Viewing photos stored in all Events") to view your photos.**

2. **Click a photo that you want to label with a keyword.**

   If you hold down the ⌘ key, you can click two or more photos to assign the same keyword to all of them.

3. **Choose Window⇨Manage My Keywords.**

   A Keywords window appears, which displays several common keywords that iPhoto provides for you, as shown in Figure 3-16.

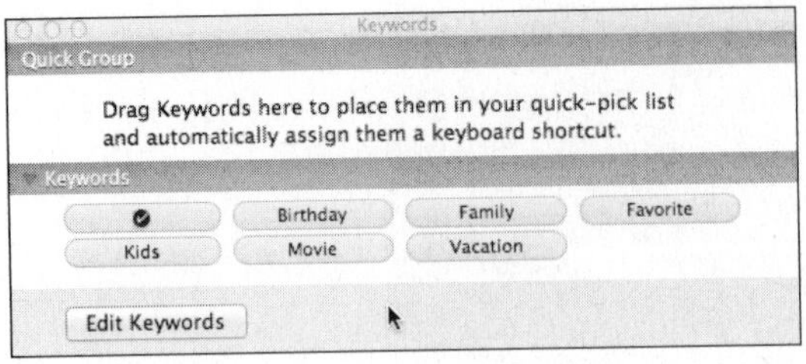

Figure 3-16: The Keywords window displays a list of keywords you can use.

4. **(Optional) To add your own keywords to the Keywords window, click the Edit Keywords button. When the Edit Keywords dialog appears, click the plus sign button to type your own keywords into the Keywords window.**

   You can also click a keyword, and then click the minus sign button to remove a keyword from the Keyword window.

   Drag a keyword from the bottom part of the Keywords window to the top part to assign a key to represent a keyword. That way you can choose View⇨Keywords to display a keywords text box underneath each photo, click that text box, and then press the shortcut key to add a keyword to that photo quickly.

5. **Click a keyword.**

   Your chosen keyword appears briefly on the photo you select.

   If you click the same keyword in the keyword window, iPhoto removes the keyword from your chosen photo.

6. **Choose View⇨Info and click the disclosure triangle next to Keyword to see the keyword(s) assigned to the photo.**

After you add keywords to photos in an Event, you can sort them by choosing View⇨Sort Photos⇨By Keyword. Then you can sort alphabetically by keyword by choosing View⇨Sort Photos⇨Ascending (or Descending).

Storing photos in albums and folders

Sorting and organizing photos into Events can be cumbersome. For example, you might have dozens of birthday photos stored in separate Events. Although you can store all these birthday photos in the same Event, you might also want to keep them grouped with other photos in separate Events that represent different years.

To keep photos stored in separate Events while grouping them at the same time, you can create an *album*. An album groups related photos without removing them from the Events they're stored in. Essentially, a photo is in only one event, but can be in as many albums as you want.

Creating albums and organizing photos manually

To create an album and store photos in it, follow these steps:

1. **Open the event that has some photos you want to put in the album.**

2. **Choose File⇨New Album.**

A New Album item appears under the Albums category in the Source List; above the pane where you see your Event photos, you see the title New Album, as shown in Figure 3-17. If you create an album in full-screen view, you can edit the name of the album where "New Album" appears across the top of the screen.

Figure 3-17: Name your album in the Albums category of the Source List or in the title of the full-screen view.

Book IV
Chapter 3

Importing, Viewing, Organizing, and Sharing Photos

3. **Type a descriptive name for your album and press Return.**

   Your album name appears under the Albums category in the iPhoto Source List and at the top of the viewing pane.

4. **Click and drag photos you want to add to your album from other events to the album folder in the iPhoto Source List.**

   You can select multiple photos by holding down the ⌘ key and clicking each photo you want to add to an album.

5. **Release the mouse button to copy your photo(s) to the album.**

6. **Repeat Steps 4 and 5 for each additional photo you want to copy to the album.**

7. **To remove a photo from the album (but not from iPhoto), click the photo and choose Edit⇨Cut.**

   Now, if you click the album name in the iPhoto Source List, you can see all the photos in that album.

To access the menus from full-screen view, hover the pointer over the top of the screen.

Creating albums and organizing photos automatically

If manually dragging photos in and out of albums is too tedious, you can set up a Smart Album from within iPhoto that will store photos automatically.

To create a Smart Album that can store photos automatically, follow these steps:

1. **Choose File⇨New Smart Album (or press Option and click the Plus "+" icon in the lower-left corner of the iPhoto window).**

   A dialog appears, asking for a name for your Smart Album.

2. **Type a descriptive name for your album in the Smart Album Name text box.**

3. **Click the first pop-up menu and choose a criterion, such as Keyword or Rating.**

4. **Click the second and third pop-up menus to refine the criterion you choose in Step 3, such as choosing only photos with a rating of four stars or with the Birthday keyword.**

5. **(Optional) Click the plus sign button to define another criterion and repeat Steps 3 and 4.**

6. **Click OK.**

   Your Smart Album now stores photos based on your chosen criteria.

If you create too many albums, you can organize them into folders by choosing File⇨New Folder and dragging each album into that folder.

Deleting photos, albums, and folders

Many times, you'll import photos into iPhoto and decide that the photo isn't worth saving after all. To keep your iPhoto Library from becoming too cluttered, you can delete the photos you don't need.

Besides deleting individual photos, you can also delete albums and folders that contain photos you don't want. When you delete an album or folder (which contains albums), you don't physically delete the photos; you just delete the folder or album that contains the photos. The original photos are still stored in the iPhoto Library.

To delete a photo, album, or folder, click the photo in Photos or Events, album, or folder you want to delete and press the Delete key or drag it to the Trash icon in the iPhoto Source List. If you delete a photo from an album, it's deleted only from that album, not from iPhoto.

Press ⌘+Z or choose Edit⇨Undo Delete right away if you want to recover your deleted items.

Choosing and Organizing Photos with Faces and Places

Two more ways to organize and view photos in your iPhoto Library are the Faces and Places features.

The Faces feature lets you add names to the faces of people in your photos and, over time, iPhoto automatically recognizes and labels the faces of people in new photos you import into your iPhoto Library.

The Places feature automatically tags and sorts photos you import that contain GPS information that your GPS-capable smartphone or camera adds to photos when you snap the photos with the GPS-tagging feature (referred to as *geotagging*) turned on.

You can use the Places feature even if you don't have a GPS-capable smartphone or camera by selecting and tagging individual photos, or a group of photos, with information that you type about the location where you captured the photos.

Using Faces to organize photos

You can organize photos in your iPhoto Library based on the faces of people in the photos.

To organize photos by using the Faces feature, follow these steps:

1. **Click the Find Faces button in the toolbar at the bottom of the full-screen view or in the Source List in normal view.**

A selection of faces to identify appears, as shown in Figure 3-18.

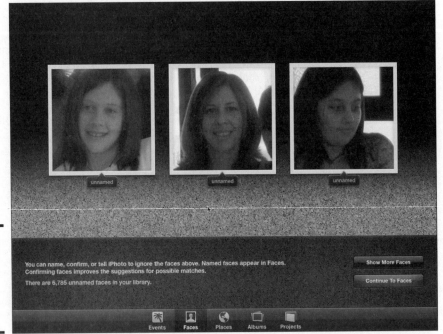

Figure 3-18:
Find Faces
shows you
a selection
of faces to
identify.

2. **Click in the field under the photo that reads "unnamed" and begin typing the name of the person.**

iPhoto displays a list of matches from your Address Book. The more letters you type, the narrower the results. If the name of the person of the photo appears, click that. If not, continue typing the correct name.

3. **Repeat Step 2 for the other photos.**

4. **Click Show More Faces to continue identifying people.**

When iPhoto finds a face that it recognizes, the name field reads "Is this Barbara Boyd?" (See Figure 3-19.) Click the check mark if the name is correct. Click the "x" if the name is wrong and enter the correct name.

When you name a person in Faces, it automatically tags that person in Facebook when you share photos from iPhoto to Facebook, as explained in the section "Other sharing options."

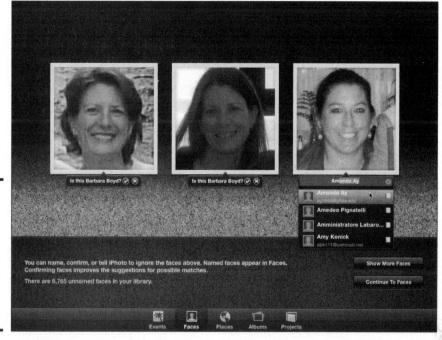

Figure 3-19:
Faces
uses your
Address
Book
contacts to
match the
name you
type.

5. **When you tire of playing the faces identification game, click Go To Faces.**

    iPhoto displays a corkboard with the named faces of people you have identified so far. The more photos you identify for each person, the better iPhoto becomes at identifying faces correctly. Double-click the person's group of photos to see all your photos of that person. Click the All Faces button in the upper-left corner to return to the Faces view.

After you identify a good selection of faces, you can instruct iPhoto to search for matches by choosing Photos➪Detect Missing Faces.

To view photos organized by Faces in your iPhoto library, click the Faces category under Library in the iPhoto Source List, and then double-click the snapshot of the person whose photos you want to look at.

Organizing photos with Places

You can view photos in your iPhoto Library based on the locations where you snapped the photos.

If your camera or smartphone has a GPS feature turned on, photos you import into your iPhoto Library will automatically contain information about the location where you captured the photos.

Viewing photos organized by places

You can view photos organized by the places where the photos were captured by clicking pushpins on a map of the world, or by clicking a display listing photos by country, region, state, and city.

To view photos organized by the Places feature in your iPhoto Library, follow these steps:

1. **Click the Places category under Library in the iPhoto Source List or click the Places button in the toolbar at the bottom of the window in full-screen view.**

   iPhoto displays a map of the world with red pushpins that indicate locations where your photos were captured. Moving the mouse pointer to a pushpin displays the name of the location where you captured the photos, as shown in Figure 3-20.

   You must enable Places for iPhoto to assign locations to your photos. Choose iPhoto⇨Preferences and click the Advanced tab. Select Automatically in the Look Up Places pop-up menu.

Figure 3-20: Pushpins represent the places where you captured your photos.

2. **To view the photos for a location, move the mouse pointer to a push-pin to display the location name and click the arrow to the right of the location name.**

   iPhoto displays the photos you captured (or manually tagged, as described in the next section) at the selected location.

3. **(Optional) From the World Map view, you can do these additional things:**

   - *Zoom In/Out:* Click and drag the slider button in the lower-right corner to zoom in and out of the World Map view. If you're using a mouse with a scroll wheel, you can zoom in and out on the map by rolling the scroll wheel forward and backward. If you're using a new or recent MacBook, you can zoom in and out on the map by pinching two fingertips together and apart on the trackpad.

   - *Terrain, Satellite, Hybrid view:* Click one of these three buttons to change the World Map view. Terrain shows a topographic view. Satellite displays an eye-in-the-sky view based on actual satellite imagery. Hybrid combines both the Terrain and Satellite views into a single view.

   - *Country, State, Cities, Place view:* Click one of these four buttons which becomes a pull-down menu to narrow your view by location, as shown in Figure 3-21.

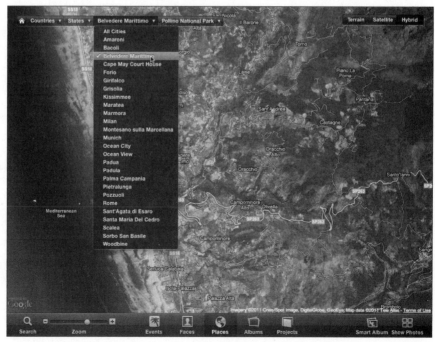

Figure 3-21: Choose country, state, city, or place to zoom in on a location.

Manually identifying locations for photos

If your camera or smartphone doesn't have a GPS feature that automatically adds a location to photos you capture, you can still add location information to photos in your iPhoto collection by selecting and typing location names for your photos.

To add location names to photos in your iPhoto Library so you can view them with the Places feature, follow these steps:

1. **Choose one of the methods mentioned earlier (in the section "Viewing photos stored in a single Event" or "Viewing photos stored in all Events") to view your photos.**

2. **Click a photo that you want to identify by location.**

   If you hold down the ⌘ key, you can click two or more photos to assign the same location to all of them.

3. **Click View⇨Info to display an information window for the selected photo (or photos), as shown in Figure 3-22.**

Figure 3-22: The View Info window lets you add or change a photo's location information.

4. **Click the name to the right of the Location check box, type or edit the name of the location where the photo was captured, and press Return.**

   While you type, a list beneath the location name appears with suggestions of locations that might match the location you want to assign to the photo.

5. **(Optional) You can add or edit the following information for the photo (or photos) by using the following check boxes:**

   - *Title:* Edit or type a title for the selected photo.

   - *Rating:* Click the dots to choose the number of stars you want to give the photo (from one to five stars).

   - *Description:* Edit or type a descriptive word or words to describe the photo so you can search for it when you want to find it again.

6. **Choose View⇨Info to hide the Info pane.**

Editing Photos

Besides organizing your photos, iPhoto lets you edit them. Such editing can be as simple as rotating or cropping a photo, or it can be as intricate as removing red-eye from a photograph or modifying colors. To edit a photo, follow these steps:

1. **Choose one of the methods mentioned earlier (in the section "Viewing photos stored in a single Event" or "Viewing photos stored in all Events") to view your photos.**

2. **Click a photo and click the Edit button in the lower-right corner.**

   iPhoto displays your selected photo in the center pane, and an editing pane opens to the right of your photo, as shown in Figure 3-23.

3. **Click the Quick Fixes tab at the top of the editing pane and click the buttons to do the following:**

   - *Rotate:* Rotates your photo 180 degrees clockwise or counterclockwise.

   - *Enhance:* Magically fixes brightness and contrast problems and improves your photo.

   - *Fix Red-Eye:* Gets rid of those vampiric red pupils that show up when the flash is too strong. Click the red pupils and drag the slider bar in the Edit pane to match the size of the pupil. Click Done when the redness is blackened.

Figure 3-23:
The editing tools appear in a pane to the right of your photo.

- *Straighten:* Changes the angle when you drag the slider. Perhaps you got a little too artistic or want to add an interesting angle to your photo. If you click the Decrease/Increase angle of photo icons that appear on opposite ends of the slider, you can adjust the angle of your photo by 0.1 of a degree. Click Done when the photo is in a position you like.

- *Crop:* Lets you select only the part of the photo you want to keep. Grabber corners let you shift the border of the photo to show only the part you want. Use the Constrain pop-up menu to choose the photo proportions you want, for example 2 x 3 for iPhone or 4 x 6 for a postcard, and move the frame around on the image to crop that best part to the selected size. Click Done when you're satisfied.

- *Retouch:* Gives you a tool to correct minor blemishes, scars, and wrinkles. Click and drag the tool over the discolored area to create a blemish-free photo. Click Done when you're pleased.

4. **Click the Effects tab of the Edit pane and click the effect you want, such as cooler colors, sepia tones, or a matte finish, as shown in Figure 3-24.**

Figure 3-24: The Effects tools let you choose a way to modify your picture.

5. **Click the Adjust tab of the Edit pane to do the following, as shown in Figure 3-25:**

   • *Exposure:* Lightens or darkens a photo.

   • *Contrast:* Alters the differences between light and dark areas.

   • *Saturation:* Alters the intensity of colors in a photo.

   • *Definition:* Reduces haze and improves clarity without adding too much contrast.

   • *Highlights:* Increases detail in a photo by lightening or darkening areas.

   • *Shadows:* Lightens or darkens shadow areas of a photo.

   • *Sharpness:* Adjusts the focus of a photo.

   • *De-noise:* Alters the graininess of a photo.

   • *Temperature:* Alters colors by making them dimmer (colder) or brighter (hotter).

   • *Tint:* Adjusts the red/green colors in a photo.

   Select the Avoid Saturating the Skin Tones check box if you want to try to make skin coloration look more natural.

Figure 3-25:
Improve
your photo
with the
options on
the Adjust
tab.

6. **Your image changes as you adjust any of these settings.**

   Click Undo to undo the last adjustment you made.

   If you decide that your original photo looked better without any adjusted settings, click the Revert to Original button.

7. **(Optional) Choose Edit⇨Copy Adjustments to copy your adjusted settings so you can use the same settings to adjust another photo, which you can open and then select Edit⇨Paste Adjustments to apply the adjusted settings.**

8. **Click the Edit button to close the Edit pane.**

Sharing Photos

There's no point in taking photos if you don't share them with others. To help you publicize your photos to the world, you can print them, post them on a web page, upload them directly to Facebook or Flickr, e-mail them to others, or burn them to a CD/DVD. For an added fee, you can print your photos as books, calendars, or greeting cards.

Printing photos

You can print individual photos or groups of photos on your home printer by following these steps:

1. **Choose one of the methods mentioned earlier (in the section "Viewing photos stored in a single Event" or "Viewing photos stored in all Events") to view your photos.**

2. **Hold down the ⌘ key and click all the photos you want to print.**

3. **Click the Print button or choose File⇨Print.**

   A Print dialog appears, as shown in Figure 3-26.

Figure 3-26: The Print dialog lets you choose different ways to print your photos.

4. **Click one of the following print styles:**

   - *Standard:* Prints photos to fill the entire page.

   - *Contact Sheet:* Prints thumbnail images of multiple photos on a single page.

   - *Simple Border:* Prints one photo per page with a plain border around the edge.

   - *Simple Mat:* Prints one photo per page with a tinted border around the edge.

   - *Double Mat:* Prints one photo per page with two borders around the edges.

**Book IV
Chapter 3**

Importing, Viewing, Organizing, and Sharing Photos

5. **Choose the following pop-up menu options:**

- *Printer:* Defines which printer to use (if you have more than one printer).

- *Paper Size:* Defines what size paper to use.

- *Presets:* Provides predefined printing settings.

- *Print Size:* Defines the size to print each photo, such as 3 x 5 or 8 x 10.

6. **Click the Print button.**

You can click the Order Prints button in the bottom-right corner of the iPhoto window to have your photos sent to Apple for printing (Kodak actually does the printing). The cost to print a 4-x-6 photo is less than what it would cost you in paper and ink on your printer, and the quality is as good — usually better — than the top photo printers. You can also click the Book, Calendar, or Card button to create photo books, calendars, or greeting cards from your photos.

E-mailing photos

If you want to share photos with family members or friends who have an e-mail address, you can e-mail photos by using the Mail application. If you use a different e-mail application, such as Outlook, you can configure iPhoto to work with your e-mail application by following these steps:

1. **Choose iPhoto⬄Preferences.**

   A Preferences window appears.

2. **Click the General button.**

3. **Click the Email Photos Using pop-up menu and choose your e-mail application or service.**

4. **Click the Close button of the Preferences window.**

After you configure your e-mail application to work with iPhoto, you can send a photo by following these steps:

1. **Choose one of the methods mentioned earlier (in the section "Viewing photos stored in a single Event" or "Viewing photos stored in all Events") to view your photos.**

2. **Hold down the ⌘ key and click the photo you want to send. You can click up to ten photos to send in one e-mail.**

3. **Click the Share button and choose Email or choose Share⬄Email.**

   Your photo appears in an e-mail message, as shown in Figure 3-27.

You can apply one of the themes that appears in the chooser on the right side. Click on the text placeholders to type in your own text. Choose Edit➪Font to change the typeface.

At the bottom of the chooser pane, a pop-up menu lets you select the size image you want to insert in the e-mail or choose Optimize so the e-mail file isn't too large to send.

4. **Enter an e-mail address or addresses in the To text box.**

    To add an e-mail address to iPhoto, choose iPhoto➪Preferences and click the Accounts tab. Click the plus sign at the bottom of the pane and choose Email from the pop-up list and click Add. Choose the type of e-mail service you use, such as Google Mail, iCloud, AOL, or Yahoo!, and click OK. Type in your account information in the appropriate fields, and click the Close button.

5. **Use the pop-up menu to choose the outgoing e-mail address (if you have more than one) and then click Send.**

Other sharing options

You can upload your photos directly to Flickr and Facebook from iPhoto by doing the following:

1. **Choose one of the methods mentioned earlier (in the section "Viewing photos stored in a single Event" or "Viewing photos stored in all Events") to view your photos.**

2. **Hold down the ⌘ key and click the photo or photos you want to upload.**

3. **Click the Share button and choose Flickr or Facebook from the pop-up menu (or choose Share➪Flickr/Facebook).**

4. **Sign in to your account with your profile name and password.**

   Alternatively, choose iPhoto➪Preferences and click the Accounts tab. Click the plus sign at the bottom of the pane and choose Facebook or Flickr from the pop-up list and click Add. Type in your profile name and password in the appropriate fields, and click Login.

5. **Choose the location where you want to use the photo; for example, for your profile or in an existing album.**

   Figure 3-28 shows the locations for Facebook.

6. **A dialog asks you to select viewing privileges from a pop-up menu. If you choose New Album, you can type in a name for the album.**

Figure 3-28: Upload your photos to Facebook or Flickr directly from iPhoto.

7. Click Publish.

Your photo or photos are uploaded to Facebook or Flickr. Comments made about your photo on Facebook appear in the Info pane of the photo in iPhoto.

Using Photo Stream

Photo Stream is part of Apple's iCloud service. If you activate Photo Stream, 1,000 of your most recent photos are uploaded to Photo Stream for 30 days. If you add more photos in a 30-day period, the new ones are uploaded and the same quantity of old ones are deleted. To activate Photo Stream in iPhoto, choose iPhoto⇨Preferences and click the Photo Stream tab. Select the Enable Photo Stream check box, as shown in Figure 3-29.

Figure 3-29: Keep up to 1,000 photos on Photo Stream.

All the photos are synced to the devices you have connected to iCloud, such as your iPhone, iPad, or iPod touch. See Book III, Chapter 2 to find out more about using iCloud.

Saving photos to a CD/DVD

If you want to give someone a copy of your photos, you can store them on CD/DVD so they can pop the CD/DVD into their own computer. To save photos on CD/DVD, follow these steps:

1. Choose one of the methods mentioned earlier (in the section "Viewing photos stored in a single Event" or "Viewing photos stored in all Events") to view your photos.

2. Hold down the ⌘ key and click all the photos you want to save.

3. Choose Share⇨Burn.

A dialog appears, prompting you to insert a blank CD/DVD into your Mac.

4. Insert a blank CD/DVD and click OK.

Your photos burn to your CD/DVD.

Using photos in iWeb and iDVD

After you store photos in iPhoto, you can import them directly into iDVD (to burn them to a DVD, complete with fancy menus and music) or into iWeb (to place on web pages). To transfer photos from iPhoto to iDVD or iWeb, follow these steps:

1. **Choose one of the methods mentioned earlier (in the section "Viewing photos stored in a single Event" or "Viewing photos stored in all Events") to view your photos.**

2. **Hold down the ⌘ key and click all the photos you want to use.**

3. **Choose one of the following:**

   - Share⇨Send to iWeb⇨Photo Page (or Blog). This loads iWeb and creates a photo album page displaying all your chosen photos.

   - Share⇨Send to iDVD. This loads the iDVD application and your chosen photographs so you can arrange them in the order you want, although the resolution of the photos is significantly reduced to comply with DVD resolution.

Ordering books, calendars, and cards

For a fee, you can have your favorite iPhoto photos printed as books, calendars, or greeting cards. To choose to print your photos on a book, calendar, or greeting card, follow these steps:

1. **Choose one of the methods mentioned earlier (in the section "Viewing photos stored in a single Event" or "Viewing photos stored in all Events") to view your photos.**

2. **Hold down the ⌘ key and click all the photos you want to use or click an Event.**

3. **Click the Create button at the bottom of the iPhoto window and choose Book, Calendar, or Card from the pop-up menu.**

   The Carousel view appears, which you can "spin" through to see the printing options. Use the tabs at the top to choose format options of the printed material, such as hard cover, soft cover, or wirebound for books. Click the buttons near the Carousel samples to choose options such as colors and size. The estimated price appears on the lower left. Scroll through the different styles (or use the pop-up menu at the top) and see how your photos will look with each style applied. See Figure 3-30.

Figure 3-30: You can choose a specific style of book, calendar, or card to create.

4. **Click a style and click Create.**

iPhoto distributes the photos you chose in the book or calendar, as shown in Figure 3-31. Double-click a page to edit the photos. Click and drag the photos to move them from one page to another. Use the buttons at the bottom to add pages or change the layout of a page. Photos on pages with "full-bleed" fill the entire page and have no borders around the photos.

iPhoto distributes the photos by using the Autoflow feature. iPhotos puts together photos that were taken on the same day and uses ratings to choose featured photos. iPhoto also detects faces and crops and frames the subject as it deems best.

5. **When you're satisfied with the layout of your book or calendar, click the Buy button.**

A summary of your order appears with the total. Prices for books and calendars typically cost $10 to $30, and greeting cards cost $2 each. Apple's letterpressed cards combine your digital photos with letterpress printing. Choose from 15 themes and order one card or a whole box of cards, which come with matching letterpressed envelopes.

Figure 3-31:
iPhoto can automatically enter photos from an event.

6. **Click the checkout button to proceed to pay online and enter your shipping information.**

   Your order goes directly to Apple, is dispatched to their service provider, and is then delivered to your doorstep a few days later.

Even if you don't plan to print books, it's a nice way to organize and view your photos on your computer. In full-screen view, click the Projects button at the bottom of the window to see all your projects arranged as books on a bookshelf. Double-click a project to open it, or click it, and then click the Slideshow button to view the book as an automatic slideshow.

Chapter 4: Making Movies with iMovie

In This Chapter

✔ **Discovering how iMovie works**

✔ **Importing and storing video**

✔ **Creating an iMovie project**

✔ **Inserting and editing video clips**

✔ **Adding titles, transitions, and sound**

✔ **Using special effects**

✔ **Making a trailer for your movie**

✔ **Saving and sharing videos**

*N*ow that video capture is commonplace on both digital cameras and smartphones, making movies has descended from the realm of Super 8 aficionados to everyday use. If you have a digital video camcorder, a digital camera, or smartphone that captures video, you can create movies with iMovie, the video-editing application that's part of Apple's iLife suite.

You can also use video from a DVD that someone gives you. If, for example, you go river rafting or hang gliding, the company you go with may record your adventure and give or sell you the video on a DVD; you can then use the video footage (that's what we call the *recording*) as part of your movie. Often when you make a presentation at a conference, the conference organizers record your presentation and give you a copy on DVD, which you can then edit and incorporate into your professional curriculum or upload to your company's website.

You can just take the raw, unedited video, also known as *source video,* copy it to a DVD with iDVD (which we explain in Book IV, Chapter 6), and share it with family, friends, and colleagues. Or, with iMovie, you can take a little time to edit your source video, add a voiceover or background music, transitions, still images, and a few special effects to create a movie that tells a story and is compelling to watch.

In this chapter, we take you through the creation of a movie with iMovie. First we show you how to import source video and explain some of the different resolution and frames per second standards. Next, we give you tips for enhancing your movie with transitions, voiceovers, music, and special effects. At the end of the chapter, we give you the steps for sharing your movie online or exporting it to a playable format.

How iMovie Works

To get the most out of iMovie, take a second to understand how the window is set up and some of the movie-making terms we use. When you first open iMovie, there are three panes in the window:

+ **Project Pane, top left:** Holds the Project Library and Project browser, where you work on editing your movie.

+ **Event Pane, lower left:** Holds the Event Library and the Event browser; *events* are your source video.

+ **Preview Pane, top right:** The viewer pane, where you preview video from either the Event or Project browser as you work on your movie.

A *library* is where you see a list of projects or events, and the *browser* is where you see the parts of your video, referred to as *clips*. Clips are made up of *frames*. Video speed is referred to as *frames per second (fps)*.

The *toolbar* runs between the upper Project and Preview panes and the lower Event pane.

The basic steps for using iMovie are

1. Import, store, and organize video in the Event Library.

2. Copy video footage from the Event browser to a project in the Project browser.

3. Edit your video clips in the Project pane.

4. Save your video as a digital video file for viewing on other computers, on DVD, or over the Internet.

Working with the Event Library

The Event Library holds all your source video, acting as your personal film vault. By storing videos in the Event Library, you have a handy place where you can choose footage from old videos to use in any new projects.

To store video in the Event Library, you must import video from one of the following sources:

+ A digital video camera

+ A smartphone or digital (still) camera capable of capturing video (the video is imported into iPhoto and then brought into iMovie from iPhoto)

+ Video captured directly to your Mac by using PhotoBooth, as explained in Book IV, Chapter 3

+ Video captured and edited by using QuickTime Player (refer to Book IV, Chapter 2)

+ A project created and saved using an earlier version of iMovie

+ A digital video file stored on your hard drive or a DVD

Importing from a digital video device

To *import* (that is, to copy) a video that you captured with a digital video camera to your Mac, follow these steps:

1. **Connect your device to your Mac with a USB cable or FireWire cable (if your Mac has a FireWire port and the device uses FireWire).**

   The appropriate cable usually comes with the camera or smartphone.

2. **Click the iMovie icon in the Dock or Launchpad to open iMovie.**

   The Import dialog appears, displaying all the footage recorded on your device.

3. **Choose File⇨Import from Camera if the Import dialog doesn't open, and then choose the device you want from the Camera pop-up menu at the bottom.**

4. **Select the clips you want to import.**

   • Set the Automatic/Manual switch to Automatic to import all the footage and click the Import All button.

   • Set the Automatic/Manual switch to Manual to import some clips from the footage. Deselect the clips you don't want to import and click the Import Checked button.

   The Import dialog shown in Figure 4-1 appears, giving you a choice of disks where you can save your video.

5. **From the Save To pop-up menu, choose where to store your video.**

   Video files can be large, so you may want to store them on an external hard drive rather than on your Mac.

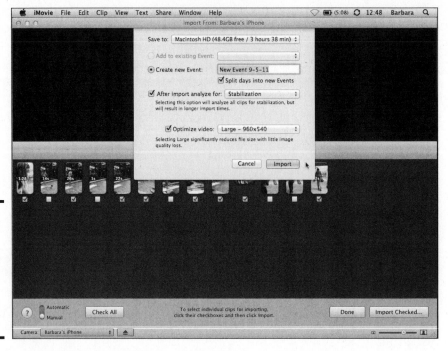

Figure 4-1:
The Import dialog lets you choose where you want to save your video file.

6. Choose how to organize your video by selecting one of the following:

- *Add to Existing Event:* Stores the video as part of an existing event in the Event Library.

- *Create New Event:* Stores the video as a new event in the Event Library. The default name for the Event will be the date, but you can always type a more descriptive name.

7. Select or deselect the Split Days into New Events check box.

Many video camcorders time-stamp any video footage you capture, so this option divides a video into parts where each part represents all video footage shot on the same day.

8. Select Analyze for Stabilization after Import if you want iMovie to attempt to detect and smooth any shaky parts.

You analyze only one time, but analyzing is time consuming, so you may want to do this when you're going to be away from your computer or overnight. You can also analyze your video later. A red squiggly line runs across the bottom of analyzed clips in both the Event and Project browsers.

You have two other choices:

- *Analyze for Stabilization and People:* iMovie stabilizes your video and searches for people in the video so you can later sort your footage and quickly find clips with people.

- *Analyze for People:* iMovie looks for people in your video without stabilizing.

9. **Choose how you want to optimize high-definition video in the Optimize Video pop-up menu.**

The Full-size option displays the frame size at 1,920 x 1,080 pixels and requires 40GB of storage for an hour of video. This option is preferred if you plan to export your video to FinalCut Pro or broadcast it on television.

The Large-size option saves your video at 960 x 540 pixels, which makes for smoother viewing on a computer, on the Internet, or in high-definition television. The video is of an imperceptibly lower quality and uses 13GB for an hour of video.

Some camcorders may have "HD" in the name, indicating high-definition recording, but don't actually record at 1,920 x 1,080. Check the documentation for your camcorder to determine the true recording resolution. Selecting Full-size is useful for 1280 x 720 HD.

10. **Click the Import button.**

When iMovie is finished importing your file, the Import window appears.

11. **Click Done.**

Your imported video appears as thumbnail images in the lower pane (the Event pane) of the iMovie window, as shown in Figure 4-2.

iMovie divides a video into separate scenes where each scene displays the first frame of a video clip. By browsing through these thumbnail images of scenes, you can see which scene is likely to contain the video footage you want to use.

After you import a video, your original video footage remains on the device you imported from, so you may want to go back and erase it.

If you have a digital video camera that records to DV or HDV tape, and which has a FireWire port, you can connect it to your Mac by using your Mac's FireWire port (if your Mac has one) and a FireWire converter cable. Follow the preceding steps. The only difference is when you set the Automatic/Manual switch. Automatic rewinds the whole tape and imports the entire video; Manual lets you rewind, fast-forward, and import the parts you want. Either way, the video plays while it's importing, so the import takes as long as the video takes to watch.

Figure 4-2:
iMovie
separates
a video into
scenes
automatically.

Importing a digital video file

When you capture video with your smartphone or a still digital camera, import the video files into iPhoto as you would still photos, and then import the digital video file as explained here. If you have digital video files stored in QuickTime, PhotoBooth, MPEG-4, or digital video (DV) lying around on your hard drive or on a DVD, you can import them into iMovie. To import a digital video file, follow these steps:

1. **Choose File⇨Import Movies.**

An Open dialog appears, as shown in Figure 4-3. You might need to navigate through drives and folders to find the file you want to import.

If the file you want to import is on a DVD, insert the DVD into the disc drive of your Mac and select the disc in the file browser.

2. **Select the digital video file you want to import.**

3. **Click the Save To pop-up menu and choose a drive to store your video.**

4. **Select one of the following radio buttons:**

- *Add to Existing Event:* Stores the video as part of an existing event in the Event Library.

- *Create New Event:* Stores the video as a new event in the iMovie Event Library.

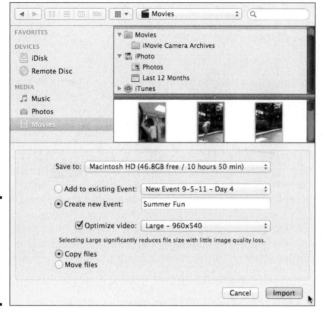

Figure 4-3:
The Open dialog lets you import digital video files.

5. **Choose how you want to optimize high-definition video in the Optimize Video pop-up menu.**

6. **Select the Copy Files or Move Files radio button.**

   The Copy Files option leaves your original file and creates a duplicate file to store in iMovie. The Move Files option physically transfers your chosen video file and moves it into iMovie; if you're using video from a DVD, you want to choose Copy Files so the original files remain on the DVD.

7. **Click Import.**

   Your imported movie appears as thumbnail images in the iMovie window.

Organizing the Event Library

The more videos you store, the more crowded the Event Library becomes, and the harder it is to find what you want. When you store a new video in the Event Library, iMovie gives you the option of creating an event folder, which identifies the date you imported the video file into iMovie.

Organizing videos in the Event Library by date can be helpful, but you may prefer identifying Events with a descriptive name. To rename an Event, follow these steps:

1. **Double-click an Event in the Event Library pane in the bottom-left corner of the iMovie window. (Choose Window⇨Show Event Library if the Event Library is not visible.)**

   Your chosen Event name appears highlighted.

2. **Type a descriptive name for your Event and press Return.**

Storing video in different Event folders can help you find the video you want. If you want to edit video of your family vacation, just click the Event folder for that day or span of days to display your video.

The Event Library displays each video file as a series of thumbnail images. To define how to divide a video into multiple thumbnail images, drag the slider in the bottom-right corner of the iMovie window. Dragging this slider to the left divides your video into more thumbnail images, whereas dragging this slider to the right divides your video into fewer thumbnail images. The number on the right of the slider indicates the duration of the clip from a half a second up to 30 seconds or All, which means no divisions.

Working with the Project Library

The Event Library lists the titles of the video you see in the Event browser, which contains your raw, unedited video. The Project Library appears in the upper-left portion of the iMovie window by default and lists your projects by title. A filmstrip displayed next to each project title lets you preview your movie. Double-click a project or click and then click Edit Project to view the Project browser, which is where you edit your movie. To view (or hide) the Event Library or Project Library (the lists in the Event and Project panes), choose Window⇨Show/Hide Project/Event Library.

Projects contain still images or video clips from source video and images stored in the Event Library. In the Project browser, you can rearrange, trim, and delete video clips to create your movie. This is where you can add titles, transitions, audio, or special effects to your edited movie. If you accidentally erase or mess up a movie in the Project browser, just retrieve the original footage from the Event Library and start over. You can copy and store the same video footage in two or more projects.

Creating an iMovie project

To create a project, follow these steps:

1. **Choose File⇨New Project.**

   The New Project dialog appears, as shown in Figure 4-4.

Figure 4-4:
Choose
a name,
aspect
ratio, and
theme for
your video
project.

2. **Enter a descriptive name for your project in the Project Name text box.**

3. **Choose Standard (4:3) or Widescreen (16:9) from the Aspect Ratio pop-up menu.**

   The aspect ratio optimizes your movie project for displaying on different devices. If you want to view your movie on a TV set, choose Standard or Widescreen.

4. **Choose a Frame Rate for your project; this number should correspond to the frame rate at which you shot your video.**

   • 30 fps (frames per second) NTSC is the standard used in the United States.

   • 25 fps PAL is the European standard.

   • 24 fps Cinema is an option that newer digital cameras have and is the rate at which film was historically shot.

5. **Choose a theme if you want iMovie to apply stylized transitions and titles to your project; choose None if you want to do the work yourself.**

   You can choose to work with a theme and then manually add or change transitions. You can also add a theme when you are already in the middle of editing a project.

   With the release of iMovie '11, two themes offer particularly enhanced movie possibilities: Sports and Newscast. Sports has a Sports Team Editor where you type in the players' names and stats. Newscast makes your reporting ready for the 6 o'clock broadcast with dynamic animated titles.

6. **(Optional) To add a particular transition effect to your movie automatically, click the Automatically Add check box, click the pop-up menu that appears, and choose the transition effect you want.**

iMovie will insert transitions automatically whenever it finds shifts from one piece of video to another. This is useful as a way to insert transitions quickly, and you can then delete or substitute transitions when you edit your video.

7. **Click the Create button.**

   A Project browser opens, and you see `To start a new project, select video or photos and drag them to this area` in the Project pane of the iMovie window, as shown in Figure 4-5.

   The stage is set for your cinematic masterpiece.

Selecting video clips

Whether you want to create a new project or edit an existing one, you need to add video clips from the Event Library and place them in a project stored in the Project Library.

Before you can select a video clip to store in a project, you need to see exactly what part of a video you want to use as a clip. To help you find any part of a video, iMovie displays an entire video as a series of images that appear like individual frames of a filmstrip. To find a specific part of a video, you can skim through a video. When you find the part of a video to use, just click and drag it into a project.

Figure 4-5: The Project browser is where you arrange video clips.

Skimming a video

Skimming a video lets you see the video footage just by moving the mouse pointer over the video images. To view a video by skimming, follow these steps:

1. **Move the pointer over any of the thumbnail images of a video file displayed in the Event browser.**

   A red vertical line appears over the thumbnail image, as shown in Figure 4-6.

2. **Move the mouse left and right to watch your video in the preview pane (upper-right section) of the iMovie window.**

   The faster you move the mouse, the faster the video plays. Moving the mouse to the left plays the video backward. Moving the mouse to the right plays the video forward.

Click anywhere in a clip to place the red vertical line at a starting point, and then press the spacebar. Your video will play from that point forward. Press the spacebar again to stop the video.

Figure 4-6: A red vertical line shows you the position of the current image in a video file.

Selecting a video clip

After you see the part of a video you want to use, you need to select the video clip by following these steps:

1. **In the Event browser, move the pointer to the beginning of the part of the video that you want to use.**

2. **Click and drag to the right.**

A yellow rectangle appears to define the size of your clip, as shown in Figure 4-7. Drag the handles to define the exact frame to start and end your video clip.

3. **Release the mouse or trackpad button when you're happy with the portion of the video that your clip contains.**

Placing a video clip in a project

After selecting a video clip, you can place it in a project. To place a video clip in a project, follow these steps:

1. **Click the project in the Project Library list.**

2. **Click the Edit Project button above the list.**

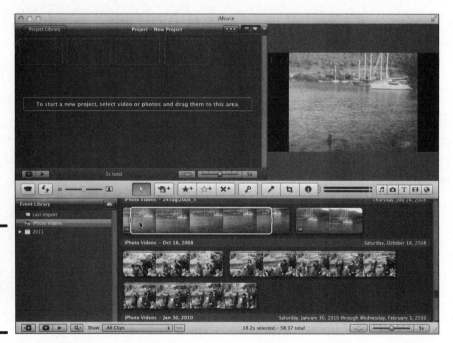

Figure 4-7:
A yellow rectangle defines the size of a video clip.

Thumbnail images of any video clips already stored in the project appear.

Note: If you haven't added any video clips to a project, you see a `To start a new project, select video or photos and drag them to this area` message, along with dotted rectangles (refer to Figure 4-5).

3. **Move the pointer inside the yellow rectangle of the video clip you selected.**

   The pointer turns into a hand icon.

4. **Click and drag the selected video clip to one of the dotted rectangles in the Project pane and then release the mouse or trackpad button, as shown in Figure 4-8.**

   Your selected video clip appears as a thumbnail image in the Project Library section of the iMovie window.

To edit a project, click the project in the Project Library list and click the Edit Project button above the list. To return to the Project Library, click the Project Library button.

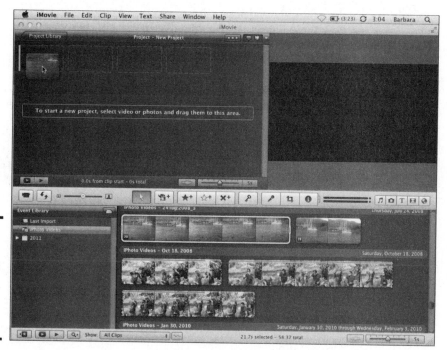

Figure 4-8: Dragging a video clip to the Project browser adds it to your movie.

Book IV
Chapter 4

Making Movies
with iMovie

Deleting video clips

In case you store a video clip in a project and later decide that you don't need that video clip, you can delete it from that project.

Deleting a video clip from a project does not delete the video clip from the Event Library.

To delete a video clip from a project, follow these steps:

1. **Click a project in the Project Library list and click the Edit Project button.**

The Project browser displays all the video clips stored in the selected project.

2. **In the Project browser, click the video clip that you want to delete.**

3. **Choose Edit⟳Delete Selection (or press Delete).**

Deleting a project

When you finish a project or decide you don't want it anymore, you can delete an entire project.

When you delete a project, you also delete any video clips stored inside that project. However, the original videos (from which you copied clips to add to the project) remain in the Event Library.

To delete a project, follow these steps:

1. **Click the project you want to delete in the Project Library list.**

2. **Choose File⟳Move Project to Trash.**

If you accidentally delete a project, you can retrieve it by pressing ⌘+Z or choosing Edit⟳Undo Delete Project.

Printing a project

Although an iMovie project is intended to be viewed onscreen, sometimes it helps during the editing stage to have a printed copy of your project. Each project displays thumbnail images of one or more video clips. If you want to review the order and images of the video clips stored in a project, you can print these images on paper. Obviously, this printout of your project thumbnails can't show you the moving images of your video, but it can show you the organization of your video clips.

To print the thumbnail images of video clips stored in a project, follow these steps:

1. **Click a project in the Project Library list.**

2. **Choose File➪Print Project.**

A Print dialog appears.

3. **(Optional) Drag the slider in the bottom-right corner of the Project pane to define how many thumbnail images to display.**

If you drag the slider to the right, you display fewer thumbnail images. Drag the slider to the left, and you display more thumbnail images.

4. **Choose PDF➪Open PDF in Preview to see how your project will appear on paper.**

5. **Click Print.**

Organizing the Project Library

You can divide the Project Library into different folders, where one folder might contain your family vacation video, and a second folder might contain the footage you captured of a UFO you spotted hovering over a mesa in New Mexico. To create a folder, follow these steps:

1. **In the Project pane, click the Project Library button.**

The Project Library list appears.

2. **Choose File➪New Folder.**

Type the name you want for the folder in the dialog that appears.

3. **Click Create.**

The folder appears in the Project Library.

4. **Click and drag the projects to the folder.**

Editing Video Clips in a Project

After you place one or more video clips in a project, you usually want to edit those video clips to put them in the best order, trim unnecessary footage, and add titles and audio to create an entertaining or informative movie. In the following sections, we take you through movie-making basics; starting in the "Using Special Effects" section, we go a step farther and show you how to add special effects.

Before you begin editing, turn on Advanced Tools and Fine Tuning so you have the full capacity of iMovie. Choose iMovie➪Preferences➪General and click Show Advanced Tools; choose iMovie➪Preferences➪Browser and click Show Fine Tuning controls.

Rearranging the order of video clips

A project plays video clips in the sequence you create, but you may want to change the order of your video clips. To rearrange the order of your video clips in a project, follow these steps:

1. **Click a project in the Project Library list.**

2. **Click the Edit Project button at the top of the pane.**

   The Project browser opens.

3. **Click the video clip you want to move and keep the pointer over the clip.**

   The pointer turns into a hand icon.

4. **Click and drag the selected video clip behind another video clip.**

   Vertical lines appear: Green shows where you can insert the clip; red shows where your video clip will appear.

5. **Release the mouse or trackpad button.**

   Your video clip now appears in its new location.

Adjusting the size of a video clip

Sometimes a video clip contains a little too much footage that you need to trim. Other times, you might have trimmed a video clip a little too much and need to add more footage. In either case, you can fix this problem and change the size of your video clip by following these steps:

1. **Click a project in the Project Library list and click the Edit Project button.**

2. **Move the pointer over a video clip and click the lower-left corner of the clip.**

   A gear icon appears.

3. **Click the gear icon and choose Clip Trimmer from the pop-up menu, as shown in Figure 4-9.**

   A Clip Trimmer pane opens at the bottom of the window, covering the Event Library and browser, as shown in Figure 4-10. The yellow rectangle contains the size of your video clip. The dimmed frames before and/or after the yellow rectangle show the original video that you used to copy the video clip.

4. **Move the pointer over the left or right side of the rectangle that defines the size of your video clip.**

   The pointer turns into a two-way pointing arrow.

Figure 4-9:
The pop-up menu for adjusting your project.

5. **Click and drag a handle to increase or decrease the size of your video clip. The number on the right indicates how many seconds your clip lasts.**

   When you increase the video, the original footage from before or after the clip you are working on is added.

6. **Click the Play button or press the spacebar to view your edited video clip.**

7. **Click Done when you're happy with the images stored in your video clip.**

   The Clip Trimmer closes, and you see the Event Library and browser again.

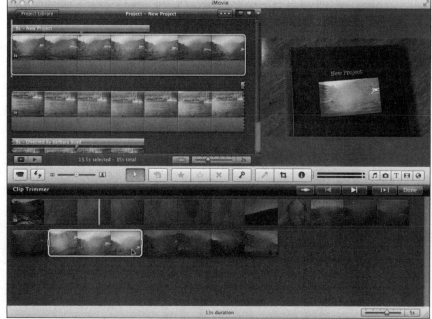

Figure 4-10:
A yellow outline defines your clip; dimmed frames before and after show the original video.

TIP

If a clip looks blurry, even though you stabilized the video when you did your import, you can try one other trick. In the Project browser, double-click the clip that looks blurry. The Clip Inspector opens. Select Reduce Motion Distortion next to Rolling Shutter, and then select the amount. Medium is right for video taken with a camcorder, High or Extra High are good settings for video shot with a Flip video camera or smartphone.

Adding titles

Titles tell your viewer what your movie is about. Opening titles can display the video's name and purpose, and the closing titles can list the credits of the people who appeared in the video and put it together. Transition titles can indicate a time or subject change in the movie.

Titles can appear by themselves or be superimposed over part of your video. To create titles for a project, follow these steps:

1. **Click a project in the Project Library list.**

2. **Click the Titles button on the iMovie toolbar (it looks like a "T" in the group of buttons on the right side) or choose Window⇨Titles.**

   The Titles browser opens, as shown in Figure 4-11. If you are using a theme, the name of the theme appears, otherwise you see No Theme.

Figure 4-11: The Titles button shows (or hides) title styles you can use.

3. **Click and drag a title from the Titles browser to a video clip or in between two clips.**

   If you are working with a theme and try to place a title in a location that the theme doesn't use, a message as shown in Figure 4-12 appears. Turn off automatic transitions to insert the title where you want. Any titles or transitions created by the theme remain in place. In fact, you can't change titles used by a theme — you can add additional titles, but those associated with the theme remain. You can edit the text in a themed title but not the appearance.

   Titles associated with a theme appear in a gold balloon above the film-strip in the Project browser; non-themed titles appear in a blue balloon.

Figure 4-12:
Turn off automatic transitions if you're using a theme.

Automatic transitions and titles are turned on

You must turn off automatic transitions and titles to make changes to individual transitions or titles. All of the transitions and titles currently in your project will remain in your project.

| Cancel | Turn Off Automatic Transitions |

4. **Release the mouse or trackpad button.**

   If you release the mouse or trackpad button over a video clip, your title appears superimposed over the video image, as shown in Figure 4-13.

   If you release the mouse or trackpad button in between video clips, your title appears as a separate video clip between those two video clips. A background chooser opens where you choose the texture or color of the background that appears behind your title.

5. **Click the title balloon that appears over a video clip.**

   Your chosen title format appears in the Preview pane.

6. **In the Preview pane, double-click the text you want to edit and type new text, or use the arrow and Delete keys to edit the existing title.**

7. **If you are working with a non-themed title, click the Show Fonts button to display a Fonts window that lets you choose a different color, font size, and typeface for your text.**

8. **Click the Play button to preview how your titles appear.**

9. **(Optional) To change the duration of time your title is onscreen, double-click the title balloon to open the Title Inspector, shown in Figure 4-14, and change the number of seconds by typing an new number in the Duration text box.**

   You can also adjust the fade in and fade out time manually or leave the automatic setting.

Figure 4-13:
Titles can appear as separate clips or super-imposed over existing video clips.

Figure 4-14:
Change the number of seconds your title appears onscreen.

10. **Click Done.**

11. **Click the Titles button to hide the list of available title styles from view.**

To delete a title, click the title balloon and press Delete, or choose Edit⇨ Delete Selection.

If you want to change the title style for a non-themed title, double-click the title to open the title Inspector and click the button next to Title to open the Title chooser.

Adding transitions

Normally, when you place video clips in a project, those video clips play one after another. Instead of abruptly cutting from one video clip to another, you can add transitions that appear in between video clips. Themes come with stylized transitions that relate to the theme. You can change themed transitions if you wish. Themed transitions last two seconds and standard transitions last half a second; however, this is changeable. To add a transition, follow these steps:

1. **Click a project in the Project Library list and click the Edit Project button.**

   The Project browser shows thumbnail images of your selected project.

2. **Click the Transitions button on the iMovie toolbar (it looks like an hourglass, to the right of the Titles button) or choose Window⇨ Transitions.**

   A list of transitions appears in the Transitions browser, as shown in Figure 4-15.

3. **Click and drag a transition from the Transitions browser to a space between two video clips in the Project pane. If you are using a theme, the theme transitions appear in the first row.**

Figure 4-15: Transitions let you create unique visual effects in between video clips.

Some different types of transitions include Cube (which spins a cube on the screen where a different video clip appears on each side of the cube) and Page Curl (which peels away one video clip like a piece of paper).

4. **A green vertical line appears when you hover over a space where a transition can be inserted. Release the mouse or trackpad button when the green vertical line appears between two video clips.**

5. **Move the pointer over the transition.**

   Move the pointer to the right and the transition plays forward. To move the transition backward, move the pointer to the left.

6. **(Optional) To change the duration, overlap, or style of a non-theme transition, double-click the transition icon within your project in the Project browser.**

   The Transition Inspector opens, as shown in Figure 4-16.

Figure 4-16: Change the duration, overlap, and style of transitions.

7. **Change the duration of the transition by typing a new value in the Transitions text box.**

8. **Choose the type of overlap you want:**

   - *All:* The two clips overlap by the length of the transition and your project time decreases by the transition length.

   - *Half:* The transition spans the two clips and the total project time remains the same.

9. **Click the button next to Transitions to open the Transitions chooser and change the style of the transition.**

10. **Click the Transitions button to hide the Transitions browser.**

If you choose a theme when you create your new project, the title and transition choices in the first row of the title and transitions browsers are those associated with the theme. You can choose a transition that isn't part of the theme; you will be prompted to turn off automatic transitions when you click and drag it to your project.

Adding still images

You don't have to limit your movie content to video, titles, and transitions. Still images such as photos, scanned documents, and graphics can add depth to your subject matter. To add still images, follow these steps:

1. **Click a project in the Project Library and click Edit Project.**

2. **Click the Photos button in the Toolbar (it looks like a camera, over on the right side).**

   The Photos browser opens.

3. **Scroll through your Events, Photos, and Albums in iPhoto to find the photo you want to add to your movie.**

4. **Click and drag the image from the Photos browser to the Project browser.**

   If you drag the image over a part of a clip, a pop-up menu appears, shown in Figure 4-17, which gives you choices of what to do with the image. The simplest options are Replace, which replaces the frame with the still image, or Insert, which inserts the still image between the two frames of the clip where you placed it. The other options are explained in the "Using Special Effects" section, later in this chapter.

Figure 4-17: Drag a still image to a clip.

5. **Choose the option you want, probably Insert.**

   Your clip is divided and the still image now rests between the two parts of the clip, as shown in Figure 4-18.

   A still image is given four seconds of video time.

6. **Click the Photos button again to close the Photos browser.**

The photos you see in the Photos browser are in iPhoto on your Mac. If you want to use a scanned document or other image, drag the image into iPhoto so you can find it in the Photos browser in iMovie.

Figure 4-18:
The clip
is divided
before and
after the still
image you
inserted.

Adding maps and globes

Maps add visual interest to your movie, especially if you are making a movie about a journey or just want to show where the events of your movie take place. iMovie comes with several maps and globes that you can place in your movie. To add a map or globe to your movie, do the following:

1. **Click a project in the Project Library and click Edit Project.**

2. **Click the Maps, Backgrounds, and Animatics button in the Toolbar (it looks like a globe, over on the right-hand side).**

   The Maps, Backgrounds, and Animatics browser opens. The first row shows four animated globes, the second row shows four animated maps, and the third row shows four still map images.

3. **Click and drag the map or globe you want to use to the place in your movie where you want it to appear.**

   A green vertical line indicates where you can insert the map or globe. You have to insert it before or after a clip; it can't replace a clip.

4. **Your map appears in the preview window and the Map Inspector opens, as shown in Figure 4-19.**

Figure 4-19:
The Map
Inspector
opens when
you insert
a globe or
map into
your movie.

5. **Click the button next to Video Effect to choose one of 20 effects for your map or globe.**

   Video Effects change the appearance of the map.

6. **Click the button next to Start Location to choose a starting point for the map animation.**

   The Inspector flips over, and you can type in the city you want to use as your starting point.

7. **Repeat Step 6 for the End Location.**

8. **Click Done.**

9. **Move the pointer across the map or globe clip to see how it will appear in your video.**

10. **Click the Maps, Backgrounds, and Animatics button to close the browser.**

You may have to split a clip to insert a globe or map exactly where you want it. Double-click at the point where you want to divide the clip. Choose Clip⇨Split Clip. Your clip is now divided into two parts, and you can insert a globe or map in between the two parts of the clip.

When you insert still images or moving maps, you probably want to add a transition in the spaces between your video and the still image or map.

Adding audio files

To enliven your movie, you can add audio files that play background music or sound effects to match the video that's playing — a car honking, say, or maybe a telephone ringing. You can also record a voiceover directly in iMovie with your Mac's built-in microphone or an external microphone connected to the USB or FireWire port.

To add an audio file to a project, follow these steps:

1. **Click a project in the Project Library list and click the Edit Project button.**

2. **Click the Music and Sound Effects button on the iMovie toolbar (it looks like a pair of musical notes).**

    A list of audio files appears in the Music and Sound Effects browser, as shown in Figure 4-20.

3. **In the Music and Sound Effects browser, click an audio file library to use, such as iTunes, GarageBand, or iLife Sound Effects.**

    A list of audio files appears. Note the time to the right of each audio file.

4. **Click and drag an audio file to a video clip in the Project pane.**

Figure 4-20: Audio files can add music or sound effects to your videos.

A red vertical line appears over the video clip to show you where the audio file will start playing.

5. **Release the mouse or trackpad button.**

   The name of the audio file appears in a balloon under the clip you attached it to.

6. **Move the pointer over the audio file until it becomes a hand, and then move the audio file backward or forward to accompany a different part of your movie.**

7. **Click the gear icon on the audio file to open the Clip Trimmer.**

   The Clip Trimmer opens beneath the Project pane. The audio file has yellow handles on both ends.

8. **Click and drag the yellow handle to shorten the audio file from the beginning (left) or the end (right).**

9. **Click Done to close the Clip Trimmer.**

Adding background audio

Background audio plays throughout your movie, behind other audio. You can adjust the volume of the background audio so it doesn't disturb other audio in your movie, and you can have more than one background audio file so different background audio plays during different moments of your movie. For example, you may begin with background music to play during the opening title of your movie, and then the music may fade and a different song plays more quietly while there is talking, and at one point you may want to add a thunderstorm as background audio. You can pin the background audio to a specific video clip, so if you move clips around, the background music stays with the clip. Here's how to add background audio:

1. **Repeat Steps 1 through 3 from the previous instructions.**

   The drop well for background audio is after the last clip in the Project browser.

2. **Click and drag the audio file you want to use for background to the Project pane, after the last clip in the Project browser.**

   The area behind your clips turns green, as shown in Figure 4-21.

3. **To pin the background to a specific clip, move the pointer over the title of the audio file until it becomes a hand.**

4. **Click and drag to the right until the background turns purple and a pin appears in the upper-left corner.**

5. **Release the mouse or trackpad button when the pin is over the frame you want to attach the audio file to.**

   To unpin a background audio file, click in the purple area. The background is outlined in yellow. Choose Clip⇨Unpin Music Track.

Figure 4-21:
The area
behind the
Project
browser
turns green
or purple
when
you add
background
audio.

6. **Double-click the green or purple background audio area to open the Inspector.**

7. **Click Audio.**

8. **Adjust the volume of the background audio by moving the Volume slider left or right.**

9. **Click Done to close the Inspector.**

To add more than one background audio file to your movie, begin with the last audio file and pin it to the frame where you want it to begin playing, and then drag the audio file you want to play before that one, and so on until you reach the beginning of your movie.

When you pin the background audio to a frame, even if you move the clip that contains the pinned frame, the audio remains with it. A purple background indicates pinned audio; a green background indicates unpinned background audio.

Adding a voiceover

Voiceovers can narrate the action in your movie or accompany still images, making them seem more "active." To add a voiceover to your movie, follow these steps:

1. **Click a project in the Project Library list and click the Edit Project button.**

2. **Click the Voiceover button (it looks like a microphone) or the press the O key.**

   The Voiceover Inspector opens, as shown in Figure 4-22.

3. **Choose the device you want to use to record in the Record From pop-up menu.**

4. **Select Play Project Audio While Recording if you want to hear the other audio while you speak.**

   Wear headphones if you choose this option so you hear the audio, but the microphone you're speaking into doesn't record it.

5. **Click the clip where you want the voiceover to begin.**

   The clip begins playing in the Preview pane, a few seconds before where you want to begin your voiceover, and a countdown lets you know when to begin speaking. This way you can watch your video while you are recording.

6. **Press any key to stop recording.**

Figure 4-22:
Use the Voiceover feature to add narration to your iMovie project.

Using the Audio Inspector

You can make adjustments to any audio you add to your movie with the Audio Inspector. Double-click the audio balloon or background audio to open the Inspector. Click the Audio tab to see the Inspector, as shown in Figure 4-23. The adjustments you can make are as follows:

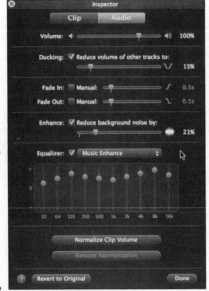

Figure 4-23:
The Audio Inspector lets you make adjustments to audio clips.

✦ **Volume slider:** Adjust volume for the selected audio clip. This is useful when you have background audio, audio associated with the source video, and sound effects.

✦ **Ducking:** Gives prevalence to the selected audio clip and reduces or "ducks" the volume of other tracks to the percentage you choose.

✦ **Fade In/Out:** Establishes how long your audio will fade in at the beginning or out at the end of when it's played.

✦ **Enhance:** Enhances your selected audio by reducing background noise by the percentage you choose.

✦ **Equalizer:** Balances the highs and lows of the audio. Choose an equalizer that matches your type of audio, such as voice or music, or choose Custom to adjust the settings yourself.

✦ **Normalize Clip Volume:** Click this button to adjust all audio associated with the clip to an optimal listening level.

Who is Ken Burns?

Ken Burns is a documentary filmmaker. There are two *Ken Burns effects*: One is the zooming and panning of a still image, which Mr. Burns uses to make inanimate objects interesting in a documentary, bringing things like photos of civil war memorabilia to life when motion film is unavailable. The second Ken Burns effect is the fame one gains after appearing in one of Mr. Burns's documentaries. iMovie can only help you with the first Ken Burns effect.

Using Special Effects

With iMovie, you can make your movie unique and memorable with special effects. There are four categories of adjustments you can make to add special effects to your original video or still images. The first three are controlled through the Inspector dialog, the last is adjusted in the Preview pane:

✦ **Clip Adjustments:** Make changes to the speed and direction of the clip, choose preset video and audio effects, and control stabilization and motion distortion.

✦ **Video Adjustments:** Allows you to make changes to brightness, contrast, exposure, and the like.

✦ **Audio Adjustments:** Set the volume, activate *ducking* (that's giving prevalence to one audio file over another), and reduce background noise. (Refer to the previous section, "Using the Audio Inspector.")

✦ **Cropping and Rotation:** Zoom in on a frame or frames of your clip to rotate or apply the Ken Burns effect (see the nearby sidebar, "Who is Ken Burns?").

Applying special effects

To apply special effects to one or more clips in your movie, do the following:

1. **Click a project in the Project Library and click Edit Project.**

2. **Move the pointer over the clip you want to adjust and click the action button (the gear).**

A menu pops up.

3. **Choose Clip Adjustments.**

The Clip Inspector opens, as shown in Figure 4-24.

Figure 4-24:
Choose
video and
audio
effects in
the Clip
Inspector.

4. **Make changes as you want:**

   • *Video Effect:* Choose one of 20 effects, such as Sepia, Dream, or X-ray.

   • *Audio Effect:* Choose one of 20 effects, for example Echo, Robot, or Cathedral.

   • *Speed:* Move the slider toward the turtle on the left to play your clip in slow motion, or toward the rabbit on the right to fast-forward. Click Reverse to run the video backward. The percentage of the original speed and the duration appear in the boxes to the right.

   • *Stabilization and Maximum Zoom:* Select the Smooth Clip Motion check box to automatically stabilize any shakiness in the video clip. Move the slider to zoom in or out.

   • *Rolling Shutter:* Select the Reduce Motion Distortion check box to correct blurriness of the clip. Choose Medium if the video was shot with a camcorder; choose High or Extra High if a Flip camera or smartphone was used to capture the video.

5. **Press the spacebar to play your clip and see the changes you made in the Preview pane.**

6. **Try other effects and repeat Step 5 to see the results.**

7. **Click Done when you're satisfied with the effects.**

You can also apply Slow Motion, Fast Forward, Instant Replay, and Rewind effects from the Clip menu.

Adjusting the quality of a clip

The Clip adjustments change the appearance and motion of your clip; however, you can also adjust the quality of the video in your clip. Follow these steps:

1. **Click a project in the Project Library and click Edit Project.**

2. **Move the pointer over the clip you want to adjust and click the action button (the gear).**

A menu pops up.

3. **Choose Video Adjustments.**

The Video Inspector opens, as shown in Figure 4-25.

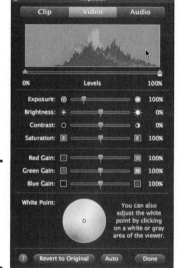

Figure 4-25: Adjust the quality of the video in the Video Inspector.

4. **Make changes as you want to the following:**

- *Exposure:* The higher the exposure, the higher the highlights and lesser the shadows.

- *Brightness:* Affects the overall light level; increasing makes the image lighter.

- *Contrast:* Increasing the contrast makes the difference between dark and light areas more pronounced.

- *Saturation:* Affects the amount of color: dragging to the right intensifies color, dragging to the far left makes a black-and-white image.

- *Red, Green, Blue Gain:* Increases the intensity of each of these colors.

- *White Point:* Because white is the reference point for all the other colors, changing the white point changes the colors. Drag the point around on the Inspector and notice the changes in the Preview pane, or click a point in Preview to see where the white point is on the Inspector.

**Book IV
Chapter 4**

**Making Movies
with iMovie**

5. **Press the spacebar to play your clip and see the changes you made in the Preview pane.**

6. **Try other effects and repeat Step 4 to see the results.**

7. **Click Done when you are satisfied with the effects.**

Cropping, rotating, panning, and zooming

Cropping, rotating, panning, and zooming a specific frame or still image are useful effects to emphasize something in your movie. To crop, rotate, or apply the Ken Burns effect, follow these steps:

1. **Click a project in the Project Library and click Edit Project.**

2. **Move the pointer over the clip you want to adjust and click the action button (the gear).**

    A menu pops up.

3. **Choose Cropping and Rotation (still images will have Cropping, Ken Burns, and Rotation).**

    The still image or the first frame of your selected clip appears in the Preview pane, as shown in Figure 4-26.

Figure 4-26:
Use the image in the Preview pane to apply Cropping, Rotation, and Ken Burns effects.

4. **Select one of the three choices:**

    • *Fit:* iMovie adjusts the image to fill the screen size.

    • *Crop:* Click and drag the corners to resize the image as you want.

    • *Ken Burns:* Apply a zoom and pan effect to the image.

5. **Use the arrows at the top to rotate the image.**

6. **Click the Play button to see the effect.**

7. **Click Done when you are satisfied with the effect.**

Two-image video effects

iMovie's two-image video effects take your movie from good to fabulous. Sounds complicated, but it's not. Have two images in mind that would look great and have an awesome impact if they could be shown at once? Follow these steps:

1. **Click a project in the Project Library and click Edit Project.**

2. **Click and drag the first of two clips into the Project browser.**

3. **Click and drag the second of the two clips over the first clip in the Project browser.**

   Essentially, you are merging the two clips. A pop-up menu appears, as shown in Figure 4-27.

Figure 4-27: Choose from three two-image effects.

4. **Choose one of the options:**

   • *Cutaway:* The first clip cuts away to expose the second clip.

   • *Picture in Picture:* The second clip plays in a box superimposed on the first clip.

   • *Side by Side:* The two clips play next to each other in a split-screen effect.

5. **Move the playhead (the red vertical line) to the beginning of your clip and press the spacebar to see your effect play in the Preview pane.**

6. **Press the spacebar again to stop playing.**

Any time you want to show or hide a pane, inspector, or browser, you can go to the Window menu and choose what you want to show or hide.

Making a Trailer for Your Movie

With iMovie '11, Apple added some great features; not the least is the possibility of making a trailer for your movie. To create a trailer, follow these steps:

1. **Click the iMovie icon in the Dock or Launchpad.**

2. **Choose File⇨New Project.**

3. **Choose one of the Trailer themes in the chooser that appears.**

4. **Click Create.**

The Trailer window opens, as shown in Figure 4-28.

5. **Replace the text in the outline with your own information.**

Give your movie a name and a release date. Add actors. Make up a production company name. Fill in the credits with the names of people who helped make your movie.

6. **Click the Storyboard tab.**

The Storyboard shows the sequence of the trailer. Empty drop wells show you the type of images to put in the storyboard. Banners in between indicate the text that will play.

7. **Click frames in the Event browser that correspond to the images in the Storyboard.**

Figure 4-28: Add your own text to your movie trailer.

The frame you click is placed in the first drop well, the second frame goes in the second drop well, and so on, until all the drop wells are filled. iMovie adds transitions, titles, and effects.

8. **Click the Play button to see your trailer in the Preview pane.**

You can convert a trailer to a project and edit it as a normal project, but you can't revert it to a trailer. So it's a good idea to copy the trailer before you convert it to a project, if you choose to do so.

Saving a Video

The point of organizing video clips in a project is to create a polished movie. With iMovie, you can save your project to view on a computer, in iTunes, on an iPod, iPad, or iPhone, or on a website such as YouTube or Vimeo. You can save the same video project to different formats in case you want to view your video on your Mac but also want to post a copy on Facebook for other people to enjoy.

If you create an interesting movie that you want to add to other applications, such as a presentation application, you can save a copy in the Media Browser to use in other applications.

Finalizing a project

Before you go any farther, congratulate yourself — you've made a movie. When you are absolutely sure that you don't want to tweak your movie any more, you want to finalize it. iMovie *renders* (prepares) your movie in all possible file configurations so you can share it in different formats and watch it on different devices. To finalize your project, do the following:

1. **Click your Project in the Project Library.**

2. **Choose File⇨Finalize Project.**

3. **iMovie begins finalizing your movie.**

   A dialog appears. Rendering may take a while, so you may want to go do something else.

4. **Your project is finalized when the dialog disappears.**

Saving a project to iDVD

If you want to burn your movie to a DVD, the easiest way to do that is to save it to iDVD. From there, you can modify your project or simply burn it to a disc. To save to iDVD, choose Share⇨iDVD. iMovie prepares the movie and opens iDVD. See Book IV, Chapter 6 for the details on using iDVD.

**Book IV
Chapter 4**

**Making Movies
with iMovie**

Saving a project as a digital video file

You may want to save your iMovie project as a digital video file so you can burn it to DVD later (using iDVD) or give a copy to someone who wants to view it on their computer. When you save a project as a digital video file, you can save it as an MPEG-4, AVI, QuickTime, or one of 11 other types of files. See Book IV, Chapter 2 for more information about digital video file formats.

To save a project in a different format, follow these steps:

1. **Click a project in the Project Library list.**

2. **Choose Share⇨Export Using QuickTime.**

The Save Exported File As dialog appears, as shown in Figure 4-29.

3. **Choose the location to save your project from the Where pop-up menu.**

You can expand the menu by clicking the disclosure triangle to the right of the Save As field.

4. **Select an option from the Export pop-up menu; refer to Figure 4-29.**

5. **Click Save.**

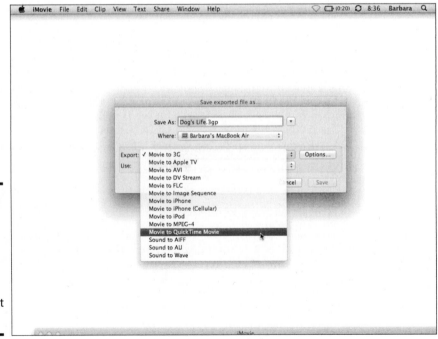

Figure 4-29: The Save Exported File As dialog lets you save your movie in a different file format.

Saving (and removing) a video for iTunes or Media Browser

If you create a particularly interesting video and store it on your hard drive or play it on an iPod touch, iPhone, or iPad, you might later have trouble finding it. To fix this problem, save your videos in your iTunes library. This way, you can quickly find and play videos later.

If you think you'll want to insert your movie into another application such as Keynote or iWeb, save your movie in the Media Browser. From there, you can access and insert that movie into any application that uses the Media Browser, such as the iWork suite, many iLife applications (such as iDVD and iWeb), and non-Apple software, such as Toast (www.roxio.com). To save a project in iTunes or Media Browser, follow these steps:

1. **Click a project in the Project Library list.**

2. **Choose Share⇨Media Browser/iTunes.**

   The Publish to Media Browser/iTunes dialog appears.

3. **Select or deselect one or more check boxes (such as Medium or Tiny), and then click Publish.**

   The sizes define the frame size of your video. Smaller sizes make your video look best on small screens, such as on mobile phones. Larger sizes make your video look best on larger screens, such as on a TV set. Your movie now appears in the Media Browser or your iTunes library on your hard drive.

After you save a movie to Media Browser or iTunes, you can remove it by choosing Share⇨Remove from Media Browser/iTunes.

Saving (and removing) a project for the Internet

One way to show off your movie is by uploading it to the web so others can watch it online or download it and watch it whenever they want. The most well-known (and well-trafficked!) video-sharing site is YouTube, but iMovie gives you options for uploading to Vimeo, Facebook, and CNN iReport.

Some services limit video files you upload to a maximum file size (YouTube is 100MB and a maximum time length of ten minutes, whichever comes first), so make sure that your video doesn't overrun the limits imposed by the service you choose to post to.

Each of the Internet sites requires you to have an account. Before you can upload your video, you have to set up an account at one or all of the following:

✦ www.youtube.com

✦ www.facebook.com

✦ www.icloud.com

✦ www.vimeo.com

✦ www.cnn.com

You can upload a video from iMovie to these services by following these steps:

1. **Click a project in the Project Library list.**

2. **Choose Share⇨YouTube/Facebook/Vimeo/CNN iReport.**

A dialog similar to Figure 4-30 appears.

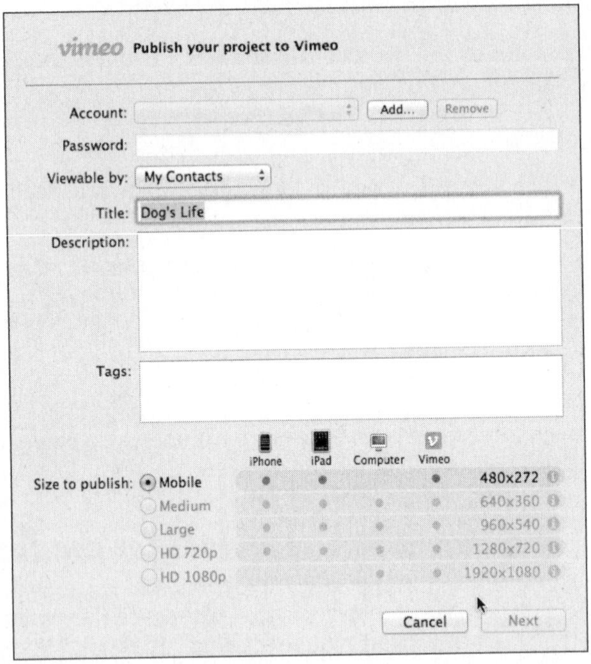

Figure 4-30: Choose an account, category, and resolution size to upload your video to the web.

3. **Enter your account name and password in the Account and Password text boxes. Identify a category and who has viewing privileges if available.**

4. **Enter information to identify your video in the appropriate text boxes (Title, Subject, Description, Tags, and so on).**

The information you type to identify your video can help others find it.

5. **Select one of the Size to Publish radio buttons and then click Next.**

Choose Mobile if you want to create a video frame size of 480 x 272 pixels, which is designed for viewing on small screens, such as an iPhone. Choose Medium or Large if you want to create a video frame size for viewing on an ordinary TV or computer screen.

After you click Next, a dialog appears, warning about copyright infringement.

6. **Click the Publish button.**

Presto! You're an Internet Video Superstar!

After you save a movie to one of the Internet services, you can remove it by choosing Share➪Remove from *service name*.

Book IV
Chapter 4

Making Movies with iMovie

Chapter 5: Making Your Own Kind of Music with GarageBand

In This Chapter

✔ Playing instruments with Magic GarageBand

✔ Recording your music

✔ Editing your recordings

✔ Saving your music

✔ Saving ringtones

✔ Learning to play the guitar and piano

✔ Recording podcasts

✔ Checking out GarageBand accessories

*W*hen you mention that you use a Mac to a group of non-Mac users, one of the first things you hear is "oh, yeah, Macs are great for graphics." While that's true, your Mac is a pretty terrific music-making and podcast-generating machine too — and we're not talking iTunes here (although we do talk about iTunes at length in Book IV, Chapter 1).

With GarageBand, which is part of Apple's iLife suite, you can record music, podcasts, and ringtones. In its simplest form, GarageBand provides instruments (such as drums, keyboards, and guitars) and prerecorded tracks that you mix up to create a virtual one-person band. You arrange the separate audio tracks and put them together to create your own songs.

GarageBand really sings when you record your own music. You have the option of using your Mac's built-in microphone or connecting your instruments and hand-held microphone to your Mac and recording directly. After you lay down the individual tracks, you can clean up the sound, alter the rhythms and timing, and cut and splice the best performances to generate a CD or iTunes quality recordings.

If you want to learn to play an instrument or brush up on your childhood music lessons, GarageBand offers guitar and piano lessons to get you started. You have the option of playing along and GarageBand will evaluate your progress.

Although designed for recording, modifying, and playing music, GarageBand can also record, modify, and save audio files in a number of audio file formats. If you're not interested in making music, you can use GarageBand to clean up a recorded speech and save it as a podcast that you can send directly from GarageBand to the website you created with iWeb or to any other podcast outlet.

In this chapter, we explain the basic functions of GarageBand along with some tips. We recommend you learn the basics and then play around. The more you use it, the more you see how powerful and flexible an application GarageBand truly is.

Recording Audio

Because GarageBand works with audio, the first task is to record audio into GarageBand by using your Mac's built-in microphone, an external microphone, or audio input (such as a keyboard or guitar plugged directly into your Mac).

If you don't have a real instrument, GarageBand provides a variety of software instruments — virtual musical instruments, such as pianos, guitars, and drums — that you can play and control through your Mac. All you have to do is specify the notes to play and the tempo, and the software instruments let you hear your music played by the instruments you choose.

Recording audio through Magic GarageBand

Magic GarageBand is great for creating background music quickly and easily. For example, if you're creating a Keynote presentation to present to cowboys, you may want country music playing in the background. Rather than hunt down a country song, just fire up Magic GarageBand, pick the Country genre, modify the song by choosing different instruments, and you git yourself an instant country song without even knowing how to play the "gee-tar." Wee-haw!

Each genre in Magic GarageBand only plays one stock song that you can modify. If you want a country song, Magic GarageBand creates the same country song. It's up to you to customize this song to make it different. If you want to create your own country song, you have to create a new music project rather than use Magic GarageBand.

To create a Magic GarageBand song, follow these steps:

1. **Click the GarageBand icon in the Dock or Launchpad.**

The GarageBand chooser opens, as shown in Figure 5-1.

Figure 5-1:
The GarageBand chooser lets you choose the type of project to create.

2. **Click Magic GarageBand in the sidebar on the left.**

   Magic GarageBand shows different genre icons, such as Rock, Jazz, or Funk, as shown in Figure 5-2.

Figure 5-2:
The Magic GarageBand icons provide different music genres.

   Move the pointer over a genre icon to make the Preview button appear (refer to Figure 5-2), and then click the Preview button to hear a snippet or entire song played in your chosen genre. (Click the Preview radio button again to stop the song.)

3. **Click a genre, such as Blues or Country, and then click Choose (or just double-click on the genre you want to choose).**

The Magic GarageBand window displays a stage and instruments, as shown in Figure 5-3.

4. **Click an instrument on the stage.**

    The bottom of the Magic GarageBand window displays all available variations of that instrument.

5. **Click the instrument variant you want, in the bottom of the Magic GarageBand window.**

    Your chosen instrument variant appears on the stage.

6. **Click the Play button to hear how the song or snippet sounds with your new instrument(s).**

    Essentially, Magic GarageBand plays one stock song that you can modify by choosing the types of instruments to play.

7. **Repeat Steps 4 through 6 for any additional instruments you want to change.**

8. **Click Open in GarageBand when you're happy with the instruments in your band.**

Figure 5-3: Magic GarageBand displays all the instruments of the band.

GarageBand displays a window that contains all your instruments arranged in separate tracks, as shown in Figure 5-4. At this point, you can modify the song.

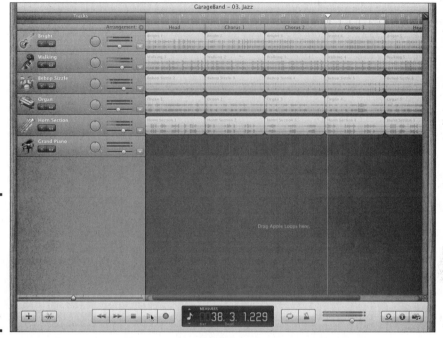

Figure 5-4:
The Project window displays separate controllers for all your instruments.

Creating music with software instruments

Magic GarageBand is great for quickly creating a song from a specific genre, but you can also specify the notes that GarageBand's software instruments will play.

With software instruments, you create one instrumental track at a time, gradually layering additional tracks until you've defined the parts for an entire band. To use software instruments, you specify the instrument you want to use, such as a baby grand piano or a steel-string acoustic guitar, and then define the notes you want that instrument to play by using a virtual keyboard — using either the keyboard on your Mac or an external keyboard that you connect to the USB port — to play the notes.

To create a software instrument, follow these steps:

1. **Open GarageBand by clicking on the GarageBand icon in the Dock or on the Launchpad.**

The GarageBand chooser opens. (Refer to Figure 5-1.)

2. **Choose File⇨New (or double-click New Project in the sidebar).**

   Ignore the instrument icons for now; we get to those a little later.

   A New Project dialog appears, as shown in Figure 5-5.

Figure 5-5: The New Project dialog lets you define your project.

3. **Enter a descriptive name for your project in the Save As text box and choose a location for storing your project from the pop-up menu.**

   The GarageBand folder (inside your Music folder) is the default location.

4. **(Optional) Change the Tempo, Time, BPM (beats per minute), and Key options.**

   You can always change these options later.

5. **Click Create.**

   A window appears, displaying a virtual keyboard and a single audio track for a grand piano.

6. **To change the instrument for your single track, choose Track⇨Show Track Info, or click the View/Hide Track Info button ("i") in the bottom-right corner of the GarageBand window.**

   The Track Info pane appears, as shown in Figure 5-6.

7. **Click an instrument category (such as Strings or Bass) and then click the specific instrument to use (such as Trance Bass or Electric Piano).**

8. **Click the virtual keyboard to hear how your chosen instrument sounds.**

Figure 5-6:
The Track
Info pane
displays
a list of
different
instruments
you can
choose.

9. **(Optional) Click the Musical Typing button on the virtual keyboard, or choose Windows⊅Musical Typing.**

The Musical Typing keyboard appears, as shown in Figure 5-7. The Musical Typing keyboard allows you to press keys on your Mac keyboard to play certain notes, which you might find more convenient than using your mouse to click keys on the virtual keyboard.

Figure 5-7:
The Musical
Typing
keyboard
lets you
use the
keyboard as
a musical
instrument.

**Book IV
Chapter 5**

Making Your Own
Kind of Music with
GarageBand

10. **Click the Record button (the red dot inside a black circle at the bottom of the GarageBand window) and click the virtual keyboard or type on the Musical Typing keyboard to record the notes you play.**

11. **Click the Record button again to stop recording.**

12. **Click the Go to Beginning button (the line and triangle icon to the right of the Record button) to return to the beginning of your recording, and then click Play to hear the notes you recorded.**

To add another software instrument, follow these steps:

1. **Click the plus sign button in the lower-left corner of the GarageBand window or choose Track⇨New Track.**

A dialog appears, asking whether you want to create a track by using a real or software instrument or plug in an instrument, such as an electric guitar or piano.

2. **Click the Software Instrument radio button and click Create.**

The new instrument track appears in the GarageBand window.

3. **Choose Track⇨Show Track Info to display the Track Info pane.**

If this window already appears, skip this step.

4. **Click the Software Instrument button.**

A list of instruments appears, such as Organs, Guitars, and Drum Kits.

5. **Click an instrument type.**

The right column displays specific types of instruments.

6. **Click a specific instrument in the right column, such as Electric Piano.**

Your newly added instrument track will now play, using your chosen instrument.

GarageBand comes with a lot of sounds to choose from, but there are more online. An arrow to the right of the specific type of instrument means that you have to download that style. A dialog appears, giving you the option of downloading the complete GarageBand software instrument suite. This occupies over 1GB of storage on your Mac, so you have to decide if you have the space and desire for additional sound options.

Playing with a real instrument

The easiest way to record on GarageBand is to sing or play an instrument within hearing range of your Mac's built-in microphone. For better quality, connect a hand-held microphone or instrument to your Mac's audio input, FireWire, or USB port. By playing with a real instrument, you can record yourself or your whole band, edit the sound, and save your recording. You can play or sing along with your own recording. Record other single tracks while playing different instruments and mix them together, and your recording sounds like a multi-piece band or orchestra.

To record a real instrument connected to your Mac, follow these steps:

1. **Click the GarageBand icon in the Dock or on the Launchpad.**

2. **Double-click the Electric Guitar, Voice, or Acoustic Instrument icon, whichever is closest to the instrument you want to use.**

   A New Project from Template dialog appears.

3. **Enter a descriptive name for your project in the Save As text box and choose a location for storing your project from the pop-up menu.**

4. **Click Create.**

   A window appears, displaying tracks associated with your chosen instrument alongside the Track Info pane, as shown in Figure 5-8.

5. **(Optional) If you chose Voice, specify Male or Female and then choose an effect, such as Epic Diva or Male Rock, in the Track Info pane.**

6. **(Optional) If you chose Acoustic Instrument, click a specific instrument type in the list on the right of the Track Info pane, such as Classic Rock or Metal.**

   The instrument you choose in this step defines how GarageBand plays your real instrument. For example, if you have a keyboard hooked up to your Mac, you can use this step to make your keyboard sound like horns, drums, or guitars.

Figure 5-8:
The Track Info pane lets you define the type of instrument you're using.

TIP

GarageBand includes a metronome (choose Control⇨Metronome) that you can toggle on and off. If you want to play along with previously recorded tracks, choose Control⇨Count In so you know when to start playing.

7. **(Optional) If you chose Electric Guitar, click the type of amp you want to use, as shown in Figure 5-9.**

   Click the arrows to the right or left of the amp to move through the selection of 12 types of amps. After choosing an amp, double-click the amp to switch between the sound controls, such as the bass and treble, and the input controls for the compressor and equalizer.

   Click one of the stomp boxes (foot pedals) under the amp to adjust the stomp box settings. Double-click one of the stomp boxes to open the selection of 15 stomp boxes. Click and drag the stomp box you want to use into the spaces that appear beneath the amp; you can have up to five stomp boxes.

8. **Click the Input Source pop-up menu and choose how your instrument is connected to your Mac (such as through a USB port or other type of connection).**

Figure 5-9: Choose from 12 different types of amps to enhance your electric guitar playing and recording.

9. **Click the Monitor pop-up menu and define whether you want to hear audio through the speakers while you play.**

If you turn the monitor on, you hear your performance while you record. (Note that this may cause feedback.) If GarageBand detects too much feedback, the dialog shown in Figure 5-10 appears, giving you a choice to fix the problem by clicking Monitor Off or accepting the feedback by turning feedback protection off.

Figure 5-10:
When GarageBand detects feedback, a dialog of solutions appears.

GarageBand has detected feedback

You have three choices:

Monitor Off
Mutes your speakers while you record to prevent feedback.

Monitor On
Lets you hear your performance while you record. Each time feedback occurs, GarageBand will mute the performance and alert you by showing you this dialog. To avoid feedback, try reducing the playback volume, avoid pointing your microphone towards your speakers, or use headphones to monitor your performance.

No Feedback Protection
Lets you hear your performance while you record. Each time feedback occurs, it will be audible.

Monitor Off | Monitor On | No Feedback Protection

10. **Drag the Recording Level slider to set the recording level, or click the Automatic Level Control check box to let GarageBand set the level.**

Lowering the recording level can reduce feedback. If you select the Automatic Level Control check box, the Monitor option is disabled.

11. **Click the Record button on your track and start playing away.**

When you finish playing, click the Record button again.

12. **(Optional) If you want to add more instruments, choose Track⇨New Track or click the Add Track button (the plus sign) in the lower-left corner.**

A dialog opens, asking whether you want to use a Software Instrument, a Real Instrument, or an Electric Guitar, as shown in Figure 5-11.

13. **Choose Real Instrument, click Create, and then repeat Steps 8 through 11.**

For the best recording quality, connect an audio interface to your Mac's USB or FireWire port. Then connect your instruments to the audio interface. Make sure that the audio interface is compatible with Mac OS X.

Book IV
Chapter 5

Making Your Own
Kind of Music with
GarageBand

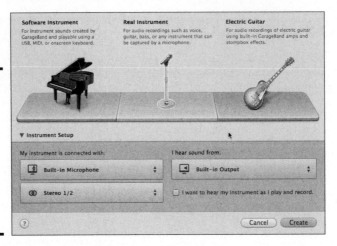

Software Instrument
For instrument sounds created by GarageBand and playable using a USB, MIDI, or onscreen keyboard.

Real Instrument
For audio recordings such as voice, guitar, bass, or any instrument that can be captured by a microphone.

Electric Guitar
For audio recordings of electric guitar using built-in GarageBand amps and stompbox effects.

▼ Instrument Setup

My instrument is connected with:

Built-in Microphone

Stereo 1/2

I hear sound from:

Built-in Output

☐ I want to hear my instrument as I play and record.

Cancel   Create

Figure 5-11:
Choose among a real instrument, a software instrument, or an electric guitar.

Using Loops

Say you want to add a song to your web page or an intro to your podcast but don't want to play "Twinkle, Twinkle, Little Star" with the S-S F-F H-H G combination on your keyboard, nor do you have a Fender Stratocaster for an attention-grabbing riff. To easily create your own little ditty, you can use the Loops that come with GarageBand. You choose the instruments and the style effects and then combine the two into short jingles or even full-length songs.

To create a song by using Loops, follow these steps:

1. **Click the GarageBand icon in the Dock or on the Launchpad.**

2. **Double-click Loops from the GarageBand chooser.**

3. **Enter a descriptive name for your project in the Save As text box and choose a location for storing your project from the pop-up menu.**

Click the disclosure triangle to expand the Save dialog, and then navigate to another location.

4. **Click Create.**

The Loops browser opens.

5. **Choose the style you want from the first column, such as Urban or Cinematic.**

6. **Choose the instrument you want to use from the second column.**

7. **Choose the adjectives that describe the type of music you want from the third and fourth column.**

The audio files that meet your criteria appear, showing the name, the tempo, and the key of the selection.

8. **Click the filenames to hear samples of the songs listed.**

9. **When you find one you like, click and drag the file to the Tracks pane on the left of the window, as shown in Figure 5-12.**

10. **To add other music clips and create a song with multiple instruments, click Reset and then repeat Steps 5 through 9.**

11. **Click the Play button to hear your composition.**

Figure 5-12:
The Loops browser lets you create songs by using prerecorded instruments.

Editing Audio

One of the great things about recording with GarageBand is that you can edit your audio. If you lay down multiple tracks and find that the timing is off between them, you can use one as the base and correct the others. If you play a riff off-key, delete that section and even replace it with a riff from a different part of the track. If you want the song you recorded in your basement to sound like you were in a stadium, add a concert-hall sound effect. You get the idea — the options are virtually endless. Here we explain the editing basics, but we encourage you to be adventurous and play around with GarageBand to develop your own particular performing style.

Splitting a track

When you first record an instrument, GarageBand saves it as a single, long track. To make it easier to edit this track, you can split a track into parts that you can modify individually, save and reuse, delete, or rearrange in a new position. The parts of a track are called audio regions, sometimes referred to as just "regions."

To split a track, follow these steps:

1. **Select a track that you want to split.**

GarageBand highlights your chosen instrument.

2. **Drag the slider (which displays a vertical red line) to where you want to split the track.**

If you can't find the slider, click the Go to Beginning button to move the slider to the beginning of your track.

3. **Choose Edit⇨Split or press ⌘+T.**

GarageBand splits your track, as shown in Figure 5-13.

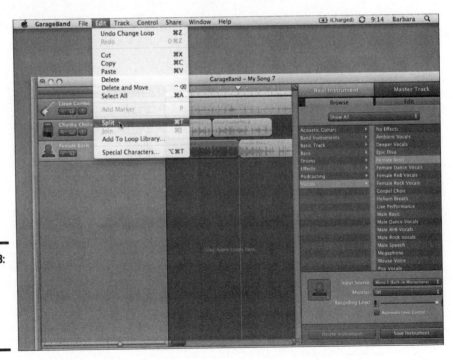

Figure 5-13: Splitting a track can make it easier to edit.

4. **Double-click any track, or select a track and click the Track Editor button (it looks like a pair of scissors), to bring up the Track Editor pane.**

   The Track Editor zooms in on an audio region of the track so you can split a more defined point.

You can zoom on all the tracks at once by moving the slider bar at the bottom of the track list, just above the Add and Track Editor buttons at bottom left.

Joining a track

If you split a track, you can always join the parts again later. To join two adjacent audio regions of a track, follow these steps:

1. **Click the first part of the track that you want to join.**

2. **Hold down the Shift key and click the second part of the track you want to join.**

3. **Choose Edit⇨Join or press ⌘+J.**

   GarageBand connects the two parts.

Moving tracks

After you record two or more tracks, you may want to adjust how each track plays relative to one another. For example, you can make one track play before or after a second track to create interesting audio effects. To move tracks, follow these steps:

1. **Click the track that you want to move.**

   GarageBand highlights your selected instrument track.

   For more flexibility, split a track into multiple regions so you can move each region separately.

2. **Click and drag the track to the left or right to adjust the relative positions of the two tracks.**

3. **Release the left mouse button when you're happy with the new arrangement of the tracks and regions.**

Quantize the times of Real and Software Instruments

You can *quantize*, or automatically correct and regularize, the timing of regions of the tracks in recordings done with both Real and Software Instruments. The sequence is slightly different between the two types of instruments.

✦ **In tracks recorded with real instruments, you can use Flex Time to adjust the timing of individual notes.** Click the Flex Time button (the wave form next to the words "Audio Region") to turn on Flex Time.

Move the pointer over the zoomed track in the Track Editor and it becomes a wave symbol. Click and drag to shorten or stretch notes within the track, as shown in Figure 5-14. Click the Flex Time button to see the difference between the two versions.

✦ **With Software Instruments, you can set the Quantize Note Timing slider before recording, in which case the region is quantized automatically.** To quantize after you record, double-click the Software Instrument track you want to quantize; the Track Editor pane opens, as shown in Figure 5-15. Choose the note value you want from the Quantize Note Timing pop-up menu or drag the Timing slider to set the quantization value you want.

Software Instruments are the instruments you connect to your Mac with one of the ports. Using the computer keyboard to play piano notes is also a form of Software Instrument.

Figure 5-14: Double-click a track or region to zoom in; use FlexTime to improve rhythm, fix timing, or shorten or stretch notes.

Figure 5-15:
Use the
Quantize
Note Timing
pop-up
menu adjust
timing of
regions
of tracks
recorded
with
Software
Instruments.

Groove matching

When you record your instruments separately, the timing within each might be fine but they aren't synchronized with each other. GarageBand saves you from painstakingly matching each track or re-recording by giving you a feature called Groove Tracks. Here's how it works:

1. **Identify the track you want to use as the groove standard for your song.**

2. **Hover over the left side of the track name until you see the outline of a star, and then click that track.**

   A dialog appears, letting you know that GarageBand will analyze the audio material of your recording to set up Groove Tracks.

3. **Click Continue in the dialog.**

   After a few seconds, the star turns yellow and a check mark appears to the left of the other track names in your recording. (See Figure 5-16.) If you don't want one of the tracks matched, click the check mark to remove it.

4. **To make a different track the Groove Track, drag the star from one track to another.**

You can't use groove matching if a track is automatically quantized.

Figure 5-16: Groove Tracks sets one track as the groove standard and matches the other tracks to it; the yellow star identifies the Groove Track.

Modifying the key and tempo

You can move tracks and/or regions in a GarageBand song to radically change how a song sounds, but you can also change the key or tempo to introduce a slight (or maybe even a major) change. Changing the key can modify how a song sounds, whereas changing the tempo speeds or slows a song without making the song sound high pitched or running down.

To change the time, key, and tempo, you use the LCD (liquid crystal display) feature at the bottom of the GarageBand window. By choosing different LCD display modes, you can modify the key and tempo of your tracks.

To change both the key and tempo, follow these steps:

1. **Click the pop-up menu in the LCD and choose Project.**

   The LCD displays the current key and tempo of your track.

2. **Click the Go to Beginning button and click Play to hear your song.**

   By playing your song, you can adjust the key, tempo, or signature and hear your changes in real time as they occur.

3. **Click the Key pop-up menu and choose a key, such as F or G.**

4. **Click the Tempo pop-up menu.**

A vertical slider appears.

5. **Drag the vertical slider up or down to speed or slow the tempo of your song.**

6. **Click the Signature pop-up menu and drag the vertical slider up or down to change the signature of your song.**

Saving Music

After you finish arranging and modifying your song, you can choose File⇨Save to save your GarageBand project (so you can edit it later). However, if you want to share your creation with others, the most common ways you can save your audio file to make it sharable are

✦ As a song or ringtone in the iTunes library

✦ As a song stored anywhere on your hard drive

✦ On a CD

We show you the steps for sharing your song by saving it as a song or ringtone in iTunes, and to a hard drive or CD, in the following sections.

Saving a song in iTunes

If you create a song that you want to save and play later, you can store that song in iTunes by following these steps:

1. **Choose Share⇨Send Song to iTunes.**

A dialog appears, as shown in Figure 5-17.

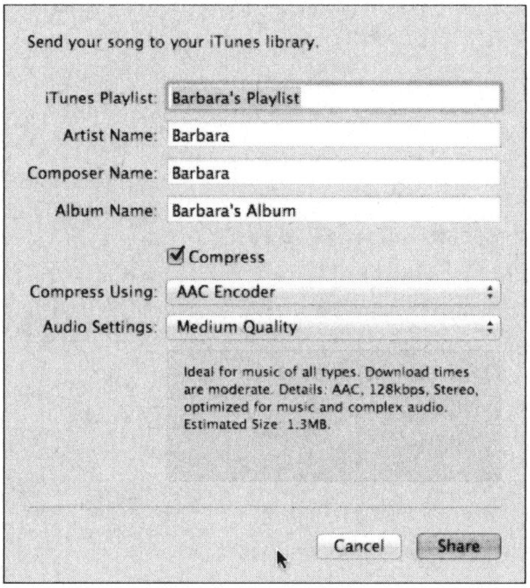

Figure 5-17:
GarageBand
lets you
choose a
playlist,
artist name,
and audio
setting for
your song.

Send your song to your iTunes library.

iTunes Playlist:	Barbara's Playlist
Artist Name:	Barbara
Composer Name:	Barbara
Album Name:	Barbara's Album

☑ Compress

Compress Using: AAC Encoder

Audio Settings: Medium Quality

Ideal for music of all types. Download times are moderate. Details: AAC, 128kbps, Stereo, optimized for music and complex audio. Estimated Size: 1.3MB.

Cancel   Share

2. **Click the iTunes Playlist, Artist Name, Composer Name, and Album Name text boxes and enter any information you want to store.**

   By default, GarageBand uses your name in each text box.

3. **Make sure that the Compress check box is selected, and then choose either AAC or MP3 Encoder from the Compress Using pop-up menu.**

   The Compress option compresses your audio file as small as possible, while retaining audio quality. If, however, you plan to compile a collection of songs that you want to burn to a CD, deselect the Compress check box so that your compilation is saved at the highest-quality sound level, which provides the best listening experience when you play the CD with a CD player or on a computer.

4. **Choose Good, High, or Higher Quality from the Audio Settings pop-up menu.**

5. **Click Share.**

   Your song appears in your iTunes library.

Saving a song as a ringtone

Any of the songs you create can be used as ringtones for your iPhone. Just follow these steps:

1. **Choose Share⇨Send Ringtone to iTunes.**

2. **GarageBand automatically converts your song and opens the iTunes application.**

3. **Your song appears in the Ringtones library on iTunes, ready to be synched to your iPhone.**

 Ringtones can't be more than 40 seconds. If your selection is too long, a dialog asks whether you want to adjust it. Click Adjust, and then drag your selection left or right so the start and end points for your selection include the segment you want to hear as a ringtone on your iPhone, or as a Facetime notification on your iPod touch or iPad, or as a text tone with iMessage on any iOS device.

Saving a song to your hard drive

If you don't want to store your song in iTunes, you can save your song as a separate audio file that you can store anywhere, such as on an external hard drive or a USB flash drive. To save your song as an audio file, follow these steps:

1. **Choose Share⇨Export Song to Disk.**

   A dialog appears.

2. **Make sure that the Compress check box is selected, and then choose either AAC or MP3 Encoder from the Compress Using pop-up menu.**

   The Compress option compresses your audio file as small as possible, while retaining audio quality. If, however, you plan to compile a collection of songs that you want to burn to a CD, deselect the Compress check box so that your compilation is saved at the highest-quality sound level, which provides the best listening experience when you play the CD on a CD player or a computer.

3. **Click the Audio Settings pop-up menu and choose Good, High, or Higher Quality.**

4. **Click Export.**

   An Export to Disk dialog appears.

5. **Enter a name for your audio file in the Save As text box.**

6. **Choose a location for storing your project from the Where pop-up menu.**

   Click the disclosure triangle to expand the Save dialog and scroll through the directories to save your project in a different location.

7. **Click Save.**

Burning a song to CD

If you create a song that you want to share with others, you can burn it to a CD and then give the CD away. To burn a song to a CD, follow these steps:

1. **Choose Share⇨Burn Song to CD.**

   A dialog appears, telling you that it's waiting for a blank CD-R or CD-RW.

2. **Insert a blank CD-R or CD-RW into your Mac and click Burn.**

Learning to Play the Guitar and Piano

You can learn piano or guitar basics with GarageBand music lessons. GarageBand provides 40 free lessons for learning piano and guitar.

Your first two free lessons are preloaded in GarageBand, and the remaining 38 free lessons can be downloaded by clicking the Lesson Store in the GarageBand chooser window, and then clicking the Basic Lessons tab and clicking each additional lesson you want to download. Additionally, you can click the Artist Lessons tab to purchase and download lessons taught by distinguished musicians including Sting, Norah Jones, John Fogerty, and Sarah McLachlan.

**Book IV
Chapter 5**

Making Your Own
Kind of Music with
GarageBand

You can follow the lesson with your free-standing piano or guitar or with a keyboard or guitar hooked up to your Mac. To take a music lesson, follow these steps:

1. **Click the GarageBand icon in the Dock or on the Launchpad.**

   The GarageBand chooser appears.

2. **Click Learn to Play in the sidebar on the left.**

3. **Double-click Piano Lesson 1 or Guitar Lesson 1.**

   A window opens with an instruction video and a keyboard or guitar, and the lesson begins.

   Notice the buttons in the top-right corner of the lesson window:

   - *Glossary* gives you a reference tool for musical words and definitions.

   - *Mixer* lists options for what you hear while you're taking the lesson.

   - *Setup* lets you customize your learning interface.

   - *Notes* lets you choose what kind of musical notation you see on the lesson window.

4. **Click the Play button (the large triangle in the middle, like you see on a CD player).**

   The lesson begins. Click the Play button again to stop the lesson. At the bottom of the lesson window, a bar is divided into the lesson chapters. You can click on their titles to jump from one section of the lesson to the next, or drag the slider to the point you want to review. Click the Cycle button (the two arrows that are chasing each other in a circle) to highlight the chapters. With the Cycle button on, you can highlight a chapter, and the Rewind button takes you back to the highlighted chapter if you move to a different point in the lesson. When the Cycle button is off, clicking the Rewind button takes you to the beginning of the lesson. You can also adjust the speed of the lesson with the slider to the left of the playback controls, although with slower speeds, the instructor's voice is muted.

5. **After you take the lesson, you can play along. Hover with the pointer to the left of your instructor to see two chapters: Learn and Play. Click Play.**

6. **If you are using an acoustic instrument, position yourself near your Mac so the microphone picks up your practice. If you are using an electronic keyboard or guitar, plug it in to the USB or FireWire port on your Mac.**

7. **Click the Record button and play along.**

   GarageBand records your practice and tells you the percentage you got right with the How Did I Play feature. GarageBand also keeps a history of your practices so you can track your progress. Click the My Results or History buttons in the lower-right corner to see how you did.

Recording Podcasts

Perhaps you're more talkative than musical. GarageBand has something for you too — podcasts. Podcasts used to be limited to recorded audio files that contain speech, such as interviews, radio talk show broadcasts, homemade audiobooks of children's stories, or just monologues of a single person talking about anything. Today, podcasts can have photos and video too. With the Media Browser, GarageBand lets you mix your media and create a captivating podcast. If you store your podcast on a website, anyone in the world can stream or download and listen to your podcast.

Recording speech

The most important part about a podcast is recording spoken words, either through the internal microphone in your Mac, an external microphone plugged into your Mac, or even a recording of an iChat audio conversation using a program, such as Conference Recorder (www.ecamm.com), Audio Hijack Pro (www.rogueamoeba.com), or WireTap Studio (www.AmbrosiaSW.com).

To record a podcast, follow these steps:

1. **Open GarageBand.**

The now-familiar GarageBand chooser opens.

2. **Click New Project in the sidebar on the left and double-click the Podcast icon from the chooser.**

A New Project from Template dialog appears.

3. **Enter a descriptive name for your podcast in the Save As text box.**

4. **Choose a location for storing your project from the Where pop-up menu.**

Click the disclosure triangle to expand the Save dialog and choose a different location by scrolling through the directories.

5. **Click Create.**

The GarageBand window appears, as shown in Figure 5-18.

6. **Click the Male Voice or Female Voice track, click the Record button, and start speaking.**

Choosing a male or female voice track makes GarageBand optimize recording for males or females.

If you already captured audio and stored it in iTunes or GarageBand, click the Audio button in the Media Browser pane, click GarageBand or iTunes, and then drag an audio file to the Male Voice or Female Voice track. In Figure 5-18, you see a list of voice memos, which Barbara recorded on her iPhone at a conference.

Figure 5-18:
The GarageBand window displays male and female voice tracks along with a jingles track.

Likewise, if you captured video stored in iMovie or iPhoto, you can click and drag that to the podcast space, at which point the Podcast track becomes two tracks: Movie Track and Movie Sound. You can't have both a Movie Track and a Podcast, but you can have a voice track, which can be recorded in GarageBand or placed from the media browser into the Male or Female Voice track.

7. **Click the Record button and start talking.**

8. **Click the Stop button when you finish talking.**

Refer to the earlier section, "Editing Audio," for instructions on editing your podcast audio file.

Adding jingles and audio effects

After recording yourself or someone else speaking, you may want to add music or sound effects to enhance your podcast. For example, you could have introductory music that fades when you start speaking.

To prevent any background jingles or audio effects from drowning out the spoken portion of your audio, GarageBand offers Ducking, a feature that reduces the background music volume level to 15 percent when the Male

Voice or Female Voice track starts playing. To turn Ducking on or off, choose Control➪Ducking.

To add audio effects, follow these steps:

1. **Choose Control➪Show Loop Browser or click the View/Hide Loop Browser button in the lower-right corner of the GarageBand window (it's the button with the icon that looks like Hot Wheels track).**

   The Loop Browser appears, as shown in Figure 5-19.

2. **Click an Effects category, such as Jingles or Sound Effects.**

3. **Click and drag an audio effect to the Jingles track.**

4. **Release the mouse button.**

Figure 5-19: The Loop Browser provides categories of music, jingles, and sound effects.

Adding pictures

Although podcasts are heard, you can add pictures to your podcast that represent your entire recording or individual parts of your podcast.

Adding pictures to a podcast is only useful when listening to your podcast on a device that can also display pictures, such as an iPad, iPhone, an iPod Classic, iPod touch, iPod nano, or a computer.

To add pictures to a podcast, follow these steps:

1. **Click the Podcast Track in the track list.**

2. **Choose Control⇨Show Editor or click the View/Hide Track Editor button — the one sporting a pair of scissors — near the bottom-left corner of the GarageBand window.**

The Track Editor pane appears at the bottom of the GarageBand window.

3. **Choose Control⇨Show Media Browser.**

The Media Browser pane appears, as shown in Figure 5-20.

4. **Click the Photos button in the Media Browser.**

5. **Click and drag a picture from the Media Browser to either the Episode Artwork box or the Artwork column in the Track Editor pane and release the mouse button.**

Figure 5-20:
The Media Browser pane lists all pictures stored in iPhoto; the Track Editor pane displays blank areas for adding pictures.

The Episode Artwork box is where you can place a picture to represent your entire podcast. The Artwork column is where you can place a picture to represent separate chapters (parts) of your podcast. You can have only one picture in the Episode Artwork box, but you can have multiple pictures in the Artwork column.

6. **(Optional) For each picture you place in the Artwork column, click the Time column and define when you want each picture to appear during your podcast.**

7. **To post your podcast to the website you created in iWeb, choose Share⇨Send Podcast to iWeb.**

   A dialog opens, which gives you options to choose AAC or MP3 compression encoding and an audio setting that best relates to your recording: mono, spoken, or musical podcast, higher quality, or iTunes Plus. You also have a custom option that lets you set the bit rate, quality, and channels.

8. **To save your podcast in a format that can be uploaded to another website or distributed on a CD, choose Share⇨Export Podcast to Disk.**

   Choose your compression settings, AAC or MP3, in the dialog that appears.

9. **Click Export.**

   Name and save your podcast in the GarageBand or iTunes folder, where you can later access the file and upload your podcast where you want or burn a copy onto a CD or DVD. (We explain burning CDs and DVDs in Book I, Chapter 4, as well as in Book IV, Chapter 6.)

As great as podcasts are, keep in mind that you can use iMovie to create lively videos featuring you as the star of the show while you sing along to music you create with GarageBand — which you can also post on YouTube so others can enjoy your talents. We show you how to use iMovie in Book IV, Chapter 4.

Enhancing GarageBand

You can do a lot with GarageBand on its own, with the typing keyboard and your Mac's built-in microphone, but there are many ways to enhance GarageBand with third-party instruments, microphones, and apps. Here we list a few just to pique your interest:

✦ **MidiKeys** (www.manyetas.com): Feeling like the band bus left without you because you don't have a USB or MIDI keyboard? Or maybe your arm is tired from strumming chords or fingering the keys with your mouse or trackpad? Either way, check out a handy little app called

**Book IV
Chapter 5**

Making Your Own Kind of Music with GarageBand

MidiKeys. With it, you can turn your Mac's keyboard into a Midi keyboard that lets you pull off neat tricks like playing multiple notes at the same time.

✦ **Apogee JAM Guitar Input** (www.apogeedigital.com)**:** Plug your Mac (or iPhone or iPad) into the pocket-size Apogee Jam Guitar Input peripheral and start jammin' with studio-quality sound. A control knob makes adjusting input levels a cinch, and a status light on the top panel makes it easy to keep an eye on whether you're properly tapped in for the best pickup performance — green means you're good to go and red is your warning sign that you ought to kick it down a few notches. Armed with this handy hardware add-on and your real guitar in your hands, going back to playing air guitar would seem like torture!

✦ **M-Audio Sustain Pedal and 49-Key USB Controller Keyboard** (www.m-audio.com)**:** Featuring eight assignable knobs and nine assignable sliders, the Oxygen 49 USB MIDI Controller keyboard can handle whatever your fast-flying fingers can throw at it. Built-in presets offer virtual instrument choices without any fuss, and velocity-sensitive keys make this keyboard ideal for both production and performance settings. Toss in the M-Audio SP-2 Professional Piano Style Pedal to round out the mix — and to put your foot to good use instead of just tapping the floor to the beat.

✦ **iDrum** (www.emediamusic.com)**:** Boost your drum selection from ho-hum to yuh-huhmmmm with the iDrum drum-machine program. With seamless GarageBand integration, iDrum provides hundreds of preprogrammed patterns, rhythms, and drum sounds to satisfy your every mix and match desire. The Song Editor mode makes assembling your compositions a snap even if you don't know the difference between a sequence and seaweed salad. From laying drum patterns alongside your existing tracks, or creating a backbeat for new tracks you're laying down, iDrum is anything but humdrum.

Chapter 6: Burning DVDs

In This Chapter

✔ Burning a DVD directly from a video camcorder

✔ Creating a Magic iDVD

✔ Working with iDVD projects

✔ Saving your iDVD project to a file or DVD

In Book I, Chapter 4 we explain burning CDs and DVDs from the Finder, and in Book IV, Chapter 1 we give you details for burning CDs from iTunes. In this chapter, we conclude our burning instructions with iDVD, which lets you add menus and graphics to your digital slideshows or videos. To burn DVDs, you need a Mac with an internal or external DVD drive that can write to DVD discs. If your Mac has an internal or external SuperDrive, it's capable of burning double-layer DVDs. That means you can burn 8.5GB (gigabytes) onto a double-layer disc, which is roughly 120 minutes of video. A single-layer disc holds 4.7GB, or 60 minutes of video, although by adjusting the quality settings, you can burn up to 120 minutes on a single-layer disc.

Using iDVD

Between social networks like Facebook and video outlets such as YouTube, sharing photos, videos, and movies has become quick and simple over the Internet. Think of the vast number of people you reach — your photos and home movies can be viewed by all 537 of your friends — but you probably wouldn't burn 537 DVDs and send them to all those friends.

That said, there are times when you want to create a digital slideshow or movie and save a copy on a disc. There are situations where you don't have a computer or Internet service but do have a DVD player and television. A DVD is a great way to share digital photos, videos, and music. With iDVD, you can add menus and graphics to your digital slideshows or videos so familiar controls appear when you insert the disc into a DVD player.

To create a DVD, iDVD gives you three choices:

+ **OneStep DVD:** Transfers a video directly from a FireWire-based mini digital videotape camcorder or movie file to a DVD.

+ **Magic iDVD:** Provides a variety of DVD templates that you can modify for creating menus to organize the content of digital photographs and movies stored on the DVD.

+ **A DVD project:** Lets you create custom DVD menus and graphics for storing and presenting digital photographs and movies.

Burning a Video Straight to DVD

The OneStep DVD option lets you burn digital video from your FireWire-enabled video camcorder, or from a movie file on your hard drive, to a recordable DVD in your Mac. When you insert your finished DVD into a DVD player, your video starts playing immediately, with no DVD menus.

USB-enabled camcorders, digital cameras, and smartphones don't work directly with OneStep DVD; however, video captured from digital cameras and smartphones will import directly to iPhoto, and you can move camcorder video to iPhoto. From iPhoto, choose those files when you select the files you want to use to create your OneStep DVD.

To burn a video from your video-capturing device to a DVD with the OneStep DVD option, follow these steps:

1. **Click the iDVD icon in the Dock or Launchpad (or double-click the iDVD icon in the Applications folder).**

The iDVD opening window appears, as shown in Figure 6-1.

Figure 6-1:
The iDVD opening window displays your options for creating a DVD.

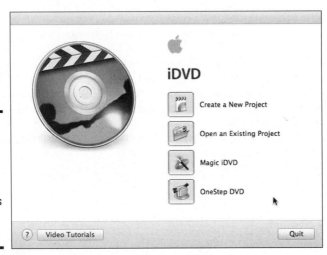

2. **Click OneStep DVD.**

   An alert appears, prompting you to connect your video camcorder to your Mac and insert a recordable DVD.

3. **Connect your video camcorder to your Mac with a FireWire cable.**

4. **Insert a recordable DVD in your Mac and then click the OK button.**

   iDVD rewinds the tape and starts importing the video, displaying a progress dialog.

   You can cancel the process at any desired endpoint before the entire video file is imported by clicking the Stop button in the progress dialog.

   A dialog appears to let you know that the DVD has finished burning.

5. **Click Done.**

   The DVD remains in your Mac so you can either view it by using the DVD Player or eject it.

OneStep DVD only works with digital video (DV); it doesn't work with high-definition video (HDV). If your camcorder records in HDV, you have to transfer the video to iMovie and then follow the following procedure.

To burn a DVD from a movie file on your hard drive, follow these steps:

1. **Choose File⇨OneStep DVD from Movie.**

2. **Select your movie file from the dialog that appears.**

3. **Click Import.**

4. **Insert a recordable DVD in your Mac.**

   A dialog appears to let you know when the DVD has finished burning.

5. **Click Done.**

Creating a DVD with the Magic iDVD Option

The Magic iDVD option provides predesigned templates that you can customize to create DVD menus. To use the Magic iDVD option, follow these steps:

1. **Click the iDVD icon in the Dock or Launchpad (or double-click the iDVD icon in the Applications folder).**

   The iDVD opening window appears (refer to Figure 6-1).

2. **Click Magic iDVD.**

   The Magic iDVD window appears, as shown in Figure 6-2.

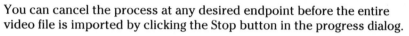

**Book IV
Chapter 6**

Burning DVDs

Figure 6-2:
The Magic
iDVD
window
lets you
choose the
template,
pictures,
and video
files to
include on
your DVD.

3. **Type a descriptive name for your DVD in the DVD Title text box.**

4. **Select a theme, such as Vintage Vinyl or Sunflower, from the Choose a Theme browser.**

   Each theme offers a different appearance for your DVD menus. The theme name describes its appearance, so Sunflower displays a big sunflower and Vintage Vinyl displays an old turntable and vinyl record.

5. **In the right pane of the Magic iDVD window — the Media pane — click the Movies tab.**

   A list of movies stored in your Movies folder appears. Some video, such as video you take with your cellphone or digital camera, will be in the iPhoto folder rather than in the Movies folder.

6. **Click and drag a movie that you want to add to your DVD onto the Drop Movies Here drop well.**

   To select multiple movies, hold down the ⌘ key and click each movie you want to add to your DVD.

   If you click a movie and click the Play button, you can see a thumbnail image of your movie.

7. **In the Media pane, click the Photos tab.**

   A list of photos stored in iPhoto appears.

8. **Click and drag a photo that you want to add to your DVD onto the Drop Photos Here well.**

To select multiple photos, hold down the ⌘ key and click each photo you want to add to your DVD.

Each well represents a separate slideshow. Generally, you want to put several photos in the same well to create a slideshow of multiple photos. Underneath each well, iDVD lists the number of slides currently stored.

9. **In the Media pane, click the Audio tab.**

A list of audio files stored in iTunes and GarageBand appears.

10. **Click and drag an audio file that you want to play during a photo slideshow onto the Drop Photos Here well.**

Photos that include audio appear with an audio icon over them, as shown in Figure 6-3.

Keep in mind that if you add a 3-minute audio file over a slideshow (well) that contains three slides, each slide will appear for 1 minute until the entire audio file finishes playing. If you add a 3-minute audio file to a slideshow of 30 slides, each slide will appear for 0.1 minutes. So the more slides (photos) you add, the faster the images pop up and disappear while the audio file plays.

Figure 6-3:
An audio icon identifies photos that include an audio file.

Audio icon

Book IV
Chapter 6

Burning DVDs

11. **Click the Preview icon in the lower-left corner.**

    An iDVD Preview window appears with a controller (which mimics a typical remote control) so you can take your DVD through its paces to make sure that it works the way you want, as shown in Figure 6-4. On the controller, click the Menu button to display the main menu or the Title button to see a list of the contents in a category. Double-clicking the items on the main menu and title menu open the corresponding content, just like on a purchased DVD.

    The titles appear onscreen with the same names that the original files have — so be sure to name your files appropriately in iMovie or iPhoto before dropping them into the wells. Otherwise your menu will have items with obscure names like PICT075.

12. **Click Exit on the Controller on the screen.**

    The Magic iDVD window appears again.

13. **Select one of the following:**

    - *Create Project:* Lets you save your DVD design to modify it later.

    - *Burn:* Burns your music, photos, and movies by using the theme you selected. If you choose this option, you need to insert a recordable DVD in your Mac's optical drive.

You don't have to fill all the wells. If you want to burn a DVD that contains only slideshows with photos, place only photos in the photo wells.

Figure 6-4: The iDVD Preview window shows you how your DVD will look when played.

Working with iDVD Projects

For maximum flexibility, you can design your own DVD menus and add graphics to give your DVD a polished, professional look. When you create your own DVD project, you can save it and edit it later.

The following list explains the different parts of an iDVD project:

✦ **Title menu:** Displays a list of the DVD contents, such as movies or slideshows.

✦ **Slideshows:** Displays a slideshow of digital photographs.

✦ **Movies:** Displays a movie.

✦ **Text:** Displays text — useful for providing instructions or descriptions about the DVD.

✦ **Submenus:** Displays another menu where you can offer additional slideshows or movies.

✦ **Opening content:** Displays a photo or movie that appears as soon as someone inserts the DVD into a DVD player. In many commercial DVDs, the opening content is usually an FBI warning about copyright infringement followed by previews or trailers for other videos.

Not every iDVD project uses all the parts just mentioned. At the very least, an iDVD project needs a title menu and one slideshow or movie.

To create a DVD project, follow these steps:

1. **Click the iDVD icon in the Dock or on the Launchpad (or double-click the iDVD icon in the Applications folder).**

2. **Click Create a New Project.**

A Create Project dialog appears.

If you already created a project and want to edit it, all you need to do is click Open an Existing Project.

3. **Enter a descriptive name for your project into the Save As text box and then choose where you want to save your project from the Where pop-up menu, as shown in Figure 6-5.**

4. **Next to Aspect Ratio, click the Standard (for ordinary TV screens) or Widescreen (for widescreen TVs) radio button.**

Choosing Standard optimizes your DVD project for an ordinary TV set, although it will still play on a widescreen with borders on either side in order to maintain the video's proper resolution and aspect ratio (this is called *pillar-boxing*). Likewise, choosing Widescreen lets a DVD project play on an ordinary TV set with black borders at the top and bottom (called *letter-boxing*), but it will have a lower resolution than that seen on a widescreen TV.

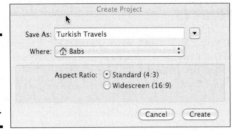

Figure 6-5:
Name your
DVD and
define the
aspect ratio.

5. **Click Create.**

   An iDVD project window appears with the Themes browser in the right pane, as shown in Figure 6-6.

6. **Scroll through the Themes browser to find a theme you like.**

   Each theme offers a different appearance for your DVD menus. When you click a theme, a preview appears in the iDVD window. Depending on the theme you choose, you might see Drop Zones where you can place photos or video.

   Most themes have a triangle to the left of the theme; clicking it expands the theme to show how it is applied to the Main, Chapters, and Extras menus of your DVD. Clicking the arrow again compresses the selection. Older themes have only one menu possibility.

Figure 6-6:
The iDVD
project
window
opens with
the Themes
browser
in the right
pane.

7. **Double-click the title placeholder in the iDVD Project pane and type the title of your movie or slideshow, as shown in Figure 6-7.**

   The font family, style, and size are pre-established to coordinate nicely with the theme; however, you can change the font by using the menus that appear when you double-click the title. If you click a different theme, your title remains.

8. **Choose File⊏>Save.**

   After saving your iDVD project, you can quit iDVD or continue with the next sections to add photos to your title menus, and to add movies and slideshows to your project.

Adding photos to the title menu

Some themes just display a colorful graphic background, while others provide placeholders for adding your own photos to customize the theme further. To use your own photos as a background, follow these steps:

1. **Open the iDVD project you want to add photos to.**

   You can open a previously saved project by choosing File⊏>Open or by clicking Open an Existing Project when iDVD first loads.

Figure 6-7:
Type the title of your movie or slideshow in the iDVD Project pane.

2. **Click the Media button in the bottom-right corner of the iDVD project window.**

   The Media pane opens showing Audio, Photos, and Movies tabs on the right side of the iDVD window.

3. **Click the Photos button.**

   A list of photos stored in iPhoto appears, which you can add to your title menu.

4. **Click the Edit Drop Zones button (the dotted square with the arrow at the bottom).**

   A list of Drop Zones appears.

5. **Click and drag a photo to a Drop Zone and then release the mouse button.**

   Your chosen photo now appears. If you drop a photo in the Menu Drop Zone, your photo replaces the image that the theme uses, as shown in Figure 6-8.

6. **Repeat Step 5 to add photos to the other Drop Zones.**

7. **Choose File⇨Save.**

   After saving your iDVD project, you can quit iDVD or continue working on your project.

Figure 6-8: You can drag and drop photos to customize a DVD menu.

Adding options to the title menu

After you define a theme and possibly add some photos for your title menu, you can add viewer options. The four types of options you can display on the title menu are:

+ Slideshow

+ Movie

+ Submenus

+ Text

The first three can be added by clicking the Add button in the bottom-left corner of the toolbar. Next, we explain how to add each option.

Creating a Slideshow

When a viewer selects a slideshow menu option, the DVD displays one or more digital photographs. To add a slideshow option to the title menu, you need to create a menu item that allows viewers to choose your slideshow, and then you create the slideshow. Follow these steps:

1. **Click the Add button (the plus sign in the lower-left corner) and choose Add Slideshow. If you prefer using the menus or keyboard commands, choose Project⇨Add Slideshow or press ⌘+L.**

   A My Slideshow button appears on your title menu, as shown in Figure 6-9. We added a slideshow.

2. **Click the My Slideshow button.**

   The My Slideshow text appears highlighted and displays Font, Style, and Font Size pop-up menus.

3. **Type descriptive text for your slideshow button.**

4. **(Optional) Click the Font, Style, or Font Size pop-up menus to choose how to format your text.**

5. **Double-click your slideshow button.**

   The iDVD project window displays a Drag Images Here box. Now you can start building the slideshow.

6. **Click and drag a photo from the right pane to the Drag Images Here box and then release the mouse button.**

   To select multiple photos, hold down the ⌘ key and then click each photo you want to select. A slideshow can hold up to 99 photos and a DVD project can have 99 slideshows.

Figure 6-9:
Use the
Add button
to add
submenus,
movies, and
slideshows.

Your selected photos appear in the Slideshow window, numbered to show you the order in which your photos will appear, as shown in Figure 6-10.

7. **(Optional) Change the slide duration, the transition style between slides, and a background music as follows:**

   a. *Click the Slide Duration pop-up menu and choose how long a slide stays onscreen, such as 1 or 10 seconds.*

   b. *Click the Transition pop-up menu and choose a transition to display between slides, such as Dissolve or Twirl.*

   c. *Click the Audio button, click and drag an audio file from the listing in the right pane onto the Audio well (it looks like an iTunes music-track icon to the left of the Slideshow volume slider), and then release the mouse button.*

   d. *If you add an audio file to a slideshow, click the Slide Duration pop-up menu and choose how long you want the audio file to play (for example, 10 seconds).*

If you add an audio file to a slideshow, the slide duration defaults to the Fit To Audio option, which means that your photos appear until the audio file finishes playing.

Figure 6-10:
A slideshow consists of multiple photos.

8. **Click the Return button.**

   Your DVD title menu appears again.

REMEMBER

9. **Choose File⇨Save.**

   You need to create a different slideshow menu option for each slideshow you want to include on your DVD.

Creating a Movie menu option

When a viewer selects a Movie menu option, the DVD plays a movie. To create a Movie menu option on the title menu, follow these steps:

1. **Click the Add button and choose Add Movie or choose Project⇨ Add Movie.**

   An Add Movie Here button appears, as shown in Figure 6-11.

2. **Click the Media button to open the Media pane and then choose Movie.**

   The movie files stored on your Mac appear.

Figure 6-11:
An Add
Movie Here
button
provides
a link to a
movie.

3. **Click and drag the movie file of the movie you want on your DVD to the Add Movie Here button.**

The menu item now displays the name of the movie file you placed. Click once on the text to edit the name. Double-click to view your movie.

4. **Choose File⇨Save.**

For a faster way to create Movie menu buttons, click and drag a movie shown in the Media pane anywhere onto your title menu and then release the mouse button to create a button that will play your chosen movie.

Creating a submenu

If you have too many options on the title menu, it can look cluttered. Submenus simplify the title menu because you see top-level menus; clicking one of those opens one submenu at a time. To create a submenu, follow these steps:

1. **Click the Add button and choose Add Submenu or choose Project⇨ Add Submenu.**

A My Submenu button appears.

2. **Click the My Submenu button.**

Font, Style, and Font Size pop-up menus appear.

3. **Type descriptive text for your submenu button.**

4. **(Optional) Click the Font, Style, or Font Size pop-up menus to choose how to format your text.**

5. **Double-click the submenu button.**

   The iDVD window displays a new menu where you can add slideshows, movies, text, or even additional submenus.

6. **Choose Project⇨Add Title Menu Button.**

   The Title Menu button lets viewers jump back to the title menu from your submenu. At this point, you add Slideshow or Movie menu options to your submenu. Follow the steps outlined in the previous pages for the title menu.

7. **(Optional) If the theme you choose has additional menu options, such as Extras or Chapters, use them for your submenu.**

   Choose the menu option you want from the Themes browser; the submenu changes to that option and keeps the titles, slideshows, or movies you've added.

Creating text

Sometimes you may want to add text on a title menu to provide additional descriptions or instructions. To add text on the title menu, follow these steps:

1. **Choose Project⇨Add Text (or press ⌘+K).**

   A Click to Edit text box appears.

2. **Click the Click to Edit text box.**

   Font, Style, and Font Size pop-up menus appear, as shown in Figure 6-12.

3. **Type descriptive text for your slideshow button.**

4. **(Optional) Click the Font, Style, or Font Size pop-up menus to choose how to format your text.**

5. **Choose File⇨Save.**

Moving and deleting buttons

After you create a Slideshow, Movie, Submenu, or Text button on a menu, you can move or delete it as follows:

✦ **Moving buttons:** Click and drag the button you want where you want it.

✦ **Deleting buttons:** Click the button you want to delete and then press the Delete key. Your button — and any slideshows, movies, or submenus linked to it — disappears in an animated puff of smoke.

**Book IV
Chapter 6**

Burning DVDs

Figure 6-12:
A Click to Edit text box lets you type text that appears on the title menu.

Defining opening content for your DVD

Opening content is what begins playing when your DVD is inserted into a DVD player. Opening content appears before the title menu. To define a photo or movie as the opening content, follow these steps:

1. **Choose View⇨Show Map (or click the Show the DVD Map icon in the toolbar, which looks like a miniature organization chart).**

   The iDVD window displays a blank content box with the message Drag Content Here to Automatically Play When the Disc Is Inserted, as shown in Figure 6-13.

2. **Click the Photos or Movies button in the Media pane to display your iPhoto photos or the movies stored in your Movies folder.**

3. **Click and drag a photo or movie to the blank content box.**

4. **Release the mouse button.**

The Show Map command is particularly useful to see the layout of your entire iDVD project.

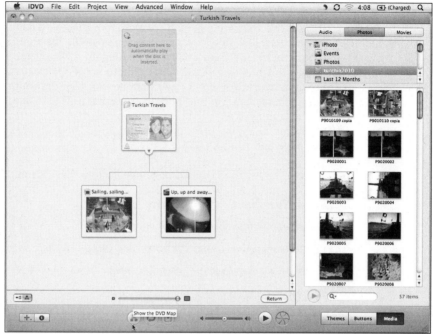

Figure 6-13:
The map
view of your
iDVD project
displays
the blank
content box.

Saving your iDVD project

After you design your DVD project, you can save your entire project in one
of three ways:

✦ As a DVD

✦ As a disc image (.img) file

✦ As files stored in a VIDEO_TS folder

Burning to a DVD

When you save your iDVD project to a DVD, you create a DVD that you can
give to anyone to play on any DVD player. To burn an iDVD project to a DVD,
follow these steps:

1. **Insert a blank DVD into your Mac.**

2. **Click the Burn button in the toolbar or choose File⇨Burn DVD.**

You can burn files to a DVD directly from the Finder. Click the file or folder
you want to burn and choose File⇨Burn *file or folder name*.

**Book IV
Chapter 6**

Burning DVDs

Saving to a disc image

As an alternative to saving an iDVD project to a DVD, you can also save an iDVD project to a disc image. A *disc image* is a single file that contains the entire contents of a drive or folder. By storing an iDVD project as a disc image, you can transfer a single (large) file to someone over the Internet; if you're on a network, you can copy the file to another computer for storing or burning to a DVD. Then that person can open that disc image to retrieve the entire contents of your iDVD project and burn the disc image contents to a DVD. You can also play the video directly from the disc image by opening the disc image and running DVD Player.

To save your iDVD project to a disc image, follow these steps:

1. **Choose File⇨Save as Disc Image.**

   A Save Disc Image As dialog appears.

2. **Type a descriptive name for your disc image in the Save As text box.**

3. **Choose a location to store your disc image from the Where pop-up menu.**

4. **Click Save.**

Saving to a VIDEO_TS folder

You can also save your entire iDVD project inside a `VIDEO_TS` folder, which essentially lets you store the contents of your iDVD project as separate files stored in a folder. By storing a DVD in a folder, you can play your DVD directly off the hard drive.

To save your iDVD project to a folder, follow these steps:

1. **Choose File⇨Save as VIDEO_TS Folder.**

   A Save VIDEO_TS Folder As dialog appears.

2. **Type a descriptive name for your folder in the Save As text box.**

3. **Choose a location to store your folder from the Where pop-up menu.**

4. **Click Save.**

When you save an iDVD project as a `VIDEO_TS` folder, you can open and play the contents of that VIDEO_TS folder by using the DVD Player application in the Applications folder of any Mac. If you later decide to burn the contents of a `VIDEO_TS` folder to a DVD, make sure that you burn the DVD in UDF format to create a DVD that can play in other DVD players.

Book V

Taking Care of Business

The 5th Wave   By Rich Tennant

"The top line represents our revenue, the middle
line is our inventory, and the bottom line shows
the rate of my hair loss over the same period."

Contents at a Glance

Chapter 1: Managing Contacts with Address Book

In This Chapter

✔ **Setting up Address Book**

✔ **Adding, editing, and searching contacts**

✔ **Organizing names in groups**

✔ **Using Shortcut menus**

✔ **Archiving and printing your Address Book**

✔ **Importing and exporting contacts**

*Y*our Mac comes with a contact management application called (surprise!) Address Book. You may write down important names and contact information in an address book or keep an electronic version on your mobile phone — but Address Book takes recording contacts to another level. Besides storing contact names and related contact information, Address Book also connects with other applications so you can click someone's e-mail address and immediately

✦ Write and send a message to that person.

✦ Open a FaceTime conversation.

✦ Click a street address and see it in Google Maps.

You can also print envelopes, mailing labels, and address books directly from Address Book — which you can't do from your handwritten address book.

Address Book is integrated with the other applications on your Mac that use addresses including Mail (refer to Book II, Chapter 2), iChat (Book II, Chapter 3), and iCal (Book V, Chapter 2). When you type in or search for an address in those applications, they refer to Address Book. This way, you only have to enter contact information one time.

This chapter explains how to set up Address Book by customizing the contact template with fields you use most frequently. Then it outlines two ways to enter information: typing it in manually or importing data from another contact management source. Next we explain setting up groups of contacts and, at the end of the chapter, printing and exporting your Address Book contacts.

Setting Up Address Book

The Address Book acts like a giant stack of cards. You save information about a person on a contact card so you can find that information again.

Each card — referred to as a *contact card* — contains traditional contact information, such as telephone numbers and postal addresses, along with more modern information such as e-mail addresses, URLs, birthdays, profile addresses, and photos. Most contact information links to something else: Click an address and Google Maps opens to show you a map of that address; click an e-mail address and choose to open an outgoing e-mail message addressed to that person or start a FaceTime conversation.

Address Book views

Address Book looks like the book that might have held your handwritten addresses sometime in the past: two facing pages with a leatherlike border. Address Book offers three views, which you choose from the View menu:

- ✦ **List and Card:** Shows two facing pages with an alphabetical list of your contacts on the left page and the active contact card on the right page. The Card Only button (it looks like a single page) at the bottom of the List page switches to Card Only view.

- ✦ **Card Only:** Shows one page of the active contact card. The List and Card button (it looks like an open book) at the bottom of the Card page switches to List and Card view.

- ✦ **Groups:** Displays a list of groups (we explain those in the second half of this chapter) on the left side; an alphabetical list of the contacts in the selected group appears on the right side.

The red bookmark at the top of the List page switches between List and Card view and Groups view.

Computer-based tools that look like their paper-based counterparts, such as Address Book or iCal in Mac OS X Lion, are called *skeuomorphic*. The idea is that it's easier to make the transition from paper based to electronic when the electronic version looks familiar.

Contact card appearance

You have a few options for how information on you contact card is displayed:

✦ When you create a new contact card, Address Book assumes that you want to display that card by a person's name. To make a card appear in Address Book by company name instead, click the card and choose Card⇨Mark as a Company (or select the Company check box when you're creating a new contact card; see Figure 1-4). Your chosen card now displays a company name and icon. To change from a company name back to a person's name, choose Card⇨Mark as a Person.

✦ To set whether your cards are sorted by first or last name, select Address Book ⇨Preferences⇨General and select the sort and display options you prefer.

✦ To change the first-name-last-name order for one card only, select Card⇨Reorder First/Last Name Before Last/First. That card only will change regardless of the General Preferences you set.

You can view multiple cards at once by clicking a name in the Contacts List in List and Card view, and then choosing Card⇨Open in Separate Window. Repeat until all the cards you want to see are open.

Designing a template

Each time you add a contact, Address Book displays blank fields, with each field representing a piece of information to fill in about that person, such as company, first and last name, title, and e-mail address. You may not want or need to store all that information about everyone, so you can define the Address Book template to list only the fields you want to use, such as name and e-mail address. To modify the Address Book template, follow these steps:

1. **Click the Address Book icon in the Dock or on the Launchpad.**

2. **Choose Address Book⇨Preferences.**

   A Preferences window appears.

3. **Click the Template icon.**

   The Template pane appears, as shown in Figure 1-1.

4. **Remove a field you don't want by clicking the minus sign to the left of the field and then repeating this for every field you want to remove.**

5. **Click the Add Field pop-up menu and choose a field to add, such as URL or Birthday (see Figure 1-2), repeating this for each field you want to add.**

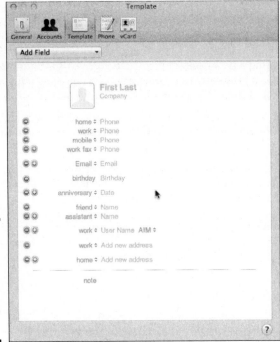

Figure 1-1:
The
Template
pane shows
all the fields
that you can
store.

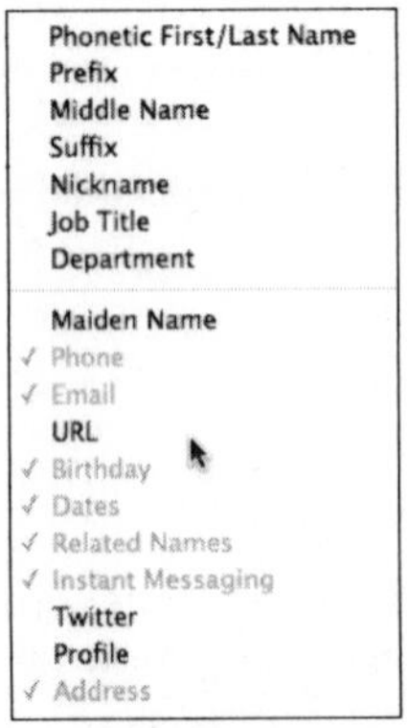

Figure 1-2:
The Add
Field menu
provides
more fields
you can
add to a
template.

6. **(Optional) Click the Work or Home address field and choose Change Address Format to select the address format of a particular country.**

Doing so affects the address format of your entire Address Book. You can make this change on individual cards, as explained in Step 2 in the "Creating a new contact" section.

7. **(Optional) Click the Phone icon to make the Phone pane appear, as shown in Figure 1-3.**

8. **Click the Formats pop-up menu and then choose the way you want phone numbers to appear.**

   - You can also choose Custom and then type your custom format, or use the down arrow and choose another provided telephone format.

   - You can deselect the Automatically Format Phone Numbers check box if you don't want Address Book to format your phone numbers automatically.

9. **Click the Close button of the Address Book preferences window.**

The template defines only the fields you know you want to use for storing contacts you'll save in the Address Book. You can always add fields to individual cards later. We show you how in Step 4 of the "Creating a new contact" section.

Figure 1-3:
The Phone pane defines a specific format for displaying telephone numbers.

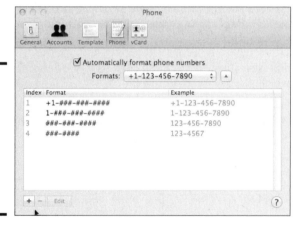

Entering contacts

After you define a template for your Address Book, the next step is to enter actual contact names and information by creating contact cards, referred to as *contacts*.

Address Book comes with two contact cards: one for Apple Inc. and one for you. Called My Card, this contact card always represents you. It contains your e-mail address, phone number, address, photo or representative image, and any other information you want to put on it. If you want to send your information to someone, say a new business associate, you send this card by clicking the Share button at the bottom of the contact card. A check box appears next to each field you fill in; deselect the check box next to any information you don't want to send out.

✦ To define a different card to represent you, click that card and choose Card⇨Make This My Card.

✦ To view your card at any time, choose Card⇨Go to My Card.

There are two ways to enter contacts into Address Book, which we explain in the upcoming subsections:

✦ Create new contacts and type in information.

✦ Import contacts from an older address-book application.

Creating a new contact

Follow these steps whenever you want to add a new contact, either when you are creating your entire Address Book for the first time or when you want to add a new contact to your existing Address Book. To create a new contact, follow these steps:

1. **Choose File⇨New Card or click the plus sign at the bottom of the Contacts window.**

The Address Book window displays a blank card for you to fill in by clicking the fields that appear in this contact edit view, as shown in Figure 1-4.

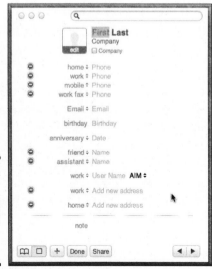

Figure 1-4:
Adding a new contact means filling out a blank card.

2. **Click the text fields, such as First, Last, or Home (for a home telephone number), and then type the information you want to save for your contact.**

   No need to fill every field. Some fields — one for birthday, for example — can have just one entry; others, such as those for phone numbers or addresses, can have many entries. When you enter data in the existing field, a new blank field appears beneath the completed one.

   To change the address field format, click the field name — Home, Work, or another — and select Change Address Format from the pop-up menu. Choose the country for that address, and the card changes to reflect the chosen country's address format.

3. **To add a photo of your contact, click Edit on the photo icon to the left of the contact's name, or select Card➪Choose Custom Image.**

   A photo pane opens. You have three ways to insert a photo:

   - Click Choose to open a chooser for your Mac. Scroll through your folders and files to find the photo you want to associate with your contact or type the name of the photo in the Spotlight search field. When you find the photo, click Open to insert your chosen photo into the photo box of the pane, as shown in Figure 1-5.

   - Click the iPhoto button at the bottom of the pane to insert a Face from iPhoto (refer to Book IV, Chapter 3 to find out more about iPhoto).

   - Click the video-capture button at the bottom of the pane to take a photo with your Mac's built-in iSight camera, if it has one, or a third-party camera you have attached to your Mac.

Figure 1-5: Adding photos to your contacts helps you connect names with faces.

4. **After you have chosen a photo, you can edit it as follows:**

   • Use the zoom slider to enlarge the portion of the photo you want to use.

   • Move the pointer over the photo until it becomes a small hand, which you use to move the photo around in the photo box until it's in a position you like.

   • Click the Special Effects button (it looks like a fan) to add special effects such as sepia tone or a controlled blurring of the photo.

5. **Click Set when you're happy with the photo.**

   The photo now appears to the left of the contact's name.

6. **(Optional) If you want to add a field only to this card, choose Card⇨ Add Field to choose a field to add on a card, as shown in Figure 1-6.**

   After you add a field to a card, you need to type information into that field.

7. **To change the name of a field, click the name of the field and choose Custom.**

   A list of field name options opens; Custom is the last choice on the list. A dialog appears, as shown in Figure 1-7.

8. **Type in the name you want for the field.**

9. **Click the Done button at the bottom of the Address Book window to save your new card.**

To help you remember how to pronounce names in unfamiliar languages, Address Book has a Phonetic First/Last Name field.

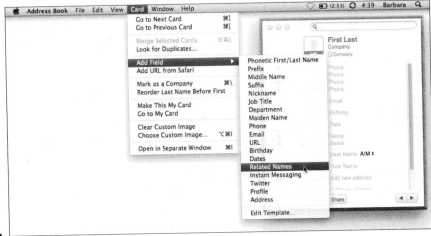

Figure 1-6:
The Add Field submenu lets you add a new field that appears only on the currently displayed card.

Figure 1-7:
Create
Custom
names for
fields.

Add custom label:

Cancel   OK

The Related Names field gives you a place to type the name of your contact's spouse, child, or assistant. Click the field name to reveal a pop-up menu of options.

Importing old contacts

If your contacts are already in another application, why retype all the data? It's easier to export the data from the old application and import the data into Address Book. Address Book understands the following four file formats:

✦ **vCards:** Standard file format that is used to store contact information; used by applications on different types of computers.

✦ **LDIF:** Standard data interchange file format; stands for Lightweight Directory Access Protocol (LDAP) Data Interchange Format.

✦ **Text File:** Tab-delimited or Comma-Separated Value (CSV) format; comes from a database, spreadsheet, or contact application.

✦ **Address Book Archive:** Standard Address Book file format useful for transferring data between Macs with Address Book.

To import a contact's data file into your Address Book, follow these steps:

1. **Choose File⇨Import.**

A dialog appears.

2. **Select the file you want to import and then click Open. Leave Text Encoding on Automatic.**

3. **Accept or review duplicate cards:**

• Click Import to automatically accept duplicates.

• Click Review if you want to see duplicates and resolve differences between the two.

4. **Click Next to continue.**

5. **(Optional) If you're importing a text or CSV file, make sure that the correct field labels are associated with the data being imported. You can change the field labels if necessary.**

When the import is finished, Address Book contains the new contact cards.

In applications that use the vCard format (such as Microsoft Exchange), you can export the contents to a vCard file and then e-mail the file to yourself. Save the attached vCard file and then double-click it to import the contact into Address Book automatically without having to bother with the steps listed here.

Your newly imported contacts will appear in both the All Contacts group and the Last Import group in the Group column.

Adding accounts

You may have access to address books on network servers, perhaps the company directory at your place of employment. You can add this remote account to Address Book so you can access the information. Because the data is in a remote location (that is not on your Mac), you need to be online to access the information. You may or may not have editing privileges. To add an account, follow these steps:

1. **Choose Address Book⇨Preferences⇨Accounts.**

2. **Click the Add button (it looks like a plus sign) in the lower-left corner of the Accounts pane.**

   A dialog opens, as shown in Figure 1-8.

3. **Select the account type and type in the requested information.**

   Address Book supports CardDAV, Exchange, LDAP, and Yahoo! accounts. You may have to ask the network administrator or someone techie in your group for the information.

Figure 1-8:
Add an account to access address books stored on remote servers.

4. **When you finish, click Create.**

Address Book finds accounts that match the information you provided and sets up your account.

Searching contacts

The more contact cards you store in your Address Book, the harder it is to find a particular contact you want. Instead of scrolling through every contact card to locate one you're looking for, you can search for specific contacts by following these steps:

1. **In List and Card view, click the Spotlight search field above the list on the left.**

2. **Type a word or phrase that you want to find, such as a person's name or the company that person works for.**

   The Address Book displays a list of contacts that match the text you typed.

3. **Click a contact to display the card for that person or company.**

To search for the occurrence of a contact's name on your Mac, Control-click the name of the contact in the List and choose Spotlight from the shortcut menu.

Editing a card

Information on cards will need to change whenever people change their address or company. To keep this information up to date, you can edit a card by following these steps:

1. **In List and Card view, type the name of the contact you want to edit in the Spotlight search field, and then click the contact you want to edit from within the list.**

2. **Click the Edit button at the bottom of the card pane.**

3. **Click the field in which you want to type or edit information, such as an e-mail address or phone number.**

4. **Click the Done button.**

   Address Book saves the updated contact information.

You can add or edit notes in the Notes field without being in Edit mode. Just click in the Notes field and type what you want.

Deleting a contact

Periodically, you can browse through your Address Book and prune the contact cards of people you don't need to save any more. To delete a name from your Address Book, just click the contact and choose Edit⇨Delete Card. If you accidentally delete a contact, press ⌘+Z or choose Edit⇨Undo to restore it.

If you hold down the ⌘ key, you can click and choose multiple contacts to delete. If you hold down the Shift key, you can click two contact cards and select those two contacts and all contacts in between as well.

Creating Groups

To help you organize the contacts you've stored, Address Book lets you create groups of contacts, such as for your co-workers, friends, family members, restaurants, and so on. For greater convenience, you can even store the same contact in multiple groups. Although you don't have to use groups, this feature can help you manage your list of important contact cards. It's also a great way to send e-mails to a group of people without having to type in each name singly.

Your Address Book initially contains one group: All Contacts. The All Contacts group automatically stores all contacts you've saved in the Address Book. Even when a contact is assigned to a group, the contact remains in All Contacts.

If your Mac is connected to a local area network, you may see a second group: Directories. The directories group contains a list of contacts of everyone connected to a local area network. If you're using a Mac at home without a local area network, you won't see the Directories group.

Creating a group

You can create as many groups as you want, but for groups to be useful, you need to add contacts to that group. To create a new group, follow these steps:

1. **Choose File⇨New Group.**

2. **Replace Group Name with a more descriptive name in the Groups pane, as shown in Figure 1-9, and then press Return.**

To add contacts to a group, follow these steps:

1. **In Groups view, click All Contacts in the Group list to see all the contacts stored in your Address Book.**

2. **Move the cursor over a contact, hold down the mouse or trackpad button, and then drag the cursor over the group name where you want to store your contact.**

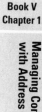

Figure 1-9:
Groups view
shows the
groups you
create in
Address
Book.

If you hold down the ⌘ key, you can click and choose multiple contacts.
If you hold down the Shift key, you can click two noncontiguous contacts to select those two contacts and all contacts in between as well.

3. **Release the mouse or trackpad button when the group name appears
highlighted.**

   Your chosen contact now appears in your newly created group and in
   the All Contacts group.

You can see which groups a contact belongs to. In Groups view, hold down the
Option key, and then click a name in the Contacts List on the right. The groups
to which that contact belongs are highlighted in the Groups list on the left.

Creating a group from a selection of contacts

If you already have a group of contacts selected that you want to organize,
you can create a new group and store those contacts at the same time. To
create a new group from a selection of contacts, follow these steps:

1. **In Groups view, click All Contacts in the Group list to see all the
names stored in your Address Book.**

2. **Hold down the ⌘ key and click each contact you want to store in
a group.**

   You can select a range of contacts by holding down the Shift key and
   clicking two noncontiguous contacts. Doing so selects those two contacts and all contacts in between.

3. **Choose File⇨New Group from Selection.**

4. **Type a more descriptive contact for your group and then press Return.**

   Your group now contains the contacts you selected in Step 2.

TIP

To send an e-mail to a group, Control-click the group name and select Send Email to *group name*.

Editing the distribution list

Often you have more than one phone number, e-mail, or street address for the same person. To choose which phone number, e-mail, or street address you want to use for each contact in a group, you edit the distribution list. You can choose the same type of address for all members of the group; for example, using the work address, or you can select the information individually for each member of the group. Follow this procedure:

1. **Choose Edit⇨Edit Distribution List.**

2. **Select the group you want to edit.**

3. **Click the column header to open a pop-up menu that lets you choose which type of data you want to manage: Email, Phone, or Address, as shown in Figure 1-10.**

4. **Select the corresponding information you want to use for each member who has more than one entry.**

   Alternatively, you can change the whole group by selecting a different label to use from the Change All Labels pop-up menu.

Figure 1-10: Using Edit Distribution List, you specify addresses or phone numbers to use when contacts in a group have more than one.

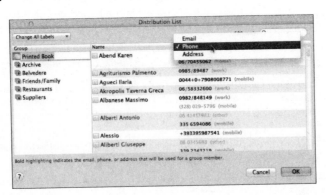

Adding contacts automatically with Smart Groups

Adding contacts manually or selecting them for a group is fine, but what if you frequently add and delete contacts? Doing all this manually can get old. To keep your group's contacts accurate and up to date more easily, you can use the Smart Group feature.

With a Smart Group, you define the types of contacts you want to store, such as contacts for everyone who works at a certain company. Then the Smart Group automatically adds any contacts to the group from your Address Book.

To create a Smart Group, follow these steps:

1. **Choose File⇨New Smart Group.**

   A dialog appears, asking for a contact and rule for storing contacts in the group. A *rule* lets you group contacts based on certain criteria. For example, you may want to group the contacts of all people who work for Apple and live in Texas.

2. **Click the Smart Group Name text box and type a descriptive name for your Smart Group.**

3. **Click the first pop-up menu and choose the criteria for including a contact in your Smart Group, such as Company or City, as shown in Figure 1-11.**

4. **Click the second pop-up menu and choose how to use the criteria you defined in Step 3, such as Contains or Was Updated After.**

5. **Click the text box and type a word or phrase for your criteria to use.**

   For example, if you want to create a Smart Group that stores only contacts of people who work at Apple, your entire Smart Group rule might look like Company Contains Apple.

6. **(Optional) Click the plus sign to the right of the text box to create any additional rules.**

   If you create any additional rules and later decide you don't want them, you can always remove them by clicking the minus sign that appears next to the rule.

7. **Click OK.**

Figure 1-11:
This pop-up menu defines the criteria for storing contacts in your Smart Group.

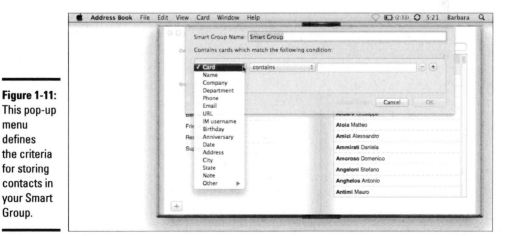

Creating a Smart Group from search results

Defining the criteria for storing names automatically in a Smart Group can be cumbersome when you aren't quite sure whether the defined criteria will work exactly the way you want. As an alternative, you can use Spotlight to search for the types of contacts you want to store, and *then* create a Smart Group based on your Spotlight search results. Using this approach, you can see exactly which types of contacts appear in your Smart Group.

To create a Smart Group from Spotlight search results, follow these steps:

1. **In List and Card view, click the Spotlight search field, type the text you want to find (such as the name of a company or part of an e-mail address), and press Return.**

   The List pane shows the contacts that Spotlight found based on the text you typed in.

2. **Choose File⇨New Smart Group from Current Search.**

   A Smart Group appears in the Group category, using the text you typed as the group name.

Deleting a Group

If you create a group and no longer need it, you can delete it. When you delete a group, you delete only the group folder; you do not delete any contact cards stored in that group. To delete a group, click the group and then choose Edit⇨Delete Group.

Using Shortcut Menus

Address Book has many more options than meet the eye. Most are revealed in pop-up or shortcut menus. Clicking field names in the Contact Card brings up shortcut menus, which present the options listed here:

✦ **Telephone Number:** Show in Large Type, FaceTime. If you have Skype installed and configured to link with Address Book, you see two more options: Call with Skype and Send SMS with Skype.

✦ **Address:** Map this Address, Copy Mailing Label, Copy Map URL.

✦ **E-mail:** Send Email, FaceTime, Send Update, Search with Spotlight.

Control-clicking a group name gives you these options: Send Email to *group* and Edit Distribution List. Regular groups also have the option of Export Group vCard, while smart groups give the option of Edit Smart Group.

To Control-click, hold down the Control key and click the item. If you click and then press the Control key, other options may open.

If you have both Address Book and iCal open, from a Contacts or Group List, you can click and drag a contact (⌘-click to select more than one invitee) to the hour of an event to which you want to invite them. See Book V, Chapter 2 to find out more about inviting contacts to an event by using iCal.

Managing Your Address Book Files

Eventually, your Address Book can hold so many important contacts that you can't afford to risk losing this information. One way to preserve your contact information is to create an archive file of your Address Book, which you then store on a backup device other than your Mac, such as a USB flash drive or external hard drive. Another way is to print your entire Address Book (although this isn't a very *green* option, especially when you have to add or remove contacts). A third way to back up your Address Book is to sync to iCloud, Apple's online storage service, which we explain in Book III, Chapter 2. Whatever way you choose, you always have access to your important contact information, even if your Mac's hard drive is wiped out.

The difference is that an archived file captures a one-time picture of your Address Book; any changes you make after you made the archive file won't be kept until the next archive file you create. iCloud keeps an up-to-date copy of Address Book because the syncing happens on a regular basis, as often as every 15 minutes if you want.

Archiving your Address Book

There're few things worse than manually retyping all your contacts if you lose them in a computer disaster. You can create an archive file of your Address Book and then back it up to an external drive or write it to a CD for safekeeping. Follow these steps:

1. **Choose File⇨Export⇨Address Book Archive.**

A Save As dialog opens.

2. **Keep the default name or type a new name in the Save As text box.**

3. **Select the location for storing your file; this can be an external drive or another folder on your Mac that you regularly back up to an external backup device.**

4. **Click Save.**

For more details on backing up files, see Book III, Chapter 1.

Sending updates

Phone numbers change. You move or change jobs and it's usually a hassle to notify everyone of your new phone number, e-mail, or physical address. In Address Book, when you change your address, phone number, or e-mail, you can quickly send an update to selected contacts and/or groups. Address Book refers to My Card to send your information. To send an update, follow these steps:

1. **Edit My Card to reflect your new information by choosing Card⇨ Go To My Card and then clicking Edit.**

2. **Make your changes, and click Done.**

3. **Choose File⇨Send Updates.**

   A dialog opens, as shown in Figure 1-12.

4. **Select the groups you want to notify in the Send Updates dialog.**

   Create a new group if you don't have one to send updates to. Send Updates only works with regular groups; it doesn't work with Smart Groups.

5. **Type in a subject line and modify the message, if you want.**

6. **Click Send.**

   The information on My Card will be sent to the group as a vCard attachment.

To send your updated information to one person at a time, use the Email shortcut menu. Click the Email field title and then choose Send Update from the pop-up menu. An outgoing e-mail addressed to that contact opens with a vCard version of My Card attached.

Figure 1-12: Send updates when your contact info changes.

Printing your Address Book

Besides printing a backup copy of your contacts, Address Book lets you print all or some of your contact information in different formats, such as mailing labels or cards that you can carry with you. To print your Address Book, follow these steps:

1. **Use one of the following methods to select the names you want to print:**

   • Click a single contact card.

   • Hold down the ⌘ key and click multiple contacts.

- Hold down the Shift key, click a contact, and then click another contact elsewhere in the list. Selecting these two contacts highlights them both and all contacts in between.

- To print all contact cards stored in a group, click the group name and then choose Edit⇨Select All or press ⌘+A.

- Use Spotlight to find names that meet a certain criteria.

2. **Choose File⇨Print.**

   A Print dialog appears.

3. **Expand the Print dialog by clicking the down arrow that appears to the right of the Printer pop-up menu.**

   You see before you the expanded Print dialog, as shown in Figure 1-13.

4. **Click the Printer pop-up menu and choose a printer to use.**

5. **Click the Style pop-up menu and choose one of the following:**

   - *Mailing Labels:* Prints names and addresses on different types of mailing labels.

   - *Envelopes:* Prints names and addresses on envelopes fed into your printer.

   - *Lists:* Prints your Address Book as a long list.

   - *Pocket Address Book:* Prints your Address Book in a condensed form suitable for carrying with you.

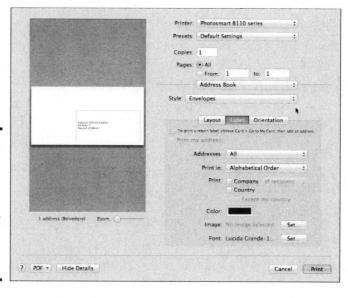

Figure 1-13: The expanded Print dialog lets you choose how to print your selected contacts.

Depending on the style that you choose in this step, you may need to pick additional options, such as defining the specific size of your mailing labels or choosing whether to print names in alphabetical order. You can also adjust other setting and options, such as number of copies and the font you want to use for your printed output.

6. **Click Print.**

Exporting your Address Book

Sometimes you may need to share contact information with others. To save one or more names from your Address Book into a file that other applications and people can use, export contact data to a vCard or archive format. A *vCard* is a standard format that many applications use to store contact information. By storing contact data as a vCard, you can copy information to another application and computer, such as a Windows PC running Outlook.

If you need to share contact information with another Mac user, you can save your Address Book data as an archive file (as detailed in the earlier section, "Archiving your Address Book") or as a vCard file.

To export contacts from your Address Book, follow these steps:

1. **Select the names you want to export.**

2. **Choose File⇨Export.**

   A submenu appears.

3. **Choose Export vCard or Address Book Archive.**

   A Save As dialog appears.

4. **Type a descriptive name for your file in the Save As text box.**

5. **Choose the location to store your file.**

6. **Click Save.**

When exporting contacts for use in another application, the application you're importing might not recognize every detail for the contact, such as a person's picture or notes you've added to a person's contact card.

Syncing with other devices

You can synchronize your Address Book contacts with your iPhone, iPad, iPod, or other mobile phone when you connect it to your Mac and open iTunes. Follow these steps:

1. **Connect your iPhone or iPod to your Mac with a USB cable.**

2. **Click your iPhone or iPod in the Devices column, click the Info tab, and then choose Sync Address Book Contacts.**

Your Address Book contacts transfer or update automatically on your iPhone or iPod.

If you have an iCloud account, your Address Book contacts (and iCal events and other information) can stay up to date automatically among your Mac and one or more other computers or devices.

Syncing with other address books

If you have a Yahoo! or Google account, you can sync Address Book with the addresses in those accounts by following these steps:

1. **Choose Address Book⇨Preferences⇨Accounts.**

The Accounts pane opens, as shown in Figure 1-14.

2. **Select the check box next to the type of account you have: Yahoo! or Google.**

Read the advisory information and click Agree to continue.

3. **Enter your account address and password, then click OK.**

Address Book syncs automatically at regular intervals.

If you have an iCloud account, syncing Address Book gives you a backup and the possibility to access your Address Book from a different computer by accessing iCloud on line. Book III, Chapter 2 gives detailed information about using iCloud. Briefly, to sync with iCloud, do the following:

1. **Choose ⌘⇨System Preferences and click the iCloud icon in the Internet and Wireless section or right-click the System Preferences icon in the Dock and choose iCloud from the shortcut menu.**

The iCloud preference pane appears.

2. **Click Sign In.**

Type your Apple ID and password in the appropriate fields.

3. **Select the Contacts check box.**

iCloud syncs the contacts from Address Book on your Mac to iCloud.

4. **When you choose Address Book⇨Preferences⇨Accounts, you see iCloud in the accounts list, as shown in Figure 1-14.**

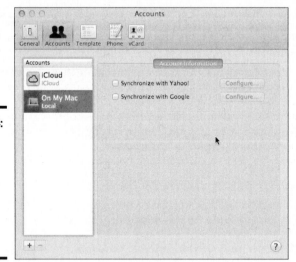

Figure 1-14:
Sync
Address
Book with
contacts
you have
in Yahoo!,
Google, or
iCloud.

You have to be connected to the Internet when using iCloud and when you are connected, any changes you make to Address Book will automatically be pulled to iCloud and then be pushed to other devices on which you activated iCloud with the same account, such as an iPhone, iPad, or another computer.

Chapter 2: Staying on Schedule with iCal

In This Chapter

✓ Understanding the iCal window

✓ Viewing calendars

✓ Creating and storing events

✓ Organizing tasks with Reminders

✓ Subscribing to calendars

✓ Printing, saving, and sharing calendars

*Y*ou're busy. You may rely on a planner, random scraps of paper, or your memory to keep track of obligations, appointments, and commitments. Your Mac comes with an alternative: iCal, Apple's calendar application. iCal lets you track appointments you need to attend and reminds you of tasks you want to complete or deadlines you have to meet.

In this chapter, first we introduce the iCal interface. Then we show you how to create multiple calendars — for example, a work calendar and a home calendar. Next, we explain how to put *events* (that's what iCal calls anything such as an appointment, birthday, or whatever else that requires a time/ date reference) and reminders on your calendars. At the end of the chapter, we talk about sharing your calendar both online and in print.

Understanding iCal

The iCal toolbar displays the following items, as shown in Figure 2-1:

✦ **Calendars:** The pop-up menu lets you choose which calendars you want to view.

✦ **Add (+) button:** Clicking this button adds an event.

✦ **Inbox:** Displays how many invitations you have.

✦ **Views:** The buttons in the center give you access to the four iCal views: Day, Week, Month, and Year.

✦ **Spotlight Search:** iCal looks for matches of text typed in the search field.

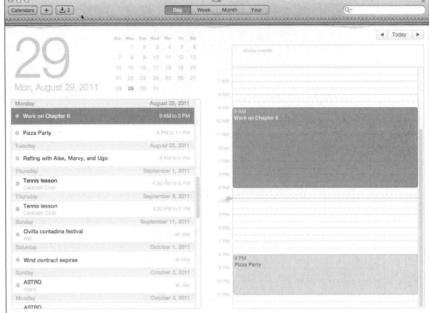

Figure 2-1:
The iCal
toolbar
helps
you view
different
calendars
and choose
the view you
want.

✦ **Full-screen:** The button takes you to a full-screen view of iCal.

✦ **Today:** In the upper-right corner, just under the toolbar, the Today button takes you to the current day in the view you're using. The arrows to the left and right move one unit (day, week, month, or year) into the past or into the future from the date where you are.

Any scheduled activity, such as a doctor's appointment, a business meeting, or your daughter's soccer practice, is an *event*.

iCal offers four types of calendar views, each an electronic version of a familiar paper-based layout:

✦ **Day:** Shows a mini-month at the top, a list of eight to ten upcoming events on the left, and a day-at-a-glance for the active day on the right (refer to Figure 2-1).

✦ **Week:** Displays a week-at-a-glance version of your calendar, as shown in Figure 2-2. A column for each day is divided into half-hour time slots. You establish how many hours of the day you want to see.

When you are viewing the current day in either Day or Week view, a line with a red ball at the left end indicates the current time of day.

Figure 2-2:
Days are
divided into
half-hour
segments in
Week view.

✦ **Month:** Shows a month-at-a-glance with as much of the text of your
events as possible on each day.

✦ **Year:** Displays the whole year in one pane, as shown in Figure 2-3. The
days are color-coded according to how full they are. The current day
is blue. The other days are white, yellow, gold, orange, or red. White is
the color for a day with no events. Colors ranging from yellow through
orange to red are for days with appointments: yellow days have the
fewest appointments and red days have the most.

You can move from one view and date to the next in the following ways:

✦ **Mini-month:** Double-click a date in the mini-month in Day view to go to
the date clicked, remaining in Day view.

✦ **Month:** Double-click a date in Month view to open that date in Day view.

✦ **Week:** Double-click a date in Week view to open that date in Day view.

✦ **Year:** Double-click a date in Year view to open that date in Day view.
Double-click a month in Year view to open that month in Month view.

Figure 2-3:
Days are
color-coded
in Year view
to show
which are
busiest.

Working with Calendars

The iCal application initially includes Home and Work calendars, but you can always create additional calendars and rename existing ones if you want. You may want an additional calendar for a specific work or home-related project, or you might need a separate calendar to keep track of your children's scheduled activities.

The Calendars list pops up when you click the Calendars button in the toolbar (look ahead to Figure 2-4). Calendars stored on remote servers such as iCloud or Google appear below the calendars you keep on your Mac. Calendars you subscribe to (which we explain later in this chapter) are shown at the bottom of the list.

When you create an event, you must first choose which calendar to use. The main reason to have separate calendars is to organize your events into calendar types. For example, the Home calendar is for storing personal events, and the Work calendar is for storing business-related events.

By selecting or deselecting the check box next to each calendar in the Calendars list, you can selectively view specific events (say, only business events) or you can view business and personal events together.

You can collapse or expand the list of calendars stored on your Mac or remote servers by clicking Show or Hide to the right of the computer or server name. The following sections explain managing your calendars in iCal.

Creating a new calendar

Although iCal provides a Home and Work calendar, you might need to create additional calendars for other purposes. To create a new calendar, follow these steps:

1. **Click the iCal icon in the Dock or on the Launchpad.**

2. **Choose File⇨New Calendar and choose where you want to store the new calendar: On My Mac or on one of the remote servers where you keep calendars (if you use remote servers).**

   An Untitled calendar appears in the Calendars pop-up list, as shown in Figure 2-4.

3. **Type a descriptive name for your calendar and press Return.**

4. **Click a calendar in the Calendars list and choose Edit⇨Get Info.**

   Doing so prepares you to assign a color to your calendar so you can distinguish events from different calendars on the calendar you view.

5. **In the Info dialog that appears, click the color pop-up menu, choose a color, and then click OK.**

   Events stored on that calendar appear in the color you chose.

If you already have calendar information in a different calendar application, see the later section, "Importing iCal data."

Figure 2-4:
See the calendars on your Mac and on remote servers.

Creating a new calendar group

Rather than create a bunch of separate calendars, you may want to organize multiple calendars in a group. For example, if you had a calendar to schedule events for your son's and daughter's school and sporting events and your father's doctor's appointments, you could put all three of those calendars into a Family group. You might wonder, "Why not just create one Family calendar?" The reason we suggest creating separate calendars is because you can then print each one for the person it pertains to, you can give your children access to their unique calendars, and they can add events to their calendars as well.

Grouping helps you to see the relationships between calendars, and it lets you hide grouped calendars to avoid cluttering the Calendar List. When you hide a calendar group, you hide all calendars stored within that group.

A calendar group can't store events; it simply stores one or more calendars.

To create a calendar group, follow these steps:

1. **Click the iCal icon in the Dock or on the Launchpad.**

2. **Choose File⇨New Calendar Group.**

   A calendar group appears in the Calendars pop-up menu with a triangle to its left, which you click to hide or show any grouped calendars.

3. **Type a descriptive name for your group and press Return.**

Adding a new calendar to a group

After you create a group, you can add new calendars to the group by following these steps:

1. **Choose File⇨New Calendar⇨On My Mac.**

   The Calendars pop-up list opens. An Untitled Calendar appears at the bottom of the On My Mac section.

2. **Type a descriptive name for your new calendar and press Return.**

3. **Move the pointer over the new calendar.**

4. **Click and drag the new calendar to the group you want to place the calendar in, and then release the mouse or trackpad button.**

   The name of your calendar now appears indented under the group.

Follow Steps 3 and 4 to move existing calendars to a group.

Moving a calendar out of a group

In case you don't want a calendar in a group, you can move it out of a group by following these steps:

1. **Click the Calendars button to open the Calendars pop-up menu.**

2. **Move the cursor over the calendar you want to remove from a group.**

3. **Click and drag the calendar toward the left and up (or down) until it's out of the group.**

4. **Release the mouse or trackpad button.**

   Your existing calendar now appears outside any groups.

Moving a calendar or group

To help organize your calendars and groups, you may want to rearrange their order in the Calendar List by following these steps:

1. **Move the cursor to the calendar or group you want to move.**

2. **Hold down the mouse or trackpad button and drag the mouse or trackpad pointer up or down.**

   A thick horizontal line appears where your calendar or group will appear in the Calendar List, as shown in Figure 2-5.

3. **Release the mouse or trackpad button when you're happy with the new location of your calendar or group.**

Figure 2-5:
A horizontal line shows where your calendar or group will appear when you release the mouse button.

Renaming and deleting calendars and groups

At any time, you can rename a calendar or group. The name of a calendar or group is for your benefit and has no effect on the way iCal works. To rename a calendar or group, double-click a calendar or group name, which highlights that name. Type a new name and press Return.

If you find that you no longer need a particular calendar or group, click the one you want to delete and choose Edit⇨Delete. If you have any events stored on a calendar, a dialog appears, asking whether you really want to delete that calendar or group. Click Delete. If you delete a calendar or group by mistake, choose Edit⇨Undo or press ⌘+Z.

When you delete a calendar, you also delete any events stored on that calendar. When you delete a group, you delete all calendars stored in that group along with all events stored on those calendars. Make sure that you really want to delete a calendar or group of calendars. You can also archive a copy before deleting so you have the reference without cluttering your calendar.

Creating and Modifying Events

An event is any occurrence that has a specific time and date associated with it. Some common types of events are meetings, appointments with clients, times when you need to pick someone up (as at the airport), or recreational time (such as a concert or a two-week vacation). If you know that a particular event will occur on a specific date and time, you can store that event in an iCal calendar so you won't forget or schedule a conflicting activity at that time.

Viewing events

As we list at the beginning of this chapter, iCal lets you display time frames by day, week, month, or year and shows all the events you've scheduled for the day, week, month, or year you choose to view. The amount of detail varies, depending on the view you choose. To change the time frame of your displayed events, click the Day, Week, Month, or Year button at the top of the iCal window.

Creating an event

To create an event, you need to decide which calendar to store the event on, the date and time to schedule the event, and the event's duration. You have options to create an alert so iCal lets you know when the event is getting close, and whether to invite others to the event. Here's where we show you how to create an event; in the next section, we explain your options. There are several ways to create an event:

✦ To create a Quick Event, here's the drill: Click the Add Event button (the plus sign in the toolbar) or choose File➪New Event. Then type in a phrase that defines your event in the Create Quick Event dialog that opens, as shown in Figure 2-6.

iCal understands regular phrases such as "dinner on Tuesday" or "staff meeting Thursday from 9:00 a.m. – 1:00 p.m." iCal uses the current date as the point of reference. The default duration for an event is one hour. "Breakfast" or "morning" starts at 9:00 a.m. "Lunch" or "noon" begins at 12:00 p.m. "Dinner" or "night" starts at 8:00 p.m.

✦ In Day or Week view, double-click the hour you want the event to begin, and then type in a title for your event.

✦ Click and drag from the starting time to the ending time in Day or Week view, and then type a title for your event.

✦ Double-click the date of the event in Month view, type in the title and time, such as **Movie 7:00 p.m. – 9:00 p.m.**

✦ In Week or Month view, click and drag from the beginning to ending date for a multi-day event.

You can change the start and end time of an event by moving the pointer to the top or bottom of an event until it turns into a two-way-pointing arrow. Then hold down the mouse or trackpad button and move it up or down to change your start and end times by 15-minute increments.

Figure 2-6:
Quickly
create an
event.

Create Quick Event

dinner on wednesday

Editing an event

Sometimes a title, time, and date are enough for an event. Other times, you want to add more information, or something changes and you have to change the date or time of an event. Editing an event lets you change the time, the date, or the description of an event. You can also add features to an event, such as setting an alarm, inviting people to your event, or automatically opening a file.

Changing the description of an event

Each time you create an event, you type in a description of that event. To modify this description, follow these steps:

1. **Double-click the event you want to modify and then click the Edit button.**

   Alternatively, click the event and choose Edit⇨Edit Event or press ⌘+E. The Edit pane opens, as shown in Figure 2-7.

2. **Click the event description (in Figure 2-7, this is *Work on Chapter 6*).**

   A text box appears around the event description.

3. **Use the arrow and Delete keys to edit the event description and type any new text.**

   - Click the Location field to type a location where the event takes place.

   - Select the All Day check box to create an event that lasts all day, like a birthday or vacation day. The From and To fields disappear if All Day is selected.

4. **Click Done when you're finished.**

Figure 2-7: In the Edit pane, you define details for your event, create alerts, and invite others.

Creating a recurring event

For an event that occurs regularly, such as every Monday or on the same day every month, you can create an event one time and then tell iCal to display that event on a recurring basis. To create a recurring event, follow these steps:

1. **Double-click the event you want to modify and click the Edit button.**

   Alternatively, click the event and choose Edit⇨Edit Event or press ⌘+E.

2. **Click the Repeat pop-up menu and choose an option, such as Every Day or Every Month.**

3. **(Optional) In the Repeat pop-up menu, click Custom.**

   A dialog appears, shown in Figure 2-8, letting you define specific days for the recurring event, such as every Monday and Thursday or the first Wednesday of every month. Click OK when you finish creating your custom recurring event.

Figure 2-8:
The Custom
option lets
you define
parameters
for a
recurring
event.

If you share your iCal calendar with other iOS devices, use the Custom
option on your Mac because the other iOS devices don't offer the same
flexibility.

4. **In the Edit Event dialog, click Done.**

   iCal automatically displays your recurring event throughout the rest of
   the calendar until you modify the event.

Indicating your availability

If you share your calendar with others, you may want to indicate your availability during certain events. You can choose Busy or Free by selecting the
pop-up menu next to Show As. Usually iCal considers you Busy when you have
an appointment, but if you show your attendance for three days at a conference, you may want to put Free so those who view your calendar know that
you're at the conference but are free for appointments during that time.

Setting an alert for an event

Scheduling an event is useless if you forget about it. That's why iCal gives
you the option of setting an alert that can notify you of upcoming events. To
set an alert, first you have to decide how you want the alert to notify you —
say, by displaying a message onscreen.

To set an alert for an event, follow these steps:

1. **Click an event you want reminded about and then choose Edit⇨Edit**
   Event or press ⌘+E.

   An Edit dialog appears (refer to Figure 2-7).

2. **Click the Alert pop-up menu.**

   You can choose any of the following options:

   • *None:* Removes any alerts you've already set for the event.

   • *Message:* Displays a message on the screen to alert you of an event.

- *Message with Sound:* Displays a message on the screen and plays a sound to alert you of an event.

- *Email:* Sends an e-mail message to you.

- *Open File:* Loads and displays a file, such as a report that you can review for an upcoming meeting.

- *Run Script:* Runs an AppleScript file that can control your Mac.

3. **Click the Time pop-up menu to define when you want the alert to trigger — for example, 15 minutes or 1 hour before the event.**

4. **(Optional) Depending on the alert type you choose, other pop-up menus might appear and offer choices of how to use your alert. Adjust the settings as desired.**

   You can add another alert (or many additional alerts) to an event by clicking the Alert pop-up menu that appears automatically beneath a new or existing alert.

5. **Click Done.**

Moving an event to another calendar

You can always move an event from one calendar to another, such as from your Work calendar to your Home calendar. To move an event to another calendar, follow these steps:

1. **Click an event that you want to modify and then choose Edit⇨ Edit Event or press ⌘+E.**

2. **Click the Calendar pop-up menu and then choose the calendar name you want the event to appear in.**

3. **Click Done.**

Adding information to an event

To prepare for an event, you can also store information about that event's location, attendees, any important files related to the event (such as a presentation), a website URL, and any additional notes you want to jot down.

To add information to an event, follow these steps:

1. **Click an event that you want to modify and then choose Edit⇨ Edit Event or press ⌘+E.**

2. **Choose one or more of the following:**

   - *Location:* Remind yourself where the event will take place.

   - *Attachments:* Attach a file to an event, such as a business presentation that you need to give at the event.

- *URL:* Type a website address that's relevant to your event, such as the restaurant's website for an upcoming dinner.

  - *Note:* Type any additional notes about your event.

3. **Click Done.**

Inviting people to your event

Invitations for events ranging from staff meetings to birthday parties are often communicated electronically. Rather than type out a separate e-mail with the details of your event, you can send the invitation directly from iCal. And iCal keeps track of the responses so you can see who has accepted, declined, or is still deciding. Follow these steps:

1. **Click an event that you want to invite people to and then choose Edit⇨Edit Event or press ⌘+E.**

2. **Click Add Invitees.**

   A blank field opens.

3. **If the person you want to invite is in your Address Book, begin typing the name and iCal automatically shows you a list of possible matches.**

   The more you type, the narrower the list becomes.

4. **Choose the e-mail of the person you want to invite.**

5. **Type in other names after the first one if you want to invite more than one person.**

6. **Click Send.**

   An invitation is sent in the iCalendar or ICS file format. If the person has iCal or another calendar application associated with the e-mail address, the invitation is sent directly to iCal or the calendar application.

   ICS is the standard file type for exchanging calendar information. iCal, Outlook, Google Calendar, and Calendar (on iOS devices) support the ICS standard (unfortunately, Eudora, Entourage, Mailsmith and others do not). When you send or receive an e-mail with an invitation attached, the invitation probably has the `.ics` filename extension. To add the event automatically to iCal or the calendar application currently in use, you or the recipient simply clicks that attachment in the e-mail message.

7. **The recipients have the option to Accept, Decline, or say Maybe.**

   You receive an e-mail when recipients respond: A white check mark in a green circle appears next to the recipients who accept, a question mark in an orange circle indicates a Maybe response, and a red circle-with-slash means the recipient declined the invitation.

If you have both Address Book and iCal open, you can click and drag a contact (⌘-click to select more than one invitee) from a Contacts or Group List to the hour of the event to which you want to invite them. See Book V, Chapter 1 to discover more about Address Book.

Responding to invitations

If someone sends you an invitation in Mail and you accept, it's added to your calendar automatically. Invitations appear in the Inbox in the toolbar. The number indicates the number of invitations you have. A badge with a number appears on the iCal icon in the Dock, which also indicates the number of invitations you have in your Inbox.

When you click the Inbox, the invitations appear, as shown in Figure 2-9. Click Maybe, Decline, or Accept. The sender will be notified of your response. If you Accept, the event is added to iCal.

Figure 2-9:
Invitations
appear in
the Inbox in
the Toolbar.

Moving an event

In case you store an event at the wrong date or time, you can change the date and time in the Edit Event dialog, or move it to a new date and time by following these steps:

1. **Move the cursor to the middle of the event box.**

2. **Hold down the mouse button and drag the cursor to a new time or date.**

   The event moves with the cursor; the duration doesn't change.

3. **Release the mouse button when you're happy with the new date and time of the event.**

Duplicating an event

If a particular event occurs more than one time, you could type the event multiple times, but why spend all that effort? Instead, you can create an event, duplicate it, and then move the duplicate to another date. To duplicate an event, just click it and choose Edit⇨Duplicate or press ⌘+D (or hold down the Option key and then drag the event to the new time slot). When the duplicate appears, move the cursor to it, drag the event to a new date, and then release the mouse button.

If your event occurs at a regular interval — for example, once a month or every Tuesday and Thursday — you can make your event a recurring event in the Repeat pop-up menu of the Edit Event dialog, as explained previously in the section "Creating a recurring event."

Deleting an event

When you no longer need to remember an event, you can delete it. Just click it and choose Edit⇨Delete. If you delete an event by mistake, press ⌘+Z or choose Edit⇨Undo to retrieve your event.

Finding Events

Storing events is only useful if you can view upcoming events so you can prepare for them. To help you find and view events, iCal offers several different methods that include using colors to identify different types of events and letting you search for a specific event by name.

Color-coding events

Events in a calendar reflect the color you assign to the calendar when you create the calendar. So if you assign the color blue to your Home calendar and the color red to your Work calendar, you can quickly identify which events on your calendar are home related (blue) or work related (red).

Use contrasting colors for multiple calendars to make it easy to tell which events belong to which calendar.

Selectively hiding events

Normally, iCal displays all events, color-coding them so you can tell which events belong to which calendars. However, if you have too many events, you might find mixing Home and Work events too confusing. If you want to see only events stored on a specific calendar (such as Home or Work calendars), you can hide the events that are stored on other calendars.

To hide events stored on other calendars, deselect the check box of any of those calendars in the Calendar List. To view events stored on a calendar, make sure that a check mark appears in the check box of that calendar, as shown in Figure 2-10.

Figure 2-10:
Hiding a
calendar
hides all
events
stored
on that
calendar.

Checking for today's events

Probably the most important events you need to worry about are the ones you've scheduled for today. To see all events scheduled for today, click the Today button at the top of the iCal window.

Another quick way to review any upcoming events for today is to use the Calendar widget in Dashboard. To display today's events in the Calendar widget, click the current date (which appears in the left pane) of the Calendar widget until the events pane appears. (For more information about using widgets and the Dashboard, see Book I, Chapter 2.)

Checking events for a specific date

Sometimes you might need to know whether you have any events scheduled on a certain date. To check a specific date, choose View⇨Go to Date or double-click the date in one of the calendar views.

The Month view can show you the events scheduled for a particular date, but the Day and Week views can show you the specific times of your events for that day.

Searching for an event

If you scheduled an event several days ago, you might forget the exact date of that event. To help you find a specific event, iCal lets you search for it by typing all or part of the information stored in that event — for example, the event name, the attendee names, or any notes you stored about the event.

To search for an event, follow these steps:

1. **Click the Spotlight text box in the upper-right corner of the iCal window.**

2. **Type as much text as you can remember about the event you want to find, such as an attendee's name or the location of the event.**

   The iCal application displays a list of events that match the text you type. The list appears below the calendar, as shown in Figure 2-11.

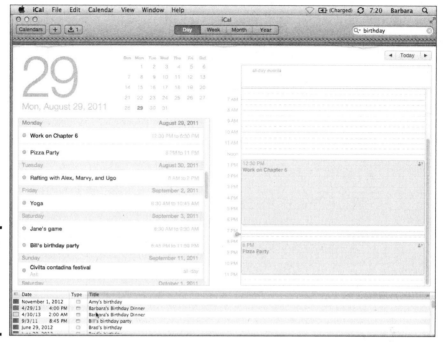

Figure 2-11:
Spotlight
can help
you search
and find
events.

3. **Double-click an event that Spotlight found.**

   Your chosen event appears.

4. **Click the Clear button in the Spotlight text box to remove the list
   of matching events from the bottom of the iCal window (or choose
   View⇨Hide Search Results).**

Organizing Tasks with Reminders

Although you can put an event on your calendar in iCal and then set an alert
so you don't forget it, not everything you need to remember is an event.
What you might think of as a to-do list (and remember as To Do in earlier
versions of iCal) is a function called Reminders in iCal. A typical Reminders
list contains goals or important tasks that you want to accomplish, usually
by a specific date or time. Reminders can help you stay focused on achieving
the goals that are most important to you so you don't waste time on tasks
that won't get you any closer to those goals.

Viewing and hiding Reminders

You can view the Reminders pane and then hide it to make more room for
viewing your events. To show Reminders, choose View⇨Show Reminders.
The Reminders pane appears on the right side of the iCal window.

To hide the Reminders pane from view, choose View⇨Hide Reminders. This tucks the Reminders pane out of sight once more. By default, iCal hides the Reminders pane.

Adding tasks to Reminders

When you add a task to Reminders, you must assign it to a calendar so that it appears color-coded, like an event. By color-coding your Reminder tasks, you can identify which tasks might be work related and which might be related to any other calendars you've created.

To add a task to Reminders, follow these steps:

1. **Choose View⇨Show Reminders.**

Skip this step if the Reminders pane is already visible.

2. **Double-click any blank space in the Reminders pane.**

A blank New Reminder task appears, color-coded to match the Home calendar, which is the default calendar.

3. **(Optional) Choose iCal⇨Preferences⇨General to change the default calendar.**

4. **Type a description of your task and press Return.**

Your new task appears in the Reminders pane.

Editing your Reminders tasks

Like Events, Reminders have an Edit dialog where you modify the details of your task. To modify the details of your Reminders task, follow these steps:

1. **Double-click a task in the Reminders pane or click a task in Reminders and choose Edit⇨Edit Reminder.**

An Edit dialog appears, as shown in Figure 2-12.

2. **To assign a priority to your task, click None next to Priority to open the pop-up menu from which you can choose None, Low, Medium, or High.**

You can also assign a priority by clicking the priority button to the right of your task; it's the circle with three bars in it. The number of high-lighted bars indicates the priority you assigned: one bar has low priority, two bars mean medium priority, and three bars mean high priority. This indicator shows you the priority of your tasks at a glance.

3. **Select the Due Date check box.**

When you select the Due Date check box, a date appears so you can type a month, day, and year for the due date.

4. **To activate an alert that reminds you of your task, click None next to Alert to open the pop-up menu.**

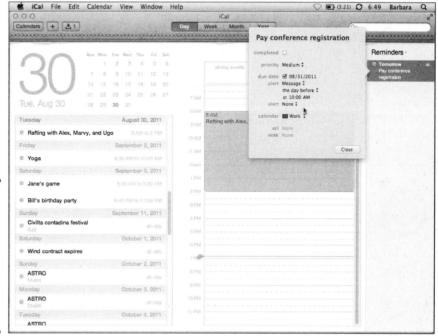

Figure 2-12:
Use the
Reminders
Editor pane
to assign
priority, due
dates, and
alerts for
your task.

Note: You have to have a Due Date in order to activate an alert.

You can choose from the following options:

- *None:* Removes any alerts you've already set for the event.
- *Message:* Displays a message on the screen to alert you of an event.
- *Message with Sound:* Displays a message onscreen and plays a sound to alert you of an event.
- *Email:* Sends an e-mail message to you.
- *Open File:* Loads and displays a file, such as a report that you can review for an upcoming meeting.
- *Run Script:* Runs an AppleScript file that can control your Mac.

5. **Click the day and time pop-up menus to define when you want the alert to trigger, such as the same day or days before.**

6:00 a.m. and 15 days are the defaults. Click the hour or number of days to change the time or number of days to what you want. The hour or number is highlighted, as shown in Figure 2-13.

Choose On Date to type in both a date and specific time for the alert.

6. **Click Close.**

Figure 2-13:
Change
the time or
day of your
Reminder.

You can establish when Reminders are visible and when they are removed by going to iCal⇨Preferences⇨Advanced.

Sorting your Reminders

You may add Reminders as they come to mind, but at some point, you may want to see them in a particular order, perhaps by priority level or by due date. Click the triangle to the right of the Reminders title to open the Sort pop-up menu (shown in Figure 2-14).

You can also click and drag Reminders in the list to manually change the order of your Reminders.

Figure 2-14:
Sort your
Reminders
as you
prefer.

Completing and deleting Reminders

Completing tasks can give you a sense of accomplishment. Rather than delete a completed task, you can mark it completed. To mark a task completed, select the check box that appears to the left of a task in the Reminders pane.

When, eventually, you want to delete a task to avoid cluttering the Reminders pane, click the task and choose Edit⇨Delete. If you delete a task accidentally, you can retrieve it by pressing ⌘+Z or by choosing Edit⇨Undo.

Subscribing to Online Calendars

The iCal application allows you to subscribe to online calendars, such as a calendar of holidays, sports team schedules, bridge tournaments, or new DVD releases. Calendars you subscribe to appear under the Subscriptions category in the Calendars pop-up list. Events that appear in these calendars are added, deleted, and modified by whoever maintains the online calendar.

To subscribe to an online calendar:

✦ Choose Calendar➪Subscribe to open the URL dialog, type the Internet URL for the calendar you want to subscribe to, such as the URL for a U.S. holidays online calendar (shown in Figure 2-15), and then click Subscribe. The name of your new online calendar appears in the Calendars column, and the online calendar's events appear in your iCal calendar window.

✦ Choose iCal➪Preferences to open the iCal Preferences window, click the Accounts tab, and then add an online calendar account, as described in the next section.

Figure 2-15:
Type the
URL to
subscribe
to an online
calendar.

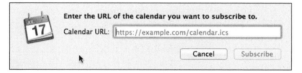

Enter the URL of the calendar you want to subscribe to.

Calendar URL: https://example.com/calendar.ics

Cancel   Subscribe

Two websites you can visit to find hundreds of useful (or just plain fun) online calendars to subscribe to are

✦ Apple iCal Calendars (www.apple.com/downloads/macosx/ calendars)

✦ iCalShare (www.icalshare.com)

Adding an Online Calendar Account

You can add *calendar accounts*, typically known as CalDAV or Exchange accounts, which can display one or more calendars you use at your workplace or a calendar you created and use with your Google or Yahoo! e-mail account. Events that you create or change at work with your company's calendar application, or events you create or change by using your Google or Yahoo! account, are added automatically to your iCal calendar, and vice versa.

1. Choose iCal⇨Preferences to open the iCal preferences window and then click the Accounts tab to open the Accounts preferences window, as shown in Figure 2-16.

2. Click the plus sign button in the lower-left corner to open the Add an Account dialog, as shown in Figure 2-17.

3. Leave the Account Type pop-up menu set to Automatic, type your online account e-mail address and password into the appropriate fields, and then click Create.

   iCal determines and configures your online calendar's account settings, and the name of your online calendar appears in the Calendars column; your online calendar's events appear in your iCal calendar window.

Figure 2-16: Accounts preferences is where you add and delete online calendar accounts.

Figure 2-17: The Add an Account dialog prompts for your online calendar account information.

4. **After the account is set up, select the account in the Accounts list.**

5. **Choose an interval next to Refresh Calendars.**

   This is the interval at which iCal will retrieve information from the account you added.

If iCal is unable to configure your online calendar account, click the Account Type pop-up menu (refer to Figure 2-17), choose CalDAV, Exchange, Google, or Yahoo!, fill the necessary fields, and then click Create.

Managing iCal Files

The iCal application stores files in a special file format called iCalendar (which uses the `.ics` filename extension). Because the iCalendar file format is a standard for storing calendar information, you can share your calendar files with any application that recognizes the iCalendar format, including Microsoft Outlook.

Importing iCal data

If you store calendar information in another application, you can export that data as an iCal file or a vCal file, and then import that file into iCal. If you're using Microsoft Entourage, you can save your Entourage calendar information as a separate file. Apple has yet to release an update for Outlook.

After you save calendar data from another application, you can import that file into iCal by following these steps:

1. **Choose File⇨Import and choose Import or Import from Entourage.**

   If you choose Import from Entourage, iCal scans your Mac's hard drive for your existing Entourage calendar data and imports those calendar events into iCal, and you can skip the remaining steps.

2. **Click the drive and/or folder that contains the file you want to import.**

3. **Click the file you want to import and then click Import.**

   iCal imports your chosen calendar file's data into iCal.

Exporting iCal data

To share your calendars with other applications (even those running on other operating systems, such as Windows or Linux), you need to export your iCal file by following these steps:

1. **Choose File⇨Export⇨Export.**

   A dialog appears, giving you a chance to choose a filename and location to store your iCal data, as shown in Figure 2-18.

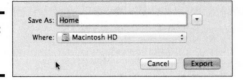

Figure 2-18:
Export your
calendars.

2. **Click the Save As text box and type a name for your file.**

3. **Choose the location to store your file from the Where pop-up menu.**

4. **Click Export.**

Sharing your calendars

You can print your calendar and hand it out to people, but an easier way is
to give others access to your calendar online. Your calendar will be a read-
only file; the people who have access can view your calendar but they can't
change it. To share your calendar, follow these steps:

1. **Click the Calendar button to open the pop-up menu that shows
   your calendars.**

2. **Click the calendar you want to share.**

3. **Choose Calendar⇨Publish.**

   A dialog opens, as shown in Figure 2-19.

4. **Type a name for your calendar that will help those who have access
   understand what the calendar represents.**

   This name is only for the shared calendar; it doesn't change the name
   of the calendar on iCal.

5. **Click the Publish On pop-up menu to choose iCloud or A Private Server.**

   If you choose A Private Server, type in the web address of the server
   along with your login and password.

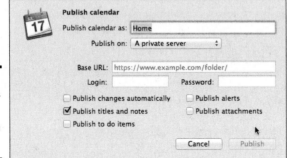

Figure 2-19:
Publish your
calendar to
share it with
others.

6. **Select the options you want from the check boxes at the bottom of the dialog, such as Publish Titles and Notes or Publish To Do Items.**

7. **Click Publish.**

   A dialog opens, confirming that your calendar has been published, as shown in Figure 2-20.

8. **Click OK.**

Figure 2-20:
A dialog
confirms
that your
calendar is
published.

Backing up iCal data and restoring a backup file

Because iCal can store all your upcoming events (appointments, meetings, and so on), disaster could strike if your hard drive fails and wipes out your iCal data. For that reason, you should always keep a backup copy of your iCal data. To do so, follow these steps:

1. **Choose File⇨Export⇨iCal Archive.**

   The Save dialog appears.

2. **Click the Save As text box and type a descriptive name for your iCal backup file.**

3. **Choose the location for storing your file from the Where pop-up menu.**

4. **Click Save.**

It's a good idea to save your iCal backup file on a separate drive, such as an external hard drive. That way if your Mac hard drive fails, you won't lose both your original iCal data and your backup file at the same time. (For more details on backing up files, see Book III, Chapter 1.)

To retrieve your schedule from a backup file that you created earlier, choose File⇨Import⇨Import. In the Open dialog that appears, click the drive and folder where you saved your backup iCal file. Then click Import. iCal imports the backed-up file; any changes you made since the last backup will be lost.

Printing an iCal file

Even if you have a laptop, you can't always have your computer with you, so you may want to print your calendar in the Day, Week, or Month view. To print a calendar, follow these steps:

1. **Choose File➪Print.**

   A Print dialog appears, as shown in Figure 2-21.

2. **Click the View pop-up menu and choose Day, Week, Month, or List, which shows a list of your events and reminders.**

3. **(Optional) Change any other settings, such as the paper size, time range, or calendars, and select the options you want.**

4. **Click Continue.**

   Another Print dialog appears.

5. **Click the Printer pop-up menu, choose a printer, and then click Print.**

Syncing with other devices

You can synchronize your iCal calendars with your iPhone or iPod when you connect it to your Mac and open iTunes. Follow these steps:

1. **Connect your iPhone, iPad, or iPod to your Mac with a USB cable, or sign in to the same Wi-Fi network from both your Mac and the iOS device to sync wirelessly.**

2. **Click the Info tab and choose Sync iCal Calendars.**

3. **Choose to synchronize all your calendars or just selected ones.**

4. **Click Apply.**

   Your iCal calendars transfer or update automatically on your iPhone, iPad, or iPod.

If you have an iCloud account, you can keep your iOS devices, Mac, and even Windows computers all synchronized automatically.

Figure 2-21:
The Print dialog shows you how your calendar will appear on paper.

Chapter 3: Building Websites with iWeb

In This Chapter

✔ **Understanding the parts of a web page**

✔ **Creating websites**

✔ **Customizing web pages**

✔ **Understanding web host services**

✔ **Publishing your website**

*I*f you visit the Internet by using a web browser, you've probably seen a website. For a Fortune 500 corporation or your Aunt Minnie, a *website* is an electronic presence that lets people reach a huge audience. There's a reason it's called the World Wide Web. Large-scale websites have all but replaced things like catalogs, newspapers, magazines, and annual reports, and small-scale websites have put the bowling-league newsletter and the holiday roundup out of business. Like many people, we're thrilled about Internet publishing from an environmental standpoint: less paper, less ink, less petroleum to move that paper and ink from one side of the country to the other. The only downside we can think of is the distraction that all these easily accessible websites create.

You may already have your own website or perhaps it's an idea you ponder. If you're a small-business owner, a website is a necessity to growing your business. If you want a creative outlet, a website is a fine place to show off your photography skills, your writing talent, or even your child's athletic ability. Whatever your motivation for creating a website, iWeb, the website-creation application that came with your Mac, makes it easy to do.

In this chapter, we show you how to use iWeb to create your own website. We begin by explaining the parts of a website, and then go into the nitty-gritty of using iWeb to create a spectacular website. In the last section of the chapter, we explain hosting services and how to *post* your website, which means moving your web pages from your Mac to the World Wide Web.

iWeb is not included in iLife '11 and isn't shipped with new Macs. You have iWeb if you have a copy of iLife '09.

The Parts of a Web Page

A website comprises web pages. Think of a web page as an endless sheet of paper that you can stretch in all directions to make it as large or as small as you want. On this sheet, you can position text, pictures, graphics, movies, songs, and even applications for others to access. To help guide people around your website, you add navigational aids called *hyperlinks,* also commonly called *links.* Clicking a link opens another section on the same web page, a different web page within the same website, or a web page on another website. Figure 3-1 shows the typical parts of a web page.

Content

The information you put on your website is called *content.* Text is the written word, which can be things like news stories, blogs, or step-by-step instructions for how to build an electric car. With today's fast Internet connections and speedy computer processors, more often than not, text is accompanied by graphics, photos, and video that *show* the inauguration of the new library, the bakery the blog raves about, or the car-building process.

Text

To make headlines stand out or make longer passages easier on your readers' eyes, you can change the fonts and font sizes, or display text in different colors and styles, such as bold and italic. Some web pages might contain lots of text, such as a news site like The New York Times (`www.nytimes.com`), whereas others might contain a minimal amount of text, such as a website displaying photographs with text simply citing the photograph's name or topic.

Graphics and media

As content, graphics can serve a purely decorative function, such as a company logo displayed in the corner of the web page, or graphics can provide information. For example, the lineup of the golf league tournament combines photos of the players and a bar graph showing scores. Graphics aren't limited to charts and graphs. Decorative text, saved as a graphic image, gives you a design option that ordinary text can't produce.

Both graphics and text can function as hyperlinks. Graphic hyperlinks offer an added measure of security — they're impossible to find with a search engine — so if you display your e-mail address as a graphic image, rather than as text, hackers can't scan the address and use it to send you junk e-mail or spam.

Audio, video, movies, and photos you add to your web page are referred to as *media.*

Navigation

Figure 3-1:
A web page
consists
of text,
graphics,
links, and
other media,
such as
video or
maps.

Hyperlink

Text

Widgets

A *widget* places content from somewhere else on the Internet onto your web-site. Common widgets are Google maps, countdown tickers, and RSS feeds. (RSS stands for Really Simple Syndication, which we explain a little later on in this chapter in the "Adding widgets" section.)

HTML

Content is what you see on a website, whereas HTML (*HyperText Markup Language*) is the unseen part; it's the motor that makes your website run. When online publishing first entered the mainstream, you had to master HTML, the markup language used to tell the computer how to create web pages. Although HTML is relatively simple, you don't have to master it to create a website. Many online service providers, such as Google and WordPress, have created applications that make creating your website as easy as click-and-drag. iWeb also simplifies this task by creating HTML code for you "behind the scenes." All you have to do is arrange objects — text, graphics, media, and widgets — on your web pages. You then upload the pages of your website to a server through an Internet host.

Creating a Website with iWeb

Every website contains one or more web pages. To design a website, you need to decide the overall appearance you want to use for your website and each web page, the purpose for each web page, and how many web pages you need. You can add or delete pages whenever you want — and we recommend that you do. Your website should be a dynamic creature, one that evolves over time by providing new, up-to-date information about the topic at hand.

The number of web pages you need can vary, depending on your website's purpose. If you're putting together an online store to sell food, books, or pet supplies, you might need dozens or even hundreds of separate web pages to display all your products. If you want a website for distant family members to see what's going on, you might only need two or three web pages. After you know (approximately) how many web pages you need, and what you want each web page to offer, the next step is to pick a theme, which defines the overall appearance of each web page, such as a background color or decorative graphic along the borders.

Picking a theme

Although you *could* create a web page starting with a blank page, it's far easier to create a website by modifying templates. With iWeb, you can choose from a variety of predesigned web page templates. Each theme applies a color scheme, font family, and style to several types of web pages, such as an About Me page, where you talk about yourself or the focus of the website; Photos, which has preset frames for placing photos; and Blog which is where you publish your blog posts. There are seven types of pages in all, plus a blank page that you can customize with text, graphics, and media as you want, while maintaining the color scheme and style of the theme.

A *theme* provides a consistent appearance for every web page that your website includes. You can have more than one theme within the same website. One part of your website might list products for sale, so you could use one theme for product listings. Another part of your website might list company news so those web pages may use a different theme. Usually, it's a good idea to use the same theme throughout with different types of web page layouts because themes help visually organize similar information.

To pick a theme or themes for your website, follow these steps:

1. **Click the iWeb icon from the Launchpad or in the Dock (or double-click the iWeb icon in the Applications folder).**

If this is the first time you open iWeb, a dialog appears, listing different themes in the Theme list on the left and displaying the appearance of specific types of web pages on the right, as shown in Figure 3-2.

If you already created a website and want to create a new one, choose iWeb⇨File⇨New Site.

2. **Click a theme in the Theme list.**

Each time you click a different theme, the web pages in the right pane show you how that new theme displays each type of web page — Welcome page, About Me page, Photos page, whatever.

If you click the pop-up menu in the upper-left corner of the iWeb dialog, you can choose to see all themes or only those used with specific versions of iWeb, such as version 3.0, 2.0, 1.1, or 1.0.

3. **Click one of the following types of web pages in the right pane:**

- *Welcome:* Introduces your website. The Welcome page is typically the first web page visitors see when they visit a specific site, such as www.dummies.com.

- *About Me:* Describes yourself or your company.

Figure 3-2:
Each iWeb theme displays web pages differently.

- *Photos:* Displays digital pictures, such as those stored in iPhoto, for everyone to see.

- *My Albums:* Displays groups of different photo categories for people to browse.

- *Movie:* Displays a digital video that people can watch directly on your web page.

- *Blog:* Provides space for typing your thoughts about different topics.

- *Podcast:* Displays lists of audio and/or video recordings (podcasts) that others can hear and/or watch directly on your web page.

- *Blank:* Provides a web page that incorporates a specific theme so you can add anything you want to it.

4. **Click Choose.**

   The web page that appears in the iWeb window is decked out in your chosen theme, as shown in Figure 3-3. You see anonymous photos and gibberish text. These are text and media *placeholders*, which you replace with your own text, graphics, and media. We explain that process in the "Customizing Your Web Pages" section, later in this chapter.

When you drag the pointer over a section of the page and lift your finger, highlighted text appears that suggests what you should write. (See Figure 3-3.)

Figure 3-3:
A Welcome page in the iWeb window with highlighted suggestion on the title.

Adding new pages

Because websites typically contain more than one web page, you need to add more web pages to your website. To add a web page, follow these steps:

1. **Click the Add Page icon at the bottom of the iWeb window or choose File⇨New Page (or press ⌘+N).**

   The list of available web page templates appears with your current theme highlighted (refer to Figure 3-2).

2. **Select the type of new page you want to add, such as Podcast or My Albums, and then click Choose.**

   Your new web page appears in the iWeb window.

Double-clicking the icon of the type of page you want to use opens it, shortening the "click page, click Choose" process.

Deleting web pages

If you find that you have more web pages than you need or you get carried away with your design and just want to start over, you can delete a web page. To delete a web page, follow these steps:

1. **Click the web page that you want to delete in the sidebar of the iWeb window.**

2. **Choose Edit⇨Delete Page.**

   Your chosen web page disappears, along with any text or media you stored on that web page.

If you accidentally delete a web page, press ⌘+Z or choose Edit⇨Undo to retrieve the deleted web page.

Customizing Your Web Pages

After you set up the skeleton of your website, you want to flesh it out with your own text, photos, graphics, podcasts, and widgets. Figure 3-4 shows an example of a website skeleton. We used the blank template for the last two pages at the end: Where's the Farm and Keep in touch. Notice that on each web page, links to each page appear under the title; the active page is highlighted. The next step is to go through each of the pages and customize them. With the exception of the Blank web page template, every iWeb template displays a web page filled with placeholder text and graphics. You replace the placeholder stuff with your own information.

Figure 3-4:
The pages
you create
appear in
the sidebar
to the left
of the iWeb
window.

Replacing placeholder text

Placeholder text gives you an idea of what the text might look like on the web page. To change placeholder text, follow these steps:

1. **In the sidebar of the iWeb window, click the web page that you want to modify.**

   Your chosen web page appears in the right pane of the iWeb window.

2. **Double-click the text you want to edit or replace.**

   The text includes titles, subtitles, even the name of the web page itself. Your chosen text appears highlighted.

3. **Type new text or press the arrow and Delete keys to edit the existing text.**

By double-clicking the web page's title — for example "About Me" — you can change that too. You should also change the title of the web page in the sidebar so that the link at the top of each web page matches the title. To do that, double-click the title in the sidebar. The words are highlighted. Type in the new title. The changes appear in the links under the title too. Refer to Figure 3-4, where we changed "About Me" to "About Us."

Replacing placeholder media

Placeholder media gives you some idea how a photo or video would work in a particular area of your page. Here we explain how to replace placeholder media with media of your own; later on in the chapter, we go through some of the settings available for photos, movies, and audio. Follow these steps:

1. **In the sidebar of the iWeb window, click the web page you want to modify.**

    Your chosen web page appears in the right pane of the iWeb window.

2. **If the Media Browser isn't open, click the Show Media button in the toolbar at the bottom of the window or choose View⇨Show Media.**

    The Media Browser appears.

3. **Click the button for the type of media you want to add: Audio, Photos, or Movies.**

    The chosen library appears in the Media Browser.

    If you choose events or faces rather than photos, you see one of the photos of that event or person. Double-click the photo you see to open a second level of the browser that shows the photos in that group, and then click and drag a single photo over the placeholder photo. Dragging the whole event creates an album on the web page.

4. **Click and drag the media you want to use to the placeholder media image you want to replace, as shown in Figure 3-5.**

    Playback controls appear at the bottom of audio and video files. A slide-show button appears automatically when a photo album is placed.

5. **Release the mouse button.**

    Your media now appears on your web page.

6. **Choose View⇨Hide Media to close the Media Browser, or click the Hide Media button (it turns into the Show Media button).**

To insert media that doesn't appear in the Media Browser, choose Insert⇨ Choose to open a file-browsing dialog, navigate to the file you want, click it, and then click the Insert button (or just double-click the file to insert it).

Dragging media to an area of the web page template that has no placeholder still places the media all the same. If you choose to add media outside of placeholders, however, pay attention to overlapping objects, which we talk about later in this chapter.

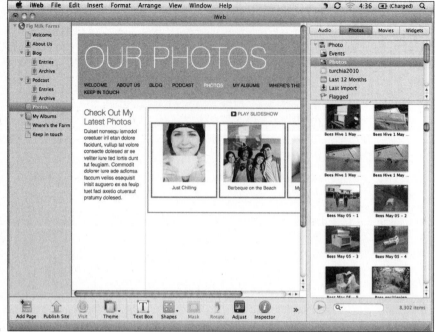

Figure 3-5: The Media Browser displays all your iPhoto photos; click the photo you want to add and drag it over the placeholder photo.

Adding widgets

As we mention at the beginning of the chapter, widgets are objects that create hyperlinks to another site, for example Google Maps or YouTube. You may want to add a widget to your web page; for example, a Google map that shows your store location or a countdown for an event that you'll be hosting. You can choose to add any or all of the widgets to your website. To add a widget to a web page, follow these steps:

1. **Click the Show Media icon at the bottom of the iWeb window.**

   The Media Browser appears.

2. **Click the Widgets tab.**

   A list of widgets appears in the Media Browser, as shown in Figure 3-6.

3. **Click and drag a widget from the Media Browser to your web page.**

4. **Release the mouse button.**

   Your chosen widget appears on your web page. You might need to move or resize the widget or specify some information as outlined in the following list of widgets.

5. **Choose View⇨Hide Media to close the Media Browser or click the Hide Media icon.**

Figure 3-6:
iWeb provides widgets to automatically create hyperlinks to other websites.

iWeb's widgets are

+ **YouTube:** Adds a YouTube video to your website. Drag this widget to the desired web page while you're connected to the Internet. Type in the URL for the video you want, or copy and paste it from YouTube. You can also select to show related videos when the video finishes playing.

+ **Google Maps:** Adds a Google Map to your website. You must have an active Internet connection to add a map. When you drag the Google Maps widget to the web page, a window opens where you type in the address you want the map to show. Select the other options, such as zoom controls and a search bar, as you want.

+ **Google AdSense:** You must have a Google AdSense account to actively use this widget; if you don't have a Google AdSense account, the first time you drag the widget to the web page, a dialog guides you through signing up. You may have up to three Google ads on a web page and place ads on any web page you want. You can decide on the position, size, and color of the ads. After your website is published, Google will place the ad content.

+ **FaceTime Photo:** After you drag the widget to your web page, click the camera icon and the photo is added to the page. You can choose to have the flash on or off.

✦ **FaceTime Movie:** To use this widget, drag it into place and then click the Camera icon. The video begins recording after a three-second count-down. Click Stop to end recording. You can move and resize the movie as you would any other object.

✦ **Countdown:** Sets up a timer that displays a countdown to a specific event. Just enter the date and time of the event and the timer begins its count-down. Choose a style for the timer by clicking the arrow next to the style shown. Specify the units to display by dragging the end brackets to high-light the units you want, such as years and days or hours and minutes.

✦ **RSS Feed:** Really Simple Syndication feeds provide up-to-date content from other websites. After you drag the RSS Feed widget to the desired web page, you can control the settings: layout, number of entries, dis-play, article length, and photo size and orientation.

If you want visitors to have the option to subscribe to an RSS Feed from your website, say to receive automatic updates of your blog or podcast, activate the subscribe buttons that appear on the Blog and Podcast web page templates.

✦ **HTML Snippet:** Lets you post content and widgets from other websites. Type in the HTML code from the other website or copy and paste it into the widget. It's best to be connected to the Internet when you do this so you can see how the live connection will appear on your website when it's loaded.

If at any time you want to delete a widget, select it and press the Delete key. The widget is removed the next time you *publish* (upload) your website.

Modifying a Template

Making an iWeb page your own by replacing placeholder text and media certainly makes creating web pages easy, but the templates don't always have the text and media positioned exactly where you want them. To further customize your web pages, here we show you how to add, move, resize, and delete, the text and graphics on your web pages.

Working with existing objects

Think of an *object* as the box for the data that's inside. Just like a box, you can make the object bigger or smaller to accommodate the text, media, or graph-ics that it holds. You can also move the object around and stack objects one on top of the other to best display the information on your web pages.

Moving an object

To move an object to another part of a web page, follow these steps:

1. **Move the pointer over the text or media object you want to move.**

2. **Click and drag the object to a new location.**

3. **Release the mouse button.**

The object stays put in its new position.

To move an object from one page to the next, cut and paste the object from the original page to a different page.

Resizing an object

To resize a text or media object to make it bigger or smaller, follow these steps:

1. **Select the object you want to resize.**

Handles appear around your chosen object, as shown in Figure 3-7.

2. **Move the pointer over a handle until the pointer turns into a two-way-pointing arrow; then click and drag the handle to change the size of your object.**

3. **Release the mouse button when you're happy with the new size of the text or media object.**

Selection handles

Figure 3-7:
Handles appear when you select an object.

Rearranging an object

If you move or resize an object, it might cover another object, as shown in Figure 3-8. To fix this problem, you have to rearrange the objects until they are no longer overlapping or they overlap in a useful or aesthetically pleasing manner.

To rearrange which object appears on top of another, follow these steps:

1. **Select the object that you want to place over (or under) another object.**

   Handles appear around your selected object.

2. **Choose one of the following:**

   - *Arrange⇨Bring Forward:* Moves the selected object over one object that might be overlapping it. If multiple objects cover your selected object, you might not see any difference.

   - *Arrange⇨Bring to Front:* Moves the selected object on top of all overlapping objects.

   - *Arrange⇨Send Backward:* Moves the selected object underneath one object that it may be covering.

   - *Arrange⇨Send to Back:* Moves the selected object underneath all other overlapping objects.

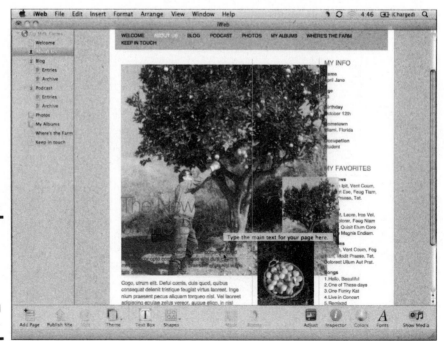

Figure 3-8:
If objects overlap, rearrange them to avoid hiding information.

Deleting an object

To delete one or more objects, follow these steps:

1. **Click the object you want to delete.**

   To select multiple objects, hold down the Shift or ⌘ key and click each object you want to delete.

2. **Press Delete or choose Edit➪Delete.**

If you delete an object by mistake, press ⌘+Z or choose Edit➪Undo.

Working with text

Text always appears inside a text box (unless the text is saved as a graphic element) — which you can move and resize on a web page. If you create a web page from a template, it has text boxes that you fill with your own text. You can edit the text in a text box and change the format by font, size, and style. If you create a blank web page, or need an additional text box, you have to create the needed text box (which we explain at the end of this section) or resize an existing one, using the steps previously outlined for resizing objects.

If you have existing objects on the web page, the text box might appear over an existing object. If you have a hard time seeing your text, press ⌘+A.

Formatting text

After you type text inside a text box, you can format it by following these steps:

1. **Double-click the text box that contains the text you want to modify.**

2. **Select the text you want to modify; alternatively, press ⌘+A (or choose Edit➪Select All) to select all the text in the text box.**

3. **Click the Font icon in the toolbar.**

   A font chooser window opens, as shown in Figure 3-9.

4. **Select the font family, typeface style, and size you want from the Family, Typeface, and Size lists, respectively.**

Figure 3-9: Clicking the Font icon in the toolbar displays different ways to format text.

Creating a text hyperlink

Besides making text look pretty inside a text box, you may also want to turn text into a *hyperlink* — the highlighted or underlined link that can jump a reader to another web page or website. To create a hyperlink, follow these steps:

1. **Double-click the text box that contains the text you want to turn into a hyperlink.**

2. **Select the text you want to turn into a hyperlink.**

3. **Choose Insert⇨Hyperlink to open the Hyperlink submenu, and then select one of the following to display a Link pane similar to the one shown in Figure 3-10:**

- *Webpage:* Links to a specific website, such as `www.dummies.com`.

- *Email Message:* Links to an e-mail address, such as `JollyOld SaintNick@gmail.com`.

- *File:* Links to a file, such as a PDF or text file, which others can download from your web page.

Figure 3-10: The Link pane lets you customize your hyperlink.

4. **Choose the options in the Link pane.**

   The options displayed in the Link pane will look different, depending on the option you choose in Step 4. For example, if you choose Webpage, you need to type the website address to link to, such as **http://www. dummies.com**. If you choose Email Message, you need to type the e-mail address, such as **babsboyd@me.com**.

5. **Click the Close button of the Link pane.**

Selecting the Make Hyperlinks Active check box in the Link Inspector lets you test your hyperlinks while you are designing your website. After you create the hyperlink, click it to make sure that it connects to the link you wanted.

Creating a text box

If you are working with a blank template or need an additional text box on an existing template, follow these steps to add a text box:

1. **Click the Text Box icon at the bottom of the iWeb window or choose Insert⇨Text Box.**

   A blinking cursor appears in the middle of your web page.

2. **Type your text.**

   Follow the previous steps to change the font and style or create a hyperlink.

3. **Click anywhere on the web page away from your newly created text box.**

4. **Click your new text box to display resizing handles.**

5. **Click and drag to move and/or resize the text box.**

If you have an existing text box that already has the fonts and styles that you want to use, it's easier to duplicate that text box and replace the text. To create a duplicate, click the existing text box, and then hold the Option key and drag out of it until a duplicate appears, or select the existing text box and choose Edit⇨Duplicate.

Working with graphics and media

You can add and place digital photographs, simple graphic shapes like arrows, or even videos anywhere on a web page — in or out of a placeholder.

Graphics and media can take time to transfer over the Internet, so the more graphics you place on a web page — and the larger the media files you use — the longer the web page takes to load and display in someone's web browser. Don't be afraid to use both graphics and media, but a good rule of thumb is to keep the size of each media file under 10MB.

Editing photos

When you click a photo that's been inserted in a placeholder, you have several editing options: You can mask the photo, rotate it, or adjust it.

Masking is a way of cropping photos without actually changing the image. In effect, you hide (*mask*) the portions of the image that you don't want to use. Follow these steps to mask an image:

1. **Click the image you want to mask.**

2. **Click the Mask button in the toolbar at the bottom of the window.**

   A rectangular mask appears over the image with a resizable area in the middle.

3. **Do one or more of the following:**
   - Drag the handles on the window to show the part of the image you want to keep.
   - Click the image so that a hand-shaped pointer appears; drag the image until the part you want is in the viewable area.
   - Zoom in or out on the image back, dragging the slider under the image to the left or right.

4. **To unmask an image, click the image and then click Unmask in the toolbar.**

5. **To mask with a shape other than a rectangle, click the image, and then choose Format⇨Mask with Shape⇨*<choose desired shape>*.**

   If the shapes are dimmed, unmask the image and repeat Step 5.

   Repeat Step 3 to edit the mask on the image.

In addition to using a mask, you can rotate and adjust an image:

✦ **To rotate an image,** click the image and then click the Rotate icon in the toolbar.

✦ **To adjust an image,** click an image and then click the Adjust icon in the toolbar. You can adjust the brightness, contrast, saturation, sharpness, and exposure levels by dragging the sliders to the left and right. If you want to return to the original image, click Reset Image.

Editing audio and movies

You can change a few settings for the audio and video you place on your web pages by doing the following:

1. **Click the media you want to edit.**

2. **Click the Inspector icon in the bar at the bottom on the window.**

3. **Click the QuickTime Inspector button (the last one on the right of the Inspector pane).**

4. **Manage the following:**

   • *Start and Stop:* Drag the start and end points to where you want the audio or video to begin or end.

   • *Poster Frame:* For movies and video only, drag the slider to the frame that is displayed before the movie or video begins playing.

   • *Autoplay:* Select this option to have the audio or video begin playing as soon as a visitor opens the web page.

   • *Loop:* Select this option for the audio or video to play repeatedly rather than just once.

   • *Show Movie Controller:* Visitors can use the playback controls to watch the movie or listen to the audio. If you deselect both this check box and the Autoplay check box, visitors double-click the image to play the audio or video.

If you record your podcast by using GarageBand, you can send the file directly to iWeb. (See Book IV, Chapter 5 for more information.)

Adding graphic effects

The Graphic Inspector gives you the possibility of adding or changing borders around photos, videos, and widgets and changing the background, or fill, color, and opacity in text boxes. Even though iWeb's templates are designed and defined, you may have an element on one of your web pages that you want to stand out. To use the Graphic Inspector, follow these steps:

1. **Click the object you want to add a graphic effect to.**

2. **Click the Inspector icon in the bar at the bottom of the window.**

3. **Click the Graphic icon, the fifth one from the left, next to the Font icon.**

   The Graphic Inspector opens, as shown in Figure 3-11.

4. **Select the options you want from the various pull-down menus:**

   • *Fill:* Choose to fill in behind an image or in a text box. Choose the color, gradient style, and angle.

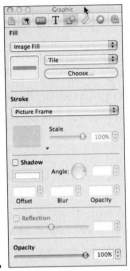

Figure 3-11:
The Graphic
Inspector
gives you
options for
adding
borders and
back-
grounds to
your text
and media.

- *Stroke:* Choose Line or Picture Frame, and then select the type of border you want by clicking the triangle on the lower-right corner, which opens a selection of border options.
- *Shadow:* Adds a shadow effect to the text box or image you have selected. You can choose the color, angle, offset, blur, and opacity.
- *Reflection:* Works with photos and videos, adding a mirror image of the bottom third of the image.
- *Opacity:* Set the percentage of opacity for the selected image or for the background fill in a text box.

Changing the web page's theme

You might modify a web page with text and graphics and suddenly realize that you don't like the theme you chose. To change a web page's theme while leaving your content (text and graphics you added) unchanged, follow these steps:

1. **In the sidebar of the iWeb window, click the web page you want to modify.**

   Your chosen web page appears in the right pane of the iWeb window.

2. **Click the Theme icon (fourth from left) that appears at the bottom of the iWeb window.**

   A pop-up menu of themes appears, as shown in Figure 3-12.

3. **Click a new theme.**

   Your web page changes to match your chosen theme.

Figure 3-12:
Choose a
new theme
by clicking
the Theme
icon.

Publishing Your Web Pages

After you create one or more web pages, they're trapped on your computer until you upload them to the Internet where others can visit your web pages with their web browser. To publish your web pages on the Internet, you typically need to transfer your web page files to a website-hosting service. This transfer is called *uploading*. If you're wondering what kind of hosting service you need, the following sections offer a quick rundown.

Types of website hosts

A website host is a bunch of computers with lots of humongous hard disks, called a *server,* connected to a really, really high-speed Internet connection (a T1 or T3 line). The main reason you need to store your web pages on a server is that the fast T1 or T3 line allows thousands of people to view your website simultaneously. A typical home Internet connection isn't fast enough to support the (potential hordes of) visitors who visit your website at the same time.

Some popular website-hosting options are

✦ Free advertiser-sponsored website hosts

✦ Free ISP (Internet service provider) website hosts

✦ Fee-based website hosts

Free advertiser-sponsored website hosts

Many companies offer free web hosting in exchange for displaying banner or pop-up ads all over your web pages. If someone wants to visit your website, he or she might have to wade through some advertisements first.

The main problem with these types of hosts is that you can't control what type of advertisements might appear on your website. If you create a website encouraging people to support the prevention of cruelty to animals, for instance, the website host might stick advertisements for fur coats or exotic animal foodstuffs all over your web pages, and you can do nothing about it. Talk about sending the wrong signal!

Another drawback of free advertiser-sponsored website hosts is that the specific website address is never anything as simple as www.joehutsko. com. Instead, free website hosts force you to use a website address that includes the website host name. So if you host your web pages on a free site called Tripod or Geocities, your website's address might look like this:

```
http://joehutsko.tripod.com
```

or this:

```
http://blogger.joehutsko.com
```

Unintuitive website addresses like these work just like the simpler, descriptive www.joehutsko.com, but they're hard to remember and even harder to type correctly. Telling someone to visit www.joe.com (or simply joe hutsko.com) is easy; telling someone to visit http://blogger.joe hutsko.com is clumsy to say or write.

By using a free web-hosting service, you can gain experience with designing and uploading your site. You can also see whether you have the stamina to maintain a website. Many people rush to create a website, furiously update it for the first week, and then gradually lose interest, eventually abandoning their site. You can use a free web-hosting service as a trial before spending money for a fee-based web-hosting service.

Not all free web-hosting services are equal. The amount of storage space and number of ads that appear on your web pages differs from one to the next, so compare these services until you find one that you like best.

Free ISP website hosts

When you pay for Internet service from an Internet Service Provider (ISP), your ISP might throw in free website hosting — not all ISPs offer free website hosting, some charge a fee, others don't offer it at all. Free ISP-provided website-hosting services don't put advertising on your website because the ISP figures you're already paying it for its service.

As a result, ISP website hosting gives you the benefits of experimenting with a free website without the drawbacks of unwanted advertisements. However, your website address might contain something convoluted and non-intuitive, such as `http://www.ispname.net/joehutsko`.

Websites hosted on free ISP websites are more often employed for personal use than for setting up online stores. Some ISPs might even restrict businesses from setting up sites because of the bandwidth problems that might occur if too many people visit the website every day.

Free website-hosting services often limit the amount of storage space you can use. The less storage space available, the fewer web pages, graphic images, and additional files (such as sound or video) you can put on your website.

Fee-based website hosts

If you want a website with no ads, more storage space, and a descriptive website address (called a *domain name*), you need to pay a fee-based website-hosting service.

Many advertiser-supported web hosts offer both a free and a subscription-based plan. These website-hosting services give you the option of experimenting with designing a website under the free plan with a lengthy site address and later transferring the site to a registered domain name (such as `www.joehutsko.com`) without having to change website-hosting companies.

The first step to using a fee-based website-hosting service is to compare prices and features. Prices vary from $1.99 per month to more than $19.99 per month, depending on what additional options you might want. (What one website-hosting service considers an option, another might throw in free as part of its basic package.) Some basic features to look for are

+ **Storage space:** The more storage space, the more web pages, pictures, videos, and animation you can post on your website. Typical storage space ranges from 10GB to 250GB or more.

+ **File transfer limitation:** Defines how much data can flow from your website between the hosting service's servers and the computers visitors use to visit your website. A high transfer rate might be necessary if you offer files for people to download, such as pictures or music files.

+ **Number of e-mail accounts:** Consider whether you need a few e-mail accounts for your family members or 50 accounts for your company.

+ **E-mail storage space:** The more storage space, the more messages all your e-mail accounts can hold. If you don't have enough e-mail storage space, you have to move them to your local disk or erase them to make room for new messages.

✦ **Domain name registration:** You need to register your particular web-site domain name so no one else can use it. Many web-hosting services include domain name registration. Otherwise, you have to register the domain name yourself.

✦ **Number of domain names:** The price might include just one domain name or several domain names.

After you pick a web-hosting service, you need to pick a domain name for your website. Many domain names are already taken (such as www.whitehouse.gov or www.dummies.com). After you decide on a descriptive domain name, you need to register it either through your website-hosting service or through a separate domain name registration service.

To check whether a domain name is already taken, do a search on a site, such as Network Solutions (www.networksolutions.com).

Registration means picking a name that no one else is using, paying a one-time fee, and then paying periodic fees to maintain that domain name. If you don't continue paying to maintain your domain name, you lose it. Registration fees typically cost $5 to $25 per year, although some website-hosting services will pay this fee for you as long as you keep using their services.

After you pick a website-hosting service and register a domain name, you can always transfer your domain name (and all your web page files) to a different website-hosting service that offers lower rates or better service.

Publishing your web pages

After you pick a web-hosting service and establish your web address or register a domain, you're ready to *publish,* or *upload,* your web pages.

iWeb has FTP capability built in, which makes uploading easy. FTP (File Transfer Protocol) is the most common way to transfer web page files from your computer to a website server. Your web-hosting service provides the server address and username that are required for FTP uploads; the web-hosting service might also provide a password and other parameters, such as a special directory, or a special communications protocol the website server requires to copy your web pages to it. To upload your web pages, follow these steps:

1. **In the sidebar of the iWeb window, click the name of the site you want to upload.**

   The Site Publishing Settings window appears, as shown in Figure 3-13.

2. **Choose FTP Server in the Publish To pop-up menu.**

3. **(Optional) Type a site name and contact e-mail in the Site Name and Contact Email text boxes.**

4. **Type the FTP server settings provided by your website-hosting service.**

Figure 3-13:
Use the Site
Publishing
Settings to
choose how
to upload
your web
pages.

5. Type your website address in the Website URL text box.

6. (Optional) If you have a Facebook account, select Update My Facebook Profile When I Publish This Site.

7. Click the Publish Site icon in the toolbar at the bottom of the iWeb window.

If you use Apple's MobileMe service to host your website, it will be active only until June 2012. Choose a new web-hosting service before that date and publish your site to the new service as explained previously in this chapter.

Making changes to your uploaded web pages

A website is a dynamic creature, and you'll probably want to change your web pages to reflect changes in your business offerings or to show off pictures of your growing puppy. To upload revised Web pages, follow these steps:

1. In the sidebar of the iWeb window, select the web page you changed.

2. Click the Publish Site icon in the toolbar at the bottom of the iWeb window.

If you made changes to many web pages and would rather re-upload the entire website, choose File⇨Publish Entire Site.

Uploaded web pages are blue in the iWeb sidebar; red indicates web pages that haven't been uploaded.

Visiting your website

After you publish your website, you probably want to see it online to make sure that it looks just the way you want. You have two ways to do so:

✦ To go to the opening page of your website, click the Visit icon in the bottom toolbar and your website opens in Safari.

✦ To go to a specific page of your website, select, in the sidebar, the page you want to view by clicking it once. Then hold down the Option key and click the Visit button in the toolbar. The page you want opens in Safari.

Chapter 4: Creating Documents with Pages

In This Chapter

✔ Using document templates

✔ Choosing Word Processing or Page Layout

✔ Creating and formatting text

✔ Inserting pages and sections

✔ Using text boxes

✔ Working with photos

✔ Checking your spelling

✔ Printing a document

*P*ages is a combination word-processing and page-layout (sometimes called "desktop publishing") application that is part of Apple's iWork suite. In word-processing mode, you type, edit, and format text to produce documents such as letters, reports, and résumés, whereas in Page Layout mode, you arrange graphics and text boxes on a page to create newsletters, brochures, menus, flyers, and the like.

In this chapter, we take you through the basics of Pages. Whether you choose to work in word-processing or page-layout mode, the functions and features are the same, so the instructions we give here apply to both. First we introduce working with templates and then we explain formatting the document and the text within. We go through the procedures for inserting text boxes, photos, charts, and tables. At the end of the chapter, we show you how to print and share your document.

In Book V, Chapter 7, we present some of the iWork features that apply to all three applications in the suite, including Pages.

Pages is part of the iWork suite. Your Mac might have a trial version of Pages that lets you play with the application to see whether it meets your needs. If your Mac doesn't have the trial version of Pages already installed, you can download it free from Apple's website (www.apple.com/iwork) for 30 days. You can purchase and download Pages from the AppStore for $19.99 or you can purchase the iWork suite ($79) from the Apple online store or your local Apple Store or authorized reseller.

Working with Document Templates

To help you start writing, Pages supplies a variety of document templates. By choosing a document template, you just enter new text and customize the appearance of the template so you don't have to create everything from scratch.

Word Processing versus Page Layout

You can quickly and easily create colorful, interesting documents on your Mac, but choosing between Word Processing and Page Layout application templates can be confusing. In general, word processing is best suited for "continuous" documents, such as letters, reports, contracts (yawn), novels, and so on. Page layout, on the other hand, targets "page-centric" documents where you have to juggle different types of content (text, photos, tables, advertisements, for example), decide where to put the various contents relative to each other, and fit it all together nicely and neatly on the same proverbial page — think flyers, brochures, newsletters, magazines, and catalogs.

The main difference between Word Processing documents and Page Layout documents is that you type directly on a page in a Word Processing document. You can insert photos or tables if you want but they complement the text and aren't the main focus of the document. If (on the other hand) you want to type text on a Page Layout document, you have to create a text box first and place that text box somewhere on your page.

The advantage of typing text directly on a page, using a Word Processing template, is that you can keep typing and Pages will create new pages automatically while you type. The disadvantage of this approach is that it's harder to define exactly where the text will appear on the page.

The advantage of using text boxes with a Page Layout template is that you can move the text boxes anywhere on a page (or to a different page). The disadvantage of typing text in text boxes is that they can display only a limited amount of text. If you need to type a larger chunk of text, you might need to link text boxes so that when your text overflows one text box, it flows automatically into another one.

Another difference between Word Processing and Page Layout is that you must manually add (or delete) pages in a Page Layout template (by choosing the Insert⇨Pages or Edit⇨Delete Page commands). With a Word Processing template, Pages adds pages automatically while you type and deletes pages as necessary when you delete text.

Generally, if the document you have in mind is to contain mostly text (as with letters or reports), start with a Word Processing template. If you need a document that consists mostly of pictures, or want to create newsletters, magazine pages, or web pages, start with a Page Layout template.

Pages offers two types of templates: Word Processing and Page Layout. Word Processing templates are designed mostly for writing (relatively) plain and simple, with the emphasis on content. Page Layout templates are designed for mixing text and graphics when content and presentation have almost equal importance. (You can always add pictures to a Word Processing template or write in a text box on a Page Layout template.)

After you create a document by using a Word Processing (or Page Layout) template, you can't switch to a new template. If you want to use a different template, you have to create another document.

To choose a document template, follow these steps:

1. Click the Pages icon in the Dock or Launchpad (or choose File⇨ New on the menu bar if Pages is already running).

A dialog appears, displaying different templates you can choose, as shown in Figure 4-1.

2. Select a template category under the Word Processing or Page Layout headings in the listing on the left.

The templates for your selected category appear in the main pane of the dialog. Figure 4-1 shows the selection for Letters under the Word Processing heading.

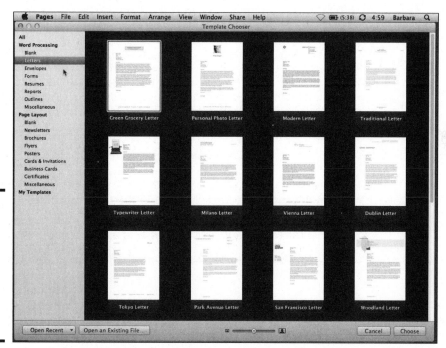

Figure 4-1: Pages provides various templates to help you create a document quickly.

3. **Select a template and then click the Choose button (or double-click the icon for the template you want to use).**

   Pages opens your chosen template as a new, untitled document.

4. **Choose File⇨Save.**

   A Save As dialog opens. Type a name for your document and choose the folder where you want to store it. Pages supports Versions, which keeps a running backup of your document each time you change it. (This is a new feature of OS X 10.7 Lion, which we explain in Book I, Chapter 4 and Book III, Chapter 1).

If you want to start with a blank document, click the Blank template category under the Word Processing or Page Layout heading.

Adding pages or sections to your document

Simple Word Processing documents, such as a letters, forms, or résumés have one style, which means that no matter how much text you type, pages are added and each page has the same layout.

Some templates in both Word Processing and Page Layout mode, however, contain more than one page or section style. For example, newsletter templates may have cover, text, photo, and mailer pages; report templates may have cover, table of contents, text, and bibliography sections; and proposal templates may have table of contents, executive summary, budget, and schedule sections.

In the Template Chooser, scroll over the template image to see thumbnails of the pages or sections available for that template. Use the slider at the bottom of the chooser to zoom — in to enlarge the thumbnail images, out to reduce the amount of screen space they occupy. The advantage of zooming in is that you see larger thumbnails but fewer at once; zooming out lets you see more thumbnails, but they are smaller.

To add different pages or sections to your document, follow these steps:

1. **Place the cursor at the beginning of the page or section that you want the additional page or section to follow.**

2. **In a Word Processing document, click the Sections button in the toolbar at the top; in a Page Layout document, click the Pages button.**

   A list of the types of sections or pages available for your template drops down, as shown in Figure 4-2.

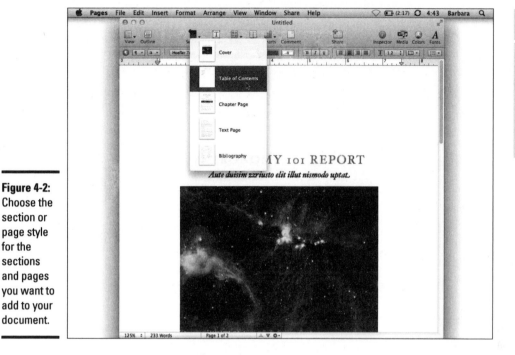

Figure 4-2:
Choose the section or page style for the sections and pages you want to add to your document.

3. **Click the section or page style you want to add. (Or click Insert⇨ Sections/Pages and select the one you want.)**

   The new section or page is added after the page or section where you placed the cursor.

4. **To see all the pages of your document, choose View⇨Page Thumbnails.**

   A left sidebar opens, showing thumbnails of the pages or sections in your document.

5. **Click and drag the thumbnails to rearrange the order in which they appear in your document, as shown in Figure 4-3.**

Word Processor documents are continuous. Pages adds any needed pages automatically as you type, so if you add one Text section but type 20 pages, all 20 will reflect the Text section style. Likewise, if your bibliography is three pages, you need insert only one bibliography section. In Page Layout, each Page you add is limited to that Page; if you have more text than will fit in the text box on that page, you have to add another Page and link the text box on the one page to another on the next page. (We explain how to do that a little later in this chapter in the "Creating linked text boxes" section.)

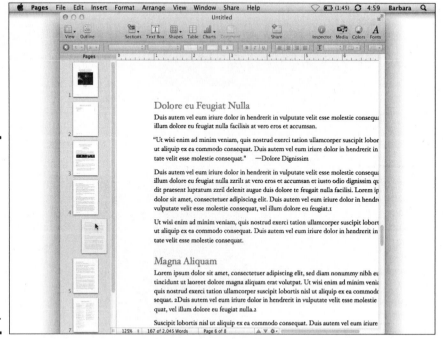

Figure 4-3:
Click and
drag the
pages or
sections
in the
thumbnail
sidebar to
rearrange
their
order of
appearance.

Moving around your document

At the bottom of the Pages window are a few tools that help you navigate your document — particularly useful when you're working with a lengthy document. You have two basic navigation methods:

✦ Click where you see Page X of X and a Go To field opens. Type a page number in the field and press Return to jump directly to that page.

✦ Click the up and down triangles to jump directly from one page to the next.

Note the two tools to the left of the navigation tools:

✦ The Resizing pop-up menu lets you zoom in or out of your document to views that range from 25 to 400 percent. You can also choose to view one or two pages at a time.

✦ The *word count* displays the number of words in your document. If you don't see the word count, choose Pages⇨Preferences and select Show Word Count at Window Bottom.

Book V
Chapter 4

Creating Documents
with Pages

Replacing placeholder text

Nearly every template, except for Blank, contains placeholder text (a mix of pseudo-Latin and gibberish that's been used in typesetting as dummy text since the 16th century) — which you replace with your own text. To change placeholder text in a template, follow these steps:

1. **Double-click the placeholder text you want to change.**

   Pages selects the entire placeholder text, which can be as short as a single sentence or as large as several paragraphs, as shown in the newsletter text selection in Figure 4-4.

2. **Type any new text you want to replace the placeholder text.**

Replacing placeholder photos and graphics

Many templates display placeholder photos and graphics. Unless you happen to like the image included with a template, you'll probably want to replace it with one of your own. Here we explain how to place photos from iPhoto, how to place images from other places on your computer, and how to insert a chart or table from Numbers, iWork's spreadsheet application.

Figure 4-4:
To replace placeholder text, double-click it and type new text.

Inserting photos from iPhoto

Follow these steps to add or replace photos in Pages documents with photos from iPhoto:

1. **Click the Media icon on the toolbar or choose View⊰Show Media Browser on the menu bar.**

   The Media Browser appears.

2. **Click the Photos tab in the Media Browser to view all the photos stored in iPhoto.**

   If, like us, you have thousands of photos, click the triangle next to iPhoto to see your photos sorted by Event, Faces, Places, or by albums you created. Then to narrow your choice, double-click the Event, Face, Place, or album, until you get to where the photo you want resides. This makes it easier to find the photo you want to add to your document.

3. **Click and drag a photo from the Media Browser to any placeholder photo in your document.**

4. **Release the mouse button.**

   Pages replaces the placeholder picture with the picture you choose from the Media Browser, as shown in Figure 4-5. Later on in this chapter in the "Moving and resizing a picture" section, we explain how to manipulate photos in your documents.

5. **Click the Close button on the Media Browser.**

Inserting other images

If the image you want to insert isn't stored in iPhoto, do the following:

1. **Click the placeholder image you want to replace.**

2. **Choose Insert⊰Choose.**

   A chooser opens, showing the folders and files on your Mac (as in Figure 4-6).

3. **Scroll through your folders and files until you find the image you want to insert.**

4. **Double-click the file.**

   Your image replaces the placeholder image.

Figure 4-5:
The Media
Browser
lets you
drag and
drop
pictures
directly
on your
document.

Figure 4-6:
Choose
the file you
want to use
to replace a
placeholder.

Inserting charts and tables from Numbers

You can insert charts or tables from Numbers (iWork's spreadsheet application, which we explore in Book V, Chapter 6) in a text or photo placeholder. (In the later section, "Creating Charts and Tables," we explain how to create a chart or table in Pages.)

1. **Open the Numbers document that has the chart or table you want to insert.**

2. **Select the chart or table you want to insert.**

3. **Choose Edit⇨Copy or press ⌘+C.**

4. **Return to your Pages document.**

5. **Click the placeholder where you want to insert the chart or table.**

6. **Choose Edit⇨Paste or press ⌘+P.**

7. **Drag the selection handles to resize the placeholder as needed to accommodate the table or chart.**

Arranging objects

In Page Layout mode, you often have multiple shapes, objects, and images that may overlap. Sometimes one object even hides another and you almost go crazy trying to find it. Arranging and aligning objects can help keep everything in view and neatly . . . well . . . arranged.

Think of the shapes, objects, and so on as a stack of paper. If the bigger or darker sheet is on top, it hides what's underneath. You have to rearrange the order of your objects in order to see them all. To reveal objects that may be hidden by others, follow these steps:

1. **Click the object that you want to be on the bottom of the stack.**

2. **Choose Arrange⇨Send to Back.**

Anything that was hidden by that object now appears on top of it.

3. **Click the other objects one at a time and choose Arrange⇨Send Back, Arrange⇨Bring to Front, or Arrange⇨Bring Forward until you're satisfied with the appearance of your page.**

Text boxes are usually the top item on the stack, so most of the time, you want to choose Arrange⇨Bring to Front for text boxes that rest on top of other shapes or images.

After you have the objects in the positions you like, you can create groups or lock the objects.

4. **To create a group of objects, select your objects and then choose Arrange⇨Group.**

The objects stay together and move together.

5. **To lock objects, select a single object, a group, or multiple objects, and then choose Arrange⇨Lock.**

   The locked objects or group are unmovable, undeleteable, and uneditable. (You can, however, copy or duplicate the locked object.) To unlock the objects, choose Arrange⇨Unlock.

Alignment refers to how objects are placed in relationship to each other. To align your shapes or objects, do the following:

1. **Hold down the Shift key and click the objects you want to align.**

   Resizing handles appear around each selected object.

2. **Choose Arrange⇨Align Objects or Arrange⇨Distribute Objects.**

   - *Align Objects* lets you align the left, right, top, or bottom sides of the objects, or the vertical or horizontal centers.

   - *Distribute Objects* evenly distributes the selected objects between the two farthest objects; choose horizontal or vertical.

Working with Text

Text can appear directly on a page or inside a text box. In a Word Processing document, whether you choose a blank document or template, you type text directly on a page. You can add text boxes and type text inside those text boxes, which you might choose to do if you want to insert a sidebar. In Page Layout templates, you can type text *only* inside text boxes. If you open a blank Page Layout document, you have to create a text box in order to type anything on the page. We explain adding text boxes later in this chapter in the "Creating and Placing Text Boxes" section.

Either way, after you type what you want to say, you probably want to make some changes. In the following subsections, we explain how to edit, format, and adjust the spacing of your text.

Editing text

Whether you're typing text directly on a page or inside a text box, you can edit text by adding, deleting, or rearranging it.

Adding text

Any new text you type appears wherever the cursor is located. To add text, just place the cursor where you want the new text to appear, click, and then type away.

Deleting text

You can delete text in two ways:

✦ **Move the cursor next to characters you want to erase and press Delete.** Press the Delete key (the one that appears to the right of the +/= key) to backspace over characters to the left of the cursor.

✦ **Select text and press Delete.** Select text by holding down the Shift key and moving the cursor with the arrow keys or by clicking and dragging the mouse over the text to select it, and then press the Delete key.

Rearranging text

After you write some text, you may need to rearrange it by copying or moving chunks of text from one location to another. You can copy and move text between two text boxes or from one part of a text page to another part of the same page — or to another page all together.

To copy and move text, you can use the Cut, Copy, and Paste commands on the Edit menu, but you might find it quicker to select and drag text with the mouse. Here's how it's done:

1. **Select the text you want to copy or move.**

2. **Drag the selected text to a new location.**

If you want to copy text, hold down the Option key while dragging the selected text. If you want to move text, you don't need to hold down any keys.

3. **Release the mouse button to finish copying or moving your text.**

Formatting text

The text styles and images you choose for your document create the tone of what you want to communicate — businesslike, fun, weird, and so on. You can format text by using fonts, styles, sizes, and colors. To give you fast access to the formatting options, Pages displays a Format bar (see Figure 4-7) near the top of the Pages window. To view (or hide) the Format bar, choose View⇨ Show (or Hide) Format Bar.

To format text, select the text you want to format and then do any of the following:

✦ **Click the Font pop-up menu** on the Format bar and then choose a font from the menu that appears. Pages has "what-you-see-is-what-you-get" (affectionately known as WYSIWYG, pronounced *wizzywig*) menus so you see what the font looks like in the pop-up menu.

Book V
Chapter 4

Creating Documents
with Pages

Figure 4-7:
Choose
different
fonts, sizes,
and styles.

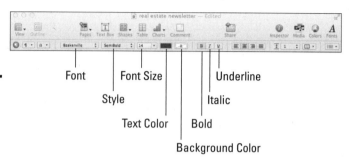

Font   Font Size   Underline

Style   Italic

Text Color   Bold

Background Color

✦ **Click the Style pop-up menu** on the Format bar and then choose a style, such as Regular or Heading 1. (Choosing Bold or Italic from the Style pop-up menu is identical to clicking the Bold or Italic icon on the Format bar.)

✦ **Click the Font Size pop-up menu** on the Format bar and then choose a size, such as 12 or 24.

✦ **Click the Text Color button** on the Format bar. A color menu appears. Click a color to change the color of your selected text.

✦ **Click the Background Color button** on the Format bar. A color menu appears, much like the one for the text color. Click a color to appear in the background of your selected text.

✦ **Click the Bold, Italic, or Underline icons** on the Format bar.

You can also click the Fonts icon in the Toolbar to format your text with the Font Panel. Click the Action icon and choose Preview to show what your text will look like, as shown in Figure 4-8.

Figure 4-8:
Clicking the
Fonts icon
opens the
Font Panel.

Adjusting line spacing, justification, and margins

You can change how letters look by playing with the font, but you can also change the way a block of text looks by changing how it's spaced on the page. In concrete terms, this means changing

+ **Line spacing:** Defines how close together lines in a paragraph appear.

+ **Text justification:** Defines how text aligns within the left and right margins.

+ **Margins:** Defines the left and right boundaries that text can't go past.

Changing line spacing

Line spacing used for most purposes typically varies from 0.5 to 2.0. (A value of 1.0 is single spacing, and a value of 2.0 is double spacing.) To change line spacing, follow these steps:

1. **Select the line or lines of text you want to modify.**

2. **Click the Line Spacing pop-up menu on the Format bar and then choose a number, such as 1.5 or 2.0.**

Click Show More in the Line Spacing pop-up menu to choose spacing beyond the 0.5–2.0 range. Line spacing values of less than 1.0, such as 0.5, can cause lines to overlap, which makes the text hard to read.

Changing justification

The four types of justification are

+ **Align Left:** Text appears flush against the left margin but ragged along the right margin.

+ **Center:** Each line of text is centered within the left and right margins, so text appears ragged on both left and right margins.

+ **Align Right:** Text appears flush against the right margin but ragged along the left margin.

+ **Justify:** Text appears flush against both the left and right margins, but extra space appears between words and characters.

Figure 4-9 shows four paragraphs. The first is aligned left, the second is centered, the third is aligned right, and the final paragraph is justified.

To set your text justification, follow these steps:

1. **Select the text you want to modify.**

2. **Click the Align Left, Center, Align Right, or Justify icons on the Format bar.**

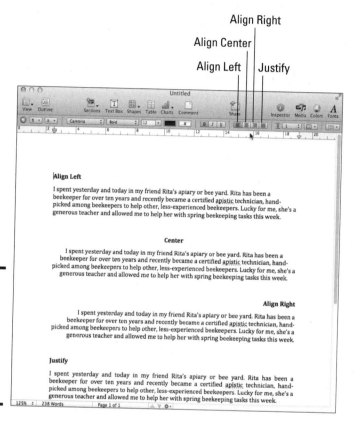

Align Right

Align Center

Align Left | Justify

Figure 4-9:
Justifying
text can
make
paragraphs
appear in
different
ways.

Defining margins for the whole document

The left and right margins only define text that appears on the page in Word Processing layout. The size of a text box as defined in the Metrics Inspector defines the left and right margins of a text box.

To define the margins for the whole document, do the following:

1. **Click the Inspector icon in the upper-right corner of the Pages window or choose View➪Show Inspector from the menu bar.**

The Inspector icon looks like a little "i" in a blue circle. When you click the icon, an Inspector window appears.

2. **Click the Document Inspector icon (the first one that looks like a piece of paper).**

3. **Click the Document tab, as shown in Figure 4-10.**

Figure 4-10: Set the margins for the entire document in the Document Inspector.

4. **Type in the values you want for your left and right margins, or use the up and down arrows to choose a value.**

 Select the Facing Pages check box if you need to set inside and outside margins.

 Set the units of measure for your rulers by choosing Pages⇨Preferences, and then click Ruler. Use the pop-up menu next to Ruler Units to choose Inches, Centimeters, Points, or Picas.

Defining margins for a portion of text

To define the left and right margins of a portion of text — say a long citation from a book — you can use the ruler, which appears at the top of the Pages window. The ruler lets you define an exact location for your margins, such as placing the left margin exactly 1.5 inches from the left edge of the page.

To define the left and right margins of selected text, follow these steps:

1. **Select the text you want to modify.**

2. **Click and drag the Left Margin marker to a new position on the ruler and then release the mouse button.**

 The Left Margin marker is the blue triangle that appears on the left side of the ruler. If only the first lines of your paragraphs move, you have selected the Indent marker, which is at the very top of the Left Margin marker; grab the Left Margin marker from the bottom.

If the ruler isn't visible, choose View➪Show Rulers.

3. To indent the first line of a paragraph or paragraphs in your selected text, click and drag the Indent marker to a new position on the ruler and then release the mouse button.

The Indent marker is the thin blue rectangle that appears over the Left Margin marker. Figure 4-11 shows the Left and Right Margin markers and the Indent marker.

If you drag the Left Margin marker after you move the Indent marker, the Indent marker moves with the Left Margin marker; dragging the Indent marker, however, moves the Indent marker by itself.

4. Click and drag the Right Margin marker to a new position on the ruler and then release the mouse button.

The Right Margin marker is the blue triangle that appears on the right side of the ruler.

Dragging the Left Margin and Right Margin markers on the ruler is a fast way to adjust the margins or first-line indents of a text selection. For a more precise way, follow these steps:

Left Margin marker

Indent marker

Right Margin marker

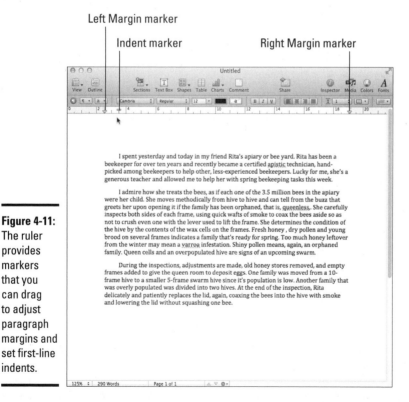

Figure 4-11:
The ruler provides markers that you can drag to adjust paragraph margins and set first-line indents.

1. **Select the text you want to modify.**

2. **Click the Inspector icon in the upper-right corner of the Pages window or choose View⇨Show Inspector.**

3. **Click the Text Inspector icon (the big T).**

4. **Click the Tabs tab, as shown in Figure 4-12.**

5. **Enter a value or click the up and down arrows to choose a value in the First Line, Left, or Right text boxes.**

   The value in the First Line adjusts the Indent marker; the Left and Right values are in relation to the margins of the overall document. This means that if the left margin of your document is 1 inch and you set the Left Indent value at .25 inches, the left margin of your selected text will be 1.25 inches.

6. **Click the Close button of the Text Inspector window.**

Adding headers and footers to a Word Processing document

In a Word Processing document, headers and footers contain text that you want repeated on each page, such as the title, author, page number, or date. Headers are at the top of the page and footers are at the bottom of the page. You can type in the text you want in the header or footer or select predetermined information. Here's how to use headers and footers:

1. **In a Word Processing document, click the Inspector button in the tool bar (it's the one that has an "I" on it).**

2. **Click the Document Inspector button, the first one on the left.**

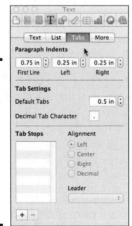

Figure 4-12:
The Text Inspector lets you choose precise values for adjusting the margins of text.

3. **Click the Document tab.**

4. **Select the Header check box, the Footer check box, or both.**

5. **Choose how far from the edge of the page you want the header and footer to appear; type in a number or use the up and down arrows.**

   The header or footer text box moves according to value you set. The top and bottom margins must be greater than the header and footer distance; otherwise, the document text will cover the header and footer.

6. **Move the pointer near the top or bottom of the page, more or less where the header or footer should be, until an empty box appears.**

7. **Click in the empty box.**

   The cursor flashes in the empty box.

8. **Type the text you want to appear at the top or bottom of each page.**

   Format the text as you would any other text, setting the font type, size, and style.

9. **To add the date, page number, or filename automatically, position the cursor where you want the text to appear, and then choose Insert⇨Page Number, Insert⇨Page Count, Insert⇨Date & Time, or Insert⇨Filename.**

   To format the Date & Time, double-click the inserted text. A window opens, shown in Figure 4-13, giving you format choices and the option to update the date whenever the file is opened.

10. **Click anywhere in the document to exit the header or footer.**

Figure 4-13: Enter the date and time automatically in the header or footer.

Using Formatting Styles

You may have a favorite way to format text. Although you could manually change each formatting feature, you might find it faster and easier to use styles instead. Formatting styles store different types of formatting that you can apply to text. In Pages, the Word Processing and Page Layout templates have formatting styles stored already. When you create your own documents, you can create formatting styles, too. By using formatting styles, you can format text quickly and consistently with minimum effort.

Applying styles

The following are the types of styles you can apply to text:

✦ **Paragraph styles** affect an entire paragraph where the end of a paragraph is defined by a line that ends where you press Return.

✦ **Character styles** affect characters or words.

✦ **List styles** affect multiple lines of text where each line of text ends where you press Return. (Think to-do lists, outlines, or bullet points.)

Using a paragraph style

To apply a paragraph style, follow these steps:

1. **Click the text (or move the cursor inside the text box) you want to modify.**

2. **Click the Styles button.**

It's a blue button with a paragraph symbol on the far left of the Format bar. The Styles drawer opens, displaying the styles used in the document. The style of the selected text is highlighted, as shown in Figure 4-14.

If you can't see the Format bar, choose View➪Show Format Bar.

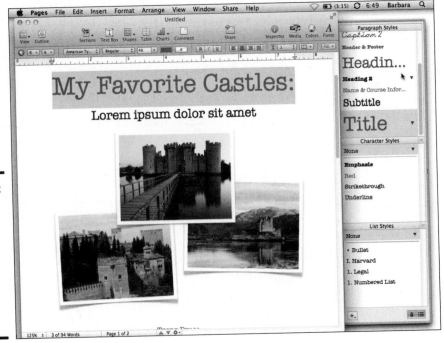

Figure 4-14:
The Styles pane shows the paragraph, character, and list styles used in the document.

3. **Choose a style that you want to use for your selected text.**

   Pages formats your selected text.

Using a character style

To apply a character style, such as **emphasis**, *italic*, <u>underline</u>, or ~~strikethrough~~, follow these steps:

1. **Select the text you want to modify.**

2. **Click the Styles button to open the Styles drawer.**

3. **Choose a character style.**

   Pages formats your selected text.

Some character styles, such as Emphasis and Italic, work the same as the Bold and Italic buttons at the far right of the Format bar.

Using a list style

To apply a list style, follow these steps:

1. **Move the cursor where you want to start typing a list.**

2. **Click the Styles button to open the Styles drawer.**

3. **Choose a style, such as Harvard or Bullet.**

4. **Type some text and press Return.**

   Pages displays your list in your chosen style, such as a numbered list or a bulleted list.

5. **Repeat Step 4 for each additional line of your list.**

6. **Turn off List mode by choosing None from the List Styles selection.**

7. **Click the Styles button to close the Styles drawer.**

There are individual buttons for Paragraph Style, Character Style, and List Style that reveal pull-down menus. The Paragraph and Character Style buttons are to the immediate right of the Styles button; the List Style button is on the far right of the Format bar.

Creating temporary styles

Pages provides paragraph, character, and list styles with each template, but you might need to format text in a certain way that Pages doesn't offer. In that case, you can copy the style from existing text and paste that style to format other text automatically.

Copying and pasting formatting

To copy and paste formatting from existing text, follow these steps:

1. **Format text in a certain way, such as changing the fonts and font size.**

2. **Click (or move the cursor) inside the formatted text.**

3. **On the menu bar, choose Format⇨Copy Character Style (or Copy Paragraph Style).**

4. **Select text that you want to format the same way as the text you choose in Step 1.**

5. **On the menu bar, choose Format⇨Paste Character Style (or Paste Paragraph Style).**

   Pages copies your style to the text you select in Step 4.

Adding or deleting a formatting style

If you format text a certain way repeatedly, you may want to save your formatting as a style that appears in the Styles Drawer. You can choose that style later by clicking the name of your saved style.

To add your own style to the Styles Drawer, follow these steps:

1. **Format text in a certain way, such as changing the fonts and font size.**

2. **Click (or move the cursor) inside the formatted text.**

3. **Choose View⇨Show Styles Drawer to open the Styles Drawer.**

4. **Click the plus sign button in the bottom-left corner of the Styles Drawer.**

   A New Paragraph Style dialog appears.

5. **Type a descriptive name for your style and click OK.**

   Your style name now appears in the Styles Drawer. The next time you need to use this style, select some text and click this style name in the Styles Drawer.

To delete a style from the Styles Drawer, right-click (two-finger tap on a trackpad) the style and choose Delete Style. When a dialog appears, click the pop-up menu to choose a style to format text currently formatted by the style you want to delete. Then click Replace.

Creating and Placing Text Boxes

Text boxes hold text that you can place anywhere on a page (even in the middle of other text). You can create and place text boxes on both Word Processing and Page Layout documents.

Creating a text box

To create a text box, follow these steps:

1. **Choose Insert⇨Text Box on the menu bar or click the Text Box icon.**

   Pages displays a text box, as shown in Figure 4-15.

2. **Type new text inside the text box.**

   Pages keeps your text within the boundaries of the text box.

Moving a text box

After you create a text box, you may want to move it. To move a text box, follow these steps:

1. **Click a text box to select it.**

   A border with handles appears around the text box. (Refer to Figure 4-15.)

2. **Click and hold down on the text box border and drag the text box to its new location.**

3. **Release the mouse button when you arrive at your destination.**

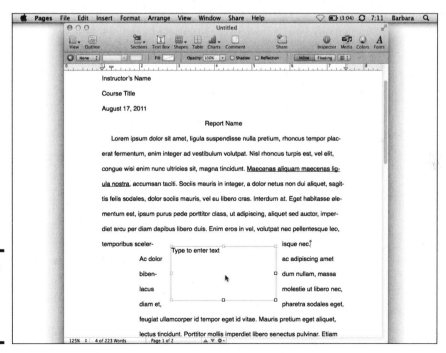

Figure 4-15:
A text box
appears in
the middle
of a page.

Resizing a text box

Sometimes a text box is too large or small for the text you type inside. To fix this problem, you can resize a text box by following these steps:

1. **Click anywhere inside the text box.**

2. **Move the pointer to a handle until the pointer turns into a two-way arrow.**

If the handle doesn't turn into a two-way arrow, make sure that it's a black handle — not all handles become resizing handles.

3. **Click and drag a handle to resize the text box.**

4. **Release the mouse button when you're happy with the size of the text box.**

Creating linked text boxes

If you type more text than a text box can display, you see a *Clipping Indicator* icon — it appears as a plus sign inside a square at the bottom of the text box.

When you see the Clipping Indicator at the bottom of a text box, you have two choices.

✦ You can resize the text box so it can display more text, as described in the preceding section. This might not always be practical because you might not want to expand a text box.

✦ Alternatively, you can link text boxes. Linked text boxes allow text from one text box to flow into another text box. The next section shows how.

Linking text boxes

To link text boxes, follow these steps:

1. **Click a text box that displays a Clipping Indicator at the bottom.**

Blue tabs appear on the sides of the text box.

2. **Click the blue tab on the right of the text box.**

A message appears, telling you to click an existing text box or anywhere on the page to create a new text box, as shown in Figure 4-16.

3. **Click an existing text box or click anywhere on the page to create a new text box.**

Pages displays a blue line linking your two text boxes and moves overflowing text from the first text box to the linked second text box, as shown in Figure 4-17.

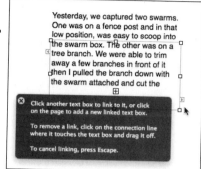

Figure 4-16:
To link a
text box,
click a
text box
or create
one auto-
matically.

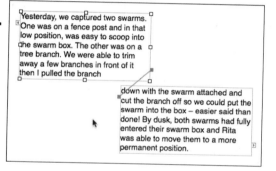

Figure 4-17:
Pages
identifies
linked text
boxes with
a blue
connecting
line.

Depending on how much text you have, you can (and might need to) link
multiple text boxes.

Unlinking text boxes

After you link two or more text boxes, you may decide that you don't want
linked text boxes after all. To unlink text boxes, follow these steps:

1. **Click the text box that you want to unlink from another text box.**

2. **Do one of the following:**

- On the menu bar, choose Format⇨Text Box⇨Break Connection into
  Text Box.

- Move the pointer to the end of the connection line, hold down the
  mouse button, drag the mouse away from the text box, and then
  release the mouse button.

When you unlink text boxes, the text fills (and overflows) the first text box,
leaving the unlinked text box empty.

Wrapping text around a text box

A new text box often appears near other text box. To prevent a text box you're adding from covering other text, you have to wrap the (already present) text around the new text box. To define how to wrap text around a text box, follow these steps:

1. **Click a text box.**

2. **Click the Inspector icon or choose View⇨Show Inspector on the menu bar.**

   The Inspector icon looks like a little "i" in a blue circle in the upper-right corner of the Pages window. The Inspector window appears.

3. **Click the Wrap Inspector button.**

   It appears to the left of the big "T" button. The Wrap Inspector options appear, as shown in Figure 4-18.

4. **Select the Object Causes Wrap check box.**

5. **Click a text-wrap button.**

   Text can wrap in various ways (six total), as indicated on the buttons:

   • Around the box on three sides, to the left or right

   • Completely around the box

   • Above and below the box, with the box to the left, right, or center

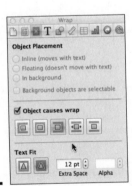

Figure 4-18: The Wrap Inspector offers different ways text can appear around a text box.

Creating Charts and Tables

As we mention earlier in this chapter, you can insert charts and tables directly from Numbers, which is great when you already have the charts and tables prepared or if you have complex data that's more easily worked with in Numbers. If you're starting from scratch, it may be quicker to build your chart or table directly in Pages. *Charts* are things like pie charts or bar charts that graphically represent data. *Tables* are rows and columns of information where the intersection of a row and column is called a *cell*.

Adding a chart

Sometimes presenting your information as a chart makes your information easier to understand. To add a chart to a Pages document, follow these steps:

1. **Choose Insert⇨Chart from the menu bar, or click the Charts icon on the Pages toolbar, and then choose the type of chart you want to create — bar, pie, 2-D or 3-D, for example.**

   A chart appears and the Chart Inspector opens along with the Chart Data Editor, as shown in Figure 4-19.

2. **Click the chart and the Inspector and Chart Data Editor become active.**

3. **Double-click the Row and Column field headers of the Chart Data Editor to select the placeholder text and enter the information you want on your chart.**

4. **Click the cells below the headers to enter the number values you want the chart to show.**

   The data entered appears in the chart and titles.

Figure 4-19:
The Inspector and Chart Data Editor open when you insert a chart in your Word Processing or Page Layout document.

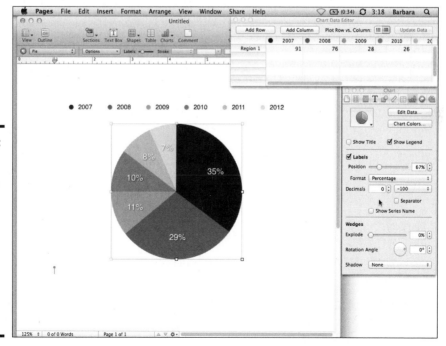

5. **Click the Format pop-up menu of the Chart Inspector to choose how you want the data to appear, such as a number or a percentage.**

If you decide that you want to remove a chart, click it and press Delete.

Adding a table

Tables in Pages are calculable — which means that you can write formulas or insert functions in much the same way you would in Numbers. These are the steps for adding a table to your document:

1. **Choose Insert⇨Table from the menu bar, or click the Table icon on the Pages toolbar.**

A blank table appears on your slide and the Table Inspector opens, as shown in Figure 4-20.

2. **Edit the size and appearance of your table with the fields in the Table Inspector.**

Set the number of rows and columns with the body rows and columns menus at the top or with the Edit Rows and Columns action menu (refer to Figure 4-20). Set the row height and column width and the appearance of the table with cell borders and backgrounds.

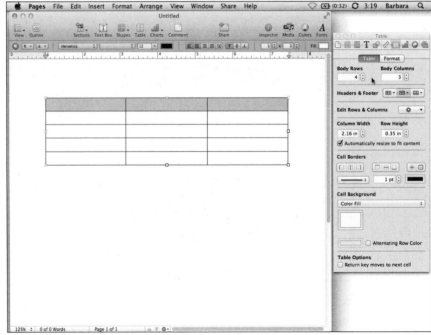

Figure 4-20:
Use the Table Inspector to edit the appearance of your table.

3. **Click the Format tab to edit the cell format; for example, make the numbers appear as currency or fractions.**

4. **Set up functions and conditional formats by entering numerical data in a row or column of cells and then assigning a function, for example sum or average, to the cell at the end of the row or column.**

Working with Digital Photographs

If you have digital photographs stored in iPhoto, you can place those photos directly into a Pages document and manipulate those photos as well. We explain inserting photos earlier in this chapter in the "Inserting photos from iPhoto" section. Here's a quick reference.

Adding a photo

To add a picture from iPhoto into a document, follow these steps:

1. **Click the Media icon on the toolbar.**

   The Media Browser appears.

2. **Click the Photos tab.**

3. **Click and drag a photo from the Media Browser to your document.**

4. **Release the mouse button.**

   Pages displays your chosen image in the document.

Moving and resizing a picture

After you place a photo in a document, you may need to resize or move it. To move a photo, follow these steps:

1. **Click and drag the photo to a new position.**

2. **Release the mouse button or trackpad when you're happy with the new location of the photo.**

To resize a photo, follow these steps:

1. **Click the photo you want to resize.**

   Handles appear around your chosen picture.

2. **Move the pointer to a handle until the pointer turns into a two-way pointing arrow.**

3. **Click and drag the handle to resize your photo.**

4. **Release the mouse button when you're happy with the new size of the photo.**

Polishing Your Document

When you finish designing your document, you're ready to show it to the world. Of course, before you show your document to others, you should proofread your document for grammar and spelling. Fortunately, Pages is happy to help you check a document's spelling. Read on . . .

Spell checking a document

Pages can spell check your entire document, including text trapped inside text boxes and shapes. To spell check an entire document, follow these steps:

1. **Choose Edit⇨Spelling⇨Spelling on the menu bar.**

(If you choose Edit⇨Spelling⇨Check Spelling, Pages highlights misspelled words but doesn't offer any suggestions.)

A dialog appears, highlighting misspelled words and offering possible corrections, as shown in Figure 4-21.

2. **Click one of the following:**

- *Change:* Changes the misspelled word with the word selected in the list box.

- *Find Next:* Looks for the next misspelled word.

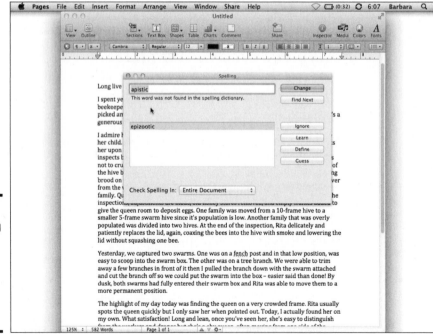

Figure 4-21:
The Spelling dialog lets you pick from a list of correctly spelled words.

- *Ignore:* Skips the misspelled word.
- *Learn:* Stores the selected word in the Pages dictionary
- *Define:* Launches Mac's Dictionary application and displays the word's definition in the Dictionary's main window.
- *Guess:* Offers best-guess word choices.

3. **Click the Close button of the Spelling dialog at any time to make it go away.**

Pages can check your spelling while you type. The moment Pages identifies a misspelled word, it underlines it with a red dotted line. If you Control-click any word underlined with a red dotted line, Pages displays a shortcut menu of correctly spelled words that you can choose. If you want to turn off spell checking while you type, choose Edit⇨Spelling⇨Check Spelling as You Type to clear the check mark in front of this command.

It's a good idea to proofread your document even after spell checking because the spell checker only makes sure that the word is correctly spelled. If you type, "I have to dogs," when you really meant to type, "I have two dogs," no spell checker on earth is going to flag that.

Finding and replacing text

Pages can also find and replace words or phrases. Say you're writing an article about a person named Swanson, only to realize that just before you send the article to your editor that the name is spelled Swansen. Pages will search your entire document and replace Swanson with Swansen. To find and replace a word or phrase, do the following:

1. **Choose Edit⇨Find⇨Find.**

   The Find dialog opens, as shown in Figure 4-22. We clicked the Advanced tab to show all the options.

2. **Type the word or phrase you want to find in the Find field.**

3. **Type the word or phrase you want to replace the found text with in the Replace field.**

4. **Click Replace All to replace all occurrences of the old word with the new word, or click Next to find the first occurrence of the word or phrase, and then do one of the following:**

   - *Click Replace* to replace the old word with the new one. You have to click Next to highlight the next occurrence.

   - *Click Replace and Find* to replace the highlighted word and find the next occurrence. (This saves you from having to click Replace and then click Next.)

5. **Continue reviewing the occurrences by repeating Step 4.**

The Advanced options let you do the following:

✦ **Insert:** The pop-up menu displays breaks such as tabs, paragraph breaks, and section breaks.

✦ **Match Case:** Select this check box to have Pages distinguish uppercase and lowercase letters and find text *exactly* as you type it.

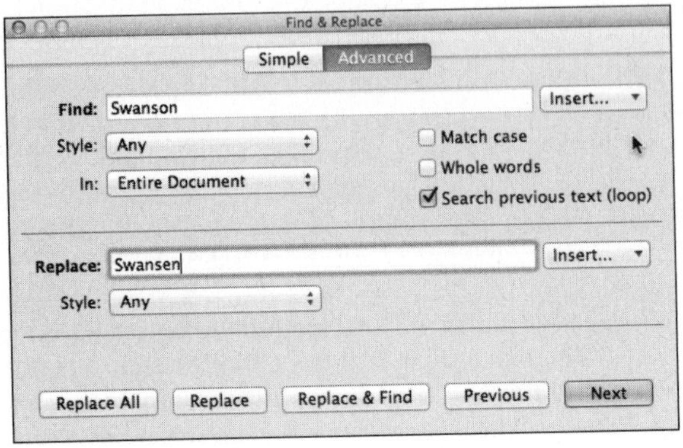

Figure 4-22:
Use Find
and Replace
to substitute
words or
phrases.

✦ **Whole Words:** Select this check box to ignore whole words that contain your text. If, for example, you search for *place* and select this option, *placemat* or *placement* won't be highlighted.

✦ **Search Previous Text (Loop):** You can begin Find and Replace from any point in your document and when Pages reaches the end of the document, it continues to search from the beginning until reaching the point where the search began.

✦ **In:** The options in this pop-up menu are Entire Document and Main Text Body. Entire Document searches everything, including headers, footers, footnotes, charts, and so on. Choose Main Text Body to search only in the main text.

Printing and Sharing Your Documents

You can print and distribute your document in the traditional way — as good old-fashioned hard copy — by following these steps:

1. **Choose File⇨Print.**

2. **Choose your printer, settings, number of copies, and page range.**

3. **Click the Print button.**

When your document comes out of the printer, you can hand it to someone, hang it up, or put a stamp on it, and drop it in your local mailbox.

Chances are that you'll want to share your document electronically, too. However, as much as you love your Mac and Pages, not everyone uses the same types of computers or applications. Don't let that stop you from sharing your document files; Pages can export files in diverse formats.

Exporting to a different file format

Although Pages saves documents in its own proprietary file format when you choose File➪Save, if you want to share your Pages documents with others who don't have the Pages application, you can export your document into another file format by using these options:

- **PDF:** Saves your document as a series of static pages stored in the PDF Adobe Acrobat file format that can be viewed (but not necessarily edited) by any computer with a PDF viewing application.

- **Word:** Saves your document as a Microsoft Word file, which can be opened by any word processor that can read and edit Microsoft Word files.

- **RTF:** Saves your document as a Rich Text Format (RTF) file, which many applications can open and edit.

- **Plain Text:** Saves your document as text without any formatting or graphic effects.

- **ePub:** Saves your document in a format that can be read in iBooks on an iPad, iPod touch, or iPhone and on many electronic readers.

The PDF file format preserves formatting 100 percent, but doesn't let anyone edit that file unless they use a separate PDF editing application, such as Acrobat Pro. If someone needs to edit your document, both the Word and RTF options preserve Pages documents well. The Plain Text option is useful only if you can't transfer your Pages document to another application as a Word or RTF file.

To export a Pages document, follow these steps:

1. **Choose File➪Export on the menu bar.**

   A dialog appears, as shown in Figure 4-23.

2. **Select an option, such as Word or ePub, and then click Next.**

3. **In the new dialog that appears, enter a name for your exported document in the Save As text box.**

4. **Select the folder in which you want to store your document.**

   You may need to switch drives or folders until you find where you want to save your file.

5. **Click Export.**

When you export a document, your original Pages document remains untouched in its original location.

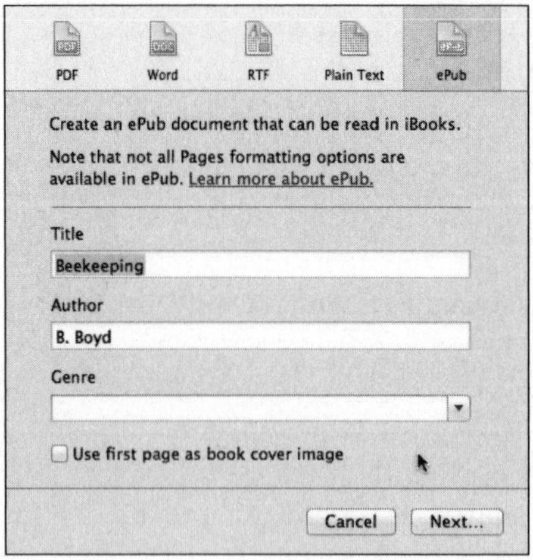

Figure 4-23: The Export dialog lets you choose a format to save your Pages document.

PDF | Word | RTF | Plain Text | ePub

Create an ePub document that can be read in iBooks.

Note that not all Pages formatting options are available in ePub. Learn more about ePub.

Title
Beekeeping

Author
B. Boyd

Genre

☐ Use first page as book cover image

Cancel | Next...

Sending files via Mail

Instead of exporting your Pages document to another format and then attaching the exported file to an e-mail message, you can send the file directly from Pages via Mail. (Book II, Chapter 2 explains Mail, the e-mail application that came with your Mac.) Here's how this option works:

1. **Choose Share⇨Send via Mail.**

2. **Select the format you want to use: Pages, Word, or PDF.**

A New Message window in Mail opens.

3. **Fill in the To, CC, and Subject fields.**

4. **Type a message to accompany your file.**

5. **Click the Send button.**

Chapter 5: Presenting with Keynote

In This Chapter

✔ Creating a presentation

✔ Adding and deleting slides

✔ Adding, editing, and formatting text

✔ Working with graphics

✔ Inserting photos and movies

✔ Using transitions and effects

✔ Giving a presentation

*P*resentations used to be confined to the realm of professional conferences and shareholder meetings. With or without a projector, the
combination of your Mac and Keynote (Apple's electronic slide-presentation
application that's part of iWork), makes it cost effective and time efficient
to give presentations at weekly staff meetings, set up an interactive kiosk
at the local small-business fair, or even post your presentation on your
website. Keynote can take the hassle out of creating, organizing, and giving
a presentation so you can concentrate more of your time on talking to an
audience and less of your time fumbling around with jammed slide projec-
tors, whiteboards, and felt markers that stain your fingertips.

Best of all, Keynote can spice up your presentation by including tables,
charts, and audio and visual effects, from playing music and movies to
showing visually interesting effects — stuff like text sliding across the display or dissolving away into nothingness. Such effects help get your point
across and hold an audience's attention.

In this chapter, we begin our presentation (pardon the pun) with the Keynote
basics: working with themes, replacing placeholder text and media with your
text and media, adding charts, tables, and animation. At the end of the chapter, we give you tips for practicing your presentation and tell you about the
options you have for running the presentation even without being present.
When you're up to speed on the basics, check out Book V, Chapter 7, which
shows you some nifty tricks that work across all three iWork applications.

Keynote comes as part of the iWork suite. You can download a trial copy
from Apple's website (www.apple.com/iwork) for 30 days. If you like it,
you can purchase and download Keynote from the AppStore for $19.99, or
you can purchase the entire iWork suite for $79 from the Apple online store
or your local Apple Store or authorized reseller.

Creating a Presentation

A Keynote presentation consists of one or more slides, where typically each slide displays information to make a single point. Slides usually contain text, shown in Figure 5-1, although graphics, video, and audio can make an appearance as well.

To make your presentation more interesting to watch, you can add *transition* effects that appear when you switch from one slide to another. To emphasize the information on a particular slide, you can add individual visual effects to specific items, such as making text rotate or making a graphic image glide across the screen and halt in place. (We explain how to do that later in this chapter.)

The basic steps to creating a presentation in Keynote are:

1. Pick a theme to use for your presentation.

2. Create one or more slides.

3. Type text or placing graphics on each slide.

4. (Optional) Add an audio or video file to each slide.

5. (Optional) Add visual effects to animate an entire slide or just the text or graphics that appear on that slide.

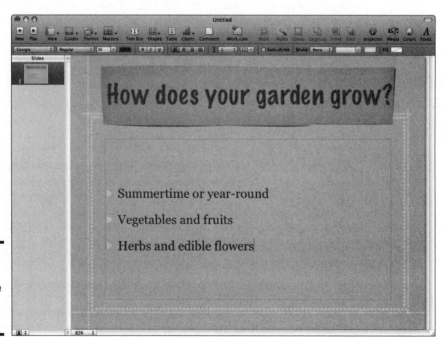

Figure 5-1:
The appearance of a typical slide.

Choosing a Theme for a New Presentation

A presentation consists of multiple slides. Although a black-and-white presentation can be elegant in a retro sort of way, color helps attract and keep
your audience's attention. To spice up your presentation, Keynote provides
predesigned background graphics called *themes* that provide a consistent
appearance for your slides, such as the font, size, style, and background
color. Within each of the 44 themes, there are multiple *master slides,* which
are templates for your slides. Most themes have the following master slides:

+ Title, top or center

+ Title and subtitle

+ Title and bullets, one- or two-column layout

+ Title, bullets, and photo

+ Bullet list

+ Photo, horizontal or vertical

+ Blank

If you want to create a presentation without using a theme — say you want your
presentation to reflect your corporate color scheme and font family — pick a
simple theme to start so you have multiple master-slide layouts to which you
can apply your desired color scheme, fonts, and so on.

To pick a theme, follow these steps:

1. **Click the Keynote icon in the Dock or on the Launchpad (or choose
File⇨New on the menu bar if Keynote is already running).**

The Theme Chooser dialog opens, as shown in Figure 5-2. Slowly drag
the pointer across the theme icon to see the master slides included with
that theme. The slider bar at the bottom of the Theme Chooser lets you
zoom in (enlarge) to make the icons bigger.

2. **Choose the slide size from the pop-up menu in the lower-right corner.**

640 x 480 was the original VGA resolution standard; 800 x 600 is the SVGA
standard; new projection systems support 1024 x 768; beyond that is high
definition (HD).

3. **Click a theme and click the Choose button or double-click a theme.**

Keynote creates the first slide of your presentation, using your chosen
theme. At this point, you can add text, graphics, audio, or video to the
slide or you can add new slides.

4. **Choose File⇨Save.**

A Save As dialog opens.

Figure 5-2:
Keynote provides a variety of themes for your presentations.

Opening an existing file in a different format

You may have presentations that were created in a different application, such as Microsoft's PowerPoint or Keynote 2008. You can open the file in Keynote, use it as is, make changes, even save it as a Keynote file.

To open a non-Keynote presentation, drag the file you want to open over the Keynote icon in the Dock. You can also open a non-Keynote presentation by following these steps:

1. **Click the Keynote icon in the Dock or Launchpad.**

2. **Click Open an Existing File. If Keynote is already running, choose File⇨Open.**

   A dialog showing the folders and files on your Mac opens.

3. **Scroll through or search to find the file you want.**

4. **Click the file you want to open.**

5. **Click Open.**

   Your presentation opens in Keynote. If there are any problems with the conversion, a Document Warning window opens. Make note of whatever tweaks you have to make. You can Hide or Show the Document Warning by choosing View⇨Hide/Show Document Warning.

6. **Work with your document as you would a document created in Keynote.**

5. **Type a name for your presentation and choose the folder where you want to store it on your Mac.**

   With Mac OS X 10.7 Lion, Keynote supports Versions, which we explain in Book I, Chapter 4 and Book III, Chapter 1.

If you want to change your theme after you open a new presentation, click the Themes icon on the Keynote toolbar and choose a different theme.

Changing Presentation Views

After you create a presentation, Keynote offers four ways to view the presentation you're working on:

✦ **Navigator:** Useful for editing individual slides and manipulating all the slides in an entire presentation. Thumbnails of your slides are displayed in the Slide Navigator on the left; the slide you are editing takes up most of the rest of the Keynote window.

✦ **Outline:** Useful for viewing and editing just the text that appears on slides, as shown in Figure 5-3. The text of your slides is displayed in the Slide Navigator. Choose Keynote⇨Preferences⇨General to choose the font you want to use in Outline View.

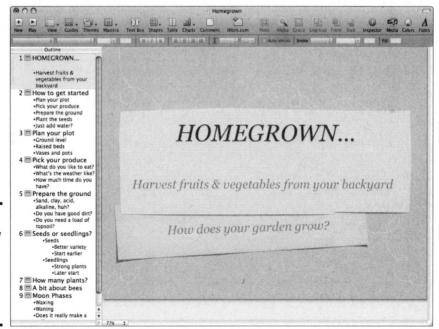

Figure 5-3:
Outline view helps you edit text without the distraction of graphics.

✦ **Slide Only:** Useful for editing the text and graphics of a single slide, as shown in Figure 5-4.

✦ **Light Table:** Useful for manipulating a large number of slides in a presentation, as shown in Figure 5-5. When you double-click a slide in Light Table, it opens in the most recent of the three other views you used.

To switch to a different view, choose the View icon on the Keynote toolbar and then choose Navigator, Outline, Slide Only, or Light Table.

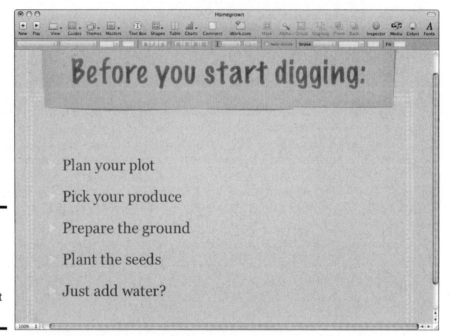

Figure 5-4:
Slide Only view helps you focus on editing one slide at a time.

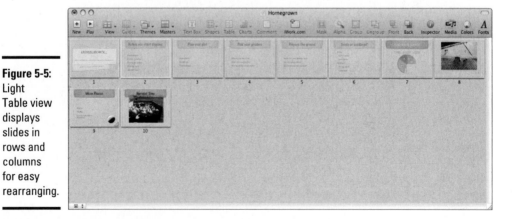

Figure 5-5:
Light Table view displays slides in rows and columns for easy rearranging.

Across the top of the Keynote window, you see the Toolbar, which holds buttons for the most frequently used functions. Below the Toolbar is the Format bar, which has pop-up menus for formatting the text and objects on your slides.

Working with Slides

When you create a new presentation, that presentation starts out containing just one slide. Because getting your idea across usually needs more than one slide, you probably want to add more slides. If you go overboard and add too many slides, you can always winnow a few.

Adding a slide

To add a slide to a presentation, follow these steps:

1. **Click a slide in the Slide Navigator pane or the Light Table view.**

   Your new slide will appear directly after the slide that you click and have the same theme.

2. **Choose one of the following to add a new slide:**

   - Click the New (+) icon.
   - Choose Slide⇨New Slide on the menu bar.
   - Click a slide in the Slide Navigator or Light Table view and press Return.
   - Control-click a slide in the Slide Navigator and choose New Slide.
   - To duplicate an existing slide, click the slide you want to duplicate and choose Edit⇨Duplicate.

Using Masters

Each Keynote theme has a selection of slide Masters (formatted slide layouts that don't have content), to which the colors, style, and fonts of the theme have been applied. To use Masters associated with a theme, follow these steps:

1. **Click a slide in any of the views.**

2. **Click the Masters icon on the Keynote toolbar, as shown in Figure 5-6, and choose the template for the type of slide you want to create.**

   For example, you might choose Title & Bullets or Photo – Vertical.

To see the Masters in the Slide Navigator panel — which can be helpful when you are initially creating your presentation — pull down the handle next to Slides; the Masters are underneath. Drag the handle up to cover them with your slides.

Figure 5-6:
The Masters
menu
shows you
all Masters
associated
with the
theme you
chose.

You zoom in or out on the slides in the Slide Navigator by choosing Small, Medium, or Large from the pull-down menu that opens from the arrows at the very bottom-left corner of the Slide Navigator window.

Rearranging slides

Keynote displays slides in the order they appear in the Slide Navigator. The top slide appears first, followed by the slide directly beneath it, and so on. After you create two or more slides in a presentation, you may want to rearrange their positions.

To rearrange slides in a presentation, follow these steps:

1. **Choose one of the following:**

   - View➪Navigator (displays slides vertically in the Slide Organizer pane.)

   - View➪Light Table (displays slides in rows and columns.)

2. **Click and drag a slide in either the Slide Navigator or Light Table to its new position.**

   In Navigator view, Keynote displays a horizontal line with a downward-pointing arrow to show you where your slide will appear when you release the mouse button. In Light Table view, Keynote moves slide icons out of the way to show you where your new slide will appear.

3. **Release the mouse button when you're happy with the new position of the slide in your presentation.**

Deleting a slide

Eventually, you may find that you don't need a slide anymore. To delete a slide, go to the Slide Navigator or Light Table view, select the slide(s) that you want to delete, and then do one of the following:

✦ Press Delete.

✦ Choose Edit⇨Delete on the menu bar.

✦ Control-click a slide in the Slide Navigator and choose Delete.

If you delete a slide by mistake, choose Edit⇨Undo Delete on the menu bar (or press ⌘+Z).

Creating groups of slides

Keynote offers you the possibility of creating groups of slides, which Apple refers to as *families,* within your presentation. You may want to create a family to group related slides, much like an outline that has topics and sub-topics. Families can make editing your presentation easier because you can move a family of related slides from one place to another without losing the order of the individual slides within the family.

To create a family, follow these steps:

1. **Choose View⇨Navigator.**

2. **Click the slide you want to be the "parent" of the family.**

3. **Add a new slide as explained previously in the "Adding a slide" section.**

4. **Click the slide you just created and press Tab or click and drag the slide toward the right.**

   The "child" slide is indented to the right and a disclosure triangle appears next to the "parent" of the family. You can also have, um, "grandchildren," as shown in Figure 5-7: Slide 3 is the parent, Slides 4 and 5 are the children, and Slide 6 is the child of 5.

   Clicking the disclosure triangle opens and closes the group.

   To move a slide out of a group, click the slide and then hold down the Shift key and press Tab; the slide moves to the left.

In groups, if you delete the parent slide when the group is closed, the entire group is deleted. If you delete the parent slide when the group is open, only the parent is deleted; its children and grandchildren move one step to the left.

Figure 5-7:
Create
groups and
subgroups
of slides
within your
presentation.

Manipulating Text

Text appears on a slide in a text box. Most slides contain at least two text boxes, where the top text box defines the title of a slide and the bottom text box displays the bullet points of a slide (refer to Figure 5-1).

The title of a slide typically defines the purpose of the slide, and the bullet points underneath provide supporting ideas. A slide can have only one Title text box but can have multiple text boxes, each of which can have paragraphs, bullets, single lines — whatever you want.

Entering text

When you create a new slide, unless you choose the blank master slide, the slide has text placeholders in text boxes and perhaps placeholder media, depending on the master you choose. You replace the placeholders with your own words and images. For now, we're going to talk about text. To place text on a slide, follow these steps:

1. **Choose View⇨Navigator on the menu bar.**

2. **In the Slide Navigator, click the slide that you want to edit.**

   Your chosen slide appears.

3. **Double-click the placeholder text that appears in the Title, Subtitle, or Bullet Point text box.**

4. **Type text or use the arrow keys and Delete key to edit existing text.**

If you want to add a text box, click the Text Box icon in the Toolbar. A text box appears on the slide. Resize the text box by clicking and dragging the resizing handles (those small boxes that appear on the corners and in the middle of each edge). You can also click and drag the text box to the position you want on the slide.

Editing text

To edit text that you've already entered, you have two choices:

✦ **In Outline view:** Select the text you want to edit in the Slide Navigator, as shown in Figure 5-8. You can change the titles, and add and delete bullets. Select a bulleted item and click and drag it by the bullet to move it up or down in the list or move it to another slide. Double-click the slide icon to hide the text. Changes you make in the Slide Navigator will be reflected in the slide(s).

✦ **In Navigator or Slide Only view:** Select the text you want to edit within the text boxes on the slide. Make the changes you want.

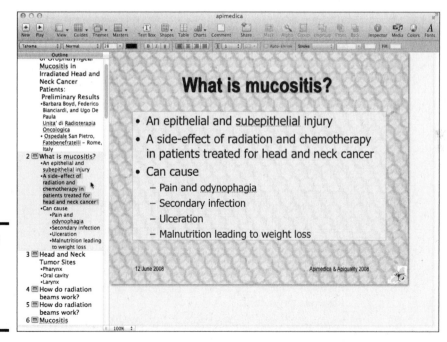

Figure 5-8: Edit text in the Slide Navigator in Outline view.

To ensure that you don't give a presentation filled with typos and misspelled words, check the spelling in your presentation by choosing Edit⇨ Spelling⇨Spelling.

Formatting text

Themes have predefined fonts, font sizes, and colors that create a coordinated design throughout the presentation, and quite frankly make creating a presentation a snap. Nonetheless, you can format the text if you want by changing fonts, font size, or color. Formatting sets the tone of your presentation — upbeat, serious, fun, or businesslike.

Use fonts and colors sparingly. Using too many fonts or colors can make text harder to read. When choosing text colors, make sure that you use colors that contrast with the slide's background color. For instance, light yellow text against a white background is nearly impossible to read.

Changing fonts

When you change a font on a Master slide, all slides that use that Master will reflect the change. Changing a font on a normal slide will change only that slide. To change the font, follow these steps:

1. **In the Slide Navigator, select the slide that contains the text you want to modify.**

2. **Double-click the text box that contains the text you want to modify.**

3. **Click and drag, or hold down the Shift key while pressing the arrow keys, to highlight the text you want to format.**

4. **Click the Fonts icon on the Keynote toolbar.**

   The Fonts panel appears. Click the Action button (it's the gear at the bottom of the pane) and select Show Preview to see a sample of the font you choose, as shown in Figure 5-9.

5. **Scroll through the Collection, Family, Typeface, and Size lists to select the font you want.**

   If you know the name of the font family, you can type it into the search box at the bottom of the pane. The Family list narrows as you type more letters.

6. **Click the font when you find it, change the typeface and size if you like.**

   The text on your slide changes to reflect the font, typeface, and size.

7. **(Optional) Click the arrows next to the underline or strikethrough icons to choose the style of underline or strikethrough you want to apply to your text.**

8. **(Optional) Click the Colors icon to change the color of the font.**

   See Steps 5 through 9 in the next section for details.

9. **(Optional) Click the Document Color button to change the color of the space behind your text.**

Follow Steps 5 through 9 in the next section. Note that changing the Document Color doesn't change the slide background.

You can also edit fonts from the menus in the Format bar below the Toolbar.

Fonts are not part of your presentation but reside on the computer from which you give the presentation. If you intend to use your presentation on a different computer, make sure that the fonts you use in your presentation are installed on the other computer or Keynote will choose the closest font. So not only could the substitute font be ugly, words may not fit within text boxes and be either cut off or dropped to a second line that could push lower text off the slide. If you use symbols or special characters, and they aren't available in the substitute font, they will be replaced by a different symbol or an empty square.

Figure 5-9:
The Fonts panel lets you choose a font to modify text.

Changing font colors

To change the color of text, follow these steps:

1. **In the Slide Navigator, click the slide that contains the text you want to modify.**

2. **Double-click the text box that contains the text you want to color.**

3. **Click and drag, or hold down the Shift key while pressing the arrow keys, to highlight the text you want to format.**

4. **Click the Colors icon on the Keynote toolbar.**

5. **At the top of the Colors window, click the color model you prefer: Wheel, (which is the default), Slider, Palette, Spectrum, or Crayons.**

The Colors window appears, as shown in Figure 5-10.

6. **Click the desired color in the color model that appears in the Colors window.**

Figure 5-10:
The Colors
window lets
you choose
a text color.

7. **(Optional) In the color wheel, make the color lighter or darker by dragging the slider on the right side up and down.**

8. **(Optional) In any of the color models, adjust the opacity by dragging the opacity slider left and right or type in a precise percentage in the text box to the right.**

   Keynote immediately uses your selected color to color the text you selected in Step 3. You can play around until you find a color you like.

9. **When you have a color you like, drag the color from the color box at the top to the color palette at the bottom. You color is saved in the palette for future use.**

10. **Click the red close window button or choose View⇨Close Colors.**

Three font tips to give your presentation that something extra are

✦ Capitalizing whole words or phrases in your presentation, especially in titles, is EYE-CATCHING. With Keynote, you don't have to use Caps Lock and retype everything if you change your mind. Choose Format⇨Font⇨ Capitalization, then choose one of the following

   • *Title* capitalizes the first letter of each word in your selected text, including articles and prepositions.

   • *All Caps* capitalizes all the letters in your selected text.

   • *Small Caps* capitalizes all the letters in your selected text — but in a small size. Any letters you type while holding the Shift key will be big capital letters. (This is one of Barbara's favorite typographical tricks when a Small Caps typeface isn't available.)

✦ If your text is just a little too long for the space it's in, you can scrunch it together, just barely, so that it fits without using a smaller font size. Choose Format⇨Font⇨Tracking⇨Tighten. (Barbara's second favorite trick.) If the typeface has a condensed variant, choose that for the best results.

✦ Turn on font smoothing. Choose ⌘⇨System Preferences⇨General and select the Use LCD Font Smoothing when Available option.

Formatting bullets

As we mention earlier in this chapter, themes come with predefined fonts, colors, styles, and bullets as part of the package. But Keynote offers such a variety of bullets, you may want to have some fun and change them. Here's how to change bullets:

1. **In the Slide Navigator, click the slide that contains the text you want to modify.**

2. **Double-click the text box that contains the list where you want to add or change bullets.**

3. **Click and drag, or hold down the Shift key while pressing the arrow keys, to highlight the text you want to bullet.**

4. **Click the Inspector icon in the Toolbar.**

   The Inspector window opens.

5. **Click the Text icon; it's the "T."**

6. **Click the Bullets tab.**

7. **Click the Bullets and Numbering pull-down menu to choose the bullet family you want: Text, Image, or Numbered.**

8. **Click the next menu down on the left to choose the bullet style, as shown in Figure 5-11.**

9. **Use the other pop-up menus to make adjustments:**

   • *Align:* Sets the vertical position of the bullet in relation to the text.

   • *Size:* Alters the size of the bullet.

   • *Bullet Indent:* Adjusts the distance from the outer edge of the text box and the bullet. The text moves with the bullet.

   • *Text Indent:* Adjusts the distance from the outer edge of the text box and the text. The greater the difference between the bullet indent and the text indent, the farther the text is from the bullet.

10. **Click the red close button to close the Inspector window or choose View⇨Hide Inspector.**

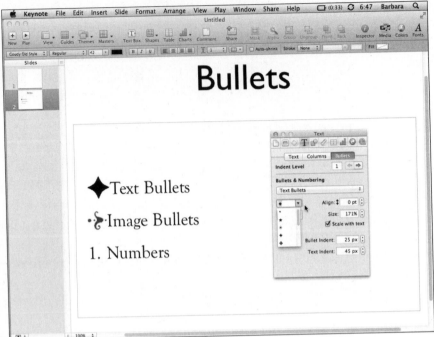

Figure 5-11:
Choose a
bullet style
for your
bulleted list.

Text alignment and spacing

You can change the horizontal alignment and vertical spacing of the text in your text boxes. Follow these steps:

1. **Select the text for which you want to change the alignment or spacing.**

2. **Click the horizontal alignment buttons in the Format bar and choose one of the following**

   - *Left Alignment* is the default: Text is aligned on the left and has a ragged edge on the right.

   - *Center Alignment* moves your text to the center but any bullets you have remain at left edge of the text box.

   - *Right Alignment* aligns your text on the right and the left edge is ragged; bullets remain on the left edge of the text box.

   - *Justified* adjusts the text to have straight edges on the left and right.

3. **To change the vertical spacing between the lines of your text, click the Spacing pop-up menu, shown in Figure 5-12, and choose the distance you want between the lines.**

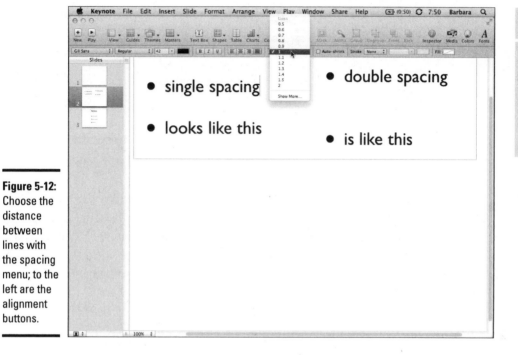

Figure 5-12:
Choose the
distance
between
lines with
the spacing
menu; to the
left are the
alignment
buttons.

If you see a small blue square with a white plus sign at the bottom of your
text box, there is text that isn't visible in the text box. You have three ways
to resolve the problem

✦ **Delete some of the text**.

✦ **Make the text box larger.** Click once in the area of the text to activate
resizing handles around the text box, and then click and drag a right-
side handle (to make the text box wider) or a bottom handle (to make
the text box longer).

✦ **Autoshrink the text.** Double-click in the text box. Click the Inspector icon
in the Toolbar and then click the Text Inspector button. Click the text tab
and select the Automatically Shrink Text check box. Your text will shrink
to fit in the text box; however, the indicated font size doesn't change.

Adding Shapes, Charts, and Tables

One basic principle of a good presentation is giving the audience something
interesting to look at. Here's where you get a look at how to use the visual-
aid options offered in Keynote.

Inserting predrawn shapes

Shapes can help draw your viewers' eyes to the thing you want them to notice. An arrow can connect your first point to your second; a star makes a key success stand out visually. Keynote comes with three types of simple, straightforward lines — and 12 ready-to-go shapes that you can stretch, shrink, and twist like Silly Putty. If you're an artistic type, there's also a tool for drawing your own shape. Follow these steps to insert a shape on your slide:

1. **Create a new slide or select the slide you want to put the shape on.**

2. **Click the Shapes icon in the Toolbar and select the shape you want, as shown in Figure 5-13.**

   Your selected shape appears on the slide with active resizing handles.

   The star and polygon shapes have sliders under them that you use to select the number of points on the star and the number of sides on the polygon (see Figure 5-13).

3. **Grab a resizing handle to enlarge or reduce the shape to the size you want.**

4. **Click and drag the shape to where you want it on your slide.**

5. **Click the Inspector icon in the Toolbar and choose the Graphic Inspector, as shown in Figure 5-14.**

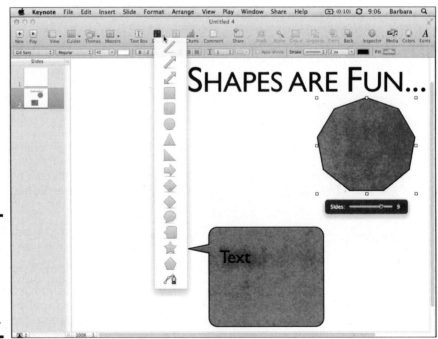

Figure 5-13: Keynote offers a dozen shapes to add to your presentation.

Figure 5-14:
Use the
Graphic
Inspector
to define
aspects of
your shape.

6. **Click the shape.**

   The Inspector shows details about the shape, such as the color.

7. **Use the menus on the Graphics Inspector to change the color of the shape, to add an outline, shadow, and/or reflection.**

To add text to your shape, create a text box as explained previously and drag it over your shape, and then edit the text.

Aligning objects

When working with multiple shapes, objects, images, and text boxes, you may want to align them or have them overlap. To align your shapes or objects, do the following:

1. **Hold down the Shift key and click the objects you want to align.**

   Resizing handles appear around each selected object.

2. **Choose Arrange➪Align Objects to align the left, right, top, or bottom sides of the objects, or the vertical or horizontal centers.**

3. **Choose Arrange➪Distribute Objects to evenly distribute the centers of the selected objects (whatever their size) between the two farthest objects; choose horizontal or vertical.**

Think about the objects on your slide as single pieces of paper, one on top of the other. If the largest piece is on top of the others, you can't see the others. On the other hand, if the largest piece is transparent, you can see what's underneath. You have to rearrange the order they're in. To reveal objects that may be hidden by others, follow these steps:

1. **Click the object that you want to be on the bottom of the stack.**

2. **Choose Arrange⇨Send to Back.**

   Anything that was hidden by that object now appears on top of it.

3. **Click the other objects one at a time and choose Arrange⇨Send Back or Arrange⇨Bring to Front, or Arrange⇨Bring Forward until you're satisfied with the appearance of your slide.**

   Text boxes are usually the top item on the stack, so most of the time you want to choose Arrange⇨Bring to Front for text boxes that rest on top of other shapes or images.

4. **After you have the objects in the positions you like, you can create groups or lock the objects.**

   You have these options:

   - *Select your objects, and then choose Arrange⇨Group.*

     The objects stay together and move together.

   - *Select a single object, a group, or multiple objects, and then choose Arrange⇨Lock.*

   The objects become unmovable, undeleteable, and uneditable. You can, however, copy or duplicate the locked object.

Choose Arrange⇨Unlock to unlock previously locked objects.

Use the Group, Ungroup, Front, and Back buttons in the Toolbar for quick adjustments.

Adding a chart

Sometimes presenting your information as a chart makes your information easier to understand. To add a chart to a presentation, follow these steps:

1. **Create a new slide or click an existing slide in the Slide Navigator or Light Table view.**

2. **Choose Insert⇨Chart from the menu bar, or click the Charts icon on the Keynote toolbar, and then choose the type of chart you want to create — Bar, Pie, 2-D or 3-D, for example.**

   A chart appears and the Chart Inspector opens, along with the Chart Data Editor.

3. **Click the chart on the slide and the Inspector and Chart Data Editor become active.**

4. **Double-click the Row and Column field headers of the Chart Data Editor to select the placeholder text and enter the information you want on your chart.**

5. **Click the cells below the headers to enter the number values you want the chart to show.**

   The data entered appears in the chart and titles on the slide.

6. **Click the Format pop-up menu of the Chart Inspector to choose how you want the data to appear, such as a number or a percentage.**

   If you decide that you want to remove a chart, click it and press Delete.

Adding a table

When you add a table in Keynote, it is a fully functioning, calculable table, much as if it had been created in Numbers. These are the steps for adding a table to your presentation:

1. **Create a new slide or click an existing slide in the Slide Navigator or Light Table view.**

2. **Choose Insert⇨Table from the menu bar, or click the Table icon on the Keynote toolbar.**

   A blank table appears on your slide and the Table Inspector opens, as shown in Figure 5-15.

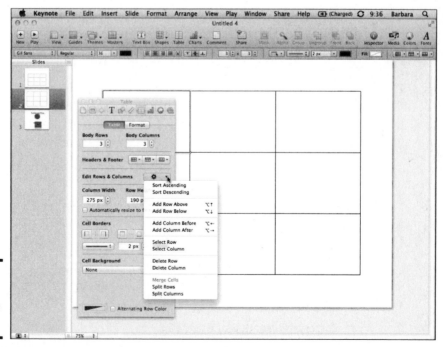

Figure 5-15:
Tables in
Keynote are
calculable.

3. **Edit the size and appearance of your table with the fields in the Table Inspector.**

   Set the number of rows and columns with the body rows and columns menus at the top or with the Edit Rows and Columns action menu (refer to Figure 5-15). Set the row height and column width and the appearance of the table with cell borders and backgrounds.

4. **Click the Format tab to edit the cell format; for example, make the numbers appear as currency or fractions.**

5. **Set up functions and conditional formats by entering numerical data in a row or column of cells and assigning a function (for example Sum or Average) to the cell at the end of the row or column.**

Adding Media Files

Text by itself can be as monotonous and confusing to read as the flight arrival and departure displays at an airport. Adding sound, still images, and movies makes your presentation appealing and communicative. Sound can be an audio recording of a song stored in iTunes or edited in GarageBand; photos can be digital photographs stored in iPhoto; and movies can be short video clips you've edited and stored in iMovie.

If you plan to hand out slides of your presentation, you probably don't want audio or video to be essential to the presentation. However, captivating and compelling audio and video can make the difference between people who stop and watch your kiosk-style presentation or just walk on by.

Adding sound

You can add any audio file stored in iTunes or GarageBand to your presentation. To add sound to a slide, follow these steps:

1. **In the Slide Navigator, click the slide with which you want to play an audio file.**

2. **Click the Media icon on the Keynote toolbar.**

   The Media Browser appears.

3. **Click the Audio tab.**

   The Media Browser displays the iTunes and GarageBand folders, as shown in Figure 5-16.

4. **Click the iTunes or GarageBand folder.**

   The bottom section of the Media Browser displays all the available files you can choose.

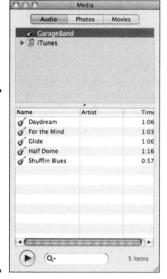

Figure 5-16:
The Audio
pane in
the Media
Browser
lets you
choose an
audio file
from iTunes
or Garage-
Band.

5. Click and drag an audio file from the Media Browser to your slide and release the mouse or trackpad button.

Keynote displays an audio icon directly on your slide to let you know that when this slide appears in your presentation, it will play your chosen audio file automatically.

6. Click the Close button of the Media Browser.

Although the audio icon appears when you edit a Keynote presentation, it won't appear when you show your presentation.

You can add voiceover to accompany your presentation so when someone views it without you, they have the benefit of hearing what you want to say about each slide. Choose Play➪Record Slideshow and begin speaking. Click the right arrow to move to the next slide. Click the Esc key when you finish. Choose Play➪Play Slideshow to hear how you did.

Adding iPhoto photos

If you store digital photos in iPhoto, you can place those photos on any slide in a Keynote presentation by following these steps:

1. In the Slide Navigator, click the slide where you want to add a photo.

2. Click the Media icon on the Keynote toolbar.

The Media Browser appears.

3. **Click the Photos tab.**

   The Media Browser displays all the pictures stored in iPhoto, as shown in Figure 5-17.

4. **Click and drag a photo from the Media Browser over placeholder media on your slide and release the mouse or trackpad.**

   If there is no placeholder media, position the photo where you want. Your chosen photo appears on your slide.

5. **Click the Close button of the Media Browser or choose View⇨ Hide Media Browser.**

Figure 5-17: Use the Photos pane in the Media Browser to choose a picture from iPhoto.

Adding iMovie videos

If you download, edit, and save digital videos, you can paste those movies on any slide. When you give your presentation, the movie will play automatically. To add a movie to a slide, follow these steps:

1. **In the Slide Navigator, click the slide on which you want to play a video.**

2. **Click the Media icon on the Keynote toolbar.**

   The Media Browser appears.

3. **Click the Movies tab.**

   The Media Browser displays all the movies stored in your Movies folder, as shown in Figure 5-18.

Figure 5-18:
The Movies pane in the Media Browser lets you add a movie to a slide.

4. **Click and drag a movie file from the Media Browser to your slide and release the mouse or trackpad.**

Your chosen movie appears on your slide.

5. **Click the Close button of the Media Browser.**

If you plan to use your presentation on a different computer, when you save the presentation, click the disclosure triangle next to Advanced Options (toward the bottom of the Save window) and select the Copy Audio and Movies into Document check box so your media files are part of the presentation.

Moving and Resizing Photos and Movies

After you paste a photo or movie on a slide, you can always move, resize, or modify that addition. Moving and resizing a photo or movie lets you place a photo or movie in the exact spot you want it to appear on a slide. Modifying the photo lets you correct an image and create unusual visual effects.

To move or resize a photo or movie, follow these steps:

1. **In the Slide Navigator, click the slide where you want to move or resize a photo or movie.**

2. **Click the photo or movie.**

Handles appear around your chosen photo or movie.

3. **To move a photo or movie, place the cursor over the middle of the image, click and drag the photo or movie to a new location on the slide, and then release the mouse or trackpad button.**

4. **To resize a photo or movie, click and drag a handle to resize the photo or movie, and then release the mouse button.**

Holding down the Shift key while resizing a photo or movie retains the height and width proportions.

Creating Transitions and Effects

To make your presentations visually interesting to watch, you can add transitions and effects. *Slide transitions* define how a slide appears and disappears from the display. *Text and graphic effects* define how the text or graphic initially appears on or disappears from the slide and how it moves around a slide.

Creating a slide transition

To create a slide transition, follow these steps:

1. **Choose View⇨Navigator on the menu bar.**

2. **In the Slide Navigator, click the slide that you want to display with a transition.**

3. **Click the Inspector icon.**

4. **Click the Slide Inspector icon (shown in Figure 5-19) in the Inspector window, and then click the Transition tab.**

5. **Click the Effect pop-up menu and choose an effect, such as Shimmer or Confetti.**

   The Magic Move effect animates an object, moving it from its location on one slide to a new location on the next slide. The object must be the same on both slides. Place the object at the starting point on the first slide and then on the end point on the second slide. The Magic Move feature moves the object when the slide transitions from the first slide to the second slide.

   The Slide Inspector gives you a preview of what your transition will look like.

   Choose None in the Effect pop-up menu to remove a transition.

6. **(Optional) Depending on the transition effect you choose, you may need to define other options, such as the direction or duration of your transition.**

7. **Click the Close button of the Inspector window.**

Slide Inspector icon

Figure 5-19:
Use the
Transition
tab in
the Slide
Inspector
to define a
transition.

Creating text and graphic effects

Sometimes you want your bullets to show up one at a time. Instead of creating separate slides — the first with one bullet, the second with two bullets, the third with three, and so on — create your slide with the bullets you want, and then choose how Keynote "builds" your slide during your presentation. Keynote offers three ways to create text and graphic effects in over 25 types of transitions:

✦ **Build In:** Defines how text and graphics enter a slide. (If you choose the Build In transition, initially, the text and graphics won't appear on the slide.)

✦ **Build Out:** Defines how text and graphics exit a slide.

✦ **Action:** Defines how text and graphics move on a slide.

To define an effect for text or graphics, follow these steps:

1. **Choose View⟹Navigator on the menu bar.**

2. **In the Slide Navigator, click the slide that contains the text or graphic you want to display with a visual effect.**

3. **Click the text or graphic you want to modify; for example, a text box with a bulleted list, a table with several rows, or a pie chart.**

Handles appear around your chosen text or graphic.

4. **Choose View⟹Show Inspector on the menu bar or click the Inspector icon.**

An Inspector window appears.

5. **Click the Build Inspector tab in the Inspector window.**

   The Build Inspector appears, as shown in Figure 5-20.

6. **Click the Build In, Build Out, or Action tab.**

7. **Choose an option from the Effect pop-up menu.**

   Rotate and Opacity are nice choices.

8. **Set the Delivery options to build your bullet list, chart, or table, one item at a time.**

   You see how your slide will build in the small display in the Build Inspector.

9. **Click the Close button of the Inspector window.**

Figure 5-20: The Build Inspector pane lets you choose an effect for text or graphics on a slide.

Making text and graphics move on a slide

If you choose the Action button for text or graphics, you can choose the Move Effect, which lets you define a line that the text or graphic follows as it moves across a slide. To define a line to move text or graphics on a slide, follow these steps:

1. **Choose View⇨Navigator on the menu bar.**

2. **In the Slide Navigator, click the slide that contains the text or graphic you want to display with a visual effect.**

3. **Click the text or graphic you want to modify.**

   Handles appear around your chosen text or graphic.

4. **Choose View⇨Show Inspector on the menu bar or click the Inspector icon.**

   An Inspector window appears.

5. **Click the Build Inspector tab.**

6. **Click the Action tab.**

7. **Choose Move from the Effect pop-up menu.**

   Keynote displays a red line that shows how your chosen text or graphic will move, as shown in Figure 5-21.

8. **(Optional) Click and drag the handle at the beginning or end of the red line to move the line or change the line length.**

   Moving the red line changes the direction your chosen text or graphic moves. Changing the line length determines how far your chosen text or graphic moves.

9. **(Optional) Click the Straight Line or Curved Line button under the Path heading in the Inspector window to change how your object moves.**

10. **Click the Close button of the Inspector window.**

REMEMBER

The Action feature moves an object or text on a slide. The Magic Move feature animates objects or text from one slide to the next during the slide transition.

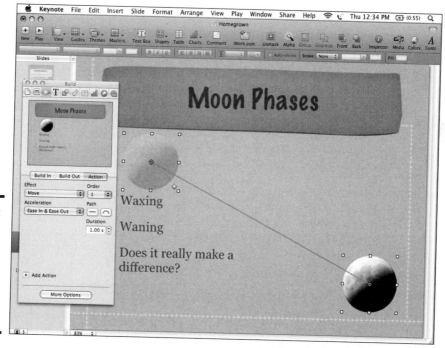

Figure 5-21: Keynote displays the path connecting text or graphics on a slide.

Adding hyperlinks to your presentation

Like links in a web page, hyperlinks within your presentation connect to another point in the presentation, connect to a website, or open an outgoing e-mail message. They are particularly useful for creating presentations which a viewer will watch alone — say, at a kiosk or even on your website — you don't even have to be present for the viewer to see your presentation. Here's how to create a hyperlink:

1. **Choose View⇨Navigator on the menu bar.**

2. **In the Slide Navigator, click the slide that contains the text or graphic you want to use as the departure point for the hyperlink.**

3. **Select the text or graphic that will act as the hyperlink button.**

4. **Click the Inspector icon in the Toolbar.**

5. **Click the Hyperlink tab.**

   The Hyperlink Inspector opens, as shown in Figure 5-22.

6. **Select the Enable as a Hyperlink check box.**

   This makes the Link To menu active.

7. **Click the Link To pop-up menu to choose what you want the hyperlink to link to:**

   • *Slide:* Use the check boxes to choose another slide within the presentation, or fill in the slide number.

   • *Webpage:* Type in the URL of the web page you want to link to.

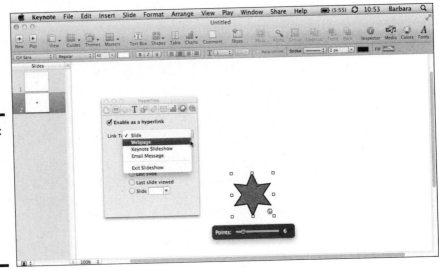

Figure 5-22: Hyperlinks use text or graphics as buttons to link to another slide or website.

- *Keynote Slideshow:* Choose the location on your Mac of a different slide show that you want to link to.

- *Email Message:* Type in the address to whom the message should be sent, along with a subject line.

- *Exit Slideshow:* Clicking the hyperlink will close the presentation.

Polishing Your Presentation

When you finish modifying the slides in your presentation, you need to show your presentation to others. You might give a presentation in person or post it on YouTube or your website so they can view it at their leisure.

Viewing a presentation

After you finish creating a presentation, you need to view it to see how it actually looks. The slide order or visual effects might have looked good when you put your presentation together, but when viewed in its entirety, you may suddenly notice gaps in your presentation. To view a presentation, follow these steps:

1. **In the Slide Navigator, click the first slide you want to view.**

   If you click the first slide of your presentation, you'll view your entire presentation. If you click a slide in the middle of your presentation, your slide show begins from that slide and proceeds until it reaches the last slide.

2. **Click the Play icon on the Keynote toolbar or choose Play⇨Play Slideshow on the menu bar.**

   The slide you chose in Step 1 appears.

3. **Click the mouse button or trackpad or press the spacebar to view each successive slide.**

   If you're at the last slide of your presentation, click the mouse button or trackpad, or press the spacebar, to exit your presentation.

4. **(Optional) Press Esc if you want to stop viewing your presentation before reaching the last slide.**

Rehearsing a presentation

Viewing a presentation lets you make sure that all the slides are in the right order and that all effects and transitions work as you expect. Before giving your presentation, you may want to rehearse it and let Keynote approximate how much time you spend on each slide.

Rehearsing can give you only a general estimate of the time needed to give your presentation. In real life, various conditions — for example, an impatient audience sitting in a stuffy conference room where the air conditioning suddenly breaks down — might make you nervous or speed up your timing.

To rehearse a presentation, follow these steps:

1. **Choose View➪Navigator on the menu bar.**

2. **In the Slide Navigator, click the first slide you want to view.**

3. **Choose Play➪Rehearse Slideshow on the menu bar.**

    Keynote displays your slides with a timer underneath, as shown in Figure 5-23.

4. **Practice what you're going to say when presenting each slide and press the spacebar or click the mouse button to advance to the next slide.**

Giving your presentation

When the day arrives that you have to give your presentation, Keynote has some tools to help you there too. As long as your presentation will be presented with a second projection system; that is, not viewed directly on your Mac while you're giving it, you can have your notes and stopwatch next to your slides on your Mac while the audience sees only your slides. To set up the Presenter Display:

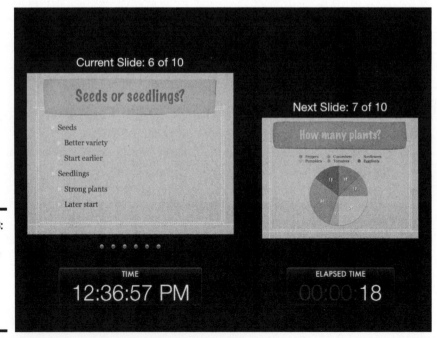

Figure 5-23: Keynote tracks how much time you spend on each slide.

1. **Choose Keynote⇨Preferences.**
2. **Select the Presenter Display tab.**
3. **Click Use Alternate Display to View Presenter Information.**
4. **Select the other items you want to see while you give your presentation, such as Notes or Timer, as shown in Figure 5-24.**
5. **Click the close button on the preferences window.**

Using Keynote Remote on your iOS device

If you have an iPhone, iPad, or iPod ouch, you can use the device as a remote control for your Keynote presentation. Download the Keynote Remote App to your iPhone, iPad, or iPod touch from the iTunes Store for $0.99. To set up Keynote Remote, do the following:

1. **Turn on Wi-Fi or Bluetooth on both your iPhone, iPad, or iPod touch, and your Mac.**

   See Book VI, Chapter 1 to find out how to set up a Wi-Fi network and Book VI, Chapter 3 to discover how to use Bluetooth on your Mac.

2. **Tap the Keynote Remote icon on your iPhone, iPad, or iPod touch.**
3. **Tap the Setup Keynote Link at the bottom of the screen.**

   A passcode appears.

4. **On your Mac, open the Keynote presentation you want to give.**
5. **Choose Keynote⇨Preferences⇨Remote.**

   Keynote searches for iPhones, iPads, and iPods on the same network as your Mac.

Figure 5-24: The Presenter Display shows tools that help you keep your presentation running smoothly.

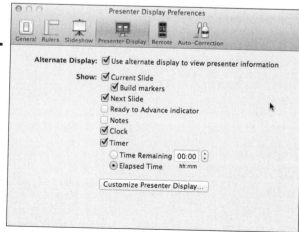

6. **Click your iPhone, iPad, or iPod touch when it appears in the list, as shown in Figure 5-25.**

7. **Enter the passcode that is on your iPhone, iPad, or iPod touch.**

8. **Close the Preferences pane.**

9. **The Keynote screen on your iPhone, iPad, or iPod touch appears, as shown in Figure 5-26.**

10. **Tap Play Slideshow.**

    You see the first two slides of your presentation on your iPhone, iPad, or iPod touch.

11. **Swipe the presentation on your iPhone, iPad, or iPod touch to move to the next slide.**

    Your presentation advances one slide on your Mac.

12. **When you're done with the presentation, press the Home button on your iPhone, iPad, or iPod touch to exit Keynote Remote, and then double-click the Home button to open the open apps bar.**

13. **Tap and hold the Keynote Remote icon until it jiggles and an "X" appears in the corner. Tap the "X" to close Keynote Remote.**

Sharing your presentation

When you give a presentation, you'll probably do it directly from your Mac. However, there might come a time when you need to save your presentation to run on a different type of computer or when you want to give others the opportunity to see your presentation on your website or on YouTube. Fortunately, Keynote lets you *export* a Keynote presentation in six different formats and send your presentation to five other applications.

Figure 5-25:
If your iPhone, iPad, iPod touch, and Mac are on the same Wi-Fi network, you see it in the Remote list in Keynote Preferences.

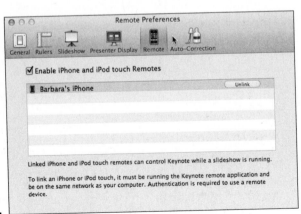

Figure 5-26:
Play your
slideshow
from your
iPhone,
iPad, or iPod
touch.

To export a Keynote presentation, follow these steps:

1. **Choose Share⇨Export on the menu bar.**

A dialog appears, as shown in Figure 5-27.

2. **Click one of the following options:**

- *QuickTime:* Saves your presentation as a movie that can play on a
  Windows PC or Mac computer that has the free QuickTime player.
  This movie preserves all transitions and visual effects.

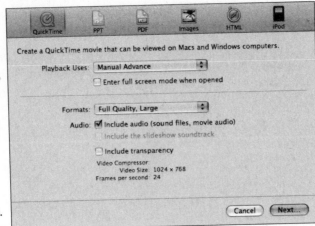

Figure 5-27:
Use the
Export dialog
to choose a
format in
which to
save your
Keynote
presentation.

- *PowerPoint:* Saves your presentation as a PowerPoint file that you can edit and run on any computer that runs PowerPoint. (Certain visual effects and transitions might not work in PowerPoint.)

- *PDF:* Saves your presentation as a series of static images stored in the Adobe Acrobat portable document file format that can be viewed by any computer with a PDF viewing application. Any interesting visual or transition effects between slides will be lost.

- *Images:* Saves each slide as a separate graphic file.

- *HTML:* Saves each slide as a separate web page. Any interesting visual or transition effects between slides will be lost.

- *iPod:* Saves your presentation as a movie specially designed to play on an iPod.

If you want to preserve your visual effects and transitions, save your presentation as a QuickTime or iPod movie, which also allows you to play your presentation on a TV connected to an iOS device. If you want to preserve and edit your presentation on a Windows PC running Microsoft PowerPoint, save your presentation as a PowerPoint file.

3. **(Optional) Depending on the option you choose in Step 2, you might see additional ways to customize your presentation.**

4. **Click Next.**

   Another dialog appears, showing all the drives and folders on your hard drive.

5. **Click the folder where you want to store your presentation.**

   You may need to switch drives or folders until you find where you want to save your file.

6. **Click the Export button.**

When you export a presentation, your original Keynote presentation remains untouched in its original location.

To send your Keynote presentation to another application, follow these steps:

1. **Choose Share⇨Send To and choose one of the following**

   • iDVD

   • iPhoto

   • iTunes

   • iWeb

   • GarageBand

   • YouTube

2. **Whichever you choose, a dialog opens that asks for formatting information specific to the application you choose.**

   For example, set the video size for iDVD or the file type for iWeb.

3. **Click Send.**

   An export window opens. Depending on the application you choose, you may have to type in a name for the presentation or save it to a folder. If so, there will be an Export button to click after you enter the requested information.

   YouTube requires a YouTube account.

4. **The application you chose opens and your presentation appears there.**

For more tips on using iWork and Keynote, go to Book V, Chapter 7.

Chapter 6: Crunching with Numbers

In This Chapter

✐ **Getting to know the Numbers spreadsheet**

✐ **Creating a spreadsheet**

✐ **Using sheets**

✐ **Working with tables**

✐ **Working with charts**

✐ **Polishing a spreadsheet**

✐ **Printing and sharing your spreadsheet efforts**

*N*umbers is a spreadsheet application designed to help you manipulate and calculate numbers for a wide variety of tasks, such as balancing a budget, calculating a loan, and creating an invoice. The Numbers application also lets you create line, bar, and pie charts that help you analyze your data graphically and understand what it means.

In this chapter, first we explain the parts of a spreadsheet; then we explain how to create a new spreadsheet or open an existing spreadsheet that was created in a different application. We show you how to work with your data on a spreadsheet — set up tables, enter your data, and use formulas. We give you some tips for personalizing a spreadsheet to make it aesthetically pleasing. At the end of the chapter, we go over printing and sharing your spreadsheet, even if the person you want to share with doesn't use Numbers.

Understanding the Parts of a Numbers Spreadsheet

A Numbers spreadsheet consists of one or more *sheets,* which are completely blank like an empty sheet of grid paper. The active sheet occupies the largest part of the Numbers window. Across the top is the Toolbar, which has buttons for frequently performed tasks. Immediately under the Toolbar is the Format bar, where you set the style, fonts, and colors for the text and objects on your spreadsheet. On the left side is the Sheets pane, which is a hierarchical thumbnail view of all the sheets on your spreadsheet, and the tables and charts that are on each sheet. Under the Sheets pane is the Styles pane that offers predefined color schemes for your tables. Below the Styles pane is the Instant Calculation Results pane, which displays results for calculations in selected cells.

A sheet may have one or more *tables* — distinct gridworks made up of horizontal *rows* (identified by numbers listed down the left margin), and vertical *columns* (in alphabetical order, each identified by a letter at the top). The intersection of a row and column is a *cell,* and that's where you type and store numbers, text, and formulas, as shown in Figure 6-1. A cell has the coordinates of the row and column; E4 (for example) is the intersection of the fifth column (E) and the fourth row.

Besides the mundane-but-fundamental cells that form the backbone of any spreadsheet, you can also place the following eye-catching (and useful) items in your spreadsheets, as shown in Figure 6-2:

✦ **Tables:** A *table* consists of rows and columns that can contain words, numbers, calculated results, or a combination of these types of contents.

✦ **Charts:** A *chart* displays data stored in a table. Common types of charts are line, bar, pie, and column charts. With Numbers, you can build 2-axis and mixed charts, too.

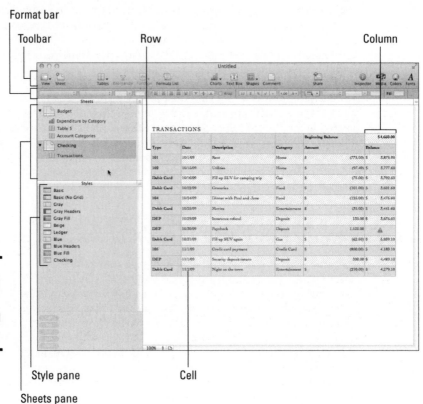

Figure 6-1:
The parts of a Numbers window and table.

✦ **Text boxes:** *Text boxes* serve mostly decorative functions. In a text box, you type and store text independent of the rows and columns in a table.

✦ **Images:** *Images* also serve mostly decorative functions. With images, you add photos or graphics on a sheet, such as a company logo.

Numbers helps you manipulate numbers and communicate your information in a visually appealing and effective way.

Putting together a spreadsheet is a simple process. The following list points out the basic steps:

✦ **Start with a sheet.** When you create a new Numbers file, either from scratch or by using a template, Numbers automatically creates one sheet with one table on it. Your job is to fill that table with data. Add more tables — yes, a sheet can hold multiple tables — or start spicing up your data presentation with charts or pictures. (More on that later.)

✦ **Fill a table with numbers and text.** After setting up at least one table on a sheet, you can move the table around on the sheet and/or resize it. When you're happy with the table's position on the sheet and the table's size, you can start typing numbers into the table's rows and columns. Add titles to the rows and columns to identify what those numbers mean, such as "August Sales" or "Screwdrivers Sold."

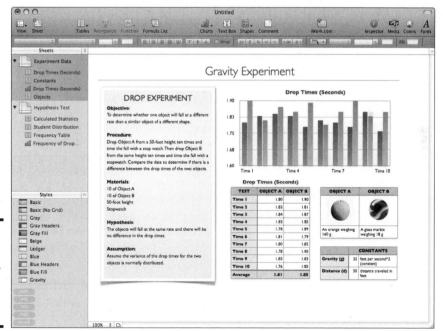

Figure 6-2:
A sheet can have tables, charts, text boxes, and images.

✦ **Create formulas and use functions.** After you type numbers in a table, you'll want to manipulate one or more numbers in certain ways, such as adding a column of numbers. Numbers offers 250 predefined functions to take your numbers or text and calculate a result, such as how much your company made in sales last month or how a salesperson's sales results have changed.

Formulas not only calculate useful results, but they also let you enter hypothetical numbers to see possible results. For example, if every salesperson improved his or her sales results by 5 percent every month, how much profit increase would that bring to the company? By typing in different values, you can ask, "What if?" questions with your data and formulas.

✦ **Visualizing data with charts.** Just glancing at a dozen numbers in a row or column might not show you much of anything. By turning numeric data into line, bar, or pie charts, Numbers can help you spot trends in your data.

✦ **Polish your sheets.** Most spreadsheets consist of rows and columns of numbers with a bit of descriptive text thrown in for good measure. Although functional, such spreadsheets are boring to look at. That's why Numbers gives you the chance to place text boxes and images on your sheets to make your information (tables and charts) compelling.

Creating a Numbers Spreadsheet

To help you create a spreadsheet, Numbers provides 30 templates that you can use as-is or modify. Templates contain preset tables with formulas, which calculate the task at hand. For example, in the Savings Tracker template, you enter your goal, the length of time for your investment, and the interest rate, and the template calculates how much you have to save each month to reach your goal. Changing those values changes the results.

Templates also have predefined font styles and color schemes. You can alter anything you want in a template — tables, charts, colors — but finding a template that is close to what you want to do gives you a head start; you don't have to spend time designing, so you can concentrate on your figures.

If you prefer, you can use the Blank template to create a spreadsheet (one sheet with one table) from scratch. If you design a particularly useful spreadsheet, you can even save it as a template (by choosing File➪Save as Template) to use in the future.

Creating a new spreadsheet with a template

To create a spreadsheet based on a template, follow these steps:

1. **Double-click the Numbers icon in the Launchpad or click the Numbers icon in the Dock (or choose File⇨New on the menu bar if Numbers is already running).**

The Template Chooser dialog opens, as shown in Figure 6-3.

2. **Click a template category in the list on the left (or click All if you want to see all 30).**

- Choose a template that is closest to what you want to do; for example, a household budget or a workout tracker.

- Most templates have more than one sheet. Move the pointer over the template image to see other sheets associated with that template.

Click and drag the slider at the bottom of the template chooser to zoom in on the icons and get a better view of their layouts.

3. **Double-click the template that you want to use, or click the template you like in the main pane, and then click Choose.**

Numbers opens your chosen template, which you can fill in with rows and columns of numbers you want to calculate, or text you want to associate with numbers that you want to sort by alphabetical order, or by highest to lowest number, or the other way around.

If you want to start with a blank spreadsheet, click Blank in the list on the left.

4. **Choose File⇨Save.**

A Save As dialog opens.

Figure 6-3:
Numbers provides spreadsheet templates organized in categories, such as Personal or Business.

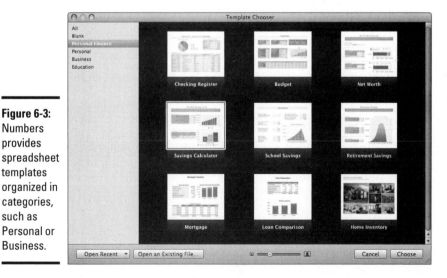

5. **Type a name for your spreadsheet and choose the folder where you want to store it on your Mac.**

   With Mac OS X 10.7 Lion, Numbers supports Versions, which we explain in Book I, Chapter 4 and Book III, Chapter 1.

Opening an existing file in a different format

You may have spreadsheets that were created in a different application, such as Microsoft Excel, Quicken's Open Financial Exchange (OFX), or AppleWorks 6, or you may have raw data that you want to bring into Numbers, such as comma-separated-values (CSV) or tab-delimited text. You can open the file in Numbers and Numbers will create sheets and tables with the data supplied.

To open non-Numbers spreadsheets, drag the file from the Desktop over the Numbers icon on the Dock. You can also open a non-Numbers spreadsheet as follows:

1. **Click the Numbers icon in the Dock or Launchpad.**

2. **Click Open an Existing File. If Numbers is already running, choose File⇨Open.**

   A window showing the folders and files on your Mac opens.

3. **Scroll through the list or use the Search field to find the file you want.**

4. **Click the file you want to open.**

5. **Click Open.**

   Your file opens in a Numbers spreadsheet. If there are any problems with the conversion, a Document Warning window opens, as shown in Figure 6-4. Make note of whatever tweaks you have to make. With our example in the figure, we have to reset the print area. You can Hide or Show the Document Warning by choosing View⇨Hide/Show Document Warning.

6. **Work with your document as you would a document created in Numbers.**

Figure 6-4: Numbers warns you of any problems with files opened from other applications.

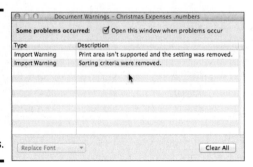

Working with Sheets

Every Numbers spreadsheet needs at least one sheet. A sheet acts like a limitless page that can hold any number of tables and charts. You want to use sheets to organize the information in your spreadsheet, such as using one sheet to hold January sales results, a second sheet to hold February sales results, and a third sheet to hold a line chart that shows each salesperson's results for the first two months.

To help organize your sheets, Numbers stores the names of all your sheets in the Sheets pane on the left. Indented underneath each sheet is a list of all tables and charts stored on that particular sheet.

To view the contents of a specific sheet, click that sheet name in the Sheets pane. To view a particular table or chart, find the sheet that contains that table or chart. Then click that specific table or chart.

Adding a sheet

You can always add another sheet if you need one. When you add a sheet, Numbers creates one table on that sheet automatically. To add a sheet, choose one of the following:

✦ Choose Insert⇨Sheet on the menu bar.

✦ Right-click (two-finger tap on a trackpad) anywhere inside the Sheets pane and choose New Sheet.

✦ Click the Sheet icon that appears above the Sheets pane.

Deleting a sheet

If you need a sheet to go away, clear out, disappear, whatever, you can delete it. When you delete a sheet, you also delete any tables or charts stored on that sheet. To delete a sheet, follow these steps:

1. **Click the sheet you want to delete in the Sheets pane.**

2. **Choose one of the following:**

   • Press the Delete key.

   • Right-click a sheet name and then choose Delete Sheet.

   • Choose Edit⇨Delete on the menu bar.

   A dialog appears, asking whether you really want to delete the sheet.

3. **Click Delete (or Cancel).**

Adding a table or chart

A sheet can hold one or more tables and charts. When you add a table or chart, the table or chart is blank. If you are working with a template, the tables or charts you add reflect the style of the template.

To add a table or chart, click the sheet where you want to add a table or chart. Then do one of the following:

✦ **To insert a table, click the Tables icon (or choose Insert⇨Table on the menu bar).** The Tables menu appears, as shown in Figure 6-5. You have the following options:

- *Headers:* Row one and column A are set aside for adding headings.

- *Basic:* Row one is highlighted for inserting column headings.

- *Sums:* Cells in the last row contain sum functions to tally the numbers in each column.

- *Plain:* Just rows and columns, no headers or sums.

- *Checklist:* Column A contains check boxes.

- *Sums Checklist:* Column A contains check boxes and cells in the last row contain sum functions.

✦ **To insert a chart, click the Charts icon (or choose Insert⇨Chart on the menu bar).** The Charts menu appears, as shown in Figure 6-6. Your options include column, bar, line, area, pie, scatter, 2-axis, and mixed charts. There are two- and three-dimensional charts.

Figure 6-5: The Tables menu lists different types of tables you can add.

Deleting a table or chart

When you create a table or chart, you don't have to keep it forever. Keep in mind, though, that when you delete a table, Numbers deletes all data (numbers, text, and formulas) stored on that table. If you created a chart that depends on those numbers you deleted, your chart will no longer display whatever information it displayed before you deleted the table.

Figure 6-6:
The Charts
menu lists
different
types of
charts you
can add.

To delete a table or chart, follow these steps:

1. **In the Sheets pane, click the table or chart you want to delete.**

2. **Choose one of the following:**

- Press the Delete key.

- Right-click a table or chart and then choose Delete.

- Choose Edit⇨Delete on the menu bar.

Naming sheets, tables, and charts

Numbers gives each sheet, table, and chart a generic name, such as Sheet 2, Table 1, or Chart 3. To help you better understand the type of information stored on each sheet, table, and chart, use more descriptive names, especially when you add multiple tables and charts (which you find out about later in this chapter). The sheet, table, and chart names don't show up on your sheet, just on the Sheets pane to help you navigate your spreadsheet.

To name a sheet, table, or chart in the Sheets pane, follow these steps:

1. **Double-click a sheet, table, or chart name, or Right-click (two-finger tap on a trackpad) a sheet, table, or chart name and then choose Rename.**

The name is highlighted.

2. **Type a new name or use the arrow keys and the Delete key to edit an existing name.**

Setting Up Tables

Just as you set the dinner table to accommodate the number and size of your guests, you set your Numbers table to accommodate your data. You define the number of rows and columns your table needs based on the quantity of data you have to enter. You set the row height and column width based on the kind of data you have, as well as the font style and size you choose.

Adding rows and columns

When you add a table to a sheet, Numbers opens a standard table in the format that you choose. This may be too small, or too big, for your data. If you know you want a bigger — or smaller — table, you use the Resize corner to add or subtract rows and columns. Just follow these steps:

1. **In the Sheets pane, click the table that you want to resize.**

Numbers displays your selected table with handles around it.

2. **Click anywhere inside the table.**

The table displays column and row headings, a Move corner (in the upper-left corner of the table), and a Resize corner (in the bottom-right corner of the table), as shown in Figure 6-7.

3. **Move the pointer to the Resize corner in the bottom-right corner of the table.**

4. **Click and drag the Resize corner to resize the table on the sheet.**

While you drag the Resize corner, you add (or delete) rows or columns or both.

5. **Release the mouse button when you're happy with the table's number of rows and columns.**

When you click inside the table, the Resize corner appears and adds rows and columns. Selecting the table in the Sheets pane or clicking the outer edge of the table brings up resizing handles. Grab any of these with the mouse pointer to enlarge or shrink the overall table, affecting the row heights and column widths; the number of rows and columns is unchanged.

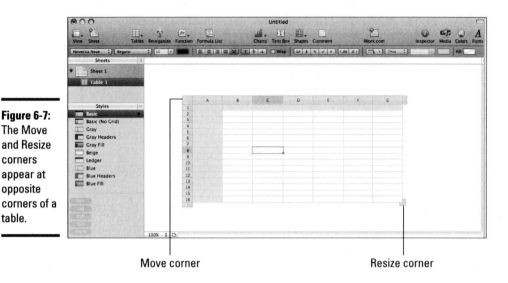

Figure 6-7:
The Move
and Resize
corners
appear at
opposite
corners of a
table.

Move corner   Resize corner

Inserting header rows and columns

Headers are the first rows and columns of your table, where you usually type
the names of the rows and columns. You can have header rows and columns
that comprise up to five rows or columns. This lets you have titles and subtitles
for each row or column. To insert header rows and columns, do the following:

1. **Click the Table menu and click Header Rows or Header Columns.**

   Select the number of rows or columns you want, between one and five. If
   you choose zero, your table has no headers. Header rows and columns
   are shaded on your table.

   If you want a footer row, choose Table➪Footer Rows and choose the
   number you want, from one to five.

2. **To make your header rows and columns stay put while you scroll
   through the rest of your table, choose Table➪Freeze Header Columns
   and/or Table➪Freeze Header Rows.**

To add more header rows or columns, do the following:

1. **Click a cell in one of the header rows or columns, either before or
   after where you want to insert another header row or column.**

2. **Click the Table menu and choose from the following:**

   • *Add Header Row Above:* Inserts an additional header row directly
     above the selected cell.

- *Add Header Row Below:* Inserts an additional header row directly below the selected cell.

- *Add Header Column Before:* Inserts an additional header column to the left of the selected cell.

- *Add Header Column After:* Inserts a new column to the right of the selected cell.

Inserting a row or column

You're entering your data and suddenly you realize you need to add a row or column in the middle of your table. No sweat.

To add a row or column in the middle of a table, click a cell where you want to insert another row or column, click the Table menu and then choose one of the following:

✦ **Add Row Above:** Inserts a new row directly above the selected cell.

✦ **Add Row Below:** Inserts a new row directly below the selected cell.

✦ **Add Column Before:** Inserts a new column to the left of the selected cell.

✦ **Add Column After:** Inserts a new column to the right of the selected cell.

To insert multiple columns or rows, highlight two or more column or row headings to equal the number of rows and columns you want to add, click the Table menu, and then choose Add Columns Before/After or Add Rows Above/Below.

If you move the pointer to a row or column heading (such as D for a column or 5 for a row), a downward-pointing arrow appears. You can click the arrow to display a menu from which you can choose any option in the preceding list.

Deleting a row or column

To delete any type of row or column — simple, header, or footer — choose one of the following:

✦ Click a cell inside the row or column you want to delete and then choose Table⇨Delete Row (or Delete Column).

✦ Right-click a cell inside the row or column you want to delete, and then choose Delete Row (or Delete Column) from the shortcut menu.

✦ Move the pointer over the row or column heading (such as column A or row 3), click the downward-pointing arrow that appears, and then choose Delete Row (or Delete column).

You can delete multiple columns or rows by highlighting those column or row headings, clicking the Table menu, and then choosing Delete Columns or Delete Rows.

Resizing rows and columns

Just as a new table opens with ten rows and four columns, the cells in those rows and columns have preset widths and heights. However, a small cell might not show all the information stored in that cell. To fix this problem, you can resize rows and columns.

Resizing the fast way

To resize a row or column with the mouse, follow these steps:

1. **Click inside the table you want to alter.**

   The row and column headings appear.

2. **Move the pointer to the border between two row or column headings, such as between columns A and B.**

   The pointer turns into a two-way pointing arrow around a vertical or horizontal line.

3. **Click and drag the mouse or trackpad up/down or right/left to resize the row or column.**

4. **Release the mouse button or trackpad when you're happy with the size of your row or column.**

If you have data stored inside a row or column, Numbers can resize the row or column automatically to fit the largest item stored in that row or column. To resize a row or column, click a cell inside the row or column you want to resize and choose Table⇨Resize Columns to Fit Content (or Resize Rows to Fit Content).

Resizing the precise way

If you want to resize a row or column to a specific height or width, follow these steps:

1. **Click a cell inside the row or column you want to resize.**

2. **Choose View⇨Inspector on the menu bar or click the Inspector icon on the Toolbar.**

   An Inspector window appears.

3. **Click the Table Inspector icon on the Inspector toolbar, as shown in Figure 6-8.**

Table Inspector icon

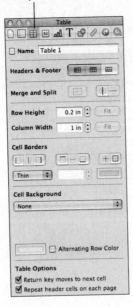

Figure 6-8:
The Table
Inspector
pane
displays
text boxes
to define a
Row Height
or Column
Width
precisely.

4. **Click the Row Height or Column Width text box and then type a value or click the up/down arrows in that text box to define a value.**

5. **Click the Close button of the Inspector window.**

Formatting a table

To make your table easier to read, you can format it with a style, which provides ways to color row and column headings of an entire table with one click of the mouse. To format a table, follow these steps:

1. **In the Sheets pane, click the table that you want to format.**

   Numbers displays your chosen table.

2. **Click a formatting style, such as Ledger or Blue Headers, in the Styles pane in the bottom-left corner of the Numbers window.**

   Numbers formats your table. If you don't like the way your table looks, choose another of the ten styles available.

Resizing a table

You may need to resize a table to fit it in a small space or to make it larger and easier to read. You can make a table larger (or smaller), while retaining the same number of rows and columns, which increases (or decreases) the height and width of rows and columns.

To stretch or shrink a table (without adding or subtracting rows or columns), follow these steps:

1. **In the Sheets pane, click the table that you want to resize.**

   Numbers displays your selected table with handles around it.

2. **Move the pointer to a handle until the pointer turns into a two-way pointing arrow.**

3. **Click and drag a handle to enlarge or shrink the table.**

   Notice that any data inside the table grows or shrinks as well.

4. **Release the mouse button when you're happy with the size of your table.**

Moving a table

After creating a table on a sheet, you can move it around to better highlight your data, especially if you have other tables, charts, or images on the sheet. When you move tables around, the surrounding objects adjust so there's no overlapping. To move a table, follow these steps:

1. **In the Sheets pane, click the table that you want to move.**

   Numbers displays your selected table.

2. **Click anywhere inside the table.**

3. **Move the pointer to the Move corner (refer to Figure 6-7) until the pointer turns into a four-way-pointing arrow underneath.**

4. **Click and drag the table to a new location on the sheet.**

5. **Release the mouse button or trackpad when you're happy with the table's new location.**

To move a table from one sheet to another, in the Sheets pane, click and drag the table from its current position to the sheet where you want it. Data and calculations remain unchanged.

Typing Data into Tables

Now we get into the numbers part of Numbers. You need to know about the three types of data you can store inside a table:

+ Numbers
+ Text
+ Formulas

To type anything into a table, follow these steps:

1. **Select a cell by clicking it or by pressing the arrow keys.**

2. **Type a number, text, or formula.**

   Be sure to precede a formula with an equal sign (=) to ensure that Numbers recognizes the contents of the cell as a formula and not as a number or text value. If you want the number to be treated as text, for example a zip code, you should enclose it in quotes.

3. **Press Return to select the cell below, press Tab to select the cell to the right, or click any cell into which you want to type new data.**

4. **Repeat Steps 2 and 3 for each additional formula or item of data you want to type into the table.**

Formatting numbers and text

When you type a number in a cell, the number will look plain — 45 or 60.3. To make your numbers more meaningful, you should format them. For example, the number 39 might mean nothing, but if you format it to appear as $39.00, your number now clearly represents a dollar amount.

To format numbers, follow these steps:

1. **Click to select one cell or click and drag to select multiple cells.**

   Numbers draws a border around your selected cell(s).

   If you select empty cells, Numbers automatically formats any numbers you type into those cells in the future.

2. **Click one of the following icons on the Format bar, as shown in Figure 6-9:**

   - *Decimal:* Displays numbers with two decimal places, such as 3.19.

   - *Currency:* Displays numbers with a currency symbol, such as $3.19.

   - *Percentage:* Displays numbers as a percentage, such as 3.19%.

   - *Increase decimal places:* Displays numbers with an additional decimal place, such as 3.190.

   - *Decrease decimal places:* Displays numbers with one less decimal place, such as 3.2.

To customize the way formatting works, such as changing the currency format from displaying dollar symbols to Euros or Swiss francs, follow these steps:

Figure 6-9:
The Format
bar displays
icons for
quickly
formatting
numbers.

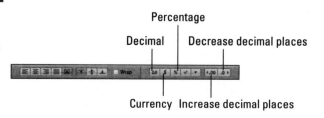

Percentage

Decimal   Decrease decimal places

Currency   Increase decimal places

1. **Select the cells that contain one or more numbers.**

2. **Click the Inspector icon or choose View⇨Show Inspector on the menu bar.**

   An Inspector window appears.

3. **Click the Cells Inspector icon on the Inspector toolbar, as shown in Figure 6-10.**

   When you click an inspector icon, the name of the inspector appears at the top of the window.

4. **Choose a format from the Cell Format pop-up menu.**

5. **Choose any options to customize your chosen format.**

   For example, if you chose the Currency format in Step 4, you can click a Symbol pop-up menu to define the type of symbol (dollar sign, Euro, and so on) that appears with each number.

6. **Click the Close button of the Inspector window.**

To make your text easier to read, you can choose different fonts and styles by following these steps:

Cells Inspector icon

Figure 6-10:
The Cells
Inspector
lets you
customize
number
formats.

1. **Select the cells that contain text.**

2. **Click one of the following on the Format bar, as shown in Figure 6-11:**

   • *Font:* Displays a variety of fonts.

   • *Style:* Displays different options, such as bold or italic.

   • *Font size:* Displays a range of sizes from 9 to 288.

   • *Text color:* Displays a color window for coloring numbers or text.

You can also set a *conditional format* so that if your data meets a certain criteria or condition, Numbers will format the number or text in a color you want. Say you create a spreadsheet to track office supply inventory and want to know when you have fewer than 5 black pens. Set the conditional formatting of the cell to "less than or equal to 5" and when there are 5 or fewer, the cell changes color. At a glance you see pertinent information. To use conditional formatting, follow these steps:

1. **Select the cell or cells where you want to use conditional formatting.**

2. **Click the Inspector icon or choose View⇨Show Inspector on the menu bar.**

3. **Click the Cells Inspector icon on the Inspector toolbar.**

4. **Click Show Rules under Conditional Formatting.**

   The Conditional Formatting window opens.

5. **Click the Choose a Rule pop-up menu and select the rule you want to use, as shown in Figure 6-12.**

   A field appears where you can type in a value.

   • If you want to refer to another cell, click the blue circle on the right end of the field and type in a cell reference, or click the cell in your sheet and its reference appears in the field.

   • To change the value, click in the field and press the Delete key, and then type another value or enter a different cell reference.

Font   Font size

Figure 6-11:
Change the
font.

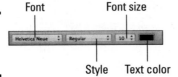

Style   Text color

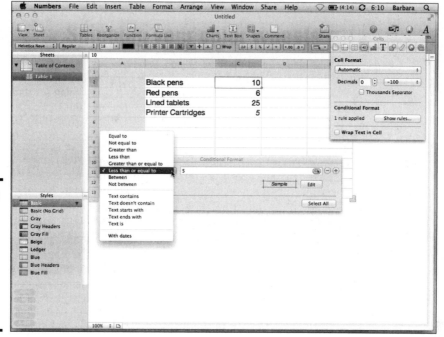

Figure 6-12:
Numbers
formats
cells that
meet
criteria
set in
Conditional
Formatting.

6. **Click the Edit button.**

   Two formatting options appear:

   - *Text*: Click the rectangle to assign a color to the text in the cell; a color picker opens where you click the color you desire for your text. You can also choose bold, italic, underline, or strikethrough by clicking the boxes with those symbols.

   - *Fill:* Click the rectangle next to Fill to assign a background color to the cell.

   The sample box shows how the cell will appear if the data in it meet the conditional rule you set.

7. **Click Done.**

8. **To add another rule, click the plus sign on the right of the window.**

9. **To delete a rule, click the minus sign to the right of the rule you want to delete.**

10. **To clear all rules, click Clear All Rules.**

Typing formulas

The main purpose of a table is to use the data (numbers, textual data, dates, and times) you store in cells to calculate a new result, such as adding a row or column of numbers. To calculate and display a result, you need to store a formula in the cell where you want the result to appear.

Numbers provides three ways to create formulas in a cell:

✦ Quick formulas

✦ Typed formulas

✦ Functions

Using Quick Formulas

To help you calculate numbers in a hurry, Numbers offers a variety of Quick Formulas that can calculate common results, such as

✦ **Sum:** Adds numbers.

✦ **Average:** Calculates the arithmetic mean.

✦ **Minimum:** Displays the smallest number.

✦ **Maximum:** Displays the largest number.

✦ **Count:** Displays how many cells you select.

✦ **Product:** Multiplies numbers.

To use a Quick Formula, follow these steps:

1. **Select two or more cells that contain numbers.**

2. **Click the Function icon, or choose Insert⇨Function on the menu bar, and then choose a Quick Formula (Sum, Average, Minimum, Maximum, Count, or Product).**

Numbers displays your calculated results.

If you highlight a row of numbers, the Quick Formula displays the result to the right. If you highlight a column of numbers, the Quick Formula displays the result at the bottom of the column. If you highlight both rows and columns of numbers, the Quick Formula displays the result at the bottom of each column.

Typing a formula

Quick Formulas are handy when they offer the formula you need, such as when you add up rows or columns of numbers with the Sum formula. Often, however, you need to create your own formulas.

Every formula consists of two parts:

✦ **Operators:** Perform calculations, such as addition (+), subtraction (–), multiplication (*), and division (/).

✦ **Cell references:** Define where to find the data to use for calculations.

A typical formula looks like this:

```
= A3 + A4
```

This formula tells Numbers to take the number stored in Column A, Row 3 and add it to the number stored in Column A, Row 4.

To type a formula, follow these steps:

1. **Click (or use the arrow keys to highlight) the cell where you want the formula results to appear.**

2. **Type =.**

The Formula Editor appears, as shown in Figure 6-13.

You can move the Formula Editor if you move the pointer to the left end of the Formula Editor. When the pointer turns into a hand, click and drag the Formula Editor to a new location.

3. **Click a cell that contains the data you want to include in your calculation.**

4. **Type an operator, such as * for multiplication or / for division.**

5. **Click another cell that contains the data you want to include in your calculation.**

6. **Repeat Steps 4 and 5 as often as necessary.**

7. **Click the Accept (or Cancel) button on the Formula Editor when you're done.**

Numbers displays the results of your formula. If you change the numbers in the cells you define in Step 3 and Step 5, Numbers calculates a new result instantly.

Figure 6-13:
The Formula
Editor lets
you create
and edit
a formula
stored in a
cell.

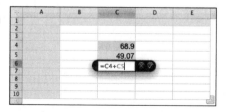

For a fast way to calculate values without having to type a formula in a cell, you can use Instant Calculations. Just select two or more cells that contain numbers and you can see the results in the Instant Calculations Results pane in the bottom-left corner of the Numbers window, as shown in Figure 6-14.

Using functions

Typing simple formulas that add or multiply is easy. However, many calculations can get more complicated, such as trying to calculate the amount of interest paid on a loan with a specific interest rate over a defined period.

To help you calculate commonly used formulas, Numbers provides a library of 250 *functions* — prebuilt formulas that you can plug into your table and define what data to use without having to create the formula yourself.

To use a function, follow these steps:

1. **Click (or use the arrow keys to highlight) the cell where you want the function results to appear.**

2. **Click the Function icon.**

   A pull-down menu appears.

3. **Choose Show Function Browser.**

   A Functions Browser opens, as shown in Figure 6-15. It displays all the available functions, along with a definition for each one.

4. **Click a function category in the left pane, such as Financial or Statistical.**

   The right pane displays only those functions stored in that category.

5. **Click a function in the right pane and click the Insert button.**

   The Formula Editor appears, containing your chosen function.

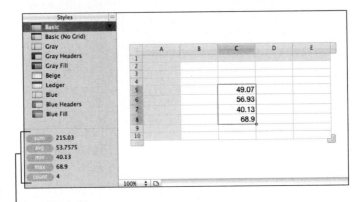

Figure 6-14: Instant calculations can show results without you typing a formula first.

Instant calculations

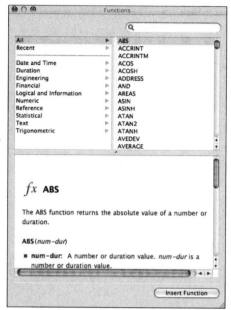

Figure 6-15:
The
Functions
Browser
displays all
available
functions
that
Numbers
provides.

6. **Edit the formula by typing the cell names (such as C4) or clicking the cells that contain the data the function needs to calculate.**

7. **Click the Accept (or Cancel) button on the Formula Editor.**

Numbers shows your result.

Choose View⇨Show Formula List to see a list of all the formulas used in a spreadsheet. You can also see the formulas used in templates in this way.

Formatting data entry cells

After you create formulas or functions in cells, you can type new data in the cells defined by a formula or function and watch Numbers calculate a new result instantly. Typing a new number in a cell is easy to do, but sometimes a formula or function requires a specific range of values. For example, if you have a formula that calculates sales tax, you may not want someone to enter a sales tax over 10% or less than 5%.

To limit the types of values someone can enter in a cell, you can use one of the following methods, as shown in Figure 6-16:

✦ **Sliders:** Lets the user drag a slider to choose a value within a fixed range.

✦ **Steppers:** Lets the user click up and down arrows to choose a value that increases or decreases in fixed increments.

✦ **Pop-up menus:** Lets the user choose from a limited range of choices.

Figure 6-16:
Sliders,
steppers,
and pop-up
menus
restrict the
types of
values a cell
can hold.

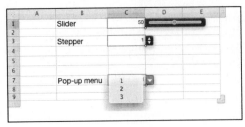

Formatting a cell with a slider or stepper

A *slider* or *stepper* is useful when you want to restrict a cell to a range of values, such as 1 to 45. The main difference between the two is that a slider appears next to a cell, whereas a stepper appears inside a cell.

To format a cell with a slider or stepper, follow these steps:

1. **Click a cell that you want to restrict to a range of values.**

2. **Click the Format button (it looks like a downward-pointing arrow) on the Format bar and choose Slider or Stepper from the pull-down menu that appears.**

   The Cells Inspector appears, as shown in Figure 6-17.

3. **Click the Minimum text box and type the minimum acceptable value.**

4. **Click the Maximum text box and type the maximum acceptable value.**

5. **Click the Increment text box and type a value to increase or decrease by when the user drags the slider or clicks the up and down arrows of the stepper.**

Figure 6-17:
The Cells
Inspector
lets you
define the
range of
values for
a slider or
stepper.

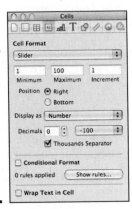

6. Click the Close button of the Inspector window.

Numbers displays a slider next to the cell. Users have a choice of typing a value or using the slider to define a value. If you choose a value outside the minimum and maximum range defined in Steps 3 and 4, the cell won't accept the invalid data.

Formatting a cell with a pop-up menu

A pop-up menu restricts a cell to a limited number of choices. To format a cell with a pop-up menu, follow these steps:

1. Click a cell that you want to restrict to a limited choice of values.

2. Click the Format button (it looks like a downward-pointing arrow) on the Format bar.

A pull-down menu appears.

3. Select Pop-up Menu from the pull-down menu.

The Cells Inspector appears, as shown in Figure 6-18.

4. In the Cells Inspector, click the list box under the Cell Format pop-up menu.

5. Click the plus (+) sign button to add an item to the pop-up menu associated with the cell, and then type in the number or text you want added.

Repeat to add other items.

6. To remove an item from the list, click the item, and then click the minus (–) sign buttons.

Repeat to delete other items.

7. Click the Close button of the Cells Inspector window.

Numbers displays a pop-up menu that lists choices when users click that cell.

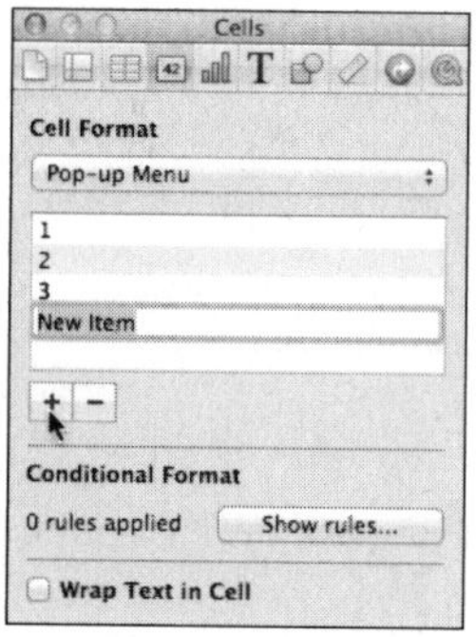

Figure 6-18: The Cells Inspector window lets you define a list of values.

Sorting data

When you type in your data, you don't always type it in the order you want to see it. For example, say you type in the data from a stack of invoices such as invoice number, date of purchase, customer name, and total. You may type the date in by invoice number but then want to sort by customer name to see which customers have more than one invoice or by total to see who spent the most. You can sort the data by one of those columns. Numbers calls this *reorganizing data* and here's how you do it:

1. **Click the table you want to sort in the Sheets pane.**

2. **To sort the entire table, do nothing. To sort a portion of the table, click and drag to select the rows and columns you want to sort.**

3. **Click the Reorganize button in the Toolbar.**

   The Reorganize window opens, as shown in Figure 6-19.

4. **Click the column pop-up menu and select the column you want to sort by.**

5. **Select Ascending or Descending to establish the order in which you want the data.**

6. **(Optional) Click the plus sign to add more sort criteria.**

   Numbers will sort your data by the column or row you chose for the first sort, and then perform a secondary sort by the column or row used as the base for the second sort.

7. **Choose Sort Entire Table or Sort Selected Rows from the pop-up menu.**

8. **Click Sort Now.**

   Your table is now reorganized to reflect the sort criteria you set.

Figure 6-19:
Use the
Reorganize
feature to
sort the
data in your
table.

Deleting data in cells

After you type data into a cell, you might later want to delete that data. Numbers provides two ways to delete data in cells:

✦ Delete data but retain any formatting.

✦ Delete data and formatting.

To delete data but retain any formatting, follow these steps:

1. **Select one or more cells that contain data you want to delete.**

2. **Press Delete or choose Edit⇨Delete on the menu bar.**

To delete both data and formatting in cells, follow these steps:

1. **Select one or more cells that contain data and formatting you want to delete.**

2. **Choose Edit⇨Clear All on the menu bar.**

Making Charts

Charts help make sense out of your numeric data by (in effect) representing numbers as images that can show trends or help you spot patterns, such as identifying which salesperson is most consistent (and which ones are consistently the best and worst).

Creating a chart

Creating a chart is a three-step process. First, you have to decide what numeric data you want to turn into a chart. Second, you need to choose a specific type of chart to create, such as a mixed bar and line chart or pie chart. Finally, you have to decide whether you want to create a two-dimensional or three-dimensional chart.

A 3-D chart might look cool, but it can often make understanding your data harder. You may need to experiment with different charts until you find one that displays your data the best.

To create a chart, follow these steps:

1. **Highlight the data you want to convert into a chart.**

   You can highlight data by dragging the mouse/trackpad or by holding down the Shift key and pressing the arrow keys.

2. **Click the Charts icon or choose Insert⇨Chart on the menu bar.**

   A pull-down menu of different chart types appears.

3. **Click a chart type.**

   Numbers creates your chart, along with a Chart Inspector window, as shown in Figure 6-20.

   If you don't like the chart type you chose, click the Chart Type icon in the Chart Inspector and choose a different chart type.

4. **Click the Close button of the Inspector window.**

Editing a chart

After you create a chart, you may need to edit it. To edit your chart, follow these steps:

1. **In the Sheets pane, click the chart name that you want to edit.**

   Numbers displays your chart with handles around its edges.

2. **Choose View⇨Show Inspector on the menu bar.**

   The Chart Inspector appears, giving you options you can modify.

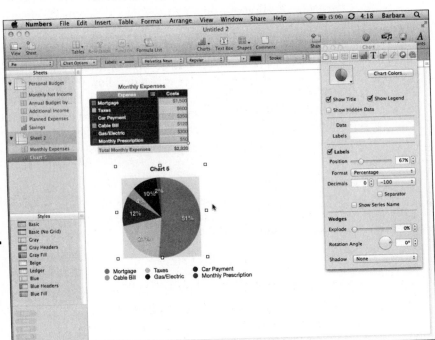

Figure 6-20: Numbers creates a chart based on the data you select.

3. **Choose any options in the Chart Inspector pane.**

   You may want to change the title of your chart or hide the legend that explains what each color represents.

4. **Click the Close button of the Inspector window.**

Manipulating a chart

A chart is just another object that you can move, resize, or delete.

Any time you resize, move, or delete a chart, you can always reverse your action by pressing ⌘+Z or choosing Edit⇨Undo.

Moving a chart on a sheet

To move a chart, follow these steps:

1. **Click a chart name in the Sheets pane.**

   Numbers displays your chart with handles around it.

2. **Click the middle of the chart, hold down the mouse or trackpad button, and drag the chart to a new location.**

3. **Release the mouse or trackpad button when you're happy with your chart's new home.**

Moving a chart from one sheet to another sheet

To move a chart to a different sheet, hold down the Option key and drag the chart from one sheet to another sheet, or follow these steps:

1. **Click and drag the chart name underneath a Sheet icon of a different sheet in the Sheets pane.**

2. **Release the mouse or trackpad button when you're happy with the location of your chart.**

   Numbers displays your chart on the other sheet. You may need to move the chart to a specific location on the sheet to make your chart look nicer.

Resizing a chart

To resize a chart, follow these steps:

1. **Click a chart name in the Sheets pane.**

   Numbers displays your chart with handles around it.

2. **Move the pointer to a handle until the pointer turns into a two-way pointing arrow.**

3. **Click and drag the handle to resize the chart.**

Release the mouse or trackpad button when you're happy with the size of your chart.

Deleting a chart

To delete a chart, choose one of the following:

✦ Click a chart name in the Sheets pane and choose Edit⇨Delete on the menu bar.

✦ Right-click a chart name in the Sheets pane and choose Delete.

Making Your Spreadsheets Pretty

Tables and charts are the two most crucial objects you can place and arrange on a sheet. However, Numbers also lets you place text boxes, shapes, and pictures on a sheet. Text boxes can contain titles or short descriptions of the information displayed on the sheet; shapes can add color or indicate navigational cues, such as arrows; and photos can make your entire sheet look more interesting — or they may be the focus of your sheet if you are creating an inventory.

Adding a text box

To add a text box to a sheet, follow these steps:

1. **In the Sheets pane, click the name of a sheet you want to add the text box to.**

Numbers displays your chosen sheet and any additional objects that might already be on that sheet, such as tables or charts.

2. **Click the Text Box icon (or choose Insert⇨Text Box on the menu bar).**

A text box appears on the sheet.

3. **Type any text that you want to appear in the text box. (Press Return to type text on a new line.)**

While you type, your text box lengthens to accommodate your text. You can widen the text box by clicking and dragging the handles on its sides.

4. **(Optional) Select any text and choose any formatting options from the Format bar, such as different fonts or font sizes.**

Adding a photo

To add a photo from iPhoto on a sheet, follow these steps:

1. **In the Sheets pane, click the name of a sheet you want to add a photo to.**

Numbers displays your chosen sheet and any additional objects that are already on that sheet, such as tables or charts.

2. **Click the Media icon.**

The Media Browser appears.

3. **Click the Photos tab, as shown in Figure 6-21.**

4. **Click and drag a picture from the Media Browser to a blank area of your sheet.**

If you drag a picture to a table, Numbers displays your picture as a tiny image inside a single cell. Consider enlarging the cell to accommodate the photo or placing the photo outside the table.

5. **Release the mouse or trackpad button.**

Numbers displays your chosen image on the sheet.

6. **Click the Close button of the Media Browser.**

You can resize your photo by clicking the photo and then using the handles to click and drag to the size you want. You can also edit your photo by choosing Format⇨Mask or Format⇨Instant Alpha, as we explain in Book V, Chapter 7.

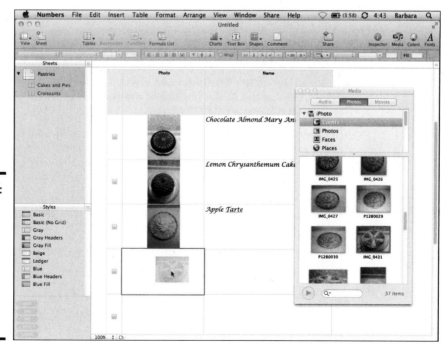

Figure 6-21:
The Photos pane in the Media Browser lets you select a photo from your iPhoto library.

Deleting text boxes, shapes, and pictures

When you want to remove an object, you can delete it by following these steps:

1. **In the Sheets pane, click the name of the sheet containing the object you want to delete.**

2. **Click the object (text box, shape, or picture) you want to delete.**

   Handles appear around your chosen object.

3. **Press the Delete key.**

Sharing Your Spreadsheet

You've put a lot of effort into making your spreadsheet presentable. When you're ready to actually *present* it, you can share your spreadsheet with others by printing it or saving it as a file for electronic distribution.

Printing a spreadsheet

In other spreadsheet applications, you can print your spreadsheet and chart — only to find that part of your chart or spreadsheet is cut off by the edge of the paper. To avoid this problem, Numbers displays a Content Slider, which lets you magnify or shrink an entire sheet so it fits and prints perfectly on a page.

To shrink or magnify a sheet to print, follow these steps:

1. **In the Sheets pane, click the name of a sheet you want to print.**

2. **Choose File⇨Show Print View or View⇨Show Print View or click the Print View button at the bottom of the page next to the pop-up magnifying menu.**

   Numbers displays a page and shows how the charts and tables on your sheet will print. If you can't see the whole page, change the view to 75% or 50% with the pop-up magnifying menu to see the borders of the page and where your tables and objects lie, as shown in Figure 6-22.

   Change between landscape (horizontal) and portrait (vertical) page orientation with the buttons at the bottom of the window.

3. **Drag the Content Slider to magnify or shrink your data until it fits exactly the way you want on the page.**

   The Content Slider is located at the bottom center of the Print view.

4. **Choose File⇨Print on the menu bar (or press ⌘+P).**

   A dialog appears asking how many copies to print, which pages to print, and which printer to use.

5. **Choose the print options you want and click Print.**

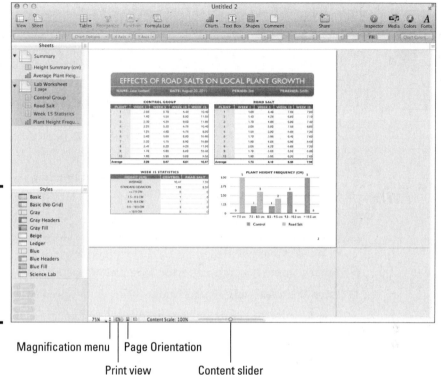

Figure 6-22:
The Print view shows you exactly how your sheet will print on paper.

Magnification menu | Page Orientation

Print view | Content slider

Exporting a spreadsheet

When you choose File⇨Save, Numbers saves your spreadsheet in its own proprietary file format. If you want to share your spreadsheets with others who don't have Numbers, you need to export your spreadsheet into another file format, such as

✦ **PDF:** Saves your spreadsheet as a series of static pages stored in the Adobe Acrobat portable document format that can be viewed by any computer with a PDF viewing application.

✦ **Excel:** Saves your spreadsheet as a Microsoft Excel file, which can be opened and edited by any spreadsheet that can read and edit Microsoft Excel files.

✦ **CSV:** Saves your spreadsheet in Comma-Separated Values format, a universal format that preserves only data, not any charts or pictures you have stored on your spreadsheet.

The PDF file format preserves formatting 100 percent, but you need extra software to edit it. Generally, if someone needs to edit your spreadsheet, choose File➪Save As and save a copy as an Excel document. The CSV option is useful only for transferring your data to another application that can't read Excel files.

To export a spreadsheet, follow these steps:

1. **Choose File➪Export on the menu bar.**

   A dialog appears, as shown in Figure 6-23.

2. **Click an icon, such as PDF or Excel.**

3. **(Optional) Click Security Options if you want to add a password to open, print, or copy the document.**

4. **Click Next.**

   A dialog appears, letting you choose a name and location to save your exported spreadsheet.

5. **Enter a name for your exported spreadsheet in the Save As text box.**

6. **Click the folder where you want to store your spreadsheet.**

   You may need to switch drives or folders until you find where you want to save your file.

7. **Click Export.**

   When you export a spreadsheet, your original Numbers spreadsheet remains untouched in its original location.

Sending files directly from Numbers

Book II, Chapter 2 explains Mail, the e-mail application that came with your Mac. You can send your files directly from Numbers via Mail by doing the following:

1. **Choose Share➪Send via Mail.**

2. **Choose the format you want to use: Numbers, Excel, PDF.**

   A New Message window in Mail opens.

3. **Fill in the To, CC, and Subject fields.**

4. **Type a message to accompany your file.**

5. **Click the Send button.**

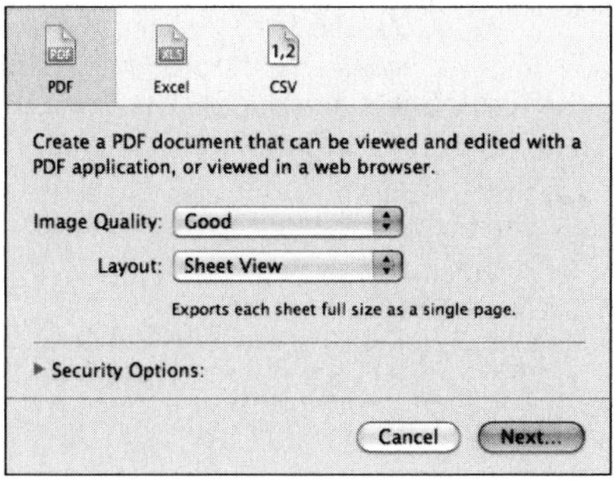

Figure 6-23:
The Export
dialog lets
you choose
a format to
save your
spread-
sheets.

Chapter 7: Getting the Most Out of iWork

In This Chapter

✔ **Customizing the Toolbar**

✔ **Opening multiple Inspector windows**

✔ **Modifying photos**

✔ **Making comments**

✔ **Sharing on iWork.com**

✔ **Finding third-party templates**

*I*f you read the last two or three chapters about using the iWork applications — Pages, Keynote, and Numbers — you may have noticed that the window layout, the commands, and the tools are similar for all of them. Some actions are exactly the same — and that's where this chapter comes in. We take you through some of the lesser-known (and, sometimes, more advanced) functions of iWork, functions that work the same whether you're writing a newsletter in Pages, preparing a presentation in Keynote, or building a budget in Numbers.

Customizing the Toolbar

One of the first things you may have noticed is that all three iWork applications have what's known as the Toolbar running across the top of the window, offering icons for (what Apple considers) the most commonly used tools. There may be some icons there that you'll never use and you might wish that you had an icon in the Toolbar for your most often used tool. Follow these steps to add and delete icons from the Toolbar and customize it to best meet your needs:

1. **Open a document in one of the iWork applications.**

2. **Choose View➪Customize Toolbar.**

   The Toolbar icon chooser window (shown in Figure 7-1) opens. Icons for all the tools for the application you opened appear. The default Toolbar runs across the bottom in case you want to reset the Toolbar.

Figure 7-1:
Customize the Toolbar to show the icons for the tools you use most.

3. **Drag icons you want to add to the Toolbar from the chooser into the position you want on the Toolbar.**

   The new icon appears in the Toolbar.

4. **Drag icons you don't want to the Toolbar icon chooser window.**

   They disappear from the Toolbar in a puff of smoke.

5. **Click Done when you're happy with the Toolbar.**

   The Toolbar remains as you customized it, even when you quit and reopen the application.

You can customize the Toolbar for each iWork application, which is probably a good idea anyway; each has some specialized tools.

Opening More Than One Inspector Window

You run into the Inspector in many Apple applications, not just iWork. Inspectors let you format parts of the document you're working on; for example, slides (in Keynote), charts, and text. There are ten Inspectors and they are slightly different in each application. Sometimes when you're working on a document, you'd like to see more than one Inspector at once; for example, the text and document Inspectors so you can change the font and margins.

The first Inspector window opens when you click on the Inspector icon in the Toolbar (the white "i" on a blue background) or choose View⇨Show Inspector. To open the second Inspector window, choose View⇨New Inspector. Repeat to open the third, fourth, or on up to the tenth Inspector window.

Modifying Photos

iWork applications (as well as iWeb and Preview) provide two ways to modify the appearance of a photo: Masking and Instant Alpha. *Masking* (sometimes called *cropping*) lets you display just a portion of an image, such as an oval or star-shaped area. *Instant Alpha* lets you make part of an image transparent, making the image seem cut-out against the background of your document.

Masking a photo

A mask acts like a cookie cutter that you plop over a photo to save anything *inside* the cookie-cutter shape but hide anything *outside* the shape. iWork applications provide a standard rectangle mask and a variety of shaped masks, such as ovals, stars, arrows, and triangles.

To apply a mask to a photo, follow these steps:

1. **Click the photo you want to mask.**

   Handles appear around your chosen photo.

2. **Click the Mask icon in the Toolbar or choose Format⇨Mask (or Format⇨ Mask with Shape) and then choose a shape, such as Polygon or Diamond.**

   Your chosen mask appears over your photo, as shown in Figure 7-2.

3. **Click and drag a mask handle to resize the mask.**

   Holding down the Shift key while dragging a mask handle retains the height and width aspect ratio.

4. **Move the pointer to the dimmed portion of the photo outside the mask and then drag the dimmed portion to adjust which part of the picture appears within the mask.**

5. **Click the Edit Mask button.**

   Keynote masks your photo.

You can apply only one mask at a time to a photo. If you want to apply a different mask over a photo, you must remove the first mask by choosing Format⇨Unmask.

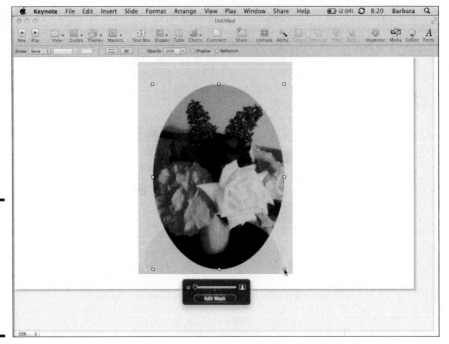

Figure 7-2:
The mask highlights the saved portion of a photo and dims the rest.

Making a picture transparent with Instant Alpha

The Instant Alpha feature lets you remove a portion of a photo. This can create unusual visual effects by stripping unwanted portions of a photo and keeping the parts you like.

To use the Instant Alpha feature, follow these steps:

1. **Click the photo you want to modify.**

   Handles appear around your chosen photo.

2. **Click the Alpha icon in the Toolbar or choose Format➪Instant Alpha on the menu bar.**

   A dialog appears over your photo, telling you how to use the Instant Alpha feature.

3. **Place the pointer over the portion of your photo that you want to make transparent and then drag the mouse or trackpad.**

   Keynote highlights all parts of your photo that are similar in color to the area that you originally pointed to, as shown in Figure 7-3.

Figure 7-3:
Dragging
the mouse
or trackpad
highlights
similar
colors to
eliminate.

4. **Release the mouse button or trackpad when you're happy with the portion of the photo that the Instant Alpha feature has highlighted and made transparent.**

You can use the Instant Alpha feature multiple times to remove different colors from the same photo. If you make a mistake, choose Edit ⇨Undo Instant Alpha on the menu bar or press ⌘+Z.

Using Adjust Image

Another way to tweak your photos is to choose View⇨Show Adjust Image, which opens the window shown in Figure 7-4. Use the sliders to adjust contrast, brightness, sharpness, and other aspects of your photo. Click Reset Image if you don't like the changes you made; doing so returns your image to its original state.

Figure 7-4:
The Adjust
Image
tool lets
you tweak
photos.

Making Comments

Comments are like putting a sticky note on your document. You can make notes to yourself, notes to someone else who may read your document, and they can make comments to you, too. To add comments, do the following:

1. **Within the document you're working on, click the Comment icon in the Toolbar or choose View⇨Show Comment.**

A yellow square appears on your document.

2. **Type the comment you want to make, as shown in Figure 7-5.**

3. **Click the Font icon in the Toolbar.**

The Font chooser opens. You can select the typeface you want to use on your comment.

4. **Resize your comment by clicking and dragging the lower-right corner.**

5. **Move your comment by clicking and dragging the comment itself.**

6. **Click the X in the upper-right corner to close the comment or choose View⇨Hide Comment.**

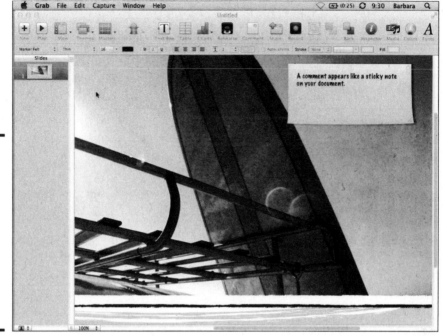

Figure 7-5:
Add comments to your documents as reminders to yourself or notes to others who share your document.

Sharing via iWork.com

iWork.com is an Apple-developed public *beta* site (that means it hasn't been officially released but is in the development stages; you can use this beta version on a provisional basis, serving as a *beta tester*). You use your Apple ID to sign on, and then upload your iWork documents to the iWork.com site. A URL is assigned to your document, which you can give to the people you want to share your document with. They then go to that URL on the Internet and can see your document, and they don't have to have a Mac or Pages to do it. Follow these steps:

1. **Choose Share⇨Share via iWork.com.**

2. **Enter your Apple ID.**

   If you don't have an Apple ID, click Create Account and follow the instructions.

   A window opens, as shown in Figure 7-6.

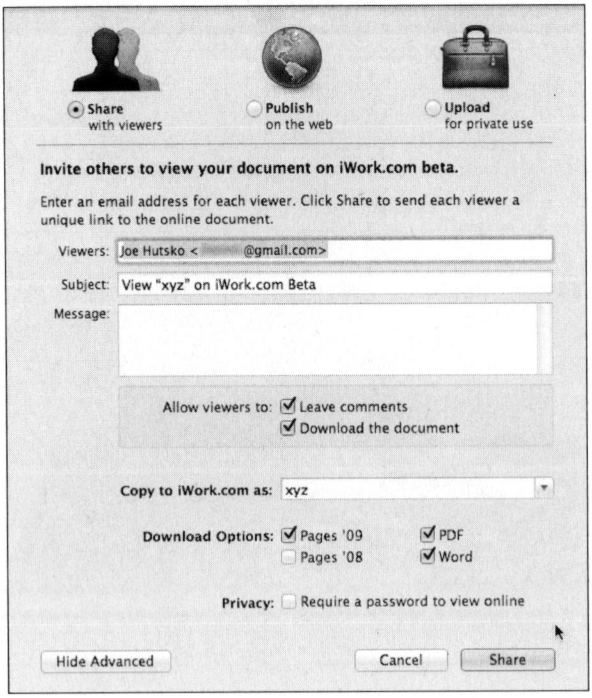

Figure 7-6:
Choose
who can
view your
document
on iWork.
com.

3. **Choose one of the following:**

   - *Share with Viewers.* Enter the e-mail addresses of the people you want to see your document. Click Show Advanced to set download and privacy options.

   - *Publish on the Web.* Puts your document on iWork.com and assigns it a URL that you can post on your preferred social network or blog and anyone can view it.

   - *Upload for Private Use.* Uploads your document to iWork.com with a name that you assign and only you have access to the document.

4. **Click Share.**

5. **You receive an e-mail with the URL of your document.**

   You can see your document on iWork.com, as shown in Figure 7-7. In iWork.com, you can also specify who can share your document after you upload it.

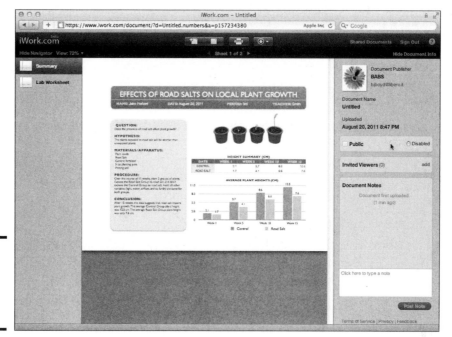

Figure 7-7:
See your
document
on iWork.
com.

Finding More Templates

If iWork's templates and typefaces don't satisfy your creative needs, several
third-party software developers give away or sell templates that work with
Pages, Keynote, and Numbers. We list a few here, but make sure to check out
the AppStore and search the Internet for others.

✦ **Design Science (**www.dessci.com**):** Offers a 30-day trial of MathType 6,
   a typeface collection of mathematical symbols; buy the full package at
   the end of 30 days, or do nothing and MathType 6 converts to MathType
   Lite, a free, streamlined version.

✦ **Facilisi (**www.facilisi.com**):** Offers over 1,600 templates for Pages.

✦ **Graphic Node (**http://graphicnode.com/products/keynote-
   quartet**):** Offers still and motion themes and animations.

✦ **iWork Community (**www.iworkcommunity.com**):** iWork users post
   templates they've designed to share with other iWork users.

✦ **Jumsoft (**www.jumsoft.com**):** Sells clip art and templates for all three
   applications.

✦ **KeynotePro** (`http://keynotepro.com`)**:** Sells stylized templates for traditional presentations and kiosks.

✦ **Keynote Theme Park** (`www.keynotethemepark.com`)**:** Offers free and fee themes.

✦ **Keynote Themes Plus** (`www.keynotethemesplus.com/home.html`)**:** Produces high-definition themes and presentations.

✦ **Numbers Templates** (`www.numberstemplates.com`)**:** The name says it all.

✦ **Stock Layouts** (`www.stocklayouts.com`)**:** Paid and free templates are available in various formats and specific to different industries such as Health Care, Sports, and Education.

Book VI

Mac Networking

The 5th Wave   By Rich Tennant

"It worked, honey! I'm connected to the network!"

Contents at a Glance

Chapter 1: Networking Your Mac and Other Peripherals

*T*oday, most households and small businesses have a few computers, a printer or two, a scanner, an Internet service, and maybe even an external drive where files are backed up from each computer. (Be sure to read about the importance of backing up in Book III, Chapter 1.) You can connect and disconnect each computer to and from the *peripheral* devices (those are your printers, scanners, and such) when you want to use them, which would be a big hassle and time waster, or you can set up a network.

A *network* allows multiple computers to share files and devices such as printers, modems, or backup hard drives. When multiple computers connect to a network, they can share files almost as quickly and easily as copying a file from one folder to another.

After you understand the concept of networking, networks aren't so difficult to set up. In this chapter, we show you how to set up a simple wired or wireless network — a few computers, a printer, and a modem.

Creating a Wired Network

The simplest wired network just connects two computers together, using either a FireWire cable or a cable that conforms to a networking cable standard called *Ethernet*. Many Macs have Ethernet ports or both Ethernet and FireWire ports. The MacBook Air, which has neither, relies on a wireless (Wi-Fi) connection or a USB-Ethernet adapter. If you plug a FireWire cable or Ethernet cable into the FireWire or Ethernet ports of two Macs, you have a simple network, as shown in Figure 1-1.

Figure 1-1:
A simple network connects two Macs via FireWire or Ethernet cable.

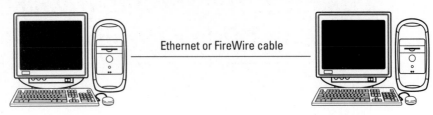

Ethernet or FireWire cable

Most Macs shipped in 2011 and later have a Thunderbolt port (as of the date of writing the MacPro does not). Thunderbolt offers two-way 10 Gbps connections, making it up to 12 times faster than FireWire and 20 times faster than USB. While the MacBook Air lacks both FireWire and Ethernet (meaning that you need a USB-Ethernet adapter), MacBook Airs shipped after July 2011 come equipped with the Thunderbolt port. Unless you have two brand-spanking-new Macs (congratulations!), you'll have to stick with FireWire or Ethernet to set up your network for now. If one of your networked Macs is a new MacBook Air, you can add either a Thunderbolt-FireWire adapter or a Thunderbolt-Ethernet adapter, both available from Sonnet (www.sonnettech.com).

Ethernet cables are often identified by the speeds at which they can send data. The earliest Ethernet cables were Category 3 (or Cat 3) cables and could transfer data at 10 megabits per second (Mbps). The next generation of Ethernet cables was Category 5 and 5e (Cat 5/5e) cables, which could transfer data at 100 Mbps. Category 6 (Cat 6) cables transfer data at 1,000 Mbps or one gigabit per second (Gbit/s). With networking, speed is everything and Category 6a (Cat 6a) and Category 7 (Cat 7) transfer data at 10 Gbit/s. Category 7a reaches transfer speeds of 100 Gbit/s.

Connecting two computers is the simplest of networks, but even a home setting today typically has a printer that is shared by two computers.

Because it's physically impossible to connect more than two devices together with a single cable, wired networks use something called a *hub*. Each device connects to the hub, which indirectly connects each device to every other device also connected to the hub, as shown in Figure 1-2.

An improved variation of a hub is called a *switch*. Physically, a hub and a switch both connect multiple devices in a single point (as shown in Figure 1-2).

With a hub, a network acts like one massive hallway that every computer shares. If many computers transfer data at the same time, the shared network can get crowded with data flowing everywhere, slowing the transfer of data throughout the network.

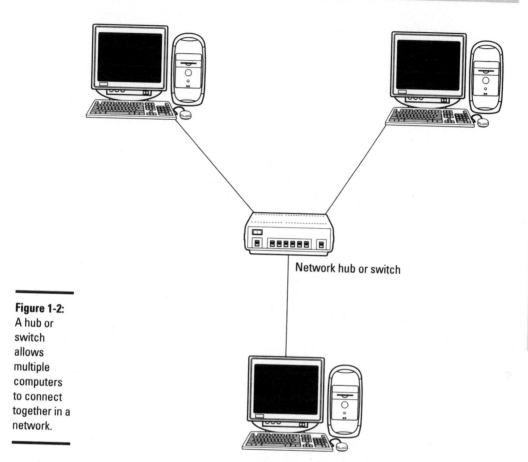

Network hub or switch

Figure 1-2:
A hub or
switch
allows
multiple
computers
to connect
together in a
network.

With a switch, the switch directs data between two devices. As a result, a switch can ensure that data transfers quickly, regardless of how much data the other devices on the network are transferring at the time.

A variation of a switch is a *router,* which often adds a firewall by using Network Address Translation (NAT) and Dynamic Host Configuration Protocol (DHCP). NAT uses one set of Internet Protocol (IP) addresses, which identify the computers and peripherals on the network for local network traffic, and another set for external traffic. This eliminates the risk of your device having the same address as another device. DHCP lets the router assign a different IP address to the same device each time it connects to the network.

Because routers cost nearly the same as ordinary hubs and switches, most wired networks rely on routers. So if you want to create a wired network of computers, you need:

✦ Two or more devices — computers, printers, scanners, modems, external drives

✦ A network switch or router with a number of ports equal to or greater than the number of devices you want to connect

✦ Enough cables to connect each device to the network switch or router

The speed of a wired network depends entirely on the slowest speed of the components used in your network. If you plan to use Cat 6 cables in your network, make sure your network switch is designed for Cat 6 cables. If not, you'll have the fastest Ethernet cables connected to a slow network switch, which will run only as fast as the slowest part of your network.

After you connect your computers and peripherals to the hub or switch and turn everything on, follow these steps to make sure that your Mac is connected:

1. **Choose ⌘⇨System Preferences.**

   The System Preferences window opens.

2. **Click the Network icon in the Internet and Wireless section.**

3. **Beside Ethernet or FireWire, whichever type of network cable you used, you should see a green light and the word Connected underneath, as shown in Figure 1-3.**

4. **To confirm that your printer is connected, click Show All to return to the main System Preferences window.**

5. **Click the Print & Scan icon in the Hardware section.**

   The Print & Scan preferences window opens, as shown in Figure 1-4. Printers and scanners connected to your network are listed on the left.

Figure 1-3: The Network System Preferences lets you connect to the network.

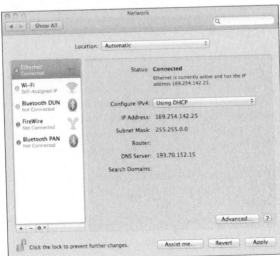

Figure 1-4:
The Print
& Scan
System
Preferences
shows
printers
that are
connected
to your
network.

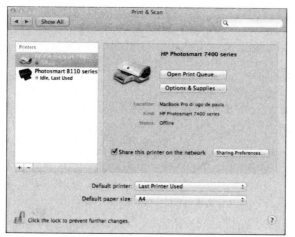

6. **Repeat these steps on other Macs and devices on your network.**

We explain how to set up file sharing in Book VI, Chapter 2. After you set up
sharing, you see other computers on your network in the Finder under the
Shared heading, as shown in Figure 1-5.

When you set up your wired network, your router may have wireless capabilities; if so, you can use an Ethernet cable to connect a computer or printer that
stays in one place to the router, and then connect to the wireless network
connection on your MacBook to work from your lawn chair in the garden, or
connect from a desktop Mac in another room in the house. To do so, you turn
on Wi-Fi and select the network as explained in the next section.

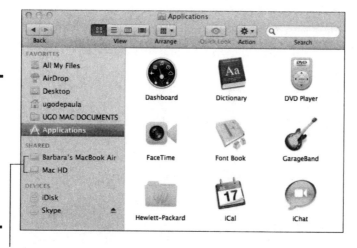

Figure 1-5:
Computers
on your
network
appear in
the Finder
under the
Shared
heading.

Computers on your network

Creating a Wireless Network

Essentially, a wireless network is no different from a wired network, except (of course) there are no wires; radio waves take their place. Wireless networks can be a bit slower than wired networks, but unless you transfer big files, wireless is probably a tidier, and more cost-effective, alternative because there are no cables to buy or tack along the baseboard. We show you how to create two types of wireless networks:

✦ A peer-to-peer or computer-to-computer network that lets two or more Macs see each other without having to connect anything other than the computers themselves

✦ A wireless network using a wireless router and eventually a cable modem or DSL modem

Setting up a computer-to-computer network

Your Mac has a built-in AirPort Card, which lets it see other Macs and Wi-Fi–enabled devices just by turning on Wi-Fi and setting up a peer-to-peer or computer-to-computer network. Do the following:

1. **Choose ⌘⇨System Preferences.**

The System Preferences window opens.

2. **Click the Network icon in the Internet and Wireless section.**

3. **Click Wi-Fi in the list on the left (refer to Figure 1-3).**

4. **Click Turn Wi-Fi On.**

5. **Click the pop-up menu by Network Name and choose Create Network.**

A dialog opens, as shown in Figure 1-6.

6. **Give your network a name, such as Home or Office.**

7. **Click the Security pop-up menu to assign a password to your network.**

Passwords are always a good idea on wireless networks because they are easily viewed by other computers in the vicinity. You can choose a 40-bit WEP, which requires a 5-character password or a 128-bit WEP, which requires a 13-character password. The longer the password, the harder it is for someone to guess what your password is.

8. **Click Create.**

Your network now appears next to Network Name.

There are two ways to connect to the wireless network you created, described in the following lists.

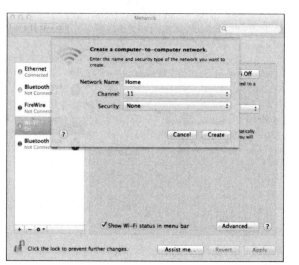

Figure 1-6:
Create a
computer-
to-computer
wireless
network in
Network
System
Preferences.

To connect to your wireless network from Network System Preferences,
follow these steps:

1. **Click Wi-Fi in the list on the left.**

2. **Click the Turn Wi-Fi On button in the upper right of the window.**

3. **Click the pop-up menu by Network Name and select the name of
    your network.**

4. **Enter the password, if you assigned one.**

5. **Click Join.**

   The Wi-Fi icon in the status bar now shows a computer rather than
   the Wi-Fi bars.

To connect to your wireless network from the Wi-Fi menu in the status bar,
follow these steps:

1. **Click the Wi-Fi pull-down menu in the status bar and drag to select
    Turn Wi-Fi On.**

2. **Click and drag the Wi-Fi pull-down menu again and select your network.**

3. **Enter the password, if you assigned one.**

4. **Click Join.**

   The Wi-Fi icon in the status bar changes to a computer.

Wireless printers also work on the computer-to-computer network. Follow the
printer manufacturer's instructions for using a wireless printer on your network.

Setting up a wireless network with a router

When you use the computer-to-computer network, your Mac can't connect to the Internet with Wi-Fi. Because your Mac has wireless capabilities, you probably want to connect to both the Internet and your network wirelessly.

As with the wired network, you need a router for your wireless network. Instead of managing physical cables, the wireless router manages signals based on the wireless network protocols. The earliest wireless networks followed a technical specification called 802.11b or 802.11a. Newer wireless equipment followed a faster wireless standard called 802.11g, and the latest (and fastest) standard (at the time of this writing) is 802.11n.

When setting up a wireless network, make sure that your router uses the same wireless standard as the built-in wireless radio or wireless adapter plugged into each of your devices. All new and recent Macs connect to Wi-Fi routers that use one to four types of the wireless 802.11 network standards.

You can buy any brand of wireless router to create a network, including Apple's Airport Extreme Base Station. Any router you choose will come with specific software and instructions for setting up your network. The basic steps are to

1. Name your network and base station so devices on the network can then find and connect to your Wi-Fi network.

2. Set up a password. (WPA2 provides the most security.)

3. Define how you connect to the Internet. (You may need information from your Internet Service Provider for this step; you can also refer to Book II, Chapter 1.)

4. Add printers and/or external hard drives.

5. Configure your Macs for sharing, as explained in Book VI, Chapter 2.

Because of physical obstacles, wireless networks don't always reach certain parts of a room or building, resulting in "dead spots" where you can't connect wirelessly. Walls or furniture can disrupt the wireless signals. You can add a device called an *access point,* which picks up the signal and rebroadcasts it beyond the reach of the Wi-Fi router, extending your wireless network range.

The difference between an access point and a router is that the router is at the center of the network, allowing the computers to share printers, Internet connections, and external hard drives. The *access point* is what allows the devices with wireless capabilities to connect to the network from a greater distance.

The hazards of wireless networking

To access a wired network, someone must physically connect a computer to the network with a cable. However, connecting to a wireless network can be done from another room, outside a building, or even across the street. As a result, wireless networks can be much less secure because a wireless network essentially shoves dozens of virtual cables out the window, so anyone can walk by and connect into the network.

The practice of connecting to unsecured wireless networks with malicious intentions is *war driving* (also war flying, war walking, or war boating, depending on how you move around). The basic idea behind war driving is to drive around a city and keep track of which areas offer an unsecured wireless network. After getting connected to an unsecured wireless network, an intruder can wipe out files, capture personal information, or interfere with the network's operation.

When you create a wireless network, you can make your network more secure by taking advantage of a variety of security measures and options. The simplest security measure is to use a password that locks out people who don't know the password. There are three types of passwords used for wireless networks:

✔ WEP (Wired Equivalent Privacy) is an older protocol and offers minimal (almost useless) protection. Being an older protocol, it may not work on all your devices. Passwords use either five or 13 characters.

✔ WPA (Wi-Fi Protected Access) is better, as it changes the encryption key for each data transmission.

✔ WPA2 is the best choice because it uses the more secure Advanced Encryption Standard (AES) to encrypt the password when it's transmitted.

For further protection, you can also use encryption. *Encryption* scrambles the data sent to and from the wireless network. Without encryption, anyone can intercept information sent through a wireless network (including passwords). Still another security measure involves configuring your wireless network to let only specific computers connect to the wireless network. By doing this, an intruder can't gain access to the wireless network because his or her computer is not approved to access the network.

Ultimately, wireless networking requires more security measures simply because it offers potential intruders the ability to access the network without physically being in the same room, house, or building. Wireless networks can be as safe as wired networks — as long as you turn on security options that can make your wireless network as secure as possible.

**Book VI
Chapter 1**

**Networking Your
Mac and Other
Peripherals**

Connecting and Choosing a Printer

Out of the box, Mac OS X comes with a number of special files called *printer drivers,* which tell your Mac how to communicate with most popular brands of printer models. When you buy a new printer, it often comes with a CD that contains a printer driver that you can install to unlock special features that the Mac's built-in drivers might not take advantage of.

Check the support section of the printer manufacturer's website to see whether a newer version of the printer installation software has become available. After you run the installer, you can check the website every now and then to see whether an even newer version (than the one you've installed) is available. Some installers place a print utility in the Dock and you may be able to set up the print utility to check automatically for updates.

Making your Mac work with your printer involves a two-step process:

1. You must connect your printer to your Mac, either physically with a USB cable or network connection (such as a USB or Ethernet connection to a router) or wirelessly to a Wi-Fi-enabled printer that is connected to the same Wi-Fi network your Mac connects to.

2. You must install the proper printer driver on your Mac (if you don't want to use the supplied driver that comes with Mac OS X, or if your Mac doesn't have a driver for it). After you connect your printer to your Mac and install or select the correct printer driver, you can then print documents and control your printer's options.

You can download additional printer drivers (and drivers for other types of hardware, such as scanners and pressure-sensitive tablets) directly from Apple's website (www.apple.com/downloads/macosx/drivers) or from the printer manufacturer's website.

After you physically or wirelessly connect a printer to your Mac and install its printer driver, you may need to take one additional step and tell your Mac that this particular printer is connected. To get your Mac to recognize a connected printer, follow these steps:

1. **Choose ⌘⇨System Preferences and click the Print & Scan icon in the Hardware section to open the Print & Scan preferences pane.**

2. **Click the Add (+) button, as shown in Figure 1-7.**

   Note: Your Mac might list local printers (printers directly attached to your Mac), as well as printers linked to your Mac via a network.

3. **Click a printer name in the Printers list and click the Default Printer pop-up menu to choose the new printer (or another) your Mac's applications will always print to (unless you specify otherwise).**

4. **Click the Close button to close the Print & Scan preferences pane.**

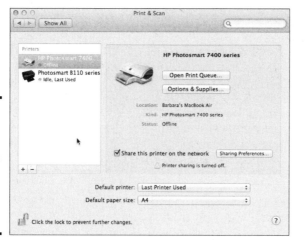

Figure 1-7:
The Print
& Scan
preferences
pane lets
you add
or delete
printers.

Chapter 2: Sharing Files and Resources on a Network

In This Chapter

✔ Using AirDrop

✔ Sharing files over a network

✔ Sharing a printer

✔ Sharing an Internet connection

*T*he benefits of sharing over a network range from swapping files quickly and easily to sharing a single printer instead of having to buy a printer for every computer. Sharing files makes it easy for several people to work on the same project. Without a network, you could give someone a copy of a file, but then you might suddenly have three different versions of the same file, and it would be difficult to decipher which file contains the most accurate information.

Although networks allow others to share your files, other persons connected to the network can't rummage through your Mac without your permission. Ideally, a network allows you to share files and equipment without risking the loss or corruption of crucial files on your own computer.

In Mac OS X Lion, Apple introduced AirDrop, a simple peer-to-peer (that means computer-to-computer) wireless network between Macs that sit near each other. In this chapter, first we talk about AirDrop, and then we explain a more traditional way of sharing files, printers, and Internet connections among computers on a network.

AirDrop

With the release of Mac OS X Lion, Apple introduced AirDrop, which is an easy way to set up a peer-to-peer network between two or more Macs that are near to each other — more or less in the same room. The caveat being you must have a Mac that supports AirDrop. If your Mac is older than those listed here, AirDrop isn't for you: MacBook or MacBookPro (late 2008) Mac Book Air (mid-2010), iMac (early 2009), Mac mini (mid-2010), MacPro (early 2009 with AirPort Extreme car or mid-2010).

Don't despair, however — there is another solution for peer-to-peer sharing even if you don't have AirDrop. Set up a peer-to-peer network as explained in Book VI, Chapter 1, and then refer to the "Sharing Files" section in this chapter, or use iChat, which we detail in Book II, Chapter 3.

You don't have to have any kind of network already set up; your Mac's internal Airport Extreme card sees other Macs. You do have to have Lion installed on any Macs you want to use AirDrop with. Here's how it works:

1. **From the Finder, choose Go⇨AirDrop.**

The AirDrop window opens, as shown in Figure 2-1. If you don't have Wi-Fi turned on, you are prompted to do so; when you do, you see the AirDrop window.

You only see the contact photo of other Mac users who have AirDrop turned on; likewise, they only see you if you have AirDrop turned on. If your Mac goes to sleep, AirDrop disconnects.

2. **Drag the file you want to transfer over the contact photo of the person you want to transfer the file to, as shown in Figure 2-2.**

3. **When you receive a file, a message appears asking what you want to do with the incoming file, as shown in Figure 2-3:**

  • *Save and Open:* This option opens the file and saves a copy of it to your Downloads folder.

  • *Decline:* Choose this option if you don't want the file; the sender receives a notice that you rejected the file.

  • *Save:* This option saves the file and you can open it later.

If you begin a download and want to cancel, open your Downloads folder and click the "x" next to the icon of the incoming file.

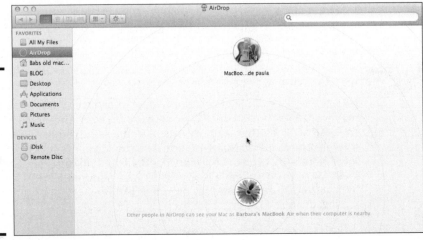

Figure 2-1:
When you open AirDrop, you see other Macs with which yours can exchange files.

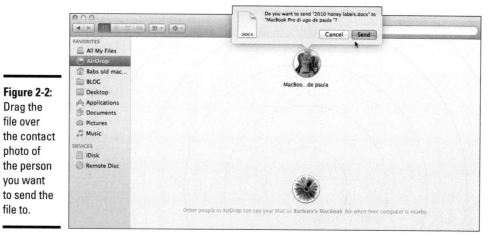

Figure 2-2:
Drag the
file over
the contact
photo of
the person
you want
to send the
file to.

Figure 2-3:
Choose
what you
want to
do with
incoming
files.

In AirDrop, you don't have to worry about security. AirDrop automatically encrypts files and creates a firewall (an impenetrable barrier) between your Mac and the Mac you're sharing the file with. Other Macs on AirDrop can only see that you are on AirDrop; they can't peek into your Mac.

Sharing Files

Sharing files over the network is different from AirDrop in a few ways:

✦ On the network, your Mac can be in a different room, a different building, even in a different country.

✦ You set up the type of access, or privileges, you want others on the network to have.

✦ Your connection to the network runs in the background where you don't see it — and even while your Mac is sleeping.

When your Mac is connected to a network, you have the option of sharing one or more folders with everyone else on the network. To share folders, you need to define different permission levels, or privileges, that allow or restrict what users can do with a folder and the files inside it:

✦ **Read & Write:** Other users have the ability to retrieve, delete, and modify files in the shared folder.

✦ **Read Only:** Other users can copy and open files, but they can't modify or delete them.

✦ **Write Only (Drop Box):** Other users can only place files in the folder; they can't copy, open, or even see any files stored in that folder.

✦ **No Access:** Specified users are blocked from accessing files on your Mac.

You decide which folder(s) to share, who can access that folder, and what access level you want others to have in accessing your shared folder.

You don't have to share folders. If you don't share folders, you can still use a network to access someone else's shared folders; you can also use devices, such as printers, that are on the network.

Turning on file sharing

The first step to sharing your files over a network is to turn on file sharing. Follow these steps:

1. **Choose ⌘⇨System Preferences to open the System Preferences window, and then click the Sharing icon or right-click (Control-click on a trackpad) the System Preferences icon on the Dock and choose Sharing from the menu that appears.**

The Sharing pane appears.

2. **Select the File Sharing check box in the leftmost Service column.**

You see a list of Public folders on your Mac. If you have more than one user account set up on your Mac, you see the public folders for each account. See Figure 2-4.

3. **Click the plus-sign button underneath the Shared Folders column.**

A dialog appears, displaying all the drives and folders on your Mac. When you select a shared file from the list, a grayed banner appears at the top that reads Shared Folder, as shown in Figure 2-5.

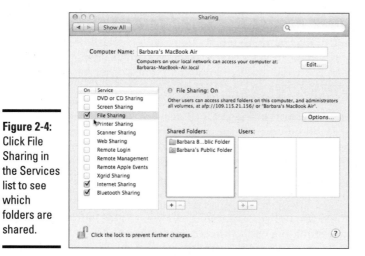

Figure 2-4:
Click File
Sharing in
the Services
list to see
which
folders are
shared.

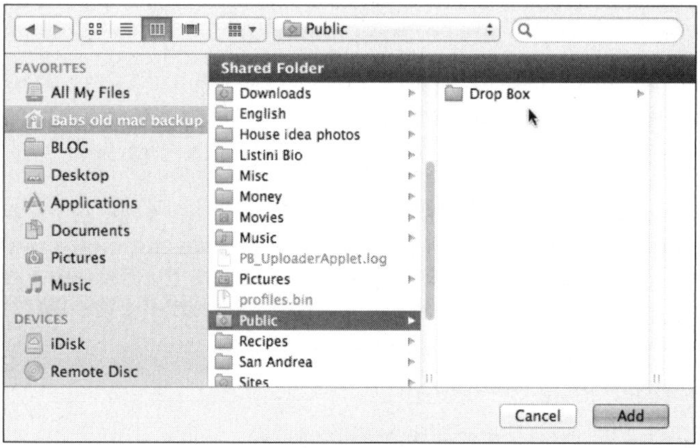

Figure 2-5:
The Public
folder
contains a
special Drop
Box folder.

4. **Click a folder, such as the Public folder, which contains the Drop Box folder.**

   The Drop Box folder is a Write Only folder that allows others to drop files in, but it doesn't allow anyone (except you) to view and retrieve files.

5. **Click Add.**

6. **Repeat Steps 4 through 6 for each additional folder you want to share via the network.**

7. **Click the Close button of the System Preferences window.**

Defining user access to shared folders

After you define one or more folders to share, you can also define the type of access people can have to your shared folders, such as giving certain people the capability to open and modify files and stopping other people from accessing your shared files.

The three types of network users are

✦ **Yourself:** Gives you Read & Write access (or else you won't be able to modify any files in your shared folders).

✦ **Everyone:** Allows others to access your shared folders as guests without requiring a password.

✦ **Names of specific network users:** Allows you to give individuals access to your shared folders with a name and password.

If you trust everyone on a network, you can give everyone Read & Write privileges to your shared folders. However, it's probably best to give everyone Read privileges and only certain people Read & Write privileges.

Defining access privileges for guests

To define access privileges for guests, follow these steps:

1. **Right-click (Control-click on a trackpad) the System Preferences icon on the Dock and choose Sharing from the menu that appears, or choose ⌘⇨System Preferences to open the System Preferences window, and then click the Sharing icon under the Internet & Wireless category.**

   The Sharing pane appears.

2. **Click File Sharing in the Services list.**

3. **Click a folder in the Shared Folders list.**

   The Users list enumerates all the people allowed to access this particular shared folder. (Refer to Figure 2-4.) By default, every shared folder lists your name with Read & Write privileges.

4. **Click Everyone (the guest account) to call up the access option pop-up menu and choose an access option, such as Read & Write, Read Only, Write Only (Drop Box), or No Access.**

5. **Repeat Steps 3 and 4 for each shared folder you want to configure.**

6. **Click the Close button of the System Preferences window.**

Giving individuals access to shared folders

The access level you give to the Everyone account for a shared folder means anyone on the network has that level of access to your files — Read & Write, Read Only, Write Only. You probably want to give Everyone the minimum access to a shared folder and give specific individuals higher levels of access.

To define a username and password to access a shared folder, follow these steps:

1. **Right-click (Control-click on a trackpad) the System Preferences icon on the Dock and choose Sharing from the menu that appears, or choose ⌘⇨System Preferences to open the System Preferences window, and then click the Sharing icon under the Internet & Wireless category.**

   The Sharing pane appears.

2. **Click File Sharing in the Services list.**

3. **Click a folder in the Shared Folders list.**

   The Users list enumerates all the people allowed to access this particular shared folder.

4. **Click the plus-sign button under the Users list, and then click the Address Book category or one of the groups from your Address Book in the left pane.**

   A dialog appears, shown in Figure 2-6, where you can choose the name of a person stored in your Address Book or create a new user.

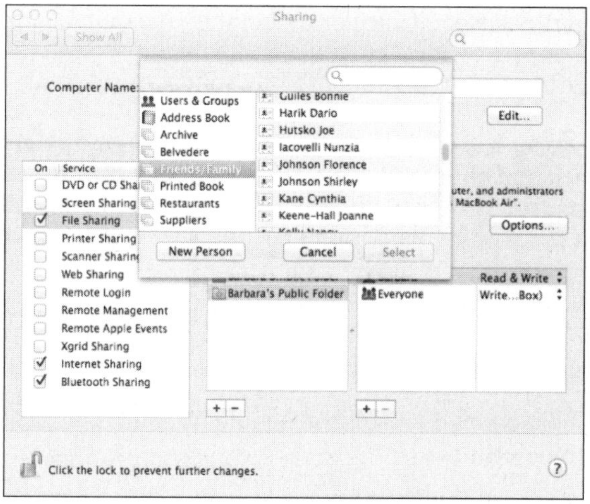

Book VI
Chapter 2

Sharing Files and Resources on a Network

Figure 2-6: A dialog lets you choose users in your Address book who can access shared folders.

5. **Click New Person.**

   A New Person dialog appears. Here you can type a username and password, as shown in Figure 2-7.

6. **Enter a name in the User Name text box.**

   The name can be an actual person or a made-up name, such as "Superman" or "John Doe." Don't forget to let the people who are going to use your folder know the username and password for that folder.

7. **Enter a password in the Password text box.**

8. **Reenter the password in the Verify text box.**

9. **Click the Create Account button.**

   Your new account name appears in the Users & Group category.

10. **Click the name of your new account in the Users & Groups category, and click Select to return to the Sharing preferences pane.**

    Your chosen account name appears in the Users box.

11. **Click the pop-up menu that appears to the right of the name you just added to the Users box, and choose Read & Write, Read Only, or Write Only (Drop Box) to assign access privileges, as shown in Figure 2-8.**

12. **Click the Close button of the System Preferences window.**

Removing accounts from shared folders

If you create an account for others to access your shared folders, you might later want to change their access privileges (such as changing their access from Read & Write to Read Only) or delete their accounts altogether.

To delete an account from a shared folder, follow these steps:

1. **Right-click (Control-click on a trackpad) the System Preferences icon on the Dock and choose Sharing from the menu that appears, or choose ⌘⇨System Preferences to open the System Preferences window, and then click the Sharing icon under the Internet & Wireless category.**

   The Sharing pane appears.

2. **Click File Sharing in the Services list.**

3. **Click a folder in the Shared Folders list.**

   The Users list enumerates all the people allowed to access this particular shared folder.

4. **Click the name of the User for whom you want to change privileges.**

5. **Click the arrows next to the name to open the Privileges pop-up menu.**

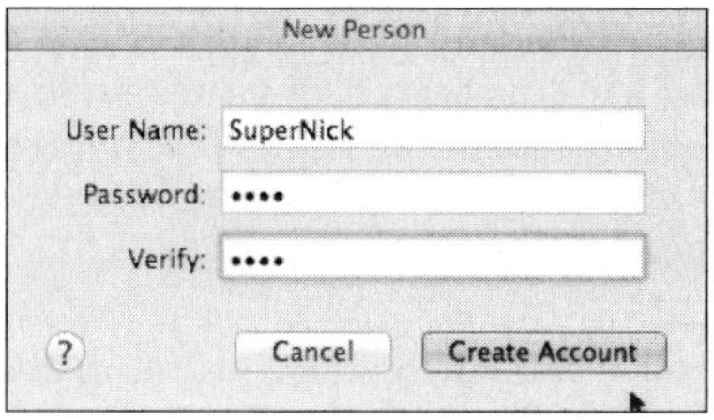

Figure 2-7:
Define
a new
user and
password
for
accessing
a shared
folder.

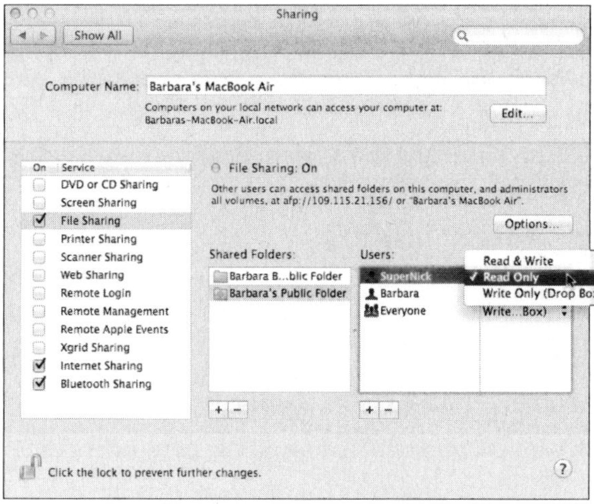

Figure 2-8:
New
network
account
names in
the Users
& Groups
category.

6. **Select the new privileges you want the user to have.**

7. **Click the Close button of the System Preferences window.**

To delete a user, follow Steps 1 through 3 in the preceding list, and then follow these steps:

1. **In the Users list, click a name that you want to delete.**

2. **Click the minus-sign button under the Users list.**

   A dialog appears, asking whether you want to keep the account from accessing your shared folder.

3. **Click OK.**

4. **Click the Close button of the System Preferences window.**

File sharing in Sleep mode

Your Mac can share files even if you set up your Mac to sleep when it's inactive for a certain time. (You can use this feature if your wireless network supports the 802.11n wireless protocol — see Book VI, Chapter 1 for a brief explanation.) If you want your Mac to wake up when another user on the network wants to access your shared files, follow these steps:

1. **Right-click (Control-click on a trackpad) the System Preferences icon on the Dock and choose Energy Saver from the menu that appears, or choose ⌘⇨System Preferences to open the System Preferences window, and then lick the Energy Saver icon in the Hardware category to open the Energy Saver pane.**

2. **Click the Power Adapter tab.**

3. **Select the Wake for Wi-Fi Network Access check box, as shown in Figure 2-9.**

4. **Click the Close button of the System Preferences window.**

Accessing shared folders

You can share your folders with others on a network, and likewise, others might want to share their folders with you. To access a shared folder on someone else's computer, follow these steps:

1. **From the Finder, choose Go⇨Network.**

   A Network window appears, listing all the computers that offer shared folders, as shown in Figure 2-10.

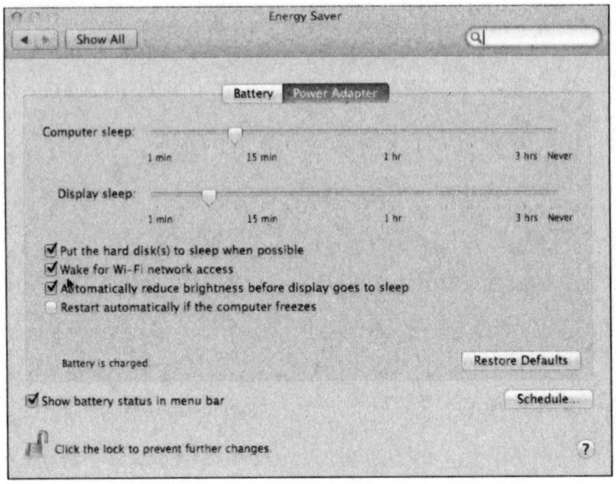

Figure 2-9:
Wake
for Wi-Fi
Network
Access
allows
sharing
when your
Mac is in
Sleep mode.

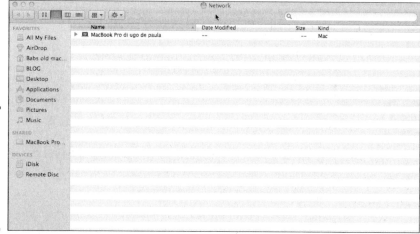

Figure 2-10:
The Network window lets you connect to other computers.

2. **Double-click the computer you want to access.**

   Another Network window appears, listing all the shared folders you can access.

3. **Click the Connect As button in the upper-right corner to display the dialog shown in Figure 2-11.**

4. **Select the Registered User (or Guest) radio button.**

   If you select the Guest radio button, skip to Step 8.

5. **Click in the Name text box and type the account name to use for accessing that shared folder.**

   The account name is the name that the computer's user created in the earlier section, "Giving individuals access to shared folders."

Figure 2-11:
The Connect As dialog lets you access a shared folder with an account name and password.

6. **Click the Password text box and type the corresponding password.**

7. **Click Connect.**

   Depending on your access to the shared folder, you might be able to copy, open, modify, or delete files.

Another way to access a shared folder is to type a shared folder's AFP (Apple Filing Protocol) address into the Safari browser address text box. To find a computer's AFP address, follow these steps:

1. **Choose ⇨System Preferences to open the System Preferences window, and then click the Sharing icon to open the Sharing pane.**

2. **Click File Sharing in the Service list.**

   Directly underneath the File Sharing: On text is the AFP address of that particular Mac, such as `afp://109.115.21.156`, as shown in Figure 2-12.

3. **Click the Close button of the System Preferences window.**

Figure 2-12: The AFP address appears in the Sharing window.

Sharing Printers

You could buy a separate printer for each computer on your network. However, this solution would be expensive and space consuming. An alternative is to connect a printer directly to one computer, and configure that computer to share its printer with any computer connected to the same network. To share a printer, follow these steps:

1. **Right-click (Control-click on a trackpad) the System Preferences icon on the Dock and choose Sharing from the menu that appears, or choose ⌘⇨System Preferences to open the System Preferences window, and click the Sharing icon under the Internet & Wireless category to open the Sharing pane.**

2. **Select the Printer Sharing check box.**

   A list of printers physically connected to your Mac appears, as shown in Figure 2-13.

3. **Select the check boxes of the printers you want to share.**

   Note that Everyone Can Print is the default in the Users column.

4. **(Optional) Add individual users just as you do for sharing files by clicking the plus-sign button beneath the Users column; choose No Access for Everyone and give selected users access to that printer.**

5. **Click the Close button of the Sharing window.**

When you choose File⇨Print in an application to print a document or photo, a Print dialog appears. If you click the Printer pop-up menu and choose Add Printer, a window appears (shown in Figure 2-14), listing all the available printers connected directly to your Mac (USB) or shared over the network (Bonjour or Bonjour Shared).

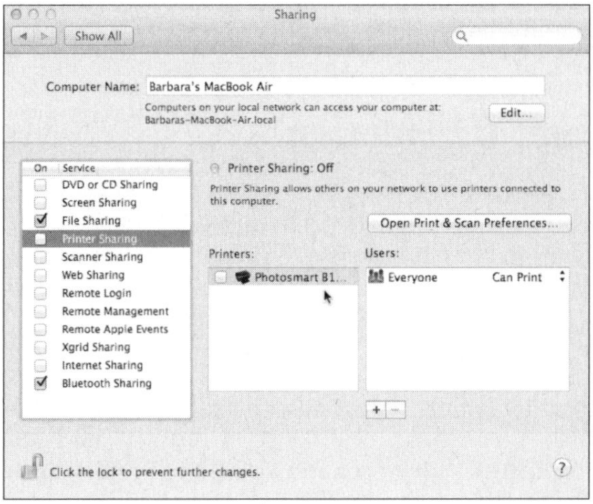

Figure 2-13:
Each physically connected printer appears with a check box in the Sharing window.

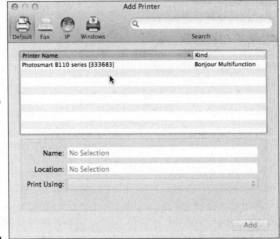

Figure 2-14:
A Printer
window lists
all available
printers
you can
use over a
network.

Bonjour is Apple's implementation of a networking standard known as
"zeroconf" (short for Zero Configuration Networking), used by most printers
to connect to other computers through Ethernet cables (wired networks)
or through wireless (Wi-Fi) connections (the number of the standard is
802.11a/b/g/n). Printer companies have written software drivers to make
their printers compatible with Bonjour/zeroconf. Windows users can download the Bonjour for Windows application free so Windows PCs can access
shared printers on a network.

Sharing an Internet Connection

Although Wi-Fi and home networks seem universal, there are situations
where only one Mac has Internet access and you'd like tap into it from other
Macs. Or one Mac might have access to the Internet through a wireless
connection, but a second, older Mac might not have a wireless or Ethernet
adapter. With Internet Sharing turned on, the second Mac can access the
Internet through the first Mac.

To share an Internet connection, follow these steps:

1. **Right-click (Control-click on a trackpad) the System Preferences
icon on the Dock and choose Sharing from the menu that appears,
or choose ➪System Preferences to open the Systems Preferences
window, and then click the Sharing icon to open the Sharing pane.**

2. **Select the Internet Sharing check box in the list box on the left.**

Internet Sharing options appear, as shown in Figure 2-15.

Figure 2-15:
To turn on Internet Sharing, you must define how to share your Internet connection.

3. **From the Share Your Connection From pop-up menu, choose how your Mac is connected to the Internet: USB Ethernet, Wi-Fi, External Modem, or Bluetooth PAN.**

4. **In the To Computers Using list, select the check box that indicates how the other computer is connected to your Mac: USB Ethernet, Wi-Fi, or Bluetooth PAN.**

   To find out more about the different connection options for connecting your Macs to create a network, see Book VI, Chapter 1.

5. **Select the Internet Sharing check box.**

   A dialog appears, asking whether you're sure that you want to turn on Internet Sharing.

6. **Click Start.**

7. **Click the Close button on the System Preferences window.**

   The second computer, connected to your Mac through Ethernet, Wi-Fi, or Bluetooth, can now access the Internet.

   To find out how to share your computer with another computer — or vice versa — using iChat, go to Book II, Chapter 3.

Chapter 3: Connecting to Bluetooth Wireless Devices and Networks

In This Chapter

✔ **Configuring Bluetooth**

✔ **Pairing devices**

✔ **Sharing files via Bluetooth**

✔ **Sharing an Internet connection over Bluetooth**

*B*luetooth is a wireless-technology standard designed primarily for connecting devices within a short distance — up to 30 feet or 10 meters — of one another. Because of its short-range nature, Bluetooth is handy for connecting computers for short periods of time and for transferring small files, unlike faster wired or wireless (Wi-Fi) networks that connect computers on a more permanent basis.

Many hand-held devices, such as mobile phones, have built-in Bluetooth capabilities, which makes it easy to wirelessly sync calendars and address books between a hand-held device and a computer (as explained in Book III, Chapter 2). Bluetooth-enabled input devices, such as wireless keyboards, mice, and game consoles, as well as wireless headsets for chatting with iChat or using Internet phone services like Skype, connect to your Mac by using your Mac's built-in Bluetooth feature.

Configuring Bluetooth

The first step to using Bluetooth is to configure your Mac's Bluetooth preferences. For example, you may not want to allow other computers to browse your hard drive through Bluetooth without your express permission. Otherwise, it's possible for someone to access your Mac and browse its hard drive from across the room, and you would never know it.

To configure how Bluetooth works on your Mac, follow these steps:

1. **Choose ⌥System Preferences to open the System Preferences window, and then click the Sharing icon (it looks like a folder in the Internet and Wireless section) to open the Sharing preferences pane.**

Alternatively, right-click (Control-click on a trackpad) the System Preferences icon on the Dock and choose Sharing from the menu that appears.

2. **Select the Bluetooth Sharing check box.**

A list of Bluetooth options appears, as shown in Figure 3-1.

3. **Choose one of the following from the When Receiving Items pop-up menu:**

   • *Accept and Save:* Automatically saves any files sent to you through Bluetooth. (Not recommended because someone can send you a malicious application, such as a virus or Trojan Horse, which can wipe out your files when opened.)

   • *Accept and Open:* Automatically saves and opens any files sent to you through Bluetooth. (Not recommended because this — like the previous option — could automatically run a malicious application sent to your Mac through Bluetooth.)

   • *Ask What to Do:* Displays a dialog that gives you the option of accepting or rejecting a file sent to you through Bluetooth — probably your best choice.

   • *Never Allow:* Always blocks anyone from sending you files through Bluetooth.

4. **Choose either Documents or Other from the Folder for Accepted Items pop-up menu.**

If you choose Other, an Open dialog appears, letting you navigate to and click a folder where you want to store any files sent to you through Bluetooth.

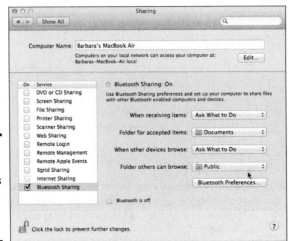

Figure 3-1: The Sharing window lists options for Bluetooth sharing.

5. **Choose one of the following from the When Other Devices Browse pop-up menu:**

    • *Always Allow:* Automatically gives another (*any*) Bluetooth device full access to the contents of your Mac. (Not recommended — this allows others to mess up your files accidentally or deliberately.)

    • *Ask What to Do:* Displays a dialog that gives you the option of accepting or rejecting another device's attempt to access your Mac through Bluetooth.

    • *Never Allow:* Always blocks anyone from browsing through your Mac by using Bluetooth.

6. **Choose either Public or Other from the Folder Others Can Browse pop-up menu.**

    If you choose Other, an Open dialog appears, letting you select a folder that you can share.

7. **Click the Close button of the System Preferences window.**

Pairing a Device

Pairing allows you to predetermine which Bluetooth-enabled devices can connect to your Mac. By pairing, you can keep strangers from trying to access your Mac without your knowledge. For additional security, paired devices require a password (also called a *passkey*) that further verifies that a specific device is allowed to connect to your Mac.

Pairing with your Mac

To pair a device with your Mac, follow these steps:

1. **Right-click (Control-click on a trackpad) the System Preferences icon on the Dock and choose Bluetooth from the menu that appears.**

    Alternatively, choose ⇨System Preferences to open the System Preferences window, and then click the Bluetooth icon.

    The Bluetooth preferences pane appears, as shown in Figure 3-2.

2. **Click the Set Up New Device button.**

    The Bluetooth Setup Assistant window appears and immediately begins searching for Bluetooth devices.

3. **While your Mac finds devices, such as mobile phones, headsets, or other computers, they appear in a list, as shown in Figure 3-3.**

Figure 3-2: Bluetooth preferences let you pair a device with your Mac.

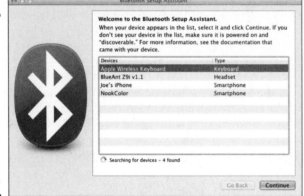

Figure 3-3: The Bluetooth Setup Assistant searches for nearby Bluetooth-enabled devices automatically.

4. **Select the device you want to pair with your Mac.**

5. **Click Continue.**

   If the other device has a keyboard or keypad, you have to enter a pass-key on that device. A Bluetooth Setup Assistant dialog appears, display-ing the passkey to use to link with the other Bluetooth device. On the other device, a dialog appears asking for the passkey. Examples of both dialog boxes are shown in Figure 3-4.

6. **Type the passkey on the other device that you want to pair with your Mac.**

   The Bluetooth Setup Assistant window informs you that the pairing has succeeded.

7. **If you want to add another device, click Set Up Another Device and follow Steps 4 through 6; otherwise, click Quit.**

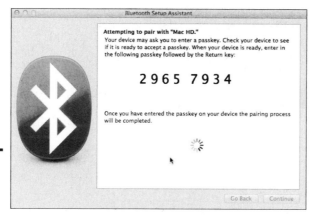

Figure 3-4:
The
Bluetooth
dialog on
your Mac
shows a
passkey;
the dialog
on the other
device has
a space to
type in the
passkey.

**Book VI
Chapter 3**

Connecting to
Bluetooth Wireless
Devices and
Networks

Bluetooth can connect devices up to 30 feet (10 meters) away, although any obstacles, such as walls, can limit the range of a Bluetooth device.

Removing a paired device from your Mac

After you pair a device with your Mac, you may want to remove it later. To remove a paired device from your Mac, follow these steps:

1. **Right-click (Control-click on a trackpad) the System Preferences icon on the Dock and choose Bluetooth from the menu that appears.**

   Alternatively, choose ⌘⇨System Preferences to open the System Preferences window, and then click the Bluetooth icon.

   A Bluetooth preferences pane appears, as shown in Figure 3-5, listing all devices paired with your Mac.

2. **Select the device you want to unlink from your Mac, and then click the minus-sign button in the bottom-left corner of the Bluetooth window.**

   A dialog appears, warning you that if you disconnect this device, it will no longer be available to your Mac.

3. **Click Remove.**

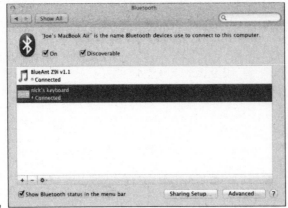

Figure 3-5:
The
Bluetooth
preferences
pane
shows you
all paired
devices on a
Mac.

If you connect Bluetooth-enabled input devices to your Mac, such as keyboards, mice, or trackpads, there are a few advanced settings that you
should consider. Choose ⌘➪System Preferences then click the Bluetooth
icon or right-click (Control-click on a trackpad) the System Preferences icon
on the Dock and choose Bluetooth. Click Advanced in the lower-right corner,
and you see the window shown in Figure 3-6. Choose the settings that apply
to the devices you use. For example, if you use a Bluetooth-enabled keyboard, you want to choose the first and third options so that you can wake
your Mac by touching the keyboard and if your Mac doesn't see the keyboard, it opens Bluetooth Preferences automatically. For a wireless mouse,
choose the second and third options. If you use an audio device, such as a
headset, you may or may not want to choose the last option. For example, if
you travel with your Mac often, you may want to turn on audio rejection so
that the Bluetooth headsets of other travelers can't connect to your Mac.

Troubleshooting connections with Bluetooth-enabled devices

Sometimes you pair a device with your Mac, but the connection doesn't
seem to hold when your Mac goes to sleep. If you connect a keyboard or
headset to your computer and experience problems with the Bluetooth
connection, power down the device by following this procedure:

1. **Shut down your Mac.**

2. **Turn off the keyboard or headset and hold the power button for
   five seconds.**

3. **Turn on your Mac.**

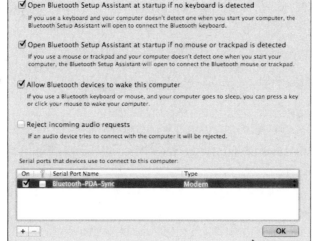

Figure 3-6:
Choose how
your Mac
interacts
with input
devices
from the
Bluetooth
Advanced
window.

4. **When your Mac says there is no keyboard connected, turn on the keyboard and hold the power button for 10 seconds.**

    Alternatively, turn on the headset and hold the power button for 10 seconds.

5. **Pair the device with your Mac as explained previously in the "Pairing with your Mac" section.**

Sharing through Bluetooth

Because Bluetooth lets you create a simple, short-range network between Macs, you can use a Bluetooth network to share files or even an Internet connection with others. Such a simple network isn't meant to share massive numbers of files or a long-term Internet connection, but it is handy for quick file copying, browsing a web page, or sending a photo or song to a mobile phone or iPod.

The speed of ordinary networks connected through Ethernet cables is 10, 100, or 1,000 megabits per second (Mbps), whereas the maximum speed of a Bluetooth network is only 1 Mbps.

Sharing files

When you want to copy a file from your Mac to another device, such as another Mac or a mobile phone, you can set up a Bluetooth connection. Sharing files through Bluetooth allows you to transfer files to another device without the hassle of using connecting cables or mutually compatible removable storage devices like portable hard drives or USB flash drives. It's also a viable option when you are out of range of a Wi-Fi network.

To share files through Bluetooth, follow these steps:

1. **From the Finder, choose Go⇨Utilities.**

   The contents of the Utilities folder appear.

2. **Double-click the Bluetooth File Exchange icon.**

   A Select File to Send window appears, as shown in Figure 3-7.

3. **Select a file.**

   To select multiple files, hold down the ⌘ key and click each file you want to send.

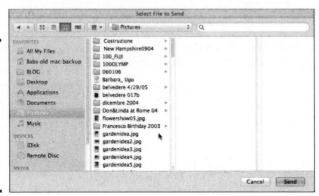

Figure 3-7: The Select File to Send window lets you choose a file to send over a Bluetooth connection.

4. **Click Send.**

   A Send File window appears, listing all Bluetooth-enabled devices near your Mac, as shown in Figure 3-8.

5. **Select a Bluetooth-enabled device and click Send.**

   If you choose another Mac or mobile phone to receive your files, a dialog might appear on the receiving device, asking the user to accept or decline the file transfer, as shown in Figure 3-9.

If the receiving device has been configured to Accept and Save or Accept and Open (transferred files), you won't see the dialog in Figure 3-9. The dialog in Figure 3-9 appears only if the user has selected Ask What to Do (the default option) when configuring Bluetooth settings.

**Book VI
Chapter 3**

Connecting to
Bluetooth Wireless
Devices and
Networks

Figure 3-8:
The Send
File window
lets you
choose a
Bluetooth-
enabled
device to
receive your
file.

Figure 3-9:
The
receiving
device can
accept or
decline a
file transfer.

Sharing an Internet connection

Sharing a Bluetooth Internet connection is great for letting someone do simple things like browse websites or retrieve e-mail by using your Mac's Internet connection, but you can't use Bluetooth for video conferencing or hosting a website because of slower Bluetooth data transfer speeds.

To share an Internet connection, follow these steps:

1. **Right-click (Control-click on a trackpad) the System Preferences icon on the Dock and choose Sharing from the menu that appears.**

Alternatively, choose ⌘⇨System Preferences to open the System Preferences window, and then click the Sharing icon to open the Sharing pane.

Make sure that Bluetooth Sharing is on. (See the earlier section, "Configuring Bluetooth.")

2. **Click Internet Sharing.**

A list of options for configuring Internet sharing appears.

3. **Click the pop-up menu next to Share Your Connection From, as shown in Figure 3-10.**

4. **Select the Internet source you want to use. Choose the Internet connection your main Mac uses.**

5. **Select the Bluetooth PAN check box in the To Computers Using section.**

6. **Select the Internet Sharing check box in the Service list on the left.**

   A dialog box asks whether you're sure that you want to turn on Internet sharing. Click Start.

   At this point, follow the steps in the earlier section, "Pairing with your Mac," to use the Bluetooth Assistant to link your Mac to a Bluetooth-enabled device, which could be another Mac or another type of computer. After you finish linking another device to your Mac, you can share your Internet connection. Pairing keeps other computers from trying to access the Internet through your Mac.

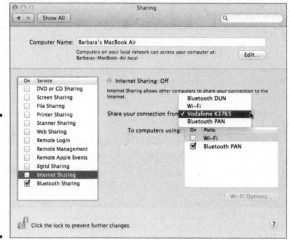

Figure 3-10: Choose the Internet connection you use on your main Mac.

Index

B

G

J

T

U

V

X

Y

Z

Apple & Mac

iPad 2 For Dummies,
3rd Edition
978-1-118-17679-5

iPhone 4S For Dummies,
5th Edition
978-1-118-03671-6

iPod touch For Dummies,
3rd Edition
978-1-118-12960-9

Mac OS X Lion
For Dummies
978-1-118-02205-4

Blogging & Social Media

CityVille For Dummies
978-1-118-08337-6

Facebook For Dummies,
4th Edition
978-1-118-09562-1

Mom Blogging
For Dummies
978-1-118-03843-7

Twitter For Dummies,
2nd Edition
978-0-470-76879-2

WordPress For Dummies,
4th Edition
978-1-118-07342-1

Business

Cash Flow For Dummies
978-1-118-01850-7

Investing For Dummies,
6th Edition
978-0-470-90545-6

Job Searching with Social
Media For Dummies
978-0-470-93072-4

QuickBooks 2012
For Dummies
978-1-118-09120-3

Resumes For Dummies,
6th Edition
978-0-470-87361-8

Starting an Etsy Business
For Dummies
978-0-470-93067-0

Cooking & Entertaining

Cooking Basics
For Dummies, 4th Edition
978-0-470-91388-8

Wine For Dummies,
4th Edition
978-0-470-04579-4

Diet & Nutrition

Kettlebells For Dummies
978-0-470-59929-7

Nutrition For Dummies,
5th Edition
978-0-470-93231-5

Restaurant Calorie Counter
For Dummies,
2nd Edition
978-0-470-64405-8

Digital Photography

Digital SLR Cameras &
Photography For Dummies,
4th Edition
978-1-118-14489-3

Digital SLR Settings
& Shortcuts
For Dummies
978-0-470-91763-3

Photoshop Elements 10
For Dummies
978-1-118-10742-3

Gardening

Gardening Basics
For Dummies
978-0-470-03749-2

Vegetable Gardening
For Dummies,
2nd Edition
978-0-470-49870-5

Green/Sustainable

Raising Chickens
For Dummies
978-0-470-46544-8

Green Cleaning
For Dummies
978-0-470-39106-8

Health

Diabetes For Dummies,
3rd Edition
978-0-470-27086-8

Food Allergies
For Dummies
978-0-470-09584-3

Living Gluten-Free
For Dummies,
2nd Edition
978-0-470-58589-4

Hobbies

Beekeeping
For Dummies,
2nd Edition
978-0-470-43065-1

Chess For Dummies,
3rd Edition
978-1-118-01695-4

Drawing For Dummies,
2nd Edition
978-0-470-61842-4

eBay For Dummies,
7th Edition
978-1-118-09806-6

Knitting For Dummies,
2nd Edition
978-0-470-28747-7

Language &
Foreign Language

English Grammar
For Dummies,
2nd Edition
978-0-470-54664-2

French For Dummies,
2nd Edition
978-1-118-00464-7

German For Dummies,
2nd Edition
978-0-470-90101-4

Spanish Essentials
For Dummies
978-0-470-63751-7

Spanish For Dummies,
2nd Edition
978-0-470-87855-2

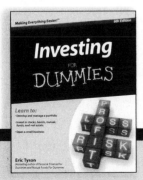

Math & Science

Algebra I For Dummies,
2nd Edition
978-0-470-55964-2

Biology For Dummies,
2nd Edition
978-0-470-59875-7

Chemistry For Dummies,
2nd Edition
978-1-1180-0730-3

Geometry For Dummies,
2nd Edition
978-0-470-08946-0

Pre-Algebra Essentials
For Dummies
978-0-470-61838-7

Microsoft Office

Excel 2010 For Dummies
978-0-470-48953-6

Office 2010 All-in-One
For Dummies
978-0-470-49748-7

Office 2011 for Mac
For Dummies
978-0-470-87869-9

Word 2010
For Dummies
978-0-470-48772-3

Music

Guitar For Dummies,
2nd Edition
978-0-7645-9904-0

Clarinet For Dummies
978-0-470-58477-4

iPod & iTunes
For Dummies,
9th Edition
978-1-118-13060-5

Pets

Cats For Dummies,
2nd Edition
978-0-7645-5275-5

Dogs All-in One
For Dummies
978-0470-52978-2

Saltwater Aquariums
For Dummies
978-0-470-06805-2

Religion & Inspiration

The Bible For Dummies
978-0-7645-5296-0

Catholicism For Dummies,
2nd Edition
978-1-118-07778-8

Spirituality For Dummies,
2nd Edition
978-0-470-19142-2

Self-Help & Relationships

Happiness For Dummies
978-0-470-28171-0

Overcoming Anxiety
For Dummies,
2nd Edition
978-0-470-57441-6

Seniors

Crosswords For Seniors
For Dummies
978-0-470-49157-7

iPad 2 For Seniors
For Dummies, 3rd Edition
978-1-118-17678-8

Laptops & Tablets
For Seniors For Dummies,
2nd Edition
978-1-118-09596-6

Smartphones & Tablets

BlackBerry For Dummies,
5th Edition
978-1-118-10035-6

Droid X2 For Dummies
978-1-118-14864-8

HTC ThunderBolt
For Dummies
978-1-118-07601-9

MOTOROLA XOOM
For Dummies
978-1-118-08835-7

Sports

Basketball For Dummies,
3rd Edition
978-1-118-07374-2

Football For Dummies,
2nd Edition
978-1-118-01261-1

Golf For Dummies,
4th Edition
978-0-470-88279-5

Test Prep

ACT For Dummies,
5th Edition
978-1-118-01259-8

ASVAB For Dummies,
3rd Edition
978-0-470-63760-9

The GRE Test For
Dummies, 7th Edition
978-0-470-00919-2

Police Officer Exam
For Dummies
978-0-470-88724-0

Series 7 Exam
For Dummies
978-0-470-09932-2

Web Development

HTML, CSS, & XHTML
For Dummies, 7th Edition
978-0-470-91659-9

Drupal For Dummies,
2nd Edition
978-1-118-08348-2

Windows 7

Windows 7
For Dummies
978-0-470-49743-2

Windows 7
For Dummies,
Book + DVD Bundle
978-0-470-52398-8

Windows 7 All-in-One
For Dummies
978-0-470-48763-1